# Annotated Bibliography of
# Southern American English

# Annotated Bibliography of Southern American English

James B. McMillan and Michael B. Montgomery

The University of Alabama Press
Tuscaloosa and London

**Library of Congress Cataloging-in-Publication Data**

McMillan, James B., 1907–
　　　Annotated bibliography of Southern American English / James B.
　　McMillan and Michael B. Montgomery.
　　　　　p.　　　cm.
　　Includes index.
　　ISBN 0-8173-0448-7
　　　1. English language—Southern States—Bibliography.　2. English
　　language—Dialects—Southern States—Bibliography.　3. English
　　language—Provincialisms—Southern States—Bibliography.
　　4. Southern States—Bibliography.　5. Americanisms—Bibliography.
　　I. Montgomery, Michael, 1950–　　. II. Title.
　　Z1251.S7M37　1989
　　[PE2922]　　　　　　　　　　　　　　　88-36856
　　016.427'975—dc19　　　　　　　　　　　　CIP

# Contents

# Preface

This work is an updated, much expanded version of the first edition, published in 1971 by the University of Miami Press. That volume was the first book-length bibliography of the speech of an American region and covered more than 1,100 items (not counting book reviews) grouped into ten chapters.

The cutoff date for the first edition was 1969. In the intervening two decades, research on American English has immensely increased the literature relevant to Southern American English and made its annotation more complicated. To be sure, local wordlists, place-name studies, and other types of conventional items continued to appear. But since the late 1960's, features of Southern American English, especially as used by blacks and whites who migrated northward or westward from Southern states in the previous two to three generations, have played a significant role in the growing discussion of variation in American English. The types of literature appearing in the past twenty years includes new types of work such as federally sponsored research reports, ERIC documents, primary and secondary studies for language arts teachers, and analyses linking pidgin and creole languages in the Caribbean and West Africa to the American South. The multi-disciplinary nature of research and commentary on Southern American English required this bibliography to draw from hundreds of technical and specialist journals and monographs and popular sources, in linguistics, speech, rhetoric, literary analysis, sociology, folklore, ethnic affairs, anthropology, state and local history, language teaching, reading, and speech and hearing science, among other fields.

Popular commentary on Southern English is more diverse and difficult to collect than the scholarly material. For two and a half centuries, nonspecialists have commented on language patterns in the Southern United States, the first recorded statements being those of Hugh Jones, whose praise of the "pure" English of the Williamsburg area in his <u>Present State of Virginia</u> (1724) aimed to promote immigration to the colony. Since the early days of the American republic, European and American travelers, journalists, and other commentators have noted what they consider unusual vocabulary and pronunciation in one locality of the South or another. Such observations are often naive, tendentious, and ignore inter-speaker differences, and are offered by non-linguists who usually represent what they have heard only very roughly, but they still frequently provide insight and put linguistic features in a cultural context better than many linguistically informed studies.

Nothing has been said about what properly does and what does not come under the rubric of "Southern English" and specifically which items are included in this bibliography. The first edition set out five principles for the inclusion of items, principles which are adhered to in the second edition, although interpreted somewhat more liberally.

The 1971 edition defines the South as "the area south of the Mason-Dixon line and the Ohio River westward to Arkansas and East Texas. The English used in the southern parts of Ohio, Indiana, Illinois, and Missouri, and in Oklahoma and West Texas shares many features with the speech of the Confederate states, but neither the natives nor linguistic geographers call this English Southern" (1971:7). This second edition includes major works on the speech of peripherally Southern areas--Central and West Texas, Oklahoma, the Missouri Ozarks, and Delaware. For our purposes, then, the South encompasses fourteen states south and west of the Mason-Dixon Line from the Delaware Bay to Texas and includes also the District of Columbia.

Second, we list items on folklore and literary language only if they discuss specific dialect features. Excluded are folklore materials per se, writings in literary dialect, and other primary documentary materials, such as the Southern Historical Collection of letters and other manuscripts at the University of North Carolina at Chapel Hill, and the Work Projects Administration ex-slave narratives. Listing such materials is beyond the scope of the present work.

Third, we include works on foreign languages spoken in the region only when they are concerned with foreign influences on Southern English, such as on place names. Extensive bibliographies on these languages--for example, William A. Read's Louisiana French (1931), Richard V. Teschner et al.'s Spanish and English of United States Hispanics: a Critical, Annotated, Linguistic Bibliography (1976), and James Crawford's Studies in Southeastern Indian Languages (1975)--cover the relevant material well.

Fourth, items in newspapers and local magazines are generally excluded. Not only are they usually quite brief, but also they are inaccessible to most users, especially those items appearing in newspapers. They are too ephemeral for bibliographers to keep track of.

Fifth, general treatments of American English, such as grammars, dictionaries, and usage books that include some commentary on Southern English, were excluded in the first edition on the grounds that users would already know them. In the second edition, they are listed if they have commentary specifically on Southern English patterns.

Since the 1960's, the advent of three new fields of sociolinguistic research has raised important questions about the definition of Southern English and about which materials to include in the second edition of this bibliography. Studies of child language patterns, the speech of ex-

Southerners, especially blacks and Appalachians migrating outside the South, and pidgin and creole languages, raise the question of whether this bibliography should restrict its coverage to studies only of adults living in the former Confederate states.

Child language studies throw light on the history and range of variation in the region's speech, and in recent years scholars have argued that some grammatical features of Southern English share an origin with features in Caribbean creole langugages. Yet the bulk of the literature in these fields, its accessibility in other bibliographies, and problems in interpreting such material have led us to exclude most of the literature in these areas.

The literature on language patterns of schoolchildren, even kindergarteners, is vast. Yet most of it concerns the receptive skills of reading and listening comprehension rather the productive skills of speech and writing. Moreover, since many of the syntactic features in these studies are common to developmental English and to nonstandard dialects, it is unclear at what age we can reasonably stop referring to one and start referring to the other. The labels "child white English" and "child black English" beg this question. The supposition by some researchers that preadolescents preserve basilectal language patterns from generation to generation is at best difficult to substantiate. As a compromise, we have decided to include only studies dealing with the speech of children above the third grade (9 years or older).

The literature on exported or migrant Southern English almost completely postdates the first edition. The relevant work of William Labov, Walt Wolfram, and J. L. Dillard on black speech in Northern cities has just begun to appear in time for inclusion. Yet the literature of this type published since that time has been immense, most prominently the Urban Language Series of studies in Detroit and Washington and other major descriptive works, but also countless smaller, derivative studies usually with a pedagogical emphasis. These latter investigations have diminished noticeably in recent years, so that most of them are annotated in Brasch and Brasch's Comprehensive Annotated Bibliography of American Black English (1974). For students of Southern English, it is important to know what happens when Southern English comes into contact with varieties of American English outside the region, but it is unclear how long an ex-Southerner must live in the North or West for the linguistic situation to no longer be one of regional language contact. The decision here, therefore, has been to include in this bibliography only the major studies.

The literature on Caribbean English pidgins and creoles clearly pertains to Gullah or Sea Island Creole and to earlier stages of Southern English, but we include such works on Jamaican, Guyanese, and other Caribbean creoles only if they mention specific features of Gullah. Except for the most recent work, such items are listed and annotated in the massive and indispensable A Bibliography of Pidgin and Creole Languages (1975) edited by Reinecke et al.

Since a broader range of specialists will consult this second edition, and in order to make it as useful as possible to such nonspecialists as local historians and folklorists and undergraduate students, this bibliography differs from the first edition in the respects listed below.

First, each item is given a longer annotation of from one to three sentences, with extensive cross-references. Annotations are with few exceptions descriptive, not evaluative. They attempt to summarize the study and to indicate the specific features examined.

Second, bracketed abbreviations appear between an entry and its annotation specifying demographic details where they are indicated in the study: number of informants, ethnicity, gender, social class, and age of informants, and location of study. A list of abbreviations used follows this introduction. These specifications allow the user of the bibliography better to gauge the character and assess the findings of each study and to compare items to one another. Unfortunately, such detail is not possible for many items, especially the anecdotal ones that make no distinctions between speakers.

Third, only materials examined by the editors are annotated. Conference papers are excluded and unpublished items are noted only if they are housed in a library and available at least through interlibrary loan. Documents from the ERIC microfiche collection are included because they are available at most research libraries and have most often not been published elsewhere. Only a few items not consultable by the editors are included, these on the basis of their inclusion in a another bibliography, particularly one listed in chapter twelve of the present work.

One of the main efforts of this edition has been to annotate master's theses. The first edition listed 114 of them; the second edition annotates well over 200. Rarely listed in standard bibliographies, and often sitting forgotten on library shelves, many of these items are potentially quite useful to researchers for a variety of comparative purposes.

**Notes on the Entries**

Because the classification of entries is not always straightforward, users of this bibliography should note the following.

Chapter one, "General Studies," includes entries that overlap more than one of the subsequent chapters. Thus, a work covering vocabulary, even one mentioning "vocabulary" in its title, appears in the first chapter if it also has a section on pronunciation or grammar. Chapter one includes anthologies and collections when they contain several items annotated separately in the bibliography and when they have been reviewed in professional journals.

Chapter two, "Historical and Creole Studies," acknowledges the inseparability of historical and creole studies, which means that most contemporary studies of Gullah (Sea Island Creole) are included. It includes entries reporting 18th- and 19th-century usage, as well as those published at least a century ago. Items dealing strictly with the etymology of words usually appear in chapter two rather than in chapter three.

Chapter three, "Lexical Studies," includes, in addition to lexical studies, works on the semantics of Southern English and compilations of dialect expressions from novels and other fiction.

Chapter six, "Place Name Studies," includes entries on the grammar and pronunciation of place names in addition to listings of glossaries and analytic studies. Because of the very large number of short items and notes in Names in South Carolina, the editors decided to list only items from this journal of at least one page in length.

Chapter seven, "Personal and Miscellaneous Names," lists works on personal names, street names, flora and fauna names, sobriquets, names of buildings and institutions, and miscellaneous appellative studies.

Chapter twelve, "Bibliographies," includes specialist bibliographies whose listings overlap with the present work as well as serial bibliographies that will continue to list items dealing with Southern American English in the future.

"See Also" listings at the ends of chapters 2-12 refer the reader to relevant items in other chapters, particularly chapter one.

In each entry, bibliographical information follows Linguistic Society of America style. Abbreviations in the list preceding the first chapter are used for most journal titles and for a number of agencies, institutes, and professional associations. Abstracts of items, especially dissertations, are noted where possible. This includes abstracts of conference papers from the Newsletter of the American Dialect Society; although many such papers are never published, the abstracts provide a useful index to work in progress. Bibliographies (in addition to the self-contained ones reported in chapter 12) are noted where potentially useful. In the annotations, the term "Southern English" in all cases refers to the English language in the Southern United States, and is preferred for its brevity.

A word or two may distinguish how types of excerpted items are handled in this work. If an entry is a chapter from a book by the same author, the title of the chapter is given immediately after the date of the work, as in the following:

Adams, Frazier B. 1970. Colloquial speech forms. Appalachia revisited: how people lived fifty years ago, 47-49. Ashland, KY: Economy. Brief presentation of archaisms.

If more than one section or chapter in a source is cited, then the titles of these will be listed after the place of publication and publisher of the work, and page numbers will follow the section titles, as in the following:

Wise, Claude Merton. 1957. Introduction to phonetics. Englewood-Cliffs, NJ: Prentice-Hall. Deviations from standard General American, Southern, and Eastern speech, 193-204; Southern American English: standard and substandard, 205-20.

If, on the other hand, an excerpt having no title is entered, the relevant page numbers and a short description of the section will follow the place of publication and publisher, as in the following:

Barker, Catherine S. 1941. Yesterday today: life in the Ozarks. Caldwell, ID: Caxton. Pp. 126-32 on dialect.

Where possible, professional reviews of books are noted. Reviews outside the professional literature are usually excluded, especially those in publicity outlets such as <u>Publishers Weekly</u>. Longer reviews--so-called "review articles"--are often listed separately as well as after the item reviewed. Given their number and their normal brevity, however, reviews are excluded from the index unless listed as separate entries. Reprintings of items are noted whenever possible because these may be easier for users to locate than the original publications. They are usually keyed to anthologies and collections entered elsewhere in the bibliography.

Some of the fine detail work, including doublechecking sources in the library, has been accomplished by student assistants, among whom we thank in particular Chin-an Chow, Belkis Fava, Joanna Garrett, Chingkwei Adrienne Lee, Daniel J. Taylor, Amoena Norcross, Hu Ming Liang, and Grady Wilkerson. Colleagues at other universities provided numerous references: Guy Bailey and Fred Tarpley on work in Texas, David Shores and Michael I. Miller on Virginia, Martha Howard on West Virginia, Philip Kolin on Mississippi, William Evans on Louisiana, Bethany Dumas on studies of Ozark speech, and Jeutonne Brewer on literary dialect studies. Librarians at several institutions, particularly the University of South Carolina, the University of Arkansas at Fayetteville, Louisiana State University, the University of Alabama, and the University of South Carolina provided generous assistance and advice. Special praise goes to Daniel Boice, Paula Swope, and Cathy Gottlieb at the last-named institution for the help in obtaining items through interlibrary loan.

The preparation of this work was supported in part by the Small Grants Program of the Southern Regional Education Board and by the Research and Productive Scholarship Program at the University of South Carolina.

# Abbreviations

AA = American Anthropologist
ADS = American Dialect Society
AJ = Appalachian Journal
AL = Alabama
AnL = Anthropological Linguistics
AR = Arkansas
AS = American Speech
ASHA = American Speech and Hearing Association
AZ = Arizona
B = Black
BC = British Columbia
BEV = Black English Vernacular
CA = California
CAL = Center for Applied Linguistics
CE = College English
CENT = Central
CJL = Canadian Journal of Linguistics
CLAJ = College Language Association Journal
CO = Colorado
CT = Connecticut
DA = Dictionary of Americanisms
DAE = Dictionary of American English
DAI = Dissertation Abstracts International
DARE = Dictionary of American Regional English
DE = Delaware
DN = Dialect Notes
E = East, Eastern
ED = ERIC Document
EDD = English Dialect Dictionary
EE = Elementary English
EJ = English Journal
EPDA = Education Profession Development Act

ERIC = Educational Resources Information Center
ETHSP = East Tennessee Historical Society Publications
EWW = English World Wide
F = Female
FFLR = Florida Foreign Language Reporter
FL = Florida
GA = Georgia
GHQ = Georgia Historical Quarterly
HEW = Health Education and Welfare
IA = Iowa
ID = Idaho
IJAL = International Journal of American Linguistics
IL = Illinois
IN = Indiana
IPA = International Phonetic Association
JAF = Journal of American Folklore
JEGP = Journal of English and Germanic Philology
JEL = Journal of English Linguistics
JMMD = Journal of Multilingual and Multicultural Development
JNE = Journal of Negro Education
JNH = Journal of Negro History
JSH = Journal of Southern History
JSHD = Journal of Speech and Hearing Disorders
JSHR = Journal of Speech and Hearing Research
KFR = Kentucky Folklore Record
KY = Kentucky
LA = Louisiana
LAGS = Linguistic Atlas of the Gulf States
LAMSAS = Linguistic Atlas of the Middle and South Atlantic States
LANCS = Linguistic Atlas of the North Central States
LAUSC = Linguistic Atlas of the United States and Canada
LC = Lower Class
LIS = Language in Society
LL = Language Learning
LLBA = Language and Language Behavior Abstracts
LMC = Lower Middle Class
LPLP = Language Problems and Language Planning
LWC = Lower Working Class
M = Male
MC = Middle Class
MD = Maryland
MFR = Mississippi Folklore Register
MLA = Modern Language Association
MLJ = Modern Language Journal
MLN = Modern Language Notes
MLR = Modern Language Review
MO = Missouri
MP = Modern Philology

MS = Mississippi
N = North or Northern
NADS = Newsletter of the American Dialect Society
NC = North Carolina
NCHR = North Carolina Historical Review
NCTE = National Council of Teachers of English
NE = Northeast
NIE = National Institute of Education
NSC = Names in South Carolina
NW = Northwest
NWAV = New Ways of Analyzing Variation
NWAVE = New Ways of Analyzing Variation in English
NY = New York
NYRB = New York Review of Books
NYTBR = New York Times Book Review
OED = Oxford English Dictionary
OH = Ohio
OK = Oklahoma
PADS = Publication of the American Dialect Society
PMLA = Publications of the Modern Language Association
QJS = Quarterly Journal of Speech
S = South, Southern
SAB = South Atlantic Bulletin
SAQ = South Atlantic Quartlery
SAR = South Atlantic Review
SC = South Carolina
SE = Southeast
SFQ = Southern Folklore Quarterly
SIL = Summer Institute of Linguistics
SLA = Special Libraries Association
SSCJ = Southern Speech Communication Journal
SSJ = Southern Speech Journal
SW = Southwest
TESOL = Teachers of English to Speakers of Other Languages
TFSB = Tennessee Folklore Society Bulletin
TN = Tennessee
TX = Texas
UC = Upper Class
UHWPL = University of Hawaii Working Papers in Linguistics
UK = United Kingdom
UMC = Upper Middle Class
USF LangQ = University of South Florida Language Quarterly
UWC = Upper Working Class
VA = Virginia
W = West, Western, or White
WC = Working Class
WI = Wisconsin
WPA = Work Projects Administration

WTHSP = West Tennessee Historical Society Publications
WV = West Virginia
YES = Yearbook of English Studies
YWES = Year's Work in English Studies
ZAA = Zeitschrift für Anglistik und Amerikanistik
ZDL = Zeitschrift für Dialektologie und Linguistik
ZFM = Zeitschrift für Mundartforschung

# Annotated Bibliography of
# Southern American English

# 1 General Studies

**1.1 Aarons, Alfred C., Barbara Y. Gordon, and William A. Stewart**, eds. 1969. Linguistic-cultural differences and American education. Special anthology issue, FFLR 7.1. Forty-three articles, many concerned with Southern dialects and black dialects. **Reviews:** Anonymous. 1970. Children's Education 46.385; Anonymous. 1971. MLJ 55.331.

**1.2 Abrahams, Roger D.** 1970-71. "Talking my talk": black English and social segmentation in black American communities. African Language Review 9.227-54. Discusses generational and sex differences in speech habits in West Indian and black American communities.

**1.3 Abrahams, Roger D., and John F. Szwed.** 1975. Black English: an essay review. AA 77.329-35. Synoptic review of eleven books on black speech.

**1.4 Abrahams, Roger D., and Rudolph Troike,** eds. 1972. Language and cultural diversity in American education. Englewood Cliffs, NJ: Prentice-Hall. 339 pp. Anthology of thirty-five articles includes many on social dialects. **Reviews:** N. Domingue. 1975. Language Sciences 35.27-31; N. Gary. 1975. Language 51.720-30; R. W. Shuy. 1975. AA 77.961-62.

**1.5 Adams, Emmett.** 1978. 'Pon honor. Ozarks Mountaineer 26.3.10. Comments on poke, you-ens, and other Ozark usages.

**1.6 Adams, Frazier B.** 1970. Colloquial speech forms. Appalachia revisited: how people lived fifty years ago, 47-49. Ashland, KY: Economy. Brief presentation of archaisms. **Review:** C. S. Guthrie. 1970. KFR 16.81.

**1.7 Adams, Minnie H.** 1940. A survey of the general characteristics of Virginia dialects. Iowa City: University of Iowa thesis. 55 pp. Surveys and compiles features from previously published research, especially Dingus (**1.200**) and Shewmake (**4.308**).

**1.8 Akers, William.** 1974. Black English: an American sociolinguistic problem. Antiquitates indogermanicae: studien zur indogermanischen altertumskunde und zur sprache- und kulturgeschichte der indogermanischen volker, ed. by Manfred Mayrhofer, et al., 505-14. Innsbruck. Overview of sociolinguistic and educational situation surrounding phenomenon of "black English."

**1.9 Alexander, Danny.** 1977. An analysis of the language of northeast Texas CB conversations. Commerce: East Texas State University thesis. 126 pp., including transcripts. A study primarily of "nonstandard" grammar and pronunciation, and slang vocabulary used by Citizens Band radio operators, especially truck drivers.

**1.10 Allen, Harold B.** 1977. Regional dialects, 1945-1974. AS 52.163-261. Bibliography, 242-61. Survey of recent research and work in progress, covering regional, urban, and feature studies, regional occupational glossaries, studies of external influences, theory and methodology, and interdisciplinary applications.

**1.11 Allen, Harold B., and Michael Linn,** eds. 1986. Dialect and language variation. New York: Academic. 616 pp. Anthology of thirty-nine previously published articles on American English.

**1.12 Allen, Harold B., and Gary N. Underwood,** eds. 1971. Readings in American dialectology. New York: Appleton Century Crofts. 584 pp. Forty-one essays on aspects of regional and social dialects. **Reviews:** J. Appleby. 1971. AS 46.158-59; N. Conklin. 1971. LL 21.269-74.

**1.13 Appleby, Jane.** 1973. Is Southern English good? SAB 35.15-19. Subjective essay defending the validity and value of regional standards of American English and argues fallacy of efforts to train speakers out of their native accents. **Reprinted** in D. Shores and C. Hines 1977(**1.689**).225-28.

**1.14 Arkansas Times staff.** 1979. Arkansas talk: plain, fancy and sometimes downright obflisticated. Arkansas Times (Mar.), pp. 35-39. Popular account of extravagant expressions and unusual language in the state.

**1.15 Armstrong, Bondie.** 1982. A study of dialect and its interference with learning to write. Memphis: Memphis State University dissertation. Abstract in DAI 43.2335A. [25 M, 5 F, ages 18-46; 15 from Memphis, TN, 6 others from elsewhere in South]. Finds little difference in error frequencies and error types in writing and speech, using Harbrace College Handbook to determine "errors"; concludes there is no direct relationship between speech and writing and therefore that "dialect" is no barrier to learning to write.

**1.16 Arnold, Oren.** 1959. Laughter is to live. This is the South, ed. by Robert W. Howard, 175-80. Chicago: Rand McNally. Vindication of humor and idiosyncrasies of Southern speech by a native.

**1.17 Arnow, Harriet Simpson.** 1963. The sounds of humankind. Flowering of the Cumberland, 121-55. New York: Macmillan. [S Appalachia]. Descriptive essay by novelist on range of language and verbal activity in Cumberland mountains.

**1.18 Atlanta model, a program for improving basic skills.** 1967. ED 018 519. 12 pp. [9 high schools in Atlanta, GA]. Reports on communication skills laboratories set up to overcome racial and social differences in speech patterns, reading ability, and social behavior.

**1.19 Atwood, E. Bagby.** 1963. The methods of American dialectology. ZFM 30.1-29. History of study of American dialects, with detailed survey of Linguistic Atlas projects and discussion of their methodology. **Reprinted** in H. Allen and G. Underwood 1971(**1.12**).5-35; in H. Allen and M. Linn 1986(**1.11**).63-97.

**1.20 Atwood, E. Bagby.** 1968. Amerikanische dialektologie. Germanische dialektologie. Festschrift für Walther Mitzka zum 80. geburtstag, 565-600. Wiesbaden: Steiner. Translation of preceding item.

**1.21 Austin, Jessie Gardner.** 1969. Syntactic maturity as an element of class dialect. Tuscaloosa: University of Alabama dissertation. Abstract in DAI 30.3442A. [5th graders, Cullman, AL]. Studies relationship between nonstandard usage, syntactic maturity, and levels of intelligence, finds syntactic maturity is an element of class dialect in writing but in speech has no determinable relationship to social class.

**1.22 Austin, William M.** 1965. Some social aspects of paralanguage. CJL 11.31-39. Presents notational system for representing paralinguistic features of different varieties of speech, including lower-class black speech. **Reprinted** in R. McDavid and W. Austin 1966(**1.468**).

**1.23 Babcock, Bernie.** 1922. The American language. Arkansas Writer 3.17-18. Reviews Mencken (**1.508**) and comments on AR speech.

**1.24 Bailey, Beryl Loftman.** 1965. Toward a new perspective in Negro English dialectology. AS 40.171-77. Finds similarities between Jamaican Creole and American black speech (using dialogue from Warren Miller's The Cool World as data for latter) and suggests that "the Southern Negro 'dialect' differs from other Southern speech because its deep structure is different, having its origins as it undoubtedly does in some proto-creole grammatical structure." **Reprinted** in H. Allen and G. Underwood 1971(**1.12**).421-27; in W. Wolfram and N. Clarke 1971(**1.853**).41-50.

**1.25 Bailey, Charles-James N.** 1968. Is there a "midland" dialect of

American English? ED 021 240. 7 pp. Opposes term "South Midland" as used by Linguistic Atlas writers and claims preponderance of phonological and grammatical evidence groups region with the South rather than with the "North Midland."

**1.26 Bailey, Charles-James N.** 1973. Variation and linguistic theory. Arlington: CAL. viii + 162 pp. Presents new "dynamic paradigm" for describing direction and rate of linguistic change and variation using a wave model; analysis based mainly on phonological data, with many examples from Southern English. **Reviews:** R. R. Butters. 1976. Language Sciences 40.32-36; V. Heeschen. 1976. Anthropos 71.298-99; A. S. Kaye. 1981. AS 56.236-38; J. Sherzer. 1975. AA 77.667-68; E. C. Traugott. 1976. Language 52.502-06; W. Wolfram. 1977. General Linguistics 17.178-85.

**1.27 Bailey, Charles-James N.** 1973. The patterning of language variation. Varieties of present-day English, ed. by Richard W. Bailey and Jay L. Robinson, 156-86. New York: Macmillan. Theoretical essay synopsizing author's wave model for language variation and change.

**1.28 Bailey, Charles-James N.** 1974. The giddy and gaudy but guileful glamor of gadfly glottometry bzw. tell me not in mirthful numbers. Lectological Newsletter 2.3.1-5. Discusses whether and how social patterns of linguistic variation are more regular than individual patterns and whether "knowledge" of this variation is available to anyone but native speakers.

**1.29 Bailey, Charles-James N.** 1975. Funny figures of Fuzz Fasold's faltering followers finally found frankly flimsy and feeble and in fact furnish futile defence for fending off fearful feeling in failing fight before fervent foes of fanciful frenzies and fitful, if not furtive, forces of unfortunate foolishness and phoney feints of few flustered flukes or: faulty findings forfeit future firstfruits in face of furious forces fatefully forestalling and fighting off frigidity of frightful follies and fake effort of unfavored fumblings and flaccid failures. Lectological Newsletter 3.1.4-8. Disagrees with Fasold (**1.234**).

**1.30 Bailey, Charles-James N.** 1980. Conceptualizing dialects as implicational constellations rather than as entities bounded by isoglossic bundles. Dialekt und dialektologie: ergebnisse des internationalen symposions "Zur theorie des dialeckte." Marban/Lahn, 5-10 September 1977, ed. by J. Goschel, P. Ivic, and K. Kehr, 234-72. Wiesbaden: Franz Steiner Verlag. Beiheft neue folge no. 26. of ZFM. Corrigenda in TUB-Arbeitspapiere zur Linguistik 10.228.

**1.31 Bailey, Charles-James N., and Roger W. Shuy,** eds. 1974. New ways of analyzing variation in English. Washington: Georgetown University Press. 373 pp. Anthology of articles on quantitative analysis of sociolinguistic variation from first NWAVE meeting. **Reviews:** R. Darnell. 1975. AA 77.119-20; R. Lass. 1976. LIS 5.219-29; G. R. Wood. 1974. AS 49.278-81.

**1.32 Bailey, Guy.** 1981. A social history of the gulf states. LAGS Working Papers 1, 2nd series. 215 pp. Addendum to Pederson, et al. 1981(**1.594**). Detailed account of settlement history and development of LAGS territory; focuses on physiography, settlement history, antebellum cultural structure, and postwar and modern developments, with discussion of each LAGS sector with reference to these topics.

**1.33 Bailey, Guy.** 1987. [Are black and white vernaculars diverging?] AS 62.32-40. Part of 1985 NWAV discussion; argues in favor of divergence, citing evidence for reanalysis of unmarked be verb for younger black speakers.

**1.34 Bailey, Guy.** 1989. Black English. Encyclopedia of Southern culture, ed. by William Ferris and Charles Wilson. Chapel Hill: University of North Carolina Press. Short essay discussing main linguistic features of the dialect and different points of view in controversies over the relation of black spech to white speech and the origin of black English.

**1.35 Bailey, Guy.** 1989. Linguistic atlas of the gulf states. Encyclopedia of Southern culture, ed. by William Ferris and Charles Wilson. Chapel Hill: University of North Carolina Press. Short history discussing history, methods, and components of LAGS project.

**1.36 Bailey, Guy.** 1989. Conch. Encyclopedia of Southern culture, ed. by William Ferris and Charles Wilson. Chapel Hill: University of North Carolina Press. [S FL]. Discusses unique sociolinguistic history and multiple sources of vocabulary of FL Keys.

**1.37 Bailey, Guy, and Natalie Maynor.** 1987. Decreolization? LIS 16.449-74. [7 B adults over 70, 20 B children ages 12-13, Brazos Valley, E CENT TX]. Challenges three assumptions behind consensus of recent research on Black English Vernacular--that grammars of children and adults are alike, that BEV is decreolizing, and that most white speech/BEV differences are result of persisting creole features; shows that younger black speakers are reanalyzing present tense of be in manner different from older black speech and all varieties of white speech.

**1.38 Bailey, Joan Smith.** 1971. Southern Appalachian non-standard speech in conflict with the standard English of the classroom. Johnson City: East Tennessee State University thesis. 50 pp. [65 high school students, 59M, 6F, with composition problems, E TN]. Explores ways to improve attitudes of failureprone speakers of Appalachian English toward their language.

**1.39 Bailey, Richard W., and Jay L. Robinson,** eds. 1973. Varieties of present-day English. New York: Macmillan. 461 pp. Collection of eighteen original and reprinted essays on English in the modern world, the English language in America, and the English language in the classroom. **Review:** G. R. Wood. 1974. AS 49.278-81.

**1.40 Baird, Scott.** 1980. Tombstone talk: multilingualism in south Texas, and consorts in North Carolina. Abstract in NADS 12.2.3-4. Discusses how cemetery data reveal minority language shift and maintenance and how usage of word consort on gravestones is more precise than in dictionaries.

**1.41 Baird, Scott.** 1984. A preliminary look at Texas LAGS. Abstract in NADS 16.3.8. [E TX]. Evaluates extent of TX dialect data in LAGS and compares this data with Arthur Norman's (**1.544**) SE TX study.

**1.42 Baird, Scott.** 1987. LAGS and the "southwest" dialect of Texas. Abstract in NADS 19.3.4. Reports eight phonological variables and vocabulary items distinctive of Southwestern English below San Antonio, TX; based on ten LAGS records.

**1.43 Baird, Scott, and Annaliese Duncan.** 1984. Variation in a German dialect: evidence from tombstone inscriptions. Methods V, ed. by H. J. Warkentyne, 93-106. Victoria, BC: University of Victoria. Abstract in NADS 16.2.10. Based on German and German-English gravestone inscriptions in NC, TX, and Germany.

**1.44 Bandy, Lewis David.** 1940. Language and beliefs. Folklore of Macon County, Tennessee, 52-63. Nashville: George Peabody College thesis. [N CENT TN]. Informal survey of unusual speech, especially lexical items.

**1.45 Baratz, Joan C.** 1969. Linguistic and cultural factors in teaching reading to ghetto children. EE 46.199-203. [Washington, DC]. Says black ghetto child speaks "a significantly different language from that of his middle class teachers."

**1.46 Baratz, Joan C.** 1969. A bi-dialectal task for determining language proficiency in economically disadvantaged Negro children. Child Development 40.889-901. ED 020 519. [B, W, 3rd, 5th graders, Washington, DC]. Finds white children have same difficulties repeating sentences in "Negro nonstandard English" as black children repeating sentences in "standard English" and that black and white children have equal difficulty in identifying speakers of other race.

**1.47 Baratz, Joan C.** 1969. Language and cognitive assessment of Negro children: assumptions and research needs. American Speech and Hearing Association 11.87-91. Says assessment must be based on a "sense of the ghetto child's culture: how he organizes his world, what his language system is, what his learning patterns are," and other considerations.

**1.48 Baratz, Joan C.** 1973. Language abilities of black Americans. Comparative studies of blacks and whites in the United States, ed. by Kent S. Miller and Ralph Mason Dreger, 125-83. New York: Seminar Press. Extensive review of linguistic, anthropological, educational, and psychological literature on black English and attitudes toward it.

**1.49 Baratz, Joan C., and Roger W. Shuy,** eds. 1969. Teaching black children to read. Washington: CAL. 219 pp. Eight essays by sociolinguists and reading specialists. **Reviews:** M. Baumkel. 1970. EE 48.90-94; J. Fishman. 1969. Science 165.1108-09; B. Y. Gordon. 1969. FFLR 7.149-50,175; M. S. Minor. 1972. Linguistics 86.94-98; L. Pederson. 1975. AS 50.98-110.

**1.50 Barker, Catherine S.** 1941. Yesterday today: life in the Ozarks. Caldwell, ID: Caxton. Pp. 126-32 on dialect. Identifies usages in Ozarks reminiscent of Chaucerian times and Old English period.

**1.51 Barnette, William.** 1980. Three variables in black and white type I speech in upper middle Tennessee. Abstract in NADS 12.3.4. [4 older speakers, 2 M, 2 F, 2 W, 2 B]. Comments on patterns of a-prefixing, final consonant cluster simplification, and oral paragraphing in Middle TN speech.

**1.52 Barnhill, Viron L., and George F. Reinecke.** 1989. Indian trade languages of the Southeast. Encyclopedia of Southern culture, ed. by William Ferris and Charles Wilson. Chapel Hill: University of North Carolina Press. Short essay on Mobilian and other American Indian lingua francas in the South.

**1.53 Bassett, Marvin.** 1981. A preliminary program for LAGS typescripting. LAGS Working Papers, 1st series, no. 16. Microfiche 1197. Addendum to Pederson, et al. 1981(**1.594**). 14 pp. Describes a method for putting LAGS field records in typed format and identifies problems in doing this.

**1.54 Bassett, Marvin, and Susan Leas.** 1981. LAGS field records: form and content. LAGS Working Papers, 1st series, no. 10. Microfiche 1191. Addendum to Pederson, et al. 1981(**1.594**). 35 pp. Describes, analyzes, and evaluates physical characteristics of LAGS collection and discusses difficulties of making professional quality recordings in the field.

**1.55 Baubkus, Lutz, and Wolfgang Viereck.** 1973. Recent American studies in sociolinguistics. Archivum Linguisticum n.s. 4.103-12. Reviews Urban Language Series studies of black speech, especially Wolfram's work (**1.835**) in Detroit.

**1.56 Baugh, John.** 1983. A survey of Afro-American English. Annual Review of Anthropology 12.335-54. Surveys educational and linguistic research on black speech and discusses needed research and emerging topics.

**1.57 Baugh, John.** 1983. Black street speech: its history, structure, and survival. Austin: University of Texas Press. x + 149 pp. Social, stylistic, and linguistic analysis of black speech, based on study in Los Angeles, Austin, Houston, Philadelphia, and Chicago; discusses implications for employment and education of blacks and deals with wider range of speech styles than other treatments. **Reviews**: R. Burling. 1985. Language 61.204-06; W. Edwards. 1986. Journal of Pragmatics 10.503-06; S. Mufwene. 1985. AS 60.161-66; A. Spears. 1985. LIS 14.101-08.

**1.58 Baugh, John, and Joel Sherzer**, eds. 1984. Language in use: readings in sociolinguistics. Englewood Cliffs, NJ: Prentice-Hall. 316 pp. Anthology of seventeen articles.

**1.59 Bauman, Richard, and Joel Sherzer**, eds. 1974. Explorations in the ethnography of speaking. New York: Cambridge University Press. vii + 501 pp. Anthology of essays on sociolinguistics and language variation. **Reviews**: R. A. Borker. 1976. Reviews in Anthropology 3.152-59; M. Bloch. 1976. LIS 5.229-34; J. Clammer. 1976. Sociology 10.157-58; J. Fishman. 1977. AA 79.160-61; E. Leach. 1976. Semiotica 16.87-97; R. B. Le Page. 1975. Times Literary Supplement 3820:568 (May 23); C. Lefebvre. 1976. IJAL 42.382-83; K. A. Watson. 1976. Language 52.745-48.

**1.60 Beckham, A. S.** 1917. Characteristics and decline of Negro dialects. Columbus: Ohio State University thesis. 28 pp. [AR, AL, KY]. Says dialect has declined in songs and poetry; using word-lists from Dialect Notes, surveys speakers in three states for generational differences in familiarity with older forms.

**1.61 Bell, Ellen Faye.** 1973. Comparison of features of black and white speech: Bradley, Ga. Chapel Hill: University of North Carolina thesis. 56 pp. [6 B, 6 W, older women, CENT GA]. Surveys phonological, morphosyntactic, and lexical features; finds zero copula and unmarked verbs three times more frequent in black speech; says whites and blacks share most features but blacks tend to use "a much broader range of variations much more frequently than did white speakers."

**1.62 Bell, W. Herman.** 1936. A better speech for Virginians? Virginia Journal of Education 29.236. Says cultivation of better speech habits depends on favorable attitudes toward good speech and on public speaking courses.

**1.63 Benardete, Delores.** 1932. Eloise. AS 7.349-64. [FL]. Represents elderly black woman's speech and comments on her phonology, grammar, and vocabulary.

**1.64 Bentley, Robert H., and Samuel D. Crawford**, eds. 1973. Black language reader. Glencoe, IL: Scott, Foresman. 256 pp. Twenty-eight essays by sociolinguists and other specialists.

**1.65 Berrey, Lester V.** 1940. Southern mountain dialect. AS 15.45-54. [S Appalachia]. General features of Appalachian phonology, morphology, syntax, dialect subregions.

**1.66 Berrian, Albert H., and Marianna Davis.** 1977. Strategies for solving problems of language acquisition: a blueprint for action. ED 147 865. 57 pp. Reports on two-day conference in Atlanta on teaching writing skills and standard English to dialectally different students in the South.

**1.67 Beveridge, Tom.** 1979. Tom Beveridge's Ozarks. Pacific Grove, CA: Boxwood Press. Sections on "Ozark Redundancies," "Idioms and Accents," and "Speech Patterns."

**1.68 Bierschwale, Margaret.** 1920. English of the Texas range. New York: Columbia University thesis. Compilation of material from dictionaries, novels, poems, and other sources.

**1.69 Billiard, Charles E.** 1972. Linguistic geography and the classroom teacher. A manual for dialect research in the Southern states, ed. by Lee Pederson et al., 77-95. Atlanta: Georgia State University. 2nd ed. 1974. University: University of Alabama Press. Same as ED 103 850. 3rd ed. 1981 published as Microfiche 0002-0004 in Pederson et al. 1981(**1.594**). Essay discussing relevance of findings on regional dialects to English teachers in the classroom.

**1.70 Billiard, Charles E.** 1975. Dialectology and the process of discovery in the classroom. ED 111 031. 15 pp. Describes graduate course for language-arts teachers at Georgia State University in Atlanta using field-work to explore and gain appreciation of language differences.

**1.71 Billiard, Charles E., and Lee Pederson.** 1979. Composition of the LAGS urban complement: Atlanta words. Orbis 28.223-41. Discusses development, initial use, and composition of 199-item LAGS supplement to worksheets used in sixteen urban centers in the Gulf States.

**1.72 Blake, Robert W., and Raven I. McDavid, Jr.** 1969. Social variety in American English: Raven McDavid at the linguistics institute. English Record 19.4.32-47. Introduction to and transcript of McDavid lecture on background to Communicative Barriers to the Culturally Deprived project (**1.468**); McDavid notes social differences in Southern speech greater than in other regions and criticizes Golden (**1.269-70**) and Lin (**1.394**) approaches to dialect remediation as uninformed about regional standards of pronunciation.

**1.73 Blanton, Linda.** 1985. Southern Appalachia: social considerations of speech. Toward a social history of American English, by J. L. Dillard, 73-90. The Hague: Mouton. Argues for existence of identifiable dialect called Southern Appalachian English "on the basis of cultural solidarity, the boundaries of this dialect [being] more social, more cultural, than geographical"; also argues that the dialect is composed of two varieties--a standard and a nonstandard, both of which have features socially stigmatized by other speakers of American English.

**1.74 Blanton, Linda.** 1989. Mountain English. Encyclopedia of Southern culture, ed. by William Ferris and Charles Wilson. Chapel Hill: University of North Carolina Press. Short essay discussing nature and major grammatical features of Southern Appalachian and Ozark speech.

**1.75 Blanton, Mackie J.-V.** 1989. New Orleans English. Encyclopedia of Southern culture, ed. by William Ferris and Charles Wilson. Chapel Hill: University of North Carolina Press. [LA]. Describes shades and varieties of English in "the Crescent City," especially with regard to vocabulary and semantics.

**1.76 Blu, Karen I.** 1980. "Talking Indian." The Lumbee problem: the making of an American Indian people, 160-62. New York: Cambridge University Press. [SE NC]. Points out function of "Indian dialect" in expressing solidarity and identity of Lumbees but cites no features of this dialect.

**1.77 Blum-West, Dina.** 1983. The need for a descriptive study of Appalachian children's language development. Abstract in Critical essays in Appalachian Life and Culture: Proceedings of the Fifth Annual Apalachian Studies Conference, ed. by Rick Simon, 108. Boone, NC: Appalachian Consortium. Says lack of research on children's language patterns in Appalachia "poses a grave problem for language assessment and educational planning in the region."

**1.78 Bond, George Foot.** 1939. A study of an Appalachian dialect. Gainesville: University of Florida thesis. 119 pp. [6M, 2F, ages 20s-90s, Broad River Valley, W NC]. Surveys pronunciation and vocabulary.

**1.79 Bondurant, Alexander.** 1895. Dialect in the United States. Dial 18.104-05. Anecdotal discussion of get shet of, adverbial right, and other forms from the South.

**1.80 Booker, Karen M., and Robert L. Rankin.** 1989. Aboriginal languages. Encyclopedia of Southern culture, ed. by William Ferris and Charles Wilson. Chapel Hill: University of North Carolina Press.

**1.81 Boone, Lalia Phipps.** 1951. The language of the oil fields. Gainesville: University of Florida dissertation. 606 pp. [Mostly TX and OK]. Analysis and glossary of terms peculiar to petroleum industry, including technical and nontechnical terms from industry literature and slang and colloquial expressions collected through fieldwork.

**1.82 Boswell, George W.** 1951. An abstract of reciprocal influences of text and tune in the Southern traditional ballad. Nashville: George Peabody College dissertation.

**1.83 Boswell, George W.** 1967. A dialect sampling of Mississippi. MFR 1.15-19. Compares speech patterns in four parts of MS.

**1.84 Boswell, George W.** 1971. Class competition in Kentucky dialect study. KFR 17.48-52. [NE KY]. Discusses generational differences in familiarity with archaic terms, with particular reference to thirteen items; finds greatest difference between 15-25 and 25-50 age groups.

**1.85 Boswell, George W.** 1973. The operation of popular etymology in folksong diction. TFSB 39.37-58. List of 221 variants of pronunciation, morphology, syntax, names, onomatopoeia, and neology in Middle TN folksongs.

**1.86 Boswell, George W.** 1979. Irony in campus speech. TFSB 45.154-60. Classifies and discusses sixty-five representative ironic locutions collected in folk literature courses at University of Mississippi.

**1.87 Boswell, George W.** 1982. Potpourri of Mississippi dialect. MFR 16.2.25-32. Unusual pronunciations, names, slang, and proverbs from Univ. of Mississippi students and from WPA archives.

**1.88 Botkin, Ben A., ed.** 1949. A treasury of Southern folklore: stories, ballads, traditions, and folksays of the people of the South. New York: Crown. **Reviews:** E. A. Davis. 1950. JSH 16.385-86; R. M. Dorson. 1950-51. Mississippi Valley Historical Review 37.354-55; F. M. Farmer. 1950. NCHR 27.374-75; J. G. Fletcher. 1950. Arkansas Historical Quarterly 9.127.

**1.89 Bountress, Nicholas.** 1977. Approximations of selected standard English sentences by speakers of black English. JSHR 20.254-62. [48 B, ages 4-9, N CENT TX]. Cross-sectional study of six features, including copula use, third person singular -s, possessive -s, and initial "th" sounds, in speech of black children.

**1.90 Bowler, Ruth.** 1957. "Ozarkian" is a language of its own. Ozarks Mountaineer 5.14-15. Says Ozark speech "is a soft-spoken easy-going language that bespeaks a kindliness that comes from an unhurried life not beset with the worries of trying to be proper" and that phonics did not work for Ozarks children for word like any, which is not in their vocabulary.

**1.91 Bowles, Philip D.** 1976. Religious language among Southern Nazarenes: a pilot study. Murfreesboro: Middle Tennessee State University thesis. [18 students at Trevecca Nazarene College, Nashville]. Study of register and semantic domains of Nazarene discourse.

**1.92 Bowman, Blanche S.** 1940. Study of a dialect employed by the people of Kentucky mountains and presented through a group of original short stories. Manhattan: Kansas State University thesis. 250 pp. Discussion of E KY speech by schoolteacher who cites forms from fiction to exemplify local patterns.

**1.93 Bowman, Elizabeth S.** 1938. Land of high horizons. Kingsport, TN:

Southern. [S Appalachia]. Pp. 45-47, discusses general qualities of mountain speech.

**1.94 Bowman, Hazel L.** 1948. Background material for the study of Florida speech. Gainesville: University of Florida thesis. 151 pp. Surveys cultural influences on and historical background and sources of evidence for FL speech; outlines contemporary FL speech patterns.

**1.95 Braddock, Clayton.** 1969. Where standard English seems foreign and is taught as if it were. Southern Education Report 4.6.18-21. Condensed in Education Digest 34.52-53. [W FL]. Discusses rationale for and presents instructional program of drills for teaching English to black school children to "erase a racial stigma by teaching English to the youngsters as if it were a foreign language."

**1.96 Bradley, Francis W.** 1952. The press as an ally in collecting folk speech. PADS 17.29-39. [SC]. Discusses rationale and procedures for collecting dialect material through a regular newspaper column that solicits and publishes popular contributions, and documents six-month effort to do this.

**1.97 Bradley, William Aspenwall.** 1915. In Shakespeare's America. Harper's 131.436-45. Antiquated speech and other relics from KY, where "the purest English on earth" is spoken.

**1.98 Brandes, Paul D., and Jeutonne Brewer.** 1977. Dialect clash in America: issues and answers. Metuchen, NJ: Scarecrow. Same as ED 144 068. Appalachian Amerenglish, 251-311. Black Amerenglish, 316-53. Southern Amerenglish, 468-521. Mainly for teachers, these chapters synopsize settlement and cultural history of the regions and give a non-technical sketch of distinctive syntactic, phonological, lexical, and nonverbal communication patterns of different groups of Southerners. Extensive bibliographies. **Reviews:** E. Jongsma. 1978. Reading Teacher 31.957-58; J. Ornstein. 1978. MLJ 62.441-42; J. C. Scott. 1978. SSCJ 43.418-20; S. M. Tsuzaki. 1978. QJS 64.353-54.

**1.99 Bray, Rose Altizer.** 1950. Disappearing dialect. Antioch Review 10.279-88. [S Appalachia]. Describes mountaineers' English as Elizabethan; lists archaisms in phonology, morphology, syntax, and lexicon.

**1.100 Brewer, Jeutonne P., and Robert W. Reising.** 1982. Tokens in the Pocosin: Lumbee English in North Carolina. AS 57.108-20. Abstract in NADS 12.3.9. **Reprinted** in Essays in Native American English, ed. by Guillermo Bartelt, Susan Penfield Jasper, and Bates L. Hoffer, 33-54. 1982. Papers in Southwest English IX. San Antonio: Trinity University. [Robeson Co., NC]. Discusses diphthong /aɪ/ and unusual and archaic vocabulary in speech of rural Indians in southeastern NC and compares findings to LAMSAS data.

**1.101 Brookes, Stella B.** 1950. Joel Chandler Harris--folklorist. Athens: University of Georgia Press. Proverbs and folk-say, 97-110, compendium of examples, little commentary; Dialect, 111-19, quotes extensively from Harris' own writings about his treatment of dialect. Reviews: S. Mandel. 1950. Saturday Review of Literature 38.41.42 (Oct. 14); C. M. Puckette. 1951. JSH 17.101-02; N. P. Tillman. 1951. Phylon 12.202-03.

**1.102 Brooks, Cleanth, Jr.** 1937. The English language in the South. A Southern treasury of life and literature, ed. by Stark Young, 350-58. New York: Scribner's. Says Southern whites and especially blacks preserve more 17th-century and other old speech features than other Americans because of isolation, a strong oral tradition, and a lack of sharp social class distinctions. Reprinted in R. C. Beatty, ed. 1944. A Vanderbilt miscellany, 179-87. Nashville: Vanderbilt University Press; in R. C. Beatty, and W. P. Fidler, eds. 1940. Contemporary Southern prose, 49-57. New York: Heath; in R. C. Beatty, et al., eds. 1968. The literature of the South, 744-50. New York: Scott-Foresman. 2nd ed. 1968, pp. 705-10; in J. Williamson and V. Burke 1971(**1.823**).136-42.

**1.103 Brooks, Cleanth.** 1980. Foreword. The run for the Elbertas, by James Still, ix-xiii. Lexington: University Press of Kentucky. Praises Still's language as "idiomatic, highly concrete, richly metaphoric," and having "the lilt of oral speech" and says it is central to Still's protrayal of a culture sharply different from contemporary urban America.

**1.104 Brooks, Cleanth.** 1985. The language of the American South. Mercer University Lamar Memorial Lectures no. 28. Athens: University of Georgia Press. 57 pp. Three subjective essays discussing and exemplifying distinctive uses of language in Southern fiction and hypothesizing that speech of lower South descends principally from Southern counties of England. Reviews: R. Bailey. 1986. EWW 7.159-61; R. Butters. 1986. SAR 51.183-85; E. J. Piacentino. 1987. Southern Humanities Review 21.88-91; J. Sledd. 1986. Southern English Newsletter 4.4-5.

**1.105 Brooks, Robert Preston.** 1952. Of murdering the language. Georgia studies: selected writings, ed. by Gregor Sebba, 184-86. Athens: University of Georgia Press. Comments that two common misconceptions of Southern usage of English are the pronunciation of I as "Ah" and the use of you-all in the singular.

**1.106 Brown, Calvin.** 1975. A glossary of Faulkner's South. New Haven: Yale University Press. 241 pp. Handbook to Faulkner's fiction; includes idioms, folk etymologies, terms of address, regionalisms, and other obscure items and expressions crucial to understanding Faulkner's fiction. Review: J. H. Hall. 1976. AS 51.238-43.

**1.107 Brown, Sterling A.** 1986. On dialect usage. The slave's narrative, ed. by Charles T. Davis and Henry Louis Gates, Jr., 37-39. New York:

Oxford University Press. Directions to WPA fieldworkers on representing dialect forms in writing down narratives of ex-slaves.

**1.108 Burghardt, Lorraine H., ed.** 1971. Dialectology: problems and perspectives. Knoxville: University of Tennessee Department of English. 142 pp. Collection of six essays, most concerning fieldwork for and editing of linguistic atlas research for TN. **Review:** R. K. O'Cain. 1971. AS 46.246-54.

**1.109 Burks, Ann, and Polly Guilford.** 1969. Wakulla County oral language project. EE 46.606-11. [NW FL]. Presents and details audiolingual program to teach black primary school children to speak "Standard English" as auxiliary dialect, not as foreign language; appends list of phonological and morphological features called "substitutions," "omissions," and "additions" that program is designed to change.

**1.110 Burling, Robbins.** 1970. Black English. Man's many voices, 117-34. New York: Holt, Rinehart and Winston. Discusses origin of social aspects of the dialect and summarizes its principal structural characteristics. **Reprinted** in H. Allen and M. Linn, eds. 1981. Readings in Applied English Linguistics, 246-58. New York: Knopf.

**1.111 Burling, Robbins.** 1973. English in black and white. New York: Holt, Rinehart and Winston. Same as ED 095 529. 178 pp. Oriented for teachers, examines pronunciation, grammar, and functions of black English, attitudes toward it, its origin, and the educational and social implications of its use. **Reviews:** R. Abrahams and J. Szwed. 1975. AA 77.329-35; R. C. Hudson. 1974. EJ 63.94-95; E. G. Pender. 1974. Educational Leadership 31.469-70; C. Pfaff. 1975. Language 51.770-76; W. Wolfram. 1974. Journal of Ethnic Studies 2.1.113-16; R. Wright. 1975. LIS 4.185-98.

**1.112 Butters, Ronald R.** 1972. Competence, performance, and variable rules. Language Sciences 20.29-32. Argues that Houston's view (**1.330**) of competence-performance distinction is too simple and that she cannot account for variation between child black and white speech on basis of performance rules alone.

**1.113 Butters, Ronald R.** 1984. When is English 'Black English'? JEL 17.29-36. Discusses criteria for defining "Black English"; mentions Southern features.

**1.114 Butters, Ronald R.** 1987. Overview: death of black English? Survey of evidence for convergence and linguistic divergence of black/white English. Abstract in NADS 19.3.9. Surveys issues on controversy over whether white and black vernacular varieties of American English are diverging and concludes "that the divergence is not nearly so extreme or alarming as some linguists . . . have proclaimed."

**1.115 Butters, Ronald R.** 1987. Linguistic convergence in a North Carolina community. Variation in language NWAV-XV at Stanford: proceedings of the fifteenth annual conference on new ways of analyzing variation, ed. by Keith M. Denning, Sharon Inkelas, Faye C. McNair-Knox, and John R. Rickford, 52-60. Stanford: Stanford University Department of Linguistics. [Wilmington, NC]. Compares two phonological and two grammatical features in speech of fifteen black adolescents and one older white in Wilmington with findings of Wolfram in Detroit and Labov in New York, concluding Wilmington is "a linguistic community where--if any generalizations can be made at all--one finds black/white convergence, not divergence."

**1.116 Butters, Ronald R., and Ruth A. Nix.** 1986. The English of blacks in Wilmington, North Carolina. Language variety in the South: perspectives in black and white, ed. by Michael Montgomery and Guy Bailey, 254-63. University: University of Alabama Press. [SE NC]. Investigates pronunciation and grammar of black teenagers in Wilmington and finds their speech much less divergent from standard speech patterns than speech of comparable black teenagers in Northern innercities.

**1.117 Byron, Gilbert.** 1965. Eastern shore idiom. Maryland English Journal 4.12-14. [E MD]. Specimens of proverbs, colorful place names, and vocabulary of Chesapeake Bay area.

**1.118 Campbell, A. A.** 1978. The influence of Southern and Midland dialects in the Huntsville area. Huntsville: Sam Houston State University. [S TX].

**1.119 Campbell, Anna L.** 1956. A study of some factors in the written language of a group of Texas land grant college freshmen to show how the nature of the language reflects the socio-economic background of these students. New York: New York University dissertation. Abstract in DAI 16.1445. [100 UC, 100 MC, 100 LC freshmen at Prairie View College, S TX]. Finds upper-class students make fewer errors in usage, sentence structure, diction, and function words, but there are no significant differences between groups otherwise.

**1.120 Campbell, John C.** 1921. The southern highlander and his homeland. New York: Russell Sage Foundation. Pp. 144-46, comments on Southern Appalachian dialect.

**1.121 Cannon, Garland.** 1968. Bilingual education and Texas. Texas College English 3.2.1-3. Argues for broad study of bilingualism in education to combat discrimination against both Latin Americans and blacks.

**1.122 Carey, George.** 1971. Folk speech and naming. A faraway time and place: lore of the Eastern shore, 233-49. Washington: Robert B. Luce. Archaic vocabulary, personal naming patterns, nicknames of places, and proverbial comparisons used in MD Chesapeake Bay communities; includes Tangier and Smith Islands, VA.

**1.123 Carpenter, Betty Owens.** 1983. Linguistic implications of variant address forms used in the classroom. Austin: University of Texas thesis. 97 pp. [CENT TX]. Compares terms that whites, blacks, and Mexican-Americans have for their own and other groups and compares other verbal behavior of these groups.

**1.124 Carpenter, Charles.** 1933. Variation in the southern mountain dialect. AS 8.22-25. Subregional differences in Appalachian vocabulary, grammar, pronunciation.

**1.125 Carpenter, Charles.** 1973. The folk-language of mid-Appalachia. Journal of the Alleghenies 9.27-31. [WV]. Essay stressing that Appalachian English is combination of old forms inherited from British dialects and new forms developed in mountain speech.

**1.126 Carpenter, Charles.** 1973. Pronunciation and grammar in mid-Appalachia. Journal of the Alleghenies 9.31-35. [WV]. Peculiarities of mountain speech, including unusual examples of contraction and assimilation.

**1.127 Carroll, William S.** 1967. Teaching a second dialect and some implications for TESOL: a teaching experiment. TESOL Quarterly 1.1.31-36. [Washington, DC]. Study based on Urban Language Survey project.

**1.128 Carter, Michael Vaughn.** 1979. Culture, language and organization. Religious language and collective action: a study of voluntarism in a rural Appalachian church, 57-70. Huntingdon: Marshall University thesis. [SW WV]. Analyzes language of the Appalachian church in terms of a "semi-autonomous symbolic cognitive system" enabling collective action.

**1.129 Carter, Michael Vaughn.** 1981. Religious language and collective action: a study of voluntarism in a rural Appalachian church. Appalachia/America: proceedings of the 1980 Appalachian studies conference, ed. by Wilson Somerville, 218-29. Johnson City, TN: Appalachian Consortium Press. [SW WV]. Examines "use of religious language in the church and the organization of the church as a voluntary organization."

**1.130 Cassidy, Frederic G.** 1973. Dialect studies, regional and social. Current trends in linguistics vol. 10, ed. by Thomas B. Sebeok, 75-100. The Hague: Mouton. History of dialect study in U.S., founding of American Dialect Society, development of dialect lexicography, linguistic atlas projects, and social dialectology.

**1.131 Cassidy, Frederic G.** 1982. Geographical variation of English in the United States. English as a world language, ed. by Richard W. Bailey and

Manfred Görlach, 177-209. Ann Arbor: University of Michigan Press. 7 maps. Overview article stressing settlement history, regional vocabulary, and the evolving conception of regional dialects areas in the U.S.

**1.132 Cassidy, Frederic G.** 1985. Language changes especially common in American folk speech. Dictionary of American Regional English, ed. by Frederic G. Cassidy, xxxvi-xl. Cambridge: Harvard University Press. Compendium of thirteen types of changes of word form, twelve grammatical changes, five types of derivational change, and four changes in pronunciation in American folk speech represented in DARE.

**1.133 Cassidy, Frederic G.** 1986. Language variation--some realities. Dialect and language variation, ed. by Harold B. Allen and Michael D. Linn, 205-11. New York: Academic Press. Explores subtleties of DARE data on catalpa and catawba.

**1.134 Chalaron, Magda.** 1918. Louisiana folklore and language. Newcomb Arcade 10.75-80. P. 76, discusses LA French creole words borrowed into English, including lagniappe, banquette, calas, cuartee, and praline.

**1.135 Chambers, John,** ed. 1983. Black English: educational equity and the law. Ann Arbor, MI: Karoma. 170 pp. Collection of eight essays on aspects of black English, motivated by Ann Arbor court decision. **Review:** J. Scott. 1985. EWW 5.292-96.

**1.136 Champion, Larry S.** 1983. "Bold to play": Shakespeare in North Carolina. Shakespeare in the South, ed. by Philip C. Kolin, 231-46. Jackson: University Press of Mississippi. P. 238, quotes theater directors and critics as testifying that Shakespearean language is more intelligible in W NC than elsewhere in country because it is allegedly close to the everyday speech there.

**1.137 Chapman, Maristan.** 1929. American speech as practiced in the southern highlands. Century 117.617-23. [S Appalachia]. Surveys characteristic southern mountain speech and compares it to earlier British usage.

**1.138 Chirich, Nancy.** 1971. Dialect country: where the flavor still is. Sandlapper 4.12.76-79. Essay praising dialect richness of SC, calling Gullah "the only true American dialect" and discussing project of state's Department of Education to enable public schoolteachers to understand and appreciate dialect diversity in SC.

**1.139 Christian, Donna, Walt Wolfram, and Nanjo Dube.** 1984. Variation and change in geographically isolated communities: Appalachian English and Ozark English. Washington: CAL. Final National Science Foundation report. 280 pp. ED 246 682. [NW AR, S WV]. Compares Ozark and Appalachian English to determine similarity between the two and examines how each preserves patterns and undergoes change; includes extended treatment of auxiliary verbs, personal datives, a-prefixing, patterns of irregular verbs, and subject-verb concord.

**1.140 Cobbs, Hamner.** 1952. Negro colloquialisms in the black belt. Alabama Review 5.203-12. Some unreported folk etymologies. [S AL]. Characteristic archaisms, colorful vocabulary, malapropisms of rural blacks whose "vivid imaginations, together with their highly developed genius for imitation, have conspired to produce for them a rich and often baffling language."

**1.141 Coleman, Wilma.** 1936. Mountain dialects in north Georgia. Athens: University of Georgia thesis. 30 pp. Sentimental study of archaic and unusual forms undertaken "with a desire to preserve a portion of this quaint old English dialect as the mountaineers in the most remote regions use it."

**1.142 Collier, Lee.** 1957. Ozarks language should become universal. Ozarks Mountaineer 5.7. Says Ozark speech is a "product of our ancestors who desired a simple and useful language to fill their simple and practical needs" and is superior to other varieties of English as well as other languages.

**1.143 Collins, Allie C.** 1956. Speech patterns of selected residents of North Biloxi, Mississippi. Hattiesburg: Mississippi Southern College thesis.

**1.144 Combs, Josiah H.** 1916. Dialect of the folk-song. DN 4.311-18. [Appalachia, WV to GA]. Dialect words; phonological and syntactic irregularities.

**1.145 Combs, Josiah H.** 1931. The language of the southern highlander. PMLA 46.1302-22. Compiles figurative expressions, colloquialisms, pronunciations, and syntax of S Appalachia.

**1.146 Combs, Josiah H.** 1943. The Kentucky highlands from a native mountaineer's viewpoint. Lexington, KY: J. L. Richardson. 44 pp. Scattered references to dialect throughout.

**1.147 Combs, Josiah H.** 1957. Spellin' 'em down in the highlands. KFR 3.69-73. [KY]. Anecdotes about unlettered techniques for spelling in spelling bees, the "proper" use of language in the mountains, how mountain residents greet one another and give directions to strangers, etc.

**1.148 Conklin, Nancy Faires, and Margaret A. Lourie.** 1983. A host of tongues: language communities in the United States. New York: Free Press. Regional dialects of American English, 72-95, scattered comments on and discussion of features of Southern and Appalachian English.

**1.149 Conrad, Earl.** 1944. The philology of Negro dialect. JNE 13.150-54. Says black speech is usually stereotyped and misrepresented in print, especially by Southern white writers who never represent their white characters as speaking dialect; argues blacks have contributed extensively to the evolution of the English language, in jazz expressions, street parlance, and other areas.

**1.150 Cooper, Horton.** 1972. North Carolina mountain folklore and miscellany. Murfreesboro, NC: Johnson. [W NC]. Riddles, 55-56; Children's rhymes, 82-85; The early vernacular of the North Carolina mountains, 87-97; Proverbs and expressions, 101-02.

**1.151 Cox, Ellen D.** 1969. A study of dialect peculiarities of Scott County, Tennessee, secondary school students. Knoxville: University of Tennessee thesis. [NE TN].

**1.152 Currie, Eva G.** 1950. Linguistic and sociological consideration of some populations of Texas. SSJ 15.286-96. Vocabulary and pronunciation of bilingual Texans and Texans who are not native English-speakers.

**1.153 Currie, Haver C.** 1952. A projection of sociolinguistics: the relationship of speech to social status. SSJ 18.28-37. Reviews early research (including McDavid's and Kurath's) on social functions and significance of speech, an emerging field author calls "socio-linguistics." **Reprinted** in J. Williamson and V. Burke 1971(**1.823**).39-47.

**1.154 Dabney, Virginius.** 1942. Below the Potomac: a book about the new South. Washington, DC: Kennikat Press. Pp. 14-16, comments on representation of a Southern accent in movies, etc.

**1.155 Damen, Louise.** 1974. Black English: anthropological and linguistic considerations in the training of teachers in black dialect patterns. Gainesville: University of Florida thesis. Discusses features of black speech of N CENT FL in a series of fourteen written texts and audio tapes designed for training of pre-service and in-service teachers.

**1.156 Damron, Shayla R.** 1977. A bidialectal approach: strategies for assimilating the mainstream dialect into the non-mainstream southern mountain dialect. ED 210 128. 29 pp. [E KY]. Instructional packet to assess an individual's language patterns and series of strategies and exercises for increasing student awareness of dialect forms.

**1.157 Davis, Alva L.**, ed. 1968. On the dialects of children. Champaign: NCTE. Reprint of five articles from EE 40 (May 1968).

**1.158 Davis, Alva L.**, et al. 1969. Recordings of standard English in the United States and Canada. Office of Education report. ED 030 668. 33 pp. Discusses preparation of set of thirty-two tape recordings of speakers of standard regional varieties of English in U.S. and Canada and set of descriptive materials to accompany them.

**1.159 Davis, Alva L., ed.** 1969. American dialects for English teachers. Urbana: NCTE. 107 pp. Anthology of articles, worksheets, checklist, speech samples, and annotated bibliography.

**1.160 Davis, A[lva] L., ed.** 1972. Culture, class, and language variety: a resource book for teachers. Urbana: NCTE. 220 pp. Collection of eleven articles by McDavid and others. **Review:** J. Appleby. 1971. AS 46.158-59.

**1.161 Davis, Alva L., and Lawrence M. Davis, eds.** 1969. Recordings of standard English. NADS 1.3.4-17. Outlines Center for American English at Illinois Institute of Technology and its standard questionnaire (with directions) to collect speech from around country.

**1.162 Davis, Alva L., Virginia G. McDavid, and Raven I. McDavid, Jr.** 1969. A compilation of the work sheets of the linguistic atlas of the United States and Canada and associated projects. Chicago: University of Chicago Press. 2nd ed. Compiles items investigated in LANE, LAMSAS, and other linguistic atlas and ancillary projects. **Reviews:** A. R. Duckert. 1972. AS 47.278-85; W. Viereck. 1973. Anglia 97.107-11.

**1.163 Davis, Boyd H.** 1986. The talking world map: eliciting Southern adolescent language. Language variety in the South: perspectives in black and white, ed. by Michael Montgomery and Guy Bailey, 359-64. University: University of Alabama Press. [Charlotte, NC]. Explores how adolescents develop notions of community and language use, and discusses method for enabling them to talk about these notions.

**1.164 Davis, Forrest, and Ernest K. Lindley.** 1942. Secretary Hull, Tennessee. Word Study 18.2.4. Praises and cites examples of downhome speech of Tennessean Cordell Hull.

**1.165 Davis, Lawrence M.** 1969. Dialect research: mythology vs. reality. Orbis 18.332-37. Questions hypothesis of creole background for dialects of American blacks and calls for further research into specific linguistic features to verify it. **Reprinted** in W. Wolfram and N. Clarke 1971 (**1.853**). 90-98.

**1.166 Davis, Lawrence M.** 1970. Some social aspects of the speech of bluegrass Kentucky. Orbis 19.337-41. [10W, 1B, E KY]. Says LANCS data for KY is insufficient for generalizing about systematic black-white differences in use of verb principal parts and in pronunciation. **Reprinted** in J. Williamson and V. Burke 1971(**1.823**).335-40.

**1.167 Davis, Lawrence M.** 1970. Social dialectology in America: a critical survey. JEL 4.46-56. Discusses and defends nature and validity of social data of LAUSC projects and chronicles conflict between the dialectologists and the creolists and sociolinguists in 1960s over LAUSC methodology.

**1.168 Davis, Lawrence M.** 1971. A study of Appalachian speech in a northern urban setting. Final report. National Center for Educational Research and Development, Washington. ED 061 205. 63 pp. [25 speakers, E KY and S WV, 19 having moved to Chicago]. Compares speech of Appalachian residents with Appalachian migrants to Chicago using "diafeature rules"; finds no significant differences in phonology and few nonstandard grammatical features in speech of any informants.

**1.169 Davis, Lawrence M.**, ed. 1972. Studies in linguistics in honor of Raven I. McDavid, Jr. University: University of Alabama Press. xviii + 461 pp. Thirty-six essays on American regional and social dialects. **Review:** W. E. Farrison. 1974. CLAJ 17.562-65.

**1.170 Davis, Lawrence M.** 1977. Dialectology and linguistics. Orbis 26.24-30. Theoretical article examining method for distinguishing dialects on basis of diafeatures, shown in an example from E KY.

**1.171 Davis, Lawrence M.** 1983. English dialectology: an introduction. University: University of Alabama Press. 151 pp. Analyzes principal developments in dialect geography in U.S. and Europe and social dialectology in U.S. **Reviews:** Anonymous. 1983. EWW 4.317-19; G. Bailey. 1985. AS 60.254-57; W. N. Francis. 1984. LIS 13.561-64; C. Hines. 1987. SECOL Review 11.205-10; R. King. 1984. Language 60.990-91; M. Wakelin. 1983. EWW 4.319-21.

**1.172 Davis, Lawrence M., and Linda L. Blanton.** 1972. Some aspects of the social stratification of English in southern Appalachia. Abstract in NADS 5.2.5. [E KY]. Suggests socioeconomic and educational differences are not most crucial factors in accounting for variation in Southern Appalachian speech.

**1.173 Dean, Patricia.** 1978. Investigating the regional dialect of north central Texas. Abstract in NADS 11.1.12. [13 counties, N TX]. Uses 126-item questionnaire and includes data from non-white groups.

**1.174 Dean, Patricia.** 1979. The speech habits of the sexes: north central Texas joins the women's movement. Abstract in NADS 11.3.4-5. [N CENT TX]. Reports usage patterns of 200 native men and women.

**1.175 Deane, Ernie.** 1976. All things changing Ozark folk speech. Proceedings of the conference on Ozark In-migration. Eureka Springs: Arkansas Humanities Committee. Compares Ozark folk speech as reported by Randolph and Wilson (**1.630**) with that of a generation later.

**1.176 Dendy, W. E.** 1927. A study in Negro dialect. Atlanta: Oglethorpe University thesis.

**1.177 Dennis, Leah A.** 1944. A word-list from Alabama and some other

Southern states. PADS 2.6-16. Word glossary and notes on eighteen features of pronunciation.

**1.178 Dent, J. J.** 1976. A dialect survey of Coldspring, Texas, and surrounding area. Huntsville: Sam Houston State University thesis. 96 pp. [San Jacinto Co., SW TX]. Compares lexicon and grammar to findings of Atwood (**3.17**) and examines effect of age, race, and level of education on speech of community; finds lexicon more influenced by race and age and grammar more by educational level of speakers.

**1.179 DeStefano, Johanna S.**, ed. 1973. Language, society, and education: a profile of black English. Worthington, OH: Charles A. Jones. 328 pp. Anthology of twenty-two essays on social, linguistic, and pedagogical aspects of black American speech. **Reviews:** J. Sledd. 1973. AS 48.258-69; L. V. Zuck. 1973. LL 23.273-76.

**1.180 DeStefano, Johanna S., and Victor M. Rentel.** 1975. Language variation: perspectives for teachers. Theory into Practice 14.328-37. Overview article for teachers covering regional and social dialects, black English, register variation, and other topics.

**1.181 Devereux, Margaret.** 1906. Plantation sketches. Cambridge, MA: Riverside Press. Pp. 33-34, notes on second-person plural pronoun yinna among Southern blacks and on given name Manuel.

**1.182 Dial, Wylene.** 1969. The dialect of the Appalachian people. West Virginia History 30.463-71. Argues with those who consider Appalachian dialect a corruption of English; says it is more accurate to consider it an archaic variety and documents ancestry of characteristic Appalachian forms from 16th-century and earlier literature. **Reprinted** in B. B. Maurer, ed. 1969. Mountain heritage, 82-91. Ripley, WV: Mountain State Art and Craft Fair, Cedar Lake; in D. N. Mielke, ed. 1978. Teaching mountain children, 49-58. Boone, NC: Appalachian Consortium.

**1.183 Dial, Wylene.** 1970. Folk speech is English, too. Mountain Life and Work 46.2.16-18 (Feb.); 46.5.15-17 (May).

**1.184 Dial, Wylene P.** 1976. Appalachian dialect. The West Virginia heritage encyclopedia, ed. by Jim Comstock, 1320-34. Richwood, WV: privately printed.

**1.185 A dialect study of St. Mary's County, Maryland.** 1982. Chronicles of St. Mary's 30.497-504,507-15.

**1.186 Dillard, J. L.** 1964. The writings of Herskovits and the study of the language of the Negro in the new world. Caribbean Studies 4.2.35-41. Says Herskovits' pioneering and prophetic analysis of Africanisms in New World language and culture has been vindicated by recent work of creolists and that popular view of distinctive American black speech is closer to accurate view of Africanisms in that variety of speech than view of traditional structural linguists and dialectologists is.

**1.187 Dillard, J. L.** 1966. The urban language study of the Center for Applied Linguistics. Linguistic Reporter 8.5.1-2. Discusses rationale and early work of the federal project and distinguishes its approach to dialect study from that of the Linguistic Atlas by its close attention to syntactic structures and its use of younger informants under fourteen years of age.

**1.188 Dillard, J. L.** 1967. Negro children's dialect in the inner city. FFLR 5.7-8,10. Pedagogical implications of recent discoveries of socio-linguistic research on systematic grammatical divergences of black children from standard English. **Reprinted** in R. Bentley and S. Crawford. 1973(**1.64**). 84-89.

**1.189 Dillard, J. L.** 1968. Non-standard Negro dialects--convergence or divergence? FFLR 6.9-10,12. Argues that Stewart's concept of relexification of earlier creole forms is more reasonable explanation for grammatical patterns in black English than that of "selective cultural differentiation" offered by traditional dialectologists; says linguistic atlas maps cannot display variation in grammatical features and therefore misrepresent degree of systematic difference between forms. **Reprinted** in N. E. Whitten, Jr. and J. F. Szwed. 1970. Afro-American anthropology: contemporary perspectives, 119-27. New York: Free Press.

**1.190 Dillard, J. L.** 1972. Black English: its history and usage in the United States. New York: Random House. 361 pp. Seminal, polemical work claiming that American black speech developed from plantation creole English based on creole originating in West Africa and that Southern white speech differs from Northern white speech largely because of heavy influence by the speech of blacks. Condensed in Stoller 1975.19-48. **Reviews:** P. Adams. 1972. Atlantic Monthly 230.3.110; M. C. Alleyne. 1974. Caribbean Studies 14.89-95; C.-J. N. Bailey. 1974. Foundations of Language 11.299-309; T. C. Bambara. 1972. NYTBR, Sept. 3, p. 3; R. L. Chapman. 1972. Nation 215.278-79 (Oct. 2); P. Christopherson. 1975. English Studies 56.79-82; S. G. D'Eloia. 1973. JEL 7.87-106; R. A. Demers. 1973. Harvard Educational Review 43.303-08; R. W. Fasold. 1975. LIS 4.198-221; J. L. Funkhouser. 1974. CE 35.625-29; I. F. Hancock. 1972. FFLR 10.1-2,21-22; K. B. Harder. 1972. TFSB 38.106; Blyden Jackson. 1973. JNH 58.90-96; Blyden Jackson. 1976. Change 8.10.34-35; M. G. Kimbrough. 1973. Negro History Bulletin 36.46; K. Lawrence. 1974. Southern Exposure 1.3-4,84-86; D. Lawton. 1974. Revista Interamericana Review 3.421-31; C. Michener. 1972. Newsweek 80.81 (Aug. 14); R. C. Olsen. 1979. Lamar Journal of the Humanities 5.66-73; M. K. Spears. 1972. New York Review of Books 19.32 (Nov. 6); G. P. Walker. 1973. JNE 42.99-101; R. W. Wescott. 1978. Word 29.186-91; W. Wolfram. 1973. Language 49.670-79; P. H. Wood. 1973. Science 179.886 (Mar. 2).

**1.191 Dillard, J. L.** 1972. On a context for dialect data: the case of black English. FFLR 10.1-2.17-18,53-54. Rebuttal to Davis 1971 (**1.167**) critique of recent creolist work on black English; argues type of data provided by linguistic atlas investigations lacks validity and is inappropriate for answering fundamental questions about distribution of American dialects.

**1.192 Dillard, J. L.** 1973. Creole studies and American dialectology. Caribbean Studies 12.4.76-91. Extended review of J. Williamson and V. Burke 1971 (**1.823**).

**1.193 Dillard, J. L.** 1974. Lay my isogloss bundle down: the contribution of black English to American dialectology. Linguistics 119.5-14. Says geographical bias of American dialectologists, their tendency to view determination of dialects in terms of bundles of isoglosses, and other practices of linguistic geographers have led to misunderstanding of black English.

**1.194 Dillard, J. L.** 1975. All-American English. New York: Random House. 369 pp. Discusses influence of language contact situations (the frontier, maritime contact, immigration) on development of American English. **Reviews:** P. J. McClung. 1977. English Studies 58.76-77; M. K. Spears. 1975. NYRB 22.34 (July 17); W. Safire. 1975. New York Times, p. 4 (May 11).

**1.195 Dillard, J. L., ed.** 1975. Perspectives on black English. The Hague: Mouton. 391 pp. Twenty-two essays on black English dialect, the history of black English, black English and the acculturation process, and black English and psycholinguistics, with extended introductions to each section by Dillard. **Reviews:** D. Bickerton. 1977. Language 53.466-69; M. M. Bryant. 1978. Word 29.191-93; R. G. Carson. 1976. Contemporary Psychology 21.443; J. M. Fayer. 1975-76. Revista Interamericana Review 5.756-59; T. Kochman. 1984. LPLP 8.212-16; C. Pfaff. 1977. Journal óf Creole Studies 1.309-17; J. H. Polsin. 1976. Sociolinguistics Newsletter 7.2.26.

**1.196 Dillard, J. L.** 1978. Bidialectal education: black English and standard English in the United States. Case studies in bilingual education, ed. by Bernard Spolsky and Robert Cooper, 293-311. Rowley, MA: Newbury House. Surveys literature providing rationale for bidialectal education for black students and reviews progress and failure of designing and implementing bidialectal programs.

**1.197 Dillard, J. L., ed.** 1980. Perspectives on American English. The Hague: Mouton. 467 pp. Twenty-seven essays, with sections (each with introductory essay by Dillard) on native English-speaking immigrants, the sea and the American frontier, immigration and migration, black English, and pidgin English. **Reviews:** K. B. Harder. 1981. TFSB 47.86-87; H. Pilch. 1982. Anglia 100.482-84; J. Sledd. 1982. EWW 3.100-02; W. Viereck. 1982. Amerikastudien 27.231-33; D. Wepman. 1983. Word 34.48-52.

**1.198 Dillard, J. L.** 1987. The ex-slave narratives: failures in interview technique. Abstract in NADS 19.3.8. Questions validity of data from ex-slave narratives because "interviewers were not only given a set of questions in a rigid order but were cued as to dialect expectations" and because editorial changes in narratives in field offices make data equivalent to literary dialect.

**1.199 Dillard, Lou.** 1974. Black English: the role it plays in the Auburn city school system. Alabama Speech and Theatre Journal 2.1.32-36. [E CENT AL]. Discusses how public school teachers in Auburn handle dialect features used by black students.

**1.200 Dingus, L. R.** 1915. A word list from Virginia. DN 4.177-93. [Scott Co., SW VA]. Discusses phonology, morphology, and syntax, and presents wordlist of 500 items.

**1.201 Dingus, L. R.** 1927. Appalachian mountain words. DN 5.468-71. [KY]. Wordlist of 100 items and shorter lists of specimen pronunciations and grammatical items from James Watt Raine's The Land of Saddle Bags (1.626).

**1.202 Doran, Edwina Bean.** 1969. Folksay. Folklore in White County, Tennessee, 97-141. Nashville: George Peabody College dissertation. Abstract in DAI 31.322A. [CENT TN]. Includes place name etymology, folk vocabulary, proverbs and phrases, and unusual personal names.

**1.203 Dorrill, George T.** 1989. Linguistic atlas of the middle and south atlantic states. Encyclopedia of Southern culture, ed. by William Ferris and Charles Wilson. Chapel Hill: University of North Carolina Press. Summary of LAMSAS history and work through 1984.

**1.204 Drinnon, Elizabeth McCants.** 1962. Picturesque Georgia speech. Georgia Magazine 5.6.9. Note on replies to greeting medianary and twixt and tween and other GA items.

**1.205 Dumas. Bethany K.** 1971. A study of the dialect of Newton County, Arkansas. Fayetteville: University of Arkansas dissertation. Abstract in DAI 31.2664A. [20 informants, NW AR]. Surveys lexical, syntactic, and phonological patterns, and identifies morphological and syntactic peculiarities; finds no social correlates to linguistic variation except nativeness to the region, which is connected to more divergent forms.

**1.206 Dumas, Bethany K.** 1974. Elicitation for linguistic diversity: guidelines for effectiveness. Southwest languages and linguistics in educational perspective, ed. by Gina Cantoni Harvey and M. F. Heiser. San Diego, CA: Institute for Cultural Pluralism. Discusses technical and methodological guidelines for effective elicitation of data in bilingual communities in the Southwest.

**1.207 Dumas, Bethany K.** 1975. Smoky Mountain speech. Pioneer Spirit 76, ed. by Dolly Berthelot, 24-29. Knoxville, TN: privately printed. [E TN]. Overview article for lay readers.

**1.208 Dumas, Bethany K.** 1975. Field methodology: ways and means of eliciting syntactic and other patterns. Orbis 24.343-49. Reports on two experiments in having minimally trained assistants conduct taped socio-linguistic interviews and proposes types of interview questions for eliciting syntactic patterns.

**1.209 Dumas, Bethany K.** 1976. Male-female conversational interaction cues: using data from dialect surveys. ED 135 216. [NW AR]. Proposes that tape-recorded interviews from dialect surveys may provide valuable information on conversational interaction, especially between men and women, and illustrates this with data from author's dissertation interviews (**1.205**).

**1.210 Dumas, Bethany K.** 1976. The Arkansas language survey: progress, problems, and prognostications. Orbis 25.249-57. Abstracts in NADS 5.2.14 and in NADS 6.1-2.31. Reports on progress and evolving methodology of Arkansas Language Survey.

**1.211 Dumas, Bethany K.** 1977. Research needs in Tennessee English. Papers in language variation: SAMLA-ADS collection, ed. by David L. Shores and Carole P. Hines, 201-08. University: University of Alabama Press. Programmatic statement of research needs and proposal for Tennessee Language Survey, with interview and goals of the project outlined.

**1.212 Dumas, Bethany K.** 1979. Regional vocabulary in the Arkansas Ozarks. Abstract in NADS 11.3.8. Reviewed in NADS 12.1.6. and NADS 12.2.15. [11 adults, Newton Co., NW AR]. Surveys lexical, syntactic, and phonological features and social correlates of speech.

**1.213 Dumas, Bethany K.** 1981. East Tennessee talk. An encyclopedia of East Tennessee, ed. by Jim Stokely and Jeff D. Johnson, 170-76. Oak Ridge, TN: Children's Museum. Survey of grammar, pronunciation, and language attitudes of region.

**1.214 Duncan, Hannibal G.** 1926. The southern highlanders. Journal of Applied Sociology 10.556-61. [S Appalachia]. Stresses isolation of mountain people, of which archaic language is one result.

**1.215 Duncan, Hannibal Gerald, and Winnie Leach Duncan.** 1929. Superstitions and sayings among the southern highlanders. JAF 42.233-37. [S Appalachia]. Includes remarks on dialects of subregions.

**1.216 Dundes, Alan,** ed. 1973. Mother wit from the laughing barrel. Englewood Cliffs, NJ: Prentice-Hall. 673 pp. **Reprinted** in 1981 by

Garland Press, Westport, CT. Anthology of articles on aspects of black folklore.

**1.217 Dunlap, A. R.** 1946. The speech of the Croatans. AS 21.231-32. Discusses a 1901 note on language of group of mixed-blood North Carolinians.

**1.218 Dunn, Durwood.** 1977. The folk culture of Cades Cove, Tennessee. TFSB 43.67-87. [Blount Co., E TN]. Reviews linguistic research done on Cades Cove residents in Smoky Mountains, 76-78.

**1.219 Dunn, Ernest F.** 1976. The black-Southern white dialect controversy: who did what to whom? Black English: a seminar, ed. by Deborah Harrison and Tom Trabasso, 105-22. Hillsdale, NJ: Erlbaum. Argues that Southern blacks preserve numerous African elements in their language and culture in order to maintain their identity and that they have had a strong innovating influence on Southern white speech that whites are reluctant to admit.

**1.220 Edmiston, William C.** 1930. The speech of the hill people of Todd County, Kentucky. Kentucky Folklore and Poetry Magazine 5.3-9. [SW KY]. Says hill residents live and speak as their ancestors did a century earlier and discusses typical words and expressions.

**1.221 Edson, Rev. H. A., and Edith M. Fairchild.** 1895. Tennessee mountains in word lists. DN 1.370-77. [Mountain areas of TN, NC, KY]. 145 words and phrases, fifteen exclamations, comments on grammar and pronunciations.

**1.222 Edwards, E. M.** 1904. The speech of Joshua or a few dialectal peculiarities of north central Texas. Norman: University of Oklahoma thesis.

**1.223 Elgin, Suzette Haden.** 1979. The red-eye gravy literacy test. Conference of Language Attitudes and Composition Newsletter 6.7-11. Test (in form of Standard Aptitude Test) of basic information on Ozark life and culture, for schoolteachers.

**1.224 Elgin, Suzette Haden.** 1981- . The lonesome node. Huntsville, AR: Ozark Center for Language Study. Quarterly newsletter with periodic brief comments and analyses of Ozark English patterns.

**1.225 Ellis, Michael E.** 1984. The relationship of Appalachian English with the British regional dialects. Johnson City: East Tennessee State University thesis. 55 pp. Compares lexical, phonological, and morphological evidence in material collected by Miller (**1.517**) and Reese (**1.645**) in E TN and material in Survey of English Dialects in Britain, but says the few correspondences found form no uniform pattern.

**1.226 Entwisle, Doris R., and Ellen Greenberger.** 1968. Differences in the language of the Negro and white grade school children. Report no. 19. Center for the study of social organization of schools. Baltimore: Johns Hopkins University.

**1.227 Epler, Blanch N.** 1933. A bit of Elizabethan England in America. National Geographic Magazine 64.695-730. [E NC]. Comments on English of isolated Outer Banks islands.

**1.228 Evertts, Eldonna L., ed.** 1967. Dimensions of dialect. Champaign: NCTE. Collection of essays on dialects for public school teachers.

**1.229 Faneuf, Mildred A.** 1939. Dialect study of Auburn, Lee County, Alabama, made as a preliminary investigation for the preparation of work sheets for the linguistic atlas. Auburn: Alabama Polytechnic Institute thesis. 351 pp. + transcripts. [7 natives, E CENT AL]. Surveys selection of phonetic, lexical, and grammatical features.

**1.230 Farmer, Roosevelt A.** 1978. Standard and nonstandard approaches to teaching language arts at Dobbs School, a juvenile correctional institution at Kinston, North Carolina. Chapel Hill: University of North Carolina thesis. Studies approaches to teaching English to minority students at juvenile correctional institution, notes persistent nonstandard grammatical features in students' writing, and demonstrates superiority of experimental, non-traditional program over traditional grammar-based approach in reducing incidence of these features.

**1.231 Farmer, Roosevelt.** 1979. An alternative approach to learning. North Carolina Education Journal. Mar.-Apr., pp. 16-17. [NC]. Report on program to teach black teenagers to overcome dialect forms in writing.

**1.232 Farrison, W. E.** 1969. Dialectology versus Negro dialect. CLAJ 13.21-26. Short review of concept of dialect and development of black literary dialect; argues there is no such thing as black spoken dialect because a dialect cannot be racially determined and because "many of the words and locutions and most of the substandard grammar which have been said to be characteristic of Negro dialect have been current at one time or another in almost every section of the United States." **Reprinted** in J. Williamson and V. Burke 1971(**1.823**).187-92.

**1.233 Fasold, Ralph W.** 1970. Distinctive linguistic characteristics of black English. Linguistics and the teaching of standard English to speakers of other languages or dialects, ed. by James E. Alatis, 233-38. Washington: Georgetown University Press. Argues against popular view that features of black English are careless deteriorations of standard English but doubts William Stewart/J. L. Dillard claim of fundamental differences between the two.

**1.234 Fasold, Ralph W.** 1974. Impish inquiries into the implausibility of immoderate insistence on intuition or, I hear Bailey has left his tree. Lectological Newsletter 2.4.1-4. Counters arguments in Bailey 1974 (**1.28**) that only native speakers can "'know' the relative power of constraints on variable, changing linguistic phenomena."

**1.235 Fasold, Ralph W.** 1981. The relation between black and white English in the South. AS 56.163-89. Synthesizes some of the important research on black-white speech relationships in the South and takes middle ground in drawing conclusions about extent and source of black-white differences. **Reprinted** in H. Allen and M. Linn 1986(**1.11**).446-73.

**1.236 Fasold, Ralph W.,** ed. 1983. Variation in the form and use of language. Washington: Georgetown University Press. 416 pp. Anthology of previously printed items from C.-J. N. Bailey and R. Shuy (**1.31**) and other Georgetown University Press volumes.

**1.237 Fasold, Ralph W.** 1987. [Are black and white vernaculars diverging?] AS 62.3-5. Introduction to NWAV panel discussion of hypothesis that black and white vernaculars are diverging.

**1.238 Fasold, Ralph W., and Roger W. Shuy,** eds. 1970. Teaching standard English in the inner city. Arlington: CAL. 141 pp. Articles by Stewart, Wolfram, Shuy, and others on teaching speech, writing, and reading primarily to black children. **Reviews:** J. M. Coady. 1971. Language Sciences 16.41-43; D. R. Entwisle. 1971. American Journal of Sociology 77.396-98; M. R. Key. 1975. IJAL 41.84-89; R. B. Le Page. 1973. Linguistics 118.119-24; L. Pederson. 1975. AS 50.98-110; J. Singleton. 1971. AA 73.1377-78.

**1.239 Ferguson, Charles, and Shirley Brice Heath,** eds. 1980. Language in the USA. New York: Cambridge University Press. xxxviii + 592 pp. **Reviews:** R. W. Bailey. 1982. EWW 3.103-06; P. Beade. 1983. Lingua 59.99; C. Cazden. 1982. Science 216.865; C. C. Eble. 1983. LIS 12.272-79; G. J. Forgue. 1983. Etudes Anglaise 37.104-05; C. R. Foster. 1982. LPLP 6.180-82; K. E. Müller. 1984. MLJ 68.63-64; J. H. Sledd. 1983. AS 58.42-46.

**1.240 Finger, Charles J.** 1931. Adventures under sapphire skies. New York: Morrow. [N AR]. Pp. 22-24, 46-47, scattered references to Ozark dialect.

**1.241 Flanagan, John T.** 1946. Texas speaks Texan. Southwest Review 31.191-92. Casual observations on lexicon, pronunciation, and grammar by newcomer to TX.

**1.242 Florida English.** 1928. AS 3.412. Brief notes on FL usages.

**1.243 Foley, Lawrence M.** 1969. A phonological and lexical study of the speech of Tuscaloosa County, Alabama. Tuscaloosa: University of Alabama dissertation. Abstract in DAI 30.4964A. Republished as PADS 58. 54 pp. [22 W, 5 B; middle-aged and older speakers, Tuscaloosa, AL]. Finds white speech in Tuscaloosa more like that in N AL and black speech more like that in S AL; finds folk pronunciations more common in black speech but that some older and socially prominent whites share features with blacks. Review: K. Hameyer. 1980. ZDL 47.108-11.

1.244 Folk, Mary Louise. 1961. A word atlas of north Louisiana. Baton Rouge: Louisiana State University dissertation. Abstract in DAI 22.3653-54A. 633 pp. [275 W, 26 counties, ages 16-87, education ranging from nothing to grad school]. Provides maps for each item. Compares findings to Kurath 1949 (3.275); finds vocabulary a mixture of Southern and South Midland but pronunciation predominantly South Midland, especially in having postvocalic /r/.

1.245 Forfeit, Karen G., and Patricia L. Donaldson. 1971. Dialect, race, and language proficiency: another dead heat on the merry-go-round. Child Development 42.1572-74. Response to Baratz (1.46).

1.246 Forgue, Guy Jean, and Raven I. McDavid, Jr. 1972. Les langue des Américains. Paris: Aubier Montaigne. 271 pp.

1.247 Fortier, Alcée. 1894. Louisiana studies: literature, customs, dialects, history and education. New Orleans: Hansell and Bro. 307 pp.

1.248 Foscue, Virginia Oden. 1966. Background and preliminary survey of the linguistic geography of Alabama. 2 vols. Madison: University of Wisconsin dissertation. Abstract in DAI 28.214A. Abstract reprinted in J. Williamson and V. Burke 1971(1.823).671-72. [50 speakers from throughout AL, half over 60, half 40-60]. Outlines settlement history of state; presents geographical and social distribution of vocabulary based on 147-item survey.

1.249 Francis, W. Nelson. 1983. Dialectology: an introduction. London: Longman. ix + 240 pp. Intensive review of field; analysis of methodology (especially sampling and collecting of data) of dialectology and relation of dialectology to linguistic theory. Reviews: G. M. Awbery. 1983. Journal of Linguistics 20.414-15; F. Chevillet. 1985. Etudes Anglaises 189.307; R. I. McDavid, Jr. 1985. SECOL Review 9.68-93; W. Viereck. 1985. JEL 18.184-88.

1.250 Fruit, John P. 1890. Kentucky words and phrases. DN 1.63-69. Glossaries of unusual words and usages and of pronunciations and grammatical forms.

1.251 Fruit, John P. 1891. Kentucky words. DN 1.229-34. Words, pronunciations, grammatical items.

1.252 Fuller, William H. 1970. A sampling of variant idiomaticity in freshman compositions at North Texas State University from 1958 to 1969. Denton: North Texas State University thesis.

**1.253 Galinsky, Hans.** 1972. "E pluribus unum"? Die antwort des sprache. Amerikastudien 17.9-55. Presents evidence on regional varieties of American English and the relationship between regional and social varieties and a national standard.

**1.254 Galinsky, Hans.** 1972. Regionalismus und einheitstreben in den Vereinigten Staaten: ein sprachwissenschaftlicher forschungsbericht. Heidelberg: Carl Winter. 55 pp. Revised version of preceding item. **Review:** E. Guillaume. 1974. Etudes Anglaises 189.351.

**1.255 Galvan, Mary M., and Rudolph C. Troike.** 1969. The Texas dialect project. FFLR 7.1.25-26,152-53. [250 B, W children and adults in 5 TX communities]. Describes project in social dialect research and teacher training carried out by TX state department of education to determine which linguistic features might have educational relevance and prepare teachers to better handle linguistic differences in the classroom. **Reprinted** in R. Abrahams and R. Troike 1972(1.4).297-304.

**1.256 Garvey, Catherine, and Ellen Dickstein.** 1970. Levels of analysis and social class differences in language. Report no. 83. Center for the Social Organization of Schools. Baltimore: Johns Hopkins University. On speech of Baltimore, MD, schoolchildren.

**1.257 Garvey, Catherine, and Paul T. McFarlane.** 1968. A preliminary study of standard English speech patterns in the Baltimore city public schools. ED 019 265. 45 pp. [158 B, W 5th-graders, Baltimore, MD]. Based on sentence-repetition task, compares speech of black and white, middle-class and inner-city children, finding that subgroups of children were similar enough to justify using some common bases of language instruction.

**1.258 Gates, Michael Foley.** 1972. Language characteristics of disadvantaged and nondisadvantaged children when engaged in problem tasks. Morgantown: West Virginia University dissertation. Abstract in DAI 33.2915-16A. [88 7th-graders]. Finds no linguistic differences between disadvantaged and nondisadvantaged children but the latter have a superior "nonverbal ability . . . to solve problem tasks."

**1.259 Genovese, Eugene D.** 1974. Roll, Jordan, roll. New York: Pantheon. The language of class and nation, 431-41 (reprinted in Urban Review 8.1.39-47); The naming of cats (personal naming practices), 443-50. Essays by historian on nature and role of English language in antebellum slave society.

**1.260 Gepp, Edward.** 1922. Essex speech in some dialects of the United States. Essex Review 31.97-104. Says dialect forms from the southeastern province of Essex are more common in American English than those from any other area of Britain, as seen in Joel Chandler Harris' Uncle Remus books and in James Russell Lowell's The Biglow Papers.

**1.261 Gibson, Frances McKinley.** 1946. The speech of the Vicksburg-Natchez area of Mississippi. Norman: University of Oklahoma thesis. [SW MS]. Outlines characteristic phonological, lexical, and morphosyntactic features.

**1.262 Gifford, Carolyn.** 1970. Black English: an introduction. Acta Symbolica 1.24-30. Outlines findings of scholarship on the structure, history, varieties, and role of black English.

**1.263 Gilbert, Glenn G.** 1965. English loanwords in the German of Fredericksburg, Texas. AS 40.102-12. [Kendall and Gillespie Cos., CENT TX]. Illustrates German influence on local English and discusses mechanisms of borrowing from English into TX German.

**1.264 Gilbert, Glenn G.** 1986. The English of the Brandywine population: a triracial isolate in southern Maryland. Language variety in the South: perspectives in black and white, ed. by Michael Montgomery and Guy Bailey, 102-10. University: University of Alabama Press. [Charles and Prince Georges Cos., SE MD]. Notes seven phonological and sixteen syntactic features of group of speakers of mixed white, black, and Piscataway Indian ancestry, and suggests connection between it and now extinct Chesapeake Bay Creole.

**1.265 Gilyard, R. Keith.** 1986. Voicing myself: a study of sociolinguistic competence. New York: New York University dissertation. Abstract in DAI 46.3636A. [1 B]. Autobiographical study of how language learning intersects with black students' sense of their own culture, therefore requiring social relations to be a vital part of their language education.

**1.266 Ginn, Doris O.** 1975. Black English: Africanisms in western culture. ED 103 863. 12 pp. Calls for understanding by educators of relationship of language and culture and says features of black dialects, especially Gullah, reflect its diverse history.

**1.267 Goerch, Carl.** 1964. Their form of speech. Ocracoke, 67-69. Winston-Salem, NC: John F. Blair. [E NC]. An outsider's comments about Banks speech; says pronunciation of diphthong /ai/ is most distinctive feature.

**1.268 Goff, John Hedges.** n.d. Ballads and dialects of the southern mountaineers. Atlanta: Oglethorpe University thesis. 34 pp. Classifies distinctive linguistic forms in mountains as 1) obsolete forms; 2) illiterate and careless forms; or 3) neologisms required by local conditions; includes word-lists from KY, NC, and TN. Much material taken from J. Combs (1.145).

**1.269 Golden, Ruth.** 1963. Effectiveness of instructional tapes for changing regional speech patterns. Detroit: Wayne State University dissertation. Abstract in DAI 24.4184-85A. Tests effectiveness of language laboratory techniques in helping black high school students in Detroit to shift from Southern rural to Northern urban pronunciation.

**1.270 Golden, Ruth.** 1964. Improving English skills of culturally different youth. Washington: U.S. Government Printing Office. P. 104, identification and unsophisticated description of features of speech of "culturally disadvantaged children" migrating from Appalachia to Detroit.

**1.271 Goodner, Jacob Beauford.** 1981. An examination of place names and presentation of lexical data for Birmingham, Alabama (based on the LAGS urban supplement). Athens: University of Georgia thesis. Study of responses to LAGS Urban Supplement questionnaire by nine speakers in the AL city.

**1.272 Grant, Hazel V.** 1967. A study of the tendency of some underprivileged high school students to use abusive terms. Baton Rouge: Louisiana State University thesis.

**1.273 Graves, John Temple.** 1938. Southern speech. SSJ 4.5-6. Essay by professional Southerner.

**1.274 Greatman, Bonnie M.** 1970. A dialect atlas of Maryland. New York: New York University dissertation. Abstract in DAI 31.6580A. [50 DARE informants]. Finds increasing education, population mobility, and urbanization are erasing original ethnic settlement patterns of dialect in MD.

**1.275 Greco, Claudia.** 1987. The care and feeding of southern men: a survival guide for the unsuspecting yankee. Chapel Hill, NC: Algonquin. Que pasa, y'all?, 19-23, anecdotes and intimate observations on use and characteristics of Southern English by men; p. 110, drawling as part of Southern bellé syndrome.

**1.276 Green, Elizabeth.** 1944. Dialect study of Mobile, Mobile County, Alabama, made as a preliminary investigation for the preparation of work sheets for the linguistic atlas. Auburn: Alabama Polytechnic Institute thesis. [8 speakers, S AL]. Outlines vowels, diphthongs, and consonants of Mobile speech and compares lexical patterns with British usage.

**1.277 Green, Gordon C.** 1963. Negro dialect, the last barrier to integration. JNE 32.81-83. Argues that blacks should get rid of their dialect.

**1.278 Green, Paul.** 1925. The dialects of North Carolina and their importance to the teachers of English. English Forum 2.1-4.1,3-5. Distinguishes four regional dialects in NC and presents case for why a schoolteacher should be a student of the state's dialects; cites usages from Cape Fear Valley area.

**1.279 Green, Paul.** 1968. Words and ways: stories and incidents from my Cape Fear Valley folklore collection. Special issue. North Carolina Folklore 16. 147 pp. [SE NC]. Localisms from the Cape Fear Valley, illustrated by stories and anecdotes. **Reviews:** J. Holm. 1983. Word 34.42-45; W. K. McNeil. 1969. TFSB 35.63.

**1.280 Greene, Susan Lutters.** 1972. A comparison of black and white speech in a rural Georgia county. Athens: University of Georgia thesis. 482 pp., including transcriptions of data. [4W, 7B adults, Walton Co., NE GA]. Finds minimal differences between black and white speech, e.g., only black speech has word-final glottal stop and white speech diphthongizes short front vowels and uses postvocalic /r/ more than black speech; finds no evidence of unmarked be.

**1.281 Greet, William Cabell.** 1934. Southern speech. Culture in the South, ed. by W. T. Couch, 594-615. Chapel Hill: University of North Carolina Press. Early survey by partisan Southern linguist, based primarily on phonograph recordings, and authoritative discussion of thirty-one features of coastal and lowland Southern pronunciation, of how Southern speech is represented on stage and in print, how Southern speech is related to varieties of British speech, and how black speech and white speech in the South are related.

**1.282 Greet, William Cabell.** 1936. Southern speech--which way? Southern Speech Bulletin 1.41-44. Notes major social changes at work in the South and discusses question of which standard should be adopted by speech teachers in region; says there is no reason Southerners should look outside their region for a standard.

**1.283 Greet, William Cabell.** 1938. A standard American language? New Republic 95.68-70. Popular essay by linguistic consultant to CBS denying existence of a national standard of speech and outlining five diverse types of regional English in the U.S.

**1.284 Guest, Charles Boyd.** 1932. A survey of the dialect of the Lee County, Alabama, Negro. Auburn: Alabama Polytechnic Institute thesis. [E CENT AL]. Surveys phonetic, lexical, and morphological features; includes extensive transcripts.

**1.285 H., S. A.** 1932. The Texas language. American Mercury 27.375. Five notes on TX usage, including assertion that you all is found in the King James Bible and is therefore not original to the American South.

**1.286 Hackenberg, Robert G.** 1975. The application of sociolinguistic techniques in rural Appalachia. Views on language, ed. by Reza Ordoubadian and Walburga von Raffler-Engel, 192-200. Murfreesboro: Middle Tennessee State University. [WV]. Discusses applicability of socioeconomic indices developed by urban sociologists for measuring social stratification in rural WV.

**1.287 Halaby, Raouf.** 1981. The influences of migratory routes on Arkansas dialects. Abstract in NADS 13.3.3. Discusses dialect differences in four corners of AR and attributes these to east-west migratory movements.

**1.288 Hall, Joe D.** 1941. A dialect study of Langdale, Chambers County, Alabama, made as a preliminary investigation for the preparation of work sheets for the linguistic atlas. Auburn: Alabama Polytechnic Institute thesis. [5M, 2F, ages 16-78, E CENT AL]. Studies lexical peculiarities and two phonological variables (postvocalic /r/ and the velar nasal); compares evidence with Guest (**1.284**) and Rash (**1.632**).

**1.289 Hall, Joseph S.** 1939. Recording speech in the Great Smokies. Regional Review 3.3-8. Richmond, VA: National Park Service, Region One. [E TN]. Account of field work for his dissertation (**4.153**).

**1.290 Hall, Joseph S.** 1941. Mountain speech in the Great Smokies. National Park Service history popular study series no. 5. Washington: United States Department of the Interior. Same as preceding item.

**1.291 Hall, Joseph S.** 1960. Smoky mountain folks and their lore. Asheville, NC: Cataloochee Press. Smokies dialect, 54-65. List of items collected by author in TN and NC mountains from 1937 to 1956.

**1.292 Hall, Mary P. F.** 1977. Description of the linguistic characteristics of the careful speech of recent high school graduates in entry-level positions of job categories of large employment in selected counties of southwest Virginia. Blacksburg: Virginia Polytechnic Institute thesis.

**1.293 Halpert, Herbert.** 1924. [Language of the Pine Mountain area]. Notes from the Pine Mountain Settlement School 2.1-2. [SE KY]. Informal essay on archaisms, especially those with a literary flavor, in mountain speech.

**1.294 Hanners, LaVerne.** 1972. A study of the effectiveness of linguistically oriented teaching methods in correcting dialectally derived errors in the writing of black college students. ED 067 701. 73 pp. [46 B college students, SE AR]. Experimental study concluding that method of teaching grammar based on linguistic analysis significantly reduces dialect errors but not nondialect errors.

**1.295 Hanners, LaVerne.** 1979. The written and spoken dialect of the southeast Arkansas black college student. Muncie: Ball State University dissertation. Abstract in DAI 41.4016A. [B college students, Pine Bluff, AR]. Studies leveled inflections, lack of phonemic differentiation, apocope, epithesis, and features of copula verb.

**1.296 Hannum, Alberta Pierson.** 1943. Words and music. The great smokies and the blue ridge, ed. by Roderick Peattie, 146-50. [E TN, W NC]. New York: Vanguard. Discusses grammar, pronunciation, Chaucerisms, and distinctive place names in the Smoky Mountains.

**1.297 Hannum, Alberta Pierson.** 1969. Shakespeare's America. Look back with love, 29-33. New York: Vanguard. Reprinting of preceding item.

**1.298 Harder, Kelsie B.** 1952. Euphemistic dilemmas in Tennessee. AS 27.156-57. [CENT TN]. Effects of taboo on goober, peanut, (wood) pecker.

**1.299 Harington, Donald.** 1976. Should the migrants learn the language? Proceedings of the Conference on Ozark In-migration. Eureka Springs: Arkansas Humanities Committee. Pp. 38-41, contrasts old-fashioned speech of older natives with that of newcomers to Ozarks from urban areas.

**1.300 Harmon, Marion F.** 1914. Negro wit and humor, also containing folk lore, folk songs, race peculiarities, race history. Louisville, KY: Harmon. Compilation of sayings, proverbs, synonyms, and other items from Southern Workman.

**1.301 Harper, Francis.** 1926. Tales of the Okefinokee. AS 1.407-20. [SE GA]. Vocabulary and pronunciation.

**1.302 Harper, Jared.** 1969. Irish traveler cant: an historical, structural, and sociolinguistic study of an argot. Athens: University of Georgia thesis.

**1.303 Harper, Jared.** 1977. Irish traveler cant. The Irish travelers of Georgia, 88-106. Athens: University of Georgia dissertation. Abstract in DAI 38.4912A. 171 pp. Discusses Shelta, or "Cant," used by itinerant Irish traders in GA.

**1.304 Harper, Jared, and Charles Hudson.** 1971. Irish traveler cant. JEL 5.78-86. Social background and notes on phonology and morphology of Irish Tinker Cant (or Shelta) in GA, whose grammar is English but whose lexicon is largely Irish Gaelic.

**1.305 Harper, Jared, and Charles Hudson.** 1973. Irish traveler cant in its social setting. SFQ 38.101-14. Functions of the cant in Irish traveler society; sample conversations with cant.

**1.306 Harris, Jesse W.** 1946. The dialect of Appalachia in southern

Illinois. AS 21.96-99. Discussion, list, and comparison of vocabulary and pronunciation of area to research on Southern Appalachian speech.

**1.307 Harrison, Deborah S., and Tom Trabasso, eds.** 1976. Black English: a seminar. Hillsdale, NJ: Lawrence Erlbaum. 301 pp. Sixteen essays on definition, historical origins, use, and implications of black English. **Reviews:** J. L. Dillard. 1983. LPLP 7.179-87; M. Hoover. 1978. Journal of Psycholinguistic Research 7.319-25.

**1.308 Hartman, James W.** 1969. Some preliminary findings from DARE. AS 44.191-99. Outlines nature and progress of Dictionary of American Regional English, presents preliminary findings from dictionary (e.g., for distribution of postvocalic /r/ in the South), and suggests areas of research for which the dictionary can provide data.

**1.309 Haskins, Jim, and Hugh F. Butts.** 1973. The psychology of black language. New York: Barnes and Noble. The genesis of black American dialects, 28-37, discusses West African pidgin, New World creole, and "universal black suffering" as possible bases for a universal black language; America's debt to the language of black Americans, 54-62.

**1.310 Heath, Shirley Brice.** 1983. Ways with words: ethnography of communication in communities and classrooms. New York: Cambridge University Press. [SC]. Pioneering ethnography of two communities, one black and one white, in the Carolina Piedmont, this volume describes and compares the linguistic environment of homes and schools of two communities in terms of oral traditions, how parents and children talk to each other, how stories are told, how language is used in the schools, and what is read and why. **Reviews:** D. Christian. 1985. AS 60.70-73; C. Feagin. 1985. Language 61.489-93; J. P. Gee. 1986. TESOL Quarterly 20.737-43; K. Walters. 1984. LIS 13.515-20; D. Bloome. 1984. Reading Teacher 37.892-94; M. Ward. 1984. AA 86.1047-48.

**1.311 Hedberg, Johannes.** 1980. The rise of black English in the United States. Moderna Sprak 74.215-18. Reviews and discusses implications of Ann Arbor "black English case."

**1.312 Hedges, James S.** 1980. Dialect and folk language: some pedagogical implications. Papers from the 1979 Mid-America Linguistics Conference, ed. by Robert S. Haller, 127-33. Lincoln: University of Nebraska. Distinguishes "folk" culture from "high culture" and "mass culture" and says such linguistic forms as phrasal verbs are typical of folk cultures.

**1.313 Hempl, George.** 1894. American speech maps. DN 1.315-18. Reprinted as American dialect. 1894. MLN 9.155-57; as Local usage in American speech. 1894. Dial 17.263; as Some American speech maps. 1895. Proceedings of the American Philological Association 26.41-42. Early dialect atlas questionnaire of eighty items, with directions for its use and request for informants.

**1.314 Hempl, George.** 1896. Grease and greasy. DN 1.438-44. Abstract in Nation 64.164 (Mar. 4, 1897). First proposal for systematic investigation of American dialects; report of author's preliminary study of 1600 informants, showing Northern, Midland, Southern, and Western dialect areas. **Reprinted** in H. Allen and G. Underwood 1971(**1.12**).154-59.

**1.315 Hench, Atcheson L.** 1938. Corbins and Nicolsons--a preliminary note. AS 13.77-79. [N VA]. Report on thirty-eight VA informants whose speech was taperecorded by Hench and Archibald Hill.

**1.316 Hendrickson, Robert.** 1986. American talk: the words and ways of American dialects. New York: Viking. 230 pp. Yawl spoken here: the sounds of the South, 86-112; Deep down in the holler where the hoot owl hollers at noon: hillbilly tawk, 113-29; "Rappin" black style: including pidgin, plantation creole, Gullah, and black English, 130-53. Popular condensation of exotic features, based on personal observations and century of published research and characterized by overstatements and anachronisms.

**1.317 Hibbard, Addison.** 1926. Aesop in Negro dialect. AS 1.495-99. Plea for serious study of black speech.

**1.318 Higgins, Cleo Surry.** 1973. The spoken English of black and white high school students of Palatka, Florida, implications for teaching and curriculum development. Madison: University of Wisconsin dissertation. Abstract in DAI 34.1244A. [20 high school students, 16 adults, N FL]. Finds that blacks and whites "differed more in phonology than in grammar and other features of usage" and that "most similarities were found at the middle class level, least at the lower class level." Surveys parents and teachers to determine most stigmatized features, finding these are "vulgarity and 'foul' language, irregular verb forms, and 'grammatical errors'."

**1.319 Hill, Archibald A.** 1935. Research in Southern speech in cooperation with the linguistic atlas. AS 10.237-40. Discusses reaction to proposed Linguistic Atlas of the South Atlantic States and research prospects and needs in region.

**1.320 Hill, Archibald A., Eston E. Ericson, Miles E. Hanley, Hans Kurath, Samuel J. McCoy, Lorenzo D. Turner, and Claude M. Wise.** 1934. A report on proposed investigations of Southern speech. DN 6.420-24. Discusses ongoing research and outline of nine types of needed research.

**1.321 Hiller, Anna K.** 1939. Means of expression. Life of the Ozarks seen through the literature of the region, 106-35. Oxford: Miami University thesis. Surveys general tendencies of Ozark speech, including extravagant word formation and naming practices, as represented in popular literature.

**1.322 Hobson, Charles D.** 1981. Language and black children: the effects of dialects in selected passages on black third graders' reading strategies as revealed by oral reading miscues. Atlanta: Georgia State University dissertation. Abstract in DAI 42.1075A. Pp. 171-201, Appendix D, Analysis of Metropolitan Atlanta Black Dialect.

**1.323 Hoff, Patricia J.** 1968. A dialect study of Faulkner County, Arkansas. Baton Rouge: Louisiana State University dissertation. Abstract in DAI 29.247A. Abstract reprinted in J. Williamson and V. Burke 1971(1.823).681-82. [28 adults, CENT AR]. Studies pronunciation and vocabulary, finding Southern, Midland, and some Northern influences; says patterns too complex for isoglosses to be drawn.

**1.324 Hoffer, Bates L.** 1982. The Alabama-Coushatta of east Texas. Essays in native American English, ed. by Guillermo Bartelt, Susan Penfield, and Bates L. Hoffer, 55-66. Discusses sociolinguistic situation and salient phonological, morphological, and syntactic features of the English spoken by the combined Muskhogean Indian group.

**1.325 Hogan, Robert F.,** ed. 1966. The English language in the school program. Urbana: NCTE. 280 pp. Anthology of articles for schoolteachers.

**1.326 Hopkins, E. W.** 1895. Dialect study in America. Dial 18.136 (Mar. 1). Points out that terms labeled by Bondurant (**1.79**) as Southern can often be found in the rural North.

**1.327 Hoskins, Conde R., Jr.** 1952. Dialect. The handbook of Texas, ed. by Walter Prescott Webb, 499. Austin: Texas State Historical Association. Encyclopedia essay summarizing work of Atwood (**3.17**), Wheatley (**4.369**), and others.

**1.328 Houston, Susan H.** 1969. Child black English in northern Florida: a sociolinguistic examination. Atlanta: Southeastern Education Laboratory. [N FL].

**1.329 Houston, Susan H.** 1969. A sociolinguistic consideration of the black English of children in northern Florida. Language 45.599-607. [22 B, ages 9-12, 5 M, 17 F, N FL]. Discusses twenty differences in phonological rules and four syntactic differences between "Child Black English" and "standard White English" and outlines sociolinguistic problems in eliciting and assessing speech of black children.

**1.330 Houston, Susan H.** 1970. Competence and performance in child black English. Language Sciences 12.9-14. Considers whether "Child Black English" differs from "Educated White English" in terms of competence or performance and decides the difference is determined "by application of systematic performance rules."

**1.331 Houston, Susan H.** 1972. More on competence and performance. Language Sciences 22.21-24. Answers Butters (**1.112**) criticisms of preceding item.

**1.332 Houston, Susan H.** 1972. Child black English: the school register. Linguistics 90.20-34. [B children, ages 10-12, N FL]. Examines difference between reading and talking and theorizes about implications for language competence.

**1.333 Howell, Benita J.** 1981. A survey of folklife along the Big South Fork of the Cumberland River: report of investigations no. 30. Knoxville: University of Tennessee Department of Anthropology. Speech, 206. [CENT TN]. Brief, general comments on Appalachian speech and report of available data from Big South Fork study.

**1.334 Howren, Robert.** 1958. The speech of Louisville, Kentucky. Bloomington: Indiana University dissertation. Abstract in DAI 19.527. Abstract reprinted in J. Williamson and V. Burke 1971(**1.823**).683. [15 natives, W and B]. Describes lexicon and segmental phonology of Louisville speech, along with miscellaneous features of its morphology and syntax; finds lexicon is primarily Midland and Northern, morphology and syntax is Midland and Southern, and phonology for whites is South Midland and for blacks is Southern. Outlines leveling of dialectal features due to urbanization.

**1.335 Howren, Robert.** 1962. The speech of Ocracoke, North Carolina. AS 37.163-75. Abstract in SAB 25.5 (1960). [E NC]. Based on more than two dozen interviews, presents pronunciation and vocabulary that distinguish oldest Outer Bank community from that of the mainland. **Reprinted** in J. Williamson and V. Burke 1971(**1.823**).280-93; in D. Shores and C. Hines 1977(**1.689**).61-72.

**1.336 Huffines, Marion Lois.** 1989. Language varieties, German. Encyclopedia of Southern culture, ed. by William Ferris and Charles Wilson. Chapel Hill: University of North Carolina Press. Short essay surveying two varieties of German spoken in the American South--in W VA and CENT TX.

**1.337 Hull, Alexander.** 1989. Language varieties, French. Encyclopedia of Southern culture, ed. by William Ferris and Charles Wilson. Chapel Hill: University of North Carolina Press. Short essay surveying history and range of French language in the South, with emphasis on three varieties of the language spoken in LA.

**1.338 Hurst, Sam N.** 1929. Mountain speech. The mountains redeemed: the romance of the mountains, 32-34. Appalachia, VA: Hurst and Company. Comments on archaicness, aptness of expression, and exactness of logic of S Appalachian speech.

**1.339 Hurston, Zora Neale.** 1970. Characteristics of Negro expression. Negro--an anthology, ed. by Nancy Cunard, 24-32. New York: Ungar. Says "the Negro's greatest contribution to the language is : 1) the use of metaphor and simile; 2) the use of double descriptions [e.g., speedy-hurry]; 3) the use of verbal nouns."

**1.340 Jackson, Blyden.** 1976. The waiting years: essays on American Negro literature. Baton Rouge: Louisiana State University Press. Pp. 146-54, review of J. L. Dillard 1972 **(1.190).**

**1.341 Jackson, Juanita, Sabra Slaughter, and J. Herman Blake.** 1974. The Sea Islands as a cultural resource. Black Scholar 5.6.32-39. Cultural and political profile of Sea Islands of SC and GA, with notes on language.

**1.342 Jackson, Sarah E.** 1975. Unusual words, expressions, and pronunciation in a North Carolina mountain community. AJ 2.148-60. [Ashe Co., W NC]. Unusual usage, idioms, names, and pronunciations collected by an outsider.

**1.343 Jacobson, Rodolfo.** 1975. Research in southwestern English and the sociolinguistic perspective: thoughts and suggestions from a newcomer to Texas. Papers in southwest English 1: research techniques and prospects. ED 111 208. 16 pp. Outlines approaches to and caveats for study of TX English.

**1.344 Jaffe, Hilda.** 1966. The speech of the central coast of North Carolina: the Carteret County version of the Banks "brogue." East Lansing: Michigan State University dissertation. Republished as PADS 60. 83 pp. Abstract in DAI 27.1355-56A. Abstract reprinted in J. Williamson and V. Burke 1971(1.823).685-86. [12 adults, E NC]. Finds no social differences among Outer Banks speakers but some differences in vowel pronunciation and verb usage between E NC mainland and Outer Banks, the latter often being more archaic. Based on taped interviews using the South Atlantic atlas worksheets. **Review:** K. Hameyer. 1980. ZDL 47.108-11.

**1.345 Johnson, Barbara Ann.** 1977. The dialect of Husser and Uneedus in Tangipahoa Parish, Louisiana: a study in generational change. Baton Rouge: Louisiana State University thesis. [12 M, 12 F, ages 13-72, SE LA]. 255 pp. Studies degree to which generational and gender groups have modified their speech to conform to outside norms; finds women have as many standard forms as men, even though their social contacts are far more limited.

**1.346 Johnson, Edwin D.** 1927. The speech of the American Negro folk. Opportunity 5.195-97. Classic argument that American blacks lack any dialect or contribution of their own to nation's speech and that their variety of English reflects survivals of archaic forms of English preserved because of cultural backwardness of blacks.

**1.347 Johnson, Guy B.** 1930. The speech of the Negro. Folk say: a regional miscellany 1930, ed. by B. A. Botkin, 346-58. Norman: University of Oklahoma Press. Says black English is American English, with varieties same as English of whites; only Gullah is different.

**1.348 Johnson, James Weldon**, ed. 1931. The book of American Negro spirituals. New York: Viking. Pp. 42-46, comments by poet stressing that black dialect "is the result of the effort of the slave to establish a medium of communication between himself and his master" and that the "soft, indolent speech" of blacks had influence on Southern whites; notes variation in black speech according to region in the South and according to grammatical environment.

**1.349 Jones, Harry L.** 1965. An approach to dialectical bilingualism: Negro folk speech in America. Maryland English Journal 4.1.50-55. Discusses phonemic, morphemic, and lexical elements of black folk speech in MD but claims none of them are exclusive to black speech.

**1.350 Jones, Mabel Jean.** 1973. The regional English of the former inhabitants of Cades Cove in the Great Smoky Mountains. Knoxville: University of Tennessee dissertation. Abstract in DAI 34.5146A. [5 elderly natives, Blount Co., E TN]. Study of pronunciation (mostly of vowels) and grammar (mostly of verb principal parts) of ex-inhabitants of Cades Cove area.

**1.351 Jones, Stephen C.** 1978. The use of foreign language methodology in teaching written edited American English to speakers of black English. Greenville: East Carolina University thesis. 102 pp. Package of lessons to teach dialect speakers "written edited American English" patterns of subject-verb agreement, negation, and use of be verb and discussion of theory of contrastive analysis behind them.

**1.352 Jordan, Terry G.** 1976. Traditional English dialects. Atlas of Texas, ed. by Stanley A. Arbingast et al. Austin: University of Texas Bureau of Business Research.

**1.353 Keener, Julia Ann.** 1973. A socio-linguistic description of nonstandard black English speakers in Wichita Falls, Texas. Wichita Falls: Midwestern University thesis. 76 pp. [6 LMC W, 6 UMC B, 6 LMC B, 6 UWC B, 6 LWC B, N CENT TX]. Finds that variation in three phonological features and two grammatical features correlates significantly with education, occupation, and sex, but not with age, style, or racial isolation.

**1.354 Kehr, Kurt.** 1979. "Deutsche" dialekte in Virginia und West Virginia (U.S.A.): zur typologie virginadeutscher Sprachinseln. ZDL 46.289-319. Discusses six locations of German language use in VA and WV, and explains their relation to and development from original settlements of Germans in

18th and 19th centuries; distinguishes VA German from PA German.

**1.355 Kent, Rosemary.** 1981. Shootin' the bull: a Texas lexicon. Genuine Texas handbook, 221-24. New York: Workman. Glossary of ninety items and nine rules of pronunciation to use to "sound like a Tejas native."

**1.356 Kent-Paxton, Laura Belle.** 1983. A linguistic analysis of the diaries of M. E. Anderson-Kent, pioneer woman. Commerce: East Texas State University dissertation. Abstract in DAI 44.1777A. 393 pp. [MO, LA]. Study of unpublished diaries written between 1896 and 1928, focusing on "colloquial words, brief forms of both words and sentences, phonetic spellings," and changes in spelling and grammar over thirty-three years; notes "a frequent loss of final 's', a joining of many previously separated morphemes, and a regularization of many verbs."

**1.357 Kephart, Horace.** 1913. The mountain dialect. Our Southern high-landers, 276-304. New York: Macmillan. Revised ed. (1922), 350-78. Reprinted in 1976 by University of Tennessee Press, Knoxville. [NC, TN mountains]. Informal, lay account of speech of Smoky Mountains; some phonology and grammar; mainly lexicon. **Reviews:** M. Bush. 1977. American Forests 83.38-39; W. K. McNeil. 1978. JAF 91.612-13; H. D. Shapiro. 1977. Book Forum 3.278-84.

**1.358 Kerr, Elizabeth M., and Ralph M. Aderman,** eds. 1971. Aspects of American English. 2nd ed. New York: Harcourt Brace Jovanovich. Thirty-seven essays on historical, regional, literary and colloquial, and social and class aspects of American English. **Review:** A. Marckwardt. 1972. MLJ 56.522-23.

**1.359 King, Florence.** 1975. Southern ladies and gentlemen. New York: Stein and Day. 216 pp. Intimate profile of Southerners and their culture, including commentary on euphemisms and other aspects of speech.

**1.360 Kochman, Thomas,** ed. 1972. Rappin' and stylin' out. Urbana: University of Illinois Press. 424 pp. Collection of twenty-seven essays on expressive verbal and nonverbal behavior, expressive role behavior, and vocabulary and culture of urban black community. **Reviews:** R. Abrahams and J. Szwed. 1975. AA 77.329-35; E. A. Folb. 1975. Language 51.243-47.

**1.361 Konold, Florence.** 1937. A workbook in speech correction for high school teachers. Baton Rouge: Louisiana State University thesis. Pp. 152-68, sectional dialect. Compiles "a list of the outstanding errors of Southern American dialect."

**1.362 Krapp, George Philip.** 1924. The English of the Negro. American Mercury 2.190-95. Argues English-dialect origin of American black speech, contending that blacks speak same kind of English as first English settlers on the continent, and that the speech of blacks retains, with exception of no more than half a dozen words, no trace of any African language influence.

**1.363 Kretzschmar, William A.** 1989. Raven I. McDavid, Jr. Encyclopedia of Southern culture, ed. by William Ferris and Charles Wilson. Chapel Hill: University of North Carolina Press. Short biography and appreciation of the linguistic geographer's contributions to the study of Southern English.

**1.364 Kroll, H. H.** 1925. A comparative study of upper and lower Southern folk speech. Nashville: George Peabody College thesis. Compiles in dictionary format dialect forms heard by author in nine disparate Southern counties.

**1.365 Kubesch, Lillian.** 1963. Dialects of southern Colorado County, Texas. Huntsville: Sam Houston State University thesis. [S CENT TX].

**1.366 Kurath, Hans.** 1934-44. Status reports of the linguistic atlas of the United States and Canada. American Council of Learned Societies Bulletin 22.88-92 (1934); 23.85-88 (1935); 25.82-85 (1938); 27.61-63 (1938); 42.68-72 (1944). Periodic progress reports on atlas project, including early development of LAMSAS.

**1.367 Kurath, Hans.** 1936. The linguistic atlas of the United States and Canada. Proceedings of the second international congress of phonetic sciences, 18-22. Cambridge, UK: Cambridge University Press. Early profile of Linguistic Atlas project showing its potential use for trans-Atlantic comparisons of speech.

**1.368 Kurath, Hans.** 1950. The American languages. Scientific American 182.48-51. Popular essay on rationale of Linguistic Atlas project, settlement history in country, and nature of dialects. **Reprinted** in C. M. Babcock, ed. 1961. The ordeal of American English, 95-99. Boston: Houghton Mifflin.

**1.369 Kurath, Hans.** 1951. Linguistic regionalism. Regionalism in America, ed. by Merril Jensen, 297-310. Madison: University of Wisconsin Press. Outlines major speech regions of Atlantic states and relates settlement history to them.

**1.370 Kurath, Hans.** 1964. Interrelation between regional and social dialects. Proceedings of the ninth international congress of linguists, Cambridge, Mass., ed. by H. G. Lunt, 135-43. The Hague: Mouton. Includes comments on vowels of book, cut, door, and tomato, and on synonyms for dragonfly in Eastern VA. **Reprinted** in H. Allen and G. Underwood 1971(**1.12**).365-74.

**1.371 Kurath, Hans.** 1966. Regionalism in American English. The English language in the school curriculum, ed. by Robert E. Hogan, 161-75. Champaign: NCTE. Discusses regional dissemination of variants in pronunciation, vocabulary, and grammar on Atlantic Seaboard and shows inadequacy of current dictionaries in listing and labeling the variants. **Reprinted** in C. Laird and R. Gorrell, eds. 1971. Reading about language, 296-98. New York: Harcourt Brace Jovanovich.

**1.372 Kurath, Hans.** 1970. The sociocultural interpretation of dialect areas [Upper South]. Studies in general and oriental linguistics, presented to Shiro Hattori on the occasion of his sixtieth birthday, ed. by Roman Jakobson and Shigeo Kawamoto, 374-77. Tokyo: TEC. 2 maps. Says boundary between Upper South and Midland dialect areas in VA, MD, and DE corresponds with settlement history rather than political boundaries or natural barriers.

**1.373 Kurath, Hans.** 1971. Regional and local words. Aspects of American English, ed. by Elizabeth M. Kerr and Ralph M. Aderman, 182-90. New York: Harcourt Brace Jovanovich. Discusses variation for nineteen grammatical and lexical terms in the Atlantic states.

**1.374 Kurath, Hans.** 1972. Studies in area linguistics. Bloomington: Indiana University Press. The structure of the Upper South, 46-51, geographical perspectives on region's speech, with emphasis on boundaries; Gullah, 118-21, summary of distinguishing features, with emphasis on "simplification" of the dialect (**Reprinted** in H. Allen and M. Linn 1986 **(1.11)**.104-10). **Reviews:** G. Gilbert. 1976. La Monda Lingvo-Problemo 6.56-61; M. F. Hopkins. 1975. SSCJ 40.213-14; R. I. McDavid, Jr. 1971. AS 47.285-92; L. A. Pederson. 1975. Foundations of Language 12.609-13; R. Shuy. 1974. LIS 3.295-97; M. S. Whitley. 1975. Linguistics 161.109-20.

**1.375 Kwachka, Patricia B.** 1970. Negro speech variation: a paralinguistic analysis of a Southern folk belief. Gainesville: University of Florida thesis. [16 B, 16 W, ages 18-45, N FL]. Explores extent to which blacks modify pitch, loudness, tempo, and precision of their speech in presence of whites and of other blacks.

**1.376 Labov, William.** 1969. The logic of nonstandard English. Linguistics and the teaching of standard English to speakers of other languages or dialects, ed. by James E. Alatis, 1-43. Washington: Georgetown University Press. Counters theory of Basil Bernstein and other educational psychologists about impoverishment and deviance of nonstandard English and argues that compensatory language arts programs, especially for blacks, are based on invalid research into native language patterns of children and erroneous assumptions. **Reprinted** in R. Bailey and J. Robinson 1973 **(1.39)**.319-54; in W. Labov 1972(**1.377**).201-40; in F. Williams 1970 **(1.814)**.153-89.

**1.377 Labov, William.** 1972. Language in the inner city: studies in the black English vernacular. Philadelphia: University of Pennsylvania Press. xiv + 412 pp. Landmark study of linguistic, educational, and social issues concerning Black English Vernacular. **Reviews:** R. Abrahams and J. Szwed. 1975. AA 77.329-35; J. J. Attinasi. 1974. The Bilingual Review/La Revista

Bilingue 1.279-304; R. Burling. 1975. Language 51.505-09; D. R. Entwisle. 1975. Social Forces 53.658-59; T. Klammer. 1974. Studies in Linguistics 24.93-98; T. Kochman. 1975. Foundation of Language 13.95; I. Lohman. 1975. Instructor 84.115 (Jan.); R. I. McDavid, Jr. 1979. AS 54.291-304; R. C. Naremore. 1974. QJS 60.260-61; J. Schultz. 1976. Urban Life 4.490-92; R. Wright. 1975. LIS 4.185-98.

**1.378 Labov, William,** ed. 1980. Locating language in time and space. New York: Academic Press. xx + 271 pp. Studies of language variation conducted within Labovian quantitative paradigm. **Reviews:** F. Anshen. 1983. AS 58.273-79; S. Gal. 1982. AA 84.853-61; L. Milroy. 1983. LIS 12.82-89; S. Romaine. 1983. Lingua 60.87-96.

**1.379 Labov, William.** 1987. [Are black and white vernaculars diverging?] AS 62.5-12,62-67. Part of NWAV panel discussion; argues two vernaculars are diverging in Philadelphia and that black speech in general is becoming less like white speech.

**1.380 Labov, William, Paul Cohen, Clarence Robins, and John Lewis.** 1968. A study of the non-standard English of Negro and Puerto Rican speakers in New York City. Volume I: phonological and grammatical analysis. Final report. Office of Education Cooperative Research Project no. 3288. ED 028 423. 397 pp. [50 pre-adolescents, 6 pre-adolescent and adolescent peer groups, 100 MC and WC adults, New York City]. Reviews related research and describes project, background, methods, and analysis of investigation of structural and functional differences between speech of Central Harlem and standard English and concludes that the former is related to the latter "by differences in low-level rules which have marked effects on surface structure." **Review:** J. Wilson. 1970. EJ 59.1299-1300,1312.

**1.381 Labov, William, Paul Cohen, Clarence Robins, and John Lewis.** 1968. A study of the non-standard English of Negro and Puerto Rican speakers in New York City. Volume II: the use of language in the speech community. Final report. Office of Education Cooperative Research Project no. 3288. ED 028 424. 366 pp. [50 pre-adolescents, 6 pre-adolescent and adolescent peer groups, 100 MC and WC adults, New York City]. Describes peer groups and vernacular culture of innercity black speakers analyzed in volume 1 above; examines verbal capacities of black children and concludes functional differences rather than structural differences between their language and that of the school system impedes their educational success. **Review:** J. Wilson. 1970. EJ 59.1299-1300,1312.

**1.382 Lance, Donald M., and Stephen V. Slemons.** 1976. The use of the computer in plotting the geographical distribution of dialect items. Computers and the Humanities 10.221-29. 7 maps. Demonstrates method to plot dialect items to produce national and regional maps with responses to individual items and with frequency counts for primary DARE responses.

**1.383 Language.** 1981. Encyclopedia of black America, ed. by W. Augustus Low and Virgil A. Clift, 23-26. New York: McGraw-Hill. Summary history of black speech in the U.S. stressing African survivals and presented from creolist point of view.

**1.384 Larmouth, Donald, and Marjorie Remsing.** 1982. "Kentuck" dialect features in the cutover region of northern Wisconsin. Abstract in NADS 14.3.4. Claims WI speakers descended from Kentuckians maintain lexical and grammatical features but have accommodated to phonology of WI regional speech.

**1.385 Lawrence, K.** 1974. Oral history of slavery. Southern Exposure 1.3-4.84-86. Review of J. L. Dillard 1972 (**1.190**).

**1.386 Leas, Susan E.** 1981. The Emory collection of the Louisiana workbooks. LAGS Working Papers, 1st series, no. 3. Microfiche 1181. Addendum to Pederson et al. 1981(**1.594**). 59 pp. Describes, assesses, and gives informant specifications for seventy-four field records made in LA under supervision of Claude Merton Wise, mostly in the 1930s.

**1.387 Leas, Susan E.** 1981. LAGS informants: social characteristics. LAGS Working Papers, 1st series, no. 12. Microfiche 1193. Addendum to Pederson, et al. 1981(**1.594**). 29 pp. Gives breakdown of LAGS informants according to ethnic origin, age, nativity, religious affiliation, and occupation.

**1.388 Leas, Susan E.** 1981. LAGS protocols: editorial procedures. LAGS Working Papers, 1st series, no. 15. Microfiche 1196. Addendum to Pederson, et al. 1981(**1.594**). 24 pp. Describes how LAGS protocols were prepared--copied, edited, and proofread.

**1.389 LeCompte, Nolan P., Jr.** 1968. Certain points of dialectal usage in South Louisiana. Louisiana Studies 7.149-58. [Lafourche and Terrebonne Parishes]. Influence of French on phonemic values and morphological, syntactic, and lexical variants of area.

**1.390 Lemotte, Justin G. T.** 1985. New Orleans talkin': a guide to yat, cajun, and some creole. New Orleans, LA: Channel Press. 58 pp. Popular dictionary dealing with social life and customs, terms and phrases, and pronunciation in the LA city.

**1.391 Levin, Norman B.** 1965. Contrived speech in Washington: the H. U. sociolect. Georgetown University Round Table 16, ed. by Charles W. Kreidler, 115-28. Washington: Georgetown University Press. [Washington, DC]. Examines morphophonemics, derivational processes for nouns and adjectives, compounding, and other features of Howard University slang for food, drink, shelter, money, and other domains; includes glossary.

**1.392 Levine, Lawrence W.** 1977. The language of freedom. Black culture and black consciousness: Afro-American folk thought from slavery to freedom, 138-55. New York: Oxford University Press. Discusses acculturation of speech and language attitudes of blacks during century following Civil War.

**1.393 Lewis, Roscoe E.** 1959. The life of Mark Thrash. Phylon 20.389-403. Extensive transcript in conventional alphabet of speech of GA black man over 100 years old.

**1.394 Lin, San-Su C.** 1965. Pattern practice in the teaching of standard English to students with a non-standard dialect. ED 002 512. [Orangeburg, SC]. Reports on three-year project at Claflin College using pattern practice to assist Southern black students to master "Standard English."

**1.395 Lollar, Michael.** 1984. A confederacy of sound: what distinguishes Mid-South speech from the rest of Southern English? Mid-South, May 20, 4-6,8-11. [W TN]. Feature article surveying current scholarly opinion in search for unique features and qualities of Memphis speech.

**1.396 Long, Richard A.** 1970. Towards a theory of Afro-American dialects. Center for Afro-American Studies Papers in Linguistics no. 1. Atlanta: Atlanta University. 11 pp. Discusses three dimensions--historical, analytical, and social--necessary to consider existence of an Afro-American dialect and its pedagogic implications.

**1.397 Lourie, Margaret A.** 1978. Black English Vernacular: a comparative description. A pluralistic nation: the language issue in the United States, ed. by Margaret A. Lourie and Nancy F. Conklin, 78-93. Rowley, MA: Newbury House. Overview of phonological and grammatical contrasts of Black English Vernacular with "Standard English."

**1.398 Lourie, Margaret A., and Nancy F. Conklin,** eds. 1978. A pluralistic nation: the language issue in the United States. Rowley, MA: Newbury House.

**1.399 Lucas, Ceil.** 1986. "I ain't got none/you don't have any": noticing and correcting variation in the classroom. Language variety in the South: perspectives in black and white, ed. by Michael Montgomery and Guy Bailey, 348-58. University: University of Alabama Press. [6th graders, Washington, DC]. Analyzes dialect features that teachers notice and correct and their strategies for correction in elementary-school classrooms in various activities.

**1.400 Lucas, Ceil, and Denise Borders.** 1987. Language diversity and classroom discourse. American Educational Research Journal 24.119-41.

**1.401 Lucas, Ceil, Denise Borders, Walt Wolfram, and Roger W. Shuy.**

1983. Language variety and classroom discourse. Final NIE report. 238 pp. + appendix. ED 246 692. [B kindergarten, 1st, 4th graders, teachers, Washington, DC]. Study of spontaneous language use by elementary school children and teachers in classroom activities to examine dialect diversity; finds more language use in situations where dialect is acceptable and raises issues about dialect use in classrooms.

**1.402 Luelsdorff, Philip A.,** ed. 1975. Linguistic perspectives on black English. Regensburg: Verlag Hans Carl. Proceedings of the first Wisconsin Symposium on Linguistic Perspectives on Black English, May 1-2, 1970. Collection of papers from conference on historical, social, and educational aspects of black English; contains transcripts of post-paper discussions. **Review:** W. Viereck. 1979. Amerikastudien 24.210-11.

**1.403 Lusk, Martha B.** 1962. The thaing in Texas. Today's Speech 10.1-2.25. Native Texan expresses chagrin and defensiveness over state's distinctive use of the English language.

**1.404 McAtee, W. L.** 1956. Some dialect of Randolph County and elsewhere in North Carolina. Chapel Hill, NC: privately printed. 59 pp. [CENT NC]. Extensive compilation of words, meanings, phrases, and expressions gleaned mainly from conversation from 1950-56 and not recorded in standard dictionaries.

**1.405 McAtee, W. L.** 1959. Oddments of speech and folklore from North Carolina. n.p. 10 pp. [Randolph Co. and Chapel Hill, NC]. Addendum to preceding item; lists popular words and phrases, rhymes, chants, superstitions, nicknames, and other items.

**1.406 McBride, John S.** 1936. Hill speech in southwestern Tennessee. New York: Columbia University thesis. 66 pp. [LC W adults, Hardeman Co.]. Study of pronunciation, morphology, and syntax based on four-year observation; includes "peculiar words, phrases, and usages."

**1.407 McCall, Mary.** 1969. Linguistic notes on two manuscript collections from Georgia. AS 44.303-05. [GA]. Sample spellings, grammatical constructions, and vocabulary items from family paper collections dating from colonial times through early 20th century.

**1.408 McCrum, Robert, William Cran, and Robert MacNeil.** 1986. The story of English. New York: Viking. 384 pp. Pp. 157-61, comments on Scotch-Irish ancestry of Appalachian speech. Black on white, 194-233, history of black speech in U.S. and its influence on white speech. **Review:** L. Todd. 1987. EWW 8.146-47.

**1.409 McDaniel, Susan L[eas].** 1989. Urban speech in the South. Encyclopedia of Southern culture, ed. by William Ferris and Charles Wilson. Chapel Hill: University of North Carolina Press. Regional and generational variation in vocabulary in LAGS territory, as revealed by responses to LAGS Urban Supplement.

**1.410 McDavid, Raven I., Jr.** 1942. Opportunity for dialect research in Louisiana. Louisiana Schools 20.2.10-11. Outlines possible directions of dialect study in LA.

**1.411 McDavid, Raven I., Jr.** 1944. Phonemic and semantic bifurcation: two examples. Studies in Linguistics 2.4.88-90. [SC Piedmont]. Heist and hoist, rear and rare.

**1.412 McDavid, Raven I., Jr.** 1946. Dialect geography and social science problems. Social Forces 25.168-72. Examines ways cultural patterns are reflected in language of region; analyzes effects of education, fashion, trade, migration, communication, settlement, urbanness, and the economy on variation in American dialects. **Reprinted** in H. Allen and G. Underwood 1971(**1.12**).357-64; in R. McDavid 1979(**1.454**).131-35.

**1.413 McDavid, Raven I., Jr.** 1948. The linguistic atlas of the south atlantic states: its history and present status. SFQ 12.231-40. Design and early work on LAMSAS project.

**1.414 McDavid, Raven I., Jr.** 1948. In search of Southern accents. South Carolina Magazine 11.11.20-21. Popular account of author's fieldwork experiences in SC; discusses progress of understanding SC dialects and says research has discovered that "dialects of SC are more various than even most scholars had hitherto suspected."

**1.415 McDavid, Raven I., Jr.** 1949. Application of the linguistic atlas method to dialect study in the south-central area. SSJ 15.1-9. Explains how linguistic atlas work proceeds and suggests how its techniques may be adapted for South-Central area of Lower Mississippi Valley.

**1.416 McDavid, Raven I., Jr.** 1951. Dialect differences and inter-group tensions. Studies in Linguistics 9.27-33. Says dialect differences in a community are index to cleavage between social groups; reports that Southern blacks learned "broad a" pronunciation to imitate prestigious Boston speech and that Michigan-born blacks aged 20-35 use Southern features while older and younger generations do not. **Reprinted** in R. McDavid 1979(**1.454**).143-45.

**1.417 McDavid, Raven I., Jr.** 1955. The position of the Charleston dialect. PADS 23.35-50. [SC]. Local features of grammar, pronunciation, and lexicon in Charleston, SC, and subsidiary areas. **Reprinted** in R. McDavid 1979(**1.454**).272-81; in J. Williamson and V. Burke 1971(**1.823**).596-609.

**1.418 McDavid, Raven I., Jr.** 1958. The dialects of American English. The structure of American English, by W. Nelson Francis, 480-543. New

York: Ronald Press. Excerpt printed in D. Shores 1972(**1.689**).26-41. Authoritative introduction to regional dialects of Atlantic states, detailing causes and development of dialect differences and chronicling formal study of regional dialects by LAUSC projects. Presents characteristic pronunciation, vocabulary, morphology, and syntax of principal and subsidiary dialect areas. Includes brief discussion of social class dialects and on influence of foreign-language communities, including French, German, and African, on Southern English.

**1.419 McDavid, Raven I., Jr.** 1960. A study in ethnolinguistics. SSJ 25.247-54. Distribution and evaluation of different pronunciations of Negro from GA to New England. **Reprinted** in R. McDavid 1979(**1.454**).146-49.

**1.420 McDavid, Raven I., Jr.** 1960. The second round in dialectology of north American English. Journal of the Canadian Linguistic Association 6.108-15. Same as following item.

**1.421 McDavid, Raven I., Jr.** 1964. The dialectology of an urban society. Communication et rapports du premier congrès international de dialectologie générale, ed. by A. J. Van Windekens, 68-80. Louvain: Centre International de Dialectologie Générale. Identifies industrialization, urbanization, and mass education as key forces in modern society and lays out a research agenda for investigating their effect on American speech. **Reprinted** in R. McDavid 1979(**1.454**).52-59.

**1.422 McDavid, Raven I., Jr.** 1965. American social dialects. CE 26.10-16. Applies findings of linguistic geography to social dialect problems; brief discussion of "Negro English." **Reprinted** in R. McDavid 1979(**1.454**).126-30.

**1.423 McDavid, Raven I., Jr.** 1965. Social dialects: cause or symptom of social maladjustment? Social dialects and language learning, ed. by Roger W. Shuy, 3-7. Urbana: NCTE. Anecdotal account of author's work on Linguistic Atlas projects mostly in the South. **Reprinted** in R. McDavid and W. Austin 1966(**1.468**); in B. Kottler and M. Light, eds. 1967. The world of words: a language reader, 158-63. Boston: Houghton Mifflin.

**1.424 McDavid, Raven I., Jr.** 1965. Dialectology and the integration of the schools. ZFM, neue folge 4.2.543-50. (Verhandlung des zweiten internationalen Dialektologenkongresses, ed. by L. E. Schmitt). Also published in Transactions of the Yorkshire Dialect Society 65.18-27. Dimensions of dialect differences in the North and how they are based on ethnic and social differences in the South; note on been and done auxiliaries in uneducated Southern speech. **Reprinted** in R. McDavid 1979(**1.454**).150-54.

**1.425 McDavid, Raven I., Jr.** 1966. Dialect differences and social differences in an urban society. Sociolinguistics: proceedings of the UCLA Sociolinguistics Conference, 1964, ed. by William Bright, 72-83. The Hague:

Mouton. Outlines social history of Greenville, SC, and Chicago, profiles socially diagnostic linguistic features, and discusses problem of acculturation of minority groups in each city. Influential essay on role of dialects in modern world and contributions an intelligent understanding of them can make to solution of educational and social problems. **Reprinted** in R. Hogan 1966(**1.325**).185-96; in R. McDavid 1979(**1.454**).60-66; in R. McDavid 1980(**1.456**).34-50.

**1.426 McDavid, Raven I., Jr.** 1966. Sense and nonsense about American dialects. PMLA 81.7-17. Warnings to students of dialects to avoid loose use of broad terms (like <u>pidgin</u> and <u>Midland</u>), categorical statements about "standard" English, racial dialects, and attitudes that some dialects are inherently superior to others. **Reprinted** in H. Allen and G. Underwood 1971(**1.12**).36-52; in E. Kerr and R. Aderman 1971(**1.358**).205-22; in R, McDavid 1979(**1.454**).67-76; in D. Shores 1972(**1.685**).134-52; in J. Williamson and V. Burke 1971(**1.823**).48-65; in W. W. Joyce and J. A. Banks. 1971. Teaching the language arts to culturally different children, 78-95. Reading, MA: Addison-Wesley.

**1.427 McDavid, Raven I., Jr.** 1966. Dialect study and English education. New trends in English education, ed. by David Stryker, 43-52. Champaign: NCTE. Cautions that focus of sociolinguists exclusively on speech of disadvantaged blacks "is likely to become a racist one, with certain features singled out and emphasized as features of 'Negro speech'."

**1.428 McDavid, Raven I., Jr.** 1967. Historical, regional, and social variation. JEL 1.25-40. Wide-ranging essay on different ways American English varies along Atlantic Coast. **Reprinted** in L. F. Dean et al., eds. 1971. The play of language, 203-18. New York: Oxford University Press; in A. L. Davis 1972(**1.160**).1-20; in R. McDavid 1979(**1.454**).33-42.

**1.429 McDavid, Raven I., Jr.** 1967. Each in his own idiom. Indiana English Journal 1.2.1-8. Characterizes himself as a member of "the largest and most neglected disadvantaged minority in the United States, the white gentile Protestant upland Southerners," and discusses social prejudice toward and linguistic misunderstanding of this group from antebellum period to contemporary compensatory education programs; distills four caveats for teachers.

**1.430 McDavid, Raven I., Jr.** 1967. Dialectology: where linguistics meets the people. Emory University Quarterly 23.203-21. Presents short history of descriptive linguistics, stressing data orientation of and his work with linguistic geography; says dialectologists can confirm or disconfirm perceptions of public about language, evaluate usage statements, and answer other public questions about language variation.

**1.431 McDavid, Raven I., Jr.** 1967. Needed research in Southern dialects. Perspectives on the South: agenda for research, ed. by Edgar T. Thompson,

113-24. Durham: Duke University Press. Outlines seven areas of needed research in the South on English and other languages, including speech of Southern migrants to the North, of isolated, relic areas, of blacks, and of French and other language enclaves in the South. **Reprinted** in R. McDavid 1979(**1.454**).288-94.

**1.432 McDavid, Raven I., Jr.** 1968. Variations in standard American English. EE 45.561-64,608. **Reprinted** in A. L. Davis 1968(**1.157**).5-9. Regional differences in pronunciation and grammar within "standard English."

**1.433 McDavid, Raven I., Jr.** 1968. Folk speech. Our living traditions, ed. by Tristram P. Coffin, 228-37. New York: Basic Books. Outlines linguistic atlas approach to dialect study, differentiates it from European approach; explains study of folk speech is the investigation of everyday speech rather than merely the search for linguistic relics.

**1.434 McDavid, Raven I., Jr.** 1969. A checklist of significant features for discriminating social dialects. American dialects for English teachers. U. S. Office of Education project HE-145; SS-12-32-67, ed. by A. L. Davis, 62-66. Urbana: Illinois Statewide Curriculum Study Center. **Reprinted** in H. Allen and G. Underwood 1971(**1.12**).468-72; in A. L. Davis 1972(**1.160**).133-39; in E. L. Evertts 1967(**1.228**).7-10.

**1.435 McDavid, Raven I., Jr.** 1969. Dialects, British and American, standard and nonstandard. Linguistics today, ed. by A. A. Hill, 79-88. New York: Basic Books. Popular essay on degree of regional dialects in English-speaking countries.

**1.436 McDavid, Raven I., Jr.** 1969. Two studies of dialects of English. Leeds Studies in English 2.23-45. In-depth comparison of two linguistic geography projects--Harold Orton's Survey of English Dialects and Hans Kurath's Linguistic Atlas of the United States and Canada. **Reprinted** in R. McDavid 1980(**1.456**).206-33.

**1.437 McDavid, Raven I., Jr.** 1969. The language of the city. Midcontinent American Studies Journal 10.48-59. Contrasts speech of Chicago, IL, and Greenville, SC, and social complexities of each city's speech patterns. **Reprinted** in R. Bentley and S. Crawford 1973(**1.64**).22-35; in J. Williamson and V. Burke 1971(**1.823**).511-24.

**1.438 McDavid, Raven I., Jr.** 1970. A theory of dialect. Linguistics and the teaching of standard English to speakers of other languages or dialects, ed. by James A. Alatis, 45-62. Washington: Georgetown University Press. Discusses features that delimit dialects and the forces that cause them; distinguishes regional and social dialects and discusses how former become the latter.

**1.439 McDavid, Raven I., Jr.** 1970. Changing patterns of Southern dialects.

Essays in honor of Claude M. Wise, ed. by Arthur J. Bronstein, Claude M. Shaver, and Cj Stevens, 206-28. New York: Speech Association of America. 10 maps. Dispels folk beliefs about origin of Southern English being due to factors of physiology and climate, analyzes main areas of Southern speech and how they have developed over past two hundred years, and discusses ongoing shifts in speech as reflections of social and economic forces in the region. **Reprinted** in R. McDavid 1979(**1.454**).295-308; revised and printed in R. McDavid 1980(**1.456**).51-77.

**1.440 McDavid, Raven I., Jr.** 1970. Language characteristics of specific groups: native whites. Readings for the disadvantaged: problems of linguistically different learners, ed. by Thomas D. Horn, 135-39. New York: Harcourt, Brace and World. Advice for the Northern teacher of students speaking Southern or South Midland English; discusses pronunciation, stress patterns, grammar of the latter.

**1.441 McDavid, Raven I., Jr.** 1970. The teacher of minorities. Nebraska English Counselor 15.3.5-15. Discusses personal, subjective views and insights regarding varieties of speech developed during youth in SC and in early teaching experiences in SC, VA, and elsewhere.

**1.442 McDavid, Raven I., Jr.** 1971. What happens in Tennessee? Dialectology: problems and perspectives, ed. by Lorraine Hall Burghardt, 119-29. Knoxville: University of Tennessee Department of English. Presents cultural and historical background for proposed linguistic research in TN and identifies crucial linguistic features to investigate.

**1.443 McDavid, Raven I., Jr.** 1972. Some notes on Acadian English. Culture, class, and language variety, ed. by A. L. Davis, 184-87. Urbana: NCTE. Brief analysis of phonological, morphological, and lexical tendencies of English spoken by LA Acadians, with social and historical notes on Acadian community.

**1.444 McDavid, Raven I., Jr.** 1972. Field procedures: instructions for investigators, linguistic atlas of the gulf states. A manual for dialect research in the Southern states, ed. by Lee Pederson et al., 33-60. Atlanta: Georgia State University. 2nd ed. 1974. University: University of Alabama Press. Same as ED 103 850. 3rd ed. published as Microfiche 0002-0004 in Pederson et al. 1981(**1.594**). General caveats for design and execution of LAGS project and personal advice for LAGS fieldworkers about finding informants and conducting interviews.

**1.445 McDavid, Raven I., Jr.** 1973. Go slow in ethnic attributions: geographic mobility and dialect prejudices. Varieties of present-day English, ed. by Richard W. Bailey and Jay L. Robinson, 258-70. New York: Macmillan. Points out how easily mobility in U.S. can disguise geographical linguistic markers as social ones and lead to misjudgments about speakers who use them.

**1.446 McDavid, Raven I., Jr.** 1975. The urbanization of American English. Philologica Pragensia 18.228-38. Discusses social and linguistic forces in America (dialect and language mixture, geographical and social mobility, industrialization, general education, urbanization, etc.) that have required the investigation of dialect in the U.S. to differ from European approaches. **Reprinted** in R. McDavid 1980(**1.456**).114-30; in revised form in Jahrbuch für Amerikastudien 16.47-59 (1971).

**1.447 McDavid, Raven I., Jr.** 1975. New directions in American dialectology. Studia Anglica Posnaniensia 5.1-2,9-25. Surveys development of dialect investigation from 19th-century European projects to the LAUSC to more recent sociolinguistic studies, with particular emphasis on methodology. **Revised** in English Studies Today 5.53-85 (1973). **Revised** further in R. McDavid 1980(**1.456**).257-95.

**1.448 McDavid, Raven I., Jr.** 1976. Language learning and dialects. Language Today 2.3-10. Recounting of personal experiences and discoveries in researching American dialects, including findings from fieldwork in KY for LANCS.

**1.449 McDavid, Raven I., Jr.** 1977. From list manuscript to isogloss. Abstract in NADS 9.3.11. [KY]. Discusses charting procedure developed for LANCS.

**1.450 McDavid, Raven I., Jr.** 1977. Evidence. Papers in language variation: SAMLA-ADS collection, ed. by David L. Shores and Carole P. Hines, 125-32. University: University of Alabama Press. Presents eight "rules of evidence, derived by common law from the linguists from whom I learned my trade," rules concerning use of direct, documentary, reported, circumstantial, and other types of evidence.

**1.451 McDavid, Raven I., Jr.** 1978. The gathering and presentation of data. JEL 12.29-37. Stresses German and French contributions to LAUSC methodology, assesses current status of regional linguistic atlases, including LAMSAS and LAGS, and describes format in which each project will present its data.

**1.452 McDavid, Raven I., Jr.** 1979. Social differences in white speech. Language and society: anthropological issues, ed. by William C. McCormack and Stephen A. Wurm, 249-61. The Hague: Mouton. Summarizes information from linguistic atlases and other dialect projects on differences in system, shape and incidence of phonemes and inflections and in syntax of "whites who are speakers of English, principally but not exclusively in the United States." **Reprinted** in R. McDavid 1980(**1.456**).164-81.

**1.453 McDavid, Raven I., Jr.** 1979. Linguistic and cultural pluralism: an American tradition. Proceedings of a symposium on American literature, ed. by Marta Sienicka, 225-40. Posnan: Adam Mickiewicz University. Surveys different immigrant European ethnic stocks which came to U.S. and points out their contributions to toponymy and vocabulary of the new nation.

**1.454 McDavid, Raven I., Jr.** 1979. Dialects in culture: essays in general dialectology, ed. by William A. Kretzschmar et al. University: University of Alabama Press. 399 pp. Collection of sixty articles and reviews spanning forty years of noted dialectologist's career and covering placenames, grammar, pronunciation, and many other aspects of American dialects, especially in South Atlantic states. **Reviews:** H. B. Allen. 1981. LIS 10.472-87; Anonymous. 1980. American Literature 52.330; J. Appleby. 1981. AA 83.443; R. R. Butters. 1981. SAQ 80.113-15; B. Crossley. 1981. Journal of American Studies 15.441-42; M. Danesi. 1981. LPLP 5.318-21; A. Duckert. 1981. JEL 15.33-35; U. Dürmüller. 1981. Language 57.499; K. Harder. 1980. TFSB 46.142-43; J. L. Idol, Jr. 1981. South Carolina Review 14.133; J. W. Hartmann. 1980. EWW 1.270-73; R. W. Shuy. 1981. LIS 10.470-72; W. Viereck. 1984. ZDL 51.104-07.

**1.455 McDavid, Raven I., Jr.** 1980. Linguistic geography. College English Association Critic 42.3.17-23. 1 map. Capsule history and profile of LAUSC. **Reprinted** in H. Allen and M. Linn 1986(**1.11**).117-22.

**1.456 McDavid, Raven I., Jr.** 1980. Varieties of American English: essays by Raven I. McDavid, Jr., selected and introduced by Anwar S. Dil. Stanford: Stanford University Press. Collection of sixteen of McDavid's longer articles including studies of regional and social dialects, lexicography, and onomastics, many of which deal with language patterns in the South Atlantic states, especially SC. **Reviews:** H. B. Allen. 1981. JEL 15.30-32; J. Appleby. 1981. AA 83.443; A. Duckert. 1981. JEL 15.33-35; U. Dürmüller. 1981. Language 57.499; J. R. Gaskin. 1981. Sewanee Review 89.298-306; R. W. Shuy. 1981. LIS 10.470-72; W. Viereck. 1984. ZDL 51.104-07.

**1.457 McDavid, Raven I., Jr.** 1980. Linguistics through the kitchen door. First person singular: papers from the conference on an oral archive for the history of American linguistics, ed. by Boyd H. Davis and Raymond O'Cain, 3-20. Amsterdam Studies in the Theory and History of Linguistic Science, Ser. 3, vol. 21. Amsterdam: John Benjamins. Autobiographical account of McDavid's early years in the field.

**1.458 McDavid, Raven I., Jr.** 1981. Southern speech: accomplishments and needs. Abstract in NADS 13.3.7. Assesses state of editorial work on Linguistic Atlas projects and comments on support of research on Southern speech by schools in the region.

**1.459 McDavid, Raven I., Jr.** 1981. The conduct of an atlas interview in the gulf states. LAGS Working Paper, 1st series, no. 8. Microfiche 1179. Ed. by Susan E. Leas. Addendum to Pederson et al., eds. 1981(**1.594**). 128 pp. Ann Arbor: University Microfilms. Transcript of tape on which McDavid proceeds through Linguistic Atlas interview questionnaire item by item and provides advice to fieldworkers on techniques for eliciting items.

**1.460 McDavid, Raven I., Jr.** 1983. Sociolinguistics and historical linguistics. Current topics in English historical linguistics: proceedings of the second international conference on English historical linguistics, held at Odense University, 13-15 April, 1981, ed. by Michael Davenport et al., 55-66. Odense, Denmark: Odense University Press. Contends recent sociolinguistic research, especially study of black speech, lacks crucial awareness of history of American society and of previous study of language differences in the country, and for this reason it has made dangerous mistakes in describing language of black Americans.

**1.461 McDavid, Raven I., Jr.** 1983. Retrospect. JEL 16.47-54. Personal view of evolution of LAUSC and related projects, with particular reference to Kurath's role.

**1.462 McDavid, Raven I., Jr.** 1984. The failure of intuition. SECOL Review 8.128-39. [SC]. Discusses and catalogs discrepancies between usage and usage judgments of lexical, pronunciation, and grammatical items by author as a LAMSAS informant in 1937; concludes half of judgments made were erroneous or doubtful, as revealed by further LAMSAS evidence.

**1.463 McDavid, Raven I., Jr.** 1984. Linguistic geography. Needed research in American English, 4-31. PADS 71. Discusses history of LAMSAS and LANCS projects, with special emphasis on recent years.

**1.464 McDavid, Raven I., Jr.** 1984. Lessons learned in a half century: experiences of a practicing dialectologist. Form and function in Chicano English, ed. by Jacob Ornstein-Galicia, 117-34. Rowley, MA: Newbury House. Essay on rationale and development of Linguistic Atlas projects in U.S., personal statement of author's role in this development, and critique of fieldwork and training of more recent work in urban "activist sociolinguists."

**1.465 McDavid, Raven I., Jr.** 1985. Dialect areas of the atlantic seaboard. American speech: 1600 to the present, ed. by Peter Benes, 14-26. Boston: Boston University. Summary of findings in Kurath 1949 (**3.275**) and Kurath and McDavid 1961(**4.197**). **Review:** J. L. Dillard. 1986. JAF 99.347-50.

**1.466 McDavid, Raven I., Jr.** 1985. Eliciting: direct, indirect, and oblique. AS 60.309-17. Pros and cons of different types of interview questions in dialect fieldwork; gives examples from research in South.

**1.467 McDavid, Raven I., Jr.** 1985. American dialectology: a historical perspective. Papers from the fifth international conference on methods in dialectology, ed. by H. J. Warkentyne, 13-34. Victoria, BC: University of Victoria. Historical essay focusing mainly on growth of American Dialect Society, work of Linguistic Atlas projects, DARE, and other projects.

**1.468 McDavid, Raven I., Jr., and William M. Austin. 1966.** Communication barriers to the culturally deprived. Cooperative research project 2107. Washington: Dept. of Health, Education, and Welfare. Collection of papers by McDavid, Austin, A. L. Davis, Pederson, and others on social and ethnic dialects; most papers deal with speech, especially pronunciation, in Chicago.

**1.469 McDavid, Raven I., Jr., and Alva L. Davis. 1973.** The linguistic atlas of the middle and south atlantic states: an editorial comment. Orbis 22.331-34. Progress report on editing LAMSAS and prospects for its publication.

**1.470 McDavid, Raven I., Jr., and Lawrence M. Davis. 1972.** The dialects of Negro Americans. Studies in linguistics in honor of George L. Trager, ed. by M. Estelle Smith, 303-12. The Hague: Mouton. Cautions that definitive judgments about distinctiveness and origin of black dialects in U.S. are "at least a generation or so" away and require "several kinds of evidence, in massive quantities . . . in short, any substantive statements about the origins of the dialects of Negro Americans will require investigations in breadth and depth far beyond what we now have"; hypothesizes that concentration of blacks in Northern inner cities may lead to "neo-creolization" of their speech. Reprinted in R. McDavid 1980(**1.456**).78-91.

**1.471 McDavid, Raven I., Jr., William A. Kretzschmar, Jr., and Gail J. Hankins., eds. 1982-86.** Linguistic atlas of the middle and south atlantic states and affiliated projects: basic materials. Microfilm MSS on Cultural Anthropology 68.360-64, 69.365-69, 71.375-80. Chicago: Joseph Regenstein Library, University of Chicago. Includes field records of LAMSAS interviews from MD, DC, VA, NC, SC, GA, and FL and Gullah interviews conducted by Turner.

**1.472 McDavid, Raven I., Jr., Hans Kurath, Raymond K. O'Cain, George Dorrill, and Sara Sanders. 1979.** Preview: the linguistic atlas of the middle and south atlantic states. JEL 13.37-47. 1 map. Announces start of publication of LAMSAS (**1.479**) and discusses plan and tabular makeup of fascicles, historical interpretation of regions, and history of project.

**1.473 McDavid, Raven I., Jr., and Virginia Glenn McDavid. 1951.** The relationship of the speech of American Negroes to the speech of whites. AS 26.3-17. Important study of black-white speech relationships debunking racially ethnocentric myths about black speech, documenting two dozen words of African origin, and suggesting that some patterns of grammar and pronunciation of blacks in the South derive from Africa. Reprinted as Bobbs-Merrill Reprint Series, Language-62; in R. Abrahams and R. Troike 1972(**1.4**).213-18; in R. McDavid 1979(**1.454**).43-51; in R. McDavid 1980 (**1.456**).15-33; in W. Wolfram and N. Clarke 1971(**1.853**).16-37 (with addendum to original version, 38-40).

**1.474 McDavid, Raven I., Jr., and Virginia G. McDavid. 1956.** Regional linguistic atlases in the United States. Orbis 5.349-86. 9 maps. Surveys current progress on Linguistic Atlas projects, presents key findings of the Atlas to date, and lists distinctive features in phonology, lexicon, morphology, and syntax for eighteen speech areas and subareas in the Atlantic states. **Reprinted in R. McDavid 1979(1.454).86-106.**

**1.475 McDavid, Raven I., Jr., and Virginia G. McDavid.** 1958. Linguistic geography and the study of folklore. New York Folklore Quarterly 14.243-62. 2 maps. Shows commonalities between two fields and comments on their parallel development; says goal of both is to document ongoing changes as well as to collect relics. **Reprinted in R. McDavid 1979(1.454).168-75.**

**1.476 McDavid, Raven I., Jr., Virginia G. McDavid, William A. Kretzschmar, Jr., Theodore K. Lerud, and Martha Ratliff.** 1986. Inside a linguistic atlas. Proceedings of the American Philosophical Society 130.390-405. 1 map. Report on current status and work of LAMSAS; includes sample pages from field notebooks and list manuscripts.

**1.477 McDavid, Raven I., Jr., and Raymond K. O'Cain.** 1973. Sociolinguistics and linguistic geography. Kansas Journal of Sociology 9.137-56. Response to Glenna Ruth Pickford and other critics of linguistic atlas methodology; discusses aims and applications of atlas work and how sociolinguists could benefit from consulting its data.

**1.478 McDavid, Raven I., Jr., and Raymond K. O'Cain.** 1977. Southern standards revisited. Papers in language variation: SAMLA-ADS collection, ed. by David L. Shores and Carole P. Hines, 229-32. University: University of Alabama Press. Defends validity of standard Southern speech and summarizes century of discussion of features of standard versus nonstandard Southern, with particular reference to Charleston, SC.

**1.479 McDavid, Raven I., Jr., Raymond K. O'Cain, and George T. Dorrill, eds.** 1980. The linguistic atlas of the middle and south atlantic states. Chicago: University of Chicago Press. Fascicles 1 and 2, x + 246 pp. [NY south to NE FL]. Fascicle 1: introductory matter, table of informants, worksheet items 1-10. Fascicle 2: worksheet items 10-23 (state names). Two of series of projected sixty lists of phonetic transcriptions of more than 800 words and phrases from interviews with 1216 informants in Middle and in South Atlantic states, conducted primarily in late 1930s and 1940s. Each list presents all transcriptions, arranged by state and informant number, for each questionnaire item. **Reviews:** H. B. Allen. 1981. JEL 15.30-32; B. Carstensen. 1981. Amerikastudien 26.453-54; E. Finegan. 1982. Language 58.244-45; K. B. Harder. 1981. Names 29.251-52; K. B. Harder. 1981. TFSB 47.38-40; J. B. McMillan. 1981. SAR 46.131-34; W. Viereck. 1981. EWW 2.115-17.

**1.480 McDavid, Raven I., Jr., and Richard C. Payne, eds., with the assistance of Duane Taylor and Evan Thomas.** 1976-78. Linguistic atlas of the north-central states. Basic materials (unaltered field records). Manuscripts on cultural anthropology series XXXVIII, no. 200-08. Microfilm. Chicago, IL: University of Chicago. Forty-three reels containing field records of phonetically recorded transcribed responses of 505 informants; volume 206 constitutes six reels with KY field records.

**1.481 McGreevy, John C.** 1977. Breathitt County, Kentucky grammar. Chicago: Illinois Institute of Technology dissertation. Abstract in DAI 38.5437A. [9 teenagers, 11 adults, E KY]. Finds no social class correlation with twenty-three grammatical and phonological features, thus concluding that "Breathitt County is a homogeneous speech community."

**1.482 McGuire, William J., Jr.** 1939. A study of Florida cracker dialect based chiefly on the prose works of Marjorie Kinnan Rawlings. Gainesville: University of Florida thesis. 191 pp. Survey of grammatical and phonological features and list of lexical elements of white dialect of N FL as presented in Rawlings' fiction.

**1.483 Mackert, C. L.** 1924. Characteristic speech trends observable at the University of Maryland. College Park: University of Maryland thesis. 35 pp. [College Park, MD]. Compiles expressions brought to university by students from their native localities and expressions that are the result of attending college.

**1.484 McLean, Leon.** 1976. They all ask'd /ækst/ for you. Abstract in NADS 8.3.4. Discusses lexical, morphological, and syntactic features of Cajun English of S LA, many of which are French-influenced, especially those likely to show up in student writing.

**1.485 McMeekin, Clark.** 1957. Old Kentucky country. New York: Duell, Sloan and Pearce. Pp. 149-50, on dialect.

**1.486 McMillan, James B.** 1968. The study of regional and social variety in American English. Language and teaching: essays in honor of Wilbur W. Hatfield, ed. by Virginia McDavid, 47-54. Chicago: Chicago State College. Chronicles scholarly efforts to document American dialects from 1873 to 1960s.

**1.487 McMillan, James B.** 1977. Naming regional dialects in America. Papers in language variation: SAMLA-ADS collection, ed. by David L. Shores and Carole P. Hines, 119-24. University: University of Alabama Press. Compiles and discusses names given to major dialect regions of U.S., based on historical dictionaries, linguistic atlas studies, and other works.

**1.488 McMillan, James B.** 1979. Dialects. The encyclopedia of Southern history, ed. by David C. Roller and Robert W. Twyman, 358-60. Baton Rouge: Louisiana State University Press. Geographical summary based on settlement history.

**1.489 McMillan, James B.** 1986. Preface. Language variety in the South: perspectives in black and white, ed. by Michael Montgomery and Guy Bailey, ix-x. University: University of Alabama Press. Brief assessment of current state of dialect research in region.

**1.490 Maguire, Robert E.** 1979. Notes on language use among English and French creole speaking blacks in Parks, Louisiana. Projet Louisiane, Document de Travail no. 6. Quebec: Université Laval. 42 pp. [15 B, ages 19-87, S CENT LA]. Anthropological study of status and dominance of French creole and English in bilingual LA community.

**1.491 Malmstrom, Jean, and Annabel Ashley.** 1963. Dialects USA. Urbana: NCTE. Pp. 39-41, summary of Midland and Southern dialect areas, condensed from R. McDavid 1958(**1.418**). **Reprinted** in A. Aarons et al. 1969(**1.1**).47-49,168. Updated and reprinted in D. Shores 1972(**1.685**).17-25. **Excerpt** in R. Abrahams and R. Troike 1972(**1.4**).130-35. **Review:** D. H. Obrecht. 1966. Linguistics 21.126-28.

**1.492 Marckwardt, Albert H.** 1957. Principal and subsidiary dialect areas in the north-central states. PADS 27.3-15. 7 maps. [Includes KY]. Preliminary report on eighteen isoglosses based on LANCS data. **Reprinted** in H. Allen and G. Underwood 1971(**1.12**).74-82.

**1.493 Marckwardt, Albert H.** 1958. American English. 2nd ed. 1980, revised by J. L. Dillard. New York: Oxford University Press. 192 pp. Classic introduction to development of American English from colonial times; includes chapter on "Social and Regional Variation" in revised edition by Dillard.

**1.494 Marshall, Howard, and John Michael Vlach.** 1973. Toward a folklife approach to American dialects. AS 48.163-91. 18 maps. Says folklife and material culture research should work in tandem with dialect research; shows how mapping of house types, barn types, and other cultural features corresponds to dialect areas and says that folklife research can explain incidences of dialect overlapping.

**1.495 Marshall, Margaret.** 1982. Language variation in the English speech codes of southern Louisiana. Abstract in NADS 14.3.4. Studies interference and code switching in phonology, syntax, and semantics of English-French bilinguals in LA.

**1.496 Marshall, Margaret.** 1983. Bilingualism in southern Louisiana: a sociolinguistic analysis. Anthropological Linguistics 24.308-24. [18 adults, ages 40-92, Vacherie, St. James Parish, SE LA]. Describes how French and English influence one another in terms of linguistic variables; identifies code switching and interference in different speech codes.

**1.497 Martin, Reginald.** 1981. The black sharecroppers of western Tennessee and their children: urban education as a catalyst of dialect change. Tennessee Linguistics 1.1.27-32. [10 rural B, ages 60-85, 10 of their offspring with high school education, Fayette and Shelby Cos., W TN]. Sketch of generational differences in grammar and pronunciation.

**1.498 Massey, Ellen Gray.** 1978. This speech of ours. Bittersweet country, ed. by E. G. Massey, 206-12. Garden City, NJ: Doubleday. Catalog of unusual terms, pronunciations, plurals, and comparisons from the Ozarks.

**1.499 Masterson, James R.** 1943. Tall tales of Arkansas. Boston: Chapman and Grimes. Pp. 180-85, discussion of name Arkansas; pp. 351-54, discussion of expressions.

**1.500 Maynor, Natalie.** 1982. Changing speech habits in Mississippi. MFR 16.17-24. Based on LAGS interviews, compares speech of elderly and teenage Mississippians and finds that their vocabulary is changing faster than pronunciation but that younger generation still maintains some characteristic Southern features.

**1.501 Maynor, Natalie.** 1987. Written records of spoken language: how reliable are they? Abstract in NADS 19.2.12. Casts doubt on validity of WPA ex-slave narrative transcripts for linguistic analysis and discusses their limitations.

**1.502 Mayo, Margot.** 1952. Kentucky talk. Promenade 8.71.

**1.503 Mayo, Margot.** 1953. More Kentucky talk. Promenade 8.8.1.

**1.504 Mead, Martha Norburn.** 1942. Asheville . . . in land of the sky. Richmond, VA: Dietz Press. [W NC]. Pp. 59-60, comments on language.

**1.505 Medford, W. Clark.** 1966. How our mountain speech became so colorful. Great smoky mountain stories and sun over ol' starlin, 65-67. Waynesville, NC: privately printed. [W NC]. Says early mountain residents often crafted new words to meet immediate needs, and lists local idioms and figures of speech not acknowledged by dictionaries.

**1.506 Mele, Joseph.** 1976. Dialect study center in Alabama. Alabama Speech and Theatre Journal 4.1.29-31. Describes purposes and plans for collection for USA Dialect Tape Depository at University of South Alabama in Mobile.

**1.507 Mele, Joseph.** 1980. University of South Alabama dialect tape center: audio tape resources. ED 199 782. 17 pp. Describes archive of more than 300 tape recordings of representative speakers of current American English throughout U.S. and of non-Americans from twenty-three countries speaking English; archive established for use by teachers, actors, sociologists, as well as linguists.

**1.508 Mencken, Henry Louis.** 1936. The American language. Fourth ed. New York: Knopf. 769 pp. Supplement one, 1945. 739 pp.; Supplement two, 1948. 890 pp. One volume ed. abridged by Raven I. McDavid, Jr., with assistance of David W. Maurer, 1963. xxv + 777 pp. Encyclopedic work synthesizing lifetime of reading and correspondence on host of topics from regional dialects to American naming practices and British-American differences. Bibliography in footnotes includes wide range of popular and scholarly articles in local magazines and newspapers. **Reviews:** W. Card. 1963. CE 25.230-31; A. Duckert. 1964. Names 12.123-26; W. C. Greet. 1965. AS 40.58-61; R. Howren. 1965. Philological Quarterly 44.133-35; L. A. Pederson. 1965. Orbis 14.63-74; R. M. Wilson. 1965. YWES 44.63-64; R. W. Wilson. 1964. CJL 10.70-72; H. B. Woolf. 1966. English Studies 47.102-18.

**1.509 Meredith, Mamie.** 1931. Negro patois and its humor. AS 6.317-21. Reviews at length discussion and anecdotes of Dodge (2.121) and says that anyone studying black speech "will be moved to admiration by its expressiveness and delighted by its rich humor."

**1.510 Midgett, L. W.** 1932. A study of the dialect of the people of northeastern North Carolina. Unpublished ms. in University of North Carolina at Chapel Hill library. 14 pp. Cites forms identical to Southern British dialect and lists 122 words and pronunciations typical of the region; comments on archaism of Outer Banks speech.

**1.511 Miles, Emma Bell.** 1905. The literature of a wolf-race. The spirit of the mountains, 172-78. **Reprinted** in 1976. Knoxville: University of Tennessee Press. Essay on literary qualities of mountain speech; cites "wild and elemental poetry" and "terse and piquant proverbs" of mountaineers.

**1.512 Miller, Michael I.** 1979. The Virginia dialect survey. Abstract in NADS 11.3.9. Reviewed in NADS 12.1.9. Reports on methodology and preliminary findings of survey to follow up DARE and LAMSAS in VA.

**1.513 Miller, Michael I.** 1984. The city as a cause of morphophonemic change. SECOL Review 8.28-59. 1 map. [17B, 20W, Augusta, GA]. Examines variants of plural formation after sibilants (in words like knife and trough) and concludes that urbanization, age, and other social factors as well as social class and ethnic caste correlate with usage.

**1.514 Miller, Michael I.** 1989. Maximilian von Schele de Vere. Encyclopedia of Southern culture, ed. by William Ferris and Charles Wilson. Chapel Hill: University of North Carolina Press. Short biography and appreciation of lexicological work of 19th-century University of Virginia philologist.

**1.515 Miller, Michael I.** 1989. Southern linguists. Encyclopedia of Southern culture, ed. by William Ferris and Charles Wilson. Chapel Hill: University of North Carolina Press. Short essay surveying general orientation and scholarly tendencies of linguists and dialectologists in the region.

**1.516 Miller, Peggy J.** 1980. Amy, Wendy, and Beth: learning language in south Baltimore. Austin: University of Texas Press. xii + 196 pp. [Baltimore, MD]. Ethnographic study of three infants and the linguistic interaction of them and their families. **Reviews:** J. W. Lindfors. 1983. LIS 12.551-56; C. E. Snow. 1983. LIS 12.381-82.

**1.517 Miller, Tracey Russell.** 1973. An investigation of the regional English of Unicoi County, Tennessee. Knoxville: University of Tennessee dissertation. Abstract in DAI 34.5147A. [6 older natives, NE TN]. Describes phonetic characteristics and relic vocabulary.

**1.518 Miller, Zell.** 1975. Mountain dialect. The mountains within me, 76-88. Toccoa, GA: Commercial. [N GA]. Autobiographical, anecdotal account of richness and archaicness of mountain speech; frequent comparison of usages of Chaucer and Shakespeare to fading usages in mountains.

**1.519 Moffat, Adeline.** 1891. The mountaineers of middle Tennessee. JAF 4.314-20. Describes mountain people, including some samples of speech, language of Cumberland Ridge area of Middle TN.

**1.520 Molloy, Robert.** 1947. How they do talk. Charleston, a gracious heritage, 239-50. New York: Appleton-Century. [SC]. Impressionistic, extravagant discussion of uniqueness of the "clear, rapid, and smooth" speech of the city.

**1.521 Montgomery, Michael.** 1980. A partial comparison of Southern Appalachian English and Vernacular Black English. Abstract in NADS 12.3.10. [E TN]. Discusses extent to which grammatical and phonological features of Vernacular Black English are present in speech of residents of small Appalachian community.

**1.522 Montgomery, Michael B.** 1982. The study of the language of blacks and whites in the American South. Tennessee Linguistics 2.1.36-45. Bibliographical review of findings and issues on black-white speech relationships from three decades of study in the South.

**1.523 Montgomery, Michael B.** 1982. Recent work in Southern English. Abstract in NADS 14.3.7. Outlines new types of studies and new sources of data in recent research on Southern English and characterizes this research as more objective and more concerned with methodology than in past.

**1.524 Montgomery, Michael.** 1985. Updating the annotated bibliography of Southern American English. Southern English Newsletter 3.1-5. Scope, goals, and progress of book-length bibliography updating McMillan (**12.19**).

**1.525 Montgomery, Michael.** 1987. A questionnaire for the study of

Tennessee English. Tennessee Linguistics 7.35-45. [TN]. Five-part questionnaire for investigating social and stylistic variation in regional speech.

**1.526 Montgomery, Michael.** 1989. The English language in the South. Encyclopedia of Southern culture, ed. by William Ferris and Charles Wilson. Chapel Hill: University of North Carolina Press. Extended essay discussing historical, cultural, and other dimensions of English in the region.

**1.527 Montgomery, Michael, and Guy Bailey.** 1986. Introduction. Language variety in the South: perspectives in black and white, 1-29. University: University of Alabama Press. Discusses development of scholarly study of relations between black and white speech in the South; reviews literature and discusses major contributions and insights of linguistic geographers, sociolinguists, creolists, and later scholars.

**1.528 Montgomery, Michael, and Guy Bailey,** eds. 1986. Language variety in the South: perspectives in black and white. University: University of Alabama Press. Collection of twenty-three original studies and an introductory review of relevant scholarship; explores complexities--historical, demographic, social, as well as linguistic--of relationship between black speech and white speech in the South. **Reviews:** J. Baugh. 1988. AS 63.265-71; M. J.-V. Blanton. 1988. South Central Review 5.121-23; M. Dressman. 1987. SECOL Review 11.78-81; W. N. Francis. 1988. Language 64.202-03; S. Mufwene. 1987. Journal of Creole and Pidgin Languages 2.93-110; E. Schneider. 1986. EWW 7.324-27; G. N. Underwood. 1988. SAR 53.142-45.

**1.529 Mooney, James.** 1889. Folk-lore of the Carolina mountains. JAF 2.95-104. [NC]. Includes remarks on mountain dialect.

**1.530 Moore, Dorothy Cox.** 1968. The dialect of Chuckatuck, Virginia. PADS 49.40. Abstract of paper on dialect of isolated farming village in Tidewater area.

**1.531 Moore, Virginia.** 1942. A sense of language. Virginia is a state of mind, 307-10. New York: E. P. Dutton. Says VA "was born with a vivid sense of language" that has been preserved by oral tradition and individualism of its citizens.

**1.532 Morgan, Lucia C.** 1960, The speech of Ocracoke, North Carolina: some observations. SSJ 25.314-22. [E NC]. Phonology; a few lexical items.

**1.533 Morgan, Lucia C.** 1967. North Carolina accents: some observations. North Carolina Journal of Speech and Drama 1.1.3-8. Based on speech of college students native to state, presents pronunciations and vocabulary, especially from Appalachians and Outer Banks, that author considers remnants of colonial speech.

**1.534 Morgan, Lucia C.** 1969. North Carolina accents. SSJ 34.174-82. Impressionistic notes on vowels; discusses three consonants and a few lexical items. **Reprinted** in J. Williamson and V. Burke 1971(**1.823**).268-79.

**1.535 Morley, Margaret W.** 1913. The speech of the mountains. The Carolina mountains, 171-81. Boston: Houghton Mifflin. [NC]. Catalogs archaisms reminiscent of Shakespeare or Chaucer in mountain speech, "the most purely 'American'" of all varieties.

**1.536 Muehl, Siegman, and Lois B. Muehl.** 1976. Comparison of differences in dialect speech among black college students grouped by standard English test performance. Language and Speech 19.28-40. Finds scores on test correlates with amount of subordination and stylistic variety in students' language; some students were from the South.

**1.537 Negro dialect.** 1924. Opportunity 2.259-60. Laments false characterization of black dialect in print as gratuitous and ridiculous; defends "haunting mellowness," "gentle humor," and literary ancestry of the dialect.

**1.538 Nelson, Agnes.** 1956. A study of the English speech of the Hungarians of Albany, Livingston Parish, Louisiana. Baton Rouge: Louisiana State University dissertation. Abstract in DAI 17.694-95. Phonology, morphology, syntax of six informants; based on atlas work sheets.

**1.539 Nelson, Joseph.** 1949. Backwoods teacher. Philadelphia: Lippincott. Scattered references on Ozark dialect.

**1.540 New Orleans voodoo.** 1957. Western Folklore 16.60-61. [LA]. Vocabulary for voodoo paraphernalia.

**1.541 Nichols, Patricia C.** 1977. A sociolinguistic perspective on reading and black children. Language Arts 54.150-57,167. [E SC]. Summarizes debate over distinctiveness of black speech and concludes from experience as teacher in rural SC that linguistic and social factors are equally important in beginning reading of black children.

**1.542 Nist, John.** 1966. A structural history of English. New York: St. Martin's. Pp. 369-70, characteristics of Southern dialect. **Reprinted** in E. Kerr and R. Aderman 1971(**1.358**).165-70.

**1.543 Nix, Ruth A.** 1980. Linguistic variation in the speech of Wilmington, North Carolina. Durham: Duke University dissertation. Abstract in DAI 41.277-78A. [8 elderly B F, 16 adolescent B M, SE NC]. Examines features of grammar and pronunciation in Labovian framework and finds factors such as age and sex correlate most closely with variation in morphological features such as use of word endings.

**1.544 Norman, Arthur M. Z.** 1955. A southeast Texas dialect study.

Austin: University of Texas dissertation. 345 pp. [12 speakers, Jefferson and other counties]. Uses Kurath-Atwood worksheets, finds predominant Southern influence on area; glossary, 61-222; condensed in following item.

**1.545 Norman, Arthur M. Z.** 1956. A southeast Texas dialect study. Orbis 5.61-79. [2 B, 10 W, 5 M, 7 F, 4 counties, SE TX]. Using Linguistic Atlas worksheets, surveys pronunciation and vocabulary patterns of area, tabulating incidence of Eastern dialect vocabulary and vocabulary of French, Spanish, and other southwestern influences; briefly notes patterns in verb principal parts. **Reprinted** in H. Allen and G. Underwood 1971(**1.12**).135-51; in J. Williamson and V. Burke 1971(**1.823**).309-28.

**1.546 Oettenger, Marion, Jr.** n.d. A linguistic survey of east Carteret County, North Carolina. Unpublished ms. in University of North Carolina at Chapel Hill library. 34 pp. [14 M, 2 F, Carteret Co., E NC]. 3 maps. Comments on terms of address, grammar, phonetics, lexicon, and semantics of Outer Banks speech.

**1.547 Oomen, Ursula.** 1982. Regionale variation: sudstaatendialekte. Die englische sprache in den USA: variation und struktur, 59-78. Teil 1. Tübingen: Niemeyer. Trends and tendencies in Southern pronunciation, especially with regard to postvocalic /r/ and diphthongs.

**1.548 Orton, Harold, and Nathalia Wright.** 1972. Questionnaire for the investigation of American regional English: based on the work sheets of the Linguistic Atlas of the United States and Canada. Knoxville: University of Tennessee Department of English. vii + 139 pp. Designed for investigation of archaic Tennessee speech.

**1.549 Owens, William A.** 1950. Big Thicket balladry. Texas folk songs. Publication of the Texas Folklore Society no. 23, 24-26. Dallas: Southern Methodist University Press. Comments on peculiarities of old-fashioned language in Big Thicket area of SE TX.

**1.550 Park, Wilmer R.** 1940. A letter from Texas. AS 15.214-15. Notes on double modals, adjective sorry, emphatic negative, and pronunciation.

**1.551 Parris, John.** 1955. Roaming the mountains. Asheville, NC: Citizen-Times. [W NC]. Mountain idiom fading, 21-23, unusual expressions in mountains; Origin of mountain county names, 179-82.

**1.552 Parris, John.** 1967. Mountain bred. Asheville, NC: Citizen-Times. [W NC]. A lavish of homespun names, 26-27; Mountain idiom fading, 120-22. Romance of mountain speech reflected in archaisms and placenames.

**1.553 Parris, John.** 1972. These storied mountains. Asheville, NC: Citizen-Times. [W NC]. Flavorsome talk, 23-24, figures of speech and similes in mountain speech; Do tongue twisters still defy diction?, 286-87.

**1.554 Parrish, C. H.** 1946. Color names and color nations. JNE 15.13-20. Affective connotations of twenty-five terms denoting skin color of blacks.

**1.555 Payne, L[eonidas]. W.** 1908-09. A word-list from east Alabama. DN 3.279-328,343-91. [Mostly W speech, Auburn, AL, area]. Glossary of nearly 2,000 words with accompanying grammar and pronunciation, compiled by Payne during twenty-year residence in Auburn. **Reprinted** in Bulletin of the University of Texas, no. 113, reprint series no. 8, Austin, 1909.

**1.556 Payne, Richard C.** 1976. The LANCS basic materials: progress report, November 4, 1976. NADS 8.4.11-12. Reports on steps necessary to standardize LANCS materials for fullscale editing.

**1.557 Pearce, J. W.** 1890. Notes from Louisiana. DN 1.69-72. Words, grammar, pronunciations.

**1.558 Pearsall, Marion.** 1966. Communicating with the educationally deprived. Mountain Life and Work 42.8-11 (Spring). **Reprinted** in F. S. Riddel, ed. 1974. Appalachia: its people, heritage, and problems, 55-62. Dubuque, IA: Kendall Hunt.

**1.559 Pederson, Lee A.** [1969]. The linguistic atlas of the gulf states: an interim report. AS 44.279-86. Chronicles early progress and gives status of project.

**1.560 Pederson, Lee A.** 1971. Southern speech and the LAGS project. Dialectology: problems and perspectives, ed. by Lorraine Hall Burghardt, 130-42. Knoxville: University of Tennessee Department of English. 3 maps. Says that systematic research on Southern speech has yet to be undertaken and therefore generalizations about it cannot be made; summarizes aims, methods, and preliminary work of LAGS project.

**1.561 Pederson, Lee A.** 1971. Southern speech and the LAGS project. Orbis 20.79-89. Revision of preceding item.

**1.562 Pederson, Lee A.** 1972. Black speech, white speech, and the Al Smith syndrome. Studies in linguistics in honor of Raven I. McDavid, Jr., ed. by Lawrence M. Davis, 123-34. University: University of Alabama Press. Finds that systematically collected and compared data from N GA do not show a homogeneous black English.

**1.563 Pederson, Lee A.** 1972. An introduction to the LAGS project. A manual for dialect research in the Southern states, ed. by Lee A. Pederson, Raven I. McDavid, Jr. Charles Foster, and Charles Billiard, 1-31. Atlanta: Georgia State University College of Education. 2nd ed. 1974. University: University of Alabama Press. Same as ED 103 850. 3rd ed. published as Microfiche 0002-0004 in Pederson et al. 1981(**1.594**). Describes aims, methods, and early plan of work for atlas project covering eight Southern states.

**1.564 Pederson, Lee A.** 1973. Dialect patterns in rural northern Georgia. Lexicography and dialect geography: festgabe for Hans Kurath, ed. by Harald Scholler and John Reidy, 195-207. Wiesbaden: Franz Steiner Verlag. Reports on preliminary study of regional distribution of phonological, grammatical, and lexical items in Dialect Survey of Rural Georgia; concludes that there are "social factors of caste and class, as well as age, education, family origins, and several other crucial aspects necessary for an adequate linguistic demography."

**1.565 Pederson, Lee A.** 1974. Tape/text and analogue. AS 49.5-23. Discusses components of LAGS project, especially role of tape recorder and taped interview.

**1.566 Pederson, Lee A.** 1974. The linguistic atlas of the gulf states: interim report two. AS 49.216-23. Discusses development of LAGS project in 1973-74, decision to add urban supplement, and current format and composition of atlas.

**1.567 Pederson, Lee A.** 1975. Basic methods of dialectic research. Trends in Southern sociolinguistics, ed. by William C. Pickens, 8-16. Lakemont, GA: CSA Printing. Discusses general principles of linguistic geography as it developed in Germany and the U.S. and how these are incorporated in Dialect Survey of Rural Georgia and LAGS.

**1.568 Pederson, Lee A.** 1975. Insular dimensions of Southern speech. Trends in Southern sociolinguistics, ed. by William C. Pickens, 26-34. Lakemont, GA: CSA Printing. Essay on historical context for main dialect areas of Southern English and how isolation has played prominent role in their development.

**1.569 Pederson, Lee A.** 1975. The Urban Language Series. AS 50.98-110. Review of first nine volumes in series published by CAL, including W. Wolfram (**1.835**) and R. Fasold (**5.95**).

**1.570 Pederson, Lee A.** 1975. The plan for a dialect survey of rural Georgia. Orbis 24.38-44. Discusses goals and program for statewide linguistic survey precursor to LAGS.

**1.571 Pederson, Lee A.** 1976. The linguistic atlas of the gulf states: interim report three. AS 51.201-07. Discusses progress of project in 1975-76, preparation of its basic materials, and current format and composition of atlas.

**1.572 Pederson, Lee A.** 1977. Toward a description of Southern speech. Papers in language variation: SAMLA-ADS collection, ed. by David L.

Shores and Carole P. Hines, 25-31. University: University of Alabama Press. Progress report after eight years of work on LAGS and discussion of goals and implications of project.

**1.573 Pederson, Lee A.** 1977. Randy sons of Nancy Whisky. AS 52.112-21. [E TN, N GA]. Shows how plentiful undocumented folk terms for illegal whiskey present problems for historical lexicographers and for semantic analysis.

**1.574 Pederson, Lee A.** 1981. The linguistic atlas of the Gulf States: interim report four. AS 56.243-59. Discusses progress of atlas from 1976 to 1978, its current format and status, and projected work on it.

**1.575 Pederson, Lee A.** 1981. A compositional guide to the LAGS project. 2nd edition ed. by Susan Leas and reprinted as LAGS Working Papers, 1st series, no. 5. Microfiche 1183-84. Addendum to Pederson et al. 1981(**1.594**). 214 pp. Originally published in 1977 by Emory University Administrative Services. Guide to methods of data gathering, written for project staff.

**1.576 Pederson, Lee A.** 1981. Introduction to the LAGS working papers, first series. Microfiche 1176. Addendum to Pederson et al. 1981(**1.594**).

**1.577 Pederson, Lee A.** 1981. A conference to plan a linguistic atlas of the southeastern states, May 16-17, 1968. LAGS Working Papers, 1st series, no. 1. Microfiche 1178. Addendum to Pederson et al. 1981(**1.594**). 27 pp. Report of two-day conference of dialectologists, teachers, and curriculum planners to organize LAGS project.

**1.578 Pederson, Lee A.** 1981. Toward the publication of the Linguistic Atlas of the Gulf States. LAGS Working Papers, 1st series, no. 4. Microfiche 1182. Addendum to Pederson et al. 1981(**1.594**). 12 pp. Progress report on LAGS, written in 1976.

**1.579 Pederson, Lee A.** 1981. The regional and social dialects of East Tennessee: a preliminary overview. LAGS Working Papers, 1st series, no. 8. Microfiche 1187-89. Addendum to Pederson et al. 1981(**1.594**). 261 pp. Final report to NCTE Research Foundation. Published later as Pederson 1983(**1.583**).

**1.580 Pederson, Lee A.** 1981. LAGS fieldworkers: styles and contributions. LAGS Working Papers, 1st series, no. 13. Microfiche 1194. Addendum to Pederson, et al. 1981(**1.594**). 55 pp. Evaluates methods and accomplishments of LAGS fieldworkers; assesses investigative skills of seventeen principal fieldworkers for project and lists other fieldworkers and indicates the interviews they conducted.

**1.581 Pederson, Lee A.** 1981. LAGS scribes: idiolects and habits of composition. LAGS Working Papers, 1st series, no. 14. Microfiche 1195. Addendum to Pederson et al. 1981(**1.594**). 64 pp. Assesses transcription skills of eight principal LAGS scribes and describes scribal practices of project.

**1.582 Pederson, Lee.** 1982. Language, culture, and the American heritage. American heritage dictionary, second college edition, 17-29. Boston: Houghton Mifflin. General essay on cultural dimensions of American English; discussion of evolution of American dialects and of African contribution to American English; relies heavily on LAGS data.

**1.583 Pederson, Lee A.** 1983. East Tennessee folk speech: a synopsis. Bamberger beiträge zur Englischen sprachwissenschaft 12. Frankfurt/Main: Peter Lang. 254 pp. [70 natives of both races and several social classes]. Presents idiolect synopsis of 137 selected features in narrow phonetic transcription for each informant; analyzes pronunciation of phonemes, incidence of phonemes and morphological and lexical variants, and regional, subregional, and social factors in area. Also includes chapters on settlement history and methodology. **Review:** E. Schneider. 1984. EWW 5.130-32.

**1.584 Pederson, Lee A.** 1986. Introduction to the LAGS working papers, second series. Addendum to Pederson, McDaniel, and Bassett 1986(**1.600**).

**1.585 Pederson, Lee A.** 1986. The LAGS grid. LAGS Working Papers, 2nd series, no. 1. Addendum to Pederson, McDaniel, and Bassett 1986 (**1.600**). 93 pp.

**1.586 Pederson, Lee A.** 1986. Introduction: a matrix for word geography. LAGS Working Papers, 3rd series. Addendum to Pederson, McDaniel, and Bassett 1986(**1.600**). 4 pp. Summary of seven papers in third series of working papers.

**1.587 Pederson, Lee A.** 1986. A graphic plotter grid. Same as LAGS Working Paper, 3rd series, no. 3. Addendum to Pederson, McDaniel, and Bassett 1986(**1.600**). 26 pp. Published as JEL 19.25-41. 6 maps. Outlines development of LAGS methods for presenting data in two-dimensional graphic fashion and demonstrates computer mapping techniques for displaying distribution of lexical data in eight-state LAGS region.

**1.588 Pederson, Lee A.** 1986. An electronic atlas in microform. LAGS Working Paper, 3rd series, no. 4. Addendum to Pederson, McDaniel, and Bassett 1986(**1.600**). 25 pp.

**1.589 Pederson, Lee A.** 1987. An automatic book code (ABC). JEL 20.48-71. 7 maps. Describes and explains "phonographically consistent alphabet in machine-readable form" used for LAGS data and illustrates how it allows mapping of lexical, grammatical, and phonological variants in eight-state region.

**1.590 Pederson, Lee A., Guy Bailey, and Marvin Bassett.** 1981. LAGS demographics. LAGS Working Papers, 1st series, no. 11. Microfiche 1191. Addendum to Pederson, et al. 1981(**1.594**). 81 pp. Summarizes population characteristics of all LAGS counties and localities from 1790 to 1970; classifies localities into eight types.

**1.591 Pederson, Lee A., and Charles E. Billiard.** 1979. The urban work sheets for the LAGS project. Orbis 28.45-62. Addendum to LAGS interview questionnaire for urban areas in Gulf States.

**1.592 Pederson, Lee A., Howard Dunlap, and Grace Rueter.** 1975. Questionnaire for a dialect survey of rural Georgia. Orbis 24.45-71. Questionnaire to accompany item **1.570** and explanation of how it was developed.

**1.593 Pederson, Lee A., and Susan Leas.** 1981. A plan for the LAGS concordance. LAGS Working Papers, 1st series, no. 9. Microfiche 1190. Addendum to Pederson, et al.(**1.594**). 1981. 49 pp. Describes prospective format of concordance; contains sample entries and progress report written in 1980.

**1.594 Pederson, Lee A., Susan Leas, Guy H. Bailey, and Marvin H. Bassett, eds.** 1981. Linguistic atlas of the gulf states: the basic materials. Microform collection. Ann Arbor: University Microfilms. Massive corpus of 128,000 pages of raw data, summary, and background from over 1,100 recorded interviews totaling over 5,000 hours and conducted in eight Southern states. Although unedited and mostly in phonetic transcription, this is the largest single collection of data on Southern speech, containing more data on speech of Southern blacks than all other collections combined.

**1.595 Pederson, Lee A., Susan Leas, Guy H. Bailey, and Marvin H. Bassett, eds.** 1981. The LAGS protocols. Ann Arbor: University Microfilms. Field notebooks containing phonetic forms of elicited and observed forms of more than 1,100 LAGS informants.

**1.596 Pederson, Lee A., Susan Leas, Guy H. Bailey, and Marvin H. Bassett, eds.** 1981. The idiolect synopses of the LAGS protocols. Ann Arbor: University Microfilms. One-page synopsis of characteristic forms of each of more than 1,100 LAGS informants.

**1.597 Pederson, Lee A., and Susan Leas McDaniel.** 1986. A reference tool for Southern folklore study. LAGS Working Papers, 3rd series, no. 6. Addendum to Pederson, McDaniel, and Bassett 1986(**1.600**). Explains LAGS microcomputer programs for analyzing vocabulary.

**1.598 Pederson, Lee A., and Susan Leas McDaniel.** 1986. Microcomputing in linguistic geography: files and maps for the LAGS project. LAGS Working Papers, 3rd series, no 7. Addendum to Pederson, McDaniel, and Bassett 1986(**1.600**). Demonstrates applications of microcomputer in editing

LAGS material, particularly in mapping phonological and lexical items.

**1.599 Pederson, Lee [A.], Susan Leas McDaniel, and Marvin [H.] Bassett.** 1984. The LAGS concordance. AS 59.332-39. Explains and gives entries showing types of phonological, intonational, morphological, syntactic, and editorial information contained in concordance to atlas project.

**1.600 Pederson, Lee A., Susan Leas McDaniel, and Marvin H. Bassett, eds.** 1986. The linguistic atlas of the gulf states: a concordance of basic materials. Ann Arbor: University Microfilms. 152 microfiche of alphabetical concordance, two series of working papers, and other material.

**1.601 Pederson, Lee A., Susan Leas McDaniel, Guy H. Bailey, and Marvin H. Bassett, eds.** 1986. The linguistic atlas of the gulf states, volume 1: handbook for the linguistic atlas of the gulf states. Athens: University of Georgia Press. 376 pp. **Reviews:** J. B. McMillan. 1987. Alabama Review 40.157-58; N. Maynor. 1988. South Central Review 5.119-21; G. N. Underwood. 1988. SAR 53.145-48; W. Viereck. 1987. JEL 20.255-57.

**1.602 Pederson, Lee A., Raven I. McDavid, Jr., Charles W. Foster, and Charles E. Billiard, eds.** 1972. A manual for dialect research in the Southern states. Atlanta: Georgia State University. 2nd ed. 1974. University: University of Alabama Press. Same as ED 103 850. 3rd ed. published as Microfiche 0002-0004 in Pederson et al. 1981(**1.594**). Questionnaire for LAGS project and useful discussions for prospective dialect collectors on field procedures, on relationship between folklore and collecting dialect, and on linguistic geography and the classroom teacher. **Reviews:** A. R. Duckert. 1972. AS 47.278-85; S. J. McCord. 1975. NADS 7.1-2.24.

**1.603 Pederson, Lee A., Grace Rueter, and Joan Hall.** 1975. Biracial dialectology: six years into the Georgia survey. JEL 9.18-25. Discusses design and goals of statewide survey preliminary to LAGS.

**1.604 Perkins, Luretha.** 1979. An investigation of communication style among five black families. Columbia: University of South Carolina thesis. 96 pp. [5 preschool B children and their parents, Columbia, SC]. Investigates styles of communication in black families, finding upper and middle classes tend to have a "person-oriented family that indulges in an elaborated and formal language mode within an open communication system" and the lower class a "position-oriented family that indulges in a restricted and public language mode within a closed communication system."

**1.605 Perrow, E. C.** 1912. Songs and rhymes from the South. JAF 25.137-55. Includes comments on dialect.

**1.606 Pfaff, Brenda Cottrell.** 1983. A critique of Appalachian sociolinguistics. Abstract in Critical essays on Appalachian life and culture: proceedings of the fifth annual Appalachian studies conference, ed. by Rick

Simon, 121. Boone, NC: Appalachian Consortium. Says sociolinguistic methods are more thorough and more detailed than linguistic atlas methods, and thus better suited to answering larger question of existence of Appalachian dialect.

**1.607 Pickens, William G.**, ed. 1975. Trends in Southern sociolinguistics: selected writings. Lakemont, GA: CSA Printing. 62 pp. Collection of seven original papers, from 1972 conference, on Gullah, black English, methods of dialect research in the South, and attitudes toward Southern language patterns used in the classroom.

**1.608 Pietras, Tom, and Helmut Esau.** 1976. Language teaching and learning: a linguistic research model. Journal of the Linguistic Association of the Southwest 2.1.1-12. [50 members of Texas A and M University faculty, 50 members of Bryan-College Station, TX, community]. Studies selected phonological, lexical, and grammatical features and finds professional status and geographical origin of speakers correlated most with dialect variation.

**1.609 Pilch, Herbert.** 1972. Structural dialectology. AS 47.165-87. Introduces structural dialectology, discussing basic terms and concepts; some illustrations from Southern English.

**1.610 Pitts, Ann H.** 1986. Is Southern English disappearing? Alabama Heritage 2.12-19. Summary of principal changes in Southern English and report on an Auburn University debate over its future.

**1.611 Polk, William T.** 1953. Uncle Remus spake Queen's English. Southern Accent: from Uncle Remus to Oak Ridge, 57-71. New York: Morrow. The old myth about preservation of Elizabethan archaisms in black speech.

**1.612 Porter, Inez M.** 1945. Qu'ar talk. Rayburn's Ozark Guide. Lonsdale, AR. Autumn, p. 156. Item reported by Randolph **12.25**, who says it reports "how the Ozarkers near Fort Smith, Arkansas are amused by the queer speech of visitors from New York."

**1.613 Posey, Darrell A.** 1981. Language variation and ethnicity in an American tri-racial group. Aspects of linguistic variation: proceedings of the conference on language varieties, July 1980, ed. by Steve Lander and Ken Reah, 1-10. Sheffield, UK: University of Sheffield.

**1.614 Posey, Meredith N.** 1962. Oral English usage. North Carolina English Teacher 19.3.6-8. Advice to teachers on dealing with speech habits of schoolchildren in NC; distinguishes between "sectional English," whose eradication "would be to make the language poorer, less colorful, less interesting" and "certain errors of grammar," which "should be drilled out of high school students."

**1.615 Presley, Delma E.** 1976. The crackers of Georgia. GHQ 60.102-16. Pp. 106-07, note on language.

**1.616 Preston, Dennis R.** 1972. Social dialectology in America: a critical rejoinder. FFLR 10.13-16,57. Responds to L. Davis (1.167) critique of recent sociolinguistic and creolist research on black English; says linguistic geographers were as subject to ongoing social and political concerns in delineating American dialects as more recent researchers have been and that Davis would require black dialect to be defined in terms of its uniqueness, which is contrary to traditional definitions of dialects.

**1.617 Preston, Dennis R., and George M. Howe.** 1987. Computerized generalizations of mental dialect maps. Variation in language NWAV-XV at Stanford: proceedings of the fifteenth annual conference on new ways of analyzing variation, ed. by Keith M. Denning, Sharon Inkelas, Faye C. McNair-Knox, and John R. Rickford, 361-78. Stanford: Stanford University Department of Linguistics. 18 maps. Demonstrates computer mapping technique for how mental maps drawn to demarcate and label different American dialects can be collapsed into consensus map for how speakers in one region of the country perceive other regions.

**1.618 Primer, Sylvester.** 1891. Dialectical studies in West Virginia. PMLA 6.3.161-70. Also published in Colorado College Studies 2.28-38. Pronunciation and notes on lexicon and grammar.

**1.619 Primer, Sylvester.** 1891. Miscellanies. DN 1.57-59. General comments on dialectology, advice to collectors, fourteen examples of rare usages, mostly from Charleston, SC.

**1.620 Puckett, Newbell Niles.** 1926. Folk beliefs of the Southern Negro. Chapel Hill: University of North Carolina Press. Pp. 13-23, notes on language, including sections on "Language and Lore," "Survivals," and "Mutilated English." **Reviews:** J. H. Cox. 1926. Saturday Review of Literature 3.52; A. Locke. 1927. JNH 12.97-98; R. E. Park. 1927-28. American Journal of Sociology 33.988-95; C. Russell. 1926. Social Forces 5.300-01.

**1.621 Putnam, George N., and Edna M. O'Hern.** 1955. The status significance of an isolated urban dialect. Language dissertation no. 53, Language 31.4.2. Catholic University of America Studies in Sociology 40. Washington: Catholic University dissertation, 1954. 32 pp. [74 B adults, Washington, DC]. Description of segmental and suprasegmental phonemes and notes on lexicon, morphology, and syntax; finds "the dialect differed most strikingly from standard English in its phonetic features"; also finds untrained speakers can accurately judge social status of taped voices. **Reviews:** E. S. Bogardus. 1956. Sociology and Social Research 41.76; M. Cohen. 1956. Bulletin de la Société de Linguistique de Paris 52.2.18; R. Evans. 1956. Language 32.822-25; H. Hoijer. 1956. American Sociological Review 21.538; R. Quirk. 1957. YWES 36.30.

**1.622 Qazilbash, Husain A.** 1972. Appalachia: people, dialect, and communication problems. Journal of Reading Behavior 5.14-25. [13 speakers from each of 9 states from NY to AL]. Claims that speech of Appalachian residents is a restricted code (in Basil Bernstein's sense).

**1.623 Qazilbash, Husain A.** 1972. A dialect survey of the Appalachian region. Tallahassee: Florida State University dissertation. Abstract in DAI 32.6085A. Also ED 052 210. Same as Atlanta: National Center for Educational Research and Development Regional Research Report 4. [13 informants from each of 9 states from NY to AL]. Claims that rustic speakers "have a small functional vocabulary" and "misuse more words" than modern and cultured speakers and that "there is a distinct pattern or linguistic structure throughout the Appalachian Region without any subregional differences within the region."

**1.624 Radford, Maude L.** 1895. Like a mountain torrent. Canadian Magazine 5.480-84. Mountain dialect.

**1.625 Rafferty, Milton D.** 1980. The Ozarks: land and life. Norman: University of Oklahoma Press. Pp. 233-34, lists Ozark archaisms but downplays their uniqueness, saying eighty percent of them would be known by rural farmers in Midwest.

**1.626 Raine, James W.** 1924. Mountain speech and song. The land of saddle-bags, 95-124. New York City: Council of Women for Home Missions. KY mountain speech.

**1.627 Randolph, Vance.** 1928. Verbal modesty in the Ozarks. DN 6.57-64. Taboos and prudish vocabulary for male animals, body parts, and sex. **Reprinted** in V. Randolph. 1931. The Ozarks, 78-86; in Miller Williams, ed. 1981. Ozark, Ozark: a hillside reader, 33-40. Columbia: University of Missouri Press.

**1.628 Randolph, Vance.** 1929. Is there an Ozark dialect? AS 4.203-04. Argues that Krapp and Mencken underestimate dialect differences in country by concentrating on pronunciation; says Ozark vocabulary is strikingly different from most of country.

**1.629 Randolph, Vance.** 1931. The Ozarks: an American survival of primitive society. New York: Vanguard. The Ozark dialect, 67-86. Popular essay based on intimate observations of Ozark people by the folklorist; says Ozark speech most distinctive in vocabulary. **Reviews:** H. A. Blaine. 1932. Mississippi Valley Historical Review 19.130-32; L. Pound. 1932. AS 7.305; R. Redfield. 1932-33. American Journal of Sociology 38.506; S. Vestal. 1931. Saturday Review of Literature 8.407-08.

**1.630 Randolph, Vance, and George P. Wilson.** 1953. Down in the holler: a gallery of Ozark folkspeech. Reprinted in 1979. Norman: University of

Oklahoma Press. Bibliography, 303-14. Comprehensive description of Ozark speech, gathering material from over thirty years of study and observation by noted folklorist, covering Ozark grammar, pronunciation, archaisms, taboos and euphemisms, and wisecracks, along with the presentation of the dialect in fiction and an extensive, scholarly glossary. Excerpted as "Backwoods Grammar" in Barnet Kottler and Martin Light, eds. 1967. The world of words: a language reader, 164-68. Boston: Houghton Mifflin. Reviews: Anonymous. 1954. Missouri Historical Review 48.204; E. H. Criswell. 1952. AS 28.285-88; C. W. Garbutt. 1953. QJS 39.374-75; R. Geist. 1954. SFQ 18.150-52; R. I. McDavid, Jr. 1953. JAF 67.327-30; C. B. Para. 1982. Mid-America Folklore 10; R. M. Wilson. 1955. YWES 40.41.

**1.631 Rascoe, Burton.** 1927. Southern accent. American Mercury 11.73-75. Subjective essay distinguishing different varieties of Southern speech.

**1.632 Rash, Coralee.** 1941. Dialect study of Kinston, Coffee County, Alabama, made as a preliminary investigation for the preparation of work sheets for the linguistic atlas. Auburn: Alabama Polytechnic Institute thesis. Surveys phonology and morphology of community and compares results with those of Faneuf (**1.229**) and Satterfield (**1.670**) and with British dialects, finding greatest similarity with northern England and Scotland.

**1.633 Ray, George Bryan.** 1983. An ethnography of speaking in an Appalachian community. Seattle: University of Washington dissertation. Abstract in DAI 44.2624A. [Jackson Co., KY]. Study of speech used in eight leisure and religious speech events in six domestic and public speech situations.

**1.634 Ray, George Bryan.** 1983. An ethnography of speaking in an Appalachian community. Abstract in Critical essays in Appalachian life and culture: proceedings of the fifth annual Appalachian studies conference, ed. by Rick Simon, 121. Boone, NC: Appalachian Consortium. [E KY]. Refers to talk on home porches, talk at stores, and testifying in church in terms of nine components of speech events.

**1.635 Rayburn, Otto Ernest.** 1930. Folk-ways. Ozark Life. Winslow, Arkansas. Aug., p. 13. Comments on "smooth" quality of Ozark speech.

**1.636 Rayburn, Otto Ernest.** 1941. Ozark country. New York: Duell, Sloan, and Pearce. Scattered comments on dialect; discusses "Anglo-Saxon" survivals and different accounts of origin of name Ozark.

**1.637 [Rayburn, Otto Ernest].** 1943. Hilly heartbeats. Rayburn's Ozark Guide 1.2.27-28. Cites reader's characterization of Ozark speech as a "queer mixture" of elements and presents story written in the dialect.

**1.638 [Rayburn, Otto Ernest].** 1944. Ex-ceptional "cawn." Rayburn's Ozark Guide 1.4.15. Says "mountain people speak with a most delightful flavor of speculative accuracy" and gives an example.

**1.639 Rayburn, Otto Ernest.** 1953. The Ozark dialect. Rayburn's Ozark Guide 11.37.59-62. Review of Randolph and Wilson (**1.630**); defends view that Ozarks have distinctive variety of speech.

**1.640 [Rayburn, Otto Ernest].** 1955. Questions and answers. Rayburn's Ozark Guide 12.44.27. Discusses uses of hillbilly, Arkansawyer, and barking a squirrel.

**1.641 Rayford, Julian Lee.** 1956. Whistlin woman and crowin hen: the true legend of Dauphin Island and the Alabama coast. Mobile, AL: Rankin Press. Notes on vocabulary and place names along AL Gulf coast.

**1.642 Raymond, James C., and I. Willis Russell,** eds. 1977. James B. McMillan: essays in linguistics by his friends and colleagues. University: University of Alabama Press. xvii + 184 pp. **Reviews:** Anonymous. 1978. Lingua 46.407-08; Anonymous. 1978. Choice 15.684; B. Davis. 1981. LIS 10.132-35; C. Eble. 1978. SECOL Bulletin 2.77-78.

**1.643 Reagan, Patty.** 1981. Generation differences in the Austin area. Abstract in NADS 13.3.3. Discusses correlations between generational differences and dialect variation in ten-county area in S CENT TX.

**1.644 Reese, James Robert.** 1975. The myth of the Southern American dialect as a mirror of the mountaineer. Voices from the hills: selected readings on Southern Appalachia, ed. by Robert J. Higgs and Ambrose N. Manning, 474-92. New York: Ungar. Questions existence of single identifiable Appalachian dialect and claims heterogeneity of mountain speech.

**1.645 Reese, James Robert.** 1977. Variation in Appalachian English: a study of the speech of elderly, rural natives of East Tennessee. Knoxville: University of Tennessee dissertation. Abstract in DAI 38.7304-05A. [12 older W, NE TN]. Investigates degree of "systematic variation" in lexicon, syntax, morphology, and phonology in speech of sociologically similar informants; finds extensive variation among the speakers, but "no general consistent sub-patterns of agreement" between areas of linguistic structure.

**1.646 Reese, James Robert.** 1978. Randomly distributed dialects in Appalachian English: syntactic and phonological variation in East Tennessee. SECOL Bulletin 2.67-76. [16 elderly W, NE TN]. Claims existence of "randomly distributed dialects" by finding "four distinct dialectal linguistic systems" in speech of sixteen sociologically and geographically similar informants.

**1.647 Reese, James Robert.** 1979. Dialectology and folklore: woodscolts in search of kin. TFSB 45.48-60. Describes American dialectology and calls for more communication between dialectologists and folklorists.

**1.648 Reese, James Robert.** 1980. Theoretical ambiguity in American dialectology. Abstract in NADS 12.3.6. Argues that ambiguity in basic terminology has resulted from lack of attention to theoretical principles.

**1.649 Reese, James Robert.** 1981. Appalachian English: reality and myth. Cross-Reference 1.3.1,6-7. Report on series of public forums in Johnson Co., TN, on issues related to Appalachian English. **Reprinted** in Tennessee Linguistics 1.1.35-36.

**1.650 Reese, James Robert.** 1981. Goals for the collection and use of Appalachian oral materials in the 1980s. Appalachia/America: proceedings of the 1980 Appalachian studies conference, ed. by Wilson Somerville, 230-35. Johnson City, TN: Appalachian Consortium Press. Argues that wealth of oral materials collected by scholars in Appalachia needs to be catalogued, analyzed, and adapted to classroom use to answer questions about Appalachian culture and language.

**1.651 Reid, Thomas B.** 1926. A philologist's paradise. Opportunity 4.21-23. English of Key West, FL, with emphasis on its multilingual flavor.

**1.652 Reinhardt, J. M.** 1926. Speech and balladry of the southern highlands. Quarterly Journal of the University of North Dakota 16.139-47. Discusses archaism, conservatism, and expressiveness of Southern Appalachian speech.

**1.653 Reirdon, Suzanne.** 1978. "How 'bout you, Bullshipper? Ya' got'cha ears on?" Ethnic names, ed. by Fred Tarpley, 97-103. Commerce, TX: Names Institute Press. Grammatical and naming patterns in Mid-South.

**1.654 Richardson, Thomas J., and Philip C. Kolin**, eds. 1982. Folk language. Special issue of MFR 16.2. **Review:** K. B. Harder. 1983. TFSB 49.191-92.

**1.655 Richert, Carol M.** 1979. A comparative study of the teaching of standard English as a second dialect to speakers of black English in college. Boca Raton: Florida Atlantic University thesis. [9 B students at Palm Beach Atlantic College, West Palm Beach, FL]. Studies effect of formal English-as-a-second-dialect course on writing of verb forms, pronouns, plurals and possessives, negative sentences, indirect questions, and complete sentences.

**1.656 Rickford, John R.** 1985. Ethnicity as a sociolinguistic boundary. AS 60.99-125. [1 older B, 1 older W, Sea Islands, SC]. Finds two informants in one community are similar phonologically but differ in three syntactic features--passivization, possessive marking, and pluralization; says "ethnicity appears to be like regional and social class boundaries insofar as it involves social distance, and like the boundary of sex or gender . . . insofar as it reflects difference in socially expected norms."

**1.657 Rickford, John R.** 1986. Some principles for the study of black and white English in the South. Language variety in the South: perspectives in black and white, ed. by Michael Montgomery and Guy Bailey, 38-62. University: University of Alabama Press. [Sea Islands, SC]. Extensive analysis of how one Gullah speaker uses plurals; outlines and exemplifies four crucial methodological principles prerequisite to making valid comparisons of black and white speech in the South but often ignored in undertaking such comparisons.

**1.658 Rickford, John R.** 1987. [Are black and white vernaculars diverging?] AS 62.55-62. Part of NWAV panel discussion; outlines linguistic and ecological aspects of divergence controversy.

**1.659 Roberts, Eleanor M.** 1977. The piedmont dialect. Sandlapper 10.2.11. [NW SC]. Claims "old English" still spoken in Piedmont area of SC and that English of settlers remains unchangd in modern-day SC; says blacks and Scots had only marginal lexical influence on SC speech.

**1.660 Rodgers, Catherine.** 1940. Dialect study of Camp Hill, Tallapoosa County, Alabama, made as a preliminary investigation for the preparation of work sheets for the linguistic atlas. Auburn: Alabama Polytechnic Institute thesis. [20 adults, Auburn, AL]. Investigates phonology, morphology, and vocabulary of community and collates results with Satterfield (1.670) and Faneuf (1.229).

**1.661 Roebuck, Julian B., and Mark Hickson, III.** 1982. The language of the redneck. The Southern redneck: a phenomenological class study, 105-20. New York: Praeger. Discussion of characteristic grammar, vocabulary, rhetoric, and nonverbal communication of white Southern blue-collar social class by sociologists. Reviews: Anonymous. 1984. Journal of Economic History 43.793; D. Blanchard. 1984. Contemporary Sociology 13.226-27; B. C. Malone. 1984. JSH 50.505-07; I. Parmley. 1984. Social Forces 62.830-31.

**1.662 Rohrer, John H., and Monro S. Edmonson.** 1960. Dialect and society. The eighth generation grows up: cultures and personalities of New Orleans Negroes, 335-41. New York: Harper and Row. [52 B, New Orleans, LA]. Finds 80% identity between black speech in New Orleans and general Southern speech and that black society "is not clearly segmented, and that only in relation to occupational class is there any clear relationship between subunits of the society and general dialect features."

**1.663 Rubrecht, August.** 1977. DARE in Louisiana. Papers in language variation: SAMLA-ADS collection, ed. by David L. Shores and Carole P. Hines, 45-59. University: University of Alabama Press. 10 maps. Relates linguistic features of vocabulary and phonology and cultural features of cuisine and type of coffee preferred to boundary between French and English speech areas in LA.

**1.664 Rudd, Mary J.** 1976. The use of third person reference in multiparty conversations in an Appalachian community. AnL 18.349-59. [E KY]. Explores functions of conversational technique in which reference made to a third party constrains that party from speaking, while allowing other parties to participate in conversation; suggests this technique varies in frequency and normative character according to region.

**1.665 Rueter, Grace S.** 1977. A dialect survey of rural Georgia: the progress. Papers in language variation: SAMLA-ADS collection, ed. by David L. Shores and Carole P. Hines, 33-43. University: University of Alabama Press. [307 B, W older natives of GA]. Summary report of fieldwork and preliminary findings of Atlas-type survey of selected features of vocabulary, grammar, and pronunciation of native Georgians.

**1.666 Rulon, Curt, M.** 1980. A linguistic outline of Texas dialects. Abstract in NADS 12.3.12. Reports on research project attempting to form linguistic rule summaries of major syntactic, semantic, and phonological features of TX dialects.

**1.667 Sackett, S. J.** 1979. Prestige dialect and the pop singer. AS 54.234-37. Says approximation of Southern accent by American and some British rock musicians has become de rigueur, and offers historical, sociological, and political reasons for this.

**1.668 Sanders, Isaiah S.** 1926. Some phases of Negro English. Chicago: University of Chicago thesis. 75 pp. Attempts to represent "the chief characteristics of Negro English pronunciation," to determine "some of the sources from which the main peculiarities of the dialect spring," and to suggest what are the "distinctive Negro elements to be found in what is called 'Negro English'."

**1.669 Sasiki, Midori.** 1979. Southern Appalachian English: the language of Faulkner's country people. Chu-Shikoku Studies in American Literature 15.37-46.

**1.670 Satterfield, Cecile.** 1939. Dialect studies of Marbury School District, Autauga County, Alabama, made as a preliminary investigation for the preparation of work sheets for the linguistic atlas. Auburn: Alabama Polytechnic Institute thesis. [7 adults, CENT AL]. Investigates phonology, morphology, and vocabulary of community, using modified atlas worksheets.

**1.671 Sawyer, Janet B.** 1957. A dialect study of San Antonio, Texas: a bilingual community. Austin: University of Texas dissertation. Abstract in DAI 18.586. Studies phonology, lexicon, and inflectional forms of seven Anglo and seven Latin natives of San Antonio, using atlas work sheets; finds Anglo speech typically Southern.

**1.672 Sawyer, Janet B.** 1959. Aloofness from Spanish influence in Texas English. Word 15.270-81. [7 native English speakers, 7 native Spanish speakers, San Antonio, TX]. Says that "English in San Antonio has not been affected by Spanish in phonology, morphology or syntax" and that there is "no evidence that Spanish contact in San Antonio is even responsible for additions to the lexicon of San Antonio English." **Reprinted** in J. Williamson and V. Burke 1971(**1.823**).570-82.

**1.673 Sawyer, Janet B.** 1964. Social aspects of bilingualism in San Antonio, Texas. PADS 41.7-15. [7 native English speakers, 7 native Spanish speakers, San Antonio, TX]. Finds strong use of Lower Southern phonological features in speech of Anglos; outlines characteristics and habits of Hispanic use of English. **Reprinted** in H. Allen and G. Underwood 1971(**1.12**).375-81; in R. Bailey and J. Robinson 1973(**1.39**).226-33.

**1.674 Scarborough, W. S.** 1897. Negro folk-lore and dialect. Arena 17.186-92. Study of forms in black speech "must be done quickly or else they will be swept away and completely obliterated. . . ."

**1.675 Scarbrough, George.** 1976. My mother language, my father tongue. AJ 4.28-34. Native Tennessean's contrast of his mother's and his father's speech habits from his childhood.

**1.676 Schnable, D. C.** 1945. Dixie is different. Printer's Ink 212.23. On local customs, including speech, that ad writers should recognize.

**1.677 Schneider, Edgar W.** 1983. Englisch in Nordamerika. Englisch-formen und funktionen einer weltsprache, 51-71. Bamberg: Universitäts-bibliothek. Chapter from exhibit catalog on varieties of English around the world; includes descriptions of several books and other items on Southern English.

**1.678 Schneider, Edgar W.** 1986. "How to speak Southern": an American English dialect stereotyped. Amerikastudien 31.4.20-33. Calls for research into linguistic stereotypes as necessary counterpart of research on language varieties and attitudes; presents analysis of Southern English as stereotyped in six popular booklets, including Mitchell (**3.340**).

**1.679 Schrock, Earl F., Jr.** 1980. A study of the dialect of the blacks in Pope County, Arkansas. Fayetteville: University of Arkansas dissertation. Abstract in DAI 41.3091A. [14 B speakers, ages 13-100, rural CENT AR]. Studies segmental phonemes, morphological and syntactic features, and attitudes of speakers about their language in relation to that of whites; finds most variation in morphology and syntax and says that features of black speech in urban North are inconsistently found in Southern black speech.

**1.680 Scott, Jerrie.** 1986. Mixed dialects in the composition classroom. Language variety in the South: perspectives in black and white, ed. by Michael Montgomery and Guy Bailey, 333-47. University: University of Alabama Press. [40 B college students, FL]. Explores idiosyncratic component of dialect mixture in writing of college freshmen and shows it is better explained by principles of second language learning than by interference from native dialect patterns.

**1.681 Shaffer, Douglas K.** 1969. EPDA institute in standard English as a second dialect. (June 23, 1969-Aug. 1, 1969). Director's report, South Florida Univ., Tampa. ED 032 288. 33 pp. Describes six-week institute for thirty-eight primary school teachers presenting introduction to modern linguistics and its implications for second dialect teaching, summary of structural similarities and differences between black dialects and "General American" English, and awareness of black part of country's heritage.

**1.682 Shands, H. A.** 1893. Some peculiarities of speech in Mississippi. Oxford, MS: privately printed. Originally University of Mississippi dissertation; synopsis in H. L. Mencken, The American Language, Supplement Two (1948), pp. 170-72. Informal but only comprehensive work devoted to the state's speech habits, this glossary is divided into cultivated white, illiterate white, and black usages and is prefaced by discussion of characteristic pronunciation of vowels and consonants in MS.

**1.683 Shearin, Hubert G.** 1927. The speech of our fathers. Kentucky Folklore and Poetry Magazine 2.2.6-7. [KY]. Discounts myth of Elizabethan English but says local speech is integral to people's heritage and will flourish despite quixotic English teachers; appends list of archaisms.

**1.684 Sherman, Samuel.** 1955. A history of speech education in New Orleans public elementary and secondary schools. Baton Rouge: Louisiana State University dissertation.

**1.685 Shores, David L.,** ed. 1972. Contemporary English: change and variation. Philadelphia: Lippincott. xvi + 380 pp. Anthology of articles on social and regional variation in American English.

**1.686 Shores, David L.** 1986. The discovery of black English: "here we go again." Abstract in NADS 18.2.6. Says recent media discussion of black speech patterns is reminiscent of the "Black English . . . enterprise" of the 1960s and early 1970s; suggests how linguists should react to situation.

**1.687 Shores, David L.** 1989. The outer bankers and their speech. Encyclopedia of Southern culture, ed. by William Ferris and Charles Wilson. Chapel Hill: University of North Carolina Press. Settlement, history, and distinctive lexical and phonological features of the isolated E NC islands.

**1.688 Shores, David L.** 1989. The islands of the Chesapeake Bay and their language. [E MD, E VA]. Encyclopedia of Southern culture, ed. by William Ferris and Charles Wilson. Chapel Hill: University of North Carolina Press. Short essay on history, culture, and distinctiveness of speech in the bay region.

**1.689 Shores, David L., and Carole P. Hines**, eds. 1977. Papers in language variation: SAMLA-ADS collection. University: University of Alabama Press. xiv + 321 pp. Collection of papers given at SAMLA meetings, many on regional and social dialects in the South. **Review:** H. Jaffe. 1978. AS 53.72-73.

**1.690 Shuy, Roger W.**, ed. 1965. Social dialects and language learning: proceedings of the Bloomington, Indiana, conference 1964. Urbana: NCTE. 157 pp. Proceedings of interdisciplinary conference of linguists, psychologists, sociologists, and educators on the "English language problems of the culturally underprivileged"; includes many papers on social dialects and has summaries of after-paper discussions.

**1.691 Shuy, Roger W.** 1968. A study of social dialects in Detroit, final report. ED 022 187. 230 pp. [702 residents of Detroit, MI]. Report on major sociolinguistic project to compare speech of whites and blacks in a Northern city; discusses goals and research design of project, field methods, analytical procedures, structural frequencies of linguistic features, computer-based phonological analysis, and sociolinguistic implications for teaching of standard English.

**1.692 Shuy, Roger W.** 1971. Some problems in studying Negro/white speech differences. English Record 21.179-85. ED 054 145. 7 pp. Problems, pitfalls, and naive expectations of conducting research on black-white speech differences.

**1.693 Shuy, Roger W., and Anna Shnukal**, eds. 1980. Language use and the uses of language. Washington: Georgetown University Press. viii + 296 pp. **Reviews:** L. D'Amico-Reisner. 1983. LIS 12.96-99; C. M. Scotton. 1983. Language 59.453-54.

**1.694 Skillman, Billie G.** 1953. Phonological and lexical features of the speech of the first generation native-born inhabitants of Cleburne County, Arkansas. Denver: University of Denver dissertation.

**1.695 Sledd, James H.** 1969. Bi-dialectalism: the linguistics of white supremacy. EJ 58.1307-15,1329. Argues that "if the majority can rid itself of its prejudices, and if the minorities can get or be given an education, differences between dialects are unlikely to hurt anybody much." **Reprinted** in D. Shores 1972(**1.685**).319-30; in Leonard F. Dean, et al., eds. 1971. The play of language, 19-25. New York: Oxford University Press; in C. Laird and R. Gorrell, eds. 1971. Reading about language, 264-74. New York: Harcourt Brace Jovanovich.

**1.696 Sledd, James.** 1972. Doublespeak: dialectology in the service of big brother. CE 33.439-56. Criticizes bidialectal approach to teaching writing as racist; says that American society will continue to discriminate against blacks whether they speak "standard English" or not. **Reprinted** in R.

Bailey and J. Robinson 1973(**1.39**).360-81; in R. Bentley and S. Crawford 1973(**1.64**).191-214.

**1.697 Sledd, James H.** 1973. Bidialectalism: a new book and some old issues. AS 48.258-69. Review of DeStefano (**1.179**).

**1.698 Sledd, James H.** 1978. What are we going to do about it now that we're number one? AS 53.171-98. Acerbic assessment of current state of research in American English and American dialects.

**1.699 Sledd, James H.** 1980. From black-white speech relationships to the ethnography of communication, or, who profits from research. ED 194 705. 22 pp. Argues that research into history of language of blacks in North America is far more complex than most linguists realize (responding to Fasold **1.235**), that research on black English cannot improve conditions of life among blacks, that opposition between creolists and dialectologists is an "oversimplified obstruction of a complex history," and that evidence for creole basis of black English has been exaggerated.

**1.700 Sledd, James H.** 1983. Introspection--yes. Abstract in NADS 15.3.5. Argues that introspection is valuable source of data for dialectologists and that methods of traditional dialectology are not suited to discover systematic phonetic conditioning.

**1.701 Smith, Arthur L.,** ed. 1972. Language, communication, and rhetoric in black America. New York: Harper and Row. 388 pp. Anthology of ten essays by sociolinguists and other authors.

**1.702 Smith, Jack A.** 1962. A survey of localisms used by the native English-speaking Key Wester. Auburn: Auburn University thesis. vii + 74 pp. Same as Kentucky Microcards, series A., no. 208 (1964). Lexington, KY. Abstract in SAB 29.4 (Jan. 1964). [18 natives, S FL]. Presents phonetics of Key West, FL, speech and glossary of characteristic words and phrases of English and Spanish origin and proper names, place names, and nicknames of town.

**1.703 Smith, Jack [A.]** 1968. Some notes on the dialect of Key West. MFR 2.2.55-64. [S FL]. Discusses distinctive Key West terms for children's games, food, weather, and other subjects, terms that differ from general Southern usage and sometimes deriving from Spanish.

**1.704 Smith, Riley B.** 1974. Research perspectives on American black English: a brief historical sketch. AS 49.24-39. Surveys principal research, researchers, and points of view in study of black speech patterns in U.S.

**1.705 Smith, Riley B.** 1979. Sociological aspects of black English dialects in the United States. Language and society: anthropological issues, ed. by William C. McCormack and Stephen A. Wurm, 137-43. The Hague: Mouton.

Outlines how sociolinguistic investigations, particularly of black speech, can reveal far more social dynamics and complexities than traditional dialect research.

**1.706 Smith, Vicki, and Jean Hoornstra., comps. 1981.** Linguistic atlas of the gulf states: the basic materials: an introduction and guide to the microfiche collection. Ann Arbor, MI: University Microfilms. 11 pp. Pamphlet to accompany Pederson et al. **(1.594)** for beginning users.

**1.707 Smith, William H. 1979.** Low-country black English. AS 54.64-67. [3 speakers, Henderson, SC]. Discusses six features of noun and verb morphology and provides narrative in modified orthography to illustrate pronunciation.

**1.708 Smitherman, Geneva. 1973.** God don't never change: black English from a black perspective. CE 34.828-33. Says that black English is a legitimate variety of English but is a style, not a dialect, and that differences between black and white speech are overdramatized, creating distractions for teachers.

**1.709 Smitherman, Geneva. 1975.** Black language and culture: sounds of soul. New York: Harper and Row. 33 pp. Popular account of sociohistorical background and linguistic elements of black speech, including extensive discussion of modes of discourse--call and response, signification, the dozens, etc.

**1.710 Smitherman, Geneva. 1977.** Talkin and testifyin: the language of black America. Boston: Houghton Mifflin. 291 pp. Popular, sometimes polemical examination of structure, origin, and use of black speech patterns in the U.S.; includes chapters on African world view and Afro-American oral tradition, black modes of discourse, and words and concepts in black English, past and present; appendices on black sounds and structure and selected glossary of black semantics. **Reviews:** C. B. Cazden. 1978. American Journal of Orthopsychiatry 48.378-79; C. Mitchell-Kernan. 1979. Contemporary Psychology 24.253-54; B. A. Sizmore. 1979. Research in Education 5.153-58.

**1.711 Smitherman, Geneva. 1980.** White English in blackface, or who do I be? The state of the language, ed. by Leonard Michaels and Christopher Ricks, 158-68. Berkeley: University of California Press. Pp. 160-61, argues against black English-white English deep structure differences, and claims black English is different lexically and stylistically, but not grammatically, from white English.

**1.712 Sommer, Elisabeth. 1980.** The course of black language in the United States. Sprachkontakt und sprachkonflikt, ed. by Peter Hans Nelde, 287-96. Wiesbaden: Franz Steiner. Surveys main issues and linguistic features discussed in literature on black speech.

**1.713 Southard, Bruce.** 1979. Will Rogers and the language of the Southwest: a centennial perspective. Will Rogers: a centennial tribute, ed. by Arrell Morgan Gibson, 113-23. Oklahoma City: Oklahoma Historical Society. Revises Atwood's (3.17) definition (that "Southwestern" speech is that of Southwest Texas) by saying Rogers' language is better model of region's language patterns; compares latter to three major dialect areas of eastern U.S. and to dictionaries, concluding Rogers' written language and pronunciation "suggests very strongly" that his speech is more Southern than Midland or Northern.

**1.714 Spalding, Henry D., ed.** 1972. Encyclopedia of black folklore and humor. Middle Village, NY: Jonathan David. Black English, 562-65. Argues "plantation dialect was the universally understood tongue in general use by the slaves and their descendants" and that "the so-called 'southern accent' is a variant of Negro dialect."

**1.715 Spears, Arthur K.** 1987. [Are black and white vernaculars diverging?] AS 62.48-55. Part of NWAV panel discussion about hypothesis that black and white speech are becoming less like each other.

**1.716 Spears, James E.** 1970. Notes on Negro folk speech. North Carolina Folklore 18.154-57. Compiles features of phonology, vocabulary, and grammar from primary sources.

**1.717 Spitzer, Nicholas.** 1977. Cajuns and creoles: the French gulf coast. Southern Exposure 5.2-3.140-51. Profiles languages spoken in modern-day LA, their status, and identity of their speakers.

**1.718 Spurlock, John Howard.** 1980. He sings for us: a sociolinguistic analysis of the Appalachian subculture and of Jesse Stuart as a major American author. Lanham, MD: University Press of America. x + 180 pp. Study of major literary elements in poetry and fiction of KY writer.

**1.719 Steadman, John M., Jr.** 1916. Old, early, and Elizabethan English in the southern mountains: addenda and corrigenda to an article by J. H. Combs. DN 4.350-52. [S Appalachia]. Critique of Combs (**2.86**).

**1.720 Stephens, J. Harold.** 1971. Echoes of a passing era (down memories lane). Orlando, FL: Daniels. Similes of a passing era, 96-104; Sayings of a passing era, 104-13; Bywords of a passing era, 113-16.

**1.721 Stephenson, Edward A.** 1958. The speech of William Faulkner. Abstract in SAB 23.5. Describes University of Virginia tapes of Faulkner speaking.

**1.722 Stewart, Penny Helen.** 1976. Linguistic signals to ethnic group and socioeconomic class among eighty ten-year-olds in Hattiesburg, Mississippi. Hattiesburg: University of Southern Mississippi dissertation. Abstract in

DAI 37.5796A. [S MS]. Studies pronunciation of <u>was</u>, existential <u>there</u> vs. <u>it</u>, and demonstrative <u>them</u> vs. <u>those;</u> finds ethnic group membership more strongly constrains frequency of linguistic variables than socioeconomic class but that white middle and upper class children use stigmatized variants more often than black counterparts.

**1.723 Stewart, William A.** 1964. Foreign language teaching methods in quasi-foreign language situations. Non-standard speech and the teaching of English, ed. by William A. Stewart, 1-15. Washington: CAL. [Washington, DC]. Says teaching of Standard English to speakers of English creoles and Black English resembles teaching of English as a foreign language in many respects; discusses features of DC nonstandard speech, 8-11.

**1.724 Stewart, William A.** 1965. Urban Negro speech: sociolinguistic factors affecting English teaching. Social dialects and language learning: proceedings of the Bloomington, Indiana, conference 1964, ed. by Roger Shuy, 10-19. Urbana: NCTE. Points out and explains neglect of study of urban black speech; calls for descriptive work and application of findings to improved English teaching; illustrates features of black speech in Washington, DC.

**1.725 Stewart, William A.** 1966. Social dialect. Research planning conference on language development in disadvantaged children, ed. by Joan Gussow and Beryl L. Bailey. New York: Ferkauf Graduate School, Yeshiva University. ED 010 777. Discusses priorities in designing instructional programs for dialect speakers.

**1.726 Stewart, William A.** 1967. Research in progress--social dialects of English. ED 012 906. 44 pp. Reports on thirty-six current, projected, and recently completed social dialect studies on English.

**1.727 Stewart, William A.** 1967. Language and communication in Southern Appalachia. Washington: CAL. 43 pp. ED 012 026. Identifies two major nonstandard dialects in Appalachia, one white and one black, and discusses their social status and pedagogical programs for dialect speakers in Appalachian schools. **Reprinted** in D. Shores 1972(**1.685**).107-22.

**1.728 Stewart, William A.** 1969. Language teaching problems in Appalachia. FFLR 7.1.58-59,161. Excerpt of preceding item.

**1.729 Stewart, William A.** 1970. Sociopolitical issues in the linguistic treatment of Negro dialect. Linguistics and the teaching of standard English to speakers of other languages or dialects, ed. by James E. Alatis, 215-23. Washington: Georgetown University Press. Discusses how sociopolitical issues have interfered with the scientific study of black speech by distorting "theoretical descriptions of Negro dialect's place in the range of dialect differences which make up 'English' in its most comprehensive sense."

**1.730 Stewart, William A.** 1970. Understanding black language. Black America, ed. by John F. Szwed, 121-31. New York: Basic Books. Calls for advancement of interracial understanding by appreciation of social history of blacks and how it produced characteristic language patterns.

**1.731 Stewart, William A.** 1971. Language learning and teaching in Appalachia. Appalachia 4.8.27-34. Discusses variation in Appalachian speech, social status of white and black varieties, and barriers to effective language teaching in region because of misunderstanding of cultural and linguistic basis of many educational problems.

**1.732 Stewart, William A.** 1971. Facts and issues concerning black dialect. English Record 21.4.121-35. Discusses cultural and educational problems of black students and how linguistic research enables educators to address them; essay written to accompany long-playing record.

**1.733 Stewart, William A.** 1971. Observations (1966) on the problems of defining Negro dialect. FFLR 9.1.47-49,57. Says that American black speech has been viewed erroneously as a version of Southern American white speech, mainly by linguistic geographers, and that consequently terms like "Negro speech" and "Negro dialect" have been widely used in ways that are "inaccurate, misleading, and socially mischievous."

**1.734 Stewart, William A.** 1971. Review of Black-white speech relationships, ed by Walt Wolfram and Nona H. Clarke. FFLR 10.1-2.25-26,55-56. Essay arguing that W. Wolfram-N. Clarke anthology (**1.853**) overrepresents Anglicist view of black speech deriving from British varieties and excludes nonacademic opinion on black-white speech relationships.

**1.735 Stewart, William A.** 1973. More on black-white speech relationships: being reflections on the occasion of Walt Wolfram's reply. FFLR 11.1-2.35-40. Answers Wolfram reply (**1.838**) to Stewart review of W. Wolfram-N. Clarke anthology.

**1.736 Stewart, William A.** 1978. The laissez-faire movement in English teaching: advance to the rear? A pluralistic nation: the language issue in the United States, ed. by Margaret A. Lourie and Nancy F. Conklin, 333-56. Rowley, MA: Newbury House. Discusses ideological considerations leading scholars to minimize black-white cultural and linguistic differences; calls for full recognition of Black English as functionally and culturally valid variety and criticizes College Conference on Composition and Communication's "Students' Right to Their Own Language" resolution for claiming only superficial differences between "Black English Vernacular" and "Standard English."

**1.737 Stoller, Paul, ed.** 1975. Black American English: its background and its usage in the schools and in literature. New York: Delta. 238 pp. Eight essays on history and structure of black speech and on black speech and education; also includes excerpts from literary works of three black authors.

**1.738 Stolz, Walter, and Garland Bills.** 1968. An investigation of the standard-nonstandard dimension of central Texan English. Part of final report, University of Texas Child Development Evaluation and Research Center. [23 speakers, ages 17-60 from rural area NW of Austin, TX]. Based on investigation of seventeen grammatical and phonological features, says "both speakers and dialect indicators could be ordered along" a linguistic continuum and highly significant correlations can be found between speaker's degree of dialect and socioeconomic status and amount of formal education.

**1.739 Stoney, Samuel Gaillard.** 1939. Charleston azaleas and old bricks. Boston: Houghton Mifflin. P. 2, notes on Charleston, SC, speech; says that there are "three distinct dialects floating about in the Charleston air."

**1.740 Stowe, William P.** 1970. Grits singular or plural? Sandlapper 3.7.34-35. Anecdote about South Dakotan's confusion over grammatical number of grits.

**1.741 Strainchamps, Ethel Reed.** 1948. An Ozarker's reaction to formal language. AS 23.262-65. [SW MO]. Observations by Ozark native on differences between local speech and language patterns of schoolbooks in her youth.

**1.742 Strainchamps, Ethel Reed.** 1957. [Comments]. Ozarks Mountaineer 5.20 (May). Response to L. Collier item (**1.142**).

**1.743 Street, Julian.** 1917. American adventures: a second trip "abroad at home." New York: Century. "You-all" and other sectional misunderstandings, 203-13. Impressions and experiences of Northern journalist touring the South; recounts occasion when he witnessed apparent singular use of expression and discusses public reaction to his publishing story reporting this with the claim and his later change of mind. Idioms and aristocracy, 214-21, discusses VA speech and how it shows character and pride of state's residents.

**1.744 Strickland, Dorothy S., and William A. Stewart.** 1976. The use of dialect readers: a dialogue. Black dialects and reading, ed. by Bernice E. Cullinan, 146-51. Urbana: NCTE. Debate over pedagogical and political advantages and drawbacks to use of beginning materials in "black nonstandard dialect" to teach dialect speakers to read.

**1.745 Stuart, Jesse.** 1959. Up the branch. This is the South, ed. by Robert West Howard. 221-28. Chicago: Rand McNally. Comments on Southern speech by the novelist.

**1.746 Stubbs, Thomas M.** 1959-70. Mountain-wise. Georgia Magazine.

Thirteen selections of monthly column that deal with language use in N GA mountains.

**1.747 Sutherland, E. J.** 1960. Folk speech on frying pan. Mountain Life and Work 36.11-14. Surveys features of Southern Appalachian speech, which author believes is full of "corruptions" and "mispronunciations."

**1.748 Tarpley, Fred.** 1971. Language development programs for Southern American Negroes. Applications of linguistics: selected papers of the second international congress of applied linguistics, Cambridge 1969, ed. by G. E. Perren and J. L. M. Trim, 407-15. Cambridge: Cambridge University Press. Presents four-step procedure for implementing "language development programs to provide standard English as a second dialect" for black students: developing a philosophy of language, analyzing features of students' speech, motivating students to learn standard English, and producing instructional materials.

**1.749 Tarpley, Fred.** 1978. A small town factory as microcosm for dialect study. Abstract in NADS 11.1.12. Contrasts speech of two groups in a factory--managers from OH and laborers from Commerce, TX.

**1.750 Taylor, Orlando L.** 1974. Black language: the research dimension. Black communication: dimensions of research and instruction, ed. by Jack L. Daniel, 145-59. New York: Speech Communication Association. Historical perspective on how views of black American speech have evolved from its being an unsystematic, childlike type of language to its being an extension of larger West African linguistic system; outlines agenda for research on issues dealing with black speech.

**1.751 Teschner, Richard V.** 1989. Language varieties, Spanish. Encyclopedia of Southern culture, ed. by William Ferris and Charles Wilson. Chapel Hill: University of North Carolina Press. Short essay on demography and strength of Spanish in TX, FL, and LA.

**1.752 They spake in divers tongues.** 1909. Atlantic 104.135-38. Popular article on speech differences written by transplanted Southerner.

**1.753 Thomas, Jean.** 1945. The changing mountain folk. American Mercury 61.43-49. [E KY]. Popular account of mountain life with many citations of Appalachian speech.

**1.754 Thomas, William J.** 1973. Black language in America. Wichita State University Bulletin 49.1.2-14. Summarizes history and structure of black English and argues that special programs to remediate black speech and view of it as disadvantaged are racist.

**1.755 Thompson, C. Lamar.** 1984. Little known facts about yesterday's impact on today's speech. Reviewed in Southeastern Conference on English in the Two-Year College Newsletter 17.1.39. Says distinctive features of black speech can be traced to English colonists and that whites no longer use them because of education and exposure to written English; claims little research has been done on speech patterns of white settlers.

**1.756 Thompson, Lawrence S.** 1956. Names in Kentucky. Kentucky tradition, 175-81. Hamden, CT: Shoe String Press. Discusses personal and place names and remarks on region's vocabulary.

**1.757 Thompson, Peggy B.** 1968. Language and the Negro child. Progressive 32.2.36-38. Review of writing of William Stewart and the Urban Language Survey publications.

**1.758 Thornborough, Laura.** 1937. The great smoky mountains. Knoxville: University of Tennessee Press. Revised edition 1962. [E TN]. Pp. 24-25, brief discussion of neologisms and Shakespearianisms of Smoky Mountains.

**1.759 Tinker, Edward Larocque.** 1953. Creole city: its past and its people. New York: Longmans, Green and Co. French, Cajun, and Gombo, 223-55. Discusses origin and status of different varieties of French in New Orleans and the relationship between them; includes basic elements of Gombo grammar and music.

**1.760 Tinkler, Mary C.** 1957. Newspaper English of Marshall County, Alabama. SFQ 21.154-59. Includes comments on vocabulary, syntax, spelling.

**1.761 Tocus, Clarence Spencer.** 1942. The Negro idiom in American musical composition. Los Angeles: University of Southern California thesis.

**1.762 Toon, Thomas E.** 1982. Appalachian English. English as a world language, ed. by Manfred Görlach and Richard W. Bailey, 239-45. Ann Arbor: University of Michigan Press. Exemplifies phonological and grammatical features of S Appalachian speech, based on Wolfram and Christian study (**1.852**).

**1.763 To save our folk-speech.** 1914. Literary Digest 48.205. (Jan. 31). Defends richness and vigor of local speech and argues that local communities "should share the scholar's respect for 'dialect regeneration'."

**1.764 Tozer, G.** 1932. The Ozark dialect. Lawrence: University of Kansas thesis. Extensive glossary of terms from fourteen areas such as"Government and Law" and "Family Ties"; includes comments on grammar and pronunciation of Ozark dialect and on Middle English survivals in region's speech.

**1.765 Traugott, Elizabeth C.** 1972. Principles in the history of American English--a reply. FFLR 10.1-2.5-6,56. Responds to Dillard's "Principles in the History of American English" (2.113) critique of traditional dialectology as Eurocentric and says study of history of varieties of American English must consider European background and theoretical principles of language change.

1.766 Tresidder, Argus. 1937. The speech of the Shenandoah Valley. AS 12.284-88. [W VA]. Surveys earlier work on VA speech; notes on phonology and lexicon.

1.767 Troike, Rudolph C. 1973. On social, regional, and age variation in black English. FFLR 11.1-2.7-8. Says preoccupation of research on black English with its differences from white English has ignored important dimensions of study--definition of standard English in black community and age differences and regional variation in black speech.

1.768 Troike, Rudolph C. 1983. The Texas dialect survey: responses from Austin, Texas. Southwest Journal of Linguistics 6.145-54. [107 7th-, 9th-, 11th-graders, Austin, TX]. Reports preliminary findings of follow-up study to Atwood 1962 investigating features in pronunciation, grammar, and lexicon; finds some regional/folk terms holding their own and others declining in use.

1.769 Trudgill, Peter. 1986. Dialects in contact. New York: Oxford University Press. viii + 174 pp. Study of how speakers accommodate and linguistic variants compete for prestige in situations of dialect contact, leading to dialect mixture and leveling and the growth of new dialects; scattered comments on features of Southern English as competing for status or as product of colonial dialect leveling. Reviews: C. Feagin. 1988. AS 81-88; M. Görlach. 1987. EWW 8.128-31; I. Smith. 1987. Language 63.675-76.

1.770 Twiggs, Robert D. 1973. Pan-African language in the Western hemisphere: Palwh [pælwh]: a re-definition of black dialect as a language and the culture of black dialect. North Quincy, MA: Christopher. 282 pp. Tendentious, nontechnical presentation of background, pronunciation, and grammar of American black speech generalized to cover entire New World; includes eleven extended lessons in "Palwh" for schoolchildren, each lesson consisting of a conversation to be studied, brief grammatical notes, and a vocabulary list. Reviews: J. D. Edwards. 1976. AA 78.457-58; R. E. Wood. 1974. MLJ 58.300; R. E. Wood. 1974. Language Sciences 30.38-39.

1.771 Tye, Billy. 1946. Our time-flavored speech. Notes from the Pine Mountain Settlement School 19.1.3. [KY]. Examples of dialect.

1.772 Underhill, David. 1975. Yukking it up at CBS. Southern Exposure 2.4.68-71. Says that network television systematically undercovers news from Appalachia and that network news personnel harbor prejudices against mountain and Southern accents which lead them not to take seriously stories reported with those accents.

**1.773 Underhill, David.** 1975. A report on CBS news and 17 million Appalachian people. Mountain Review 1.2.1-3. Expansion of preceding item; says network prejudice against Appalachian accents and people is consistent with economic paternalism in region.

**1.774 Underwood, Gary N.** 1972. The research methods of the Arkansas language survey. AS 47.211-20. ED 074 823. Procedures, objectives, and parameters of the Arkansas Language Survey, statewide project investigating speech patterns for three social classes and three generations in nine regions of AR.

**1.775 Underwood, Gary N.** 1973. Problems in the study of Arkansas dialects. Orbis 22.64-71. ED 044 698. Rationale and design for statewide linguistic survey incorporating study of social and generational variation into a regional survey.

**1.776 Underwood, Gary N.** 1974. Needs in southwest English dialectology (or, want a LASS? Thanks, but no thanks). Southwest areal linguistics, ed. by Garland Bills, 119-44. San Diego, CA: Institute for Cultural Pluralism, San Diego State University. ED 109 883. Same as following item.

**1.777 Underwood, Gary N.** 1974. American English dialectology: alternatives for the Southwest. International Journal of the Sociology of Language 2.19-40. Same as Linguistics 128.19-40. Calls for immediate halt in work of LAUSC, saying it lacks sociolinguistic validity and its "methodology is not salvageable." **Reprinted** in J. L. Dillard 1980(**1.197**).72-91.

**1.778 Underwood, Gary N.** 1974. Teacher, what do you think you are doing? ED 128 833. 11 pp. [AR]. Points out that satisfaction 4th, 5th, and 6th graders in AR have with their own speech conflicts with teachers' attempts to modify that speech, and says this conflict is mirrored in materials for teachers that both indicate value of preserving dialect diversity and stress importance of instituting standard English usage.

**1.779 Underwood, Gary N.** 1982. James Sledd on standard English: avant-garde radical or old-fashioned conservative? Journal of the Linguistic Association of the Southwest 5.234-45. Reviews views of Sledd on teaching of standard English and those of his critics; concludes Sledd's ideas "are neither radical nor revolutionary" and that Sledd himself is "an old-fashioned middle-class white Southerner whose Methodist heritage taught him the Fatherhood of God and the Brotherhood of Mankind."

**1.780 Van Nest, R. J.** 1976. Gillis ridge. AJ 3.307-10. [NE TN]. Semifictional account discussing how linguistic behavior fits into mountain culture; claims that in sound and pace of mountain speech "there is reaffirmation of the manner of their life."

**1.781 Van Riper, Mrs. William R.** 1979. The speech of the American heartland: Oklahoma. JEL 13.65-71. Describes and chronicles work on Linguistic Atlas of Oklahoma and recounts settlement history of state.

**1.782 Vaughn-Cooke, Fay Boyd.** 1987. [Are black and white vernaculars diverging?] AS 62.12-32. Part of NWAV panel discussion; opposes William Labov's hypothesis that black and white speech are becoming less like one another and argues that research of Labov had significant flaws in methodology.

**1.783 Vickers, Carol.** 1982. "Meddlin" and other words in black English. MFR 16.55-59. [B junior-high students in Newton Co., MS]. Notes on lexicon, pronunciation, and semantics characteristic of black youths.

**1.784 Vickers, Ovid S.** 1968. Word watching in red neck country. MFR 2.69-75. [E CENT MS]. Discusses language taboos, honorific designations, terms for illegal liquor, hunting, and household items; notes expressions used only by blacks.

**1.785 Viereck, Wolfgang.** 1969. Zur negersprache im den Vereinigten Staaten. Idioma 6.55-60. Presents list of features identified with American blacks, particularly lexicon, but also phonological and syntactic features, based on work of Raven McDavid.

**1.786 Viereck, Wolfgang.** 1971. Britische und amerikanische sprachatlanten. ZDL 38.167-205. Survey of major linguistic atlas projects in U.S. and in Britain.

**1.787 Viereck, Wolfgang.** 1975. Die erforschung des black English in den USA--sinn und unsinn. Grazer Linguistische Studien 2.102-18. Critique of early sociolinguistic work on black English.

**1.788 Viereck, Wolfgang.** 1978. Afro-Amerikanische aspekte der mobilität: "black" English--eine kritische auseinandersetzung. Amerikastudien 23.332-40. Chronicles quest of U.S. black minority for equality and cultural recognition and reviews dispute between linguistic geographers and other scholars over distinctiveness of black speech, an irresolvable question until more data is gathered.

**1.789 Viereck, Wolfgang.** 1980. Social dialectology: a plea for more data. Studia Anglica Posnaniensia 11.15-25. Says much research on black English is based on few informants, little data, and too much intuition. **Reprinted** in H. Allen and M. Linn 1986(1.11).415-25.

**1.790 Vinson, Mark A.** 1983. The speech of Calloway County, Kentucky. Memphis: Memphis State University thesis. [10 B, 44 W, 24 M, 30 F adults, SW KY]. Based on Linguistic Atlas methods and informant types; deals with characteristic lexicon and phonology.

**1.791 Wächtler, K.** 1978. Vom regionaldialekt zum konsensusvarietät: sozialdialektologische und sozialpsychologische aspekte der mobilität in den U.S.A. Amerikastudien 23.341-46. Says advancing urbanization of American society is reducing regional variation in American English, increasing sociolinguistic diversification in cities, and replacing the former regional standards by national standard variety of speech.

**1.792 Wagner, Martha Prentice.** 1971. The language problem. Teaching speech in an all-black senior high school, 82-107. Baton Rouge: Louisiana State University thesis. Discusses challenge for white person teaching English in all-black high school and offers recommendations for adjusting to situation.

**1.793 Walker, Raphy S.** 1939. A mountaineer looks at his own speech. TFSB 5.1-13. [E TN]. Discusses Smoky Mountain vocabulary, grammar, and pronunciation (with anecdotal account of the drawl), with five pages of transcriptions.

**1.794 Walker, Ursula.** 1968. Structural features of Negro-English of Natchitoches Parish, Louisiana. Natchitoches: Northwestern Louisiana State University thesis. 110 pp. Same as ED 022 184. [355 W, 355 B high school students, NW LA]. Compares morphological and other problems in writing of freshman students at Northwestern State College and explores challenge of black students to become bidialectal; says there is "a definite African substructure in the local Negro dialect."

**1.795 Walters, Keith.** 1985. Friendly persuasion: students as collectors of dialect data. Papers from the fifth international conference on methods in dialectology, ed. by H. J. Warkentyne, 465-76. Victoria, BC: Department of Linguistics, University of Victoria. Abstract in NADS 16.2.4. Discusses methodology for conducting dialect study among undergraduate students at University of Texas.

**1.796 Ward, Martha.** 1971. Them children: a study in language learning. New York: Holt Rinehart and Winston. 99 pp. [St. James Parish, SE LA]. Ethnographic study of language acquisition and language interaction. **Reviews:** R. W. Casson. 1974. AA 160-61; R. Macaulay. 1973. LIS 2.310-14.

**1.797 Waters, Donald J.,** ed. 1983. Strange ways and sweet dreams: Afro-American folklore from the Hampton Institute. Boston: G. K. Hall. 439 pp. Anthology of brief items on folklore and ethnology, mostly from issues of Southern Workman magazine. Scattered references to black speech.

**1.798 Weaver, Linda.** 1980. A sociolinguistic analysis of Alba, Texas. Abstract in NADS 12.3.4. [N CENT TX]. Says that social factors are correlated with nonstandard speech in a TX community.

**1.799 Weeks, Abigail E.** 1921. The speech of the Kentucky mountaineer as I know it. New York: Teachers College, Columbia University thesis. 21 pp. Discusses origin of mountain people and their speech and how mountaineers' speech habits reflect their culture and ways of thinking.

**1.800 Wentworth, Harold.** 1936. The mapping of American speech. Philological Papers 1.49-53. Relates WV to LAUSC.

**1.801 West, John Foster.** 1966. Dialect of the southern mountains. North Carolina Folklore 14.31-34. [W NC]. Reminiscences of folksy mountain speech by former resident.

**1.802 West, Roy Andre.** 1922. The songs of the mountaineers. Nashville: George Peabody College thesis. Brief comments on relic, mostly lexical, forms.

**1.803 Westover, J. Hutson.** 1960. Highland language of the Cumberland coal country. Mountain Life and Work 36.18-21. [KY]. Compilation of archaic vocabulary and pronunciations from 17th century to present, based on personal observation in physician's clinic and on reading.

**1.804 Whiteman, Marcia F.** 1976. Dialect influence and the writing of black and white working class Americans. Washington: Georgetown University dissertation. Abstract in DAI 37.3295-96A. [B, W LC 8th-graders, southern MD]. Compares writing performance on inflectional endings, copula deletion, final consonant cluster reduction, and postvocalic /r/ of MD students with performance of four ages of white and black student and adult writers from rest of country; finds absence of same inflectional suffixes in writing by both those for whom they are absent in speech and those for whom they are not, but to greater extent for former, leading to conclusion of "dialect influence" from speech on writing responsible for grammatical but not phonological patterns.

**1.805 Whitener, Rogers.** 1981. Selections from "Folk-ways and folk-speech." North Carolina Folklore Journal 29.1. Mountain sayings, 19-20; Appalachian place names, 39-40; Mountain speech, 40-42; Folk speech, 43-44; Academic lore and "ferry dittles," 60-61. Short essays on aspects of W NC mountain speech.

**1.806 Whitney, Annie Weston.** 1901. Negro American dialects. Independent 53.1979-81,2039-42. Says dialects of black Southerners differ throughout region, often from one plantation to another and consist of archaic as well as "corrupted" words from white speech; comments on language use by blacks and whites on a SC plantation.

**1.807 Whitney, Annie Weston, and Carline Canfield Bullock.** 1925. Dialect notes. Folklore from Maryland, 203-05. New York: American Folklore Society. Seventy-four notes on unusual words and expressions.

**1.808 Williams, Cratis D.** 1961. The content of mountain speech. Mountain Life and Work 37.13-17 (Winter). [S Appalachia]. Says mountain speech does have "strong language, sparkling with proverbial wisdom, sparkling with pleonasms, powerful metaphors, and vivid similes, abounding with archaisms," but that it is not, contrary to some literary treatments, qualitatively different from other varieties of American folk speech.

**1.809 Williams, Cratis D.** 1961. Rhythm and melody in mountain speech. Mountain Life and Work 37.7-10 (Fall). [S Appalachia]. Cites features of grammar, diction, and rhetoric of mountain speech. **Reprinted** in Bobbs-Merrill Reprint Series, Language-100.

**1.810 Williams, Cratis D.** 1962. Mountaineers mind their manners. Mountain Life and Work 38.19-25 (Summer). [S Appalachia]. Discussion of manners and civilities of mountain speech behavior by a native.

**1.811 Williams, Cratis D.** 1967. Subtlety in mountain speech. Mountain Life and Work 43.14-16 (Spring). [S Appalachia]. Says mountaineer "possesses subtleties in emphasis and traditional tricks in turning phrases in basic English that enable him to express himself colorfully" and presents his translation of five literary selections into mountain dialect to demonstrate this.

**1.812 Williams, Cratis D.** 1968. Mountain speech. Language and culture: a reader, ed. by Patrick Gleeson and Nancy Wakefield, 151-60. Columbus, OH: Charles E. Merrill. Revision of items **1.808** and **5.241**.

**1.813 Williams, Cratis D.** 1978. Appalachian speech. NCHR 55.174-79. Provides overview of Southern Appalachian pronunciation and grammar and presents folk tale in modified orthography to reflect these features.

**1.814 Williams, Frederick,** ed. 1970. The language of poverty: perspectives on a theme. Chicago: Markham. 459 pp. Anthology of nineteen articles and annotated bibliography of journal articles. **Reviews:** W. C. Bailey. 1971. AA 73.1375-76; J. L. Dillard. 1972. Language 48.479-87.

**1.815 Williams, Patricia Ann.** 1975. What did you say? a study concerning the vocabulary, grammatical, and pronunciation choices of Houston residents. ED 163 786. [50 adults, Houston, TX]. Explores correlations between answers to twenty-three-item linguistic survey with five social factors--age, sex, race, education, and length of residence.

**1.816 Williamson, Juanita V.** 1961. A phonological and morphological study of the speech of the Negro of Memphis, Tennessee. Ann Arbor: University of Michigan dissertation. Abstract in DAI 21.3777-78. Published with minor revisions as PADS 50. 54 pp. Excerpt in J. Williamson and V. Burke 1971.583-95. [24 B, ages 27-84, Memphis]. Finds pronunciation of blacks in Memphis is largely homogeneous and very similar to General

Southern pronunciation but that social and generational differences exist in morphology, with older and less educated black speakers often using nonstandard, and sometimes archaic, irregular verb forms.

**1.817 Williamson, Juanita V.** 1965. Report on a proposed study of the speech of Negro high school students in Memphis. Social dialectology and language learning, ed. by Roger Shuy, 23-27. Champaign: NCTE. Reports on institute for high school teachers to develop understanding of and strategies for correction of nonstandard speech in black high schools; lists grammatical features found in local black speech by practice teachers.

**1.818 Williamson, Juanita V.** 1968. The speech of Negro high school students in Memphis, Tennessee. Final report project no. 5-0592-12-1. U.S. Department of Health, Education, and Welfare. 96 pp. [18 B teenagers, Memphis]. Finds phonology of black teenagers same as that of other Southerners; grammatical patterns are generally those of standard English, though some nonstandard pronoun and verb patterns were found.

**1.819 Williamson, Juanita V.** 1970. Selected features of speech: black and white. CLAJ 13.420-33. Responds to Beryl Bailey (**1.24**) argument of distinctiveness of black speech based on literary dialect by showing that same features (zero copula, auxiliary been, negators ain't/don't, and existential they) can be found in speech of white KKK members; includes citations of same features from other white speakers. **Reprinted** in J. Williamson and V. Burke 1971(**1.823**).496-507.

**1.820 Williamson, Juanita V.** 1980. The speech of black and white Southerners: who learned from whom? Abstract in NADS 12.3.12. Reviewed in NADS 13.1.13. Argues that blacks learned English primarily from illiterate whites in 17th and 18th centuries and that whites did not learn nonstandard features from blacks.

**1.821 Williamson, Juanita.** 1980. Views on non-standard and standard English usage. Abstract in Southeastern Conference on English in the Two-Year College Newsletter 13.1.45-46. Says distinction between black speech and white speech is false one; rejects African influences on American black speech, claiming the latter reflects language learned from white overseers and owners.

**1.822 Williamson, Juanita.** 1983. Southern American English: yet a part of the whole. Abstract in NADS 15.3.5. Argues that Southern white English and English of blacks had their roots in British English like other American dialects.

**1.823 Williamson, Juanita V., and Virginia M. Burke**, eds. 1971. A various language: perspectives on American dialects. New York: Holt, Rinehart and Winston. 706 pp. Collection of fifty essays, most of them reprinted from journals, many of them on Southern American dialects.

Reviews: J. Appleby. 1971. AS 46.158-59; R. E. Cooley. 1971. LL 21.263-67; J. L. Dillard. 1973. Caribbean Studies 12.4.76-91; W. E. Farrison. 1971. CLAJ 15.245-47; C. W. McCord. 1973. SSCJ 39.197-98; P. W. Rogers. 1972. Queen's Quarterly 79.559-60.

**1.824 Wilson, Charles Morrow.** 1930. Beefsteak when I'm hungry. Virginia Quarterly Review 6.240-50. Layman's observations of English of Southern mountains.

**1.825 Wilson, Charles Morrow.** 1933. Friendly days in the Ozarks. Travel Magazine 60.18-21,45. Fifty dialect items, repeated in following item.

**1.826 Wilson, Charles Morrow.** 1934. Backwoods language. Backwoods America, 61-71. Chapel Hill: University of North Carolina Press. Sentimental essay on Ozark mountain English, calling it "a speech of illiteracy" that "carries a surprising portion of unexpectedly long or literary words."

**1.827 Wilson, Charles Morrow.** 1934. Ozarkadia. American Magazine 117.58-60,112. Extols life and language of Ozarks and relates latter to language of Sidney and Chaucer.

**1.828 Wilson, Charles Morrow.** 1959. Way folks say it. The bodacious Ozarks: true tales of the backhills, 141-49. New York: Hastings House. Catalog of archaisms and colorful expressions from Ozarks.

**1.829 [Wilson, George].** 1945. [Collecting dialect in North Carolina]. North Carolina English Teacher 3.1.23-24. Points out many locations and types of written sources from which dialect material may be collected.

**1.830 Wilson, George P., ed.** 1952. Folk speech. The Frank C. Brown collection of North Carolina folklore, 505-618. Durham: Duke University Press. List of more than 1,500 items including pronunciations, unusual meanings, names, and grammatical usages (frequently compared to British dialectal or literary usages), figurative expressions, humorous rhymes, dance calls, salutations and replies, and unusual interpretations of scripture, culled by Wilson from the folklorist Brown's collection of notes on the English language as used in NC.

**1.831 Wilson, George P.** 1960. Josiah H. Combs and folk speech. KFR 6.104-07. Obituary praising contributions of Combs as collector of folk speech and enumerating his contributions.

**1.832 Wilson, Gypsy Vera.** 1937. Language. Folklore in southeastern Kentucky, 6-38. Nashville: George Peabody College thesis. [Bell County, KY]. Surveys archaisms, names, pronunciations, and proverbial expressions, and investigates familiarity of list of latter in Blount Co., TN.

**1.833 Wise, Claude M.** 1945. The dialect atlas of Louisiana--a review of progress. Studies in Linguistics 3.2.37-42. Includes bibliography of Louisiana State University theses and dissertations on phonetics and dialectology, 1935-1943.

**1.834 Wolf, John Quincy.** 1974. Life in the leatherwoods. Edited, with an afterword, by John Quincy Wolf, Jr. Introduction and notes by F. Jack Hurley. Memphis: Memphis State University Press. [AR Ozarks]. Pp. 106-07, role of local expressions in mountain humor.

**1.835 Wolfram, Walter A.** 1969. A sociolinguistic description of Detroit Negro speech. Washington: CAL. [48 B, 4 social classes, 16 preadolescents, 16 teenagers, 16 middle-aged adults, Detroit, MI]. Investigates four phonological variables, including postvocalic /r/ and final consonant clusters, and four syntactic features, including invariant be and multiple negation, and correlates variants with style, sex, age, and isolation of speaker. **Reviews:** J. Fickett. 1969-70. Studies in Linguistics 21.141-42; J. Grillet. 1977. La Linguistique 13.156-57; R. B. LePage. 1973. Linguistics 118.119-24; R. S. Macaulay. 1970. Language 46.764-74; L. Pederson. 1975. 50.98-110.

**1.836 Wolfram, Walt.** 1969. An appraisal of ERIC documents on the manner and extent of nonstandard dialect divergence. ED 034 991. 23 pp. Evaluates recent literature in terms of deficit vs. difference of nonstandard dialects with respect to "standard English."

**1.837 Wolfram, Walt.** 1971. Black-white speech differences revisited. Viewpoints: Bulletin of the School of Education, Indiana University 47.2.27-50. [25 W, 25 B, ages 6-8, Holmes Co., MS]. Investigates patterning of third-person-singular -s and possessive -s, contraction and deletion of copula, and use of invariant be; finds both quantitative and qualitative black-white differences. **Reprinted** in W. Wolfram and N. Clarke 1971(**1.853**).139-61.

**1.838 Wolfram, Walt.** 1973. Hidden agendas and witch hunts: which is witch?: a reply to William A. Stewart. FFLR 11.1-2.33-34,45. Answers criticisms (**1.735**) raised in review of W. Wolfram and N. Clarke anthology (**1.853**).

**1.839 Wolfram, Walt.** 1974. The relationship of white Southern speech to vernacular black English. Language 50.498-527. [100+ B, W LC speakers, ages 8-17, some MC adults, Franklin Co., SW MS]. Quantitative study finding that many patterns in black speech, most notably copula deletion, are also present in white speech, although less frequently, but often pattern differently in white speech; finds "distributive be" only in black speech.

**1.840 Wolfram, Walt.** 1975. Variable constraints and rule relations. Analyzing variation in language, ed. by Ralph W. Fasold and Roger W. Shuy, 70-88. Washington: Georgetown University Press. P. 75, note on copula deletion and contraction in Southern English. **Reprinted** in R. Fasold 1983(**1.236**).

**1.841 Wolfram, Walt.** 1977. On the linguistic study of Appalachian speech. AJ 5.92-102. History of study of Appalachian speech, assessment of current knowledge, and statement of future prospects and needs for research; extensive bibliography.

**1.842 Wolfram, Walt.** 1977. Language assessment in Appalachia: a socio-linguistic perspective. AJ 4.224-34. Guidelines for testing language ability of Appalachian children and for using and interpreting results of standardized tests.

**1.843 Wolfram, Walt.** 1980. Beyond black English: implications of the Ann Arbor decision for other nonmainstream varieties. Reactions to Ann Arbor: vernacular black English and education, ed. by Marcia Farr Whiteman, 10-23. Arlington: CAL. Discusses linguistic, sociolinguistic, and educational parallels between Black English and other varieties of American English and implications of Ann Arbor "Black English case" for dealing with and testing speakers of these varieties, especially speakers of Appalachian speech.

**1.844 Wolfram, Walt.** 1980. Variation in American English. Language in the USA, ed. by Charles Ferguson and Shirley Brice Heath, 44-68. New York: Cambridge University Press. 3 maps. Overview article on main dimensions of regional and social variation.

**1.845 Wolfram, Walt.** 1982. Research conference on the English language in the Southern United States. Linguistic Reporter 24.4.10-11. Report on significance of research conference on black-white speech relationships held in Columbia, SC, whose papers were published in **1.528**.

**1.846 Wolfram, Walt.** 1984. Is there an "Appalachian English"? AJ 11.215-24. Outlines stages in study of Appalachian speech and discusses difficulty of defining "Appalachian English" and other dialects on objective basis but concludes tentatively that it can be characterized by a unique "set of co-occurring structures."

**1.847 Wolfram, Walt.** 1986. Black-white dimensions in sociolinguistic test bias. Language variety in the South: perspectives in black and white, ed. by Michael Montgomery and Guy Bailey, 373-85. University: University of Alabama Press. Explores levels on which sociolinguistic differences may be reflected in standardized tests and in testing situations for speakers of Vernacular Black English or Southern Appalachian English and relationship of these levels to issues of educational equity.

**1.848 Wolfram, Walt.** 1987. [Are black and white vernaculars diverging?] AS 62.40-48. Part of NWAV panel discussion; outlines methodological prerequisites for supporting divergence hypothesis.

**1.849 Wolfram, Walt, and Donna Christian.** 1975. Sociolinguistic variables in Appalachian dialects. Final report, NIE grant number 74-0026. ED 112 687. 413 pp. Republished as following item.

**1.850 Wolfram, Walt, and Donna Christian.** 1976. Appalachian speech. Arlington: CAL. viii + 190 pp. ED 150 811. [129 speakers, all ages, Mercer and Monroe Cos., S WV]. Detailed sociolinguistic analysis of rural Appalachian speech, presenting a sociolinguistic framework for study of Appalachian English, focusing on phonological aspects (final consonant clusters, contraction, pronunciation of initial segments, etc.) and grammatical features of verbs, adverbs, negation, nominals, prepositions, and indirect questions, and discussing educational implications of dialect diversity in region; includes interview questionnaire and sample interview. **Reviews:** R. R. Butters. 1979. Language 55.460-62; J. Coady. 1973. Language Sciences 28.27-28; M. Montgomery. 1982. AS 57.134-39; R. Payne. 1977. JEL 11.83-92.

**1.851 Wolfram, Walt, and Donna Christian.** 1977. The language frontier in Appalachia. Appalachian Notes 5.33-41. **Reprinted** in Mountain Review 3.2.1-5 (1977). Semipopular essay on variation and change in mountain speech, attitudes towards it, and implications for teachers.

**1.852 Wolfram, Walt, and Donna Christian.** 1980. On the application of sociolinguistic information: test evaluation and dialect differences in Appalachia. Standards and dialects in English, ed. by Timothy Shopen and Joseph M. Williams, 177-212. Cambridge, MA: Winthrop. Application of findings from sociolinguistic research in WV to taking and evaluation of standardized tests of "correct" language use; discusses four principles of test evaluation and how they should be applied. Appendix A, Some grammatical characteristics of Appalachian English, 205-09; Appendix B, Two illustrative narratives from West Virginia, 210-12.

**1.853 Wolfram, Walt, and Nona H. Clarke,** eds. 1971. Black-white speech relationships. Washington: CAL. xiii + 161 pp. Anthology of eight previously published essays presenting synchronic and diachronic views, including those of dialect geographers, sociolinguists, and creolists, on relation of black and white speech in the U.S. **Reviews:** J. Fickett. 1973. Studies in Linguistics 23.111-15; M. R. Key. 1975. IJAL 41.84-89; D. Lawton. 1973. Revista Interamericana Review 2.624-33; P. J. Melmed. 1973. AA 75.497-98; L. Pederson. 1975. AS 50.98-110; W. Stewart. 1972. FFLR 10.1-2,25-26,55-56.

**1.854 Wolfram, Walt, and Ralph W. Fasold.** 1974. The study of social dialects in American English. Englewood Cliffs, NJ: Prentice-Hall. 239 pp. Surveys social dialect patterns in U.S. based on sociolinguistic studies and comparing many patterns of Southern American pronunciation and grammar to those of social groups and regions elsewhere in country. **Reviews:** T. K. Crowl. 1976. Journal of Communication 26.151-53; J. L. Dillard. 1975. LIS

4.367-75; D. E. Eskey. 1976. CE 37.718-23; R. I. McDavid, Jr. and R. K. O'Cain. 1977. AA 79.947-48; S. M. Tsuzaki. 1975. TESOL Quarterly 9.438-40; W. Viereck. 1977. Studies in Linguistics 1.145-49; L. V. Zuck. 1976. LL 26.191-98.

**1.855 Wolfram, Walt, and Marcia Whiteman.** 1971. The role of dialect interference in composition. FFLR 9.1-2.34-38,59. Raises issues about study of dialect interference in writing, answers questions about nature of interference, and points out possible implications for educational strategy.

**1.856 Wood, Gordon R.** 1960. An atlas survey of the interior South. Orbis 9.7-12. Account of progress of author's project from 1957 through 1959 (final project reported in Wood 3.537).

**1.857 Wood, Gordon R.** 1961. An all-South survey. Round Table of the South Central College English Association 2.3.

**1.858 Wood, Gordon R.** 1967. Sub-regional speech variation in vocabulary, grammar, and pronunciation. Cooperative research project no. 3046 final report. ED 019 263. [33 natives of AL, E TN, NE MS, NW GA]. Investigates degree of subregional homogeneity in vocabulary, pronunciation, and sentence structure; finds generational differences greatest in vocabulary and least in grammar.

**1.859 Wood, Gordon R.** 1970. Questionable white dialects: if questionable, what then? ED 054 142. 21 pp. Discusses complexity of dialects of Southern states and difficulty of describing them as well as of distinguishing questionable uses from dialect forms.

**1.860 Words words words.** 1974. AS 49.307. Comments on selected items, including terms case quarter and case dime and pronunciation of larynx as /larniks/ in GA.

**1.861 Workman, William D., Jr.** 1960. The war of words--semantics. The case for the South, 40-61. New York: Devin-Adair. Discusses such terms as black belt, discrimination, desegregation, prejudice, darky, nigger, and pronunciation and capitalization of Negro.

**1.862 Work Projects Administration.** 1939. Florida: a guide to the southernmost state. New York: Oxford University Press. Reprinted in 1975. Pp. 128-35, notes on language of Conchs and crackers.

**1.863 Work Projects Administration.** 1939. Kentucky: a guide to the bluegrass state. New York: Harcourt Brace. Pp. 89-90, on dialect.

**1.864 Work Projects Administration.** 1939. North Carolina: a guide to the old north state. Chapel Hill: University of North Carolina Press. Pp. 97-98, on dialect.

**1.865 Work Projects Administration.** 1939. Tennessee: a guide to the state. New York: Viking Press. Pp. 134-35, notes on speech.

**1.866 Work Projects Administration.** 1941. Arkansas: a guide to the state. New York: Hastings House. 447 pp. Pp. 4, 297, comments on speech.

**1.867 Work Projects Administration.** 1941. South Carolina: a guide to the palmetto state. New York: Oxford University Press. Pp. 104-08, notes on speech in SC.

**1.868 Works Progress Administration.** 1938. Mississippi: a guide to the magnolia state. New York: Viking. P. 22, note on black speech.

# 2 Historical and Creole Studies

**2.1 A., C. H.** 1891. Tote. American Notes and Queries 6.190 (Feb. 14). Reports word used in Maine, therefore indicating it is not exclusively Southern and therefore not of African derivation.

**2.2 Adams, Edward C. L.** 1928. Nigger to nigger. New York: Scribner's. Impressions of Gullah dialect, 194. Comments by fiction writer.

**2.3 Adkins, Nelson F.** 1933. Early Americanisms. AS 8.1.75-76. Cites nineteen terms from an 1833 newspaper story, including items from VA and KY.

**2.4 Adler, Max.** 1978. Pidgins, creoles and lingua francas: a sociolinguistic study. Hamburg: Helmut Buske. Pp. 78-80, summary of Gullah. **Reviews:** R. B. Le Page. 1979. LIS 8.129-30; S. M. Tsuzaki. 1979. TESOL Quarterly 13.591-92.

**2.5 Allen, William Francis.** 1867[1929]. Slave songs of the United States. New York: Peter Smith. Pp. xxiii-xxxvi, on dialect. [Port Royal, SC]. Popular analysis of phonology and grammar of Sea Island black speech; speculates on possible Huguenot influence on it.

**2.6 Alleyne, Mervyn C.** 1971. The linguistic continuity of Africa in the Caribbean. Topics in Afro-American studies, ed. by Henry J. Richards, 119-35. Buffalo, NY: Black Academy Press. Reviews ideological debate over continuity of African cultural and linguistic patterns in New World.

**2.7 Alleyne, Mervyn C.** 1980. Comparative Afro-American: an historical comparative study of English based Afro-American dialects of the new world. Ann Arbor, MI: Karoma. 253 pp. Comparative phonology, syntax, lexicosemantics; stresses African base. **Reviews:** M. Görlach. 1983. Indogermanische Forschungen 88.382-83; J. Holm. 1981. EWW 2.121-22; S. Mufwene. 1983. Carib 3.98-113; J. Rickford. 1983. Language 59.670-76;

M. Sebba. 1981. Lingua 54.361-68; B. M. H. Strang. 1982. YES 12.264-66; L. Todd. 1982. New West Indian Guide 56.167-69.

**2.8 Ames, Susie M.** 1947. Law-in-action: the court records of Virginia's Eastern shore. William and Mary Quarterly, ser. 3, vol 4.177-91. [E VA]. Pp. 180-81, how variant spellings by county clerks indicated different local pronunciations in 17th century.

**2.9 Andrews, Eliza F.** 1896. Cracker English. Chatauquan 23.85-88. [GA]. Discusses analogues of rural Southern white speech in Chaucer, Shakespeare, and other British writers; derives cracker from corn cracker.

**2.10 Asante, Molefi.** 1975. African and African American communication continuities. New York: Council on International Studies, State University of New York at Buffalo. 24 pp. Maintains there is continuity in manner of expression between West African languages and African American English, continuity "supported in the main by serialization [of verbs] and the unique usage of tense and aspect."

**2.11 Ashby, Rickie Zayne.** 1976. Philosophical and religious language in early Kentucky wills. KFR 22.2.39-44. Typical religious phrases used in 18th- and early 19th-century KY wills.

**2.12 B., W. G.** 1894. "Tote." Nation 58.121. Says word is used in Yorkshire and Lincolnshire in same way as in VA, discounting it as Southernism or Africanism.

**2.13 Bailey, Charles-James N.** 1982. Irish English and Caribbean English: another joinder. AS 57.237-39. Argues that an Irish source for habitual be is not inconsistent with Afro-Caribbean Creole origin for American black speech and says that those who argue the latter must propose an alternative source for patterning of be in black speech.

**2.14 Baird, Keith E.** 1980. Guy B. Johnson revisited: another look at Gullah. Journal of Black Studies 10.425-35. Reviews controversy between Guy Johnson (2.222) and M. Herskovits (2.203)/Turner (2.437) on degree of African influence on Gullah and says Johnson's continuing assessment of few African retentions is misled by his misunderstanding of the barriers surrounding Sea Island culture.

**2.15 Barker, L. J.** 1855. The influence of slavery on the white population. New York: American Anti-Slavery Society. Comments on slaves' influence on Southern speech, particularly from close contact between white children and black nurses and playmates.

**2.16 Bartlett, John R.** 1848. Dictionary of Americanisms. New York: Bartlett and Welford. Pp. xv-xxvii, on American dialects. Introduction reprinted in 1931, 1963, 1973 in The beginnings of American English, ed.

by Mitford M. Mathews, 141-50. Chicago: University of Chicago Press. Discusses "peculiarity in the pronunciation of the Southern and Western people" in pronouncing vowels before /r/ differently from New England; includes thirteen words "incorrectly pronounced" in South in longer wordlist.

**2.17 Baskerville, W. M.** 1891. The etymology of English "tote." MLN 6.180-81. Says verb is used throughout South and argues for Old English origin.

**2.18 Bates-Mims, Merelyn B.** 1986. Cincinnati: University of Cincinnati dissertation. Abstract in DAI 47.2142A. Claims existence of LA Creole English in SW LA.

**2.19 Beaudry, Mary Carolyn.** 1980. "Or what else you please to call it": folk semantic domains in early Virginia probate inventories. Providence: Brown University dissertation. Abstract in DAI 41.5153A. Studies folk classification of objects related to foodways, social relationships, and other matters and discusses consequent semantic domains.

**2.20 Benmaman, Virginia D.** 1976. An investigation of reading comprehension ability of black fourth and fifth grade students who are reading below grade level utilizing materials written in Gullah and standard English. Columbia: University of South Carolina dissertation. Abstract in DAI 37.167A. ED 124 934. Review of literature on Gullah, 27-36. [120 4th and 5th graders, Low Country SC]. Finds that Gullah-speaking students with reading difficulties prefer reading materials in Standard English rather than Gullah but that they comprehend both types of materials equally well.

**2.21 Bennett, John.** 1908-09. Gullah: a Negro patois. SAQ 7.332-47; 8.39-52. Early essays on exoticness of Gullah with plentiful citations and contention that its forms are retentions from British dialects and are "good Elizabethan style."

**2.22 Berdan, Robert.** 1980. Sufficiency conditions for a prior creolization of black English. Issues in English creoles: papers from the 1975 Hawaii conference, ed. by Richard R. Day, 147-62. Heidelberg: Julius Groos Verlag. Says that "there are at least four constructions in Black English that can be viewed as simplifications of standard English grammar: relative clause reduction, multiple negation, existential sentences and auxiliary inversion" and that "the existence of some prior creole would be sufficient to explain them."

**2.23 Berger, Marshall D.** 1980. New York City and the antebellum South: the Maritime connection. Perspectives on American English, ed. by J. L. Dillard, 135-41. The Hague: Mouton. Same as Word 31.47-54 (1980). Argues that fronted and r-less pronunciation of vowels in New York in words like first resulted from close contact the city had with cotton ports of Charleston, Savannah, Mobile, and New Orleans in antebellum period.

**2.24 Bickerton, Derek.** 1975. Dynamics of a creole system. New York: Cambridge University Press. P. 62, relates Gullah <u>doz</u> to Caribbean forms.

**2.25 Birmingham, John C.** 1976. Black English near its roots: the transplanted west African creoles. ED 132 882. 20 pp. Argues that many grammatical features of Black English and Caribbean Creoles derive from "Afro-Portuguese Creole dialects that sprang up in the fifteenth century in Portuguese slave camps along the West African coast" but that others have been lost "due to contact with Standard English."

**2.26 Blok, H. P.** 1959. Annotations to Mr. Turner's <u>Africanisms in the Gullah dialect</u>. Lingua 8.306-21. Extended review criticizing Turner's methods comparing African languages with Gullah and his emphasis on naming patterns.

**2.27 Bloomfield, Leonard.** 1933. Language. New York: Holt, Rinehart Winston. Pp. 474-75, notes creolized version of English spoken by American blacks and in Caribbean.

**2.28 Bolinger, Dwight L.** 1939. Bozo. AS 14.238-39. <u>Bozo</u> possibly from <u>bozal</u>, a slave-trade term for a black recently brought from Africa.

**2.29 Bolton, Henry Carrington.** 1888. Request for information in regard to terms used to talk to domestic animals. JAF 1.81-82. Gives samples of terms from AL, VA, MD, and elsewhere.

**2.30 Boney, F. N.** 1979. Southern "cotton snobs." AS 54.80. Term from 1860 social treatise that refers to unique Southern type who was "rural, inadequately educated, arrogant, ostentatious, deceitful, irreligious, crude, and debauched."

**2.31 Botume, Elizabeth Hyde.** 1893. First days amongst the contrabands. Boston: Lee and Shepard. Reprinted in 1968. New York: Arno Press. Pp. 137-42, scattered comments and citations of Gullah expressions and naming patterns.

**2.32 Bowden, Henry M.** 1895. "Axe" and "spunky" in dialect. Dial 18.136 (Mar. 1). Responds to Bondurant (1.79); says <u>axe</u> is common in Eastern states and is found in Lowell's <u>Biglow Papers</u>; says <u>spunky</u> is Scotch-Irish term spread by migration through much of country.

**2.33 Boyette, Dora S.** 1951. Variant pronunciations from Rockingham County, North Carolina, 1829-1860. Chapel Hill: University of North Carolina thesis. xiii + 46 pp. [N CENT NC]. Analyzes variant pronunciations of eight plantation overseers as reflected in their naive spellings in monthly reports to the plantation owner.

**2.34 Brewer, Fisk P.** 1873. Peculiar usages of English--observed in North

Carolina. Nation 16.148-49 (Feb. 27). Comment from Chapel Hill on pronunciation and words; see response (Nation 16.183).

**2.35 Brewer, Jeutonne P.** 1970. Possible relationships between African languages and black English dialects: implications for teaching standard English as an alternate dialect. ED 058 184. 17 pp. Distills findings of decade of sociolinguistic research on distinctiveness and systematicness of Black English and its creole and West African connections.

**2.36 Brewer, Jeutonne P.** 1973. Subject concord of "be" in early black English. AS 48.5-21. [22 B, 15 M, 7 F, 12 from TX, 10 from MS, ages 75-101]. Surveys subject-verb concord with be in early (based on WPA ex-slave narratives) and present-day black speech; finds "high percentage of person-number disagreement of be forms with pronoun subjects" different from both standard English and present-day black English. **Reprinted** in D. Shores and C. Hines 1977(**1.689**).161-75.

**2.37 Brewer, Jeutonne P.** 1974. The verb "be" in early Black English: a study based on the WPA ex-slave narratives. Chapel Hill: University of North Carolina dissertation. Abstract in DAI 36.337A. [40 B, from SC, TN, MS, TX]. Finds grammatical similarities in narratives of ex-slaves collected by different interviewers in four regions of South and that nonagreeing am was found mainly in TX.

**2.38 Brewer, Jeutonne P.** 1979. Nonagreeing "am" and invariant "be" in early black English. SECOL Bulletin 3.81-100. [54 ex-slaves interviewed by WPA, SC]. Documents grammatical change in black English and offers an empirical assessment of its possible plantation creole origin.

**2.39 Brewer, Jeutonne P.** 1980. The WPA slave narratives as linguistic data. Orbis 29.30-54. Says data from transcripts of ex-slaves hold promise of resolving issues about origin of black English and cites unpublished correspondence between Washington and state offices in effort to validate data; says "Washington office encouraged the state officials and the interviewers in the field to record what they heard, to avoid editorializing and editing, and to conduct follow-up interviews wherever possible."

**2.40 Brewer, Jeutonne P.** 1986. Durative marker or hypercorrection?: the case of -s in the WPA ex-slave narratives. Language variety in the South: perspectives in black and white, ed. by Michael Montgomery and Guy Bailey, 131-48. University: University of Alabama Press. [69 B over 60, SC, TX]. Finds "verb -s occurs regularly and frequently in a significant number of narratives" and that it functions as a durative marker and not as hypercorrection or regularized present tense marker since it occurs with all subjects of both numbers of all persons.

**2.41 Brewer, Jeutonne P.** 1986. Camouflaged forms in early black English: evidence from the WPA ex-slave narratives. Abstract in NADS 18.2.6.

[TX]. Analyzes use of camouflaged forms--structures similar in form between dialects but different in syntactic-semantic functions--in 130 interviews of ex-slaves conducted by WPA in 1930s.

**2.42 Brinton, D. G.** 1887. On certain supposed Nanticoke words, shown to be of African origin. American Antiquarian and Oriental Journal 9.350-54. [E MD]. Identifies supposed numerals of Amerindian language as Mandingo and most likely collected from runaway slave; calls for research on languages spoken by imported slaves.

**2.43 Bronstein, Arthur J.** 1949. A study of predominant dialect variation of standard speech in the United States during the first half of the nineteenth century. New York: New York University dissertation.

**2.44 Brooks, Cleanth, Jr.** 1935. The relation of the Alabama-Georgia dialect to the provincial dialects of Great Britain. Baton Rouge: Louisiana State University Studies 20. 91 pp. Takes Southern speech as represented in Payne (**1.555**) and in Uncle Remus stories, compares it to evidence in English Dialect Dictionary, concludes that English of both blacks and whites of Alabama-Georgia border derives more from Southern and Southwestern England than any other region. **Reviews:** G. T. Flom. 1936. JEGP 35.614; G. W. Gray. 1937. QJS 23.146; K. Malone. 1938. MLN 53.39-40; R. J. Menner. 1935. AS 10.304-07; S. S. Smith. 1937. American Oxonian 24.177-80; C. L. Wrenn. 1935. YWES 16.62-63.

**2.45 Brown, Calvin S.** 1889. Dialectal survivals in Tennessee. MLN 4.205-09. Same as American Notes and Queries 4.16-18 (Nov. 9, 1889) and 4.64-66 (Dec. 7, 1889). Thirty-nine forms found in TN and in Uncle Remus stories that are identical to forms in Shakespeare.

**2.46 Brown, Calvin S.** 1891. Other dialectal forms in Tennessee. PMLA 6.171-75. Same as American Notes and Queries 8.49-50 (Dec. 5, 1891); 8.62-63 (Dec. 12, 1891); 8.75 (Dec. 19, 1891). Surveys phonological and lexical peculiarities of TN speech and compares them to Shakespeare, Pope, and William Bartlett.

**2.47 Brown, Calvin S.** 1894. Dialectal survivals from Spenser. Dial 16.40. Comments on nonstandard forms with long history.

**2.48 Brown, Calvin S.** 1897. Dialectal survivals from Chaucer. Dial 22.139-41. Compiles analogs of modern-day nonstandard forms in Chaucer; refers to preceding item.

**2.49 Brown, John Mason.** 1868. Songs of the slaves. Lippincott's Magazine 2.617-23. **Reprinted** in Bruce Jackson, ed. 1967. The Negro and his folklore, 109-19. Austin: University of Texas Press. P. 119, comments on how to read punctuation in written version of black dialect accurately.

**2.50 Brown, Thomas L.** 1904. The word "tote." Publication of the Southern Historical Association 8.294-96. Cites meaning and etymologies of word from four dictionaries and cites Latin and English etyma to discount African derivation of verb; says "very few words, if any, have been introduced into the English language through Southern Negroes, certainly no verb, and tote is a verb."

**2.51 Bruce, J. Douglas.** 1893. Tote. MLN 8.251. Disagrees with etymology of W. M. Baskerville (2.17) but agrees term most likely had English derivation rather than African one because it was used as early as 1677 in VA.

**2.52 Bruce, Philip A.** 1894. Tote. Nation 58.121. Black origin unlikely because of early use in VA; cites February, 1677.

**2.53 Bruce, Philip Alexander.** 1914. Old pronunciation. William and Mary Quarterly, ser. 1, vol. 23.126. Infers from spelling of James as Jemes that raised pronunciation of vowel in VA goes back at least 400 years.

**2.54 Burch, C. E.** 1921. The advance of English speech among Negroes in the United States. EJ 10.222-25. Commends marked improvement in use of English by blacks since 1865 and says "there is a tremendous difference between the dialect of the slave of 1864 and the English speech of the struggling Negro citizen of today."

**2.55 Burke, Emily.** 1978. Pleasure and pain: reminiscences of Georgia in the 1840's. Savannah, GA: Beehive Press. P. 77, notes on "Crackers" and etymology of term cracker.

**2.56 Burling, Robbins.** 1973. Where did it come from? English in black and white, 114-28. New York: Holt, Rinehart and Winston. Discussion of Gullah.

**2.57 Burt, N. C.** 1878. The dialects of our country. Appleton's Journal, n.s. 5.411-17. Survey of regional and local varieties of American English, with special reference to settlement history, and emphasis on pronunciation and vocabulary.

**2.58 Butler, Melvin A.** 1969. African linguistic remnants in the speech of black Louisianans. Black Experience: a Southern University Journal 55.45-52.

**2.59 Campbell, G. I.** 1746. Observations in several voyages and travels in America. London Magazine 15.321-30. Complains that many Southern colonial planters allow their children "too much to prowl amongst the young Negros, which insensibly causes them to imbibe their manners and broken speech."

**2.60 Carpenter, Charles.** 1929. The evolution of our dialect. West Virginia Review 7.9,28. [WV]. Discussion of dialect forms author says have passed out of currency within previous generation.

**2.61 Carpenter, Charles.** 1934. Remnants of archaic English in West Virginia. West Virginia Review 12.77-79,94-95. Discussion of archaisms with precedents cited from Elizabethan drama and other British literary sources.

**2.62 Carriere, Joseph Medard.** 1937. Indian and Creole "barboka," American barbecue. Language 13.148-50. Citation from 1770 letter written by French officer in AR.

**2.63 Cassidy, Frederic G.** 1955. The source of "shats." AS 30.66-68. Word reported from DE, MD, and VA.

**2.64 Cassidy, Frederic G.** 1966. "Hipsaw" and "John Canoe." AS 41.45-51. Two terms of African origin.

**2.65 Cassidy, Frederic G.** 1978. Gullah and Jamaican creole--the African connection. International dimensions of bilingual education: Georgetown University round table on languages and linguistics 1978, ed. by James E. Alatis, 621-29. Washington: Georgetown University Press. Compares development, status, and linguistic features of two creole languages.

**2.66 Cassidy, Frederic G.** 1980. The place of Gullah. AS 55.3-16. Assesses hypothesis that Gullah originated from Atlantic pidgin based on Portuguese, but concludes rather that it derives from English-based creole that developed in Barbados.

**2.67 Cassidy, Frederic G.** 1981. "OK"-is it African? AS 56.269-73. Defends Allen Walker Read's dating of term to 1839 and its spread through political association with Martin Van Buren, and contends that no plausible case for an earlier or an African origin has been made.

**2.68 Cassidy, Frederic G.** 1983. Sources of the African element in Gullah. Studies in Caribbean language, ed. by Lawrence D. Carrington, in collaboration with Dennis R. Craig and Ramon Todd-Dandare, 75-81. St. Augustine, Trinidad: Society for Caribbean Linguistics. Statistical analysis of Africanisms in word-lists and texts in Turner (2.437) with reference to African areas and languages from which they most likely derived; finds Congo-Angola element strongest in word-list and Nigerian element strongest in texts.

**2.69 Cassidy, Frederic G.** 1986. Some similarities between Gullah and Caribbean creoles. Language variety in the South: perspectives in black and white, ed. by Michael Montgomery and Guy Bailey, 30-37. University: University of Alabama Press. Discusses Gullah in light of development of

English in New World and surveys main issues in nature and change of the creole.

**2.70 Cassidy, Frederic G.** 1989. Gullah. Encyclopedia of Southern culture, ed. by William Ferris and Charles Wilson. Chapel Hill: University of North Carolina Press. [SC]. Discusses historical setting and main distinctive linguistic features of the creole language.

**2.71 Chamberlain, A[lexander] F.** 1888. Negro dialect. Science 12.23-24 (July 13). Suggests etyma in African languages for goober and buccra.

**2.72 Chamberlain, A[lexander] F.** 1889. Goober, a Negro word for peanuts. American Notes and Queries 2.120. On goober and pinder.

**2.73 Chamberlain, Alexander F.** 1894. The origin of "bayou." Nation 59.381. Cites Creek Indian etymon for word found in Gatschet's ethnological work (6.217).

**2.74 Chamberlain, Alexander F.** 1902. Algonkian words in American English: a study in the contact of the white man and the Indian. JAF 15.240-67. Extended glossary of 132 items in American English borrowed from Algonkian languages; includes terms in the Southeast.

**2.75 Cleaves, Mildred P.** 1946. King's English reigns in the Kentucky knobs. In Kentucky 10.3.35. Brief defense of mountain speech, whose speakers are "linguistic purists and sole custodians of His Majesty's diction as it was originally enunciated."

**2.76 Clemens, J. R.** 1932. George Washington's pronunciation. AS 7.438-41. Some pronunciations from Richard S. Coxe's New Critical Pronouncing Dictionary of 1813.

**2.77 Cobb, Collier.** 1910. Early English survivals on Hatteras island. University of North Carolina Magazine o.s. (Feb.), 3-9. **Reprinted** in North Carolina Review, Mar. 6, 1910; in North Carolina Booklet 14.91-99 (1914). [E NC]. Relic vocabulary (such as couthy and fleech) and pronunciations in speech of Outer Banks island preserved from Middle and Early Modern English.

**2.78 Cohen, Hennig.** 1950. The history of "poor boy," the New Orleans bargain sandwich. AS 25.67-69. Traces name of sandwich to small cafe that dates from 1921 in French Market district of LA city.

**2.79 Cohen, Hennig.** 1950. "Poor boy" as an oil field term. AS 25.233-34. Term used in LA oil fields to refer to "any cheap or makeshift mechanical device."

**2.80 Cohen, Hennig.** 1952. A Southern colonial word-list: addenda to the

DA. AS 27.282-84. List of twenty-six items earlier than or unrecorded in Dictionary of Americanisms and that derive from colonial period from geographical area in and around Charleston, SC.

**2.81 Cohen, Hennig.** 1953. A Southern colonial word-list: addenda to the DA, II. AS 28.304-06. Supplements Mitford M. Mathews' work. Thirty-eight additions to Dictionary of Americanisms from three colonial newspapers and collections of plantation records and documents about Indians, African slave system, local produce and occupations, etc.

**2.82 Cohen, Hennig.** 1954. "Old field school," "Cornfield school," and "Indian old field." AS 29.225-26. [SC]. Traces last term, referring to manmade clearing on early frontier, at least as far back as 1748 and says it is source for other terms.

**2.83 Cohen, Hennig.** 1954. Unnoticed Americanisms from Russell's Magazine. AS 29.226-27. [Charleston, SC]. Nineteen items from an 1850s periodical.

**2.84 Cohen, Hennig.** 1956. Drayton's notes on Pickering's list of Americanisms. AS 31.264-70. [SC]. Compiles marginal annotations (c. 1820) of John Drayton, one founder of University of South Carolina, in copy of Pickering's 1815 discussion of Americanisms (**2.343**).

**2.85 Cohen, Lily Young.** 1928. Lost spirituals. New York: Walter Neale. Pp. xi-xii, notes on Gullah.

**2.86 Combs, Josiah H.** 1916. Old, early, and Elizabethan English in the Southern mountains. DN 4.283-97. [Appalachians from WV to N AL]. Gives special attention to similarities between Appalachian and Shakespearean forms. Cf. Steadman (**1.719**).

**2.87 Combs, Josiah H.** 1921. Early English slang survivals in the mountains of Kentucky. DN 5.115-17. Relic vocabulary from Old, Elizabethan, and Irish English.

**2.88 Combs, Josiah H.** 1921. First warrant issued in Breathitt County, Kentucky. DN 5.119-20. Short document containing naive spellings.

**2.89 Contributor's Club.** 1891. Word-shadows. Atlantic Monthly 67.143-44. Quaint metaphorical expressions and descriptions, and modifications of pronunciation and word formation in black speech and in black stage and written dialect.

**2.90 Courlander, Harold.** 1963. Negro folk music, U.S.A. New York: Columbia University Press. Pp. 5-7, short discussion of Turner (**2.437**) findings on vocabulary and names.

**2.91 Courlander, Harold.** 1976. The Gullah speech of the coastal region. A treasury of Afro-American folklore: the oral literature, traditions, recollections, legends, tales, songs, religious beliefs, customs, sayings and humor of peoples of African descent in the Americas, 290-96. New York: Crown. Excerpt of W. F. Allen's introduction to Slave Songs of the United States (2.5).

**2.92 Cowan, John L.** 1909. Lingo of the cow country. Outing 54.620-23. Etymologies of maverick, rustler, waddy, slow elk, and other terms from TX.

**2.93 Creecy, James R.** 1860. Scenes in the south, and other miscellaneous pieces. Philadelphia: Lippincott. Pp. 18-23, on languages, dances, etc. in New Orleans, LA.

**2.94 Crum, Mason.** 1940. The Gullah dialect. Gullah: Negro life in the Carolina sea islands, 101-31. Durham: Duke University Press. Early, serious essay on Gullah that leans heavily on previous scholarship (Reed Smith 2.396, Guy Johnson 2.222) and takes openminded but inconclusive view on question of African retentions in dialect. **Review:** C. H. Wesley. 1941. Annals of the American Academy of Political and Social Science 214. 269-71.

**2.95 Cunningham, Irma Aloyce Ewing.** 1970. A syntactic analysis of Sea Island Creole ("Gullah"). Ann Arbor: University of Michigan dissertation. Abstract in DAI 31.4141-42A. [Johns, Edisto, and Yonges Islands, Low Country SC]. Using early transformational model of Beryl Bailey for Jamaican Creole, finds Sea Island Creole has syntactic system "remarkably different from that of Standard English" that cannot be described "in terms of a superficial modification of the one underlying English."

**2.96 Cunningham, Irma Aloyce Ewing.** 1987. Innovative methods employed in the collection and presentation of Sea Island Creole ("Gullah") syntactic constructions: some aspects of the Sea Island Creole verbal auxiliary. Abstract in NADS 19.2.10. [SC]. Discusses challenge of devising questionnaire for collecting syntactic material on Sea Islands.

**2.97 Dakin, Robert Ford.** 1966. The dialect vocabulary of the Ohio River valley: a survey of the distribution of selected vocabulary forms in an area of complex settlement history. Volumes I and II. Ann Arbor: University of Michigan dissertation. 1187 pp. 158 maps. Abstract in DAI 27.2139A. Abstract reprinted in J. Williamson and V. Burke 1971(1.823).667-68. Condensed as "South Midland Speech in the Old Northwest" in JEL 5.31-48 (1971). Studies distribution of variant forms of 205 expressions and words in LANCS field records from Ohio River Valley. Covers 254-county area in OH, IN, IL, and KY; presents diachronic description of vocabulary, and traces "the historical bases and development of the dialect in various sections" of the Ohio River Valley; finds that "the oldest layer of usage reflects the predominance of the southern element in most of the valley."

**2.98 Dalby, David.** 1970. Black through white: patterns of communication. Hans Wolff memorial lecture. Bloomington: Indiana University African Studies Program. Traces patterns of European-African communication since 15th century, development of pidgin forms of Portuguese, Dutch, and English in Africa and their transportation through the slave trade to the New World, current state of these pidgins and related creoles throughout the world, and possible African survivals in black American English. **Reprinted** in W. Wolfram and N. Clarke 1971(**1.853**).99-138.

**2.99 Dalby, David.** 1970-71. The place of Africa and Afro-America in the history of the English language. African Language Review 9.280-98. Chronicles social aspects of European contacts from 15th to 18th centuries and says Black Portuguese, Black English, and other creoles developed in West Africa beginning in 16th century, mainly through a process of relexification from Mandingo; summarizes factors promoting "linguistic discontinuities between networks of black and white idiolects" of New World English.

**2.100 Dalby, David.** 1972. The African element in American English. Rappin' and stylin' out: communication in urban black America, ed. by Thomas Kochman, 170-86. Urbana: University of Illinois Press. Reviews African language background of colonial American blacks; discusses Africanisms and probable Africanisms in American English and presents eighty forms in glossary (pp. 177-86) with etymological notes.

**2.101 Dale, Edward Everett.** 1947. The speech of the pioneers. Arkansas Historical Quarterly 6.117-31. Place naming patterns, contributions from American Indians, and development of "words, phrases, and expressions [i.e., for hunting, fishing, social life, and food, terms for reproach and comparison] which [the pioneers] themselves coined and which grew out of the incidents and experience of their daily lives." **Reprinted** in W. K. McNeil, ed. 1984. The charm is broken: readings in Arkansas and Missouri folklore, 48-58. Little Rock: August House.

**2.102 Dalton, Alford Paul.** 1936. Elizabethan left-overs in Allen County, Kentucky. Bowling Green: Western Kentucky University thesis. 52 pp. Condensed in Bulletin of the Kentucky Folklore Society, Jan. 1938, 13-16. Discusses obsolete words, pronunciations, grammatical features, meanings, and idioms.

**2.103 Damon, S. Foster.** 1934. The Negro in early American songsters. Papers of the Bibliographical Society of America 28.132-63. Calls minstrel speech "a cockney, Frenchified English, sprinkled with such words as buckra, banjo, massa, pickininny, . . . probably fairly close to the West Indian speech."

**2.104 Davis, Daniel Webster.** 1897. 'Weh down souf and other poems. Cleveland, OH: Helman-Taylor. Glossary of words in black literary dialect, 144-46.

**2.105 Day, E. M.** 1888. Philological curiosities. North American Review 146.709. Report of <u>brottus</u> used in Savannah, meaning "lagniappe"; speculation on possible African origin.

**2.106 Day, Richard R.,** ed. 1980. Issues in English creoles: papers from the 1975 Hawaii conference. Heidelberg: Julius Groos Verlag. xi + 185 pp. Varieties of English around the world General Series Vol. 2. **Reviews:** G. Escure. 1982. LIS 11.473-78; M. Hellinger. 1983. Archiv für das Studium des neueren Sprachen und Literaturen 220.144-47; P. Mühlhäusler. 1982. EWW 3.107-12; S. Romaine. 1983. Studia Neophilologica 55.202-04; L. Todd. 1982. Anglia 100.141-44; H. Wode. 1982. Indogermanische Forschungen 87.337-42.

**2.107 DeBose, Charles.** 1983. Samaná English: the dialect that time forgot. Proceedings of the ninth annual meeting of the Berkeley Linguistics Society, ed. by Amy Dahlstrom, et al., 47-53. Berkeley: University of California. [2 B M, ages 40, 70]. Compares speech of isolated community of black speakers who immigrated from Philadelphia and Middle Atlantic states to Dominican Republic beginning in 1824 to present-day black speech in U.S.

**2.108 DeCamp, David.** 1974. Introduction. Africanisms in the Gullah dialect by Lorenzo Dow Turner, v-xi. Ann Arbor: University of Michigan Press. Essay on Turner's achievements as a scholar and the monumental significance of his study of Gullah.

**2.109 DeCamp, David, and Ian F. Hancock,** eds. 1974. Pidgins and creoles: trends and prospects. Arlington: CAL. 137 pp. Collection of eleven essays on pidgin and creole languages from various parts of the world. **Review:** J. Voorheeve. 1977. LIS 6.95-99.

**2.110 de Graffenried, Clare.** 1891. The Georgia cracker in the cotton mills. Century Magazine 41.483-98. P. 498, comments about language.

**2.111 Dickinson, M. B.** 1951. Words from the diaries of North Carolina students. AS 26.181-84. Lexical items culled from diaries of six mid 19th-century student diaries predating citations or not recorded in American dictionaries.

**2.112 Dillard, J. L.** 1969. The DARE-ing old men on their flying isoglosses or, dialectology and dialect geography. FFLR 7.8-10,22. Argues that geographically based dialect research such as that of linguistic atlas projects is misguided and theoretically indefensible and excludes widely recognized styles and social dialects; contends that "all (100%) of dialect variation is to be accounted for in terms of social factors."

**2.113 Dillard, J. L.** 1970. Principles in the history of American English--paradox, virginity, and cafeteria. FFLR 8.1.32-33,46. Severe criticism of Linguistic Atlas research methodology, particularly its insistence that geographical variation is basis of other types of linguistic variation and its neglect of speech of minority groups.

**2.114 Dillard, J. L.** 1971. The creolist and the study of Negro non-standard dialects in the continental United States. Pidginization and creolization of languages, ed. by Dell Hymes, 393-408. New York: Cambridge University Press. Argues there is continuum of varieties of black speech in U.S., with Gullah as one extreme; points out resemblances between Jamaican Creole and American Black English.

**2.115 Dillard, J. L.** 1972. On the beginnings of black English in the New World. Orbis 21.523-36. Says view of Kurath, McDavid, and Labov that black speech is merely modified version of white speech completely ignores language contact situation of 17th and 18th centuries that led to remarkable resemblances in grammar between black American English and Caribbean creole English. **Reprinted** in P. Luelsdorff 1975(**1.402**).29-38.

**2.116 Dillard, J. L.** 1973. The historian's history and the reconstructionists' history in the tracing of linguistic variants. FFLR 11.9-10,41. Says that linguistic geography, as a branch of historical linguistics, takes a reconstructionist bias toward relationship of dialects that cannot deal with pidgin varieties of language and other types of social variation.

**2.117 Dillard, J. L.** 1973. The American koiné--origin, rise, and plateau stage. Kansas Journal of Sociology 9.157-90. Says early dialect history of British immigrants to U.S. involved leveling process, leading to striking uniformity of English of colonies and that American dialects started to develop toward end of 18th century due to social factors.

**2.118 Dillard, J. L.** 1973. The lingua franca in the American southwest. Revista Interamericana 3.278-89. Argues that Spanish-English contact in 19th-century TX led to wholesale language mixture and development of a pidgin English, contrary to conventional view of simple borrowing of selected words from Spanish.

**2.119 Dillard, J. L.** 1979. Creole English and Creole Portuguese. Readings in creole studies, ed by Ian Hancock et al., 261-68. Ghent: Story-Scientia. Provides historical background for contention that Creole Portuguese is related to New World Creole English, putative ancestor of Gullah and black American speech.

**2.120 Dillard, J. L.** 1985. Toward a social history of American English, with a chapter on Appalachian English by Linda L. Blanton. The Hague: Mouton. xii + 301 pp. Development of English in America and as international language, with particular reference to influence of frontier, migration, and language contact; repeats much information from Dillard **1.194**. **Reviews:** R. Bailey. 1987. JMMD 7.529-31; W. N. Francis. 1987. LIS 16. 257-61; K. Harder. 1985. TFSB 52.26-27; W. Stewart. 1986. EWW 7.321-23; W. Viereck. 1987. ZDL 54.85-87.

**2.121 [Dodge, N. S.]** 1870. Negro patois and its humor. Appleton's Journal of Literature, Science, and Art 3.161-62. Humorous anecdotes from slave quarters and praise for qualities of black speech, about which author says "there is no language more lucid."

**2.122 Donahue, Thomas S.** 1978. A crucial perspective on the early history of American Black English. ED 171 154. 19 pp. Consonant loss and substitutions as represented in dialogue of plays and novels, 1771-1836.

**2.123 Donahue, Thomas S.** 1979. The nature of the early American black English lingua franca. Proceedings of the eighth annual meeting of the Western conference on linguistics, October 20-21, 1978, ed. by Derry L. Malsch, James E. Hoard, and Clarence Sloat, 23-30. Edmonton, Alberta: Linguistic Research. Disagrees with view of Stewart, Dillard, and Hancock that American black speech had roots in a type of West African Pidgin English and reinterprets relations between language of dominant white society and enslaved blacks in colonial period.

**2.124 Douglas, Connie W.** 1969. A linguistic study of the English used by New Orleans speakers of creole. New Orleans: University of New Orleans thesis.

**2.125 Dreyfuss, Gail Raimi.** 1978. Pidgin and creole languages in the United States. A pluralistic nation: the language issue in the United States, ed. by Margaret A. Lourie and Nancy F. Conklin, 61-77. Rowley, MA: Newbury House. Overviews of grammatical features of Gullah (pp. 65-67) and Black English (73-75).

**2.126 Dunbar, Gary S.** 1961. A southern geographical word list. AS 36.293-96. [SC, NC, VA, GA]. Twenty-two previously unrecorded geographical words and phrases, culled from 18th- and 19th-century documents.

**2.127 Dunglison, Robley.** 1829-30. [Glossary]. Virginia Literary Museum and Journal of Belles Lettres, Arts, etc., pp. 417-20 (Dec. 16, 1829), 457-60 (Dec. 30, 1829), and 479-80 (Jan. 6, 1830). Wordlist of Americanisms, with notes on regional currency. **Reprinted** in 1931, 1963, 1973 with commentary as "Americanisms in the Virginia Literary Museum" in The beginnings of American English: essays and comments, ed. by Mitford M. Mathews, 99-112. Chicago: University of Chicago Press. Cf. A. W. Read **2.356**.

**2.128 Dunlap, A. R.** 1956. "Blue hen's chickens" in North Carolina. AS 31.223. A 1799 citation; see also Halpert (**3.204**).

**2.129 Eanes, Evelyn L.** 1939. The orthography and phonology of <u>The narrative of Robert Hancock Hunter</u>: a study in the origins of Texas speech. Austin: University of Texas thesis. 72 pp. Describes phonology of early TX speech on basis of occasional spellings in an 1860 autobiography; pp. 61-69, glossary of occasional spellings.

**2.130 Edwards, Walter F.** 1982. Some linguistic and behavioral links in the African diaspora: cultural implications. International Journal of Intercultural Relations 6.169-84. Points out lexical, phonological, grammatical, and sociolinguistic links between Guyanese Creole and West African languages; scattered references to Gullah.

**2.131 Eggleston, Edward.** 1894. Folk-speech in America. Century Magazine 48.867-75. Points out antiquity of folk usages and compares them to 16th-, 17th-, and 18th-century British citations; scattered references to Southern usages.

**2.132 Eliason, Norman E.** 1956. Tarheel talk: an historical study of the English language in North Carolina to 1860. Chapel Hill: University of North Carolina Press. 324 pp. Compendium of linguistic, historical, and cultural material from unpublished letters, diaries, plantation books, church records, legal papers, and other manuscripts in Southern Historical Collection at Univ. of North Carolina at Chapel Hill library. Surveys patterns of vocabulary, grammar, and pronunciation, as well as language attitudes and language variation, as revealed in these documents. **Reviews:** W. Barritt. 1957. Virginia Magazine of History and Biography 65.375-76; D. E. Baughan. 1957. AS 32.283-86; M. Bryant. 1958. Midwest Folklore 8.53-56; R. Burchfield. 1958. Review of English Studies n.s. 9.454; P. Christophersen. 1958. English Studies 39.183-85; H. Galinsky. 1958. Anglia 76.452-60; R. Gaskin. 1957. Carolina Quarterly 9.58-59; W. C. Greet. 1958. MLN 73.64-67; B. Kottler. 1957. SAQ 56.512-14; J. B. Lewis. 1957. North Carolina English Teacher 14.3.16-17; R. I. McDavid, Jr. 1958. JEGP 57.160-65; S. Potter. 1957. MLR 52.624; T. Pyles. 1957. Language 33.256-61; R. H. Spiro, Jr. 1957. JSH 23.375-76; C. K. Thomas. 1958. QJS 44.196; R. Walser. 1957. NCHR 34.86-87; R. M. Wilson. 1958. YWES 37.67.

**2.133 Ericson, Eston Everett.** 1937. Black belt. Notes and Queries 173.424. Gulf States term originally referred to soil, later to inhabitants.

**2.134 Ericson, Eston Everett.** 1937. Bowie knife. AS 12.77-79. Reviews accounts connecting knife to Colonel James Bowie and discusses early development of term.

**2.135 Eubanks, Seaford William.** 1940. A vocabulary study of Thomas Jefferson's <u>Notes on Virginia</u>. Columbia: University of Missouri thesis. 254 pp. Classifies vocabulary Jefferson used in book, compiles lexicon of notable terms, and lists and discusses Jefferson's use of place names and Indian names.

**2.136 Fancher, Betsy.** 1971. Gullah: the haunted land. The lost legacy of Georgia's golden isles, 41-57. Garden City, NJ: Doubleday. Popular, sentimental essay on Gullah of GA Sea Islands, a "haunting, poetic" language that "sing[s] with onomatopoeia" and "elemental rhythms." **Review:** Anonymous. 1971. GHQ 55.598-99.

**2.137 Farmer, John S.** 1889. Americanisms--old and new: a dictionary of words, phrases and colloquialisms peculiar to the United States, British America, the West Indies, etc., etc., their derivation, meaning and application, together with numerous anecdotal, historical, explanatory and folklore notes. London: Thomas Poulter and Sons. Reprinted in 1971 by Gryphon Books, Ann Arbor, MI.

**2.138 Farrand, Max.** 1913. A word-list of 1823. DN 4.46-48. Newspaper list of twenty-eight "Western Dialect" items presented "for the convenience of emigrants."

**2.139 Farrison, William Edward.** 1947. "Grapple," "grabble," and "gravel." AS 22.235-36. [Orangeburg, SC]. Says verb gravel is either folk etymology for grabble or misspelling of word's pronunciation with bilabial fricative.

**2.140 Fasold, Ralph W.** 1976. One hundred years from syntax to phonology. Papers from the parasession on diachronic syntax, ed. by Sanford B. Steever et al., 79-87. Chicago: Chicago Linguistic Society. Theorizes about evolution of copula verb in black speech during last century and argues that deletion of copula was most likely a syntactic rule at an earlier period rather than a present-day rule for deletion of the remains of contraction.

**2.141 Faust, Drew Gilpin.** 1979. The rhetoric and ritual of agriculture in antebellum South Carolina. JSH 45.541-68. Analyzes imagery and rhetorical patterns in oratorical genre of the agricultural address and focuses on how themes and terminology from declining profession of agriculture functioned in larger social context.

**2.142 Fitzhugh, Jewell K.** 1969. Old English survivals in mountain speech. EJ 58.1224-27. [S Appalachia, Ozarks]. Vocabulary and grammar typical of old-fashioned mountain speech, with analogues cited from Chaucer and Shakespeare.

**2.143 Floyd, Marmaduke, and Raven I. McDavid, Jr.** 1948. A note on the origin of "juke." Studies in Linguistics 6.36-38. Suggests word originated in S GA lumber and turpentine areas as a blend of jut and nook rather than being an Africanism.

**2.144 Follin, Maynard D.** 1933. Two notes. AS 8.1.78. African origin of goober and comment on you all.

**2.145 Forgue, Guy Jean.** 1977. American English at the time of the revolution. Revue des Langues Vivantes 43.255-68. Surveys characteristics of colonial American English and examines comments from travelers and journalists; concludes that view of many commentators that "there were no dialects in North America had no basis in reality" because "American English had begun to diverge from the mother tongue for over a century and a half through the addition of foreign terms, the application of new senses to already existing English words and phrases, and the retention of archaic or provincial features."

**2.146 Fowler, William C.** 1850. American dialects: causes of existing dialect differences. English grammar, 91-94. New York: Harper. Lists "generic dialect differences" in U.S. and notes which are characteristic of New England, Western states, or Southern states.

**2.147 Fox, John, Jr.** 1901. The southern mountaineer. Scribner's Magazine 29.385-99. Pp. 394-95, claims that "in his speech, the mountaineer touches a very remote past. . . . there are perhaps two hundred words, meanings, and pronunciations that in the mountaineer's speech go back unchanged to Chaucer" and cites examples.

**2.148 Frajzyngier, Zygmunt.** 1984. On the origin of "say" and "se" as complementizers in black English and English-based creoles. AS 59.207-10. Says that both complementizers are "a loan translation from English rather than a direct borrowing from Twi" in both black English and creoles, including Gullah.

**2.149 Funk, Charles Earle.** 1953. Bill Robinson's "copesetic." AS 28.230-31. Thinks term is from LA Creole-French coupersètique.

**2.150 G., B. W.** 1894. Tote. Nation 58.121. Argues tote is British, not Southern.

**2.151 Garrett, Romeo B.** 1966. African survivals in American culture. JNH 51.239-45. Catalogs elements of language (mainly from Turner 2.437), music, dance, food, and other aspects of culture surviving from Africa that "reveal the identity, civilization, and relative influence of the people from which most of America's 20,000,000 Negroes descend."

**2.152 Gehrke, William H.** 1935. The transition from the German to the English language in North Carolina. NCHR 12.1-19. Says German was preserved throughout 18th century and promoted well into the 19th, but had all but disappeared by 1850.

**2.153 Gehrke, William Herman.** 1937. Negro slavery among the Germans in North Carolina. NCHR 14.307-24. Notes retention of PA German expressions in speech of black slaves.

**2.154 Gerard, William R.** 1904. The Tapehanek dialect of Virginia. AA n.s. 6.313-30. Derivation of the language and some place names. **Review:** W. Tooker. 1904. AA 6.670-94.

**2.155 Gerard, William R.** 1907. Virginia's Indian contributions to English. AA 9.87-112. Also published as pamphlet (Lancaster, PA, 1907). Discusses and annotates list of common American English words from American Indian sources.

**2.156 Gilbert, Glenn.** 1985. Hugo Schuchardt and the Atlantic creoles: a newly discovered manuscript On the Negro English of West Africa. AS 60.31-63. Publishes 1892/93 essay by Schuchardt, with lengthy introduction by Gilbert, linking West African Krio with New World English creoles, including Gullah.

**2.157 Gilliam, Angela.** 1976. Sociolinguistic configurations of African language in the Americas: some educational directives. Black English: a seminar, ed. by Deborah Harrison and Tom Trabasso, 95-103. Hillsdale, NJ: Erlbaum. Says that language of subjugated peoples, including that of blacks in the U.S., should be analyzed horizontally, i.e., in comparison with that of other subjugated groups, rather than vertically, only with reference to the colonially dominant languages.

**2.158 Gilliam, Charles Edgar.** 1939. "Mr" in Virginia records before 1776. William and Mary College Quarterly Historical Magazine 19.142-45. Form of address had social significance (indicating a member of the gentry or someone of equivalent rank) when brought to the colony but was extended in early days of VA to all males "with no claim to social position by virtue of their blood or calling."

**2.159 Gilman, Caroline.** 1838. Recollections of a southern matron. New York: Harper. Account of everyday life in plantation South, including comments on black dialect and on white speech to blacks.

**2.160 Godfrey, William H., Jr.** 1974. Some features of an idiolect of a James Island, South Carolina, Gullah speaker. Atlanta: Atlanta University thesis. 85 pp. [1 M, age 61]. Phonemics and phonotactics; includes complete transcript.

**2.161 Gonzales, Ambrose E.** 1922. The black border. Columbia SC: State Company. Gullah tales with glossary, pp. 277-340. **Review:** R. Smith. 1926. AS 1.559-62. Glossary based on book only in part.

**2.162 Goodchild, C. W.** 1888. Philological puzzles. North American Review 147.475. Suggests South American etymon for lagniappe, noted in New Orleans, and French origin for brottus, noted in Savannah.

**2.163 Grade, P.** 1892. Das Neger-Englische an der westküste von Afrika.

*Anglia* 14.362-93. Historical background, phonetics, phonology, and morphology of West African creole English.

**2.164 Gray, Lewis C.** 1933. History of agriculture in the Southern United States to 1860. Washington: The Carnegie Institution. Vol 1, pp. 149, 484, discusses antebellum use of <u>cracker</u> and other terms for poor whites in the South.

**2.165 Gregg, Stuart, III.** 1982. A case of Gullah. *Hilton Head Islander* 18.1.58. Takes issue with blacks, especially those who have moved back to the Sea Islands from the North, who deny that Gullah exists.

**2.166 Hair, P. E. H.** 1965. Sierra Leone items in the Gullah dialect of American English. *Sierra Leone Language Review* 4.79-84. Says that "a remarkably large proportion of the 'Africanisms' cited by Turner are derived from a very small part of Africa, the Sierra Leone region" but expresses reservations about validity of Turner's derivation of personal names; also details historical connections between Sierra Leone and SC Sea Islands.

**2.167 Hall, Leila Maude.** 1938. Phonology and orthography of the Austin papers: a study in the origins of Texas pronunciation. Austin: University of Texas thesis. 118 pp. Isolates spellings from <u>The Austin Papers</u> (a compilation of correspondence of Stephen F. Austin) which may illuminate the pronunciation of early 19th century, in order to document "linguistic tendencies which have helped to build up the colloquial speech of Modern Texas."

**2.168 Hall, Robert A., Jr.** 1950. African substratum in Negro English. *AS* 25.51-54. Praises Turner's work (2.437) as "revolutionary" and calls for further comparison of Gullah with West African and West Indian pidgins and creoles.

**2.169 Hall, Robert A., Jr.** 1966. Pidgin and creole languages. Ithaca: Cornell University Press. Survey of pidgin and creole languages around the world, focusing on their nature and history, structure and relationships, and linguistic, social, and political significance; has sample texts (pp. 149-62), including Gullah text (pp. 154-55) from Turner (2.437). Excerpt published as Pidgin languages. 1973. Varieties of present-day English, ed. by Richard W. Bailey and Jay L. Robinson, 91-108. New York: Macmillan. **Reviews:** H. Helmcke. 1969. *Anglia* 87.66-72; T. Kaufman. 1969. *Romance Philology* 23.104-10; A. R. Keiler. 1967. *MLJ* 51.317-18; R. B. Le Page. 1967. *Journal of African Languages* 6.83-86; D. Taylor. 1967. *Language* 43.817-24; J. Voorheeve. 1967. *Lingua* 18.101-05; K. Whinnom. 1967. *AA* 69.256-57.

**2.170 Hancock, Ian F.** 1969. The English-derived Atlantic creoles: a provisional comparison. *African Language Review* 8.7-72. Wordlist of up to 570 items in eight English-derived creoles, with extensive terminological and bibliographical notes, based on hypothesis that eight creoles represent "modern descendants of a single early pidgin spoken probably with local variants along the West African coast from the early sixteenth century."

**2.171 Hancock, Ian F.** 1971. A provisional comparison of the English-derived Atlantic creoles. Pidginization and creolization of languages, ed. by Dell Hymes, 287-91. New York: Cambridge University Press. Extended abstract of preceding item.

**2.172 Hancock, Ian F.** 1971. A map and list of pidgin and creole languages. Pidginization and creolization of languages, ed. by Dell Hymes, 509-23. New York: Cambridge University Press. Includes notes on Gullah and LA Gumbo.

**2.173 Hancock, Ian F.** 1971. West Africa and Atlantic creoles. The English language in West Africa, ed. by John Spencer, 113-22. London: Longman. Discussion of relationships and wordlists of 100 items in seven creoles, including Krio, Jamaican, and Gullah.

**2.174 Hancock, Ian F.** 1972. A domestic origin for the English-derived Atlantic creoles. FFLR 10.1-2.7-8,52. Essay on author's "domestic hypothesis" that all Atlantic English-derived creoles descended from form of English are spoken by shipwrecked sailors and British expatriates and already in existence long before English commercial contact in West Africa.

**2.175 Hancock, Ian F.** 1975. Creole features in the Afro-Seminole speech of Brackettville, Texas. Society for Caribbean Linguistics Occasional Paper no. 3. 15 pp. Historical and linguistic background of community of Gullah speakers in SW TX; includes transcript of speaker and analysis of principal linguistic characteristics.

**2.176 Hancock, Ian F.** 1977. Further observations on Afro-Seminole creole. Society for Caribbean Linguistics Occasional Paper no. 7. St. Augustine, Trinidad: University of the West Indies Press. 22 pp. Addenda of social and linguistic notes to preceding item; includes extensive citations.

**2.177 Hancock, Ian F.** 1978. The relationship of black vernacular English to the Atlantic creoles. Working paper of the African and Afro-American Studies and Research Center of the University of Texas at Austin. Spring. 26 pp. Compares grammatical features of Black Vernacular English with standard English and six Atlantic English-derived creoles and concludes that "although BVE does have grammatical and historical features in common with the Atlantic creoles, it . . . cannot now be classified on the one hand either as a creole per se, or as the terminal product of a continuum having its roots in Gullah specifically nor, on the other, simply as a British-derived American nonstandard variety of English."

**2.178 Hancock, Ian F.** 1980. Texas Gullah: the creole English of the Brackettville Afro-Seminoles. Perspectives in American English, ed. by J. L. Dillard, 305-33. The Hague: Mouton. Revised version of items (2.175) and (2.176).

**2.179 Hancock, Ian F.** 1980. The Texas Seminoles and their language. Working Paper of the African and Afro-American Studies and Research Center of the University of Texas at Austin. Spring. 29 pp. Semi-popular version of preceding item, with particular emphasis on grammatical features (pp. 12-24); includes wordlist (pp. 25-28).

**2.180 Hancock, Ian F.** 1980. Gullah and Barbadian: origins and relationships. AS 55.17-35. Claims that Gullah is derived from nautical pidgin English developed by sailors along West African coast and not from any New World source. Cf. F. Cassidy **2.66**.

**2.181 Hancock, Ian F.** 1986. On the classification of Afro-Seminole Creole. Language variety in the South: perspectives in black and white, ed. by Michael Montgomery and Guy Bailey, 85-101. University: University of Alabama Press. [TX]. Discusses development of Atlantic creoles from 16th to 20th centuries; details history and principal features of Afro-Seminole creole spoken by blacks who escaped from GA to Indians in Spanish territory in 17th and 18th centuries and then migrated west to TX and OK; compares grammar and phonology of Afro-Seminole and Sea Island Creole.

**2.182 Hancock, Ian F.** 1987. A preliminary classification of the Anglophone Atlantic creoles, with syntactic data from thirty-three representative districts. Pidgin and creole languages: essays in memory of John E. Reinecke, ed. by Glenn G. Gilbert. Honolulu: University of Hawaii Press.

**2.183 Hancock, Ian F., ed.** 1979. Readings in creole studies. Ghent: Story-Scientia. **Reviews:** G. Aub-Buscher. 1981. Journal of Linguistics 17.382-83; G. Gilbert. 1982. LPLP 6.293-304; P. Mohan. 1981. Language 57.904-11; P. Mühlhäusler. 1980. EWW 1.149-51.

**2.184 Hansen, Chadwick.** 1967. Jenny's toes: Negro shaking dances in America. American Quarterly 19.554-63. Discusses word of possible African derivation in 19th-century dance and modern-day jazz lyrics.

**2.185 Harris, Beryl.** 1975. Ozark dialect: beautiful and old. School and Community 62.3.10,49-50. Schoolteacher's account of effort to defend heritage of Ozark speech to its users.

**2.186 Harris, Joel Chandler.** 1894. The sea island hurricane. Scribner's Magazine 15.267-84. [Sea Islands, SC]. Pp. 275-76, comments on verbal tendencies of Sea Island blacks, with citations.

**2.187 Harrison, James A.** 1884. Negro English. Anglia 7.232-79. Somewhat condescending but the first comprehensive discussion of Southern black speech, surveying phonetics, morphology, lexicon, neologisms, interjections, linguistic changes, and appending list of more than 800 idioms and phrases representing black speech; collection based on personal observation and literature in literary dialect.

**2.188 Harrison, James A.** 1892. Negro-English. MLN 7.62. Letter protesting P. Grade's (**2.163**) overuse of Harriet B. Stowe citations as source of information on American black speech.

**2.189 Harrison, Thomas P.** 1893. Elnyard. MLN 8.128. Discusses possible sources for term popular among Southern blacks for Orion or Seven Stars constellation.

**2.190 Hatteras, Owen III [Raven I. McDavid, Jr.]** 1980. "Pig" and "blind pig." AS 55.35. [Richmond, VA]. Cites 1858 use of term blind pig to refer to member of the Public Guard.

**2.191 Hawkins, Benjamin.** 1848. A sketch of the Creek country in the years 1798 and 1799. Georgia Historical Society Collections 3.1. Reprinted by Americus Book Co., Americus, GA, 1938. Early occurrences of Southern Indian place names.

**2.192 Hawkins, Opal W.** 1982. Southern linguistic variation as revealed through overseers' letters, 1829-1858. Chapel Hill: University of North Carolina dissertation. Abstract in DAI 43.1957A. [NC, AL]. Compares how often fourteen white overseers from antebellum period delete articles, subject pronouns, verb be, and unaccented syllables with how often present-day black speakers delete them, and finds only limited similarity between two groups, thus casting some doubt on overseers as being source of features in black English.

**2.193 Hayes, Dorothy.** 1984. Old, old English in them thar hills. Tennessee Philological Bulletin 21.80-81. [Community called "Little Smoky Ridge"]. Cites fifteen forms, including ax, ye, fotch, antic, holpt, sallett, and poke.

**2.194 Haynes, Lilith M.** 1976. Candid chimaera: Texas seminole. Southwest areal linguistics then and now: proceedings of the fifth southwest areal language and linguistics workshop, ed. by Bates L. Hoffer and Betty Lou Dubois, 280-300. San Antonio: Trinity University. [20 adults, SW TX]. Cites grammatical features observed in language of mixed Indian-black TX Seminoles and disagrees with Dillard that their language has creole features or is form of "black English."

**2.195 Hays, William S.** 1975. Mountain language and the English classics. Mountain Review 2.1.13-15. Chronicles KY mountaineer's evolution from attempt to abandon his native speech patterns while at college to defense of mountain expressions as having "ancient legitimate lineage" in works of Chaucer, Shakespeare, and Pope.

**2.196 Haywood, Charles.** 1957. Charivari. JAF 70.279. Cites 1838 New York editorial characterizing as "evil" the New Orleans custom of raucously serenading a couple after the marriage ceremony.

**2.197 Hench, Atcheson L.** 1937. Kentucky pioneers. AS 12.75-76. Twelve lexical items from 1844 document.

**2.198 Hench, Atcheson L.** 1941. Hyppo, blue devils, etc. AS 16.234-35. Cites unusual words in 1837 diary of Kentuckian traveling to New Orleans.

**2.199 Hench, Atcheson L.** 1960. The meaning of "wiglish"? AS 35.302. Cites 1862 use of term.

**2.200 Henrici, Ernst.** 1898. Westafrikanisches Negerenglisch. Anglia 20.397-403. Relates pronunciation of West African creole English to that of English by blacks in Western Hemisphere.

**2.201 Herskovits, Melville J.** 1933. On the provenience of new world Negroes. Social Forces 12.247-62. P. 261, points out similarities in speech patterns of blacks from American South, Guyana, Suriname, and Jamaica.

**2.202 Herskovits, Melville J.** 1935. What has Africa given America? New Republic 84.91-93. **Reprinted** in Frances S. Herskovits, ed. 1966. The new world Negro [essays of Melville J. Herskovits], 168-74. Bloomington: Indiana University Press. Says that pronunciation and "musical quality" of English of both blacks and white in South was heavily influenced by the speech of black slaves.

**2.203 Herskovits, Melville J.** 1941. The myth of the Negro past. Boston: Beacon Press. Pp. 190-94, naming practices; Pp. 275-91, discussion of Gullah and its antecedents, based largely on unpublished work of Turner (**2.437**). **Reviews:** I. C. Brown. 1942. Social Forces 21.110; H. Courlander. 1942. Saturday Review of Literature 14.12 (Jan. 10); W. E. B. Dubois. 1942. Annals of the American Academy 222.226; E. F. Frazier. 1942. Nation 154.195 (Feb. 14); G. B. Johnson. 1942. American Sociological Review 7.289; I. B. Lindsay. 1942. Social Services Review 16.695-96; G. Streater. 1942. Commonweal 35.570; I. C. Ward. 1942. African Affairs 41.141-44; C. G. Woodson. 1942. JNH 27.115-18.

**2.204 Herskovits, Melville J.** 1966. The new world Negro. Edited by Frances S. Herskovits. Bloomington: Indiana University Press. Scattered comments on Gullah and Africanisms in speech.

**2.205 Heydenfeldt, S.** 1888. Those queer words. North American Review 147.348. [Charleston, SC]. Offers etymologies for brottus, buccra, and goober, and says there are no African survivals in local speech. Cf. E. M. Day (2.105).

**2.206 Higginson, Thomas Wentworth.** 1870. Army life in a black regiment. Reprinted by Houghton-Mifflin Co., 1900; by Michigan State University Press, 1960; by Beacon Books, 1962; by Collier Books, 1962. Scattered comments on and citations of Sea Island creole recorded by Union soldier stationed in SC during Civil War.

**2.207 Higginson, Thomas Wentworth.** 1886. English sources of American dialect. Proceedings of the American Antiquarian Society n.s. 4.4.159-66. Cites common terms in South and in Britain recorded in Francis Grose's Provincial Glossary of 1787.

**2.208 Hill, D. H.** 1886. The battle of South Mountain or Boonsboro. Century 32.137-52. Article begins with explanation of Southerners' and Northerners' giving different names to same battle.

**2.209 Hisley, Ann Marie.** 1964. An historical analysis of the development of Baltimore dialect. College Park: University of Maryland thesis. 53 pp. [20 Baltimore natives at University of Maryland]. Compares vowels and diphthongs in Baltimore speech with "General American English"; concludes tendencies to raise and front vowels and to have postvocalic /r/ in Baltimore speech derive from original northern English and Scotch-Irish settlers.

**2.210 Holm, John.** 1983. On the relationship of Gullah and Bahamian. AS 58.303-18. Cites historical and linguistic evidence that "Gullah and Bahamian are closely related creoles sharing an immediate ancestor in the eighteenth-century creole spoken in the American South."

**2.211 Holm, John.** 1986. The spread of English in the Caribbean area. Focus on the Caribbean, ed. by Manfred Görlach and John A. Holm, 1-22. Amsterdam and Philadelphia: John Benjamins. Places Gullah and Afro-Seminole Creole in context of expansion of English throughout Caribbean in colonial period.

**2.212 Holmberg, Carl Bryan, and Gilbert D. Schneider.** 1986. Daniel Decatur Emmett's stump sermons: genuine Afro-American culture, language and rhetoric in the Negro minstrel show. Journal of Popular Culture 19.27-38. Finds resemblances between spelling of unpublished mid-19th-century sermons and phonology of West African Pidgin English.

**2.213 Hooker, Richard J., ed.** 1953. A burlesque sermon: "there was an old man, in old times who was called Abraham." The Carolina backcountry on the eve of the revolution: the journal and other writings of Charles Woodmason, Anglican itinerant, 150-61. Chapel Hill: University of North Carolina Press. A sermon translated into the "Quohee language," Hooker's characterization of speech of Scotch-Irish settlers.

**2.214 How the U.S. uses African words.** 1950. Negro Digest 8.4.79-80. Reprinted from Associated Press. Popular summary of Lorenzo Dow Turner's (**2.437**) more dramatic findings of African retentions in Sea Islands.

**2.215 Hyacinth, Socrates.** 1869. South-western slang. Overland Monthly 3.125-31. Essay on the "startling originality" and distinctive expressions of TX lexicon; notes on nicknames of Southern state residents. **Reprinted** in 1931, 1963, 1973 as "Southwestern Vernacular" in The beginnings of American English: essays and comments, ed. by Mitford M. Mathews, 151-64. Chicago: University of Chicago Press.

**2.216 Hymes, Dell S., ed.** 1971. Pidginization and creolization of language. New York: Cambridge University Press. viii + 530 pp. **Reviews:** M. Durbin. 1972. AA 74.1475-77; R. St. Clair. 1973. Linguistics 132.109-16; P. Trudgill. 1973. Journal of Linguistics 9.193-95; A. Valdman. 1973. MLJ 57.53-54.

**2.217 Jackson, Bruce,** ed. 1967. The Negro and his folklore in 19th-century periodicals. Austin: University of Texas Press. xxiii + 374 pp. Anthology of thirty-three selections on black music, superstitions, and other aspects of folk culture.

**2.218 Jackson, Giles B., and D. Webster Davis.** 1908. The industrial history of the Negro race of the United States. Richmond, VA: Virginia Press. Reprinted in 1971 by Books for Libraries Press, Freeport, NY. P. 112, says blacks used "in many instances a kind of pigeon English or dialect. The whites heard this jargon on southern plantations, and copied it, and thus the language of the whites and blacks on southern plantations had a strange similarity."

**2.219 Jeremiah, Milford A.** 1977. Linguistic roots: a brief investigation of slave speech with verb "-s." Notes from the Association of Black Anthropologists 3.2.4-8. Cites examples of verbal -s from slave speech recorded by 19th-century journalists Olmstead and Redpath and from present-day speakers in Baltimore to support argument that structure normally represents durative aspect rather than hypercorrection.

**2.220 Jeremiah, Milford A.** 1977. The linguistic relatedness of black English and Antiguan creole: evidence from the eighteenth and nineteenth centuries. Providence: Brown University dissertation. Abstract in DAI 38.4788A. Compares phonological and syntactic features and three types of speech acts in Antiguan Creole and American black speech and concludes two are dialects of an Atlantic-based creole English.

**2.221 Johnson, Guion Griffis.** 1930. A social history of the Sea Islands, with special reference to St. Helena Island, South Carolina. Chapel Hill: University of North Carolina Press. Reprinted in 1969 by Negro Universities

Press, Westport, CT. Pp. 127-28, notes on Gullah. **Review**: Anonymous. 1932. GHQ 16.321-23.

**2.222 Johnson, Guy B.** 1930. Gullah: the dialect of the Negroes of St. Helena island. Folk culture on St. Helena Island, South Carolina, 3-62. Chapel Hill: University of North Carolina Press. Most extensive analysis of Gullah before Turner; description of Gullah by sociologist, covering cultural background of the dialect, its pronunciation, grammar, vocabulary, and intonational patterns; studies in detail question of African influences on Gullah but finds little such influence. **Reviews**: Anonymous. 1933. GHQ 17.74; B. A. Botkin. 1931. AS 7.64-66; G. Herzog. 1935. JAF 48.394-97; H. H. Roberts. 1933. AA 35.176-78.

**2.223 Johnson, Guy B.** 1930. The speech of the Negro. Folk-Say 2.346-58. Classic statement that black American speech is nothing more than a copy of white speech and that all features of its phonology and grammar "have no characteristics which are not explainable on the basis of English dialect"; says that "it is no accident that practically every archaism found among the Negroes of the sea islands is also found among the whites of the Southern mountains."

**2.224 Johnson, Guy B.** 1980. The Gullah dialect revisited: a note on linguistic acculturation. Journal of Black Studies 10.417-24. Argues that Gullah on St. Helena and Edisto Islands, SC, all but disappeared between author's research in 1930 and visit in 1965 and that this casts doubt on strength of Herskovits-Turner arguments about retentions; points out major weaknesses of Herskovits' research (**2.203**).

**2.225 Johnson, H. P.** 1928. Who lost the Southern "r"? AS 3.377-83. 18th- and 19th-century literary citations and comments from orthoepists on features of pronunciation--lack of postvocalic /r/, alveolar pronunciation of final consonant in -ing, use of "y-glide" after initial consonants in car and garden, and others--all in effort to show British, and not American black, influence on Southern whites.

**2.226 Johnson, Jerah.** 1962. The "Picayune": from colonial coin to current expression. Louisiana History 3.245-50. Traces history and applications of term, originally referring to Spanish coin, from 18th century to present.

**2.227 Johnson, Mary Canice.** 1974. Two morpheme structure rules in an English proto-creole. Pidgins and creoles: current trends and prospects, ed. by David DeCamp and Ian F. Hancock, 118-29. Washington: Georgetown University Press. Builds on Hancock case (**2.170**) of syntactic similarities by finding that eight English-derived Atlantic creoles "show comparable 'simplication' of consonant clusters as words were borrowed from English can be reduced to two morpheme structure rules which must have existed in the proto-creole for which Hancock argues."

**2.228 Jones, Charles C., Jr.** 1888. Word-list. Negro myths from the Georgia coast: told in the vernacular, 185-92. Boston: Houghton-Mifflin. Reprinted 1925 by The State Co., Columbia, SC. Reissued 1969 by Singing Free Press Book Tower, Detroit. Word-list of Gullah in modified orthography to indicate pronunciation. **Review:** W. W. Newell. 1888. JAF 1.169-70.

**2.229 Jones, Hugh.** 1724. The present state of Virginia from whence is inferred a short view of Maryland and North Carolina. Reprinted in 1956 by the University of North Carolina Press, Chapel Hill. Pp. 18, 70, notes on speech of Virginians.

**2.230 Jones, James P.** 1945. "Dixie's land" in the game of tag? AS 20.238. On note in New York Weekly 28.8.6 (Dec. 30, 1872) contending Manhattan origin of term.

**2.231 [Jones-] Jackson, Patricia A.** 1978. The status of Gullah: an investigation of convergent processes. Ann Arbor: University of Michigan dissertation. Abstract in DAI 39.851A. [SC]. Studies auxiliaries, pronouns, and segmental phonology and compares them to speech of inland blacks and whites.

**2.232 Jones-Jackson, Patricia.** 1978. Gullah: on the question of Afro-American language. [SC]. AL 20.422-29. Surveys research on Gullah to show its evolving recognition as full-fledged creole; asserts distinctiveness of Gullah from English and cites pronominal case system and phonology of voiced labial and alveolar consonants in support.

**2.233 Jones-Jackson, Patricia.** 1983. Contemporary Gullah speech: some persistent linguistic features. Journal of Black Studies 13.289-303. [SC]. Nontechnical discussion contrasting use of pronouns and of noun and verb suffixes in Gullah with same features in speech of blacks in Northern inner cities; points out creole features in Gullah and shows that English of American blacks is more heterogeneous than often thought.

**2.234 Jones-Jackson, Patricia.** 1986. On the status of Gullah on the Sea Islands. Language variety in the South: perspectives in black and white, ed. by Michael Montgomery and Guy Bailey, 63-72. University: University of Alabama Press. [9 B, 6 M, 3 F, ages 45-96, Wadmalaw Island, SC]. Argues that Gullah pronoun system, which differs from inland black speech and other varieties of American English in not marking gender and in other ways, is holding its own on offshore SC islands.

**2.235 Jones-Jackson, Patricia.** 1987. The language. When roots die: endangered traditions on the Sea Islands, 132-46. Athens: University of Georgia Press. Semipopular discussion of lexical and grammatical features of Gullah and their role in changing Sea Island culture. Excerpted in National Geographic 172.6.744 (Dec. 1987).

**2.236 Joyner, Charles.** 1977. Slave folklife on the Waccamaw Neck: antebellum black culture in the South Carolina low country, 110-47. Philadelphia: University of Pennsylvania dissertation. Abstract in DAI 38.1565A. [Georgetown Co., SC].

**2.237 Joyner, Charles.** 1984. Gullah: a creole language. Down by the riverside, 196-224. Urbana: University of Illinois Press. [Georgetown Co., SC]. Essay by social historian on creole society and language of antebellum plantation slaves emphasizing variety of African sources for vocabulary, proverbs, names, and other elements of language. Reviews: R. J. Brugger. 1985. American Historical Review 90.1015; E. Genovese. 1985. GHQ 65.597-99; R. L. Hall. 1985. JSH 85.439-40; T. Minton. 1985. JAF 98.358-60; C. Perdue. 1986. Western Folklore 45.57-59; L. Schweninger. 1985. NCHR 62.93-94; F. Shivers. 1985. Southern Humanities Review 19.273-74; W. L. Van Deburg. 1985. Journal of American History 72.403-04; K. Walters. 1986. LIS 15.109-11.

**2.238 Joyner, Charles.** 1986. "If you ain't got education": slave language and slave thought in antebellum Charleston. Intellectual life in antebellum Charleston, ed. by Michael O'Brien and David Molteke-Hansen, 255-78. Knoxville: University of Tennessee Press. Discusses distinctive grammatical elements of Gullah and functions of Gullah in slave social life, particularly in religious activities.

**2.239 Kahn, Ed.** 1965. Hillbilly music: source and resource. JAF 78.257-66. On origin and diffusion of hillbilly.

**2.240 Kilham, Elizabeth.** 1869. Sketches in color. Putnam's Magazine n.s. 4.741-46, p. 743, notes on use of at to end questions and other Southern usages, especially among blacks; n.s. 5.31-38, p. 36, note on language.

**2.241 King, Edward.** 1972. The great south, ed. by W. Magruder Drake and Robert R. Jones. Baton Rouge: Louisiana State University Press. Originally published in 1875. Dialect-forms of expression--diet, 784-91. Insightful comments on Southern linguistic habits by Northerner on extensive travel throughout region; includes many examples.

**2.242 Kloe, Donald R.** 1974. Buddy Quow: an anonymous poem in Gullah-Jamaican dialect written circa 1800. SFQ 38.81-90. Reproduces and catalogs Gullah terms in anonymous poem.

**2.243 Krehbiel, Henry Edward.** 1914. Afro-American folksongs: a study in racial and national music. New York: G. Schirmer. Songs of the black creoles, 127-38. Discusses how blacks in Southeast modified English and blacks in LA modified French in creating songs and attributes modifications to ignorance and illiteracy.

**2.244 Krumpelmann, John T.** 1942. For the DAE supplement. AS 17.69-70. Banquette, neutral ground, in New Orleans.

**2.245 Krumpelmann, John T.** 1944. Some Americanisms from Texas in 1848. AS 19.69-70. Eight items in 1849 German book on TX.

**2.246 Krumpelmann, John T.** 1949. Supplementing the DAE. AS 24.149-51. Twenty-one items from Col. David Crockett's writings not recorded in DAE.

**2.247 Kuethe, J. Louis.** 1940. Words from Maryland. AS 15.451-52. Bound(ed), pockhiccory, pocosin, water oak.

**2.248 Kuhar, Kyra.** 1985. Gullah: a lowcountry experience. Gateway to historic Charleston 38.9.43,46. [Charleston, SC]. Casual essay by outsider, who argues Gullah is a language, not a dialect.

**2.249 Kuiper, Koenraad, and Frederick Tillis.** 1985. The chant of the tobacco auctioneer. AS 60.141-49. Says tobacco auctioneer chants in the South are product of two oral traditions: English auctioneering tradition from 17th-century England and West African musical traditions of black slaves.

**2.250 Kurath, Hans.** 1928. The origin of the dialectal differences in spoken American English. MP 25.385-95. Reviews forty years of research by scholars before the Linguistic Atlas and relates features of British pronunciations, especially postvocalic /r/, to Atlantic states; concludes pronunciation of lowland South derives primarily from Southeastern England and that of the piedmont and mountain South from Scotland. **Reprinted** in J. Williamson and V. Burke 1971(**1.823**).12-21.

**2.251 Kurath, Hans.** 1940. Dialect areas, settlement areas, and cultural areas in the United States. The cultural approach to history, ed. by C. F. Ware, 331-45. New York: Columbia University Press. 8 maps. Early essay showing geographic variations in New England and South Atlantic states are result of settlement history and influence of trade and culture areas.

**2.252 Kurath, Hans.** 1965. Some aspects of Atlantic seaboard English considered in their connections with British English. Communications et rapports de Premier Congrès International de Dialectologie Générale, Troisième Partie, 236-40. Louvaine: Centre Internationale de Dialectologie Générale. Says "effects of the settlement, of the post-settlement expansion from important centers across old settlement boundaries, and of formal schooling" are most important factors in tracing history of specific regional features, and that several features of Tidewater VA and Low Country SC pronunciation derive from 18th-century Southeast British speech. **Reprinted** in J. Williamson and V. Burke 1971(**1.823**).101-07.

**2.253 Kurath, Hans.** 1968. Contributions of British folk speech to American pronunciation. Leeds Studies in English 2.129-34. Discusses dynamics of formation of American dialects along Atlantic coast in 18th century and compares phonic differences in vowels and diphthongs between American dialects and "Standard British English."

**2.254 Kurath, Hans.** 1971. British sources of selected features of American pronunciation: problems and methods. In honor of Daniel Jones, ed. by David Abercrombie et al., 146-55. **Reprinted** in H. Allen and G. Underwood 1971(**1.12**).265-72. New York: Appleton Century Crofts. Outlines problems in identifying British sources of features of American pronunciation in subregions of Atlantic states, citing known British variants and Middle English reflexes.

**2.255 Kurath, Hans.** 1970. English sources of some American regional words and verb forms. AS 45.60-68. Compares data from Survey of English Dialects and other British sources with historical dictionaries of American English and Linguistic Atlas data for fourteen items from farm life and four verb principal parts; finds "New England has preserved some words that were brought over from the East Midland, while Pennsylvania and the South owe some of their expressions to the North of England--if not to Scotland and to Ulster."

**2.256 Kurath, Hans.** 1972. Relics of English folk speech in American English. Studies in linguistics in honor of Raven I. McDavid, Jr., ed. by Lawrence M. Davis, 367-75. University: University of Alabama Press. 1 map. Examines ten regional survivals of pronunciation in Atlantic States "as symptomatic of the recession of hundreds of English dialect features imported during the settlement period" and compares them to British dialects.

**2.257 Kurath, Hans.** 1972. Gullah. Studies in area linguistics, 118-21. Bloomington: Indiana University Press. Summary profile of Gullah, with syntactic, morphological, and phonemic characteristics, and discussion of sociocultural background.

**2.258 Ladd, Mary Pauline.** 1942. A vocabulary study of early Texas English. Austin: University of Texas thesis. 81 pp. Study of vocabulary of TX English during first half-century of settlement, based on six manuscripts representing colloquial language of period, including The Austin Papers; pp. 21-77, glossary.

**2.259 La Fargue, Andre.** 1941. Louisiana linguistic and folklore backgrounds. Louisiana Historical Quarterly 24.744-55. Estimates influence of French, Spanish, Indian, African, and Acadian cultures on LA; stresses vitality of French language in state.

**2.260 Lang, Henry R.** 1888. Zu den Charleston provincialisms. Phonetische Studien 2.245-86. [Charleston, SC]. Objects to Primer's (2.349) description of Charleston speech, especially his account of pronunciation of long and short mid vowels.

**2.261 Lanier, Dorothy.** 1979. Gullah: English or African? Abstract in NADS 11.3.4. Reviews arguments over English vs. African origin of Gullah.

**2.262 Larmouth, Donald W.** 1985. "Kentuck" English in the Cutover region of Wisconsin: further notes and relationships in LANCS records. Abstract in NADS 17.3.8. Discusses survey of South Midland features in northeastern WI and compares results with LANCS.

**2.263 Lee, Mary Hope.** 1972. On the origin of Gullah. Berkeley: University of California thesis.

**2.264 Legman, G.** 1950. Poontang. AS 25.234-35. Etymon is French putain, and is not African.

**2.265 Lewis, Jessie Belle.** 1939. North Carolina English as reflected in old documents. Chapel Hill: University of North Carolina thesis. 201 pp. [Halifax Co., NE NC]. Collects and classifies "heterodox" spellings, vocabulary, and grammatical usages found in early 19th-century collection of letters and documents.

**2.266 Lincoln, Lewis A.** 1946. Ozark Anglo-Saxon. Rayburn's Ozark Guide 3.323-25 (Spring).

**2.267 Lindsay, Nick.** 1974. An oral history of Edisto Island: Sam Gadsden tells the story. Goshen, IN: Pinchpenny Press. [Low Country SC]. Pp. 1-4, author explains how he represents Gullah speech forms in print.

**2.268 Littlefield, Daniel C.** 1981. Rice and slaves: ethnicity and the slave trade in colonial South Carolina. Baton Rouge: Louisiana State University Press. Pp. 156-60, on language ability of slaves.

**2.269 Long, Richard A.** n.d. From Africa to the new world: the linguistic continuum. Center for African and African American Studies Paper in Linguistics no. 2. Atlanta: Atlanta University. 8 pp. Says scholarship on American blacks must presume existence of African substratum rather than lack of it, and points out features of syllable structure and word order shared by West African languages and New World creoles.

**2.270 Lucke, Jessie R.** 1949. A study of the Virginia dialect and its origin in England. Charlottesville: University of Virginia dissertation. Abstract in University of Virginia Abstracts of Dissertations, 1949, pp. 7-10. Historical phonological study of VA speech.

**2.271 Lumiansky, Robert M.** 1948. Opium argot: New Orleans, 1887. AS 23.245-47. Thirty-two terms from the New Orleans Lantern.

**2.272 Lumiansky, Robert M.** 1950. New Orleans slang in the 1880's. AS 25.28-40. Evidence from the New Orleans Lantern, a weekly journal.

**2.273 "Lynch law."** 1859. Harper's magazine 18.794-98. Gives 1834 citation and account deriving term from judge in Pittsylvania, VA.

**2.274 M., F. E.** 1894. Tote. Nation 58.85. Cites 1816 (1803) use for hauling tobacco, recorded by Lorenzo Dow in GA.

**2.275 McAlonan, John P.** 1980. The influence of French on Louisiana legal jargon. Southern Studies 19.291-309. Attempt to reconstruct picture of bilingual LA in first half of 19th century and to examine effect of bilingualism on LA legal English.

**2.276 McCord, May Kennedy.** 1944. Landed aristocracy. Ozark Guide. Lonsdale, AR. Jan.-Feb., p. 15. Identifies Elizabethan usages in Ozark speech.

**2.277 McDavid, Raven I., Jr.** 1948. The influence of French on Southern American English. Studies in Linguistics 6.2.39-43. Says French influence on speech of SC and GA that came primarily from Huguenots is "exclusively lexical" and in no way accounts for distinctiveness of Low Country pronunciation.

**2.278 McDavid, Raven I., Jr.** 1950. Review of Africanisms in the Gullah dialect, by Lorenzo D. Turner. Language 26.223-33.

**2.279 McDavid, Raven I., Jr.** 1973. The English language in the United States. Current trends in linguistics vol. 10, ed. by Thomas B. Sebeok, 5-39. The Hague: Mouton. Historical essay on evolution of American English, focusing on its divergence from British English, its academic status, the definition of "Americanism," and characteristic developments, especially lexicological.

**2.280 McDavid, Raven I., Jr., and Theodore Lerud.** 1984. German relics in the English of South Carolina. Dialectology, linguistics, literature: festschrift for Carroll E. Reed, ed. by Wolfgang W. Moelleken, 133-49. Goppingen: Kummerle-Verlag. 4 maps. Discusses four stages of German, Austrian, and Swiss settlement in SC beginning in 17th century; finds four Germanisms (saddle horse, sawbuck, spooks, I want off) widely distributed but notes few similarities to German usages in PA.

**2.281 McGinnis, James.** 1972. Historical sketch of black English. Ebonics: the true language of black folks, ed. by Robert L. Williams, 4-10. St. Louis, MO: Robert L. Williams and Associates.

**2.282 McIver, Zadie Runkels.** 1939. Linguistic borrowings from the Spanish as reflected in writing of the Southwest. Austin: University of Texas thesis. Includes material on SW TX.

**2.283 Mack, Linda D.** 1984. A comparative analysis of linguistic stress patterns in Gullah (Sea Island Creole) and English speakers. Gainesville: University of Florida thesis. 68 pp. [19 B Gullah speakers, 19 B English speakers, 19 B code switchers, SC Sea Islands, Orangeburg, SC, N FL]. Finds significant differences between Gullah and English in phonological contrast system and in the acoustic domains of fundamental frequency and duration.

**2.284 McMillan, Hamilton.** 1888. Sir Walter Raleigh's lost colony. Wilson, NC: Advance Press. [SE NC]. P. 201, note on Lumbee English.

**2.285 McMillan, James B.** 1953. The origin of "Everglades." AS 28.200-01. Comments on McMullen (2.286); argues <u>River Glade</u> only plausible source for term.

**2.286 McMullen, Edwin Wallace.** 1953. Origin of the term "Everglades." AS 28.26-34. History of term with early 19th-century citations and theories on its derivation.

**2.287 Macon, J. A.** 1883. Essay upon the Negro dialect. Uncle Gabe Tucker: or, reflection, song, and sentiment in the quarters., 175-81. Philadelphia: Lippincott. General description and vindication of character of Southern black speech, which author says has been "subjected to such violent caricature and exaggeration."

**2.288 Mahar, William J.** 1985. Black English in early blackface minstrelsy: a new interpretation of the sources of minstrel show dialect. American Quarterly 37.260-85. Study of functions of stereotypical black dialect in antebellum minstrel shows and extent to which this dialect authentically reflected patterns of Black English Vernacular.

**2.289 "Marcel" [W. F. Allen].** 1865. The Negro dialect. Nation 1.744-45 (Dec. 14). [St. Helena Island, SC]. Cites uniqueness of black speech on Sea Island plantations and illustrates its phonetics and morphology in religious hymns and shouts. **Reprinted** in B. Jackson 1967(2.217).74-81.

**2.290 Marryatt, Frederick.** 1839. Diary in America with remarks on its institutions. 2 vols. Philadelphia. Excerpt reprinted with commentary as "English Travelers" in The beginnings of American English: essays and comments, ed. by Mitford M. Mathews, 130-40. 1931. Chicago: University of Chicago Press. Reprinted in 1963, 1973. Says <u>absquatiated</u> is heard in KY but derives from SC expression <u>absquatalized</u>; notes use of verb <u>raise</u> for rearing children in KY and VA.

**2.291 Mathews, Mitford McLeod.** 1927. Mrs. Anne Royall as an observer of dialect. AS 2.204-07. Cites comments on speech of VA, WV, TN, DC, and Northern cities by 19th-century author/journalist.

**2.292 Mathews, Mitford McLeod.** 1927. Sherwood's provincialisms. DN 5.415-21. Adiel Sherwood's 1827 word list of forty-eight items (415-16) and his 1837 list of 248 items (see **2.390** for reprint of the latter). Vocabulary and pronunciation.

**2.293 Mathews, Mitford McLeod,** ed. 1931. The beginnings of American English: essays and comments. Chicago: University of Chicago Press. Reprinted in 1963, 1973. Collection of fourteen 18th- and early 19th-century essays, comments, and wordlists on language of the young nation, including several selections from the South.

**2.294 Mathews, Mitford McLeod.** 1931. Mrs. Anne Royall (1769-1854). The beginnings of American English, 88-98. Chicago: University of Chicago Press. Reprinted in 1963, 1973. Comments on Southern American English by early 19th-century traveler.

**2.295 Mathews, Mitford McLeod.** 1931. Southwestern vernacular. The beginnings of American English: essays and comments, 151-63. Chicago: University of Chicago Press. Reprinted in 1963, 1973. 1869 description of TX English; see Socrates Hyacinth (**2.215**).

**2.296 Mathews, Mitford McLeod.** 1931. Western and Southern vernacular. The beginnings of American English: essays and comments, 113-22. Chicago: University of Chicago Press. Reprinted in 1963, 1973. Discusses and compiles short list of tall talk associated with David Crockett and his like; reprints early Sherwood word-lists (**2.390**).

**2.297 Mathews, Mitford McLeod.** 1933. Additional comment on Boucher. DN 6.360-63. Supplements A. W. Read, (**2.358**); comments on 'simmon beer and other items.

**2.298 Mathews, Mitford McLeod.** 1948. Some sources of southernisms. University: University of Alabama Press. 154 pp. Popular treatment of words and geographical nomenclature that entered Southern American English from Muskhogean, Nahuatl, and African sources. **Reviews:** K. Croft. 1950. IJAL 16.208-10; N. E. Eliason. 1949. AS 24.123-24; A. L. Hench. 1948. Alabama Review 1.294-95; T. A. Kirby. 1949. JEGP 48.422; S. B. Liljegren. 1949-50. Studia Neophilogica 22.224-25; R. I. McDavid, Jr. 1949. Studies in Linguistics 7.71-74; K. Malone. 1949. MLN 64.552; L. D. Turner. 1950. Language 26.167-70; R. M. Wilson. 1950. YWES 29.51.

**2.299 Mathews, Mitford McLeod.** 1952-60. Of matters lexicographical. AS 28-35. Jim crow, dance juba. 28.202-07 (Oct. 1952); Pavilion, punger gourd. 29.142-46 (Feb. 1953); Pine mast. 29.289-93 (Dec. 1953); Comments on McMullen's (**3.286**) topographic terms. 30.57-61 (Feb. 1955); <u>Cracker</u>, <u>lynch law</u>. 34.126-30 (May 1959); <u>Hickory horned devil</u>. 35.138-42 (May 1960).

**2.300 Matthews, Albert.** 1902. The term state-house. DN 2.199-224. Includes evidence from VA, MD, and SC.

**2.301 Menner, Robert J.** 1938. Two early comments on American dialects. AS 13.8-12. Discusses Francis Kemble Butler's remarks on and informal classification of American dialects.

**2.302 Merriam, Alan P., and Frank H. Garner.** 1968. Jazz--the word. Ethnomusicology 12.373-96. Reviews numerous and diverse accounts (including African, Creole, French, Amerindian, and Old English) of word's etymology and discusses variant spellings and euphemisms and proposed replacements for word.

**2.303 Miller, Michael I.** 1983. A Jacksonian view of American English. Revue Française d'Etudes Américaines 18.397-403. On authorship of Virginia Literary Museum papers, the so-called "Dunglison's Glossary" (cf. 2.338).

**2.304 Miller, Michael I.** 1984. Evidence for a Virginia plantation creole. Abstract in NADS 16.3.7. [Hampton, VA]. Cites unusual consonantal features in LAMSAS field record made by Guy Lowman in early 1930s.

**2.305 Miller, Michael I.** 1986. The African substratum in American English: evidence from plural formation in upcountry lower Southern. Abstract in NADS 18.2.5. [Augusta, GA]. Says that zero plural in speech of black speakers reveals structural borrowing from African languages brought by slaves.

**2.306 Miller, Michael I.** 1987. Evidence for a Virginia plantation creole? ZDL 54.184-201.

**2.307 Monie, John Ferdinand.** 1942. The trend in the use of Latin words and phrases in New Orleans newspaper editorials, 1840-1925. New Orleans: Tulane University thesis.

**2.308 Moore, Dorothy Cox.** 1965. A glimpse into records at Surry Courthouse, Virginia. AS 40.235-38. Sampling of lexical items and naive spellings from 17th- and 18th-century wills and depositions.

**2.309 Moore, Janie G.** 1980. Africanisms among blacks of the sea islands. Journal of Black Studies 10.467-80. Pp. 471-72, reviews how scholarly views of Gullah evolved from its being "bad English" to being language in its own right.

**2.310 Mufwene, Salikoko.** 1986. Number delimitation in Gullah. AS 61.33-60. [SC]. Argues that "number delimitation in Gullah is governed by a body of principles which are somewhat different" from those governing English.

**2.311 Mufwene, Salikoko.** 1986. Restrictive relativization in Gullah. Journal of Pidgin and Creole Languages 1.1-31. [SC]. Discusses three types of relative clauses and finds "the predominant role of English superstrate influence" and only minor substrate influence from African languages.

**2.312 Mufwene, Salikoko, and Charles Gilman.** 1987. How African is Gullah, and why? AS 62.120-39. Rejects extreme points of view about universalist, substratum, and English dialect origin of Gullah; says moderate viewpoints are not mutually exclusive and cites evidence for complex genesis of Gullah.

**2.313 Neal, Julia.** 1968. The language of South Union Shaker manuscripts. Filson Club Historical Quarterly 42.157-61. [KY]. Archaic and unusual diction from journals, account books, and diaries kept in archives of Shaker colony dating from 1807 to 1922.

**2.314 Neitzel, Stuart.** 1936. Tennessee expressions. AS 11.373. [S CENT TN]. "Shakespearean phrases" poke, proud, admire, stob, "drawled by the local gentry."

**2.315 Newlin, Claude M.** 1928. Philip Vickers Fithian's observations on the language of Virginia (1774). AS 4.110. Comments by NJ native while tutoring in Richmond.

**2.316 Nichols, Patricia C.** 1975. Complementizers in creoles. Working papers on language universals 19.131-35. Compares Tok Pisin with Gullah.

**2.317 Nichols, Patricia C.** 1976. Black women in the rural South: conservative and innovative. Papers in southwest English IV: proceedings of the conference on the sociology of the languages of America women, ed. by Betty L. Dubois and Isabel Crouch, 103-14. San Antonio: Trinity University. [SC]. **Reprinted** in 1978 in International Journal of the Sociology of Language 17.45-54. Finds Gullah-speaking women, especially younger ones, to be more innovative in grammatical usage than less-rural and less-isolated mainland women, a finding that is contrary to studies of women's speech in many other English-speaking communities in the U.S. and the British Isles.

**2.318 Nichols, Patricia C.** 1976. Linguistic change in Gullah: sex, age, and mobility. Stanford: Stanford University dissertation. Abstract in DAI 37.2834A. [Georgetown Co., SC]. Explores effects of social differences in replacement of Gullah complementizers, pronouns, and prepositions by standard ones; compares speech of men and women and three adult age groups and finds that younger, more mobile women are in forefront of language change and that older, less mobile women are in rear, while men, both younger and older, are in middle.

**2.319 Nichols, Patricia C.** 1980. Women in their speech communities. Language and women's lives, ed. by Sally McConnell-Ginet et al., 140-49. New York: Cambridge University Press. Suggests that sociolinguistic research has defined "women's speech" too narrowly and that sex role interacts with language use in numerous ways because of the many roles of women in their speech communities; illustrates with three studies, including author's own from coastal SC.

**2.320 Nichols, Patricia C.** 1980. Variation among Gullah speakers in rural South Carolina: implications for education. Language use and the uses of language, ed. by Roger W. Shuy and Anna Shnukal, 205-13. Washington: Georgetown University Press. [16 adults, ages 15-88, Georgetown Co., SC]. Examines prepositions, pronouns, and complementizers in Gullah and discusses implications for instruction in reading.

**2.321 Nichols, Patricia C.** 1981. Creoles in the USA. Language in the USA, ed. by Charles A, Ferguson and Shirley B. Heath, 69-91. New York: Cambridge University Press. Overview of origin and structure of three American creoles--Gullah on Sea Islands, Gumbo in LA, and Hawaiian Creole English.

**2.322 Nichols, Patricia C.** 1983. Black and white speaking in the rural South: difference in the pronominal system. AS 58.201-15. [2 communities in coastal SC, one B, one W, 13 speakers in each]. Finds significant differences in use of third-person-singular pronouns but that speakers in each community are moving toward a national standard, even if from different directions.

**2.323 Nichols, Patricia C.** 1984. Networks and hierarchies: language and social stratification. Language and power, ed. by Cheris Kramarae, Muriel Schulz, and William M. O'Barr, 23-42. Beverly Hills, CA: Sage. [SC]. Examines linguistic variation in Sea Island community in framework of three models of social organization--conflict model, interactionist model, and social network model--to test insights provided by each.

**2.324 Nichols, Patricia C.** 1984. African-American children's stories. Abstract in NADS 16.3.7. Argues that language and rhetorical devices of stories told by African-American children in SC reflect African roots and have Caribbean counterparts.

**2.325 Nies, Frederick J.** 1952. The phonology of the Globe Primitive Baptist Church minutes, 1797-1911. Chapel Hill: University of North Carolina thesis. xvi + 66 pp. [Caldwell Co., W NC]. Analysis of occasional and naive spellings of clerks in church minutes.

**2.326 Norman, Henderson D.** 1910. The English of the mountaineer. Atlantic 105.276-78. [S Appalachia]. Shakespearean (archaic) expressions in Cumberland mountains.

**2.327 Norton, Arthur A.** 1930. Linguistic persistence. AS 6.149. Says that Gullah speech of turn of 20th century "was nearly similar to the broken English of our French Canadians."

**2.328 Note on Gullah.** 1948. South Carolina Historical Magazine 49.56-57. Reprints 1794 newspaper account of anecdote in Gullah and comments on variation between "r" and "l" it shows.

**2.329 Notes.** 1873. Nation 16.183. Comments on letters received in response to Fisk P. Brewer's remarks (**2.34**) on NC usage by pointing out that most of Brewer's NC usages are common in PA; editor thinks dialects in U.S. are being leveled.

**2.330 Oke, David O.** 1977. On the genesis of new world black English. Caribbean Quarterly 23.63-79. Critical review of efforts to establish creole genesis of American black speech; points out failures of such efforts and suggests ways they might be undertaken more fruitfully.

**2.331 O'Maille, T. S.** 1966. "Sheebeen" and "shebang." AS 41.127-31. Suggests derivation of shebang from char-a-banc in the South.

**2.332 Owsley, Frank.** 1949. Plain folk of the old south. Chicago: Quadrangle. Pp. 91-94, comments on language. Points out how Southern manners of talking irritate Northerners and speculates on origin of Southern drawl.

**2.333 Page, Thomas N.** 1886. Meh lady: a story of the war. Century 32.187-205. [VA]. Short story with phonetic notes about speech of VA blacks.

**2.334 Paine, Lewis W.** 1851. Six years in a Georgia prison. New York: the author. Pp. 178-82, notes on tote, white eye, and pats juber.

**2.335 Pardoe, T. Earl.** 1937. A historical and phonetic study of Negro dialect. Baton Rouge: Louisiana State University dissertation. Abstract in Louisiana State University Bulletin 30.21 (1938). 355 pp. Chronicles history of black American speech with more than 150 written selections of the dialect, and provides transcriptions of portions of these and current selections of black speech; study undertaken to show that black dialect is primarily product of teachings of English-speaking antebellum overseers, British and American, modified by native African phonetic patterns.

**2.336 Pardoe, T. Earl.** 1939. African tonal patterns . . . extant in present day Afro-American speech. Proceedings, Third international congress of phonetic science held at the University of Ghent, 18-22 July 1938, 388-89. Ghent: Laboratory of Phonetics. Finds African tonal patterns and speech cadences of black speakers whose parents or grandparents were slaves brought over directly from Africa, showing that newly arrived Africans "adapted the new language to their African traditions and linguistic forms."

**2.337 Parrish, Lydia.** 1942. Slave songs of the Georgia sea islands. New York: Creative Age Press. Pp. 41-42, notes on African retentions in Gullah collected in fieldwork and from Turner (**2.437**).

**2.338 Pearson, Elizabeth Ware**, ed. 1906. Letters from Port Royal written at the time of the Civil War. Boston, MA: W. B. Clarke. [St. Helena, SC]. Scattered comments on language.

**2.339 Pederson, Lee A.** 1978. Sociolinguistic aspects of American mobility. Amerikastudien 23.299-319. 4 maps. Demographic and historical background, analyzed in four eras--colonization, nationalization, alienation, and integration--of spread of English across U.S.

**2.340 Peterkin, Julia.** 1927. Gullah. Ebony and topaz: a collectanea, ed. by Charles S. Johnson, 35. New York: National Urban League. Note on Gullah language, people, and region.

**2.341 Philips, Ulrich B.** 1929. Life and labor in the old South. Boston: Little Brown. Pp. 5,41,54-55, notes on language. Points out distinctiveness of Gullah and Charleston, SC, speech.

**2.342 Pickens, William.** 1975. Notes on Gullah literature. Trends in Southern sociolinguistics, ed. by William G. Pickens, 35-39. Lakemont, GA: CSA Printing and Bindery. Surveys early use of Gullah in literature from time of Gilman, Poe, and Simms and principal scholarly views on its nature.

**2.343 Pickering, John.** 1815. Memoir on the present state of the English language in the United States of America, with a vocabulary, containing various words and phrases which have been supposed to be peculiar to this country. Memoirs of the American Academy of Arts and Sciences 3.2.439-536.

**2.344 Pike, Albert.** 1836. Life in Arkansas. American Monthly Magazine 1.295-302. P. 302, describes AR dialect.

**2.345 Plair, Sally.** 1972. Something to shout about: reflections on the Gullah spiritual. Mt. Pleasant, SC: Molasses Lane. [SC]. Pp. 12-16, on language patterns.

**2.346 Platt, James, Jr.** 1900. The Negro element in English. Athenaeum 3801.283. British criticism of the Oxford, Century, and other dictionaries for poor etymologies of words from Africa such as gumbo and goober.

**2.347 Poplack, Shana, and David Sankoff.** 1984. El ingles de Samaná y la hipotesis del origen criollo. Boletín de la Academic Puertorriqueña de la lengua española 8.103-21. Examines syntactic constraints on copula deletion in speech of isolated black community in the Dominican Republic descended from immigrants from Philadelphia area in 1820s.

**2.348 Poplack, Shana, and David Sankoff.** 1987. The Philadelphia story in the Spanish Caribbean. AS 62.291-314. Study of English in Samaná enclave of the Dominican Republic, showing that the language has been resistant to Spanish influence and that it is no more creolized than current black English in America; says if Samana English is lineal descendant of 19th-century black American English, then latter may have been diverging away from white American English.

**2.349 Primer, Sylvester.** 1887. Charleston provincialisms. Transactions of the Modern Language Association [PMLA] 3.84-99. Also in American Journal of Philology 9.198-213 (1888) and in Phonetische Studien 1.227-43 (1887). [SC]. Details conservative pronunciation of Charlestonians and compares it, sound by sound, to British speech of 18th century and earlier. See MLA Transactions, 1887, pp. 19-25 for MLA discussions.

**2.350 Primer, Sylvester.** 1889. The Huguenot element in Charleston's pronunciation. PMLA 4.214-44. Also in Phonetische Studien 3.139-53, 290-308 (1890). [SC]. Insightful early study comparing pronunciation of 16th- and 17th-century French with late 19th-century Charlestonian English in speculative attempt to determine influence of Huguenots on city's speech; finds pronunciation of Huguenot surnames changed only sporadically in two centuries.

**2.351 Primer, Sylvester.** 1889. Pronunciation near Fredericksburg, Virginia. Proceedings of the American Philological Association 20.xxv-xxviii. Peculiarities of pronunciation of NE VA area that has "preserved to a remarkable degree the older English sounds brought over in the 17th century by the early settlers of this region."

**2.352 Primer, Sylvester.** 1890. The pronunciation of Fredericksburg, Virginia. PMLA 5.185-99. Discusses settlement and early history of area, renders three early 17th-century documents into broad transcription (including passage from John Smith) in order to describe pronunciation of period, and comments on contemporary patterns of pronunciation in state.

**2.353 Quattlebaum, Julian K.** 1974. Gullah. My friend, the Gullah, by Gary Black, ix-xii. Columbia, SC: Bryan. Discusses origin of Gullah in SC colony and its connection to the Caribbean.

**2.354 R., S. S.** 1891. Tote. American Notes and Queries 6.177 (Feb. 7). Reports tote from IN, KY, and along Ohio and Mississippi Rivers.

**2.355 Ravenel, Henry William.** 1936. Recollections of Southern plantation life. Yale Review n.s. 25.748-77. Ed. by Marjorie Stratford Mendenhall. Notes on SC black vocabulary recorded in 1876.

**2.356 Read, Allen Walker,** ed. 1927. Dunglison's glossary (1829-1830). DN 5.422-32. Glossary of 193 Americanisms--old words used in new sense and new words of indigenous origin; criticizes Pickering's compilation of Americanisms as too inclusive. **Reprinted** in Mathews **2.293**, pp. 99-112.

**2.357 Read, Allen Walker.** 1932. British recognition of American speech in the eighteenth century. DN 6.313-34. Surveys British comments and attitudes about American speech before 1800; says British commentators "conceded that the general level of purity in pronunciation was high, even higher than in Great Britain" but they censured new vocabulary of American colony.

**2.358 Read, Allen Walker.** 1933. Boucher's linguistic pastoral of colonial Maryland. DN 6.353-60. [MD] Reprints poem written by Jonathan Boucher around 1770 to exemplify "such words and idioms of speech, then prevalent and common in Maryland, as I conceived to be dialectal, and peculiar to those parts of America" and list of thirty-nine terms compiled by Boucher.

**2.359 Read, Allen Walker.** 1939. The speech of Negroes in colonial America. JNH 24.247-58. On basis of advertisements for runaway slaves in colonial era, concludes that "there were Negroes in all stages of proficiency in their knowledge of English . . . the Negroes born in this country invariably used, according to these records, good English."

**2.360 Read, Allen Walker.** 1961. The rebel yell as a linguistic problem. AS 36.83-92. Calls for attempts at linguistic analysis of such conventionalized sounds as yells, cheers, and shouts; from historical and biographical literature, discusses the uniqueness, possible sound pattern, origin, function, and effect of war cry used by Confederate soldiers.

**2.361 Read, William A.** 1939. Notes on A dictionary of American English, parts I-VI. AS 14.255-60. Comments on words in <u>Dictionary of American English</u> and suggests additional words, mainly Southern.

**2.362 Read, William A.** 1945. Notes on "Gaspergou." AS 20.277-80. Finds 18th-century etymology for LA-French name for fresh water drum.

**2.363 Reeves, Dick.** 1970. Gullah: some say the Carolina low-country patois is disappearing. Sandlapper 3.5.8-11. Calls Gullah "the most fascinating of all American dialects" and presents anecdotes of Gullah phrases; author is elderly white Charlestonian who tells and records stories in Gullah.

**2.364 Reeves, Henry.** 1869. Southern states. Lippincott's Magazine 3.317-18. Surveys of characteristic usages from VA, SC, FL, LA, and TN, with many citations from Civil War experiences.

**2.365 Repka, Patricia L., and Rick Evans.** 1986. The evolution of the present tense of the verb "to be": evidence from literary dialects. Abstract in NADS 18.2.5. Surveys verb be as used in literary dialects from 1767 to 1982, with special reference to six novelists.

**2.366 Rickford, John R.** 1974. The insights of the mesolect. Pidgins and creoles: current trends and prospects, ed. by David DeCamp and Ian F. Hancock, 92-117. Washington: Georgetown University Press. [SC]. Says analysis of mesolectal creole features of Sea Island Creole, such as auxiliary verb doz, provides new evidence for extent of creole origin of American black speech.

**2.367 Rickford, John R.** 1977. The question of prior creolization in black English. Pidgin and creole linguistics, ed. by Albert Valdman, 190-221. Bloomington: Indiana University Press. Discusses sociohistorical factors in creolization of languages, proposes four linguistic criteria for assessing prior creolization of a language, and considers phonological, syntactic, and lexical features of American black speech according to these criteria.

**2.368 Rickford, John R.** 1980. How does "doz" disappear? Issues in English creoles: papers from the 1975 Hawaii conference, ed. by Richard R. Day, 77-96. Heidelberg: Julius Groos Verlag. Same as ED 119 516. [SC]. Examines phonological reduction of auxiliary verb in Guyanese Creole and Sea Island Creole and concludes that he has "unearthed a subtle but widespread pan-creole rule by which initial voiced stops in auxiliaries are deleted."

**2.369 Rickford, John R.** 1986. Social contact and linguistic diffusion. Language 62.245-90. Explores interplay of internal and external factors in possible linguistic diffusion of Hiberno English (does) + be habitual auxiliary into New World black speech but concludes that "a hypothesis which involves decreolization from creole does + (be)" that incorporates possible influences from Irish and British varieties of English provides most likely explanation of development of verb form.

**2.370 Rogers, George C.** 1970. South Carolina federalists and the origins of the nullification movement. South Carolina Historical Magazine 71.17-32. Pp. 25-26, profiles multilingual, multidialectal nature of antebellum SC.

**2.371 Rogers, William Warren.** 1962. Deep South slang in the 1880's. AS 37.75-76. Excerpt of 1888 newspaper listing of "'slang' phrases dropped from the lips of the young ladies and gentlemen of Troy [AL]."

**2.372 Rogge, Heinz.** 1965. Das erbe Afrikas in sprache und kultur der

Nordamerikanischen Gullahs. Zeitschrift für Volkskunde 61.30-37. Discusses African background of Gullah culture and speech.

**2.373 Rollins, Onie.** 1978. A comparative syntactic study of Gullah and Tok Pisin. Pittsburgh: University of Pittsburgh thesis.

**2.374 Rose, Willie Lee.** 1964. Rehearsal for reconstruction: the Port Royal experiment. New York: Random House. [St. Helena Island, SC]. Pp. 96-97, comments on Gullah.

**2.375 Rowe, G. S.** 1900. The Negroes of the sea islands. Southern Workman 29.709-15. Describes SC plantation life, music, dialect.

**2.376 Roy, John D.** 1977. The origin of English creole: evidence from lexical structure. New York: Columbia University thesis. Compares idioms in Gullah, Bajan, Djuka, and Virgin Island Creole and claims four languages have a common origin.

**2.377 Ryan, Lee W.** 1939. French travelers in the southeastern United States, 1775-1809. Bloomington, IN: Principia. P. 87, note on euphemisms used in the South.

**2.378 Sauer, N. J.** 1939. American Indian words in the literature of the West and Southwest. Lubbock: Texas Technological College thesis.

**2.379 Scarborough, W. H.** 1896. Negro speech and folklore. Southern Workman 25.144-47. Examines dialect through proverbs, humor, and charms.

**2.380 Schneider, Edgar W.** 1981. Morphologische und syntaktische variablen im amerikanischen early black English. Bamberger beiträge zur Englische sprachwissenschaft 10. Frankfurt: Peter Lang. 361 pp. Translated into English and revised, 1989, University of Alabama Press, Tuscaloosa. Using transcripts of 104 interviews of ex-slaves conducted by WPA, shows regional patterning of black speech in nine Southern states and concludes that features of black speech derive from nonstandard colonial English rather than from plantation creole variety of English; investigates subject-verb agreement, verb principal parts, auxiliary verbs, noun plurals and genitives, direct and indirect questions, relative clauses, negation, existentials, and other features. **Reviews:** W.-D. Bald. 1985. Amerikastudien 30.127-28; J. Brewer. 1986. AS 61.153-59; M. Görlach. 1985. ZDL 52.244-45; U. Oomen. 1983. Anglia 101.196-98; K. Wächtler. 1982. EWW 3.106-07.

**2.381 Schneider, Edgar W.** 1982. On the history of black English in the USA: some new evidence. EWW 3.18-46. Summarizes patterns of morphological and syntactic features investigated in preceding item and concludes that "the linguistic character of [early black speech] is largely determined by its descent from the nonstandard English spoken in the colonial period, which can be established clearly for most of its linguistic forms and structures independently" and that "there are no indications that a supra-regional uniform 'Plantation Creole' throughout has ever existed."

**2.382 Schneider, Edgar W.** 1983. The origin of the verbal "-s" in black English. AS 58.99-113. [104 WPA interview records from 9 Southern states]. Argues that feature "does not derive from an originally uninflected creole system, but from the early American and basically British English pattern of colonial folk speech."

**2.383 Schneider, Edgar W.** 1983. The diachronic development of the black English perfective auxiliary phrase. JEL 16.55-64. [104 WPA interview records from 9 Southern states]. Describes geographical variation in perfective structures with have, done, and other auxiliaries in narratives with ex-slaves and says perfective auxiliary system found in South Atlantic states represents an earlier stage than system found in Southern states from AL westward.

**2.384 Schneider, Edgar W.** 1985. Regional variation in 19th century black English in the American South. Papers from the sixth international conference on historical linguistics, ed. by Jacek Fisiak, 467-85. Poznan: Adam Micklewicz University Press. 7 maps. [104 WPA ex-slave narratives from 9 Southern states]. Says "the morphosyntax of 19th century black speech seems to have been very homogeneous from South Carolina to Mississippi."

**2.385 Schneider, Gilbert D.** 1975. The black English manuscripts of Dan Emmett. Ohio University Working Papers in Applied Linguistics 3.1-4. Athens, OH. Discusses nature and background of archive of unpublished manuscripts, mostly sermons and hymns, written in black English in the 1860s and 1870s by the famous minstrel performer and composer.

**2.386 Schoonover, M. M.** 1933. "A sin to Crockett." AS 8.4.79. Cites phrase from 1844 traveler's journal as referring to a boat that is extravagantly large.

**2.387 Scypes, George S.** 1888. Notes of "we-uns" and "you-uns." Century 36.799. Says both pronouns were used in VA in 1860s.

**2.388 Seidleman, Morton.** 1937. Survivals in Negro vocabulary. AS 12.231-32. Provides etymologies and 17th-century attestations of vocabulary used by blacks in NJ, some of whom were born in the South.

**2.389 Sewell, Ernestine.** 1978. Dialect of the last frontier in Texas as found in newspapers, 1875-1880. Abstract in NADS 10.3.4. Claims slang in frontier TX newspapers helped shape the speech of the period.

**2.390 Sherwood, Adiel.** 1931. Provincialisms. The beginnings of American English, ed. by Mitford M. Mathews, 117-22. Chicago: University of Chicago Press. Reprinted in 1963, 1973. Georgia word lists of 1827 and 1837. 250-item wordlist compiled by New England minister who had moved to GA and who wished to publish words so that by "seeing them printed, we shall forbear to drag them into service."

**2.391 Shilling, Alison Watt.** 1984. Black English as a creole: some Bahamian evidence. St. Augustine, Trinidad: School of Education, University of the West Indies.

**2.392 Smallfry, Simeon.** 1837. Improprieties of speech. Southern Literary Messenger 3.222-32. Objects to "dropping r," intrusive r, and other features of speech in VA.

**2.393 Smith, Charles Forster.** 1883. On southernisms. Transactions of the American Philological Association 14.42-56. Annotated wordlist of fifty items, with extensive etymological comments; 17.34-46 (1886). Annotated wordlist of thirty-eight items, with extensive etymological notes.

**2.394 Smith, Ernie Adolphus.** 1975. The evolution and continuing presence of the African oral tradition in black America. Irvine: University of California dissertation. Abstract in DAI 35.7290A. Claims that an "ethnolinguistic continuity of Africa in Afro-America" is represented in oral tradition used most fully by inner-city youths and is responsible for continuing lack of acculturation of blacks in American society.

**2.395 Smith, Rebecca W.** 1934. A Tennessean's pronunciation in 1841. AS 9.262-63. [E TN]. Thirty-nine naive spellings of Jefferson Co. resident in 1841.

**2.396 Smith, Reed.** 1926. Gullah. Columbia: University of South Carolina Bulletin no. 190. ED 034 191. 34 pp. Short monograph by ballad expert utilizing literary representations and commenting on Gullah, focusing primarily on colorful phrases and proverbs, archaic vocabulary, and morphologically reduced grammar of Gullah.

**2.397 Smith, Robert Wayne.** 1975. Low country patois. Sandlapper 8.10.47-49. [SC]. Drawing on Turner (2.437) and other authorities, summarizes grammar and intonation of Gullah for lay audience.

**2.398 Smitherman, Geneva.** 1981. From Africa in the new world and into the the space age. Black English and the education of black children and youth: proceedings of the national invitational symposium on the King decision, ed. by Geneva Smitherman, 409-23. Detroit, MI: Harlo. Synoptic, historical account of four hundred years of speech of black Americans.

**2.399 Specimens of Kentucky slang.** 1833. Atkinson's Casket 8.335. Nineteen items used by Nimrod Wildfire in James Kirke Paulding's The Lion of the West.

**2.400 The speech of our fathers.** 1927. Kentucky Folklore and Poetry Magazine 2.6-7.

**2.401 Spitzer, Leo.** 1952. Snallygaster. AS 27.237-38. Says term for "legendary Maryland creature" originated from German schnelle geiste, ("fast-moving ghost") and reflects ancient belief in troupe of ghosts of damned souls believed to ride the air.

**2.402 Stephens, Erwin D.**, comp. 1979. How to understand clodknocker talk: a skimption of the language once used by rural folk in a central North Carolina country from way back through the first quarter of this century. Charlotte: privately printed. 36 pp. [CENT NC]. Popular glossary of unusual terms, many concerned with agriculture; defines clodknocker as homemade hoe for crushing clods of earth and, by extension, a farmer.

**2.403 Stephenson, Edward A.** 1956. Linguistic resources of the Southern Historical Collection. AS 31.271-77. Discusses value to linguistic historians of five types of original documents (arithmetic books, school papers, court records, wills, and letters) in special library collection at the University of North Carolina at Chapel Hill.

**2.404 Stephenson, Edward A.** 1958. The Anderson-Thornwall Papers: a sample of linguistic annotation. AS 33.73-74. Calls for large-scale analyses of original manuscripts to document history of American English and provides sample annotation of one collection of documents at Southern Historical Collection to show how materials can be described for scholarly use.

**2.405 Stephenson, Edward A.** 1958. Early North Carolina pronunciation. Chapel Hill: University of North Carolina dissertation. Abstract in DAI 19.2342-43A. Abstract reprinted in J. Williamson and V. Burke 1971 (1.823).695-96. Reconstructs sounds of NC speech in 18th century and determines pronunciation of hundreds of individual words, based on occasional spellings from 165 manuscripts. Finds no evidence for sectional dialects in NC in colonial times.

**2.406 Stephenson, Edward.** 1967. On the interpretation of occasional spellings. PADS 48.33-50. Describes and advocates a rigorous methodology in using spelling evidence for the reconstruction of the sounds of English from days before recording machinery, using 18th-century NC manuscripts as examples.

**2.407 Stephenson, Edward A.** 1967. Schools of modern linguistics: is a rapprochement possible? Emory University Quarterly 23.222-62. Evaluates how Chomsky and Halle's Sound Pattern of English and other models of phonology can analyze author's orthographic data from 18th-century NC documents.

**2.408 Stephenson, Edward A.** 1968. The beginnings of the loss of the post-vocalic /r/ in North Carolina. JEL 2.57-77. Abstract in SAB 31.3 (Jan. 1966). Studies spelling of words in 18th-century manuscripts in Southern Historical Collection and shows how pronunciation of r̲ was lost after vowels, especially in state's north-central counties, and speculates that it spread and became a characteristic Southern feature because it was identified with prestigious VA speech. **Reprinted** in D. Shores and C. Hines 1977(**1.689**).73-92.

**2.409 Stephenson, Edward A.** 1975. Forms like "nater" for "nature." AS 50.146-49. Six terms from 18th-century NC manuscripts reflecting lack of affricates.

**2.410 Stephenson, George M.** 1929. The effect of movements of population upon American dialects. Linguistic Society of America Bulletin 4.22-25. Surveys immigrant stocks in colonies and early republic and points out ways historians and historical information can help linguists compile a dialect atlas.

**2.411 Stevens, William Oliver.** 1940. Charleston: historic city of gardens. New York: Dodd Mead. [SC]. Pp. 75-77, on Gullah.

**2.412 Stewart, William A.** 1967. Nonstandard speech patterns. Baltimore Bulletin of Education 43.2-4,52-65. Explains American "Negro English" as descended from creolized language begun as relexified variety of West African Pidgin English that developed through isolation and multilingual background of slaves.

**2.413 Stewart, William A.** 1967. Sociolinguistic factors in the history of American Negro dialects. FFLR 5.2.1-4. Same as ED 012 435. Says that compensatory education programs for American blacks must appreciate fundamental differences in grammar from other types of American speech produced by creole background of black speech and that these differences are not clear from traditional dialect geography emphasis on pronunciation and vocabulary. **Reprinted** in R. Abrahams and R. Troike 1972(**1.4**).219-24; in H. Allen and G. Underwood 1971(**1.12**).444-53; in R. Bentley and S. Crawford 1973(**1.64**).45-55; in J. L. Dillard 1975(**1.195**).222-32; in D. Shores 1972(**1.685**).86-95; in F. Williams 1970(**1.814**).353-62; in W. Wolfram and N. Clarke 1971(**1.853**).74-89.

**2.414 Stewart, William A.** 1968. Continuity and change in American Negro dialects. FFLR 6.2.3-4,14-16,18. Same as ED 016 236. Says decreolization of lexicon of American black speech since time of Civil War has obscured deep-structure grammatical differences from standard English, since surface similarities "can camouflage functional differences between the two linguistic systems." **Reprinted** in H. Allen and G. Underwood 1971(**1.12**).454-65; in R. Bentley and S. Crawford 1973(**1.64**).55-69; in J. L. Dillard 1975(**1.195**).233-47; in D. Shores 1972(**1.685**).96-106; in F. Williams 1970(**1.814**).362-76; in W. Wolfram and N. Clarke 1971(**1.853**).51-73.

**2.415 Stewart, William A.** 1970. Historical and structural bases for the recognition of Negro dialect. Linguistics and the teaching of standard English to speakers of other languages and dialects. Monograph series on languages and linguistics, ed. by James E. Alatis, 239-47. Washington: Georgetown University Press. Presents linguistic and historical arguments for recognizing speech of blacks as variety of English distinct from speech of whites.

**2.416 Stewart, William A.** 1970. Toward a history of American Negro dialect. Language and poverty: perspectives on a theme, ed. by Frederick Williams, 351-79. Chicago: Markham. Reprinting of Stewart **2.413** and **2.414**.

**2.417 Stewart, William A.** 1972. Acculturative processes and the language of the American Negro. Language in its social setting, ed. by W. W. Gage, 1-46. Washington: Anthropological Society of Washington. Insightful analysis of academic and intellectual controversies and development of research in linguistics and social sciences over extent of retentions in culture of American blacks.

**2.418 Stoddard, Albert H.** 1939. Buh partridge outhides buh rabbit. Savannah: privately printed. One tale in dialect; preface discusses Gullah speech.

**2.419 Stoddard, Albert H.** 1940. Gulla tales and anecdotes of South Carolina sea islands. Savannah, GA: privately printed. P. 1, comment on uniqueness of Gullah; pp. 2-3, suggestions for pronunciation of Gullah words.

**2.420 Stoddard, Albert H.** 1944. Origins, dialect, beliefs, and characteristics of the Negroes of the South Carolina and Georgia coasts. GHQ 28.186-95. Layman's essay on Sea Island language and lore, which were heavily influenced by native West African habits of residents.

**2.421 Stoney, Samuel Gaillard, and Gertrude Mathews Shelby.** 1930. The family tree of Gullah folk speech and folk tales. Black genesis: a chronicle, ix-xxv. New York: Macmillan. Early essay discussing historical connections of Sea Island people and culture with the Caribbean as well as with Africa; says "the branches of the family tree of Gullah are American, the trunk is West Indian and the roots English and African" and illustrates commonalities between Sea Island and Caribbean and African speech.

**2.422 Szwed, John F.** 1970. Africa lies just off Georgia: sea islands preserve origins of Afro-American culture. Africa Report 15.29-31. Popular essay on origin and main features of Sea Island language and culture.

**2.423 Tallichet, H.** 1892. The etymology of bayou. MLN 7.198-99. [LA]. From French dialect word or Spanish bahia.

**2.424 Taylor, Orlando.** 1969. An introduction to the historical development of black English and implications for American education. Washington: CAL. ED 035 863. Also in Language, Speech and Hearing Services in Schools 3.4.5-15. Chronicles development of New World black speech from 16th century, emphasizing its creole background and arguing this history provides legitimacy and identity to American black culture.

**2.425 Thom, William T.** 1883. Some parallelisms between Shakespeare's English and the Negro-English of the U.S. Shakespeariana 1.129-35. Says "there are some things in the Negro-English so immediately representative of Shakespeare English as to be matter of interest to all students of Shakespeare philology" and illustrates common usages in the plays and in Uncle Remus stories.

**2.426 Thomas, Charles K.** 1952. American dialects--how they got that way. American Mercury 75.348.43-49. Popular essay surveying how English developed from Indo-European and how settlement history of U.S. contributed to American dialects.

**2.427 Thompson, Stith.** 1952. Killed up. AS 27.235. Kentucky usage. [Perryville, KY]. Cites 1836 and 1951 occurrences of the intensifying verb.

**2.428 Thrower, Sarah S.** 1954. The spiritual of the Gullah Negro in South Carolina. Cincinnati: Cincinnati Conservatory of Music thesis. Pp. 13-17, 63, notes on pronunciation, intonation, and voice qualities of Sea Islands speakers that lend special effects to singing of spirituals of region.

**2.429 Tillman, Nathaniel.** 1942. A possible etymology of "tote." AS 17.128-29. West African origin suggested.

**2.430 Tinker, Edward Larocque.** 1932. Louisiana gombo. Yale Review n.s. 21.566-79. Layman's essay on nature of French creole spoken by blacks in New Orleans and elsewhere in LA with examples showing influence of local dialect of English.

**2.431 Tinker, Edward Larocque.** 1935. Gombo, the creole dialect of Louisiana. Proceedings of the American Antiquarian Society 45.101-42. Survey of speech and culture of LA French creole community, with extensive bibliography.

**2.432 Traugott, Elizabeth.** 1976. Pidgins, creoles, and the origins of vernacular black English. Black English: a seminar, ed. by Deborah Harrison and Tom Trabasso, 57-93. Hillsdale, NJ: Erlbaum. Detailed typological comparison of grammatical, lexical, and phonological elements of West African Pidgin English, Tok Pisin, Jamaican Creole, Gullah, and Vernacular Black English based on representative texts; concludes that "aspects of VBE can best be explained in the light of centuries of linguistic change, and development from a pidgin to a creole, through various stages of decreolization, to a point where VBE . . . still has features which clearly distinguishes it from [other varieties of English]."

**2.433 Troubridge, Sir St. Vincent.** 1951. Notes on the DAE: VII. Negroes and slavery. AS 26.27-28. Fifteen lexical items, mostly from abolitionist writings.

**2.434 Turner, Lorenzo Dow.** 1941. Linguistic research and African survivals. The interdisciplinary aspects of Negro studies, ed. by Melville J. Herskovits. American Council of Learned Societies Bulletin 32.68-89. Discusses difficulties for researchers to establish African survivals in New World and traces common belief of no linguistic survivals to lack of knowledge of African languages, lack of documents about importation of slaves to New World, lack of ethnological studies of West African peoples, and lack of dictionaries and grammars of West African languages; includes (pp. 78-89) discussion after presentation of paper.

**2.435 Turner, Lorenzo Dow.** 1945. Notes on the sounds and vocabulary of Gullah. PADS 3.13-26. Preliminary synopsis of findings in item **2.437** below, with special attention to phonology and personal naming patterns. **Reprinted** in J. Williamson and V. Burke 1971(**1.823**).121-35.

**2.436 Turner, Lorenzo Dow.** 1948. Problems confronting the investigator of Gullah. PADS 9.74-84. Outlines requisites for valid study of Gullah, including acquaintance with African languages and close, informal relationship with informants. **Reprinted** in W. Wolfram and N. Clarke 1971(**1.853**).1-15.

**2.437 Turner, Lorenzo Dow.** 1949. Africanisms in the Gullah dialect. Chicago: University of Chicago Press. Reprinted in 1969 by Arno Press, New York; in 1974 with introduction by David DeCamp by University of Michigan Press. Bibliography, 293-99. 317 pp. [SC, GA Sea Islands]. Most significant, thorough single work on Gullah and first systematic work on dialect by black investigator, this study has sample Gullah texts and short sections on Gullah syntax, morphology, pronunciation, and intonation, as well as an exhaustive list of Gullah personal names compared to similar words in thirty languages of West Africa. **Reviews:** C. Aguirre Beltran. 1949. Boletín Bibliografico Antropologia Americana 12.205-06; H. P. Blok. 1950. Lingua 8.306-21; J. H. Greenberg. 1950. JAF 63.381-82; G. B. Johnson. 1950. Social Forces 28.458; R. A. Hall, Jr. 1950. AS 25.51-54; R. I. McDavid, Jr. 1950. Language 26.323-33; J. B. McMillan. 1950. Alabama

Review 3.148-50; E. C. Rowlands. 1950. African Affairs 49.349; M. Swadesh. 1951. Word 7.82-84; M. H. Watkins. 1950. AA 52.259; M. H. Watkins. 1950. JNE 19.485-86; G. P. Wilson. 1950. QJS 36.261-62; G. R. Wood. 1974. AS 49.279-80; C. G. Woodson. 1949. JNH 34.477-79.

**2.438 Turner, Lorenzo Dow.** 1958. African survivals in the new world with special emphasis on the arts. Africa seen by American Negroes, ed. by John A. Davis, 101-16. Paris: Presence Africaine. Reviews Africanisms found in language, folk literature, music, and other cultural areas of various countries.

**2.439 Twining, Mary A.** 1977. An examination of African retentions in the folk culture of the South Carolina and Georgia sea islands. Bloomington: Indiana University dissertation. Abstract in DAI 38.2273A. 2 vols. 464 pp. The Gullah language, 60-70. Vol. 1: Survey of Sea Island folklife, expressive behavior, material culture. Vol. 2: Folktales, games, plays, and songs, and religious services and prayers.

**2.440 Utley, Francis Lee.** 1970. Review of Gullah, a breath of the Carolina low country by Dick Reeves. SFQ 24.365-68. Says the long-playing record album has its charms but is of little value to linguists or folklorists.

**2.441 van Sertima, Ivan.** 1971. African linguistic and mythological structures in the new world. Black life and culture in the United States, ed. by Rhoda L. Goldstein, 12-35. New York: Crowell. Discusses misconceptions about varieties of black speech in the New World and points out influences African languages have had on them.

**2.442 van Sertima, Ivan.** 1976. My Gullah brother and I: exploration into a community's language and myth through its oral tradition. Black English: a seminar, ed. by Deborah Harrison and Tom Trabasso, 123-46. Hillsdale, NJ: Erlbaum. Emphasizes strength of African influence on Sea Island oral culture and its closeness to the Caribbean, particularly in folktales.

**2.443 Vass, Winifred Kellersberger.** 1971. The Bantu speaking heritage of the United States. Gainesville: University of Florida thesis. 476 pp. Reprinted in 1979 as Center for Afro-American Studies Monograph series 2. Los Angeles: University of California at Los Angeles Center for Afro-American Studies. xi + 122 pp. Explores question of "proving African content" in American culture and discusses possible Bantu place names in seven Southern states, Bantu speech survivals in folktales and songs, and Bantu-origin vocabulary in the U.S. **Reviews:** I. F. Hancock. 1981. Research in African Literature 12.412-19; R. Price. 1983. LPLP 7.108-12; B. Wald. 1983. LIS 12.106.

**2.444 Vaughan, Celina McGregor.** 1969. Pawley's . . . as it was. Columbia, SC: privately printed. [Georgetown Co., SC]. Pp. 1-3, on Gullah.

**2.445 Viereck, Wolfgang.** 1983, On the history of American English: sense and nonsense. Eigoseinen. The Rising Generation (Tokyo) 129/7.329-31.

**2.446 Viereck, Wolfgang.** 1985. On the origins and developments of American English. Papers from the 6th international conference on historical linguistics, ed. by Jacek Fisiak, 561-69. Current issues in linguistic theory vol. 34. Amsterdam/Poznan: John Benjamins. Assesses state of current knowledge and recent research on early history of American English; finds little progress in substantiating creole background for black English.

**2.447 Viereck, Wolfgang.** 1986. In need of more evidence on black English: the ex-slave narratives revisited. Abstract in NADS 18.2.7. Calls for more research on ex-slave narratives, especially with regard to third-person-singular pronouns, negation, and use of auxiliary been.

**2.448 Visit to a Negro cabin in Virginia.** 1836. The Family Magazine 3.242-45. [VA]. Reports and represents a conversation in the slave quarters.

**2.449 W., G. B.** 1894. Tote. Nation 58.121. Argues word is British, not Southern in origin.

**2.450 Wade-Lewis, Margaret.** 1986. Focus on creolists 16: Lorenzo Dow Turner. Carrier Pidgin 14.1.1-3. Account of the career and accomplishments of Turner.

**2.451 Walser, Richard.** 1962. "Buncombe." The North Carolina miscellany, 150-51. Traces term for trivial and high-sounding verbiage to early 19th-century Congressman from W NC county by the name.

**2.452 Walser, Richard.** 1957. That word "tar heel" again. North Carolina Folklore 5.3-4. Says most popular accounts of origin of the nickname for North Carolinian trace it to Civil War times but ignore fact that state residents were called "Tar-burners" as early as 1775.

**2.453 Warren, H. E.** 1889. Waste basket of words. JAF 2.229. Seven terms for pension claims from KY and TN.

**2.454 Watkins, Floyd.** 1949. The Southern mountaineers' archaic English. Georgia Review 3.219-25. Classic case surveying archaic grammar and pronunciation and saying that Chaucer and Shakespeare "would in many respects feel almost at home" in S Appalachia today.

**2.455 Westbrook, Colton R.** 1974. The dual linguistic heritage of Afro-Americans. Berkeley: University of California thesis. 96 pp. Essay on African language background of American black speech, especially with regard to influence of Cameroon Pidgin English.

**2.456 Whaley, Marcellus S.** 1925. The old types pass--Gullah sketches of the Carolina sea islands. Boston: Christopher. Glossary, 159-65; Vocabulary, 166-89; Idioms, 191-92.

**2.457 Whipple, Henry B.** 1937. Bishop Whipple's Southern Diary 1843-1844. Edited with an introduction by Lester B. Shippee. Minneapolis: University of Minnesota Press. Diary of clergyman touring the South in antebellum period; notes on intelligibility of speech of plantation blacks.

**2.458 Whiting, B. J.** 1952. William Johnson of Natchez: free Negro. SFQ 16.145-53. Cites many examples of language, often having literary flavor, from recently published diary of free antebellum black man.

**2.459 Whitney, Annie Weston.** 1897. "De los' ell an' yard." JAF 10.293-300. Disagrees with Thomas Harrison (**2.189**) and says expression for part of Orion constellation rather than being "genuine Negro" is, like most other items supposedly distinctive to blacks, a survival "with an English parentage, [that] shows a background with a perspective leading into a far distant past."

**2.460 Wightman, Orris Sage, and Margaret Davis Cate.** 1955. Early days of coastal Georgia, 205. St. Simons, GA: Fort Frederica Association.

**2.461 Wiley, Bell Irvin.** 1956. A time of greatness. JSH 23.3-35. Essay on "plain folks" of Civil War era including notes on their language.

**2.462 Wilkinson, Lupton A.** 1933. Gullah vs. grammar. North American Review 236.539-42. [SC]. Says Gullah is unsurpassed in "grammatic economy" and effectiveness and is refreshing antidote to language of academics; cites Africanisms, compounds, folk etymologies, and figures of speech.

**2.463 Williams, Cratis D.** 1961. A E I O U: Vowels and diphthongs in mountain speech. Mountain Life and Work 37.8-11. [S Appalachia]. Relates features of vowel pronunciation in mountains to 18th-century colonial American and other varieties of speech.

**2.464 Williams, Darnell.** 1973. An investigation of possible Gullah survivals in the speech and cultural patterns of black Mississippians. Columbus: Ohio State University dissertation. Abstract in DAI 34.2490A. Author disagrees with thesis that Gullah is basilect of black English in U.S. and says that features of black speech in MS are not survivals of Gullah.

**2.465 Williams, Elizabeth Joan.** 1953. The grammar of plantation overseers' letters, Rockingham County [NC]. Chapel Hill: University of North Carolina thesis. ix + 59 pp. Based on correspondence of eight overseers with plantation owner from 1829-60, studies parts of speech and sentence grammar; finds archaic usages, lack of subject-verb concord, and other features.

**2.466 Williams, John G.** 1895. A study in Gullah English. The Sunday News [Charleston, SC], Feb. 10. 13 pp. typescript. Early essay calling Gullah the "most interesting and the richest" of varieties of American black speech and surveying literary use of it by early writers.

**2.467 Williams, John G.** 1895. Is Gullah a corruption of Angola? Sunday News [Charleston, SC], Feb. 10. 1 p. typescript. Addendum to preceding item. Believes Gullah derives from the name of the West African country Angola.

**2.468 Williams, John G.** 1895. "De ole plantation": elder Coteney's sermons. Charleston, SC: Walker, Evans and Cogswell. Pp. v-xi, reprinting of preceding two items.

**2.469 Williams, Leonard,** ed. 1979. Cavorting on the Devil's Fork: the Pete Whetstone letters of C. F. M. Noland. Memphis: Memphis State University Press. Glossary of proper names, 216-38; Glossary of words and phrases, 239-45. Material drawn from letters published between 1835 and 1856.

**2.470 Wilson, Charles M.** 1929. Elizabethan America. Atlantic 144.238-44. [Appalachia, Ozarks]. Cites linguistic and cultural traits of mountains that have survived "from Elizabethan England."

**2.471 Wise, Claude M[erton].** 1939. Louisiana speech under many flags. SSJ 4.4.8-13. LA's polyglot history.

**2.472 Witherspoon, John.** 1781. The Druid. Pennsylvania Journal. Printed with comments in 1931 in The Beginnings of American English: essays and comments, ed. by Mitford M. Mathews, 13-30. Chicago: University of Chicago Press. Reprinted in 1963, 1973. Three early essays on American usages, with scattered comments on Southern usages such as tot (tote) and raw salad.

**2.473 Wood, Peter H.** 1974. Gullah speech: the roots of black English. Black majority: Negroes in colonial South Carolina from 1670 through the Stoner rebellion, 167-91. New York: Knopf. Insightful review of linguistic literature by historian, putting Gullah in context of colonial demography and the African-American social crucible of early SC coast.

**2.474 Woodson, Carter G.** 1936. The African background outlined, or handbook for the study of the Negro. Washington, DC: Association for the Study of Negro Life and History. Pp. 170-71, note on language.

**2.475 Woofter, T. J., Jr.** 1930. Black yeomanry. New York: Holt. Pp. 48-55, on Gullah. [St. Helena, SC]. Notes on phonology and grammar, with emphasis on archaisms; says "the strange dialect turns out to be little more than the peasant English of two centuries ago, modified to suit the needs of slaves."

**2.476 Work Projects Administration.** 1941. South Carolina: a guide to the palmetto state. New York: Oxford University Press. Note on Gullah, 107-08.

**2.477 Wright, J. Leitch, Jr.** 1976. Blacks in British East Florida. Florida Historical Quarterly 54.425-42. Pp. 426-27, note on languages blacks knew in late 18th century.

**2.478 Wyman, W. S.** 1894. The American word "bayou." Nation 59.361. Letter proposing etymology of word from name of group of Choctaw Indians.

**2.479 Ziegler, Douglas-Val.** 1981. Be-twi-n the lines: some Akan linguistic influences in the new world. Anthropological Linguistics 23.203-08. Analyzes complementizer se in New World English creoles and discusses its use in Sea Island Creole and Southern American black speech.

See Also

1.24 Bailey; 1.32 Bailey; 1.50 Barker; 1.57 Baugh; 1.94 Bowman; 1.97 Bradley; 1.99 Bray; 1.102 Brooks; 1.111 Burling; 1.138 Chirich; 1.182 Dial; 1.186 Dillard; 1.190 Dillard; 1.194 Dillard; 1.219 Dunn; 1.227 Epler; 1.246 Forgue; 1.247 Fortier; 1.248 Foscue; 1.254 Galinsky; 1.259 Genovese; 1.260 Gepp; 1.266 Ginn; 1.295 Halpert; 1.296 Hannum; 1.302 Harper; 1.309 Haskins; 1.345 Johnson; 1.354 Kehr; 1.355 Kent-Paxton; 1.362 Krapp; 1.369 Kurath; 1.383 Language; 1.392 Levine; 1.406 McCall; 1.408 McCrum; 1.439 McDavid; 1.452 McDavid; 1.467 McDavid; 1.473 McDavid; 1.486 McMillan; 1.490 Maguire; 1.493 Marckwardt; 1.508 Mencken; 1.518 Miller; 1.526 Montgomery; 1.527 Montgomery; 1.535 Morley; 1.543 Norman; 1.652 Reinhardt; 1.659 Roberts; 1.687-88 Shores; 1.704 Smith; 1.710 Smitherman; 1.719 Steadman; 1.750 Taylor; 1.759 Tinker; 1.764 Tozer; 1.765 Traugott; 1.770 Twiggs; 1.791 Wächtler; 1.799 Weeks; 1.803 Westover; 1.826 Wilson; 1.841 Wolfram; 3.104 Combs; 3.110 Crozier; 3.339 Miller; 3.370 Owens; 3.397 Raine; 3.405 Randolph; 4.50 G. Bailey; 4.165 Hartmann; 4.204-05 Kurath; 4.268 O'Cain; 4.287 Pilch; 4.293 Randolph; 4.319 Shewmake; 4.340 Stephenson; 4.342 Stephenson; 5.213 Smith; 6.5 Alleman; 6.18 Associated; 6.24-25 Barbour; 6.40 Berry; 6.44 Bigbee; 6.54 Bloodworth; 6.61 Boyd; 6.66 Branner; 6.82 Brannon; 6.98-99 Bull; 6.107 Butt; 6.108 Cain; 6.124 Corbitt; 6.132 Cridlin; 6.134-35 Cumming; 6.148 Detro; 6.164 Dunbar; 6.170 Dunlap; 6.193 Finnie; 6.209 Fulmore; 6.212 Gannett; 6.217 Gatschet; 6.263 Gritzner; 6.264 Grubbs; 6.280 Harris; 6.285 Heckewelder; 6.306 Indian; 6.336 Kenny; 6.370 McCampbell; 6.394 Mahr; 6.398 Martin; 6.417 Miller; 6.429 Murley; 6.437 Neuffer; 6.458 Oakley; 6.492 Powell; 6.497 Rawlings; 6.509 Read; 6.523 Reynolds; 6.535 Robinson; 6.548 Seale; 6.554 Sherwood; 6.605 Tooker; 6.610 Tooker; 6.620 Underwood; 7.4 Ames; 7.24 Bull; 7.30 Cohen; 7.32 Combs; 7.37 Darden; 7.53 Eby; 7.63 Genovese; 7.72 Gutman; 7.77 Heller; 7.86 Inscoe; 7.117 McWhiney; 7.129-30 Mockler; 7.137 Mufwene; 7.147 Oliphant; 7.149 Otto; 7.158 Powell; 7.161-62 Puckett; 7.206 West; 7.212

Zelinsky; 9.60 Harris; 9.61 Haskell; 9.80-81 McDowell; 9.90 Morris; 9.94 Nixon; 9.101 Pennekamp; 9.105 Pollard; 9.113 Rhame; 9.123 Sledge; 9.128 Smith; 9.135 Tiller; 9.140 Walser; 9.148 Zanger; 11.39 Peppin; 11.53 Vaughn-Cooke; 12.20 Meehan; 12.26-27 Reinecke; 12.31 Twining.

# 3 Lexical Studies

**3.1 Adams, Edward C. L.** 1927. Word-list. Congaree sketches: scenes from Negro life in the swamps of the Congaree and tales by Tad and Scip of heaven and hell with other miscellany, 111-16. Chapel Hill: University of North Carolina Press. [CENT SC]. Glossary for collection of short stories.

**3.2 Adams, Edward C. L.** 1928. Nigger to nigger. New York: Scribner's. [Richland Co., CENT SC]. P. 194, impressions of Gullah dialect; Pp. 263-70, glossary of Gullah. Glossary of dialect used by blacks that is "shot through and influenced by the traditions and sentiments of the African slaves."

**3.3 Adams, Edward C. L.** 1987. Glossary. Tales of the Congaree, 303-12. Chapel Hill: University of North Carolina Press. Combined glossary for volume reprinting preceding two collections.

**3.4 Adams, Homer.** 1976. Speech patterns. TFSB 42.70-71. Seventeen phrases heard in Southeast.

**3.5 Aiken, Loyce R.** 1959. An experimental study showing the effects of semantic variations on a specified group of fifth grade students. San Marcos: Southwest Texas State University thesis.

**3.6 Albright, Theresa.** 1969. The vocabulary of the younger generation in the Richmond area of Virginia. College Park: University of Maryland thesis. [48 high school students]. Examines retention of terms reported by Nixon 1946 (**3.358**) and Kurath 1949 (**3.275**) and effect of urbanization on vocabulary of younger generation in Richmond.

**3.8 Allen, F. Sturges.** 1916. Florida. DN 4.344-45. [St. Petersburg]. Twenty terms.

**3.9 Allin, Richard.** 1983. Southern legislative dictionary: words used by southern legislators. Little Rock: Arkansas Gazette. 36 pp. Popular glossary, with illustrations, of terms "taken mostly from the mouths of Arkansas's legislators" by newspaper columnist.

**3.10 Anderson, John Q.** 1956. Up salt creek without a paddle. Kentucky Historical Society Register 54.147-52. Discusses origin of expression.

**3.11 An Appalachian relic: notes on "swarp."** 1981. AJ 8.203-05. Unsigned document found in Knott County, KY, Public Library that recounts improbable tales of word's usage.

**3.12 Armstrong, Mary Sheila.** 1952. A lexical study of the vocabulary of Harriette Arnow's regional novel Hunter's Horn. Charlottesville: University of Virginia thesis. 71 pp. Study of pp. 1-150 of novel to discover how well standard dictionaries record regional language; classifies into six lists 200 terms and senses not recorded in them.

**3.13 Armstrong, Sheila.** 1953. Survivals in Kentucky. AS 27.306-07. Note based on preceding item.

**3.14 Atwood, E. Bagby.** 1945. Kentucky "windage." AS 20.238. Term refers to aiming of rifle to one side, to allow for wind or for inaccurate gun.

**3.15 Atwood, E. Bagby.** 1953. A preliminary report on Texas word geography. Orbis 2.61-66. Background and preliminary findings of lexical survey of state, reported in **3.17**.

**3.16 Atwood, E. Bagby.** 1961. Words of the Southwest. Round Table of the South Central College English Association 2.1.

**3.17 Atwood, E. Bagby.** 1962. The regional vocabulary of Texas. Austin: University of Texas Press. xiii + 273 pp. 125 maps. Lexical survey of TX; includes border areas of LA, OK, and AR. **Reviews:** Anonymous. 1952. Leuvense Bijdragen 52.179; W. Avis. 1964. CJL 9.131-33; B. Carstensen. 1964. ZFM 31.264-67; K. E. Elmquist. 1963. Arizona and the West 5.174-75; M. L. Hartley. 1963. Southwest Review 48.173-74; E. Kolb. 1970. English Studies 51.376-78; W. Labov. 1963. Word 19.266-72; R. I. McDavid, Jr. 1964. JEGP 63.841-46; D. M. McKeithan. 1963. Southwestern Historical Quarterly 67.158-63; C. E. Reed. 1964. Language 40.296-98; J. N. Tidwell. 1964. JAF 77.163; R. M. Wilson. 1964. YWES 43.50; G. Wood. 1963. AS 38.220-23.

**3.18 Atwood, E. Bagby.** 1964. Shivarees and charivaris: variations on a theme. A good tale and a bonnie tune, ed. by Mody C. Boatright, 64-71. Texas Folklore Society Publication 32. Definition of terms with examples.

**3.19 AuCoin, Bill.** 1977. Glossary. Redneck, 158-65. Matteson, IL: Greatlakes Living Press. Popular glossary of 126 terms used by Southern rural whites.

**3.20 Austin, James C., and Wayne Pike.** 1973. The language of Bill Arp. AS 48.84-97. Word-list from 19th-century GA humorist and columnist Charles Henry Smith; compares usages to dictionaries and other reference works.

**3.21 Avis, Walter S.** 1955. "Crocus bag": a problem in areal linguistics. AS 30.5-16. 3 maps. [220 LAMSAS informants in SC and GA]. Says term entered U.S. through colonial seaports and is basis for other variants--crocus sack, crocker sack, and crocker bag. **Reprinted** in H. Allen and G. Underwood 1971(1.12).185-95.

**3.22 Aycock, Etholine Grigsby.** 1940. Americanisms in the traditional ballads of the eastern United States. Columbia: University of Missouri thesis. Scattered comments on phrasings and word choices in ballads from different states and regions of eastern U.S.

**3.23 Ayres, Lucile, Mrs. Hazel McLaughlin, Mrs. Roy Mobley, and Foster Olroyd.** 1950. Expressions from rural Florida. PADS 14.74-80. Glossary of words and idiomatic sayings collected from University of Florida students.

**3.24 Babington, Mima, and E. B. Atwood.** 1961. Lexical usage in southern Louisiana. PADS 36.1-24. 13 maps. [70 speakers, 51 with French-language background, from 6 counties, SE LA]. Outlines sources of southern LA vocabulary from Atlantic dialects and from French and says area is focal region for Southwest.

**3.25 Bailey, Oran B.** 1943. Glossary of cafe terms. AS 18.307-08. Fifty-six terms used by waiters and waitresses in E and W LA.

**3.26 Baker, Howard F.** 1927. West Virginia dialect. AS 3.68. Says 210 of terms cited by Carey Woofter (**3.554**) are unfamiliar to the author in MD and questions how many of them are localisms; suggests that Woofter's word-list be supplemented by other West Virginians.

**3.27 Ball, Donald B.** 1978. Notes on the slang and folk speech of Knoxville, Knox County, Tennessee. TFSB 44.134-42. [15 adults]. Seventy items collected in 1974-75.

**3.28 Banks, Ruth.** 1938. Idioms of the present-day American Negro. AS 13.313-14. Twenty-one expressions used by urban blacks.

**3.29 Barnes, Linda S.** 1981. Rural expressions in Bedford County, Tennessee. Murfreesboro: Middle Tennessee State University thesis. [S CENT TN]. Investigates 151 words and phrases; compares speakers by age and educational level and forms according to usage and familiarity.

**3.30 Barnes, Linda S.** 1981. Rural expressions in Bedford County. Tennessee Linguistics 2.1.8-16. [S CENT TN]. Compares how familiar older and younger generations are with over 100 expressions.

**3.31 Barnhill, Viron L.** 1950. A linguistic atlas type investigation in western Louisiana. New Orleans: Tulane University thesis. Abstract in Tulane University Bulletin 51.13.71 (Oct. 1950). [21 speakers]. Surveys items borrowed from or influenced by French in vocabulary of speakers from SW LA whose primary language is English.

**3.32 Barrick, Mac E.** 1979. Texas chicken. North Carolina Folklore Journal 27.88-92. Comments on folk terms for food and on regional and ethnic slurs.

**3.33 Bassett, Marvin, and Lee Pederson.** 1983. "Press the collar." AS 58.95. [Nevada Co., SW AR]. Cites term meaning "an unmotivated poor white" from LAGS interview.

**3.34 Baum, Lorna.** 1974. Outer bank dialect. North Carolina English Teacher 36.2.9.

**3.35 Bazaar, Eugene Marion.** 1973. A dialect study of the lexicon of Lafayette County, Mississippi. Oxford: University of Mississippi thesis. 203 pp. [N CENT MS, 82 households]. Postal survey of county with 105 items from LAGS worksheets.

**3.36 Becker, E. O.** 1917. Terms from Louisiana. DN 4.421. Two word-lists--terms from New Orleans, terms from De Soto Parish (on TX border).

**3.37 Benthul, Herman F.** 1981. Wording your way through Texas. Burnet, TX: Eakin Press. Includes discussion of history, religious roots, people groups of state.

**3.38 Bentley, Harold.** 1932. A dictionary of Spanish terms in English. New York. x + 243 pp. Pp. 83-214, wordlist. **Reviews:** J. F. Dobie. 1933. Southwest Review 19.1.13; W. C. Greet. 1932. AS 8.1.66; R. D. Hussey. 1933. Pacific Historical Review 2.340.

**3.39 Berry, Edward.** 1928. Sawmill talk (East Texas). AS 3.24-25. Slang of sawmill workers.

**3.40 Betts, Leonidas.** 1966. Folk speech from Kipling. North Carolina Folklore 14.37-40. [Barnett Co., E NC]. Localisms, similes, and other expressions.

**3.41 Black, Donald Chain.** 1981. Therapeutics for the smilin' mighty Jesus: understanding East Texas lower class patients' medically-significant departures from standard English. Mid-American Folklore 13.101-12. Examines nonstandard words, phrases, and sentences employed as euphemisms and oblique references to diseases and medical conditions, used with "medically-significant ambiguity during doctor-patient and nurse-patient interviews" in rural TX.

**3.42 Boone, Lalia Phipps.** 1959. Gator (University of Florida) slang. AS 34.153-57. Examples of contemporary slang from the FL school.

**3.43 Boswell, Andrew.** 1985. Query: thaw up. AS 60.227. [CENT GA]. Term is cited as variant of thaw.

**3.44 Botkin, B. A.** 1931. Folk speech in the Kentucky mountain cycle of Percy Mackaye. AS 6.264-76. Account of metaphor, blending, functional change, compounding, folk etymology, and false analysis that occur in writing of the KY author.

**3.45 Botkin, B. A., ed.** 1978. A treasury of Mississippi River folklore. New York: Bonanza. Pp. 556-57, defines and speculates on etymology of coonjining.

**3.46 Bowman, Myrtle.** 1936. A comparative study of the vocabularies of white and colored children. Waco: Baylor University thesis. v + 91 pp. [40 W, 20 B 7th graders, Waco, TX]. Finds black children averaged fifty more total words and thirty more different words in their writing than white children.

**3.47 Bradley, Francis W.** 1950. A word-list from South Carolina. PADS 14.3-73. Extensive glossary of dialect material collected through newspaper column and correspondence it generated (cf. **1.96**).

**3.48 Bradley, Francis W.** 1954. Supplementary list of South Carolina words and phrases. PADS 21.16-41. Additions and corrections to preceding item.

**3.49 Bradley, Francis W.** 1964. Sandlappers and clay eaters. North Carolina Folklore 12.27-28. Explains the practices of ingesting sand and clay and speculates why natives of SC were given two appellations.

**3.50 Brantley, Mary E.** 1981. Colloquialisms. From cabins to mountains: gleanings from Southwest Alabama, 270-73. Huntsville, AL: Strode. Miscellaneous folk vocabulary of region, collected mostly in oral history research, but not peculiar to area.

**3.51 Broaddus, James W.** 1957. The folk vocabulary of Estill County, Kentucky. Lexington: University of Kentucky thesis. xx + 89 pp. [4 elderly, uneducated natives, E KY]. Compiles glossary of 2,000 items, but does not relate material to other localities or regions.

**3.52 Brown, B. W.** 1958. The buzzard in the folklore of Western Kentucky. KFR 4.11-12.

**3.53 Brown, Calvin S.** 1916. Tennessee. DN 3.345-46. [NW TN]. Fifteen terms from Obion County.

**3.54 Bruce, J. D.** 1913. Terms from Tennessee. DN 4.58. [SE TN]. Thirteen terms.

**3.55 Brydon, G. McLauren.** 1947. Comments on some Virginia words in Dr. Woodard's list (PADS 6). PADS 8.34-36. Adds material from Danville, VA area to Woofter material (**3.539**).

**3.56 Bryson, Artemisia B.** 1929. Some Texas dialect words. AS 4.330-31. Discusses six terms, including larripin and dogie, and speculates on their derivation.

**3.57 Bryson, Artemisia B.** 1934. Homely words in Texas. AS 9.70-71. Hissy, hush-puppy, larrup, son-of-a-gun, salmagundi, whelp.

**3.58 Burgess, Harvey.** 1981. "All ya hasta do . . . is AST": a Robeson County dictionary and guide for the tourist and newcomer to the swampland. Vol. 1. Lumberton, NC: Media and Marketing Associates. 13 pp. [SE NC]. Popular glossary of 108 terms for tourists and newcomers.

**3.59 Burns, Zed Houston.** 1982. An anthology of word origins and meanings. Hattiesburg: University of Southern Mississippi thesis. Collection of etymological comments on curious items, including some Southernisms like cracker.

**3.60 Butler, Melvin Arthur.** 1962. A vocabulary study of Negroes in Austin, TX. Austin: University of Texas thesis. 97 pp. [10 B, ages 18-60]. Uses Atwood worksheets; finds predominance of Southern forms and limited South Midland forms in Austin black speech.

**3.61 Butler, Melvin Arthur.** 1968. Lexical usage of Negroes in northeastern Louisiana. Ann Arbor: University of Michigan dissertation. Abstract in DAI 29.888A. [20 B, ages 18-82]. Says NE LA vocabulary is nearly all General Southern, with little Midland or French influence; social class membership has little influence on vocabulary and only verb choices correlate with educational level of informants.

**3.62 Butters, Ronald R.** 1980. Narrative go, "say." AS 55.304-07. [NC and elsewhere]. Cites use of <u>goes</u> in informal, narrative style of American English and speculates on origin of usage.

**3.63 Buxbaum, Katerine.** 1935. Heard in North Carolina. AS 10.156-57. Localisms noted by tourist from Iowa.

**3.64 Cabaniss, Alice.** 1986. I specken: a blend for Southerners and other logophiles. Carolina Undergraduate Review 1.1.14-17. Proposes new verb "<u>specken</u>, a combination of <u>to suspect</u> and <u>to reckon</u> in their commonality of meaning otherwise designated <u>surmise</u>."

**3.65 Campbell, Marie.** 1937. Old time sayings and old tales. The folk life of a Kentucky mountain community, 526-50. Nashville: George Peabody College thesis. [E KY]. Mostly transcripts of stories, but a few items on "doctoring" and other matters.

**3.66 Carpenter, Cal.** 1979. Southern mountain sayings. The Walton war and tales of the Great Smoky Mountains, 141-90. Lakemont, GA: Copple House. [W NC]. List of 266 "quaint and descriptive expressions" with explanatory notes to include the circumstances under which expressions were used and to analyze each "for a better understanding of its meaning and background in the language of the mountain people."

**3.67 Carpenter, Charles.** 1936. West Virginia expletives. West Virginia Review 13.346-47. Lists and discusses colorful expressions and curses for surprise, anger, and confoundment.

**3.68 Carr, Donna Humphreys.** 1966. Reflections of Atlantic coast lexical variations in three Mormon communities. Salt Lake City: University of Utah thesis. Finds Northern and Midland variants dominate lexicon of three Mormon communities and that the few Southern variants are used rarely and are decreasing.

**3.69 Carr, Joseph William.** 1904-07. A list of words from northwest Arkansas. DN 2.416-22; 3.68-103; 3.124-65; 3.205-38. Characteristic local expressions collected primarily in Washington Co.

**3.70 Carr, Joseph William, and Rupert Taylor.** 1909. A list of words from northwest Arkansas. DN 3.392-406. 400 terms.

**3.71 Carson, Sam, and A. W. Vick.** 1972. Hillbilly cookin 2: more recipes, more sayings. Thorn Hill, TN: Clinch Mountain Lookout. [E TN]. Appalachian talk, 59-60; What the old folks said, 61-62. Thirty-seven lexical and proverbial items.

**3.72 Carter, John Ray.** 1958. Folksay and folk wit. Life and lore of Reelfoot Lake, 47-51. Nashville: George Peabody College thesis. [NW TN]. List of ninety-seven expressions collected by high school students.

**3.73 Carver, Craig M.** 1987. American regional dialects: a word geography. Ann Arbor: University of Michigan Press. xiii + 317 pp. 92 maps. Comprehensive description of character of American geographical dialects, based on lexical and morphological data from LAUSC and DARE. **Review:** T. C. Frazer. 1987. AS 62.154-59.

**3.74 Cassidy, Frederic G.** 1977- . [DARE inquiries]. NADS 9- . Series of short word-lists from DARE of items about which the dictionary requests more documentation, many items from the South.

**3.75 Cassidy, Frederic G.** 1982. Lemmatization - the case of "catalpa." Language form and linguistic variation: papers dedicated to Angus McIntosh, ed. by John Anderson, 1-10. Amsterdam: Benjamins. Discusses how form of DARE headword for common American tree native to lower Mississippi basin was chosen from forty phonemically different forms that developed.

**3.76 Cassidy, Frederic G.** 1985. Dictionary of American regional English, A-C. Cambridge: Harvard University Press. clvi + 903 pp. Numerous maps. First volume of five-volume, comprehensive historical dictionary of American folk vocabulary, based on 1700 interviews and on printed sources; introduction includes explanation of mapping and regional labels, essay on changes in American folk speech, guide to pronunciation, text of questionnaire, and list of informants. **Reviews:** L. R. N. Ashley. 1986. Geolinguistics 12.79-87; M. Ching. 1987. SECOL Review 11.195-203; V. G. McDavid. 1987. JEL 20.249-54; J. B. McMillan. 1987. Alabama Review 40.157-58; T. K. Pratt. 1986. CJL 31.179-85; W. Viereck. 1986. EWW 7.317-20; W. Wolfram. 1986. AS 61.345-52.

**3.77 Cauthern, Elizabeth Greear.** 1955. A lexical study of the vocabulary of Harriette Arnow's regional novel, Hunter's Horn. Charlottesville: University of Virginia thesis. 53 pp. Continues approach of Armstrong (3.12) for second third of novel (pp. 150-300).

**3.78 Chalk, Sarah C.** 1958. A vocabulary study of Dallas County, Texas. Austin: University of Texas thesis. [8 W, 2 B, ages 21-89]. Analyzes influences on county's vocabulary, finding combined South and South Midland influence greatest; glossary, 14-164.

**3.79 Chapman, Maristan.** 1928. Glossary. The happy mountain, 311-13. New York: Literary Guild. Eighty-eight terms from novel.

**3.80 Chapman, Maristan.** 1929. Glossary. Homeplace, 273-75. New York: Viking. Eighty-six terms from novel, many the same as from preceding item.

**3.81 Chapman, Maristan.** 1932. Glossary. The weather tree, 297-98. New York: Viking. Sixty-one terms from novel.

**3.82 Chapman, Maristan.** 1933. Glossary. Glen hazard, 321-22. New York: Knopf. Twenty-three terms from novel.

**3.83 Chase, Richard.** 1943. [Glossary]. The jack tales: told by R. M. Ward and his kindred in the Beech Mountain section of western North Carolina and by other descendants of Council Harmon (1803-1896) elsewhere in the Southern mountains; with three tales from Wise Co., Virginia, ed. by Richard Chase, 201-02. Boston: Houghton-Mifflin. Twenty-nine terms.

**3.84 Ching, Marvin K. L.** 1987. How fixed is <u>fixin' to</u>? AS 62.332-45. Study based on responses of 104 informants at Memphis State University showing that Southern <u>fixin' to</u> can be interpreted from core of inherent concepts supplemented by knowledge of social context.

**3.85 Claerbaut, David.** 1972. Black jargon in white America. Grand Rapids, MI: Eerdmans. Examines genesis of black American dialects, confrontation between language of black children and teacher attitudes, and contributions of black dialect to American vocabulary, among other topics. **Reviews:** R. Abrahams and J. Szwed. 1975. AA 77.329; M. K. Spears. 1972. NYTBR 19, p. 32 (Nov. 16).

**3.86 Clark, Joe.** 1986. Explanation of Tennessee words and terms. The Tennessee sampler, ed. by Peter Jenkins et al., 276. Nashville: Thomas Nelson. Ten items.

**3.87 Clark, John F.** 1983. The vainglorious "trade-last": a reappraisal. AS 58.20-30. Uses DARE data in discussing term (meaning "a complimentary remark reported by one person to another") and its variants, one of which, <u>last-go-trade</u>, is found almost entirely in SE U.S.

**3.88 Clark, Joseph D.** 1962. Folk speech from North Carolina. SFQ 26.301-25. List of 750 items of dialect, slang, and colloquial usage collected from freshmen students at North Carolina State University and compared to dictionaries and Frank Brown collection of NC folklore materials.

**3.89 Clark, Joseph D.** 1962. Folk speech from North Carolina. North Carolina Folklore 10.6-12. List of 649 items.

**3.90 Clarke, Kenneth, and Mary Clarke.** 1974. Kentucky words and brief expressions. The harvest and the reapers: oral traditions of Kentucky, 17-31. Lexington: University Press of Kentucky. Surveys early observation of KY folkspeech by folklorists.

**3.91 Clarke, Mary Washington.** 1964. Jesse Stuart's writings preserve passing folk idiom. SFQ 28.157-98. [NE KY]. Generous sampling of vocabulary items from Stuart's fiction.

**3.92 Clarke, Mary Washington.** 1972. To dance in a hog trough: a folk expression. KFR 18.68-69. Says term still has currency in KY as humorous remark to any girl whose younger sister is likely to marry first.

**3.93 Claudel, Alice Moser.** 1975. A New Orleans postscript on "nigger." AS 50.143. Discusses crossracial catcalls and terms of derision in LA city.

**3.94 Cobb, Ida Sublette.** 1940. The silver shuttle. Little Rock, AR: Central. Pp. 117-21, list of sixty-nine AR expressions.

**3.95 Cohen, Hennig.** 1951. The terminology of mardi gras. AS 26.110-15. [New Orleans, LA]. Discusses words and phrases associated with Mardi Gras parades and balls and naming patterns of carnival organizations called "krewes."

**3.96 Col. Horsepasture's guidebook and dictionary.** 1966. Roanoke, VA: Tip 'n Twinkle. Popular dictionary.

**3.97 Combs, Josiah H.** 1918. A word-list from the South. DN 5.31-40. Mainly mountain English from AR, KY, NC, TN, and VA.

**3.98 Combs, Josiah H.** 1921. Kentucky items. DN 5.118-19. Twenty-seven words and phrases.

**3.99 Combs, Josiah H.** 1921. Transpositions and scrambled words. DN 5.119. [KY]. Eleven items, mostly metathesis.

**3.100 Combs, Josiah H.** 1922. A word-list from Georgia. DN 5.183-84. From Uncle Remus stories; words said to be used by blacks and KY mountaineers.

**3.101 Combs, Josiah H.** 1923. Addenda from Kentucky. DN 5.242-43. Twenty-one expressions.

**3.102 Combs, Josiah H.** 1944. A word-list from the Southern highlands. PADS 2.17-23. [S Appalachia]. Includes list of figures of speech and idioms.

**3.103 Combs, Josiah H.** 1959. Dialect terms in boys' games. KFR 5. 30,136. Nine terms from Knott Co, KY.

**3.104 Combs, Mona R.** 1958. Archaic words used in north eastern Kentucky. Morehead: Morehead State College thesis. iv + 60 pp. [Rowan Co.]. Compiles 679 words collected from older residents of county by high school students in effort to compare vocabulary of Shakespeare with that of KY mountains; lists 100 Middle English words (pp. 56-59), and presents statistical data on informants' knowledge and use of them.

**3.105 Conrad, John Calvin.** 1926. Some American localisms of Mexican origin. Norman: University of Oklahoma thesis.

**3.106 Coon-fest.** 1970. Metairie, LA: Jefferson Parish Recreation Department. Glossary of SE LA localisms.

**3.107 Cracker.** 1921. South Carolina Historical Magazine 22. 99-100.

**3.108 Crawford, Bernice F.** 1950. Some lexical variants in pioneer Ellis County [Texas]. Denton: North Texas State University thesis. [10 elderly, less educated natives, NE TX]. Study of old-fashioned farm vocabulary.

**3.109 Crow, C. L.** 1916. Texas. DN 4.347-48. [N CENT TX]. Thirty-eight terms from Parker County.

**3.110 Crozier, Alan.** 1984. The Scotch-Irish influence on American English. AS 59.310-31. 5 maps. Discusses problems in making cross-Atlantic comparisons and identifies thirty-three items used in Midland area of U.S. that reflect influence of Scotch-Irish immigrants.

**3.111 Cunningham, Rodger.** 1971. Appalachian /ˌpaɪtˈnaɪ/ "almost": a notice and various etymologies. AS 46.304. [WV, KY]. Believes term, equivalent to "pretty nigh," is influenced by Scotch-Irish pronunciation of Gaelic term.

**3.112 Curtiss, Laura C.** 1910. Southern expressions, reported as common to Florida and Georgia. DN 3.450. Twenty items.

**3.113 Dabney, Joseph Earl.** 1974. A chronicle of corn whiskey from King James' Ulster plantation to America's Appalachians and the moonshine life. New York: Scribner's. Pp. xix-xxvi, glossary of terms used in S Appalachian moonshining.

**3.114 Dalton, Alford P.** 1950. A word-list from southern Kentucky. PADS 13.22-23. Twenty-two miscellaneous items compared to British dialect usage.

**3.115 Daugneaux, Christine B.** 1981. Appalachia: a separate place, a unique people. Parsons, WV: McClain. Why do Appalachians talk that way?, 30-35; Polyfoxing, a lost art being revived, 63. Presents standard case that mountain English is "older in its forms and rich in unique vocabulary and in that sense at least is purer English" and explains polyfoxing as the "art of making homemade medicine."

**3.116 Davis, Alva L., and Raven I. McDavid, Jr.** 1949. "Shivaree": an example of cultural diffusion. AS 24.249-55. 1 map. Based on Linguistic Atlas, discusses terms for raucous celebration following rural weddings in Eastern U.S.; serenade dominates Southeast and South Atlantic areas, shivaree the mid-South. **Reprinted** in H. Allen and G. Underwood 1971(**1.12**).178-84.

**3.117 Davis, Hubert J.** 1973. Glossary. 'Pon my honor hit's the truth: tall tales from the mountains, 93-102. Murfreesboro, NC: Johnson. Glossary of 323 items.

**3.118 Davison, Zeta C.** 1953. A word-list from the Appalachians and the Piedmont area of North Carolina. PADS 19.8-14. [NC, KY, TN]. 113 items collected over period of 30 years.

**3.119 Deal, Borden.** 1984. Inquiry: "robelay." AS 59.339. [Langston, AL]. Reports term means "junk."

**3.120 Dean, Patricia Kay Elder.** 1980. A word atlas of north central Texas. Commerce: East Texas State University dissertation. Abstract in DAI 41.655A. [200 speakers from 13 counties]. Investigates folk expressions for 126 concepts, only three of which produce isoglosses; finds social factors important in determining word distribution and vocabulary closely similar to that of S WV, W NC, and W SC.

**3.121 Dear, Ruth.** 1960. Some queries about regionalisms. AS 35.298-300. [NC, AR]. Brief comments about three terms: doffing, weaving, slashing.

**3.122 Dearden, Elizabeth Jeanette.** 1941. A word geography of the south Atlantic states. Providence: Brown University thesis. iv + 74 pp. 32 maps. Preliminary analysis of data from Guy Lowman's fieldwork in South Atlantic States. Establishes major dialect areas of VA and NC and compares findings to Middle Atlantic states.

**3.123 Dearden, Elizabeth Jeanette.** 1943. Dialect areas of the south Atlantic states as determined by variations in vocabulary. Providence: Brown University dissertation.

**3.124 DeLaPerriere, Earleen.** 1980. "Go-long." AS 55.154-55. Term from black community for inevitable sequence of events; citations from Memphis, TN, and from Zora Neale Hurston novel.

**3.125 Dempsey, Arthur D.** 1974. I calls 'em as I eats 'em or the great pea-bean controversy. They had to call it something, ed. by Fred Tarpley, 43-44. Commerce, TX: Names Institute Press. Report from Northern immigrant confused by the maze of types of peas and beans in NE TX; says "the real test in determining a Southerner as opposed to a Northerner is the ability to distinguish between peas and beans when they are placed before him."

**3.126 DeVere, Louise A.** 1975. Bridge over semantic waters: semantic restrictions on the word "bridge" in tidewater Virginia. Abstract in NADS 8.3.10. [SE VA]. Word bridge has narrow meaning in Tidewater area, referring only to passages for motor vehicles over navigable bodies of water.

**3.127 Dickinson, Meriwether B.** 1941. A lexicographical study of the vocabulary of Greenup County, Kentucky, set forth in Jesse Stuart's <u>Beyond Dark Hills</u>. Charlottesville: University of Virginia thesis. [NE KY]. 71 pp. Lists 250 words from Stuart's autobiographical novel not in current dictionaries; points out tautological expressions, Scottish retentions, and unusual types of compounds.

**3.128 Dillard, J. L.** 1976. American talk: where our words came from. New York: Random House. 187 pp. Popular treatment of sources of American vocabulary, giving special emphasis to its multilingual background. **Reviews:** F. G. Cassidy. 1979. LIS 8.74-79; J. R. Gaskin. 1978. Sewanee Review 86.426; J. H. Hall. 1978. JEL 12.71-75; K. B. Harder. 1977. Names 25.174; L. Johnson. 1977. Language 53.494-95.

**3.129 Dillard, J. L.** 1977. Lexicon of black English. New York: Seabury. 199 pp. Discusses problems of finding and designating vocabulary associated with blacks and analyzes vocabulary in specific domains--religion, music, narcotics, root work, and others--in effort to solve these problems. **Reviews:** W. E. Farrison. 1977. CLAJ 21.321-24; J. A. Hirshberg. 1982. AS 57.52-73; K. C. Jones. 1979. Lamar Journal of the Humanities 5.74-77; R. C. Olson. 1979. Lamar Journal of the Humanities 5.66-73; R. W. Wescott. 1979. JAF 92.509-10.

**3.130 Dingus, L. R.** 1944. Tobacco words. PADS 2.63-72. [KY, E TN, SW VA]. Vocabulary of tobacco farming; additions from S VA by George P. Wilson.

**3.131 Dohan, Mary H.** 1974. Our own words. New York: Knopf. Pp. 102-05, on Southern vocabulary.

**3.132 Dollard, John.** 1949. Caste and class in a Southern town. New York: Harper and Brothers. Pp. 6-7, notes on Southern speech; cites <u>evening</u>, <u>carry</u>, <u>done</u>, <u>you-all</u>, and other usages.

**3.133 Dominick, Doris S.** 1955. A lexical study of the vocabulary of a part of Harriett Arnow's regional novel, <u>Hunter's Horn</u>. Charlottesville: University of Virginia thesis. 72 pp. Continues approach of Armstrong (**3.12**) for final third of novel.

**3.134 Doyle, Charles Clay.** 1975. Sarcastic interrogative affirmatives and negatives. Midwestern Journal of Language and Folklore 1.33-34. [CENT TX, N GA]. Discusses expressions like "Is Billy Graham Catholic?" that paraphrase "one experience or situation in terms of another, 'standard' one."

**3.135 Dressman, Michael R.** 1979. "Redd up." AS 54.141-45. Cites term from PA to Carolinas and attributes its distribution to early Scotch-Irish.

**3.136 Drums and shadows: survival studies among the Georgia coastal Negroes, produced by the Savannah unit of the Georgia Writers' Project of the Work Projects Administration.** 1940. Glossary, 251-52. Athens: University of Georgia Press. Reprinted in 1986 with introduction by Charles W. Joyner. Forty-six items, including Africanisms.

**3.137 Dudley, Fred A.** 1946. "Swarp" and some other Kentucky words. AS 21.270-73. [NE KY]. Glossary from Rowan Co.

**3.138 Dumas, Bethany K.** 1981. Appalachian glossary. An encyclopedia of East Tennessee, ed. by Jim Stokely and Jeff D. Johnson, 16-18. Oak Ridge, TN: Children's Museum. 102 items.

**3.139 Duncan, Mary Lou.** 1974/75. Mountain sayens: "dog days" to "dogwood winter." Mountain Call 2.31 (Dec.-Jan.).

**3.140 [Dunglison, Robley.]** 1931. Americanisms in the Virginia Literary Museum. The beginnings of American English, ed. by Mitford M. Mathews, 99-112. Chicago: University of Chicago Press. Reprinted 1963, 1973. Also reprinted as "Dunglison's Glossary" (1829-1830), ed. by Allen Walker Read, DN 5.422-32 (1927). Early VA word list.

**3.141 Dwyer, Paul.** 1971. Dictionary for Yankees and other uneducated people. Highlands, NC: Merry Mountaineers. 36 pp. Compendium of unusual expressions and spellings, with cartoons, for tourist trade.

**3.142 Dwyer, Paul.** 1975. Thangs Yankees don' know: dialect, lawin', greens, recipes, squar' dancin', beauty aids, wild life, remedies, signs, stills, and folks-fire things. Highlands, NC: Merry Mountaineers. 40 pp. Thangs yuh should larn!, 4-5; Yore wrong!, 15; Shor and sartain: redundancies, 17; Folk expressions, 29; The way it was said!, 31. Collection of unusual tidbits about mountain life for tourists.

**3.143 Dwyer, Paul.** 1976. Southern sayin's for Yankees and other immigrants: plus--Yankee woids that "break up" Southerners. Highlands, NC: Merry Mountaineers. 36 pp. Compendium of unusual expressions and spellings, with cartoons, for tourist trade.

**3.144 Eames, Edwin, and Howard Robboy.** 1967. The submarine sandwich: lexical variations in a cultural context. AS 42.279-88. Variant terms for the sandwich in 100 American cities.

**3.145 Eble, Connie.** 1980. Slang, productivity, and semantic theory. The sixth LACUS forum 1979, ed. by William C. McCormack and Herbert J. Izzo, 215-27. Columbia, SC: Hornbeam. [Chapel Hill, NC]. Shows productivity of semantic processes like generalization, pejoration, and metaphor and processes of word-formation like clipping and acronyming in college slang.

**3.146 Eble, Connie.** 1981. Slang, productivity, and semantic theory: a closer look. The seventh LACUS forum, ed. by James E. Copeland and Philip W. Davis, 270-75. Columbia, SC: Hornbeam. [Chapel Hill, NC]. Discusses implications of productivity of slang for theory of linguistic abilities.

**3.147 Eble, Connie.** 1981. Scenes from slang. SECOL Bulletin 5.74-78. [Chapel Hill, NC]. Says that slang is major area of semantic change and illustrates this with types of semantic shift.

**3.148 Eble, Connie.** 1983. Greetings and farewells in college slang. The ninth LACUS forum, ed. by John Morreall, 433-42. Columbia, SC: Hornbeam. [Chapel Hill, NC]. Examines semantic motivation of greetings and partings and describes kinds of words and phrases appropriate in these expressions.

**3.149 Eddins, A. W.** 1916. The state industrial school boys' slang. Round the levee, ed. by Stith Thompson, 44-46. Texas Folklore Society Publication 1. Dallas: Southern Methodist University Press. Slang terms, nicknames, and verbal insults among TX teenagers.

**3.150 Edmiston, William C.** 1929. A study of provincialisms from northern Todd County, Kentucky. Nashville: George Peabody College thesis. [SW KY]. List of 893 unusual words and expressions collected by personal observation and from school children.

**3.151 Eikel, Fred, Jr.** 1946. An Aggie vocabulary of slang. AS 21.29-36. [College Station, TX]. Extensive lexicon used by Texas A and M students, some of it general military and college slang.

**3.152 Elton, William.** 1950. "Playing the dozens." AS 25.120-33. Cites use of term by Erskine Caldwell and other writers.

**3.153 Entwisle, Doris R.** 1969. Semantic systems of minority groups. ED 030 106. 49 pp. [B, W, 1st, 3rd, 5th graders, Baltimore, MD]. Using word association research, says that black children develop more restricted semantic system during elementary school years than whites do.

**3.154 Eskew, Garnett L.** 1933. Coonjining. AS 8.77-78. Abstract of New York Herald-Tribune story about term for the peculiar gait or shuffle.

**3.155 Evans, Wiliam W.** 1979. "Office." AS 51.24. Notes use of office, "to share an office with," in TX and LA.

**3.156 Everhart, Jim.** 1967. The illustrated Texas dictionary of the English language. Vol. 1. Houston: Creative Books. 49 pp. Glossary of forty-seven terms, each with photograph of the histrionic author, in modified spellings.

**3.157 Everhart, Jim.** 1968. The illustrated Texas dictionary of the English language. Vol. 2. Houston: Creative Books. 48 pp. Forty-six terms, in modified spellings, with photographs.

**3.158 Everhart, Jim.** 1973. The illustrated Texas dictionary of the English language. Vol. 3. Houston: Creative Books. 48 pp. Forty-six terms, in modified spellings, with photographs.

**3.159 Everhart, Jim.** 1975. The illustrated Texas dictionary of the English language. Vol. 4. Houston: Creative Books. 48 pp. Forty-six terms, in modified spellings, with photographs.

**3.160 Everhart, Jim.** 1979. The illustrated Texas dictionary of the English language. Vol. 5. Houston: Creative Books. 48 pp. Forty-six terms, in modified spellings, with photographs.

**3.161 Everhart, Jim.** 1985. The illustrated Texas dictionary of the English language. Vol. 6. Houston: Creative Books. 48 pp. Forty-six terms, in modified spellings, with photographs.

**3.162 Fagan, David.** 1979. I knowed it all my life/folk expressions as geographical locators in the South. Abstract in NADS 11.3.4. Discusses variety and distribution of local folk sayings in South.

**3.163 Faries, Rachel Bernice.** 1967. A word geography of Missouri. Columbia: University of Missouri dissertation. 348 pp. 128 maps. [700 older natives of MO, 124-item checklist]. Abstract in DAI 28.4156. Abstract reprinted in J. Williamson and V. Burke 1971(1.823).670-71. Compares vocabulary to findings from dialect areas of Eastern US established in Kurath (3.275) and concludes Missouri dialect "has a strong Midland base; it is more akin to the South than to the North; a recurrent pattern of isoglosses marks off the Ozark Highland and its contingent areas."

**3.164 Farr, T. J.** 1936. Folk speech of middle Tennessee. AS 11.275-76. Reports sixty-three words and expressions used in at least five counties in Cumberland Plateau area.

**3.165 Farr, T. J.** 1939. The language of the Tennessee mountain regions. AS 14.89-92. 150 items collected in five counties of middle TN.

**3.166 Farr, T. J.** 1940. More Tennessee expressions. AS 15.446-48. Additions to earlier TN lists.

**3.167 Farrier, Ph. H.** 1936. "Few of" and "few bit." AS 11.278-79. [Giles Co., SW VA]. Reports two expressions as intensifiers equivalent to rather.

**3.168 Fink, Paul M.** 1974. Bits of mountain speech gathered between 1910 and 1965 along the mountains bordering North Carolina and Tennessee.

Boone, NC: Appalachian Consortium. 31 pp. Dictionary of 556 items, with citations. **Review**: R. Whitener. 1975. AJ 2.230-31.

**3.169 Fitzpatrick, Robert J.** 1940. Language of the tobacco market. AS 15.132-35. [KY]. Lexicon of seventy-four terms used by growers, auctioneers, and others in tobacco industry.

**3.170 Flexner, Stuart B.** 1976. I hear America talking: an illustrated treasury of American words and phrases. New York: Simon and Schuster. 505 pp. One-volume encyclopedia of short accounts of typical American words and expressions, many of them from the South. **Review**: Owen Hatteras III [R. I. McDavid, Jr.]. 1977. IJAL 44.350-51.

**3.171 Flowers, Paul.** 1944. Picturesque speech. TFSB 10.9-10. On <u>bo-dollar</u>, "silver dollar," said to be used by blacks in interior South, especially along the Mississippi River.

**3.172 Foley, Robert.** n.d. A dictionary of Ozark usage. n.p. 13 pp. manuscript in University of Georgia library. Compiles 130 terms from writings of Vance Randolph but not noted by other lexicographers.

**3.173 Forrester, Christine D.** 1952. A word geography of Kentucky. Lexington: University of Kentucky thesis. Data from questionnaire. iv + 122 pp. 49 maps. [89 speakers, 29 counties]. Based on postal survey, finds that KY "is intercepted by no main linguistic boundaries, but lies entirely within the broad Midland speech area" and that the state's vocabulary is "South Midland with restricted occurrence of occasional Southern terms."

**3.174 Foscue, Virginia O.** 1971. A preliminary survey of the vocabulary of white Alabamians. PADS 56. 46 pp. 15 maps. [52 adults from 25 representative counties]. Analyzes distribution of terms by geography and by age and education, identifies a Southern-South Midland boundary across state, and says some regional terms are being replaced by national ones. **Review**: K. Hameyer. 1975. AS 50.115-20.

**3.175 Foscue, Virginia O.** 1981. Vocabulary change in Alabama. Abstract in NADS 13.3.9-10. Follows up preceding study of generational differences in vocabulary.

**3.176 [Four words].** 1951. Ozark Folklore 1.2.2. [AR]. Note on <u>durgen</u>, <u>ramp</u>, <u>painter</u>, and <u>ing-urn</u>.

**3.177 Foushee, Isabella Lewis.** 1967. A vocabulary study of Brunswick and New Hanover Counties, North Carolina. Chapel Hill: University of North Carolina thesis. [16 older natives, SE NC]. 71 maps. Surveys distribution and use of sixty-four terms in Lower Cape Fear Valley and finds little change since Linguistic Atlas data was collected thirty years earlier; minimal differences between counties were found.

**3.178 Fowler, Ila Earle.** 1944. Humdurgan. Down in West Kentucky and other poems, 12-13. Cynthiana, KY: Hobson Book Press. [Caldwell and Christian Cos., KY]. Discusses origin of durgan and hamdurgan.

**3.179 Freeman, Dale.** n.d. How to talk . . . pure Ozark . . . in one easy lesson. Kimberling City, MO: Ozark Postcard. iv + 15 pp. Popular dictionary of pure "Ozarkese" for tourists and new residents.

**3.180 Friedman, Lillian.** 1950. Minorcan dialect words in St. Augustine, Florida. PADS 14.81. Fifteen Spanish items from descendants of 18th-century settlers.

**3.181 Fruit, John P.** 1890. [Marble terms from Russellville, Kentucky]. DN 1.24. Twenty-three terms.

**3.182 Garber, Aubrey.** 1976. Mountain-ese: basic grammar for Appalachia. Radford, VA: Commonwealth. 105 pp. Popular dictionary of Southern Appalachian speech, with illustrative citation for each entry.

**3.183 Garcia, Juliet Villareal.** 1976. The regional vocabulary of Brownsville, Texas. Austin: University of Texas dissertation. Abstract in DAI 37.4698A. [S TX]. Surveys distribution of vocabulary, based on Atwood's approach (**3.17**).

**3.184 Gaston, C. R.** 1903. Note on "stubboy." DN 4.347-48. Cites SC and TN variants of term used to call domestic animals.

**3.185 Gaston, Edwin W., Jr.** 1961. Tall timber tales. Singers and storytellers, ed. by Mody C. Boatright et al., 178-84. Texas Folklore Society Publication 30. Dallas: Southern Methodist University Press. P. 182, cites ten terms from E TX sawmill and logging industry.

**3.186 Gentry, Alice B.** 1952. [Folk expressions]. Arkansas Folklore 2.6. [Berryville, AR]. List of archaic forms and quaint sayings.

**3.187 Georgia colloquialisms.** 1940. Word Study 16.2.5. Report on Adiel Sherwood 1827 Gazetteer of the state of Georgia. Says many of terms in Sherwood's list (**2.390**) are still current in the state.

**3.188 [Gilbreth, Frank].** n.d. Lord Ashley Cooper's dictionary of Charlestonese. Charleston, SC: News and Courier. 10 pp. A popular glossary of the "perfect English" as spoken in the "Holy City."

**3.189 Gillet, Joseph E.** 1939. Lexicographical notes. AS 14.93-98. Note on lagniappe in New Orleans.

**3.190 Gilmer, Paul.** 1987. Inventiveness in college slang. Abstract in NADS 19.3.7. Discusses word-formation processes and sociolinguistic contexts for creation of new slang, based on five-year study at the University of Texas.

**3.191 Goerch, Carl.** 1943. Down home. Raleigh, NC: Edwards and Broughton. Odd words and expressions, 29-31. Origin of "tar heels," 97-100. [NC]. Glossary of twenty-nine terms characteristic of state and story of origin of tar heel, dating term to antebellum period.

**3.192 Goodspeed, John.** n.d. A fairly compleat lexicon of Baltimorese: compiled from "Mr. Peep's diary" in the Evening Sun. 2nd ed. Baltimore: Baltimore Sunpapers. 4 pp. [MD]. Short glossary of "the spoken dialect of dyed-in-the-row-house, usually native Baltimoreans"; most entries are only modified spellings to show local pronunciation.

**3.193 Green, Bennett Wood.** 1899. Word-book of Virginia folk-speech. Richmond. Revised ed. published by W. E. Jones' Sons, 1912. Reprinted in 1971 by Benjamin Blom, New York. 474 pp. Introductory sections: 5-12, notes on character, ancestry, and contributing streams to VA English; Some Virginia names spelt one way and pronounced another, 13-16; Some Virginia folk-sayings, 17-36; Word-book, 37-435.

**3.194 Gregg, Dorothy.** 1930. A linguistic study of G. W. Cable's novel The Grandissimes. Lawrence: University of Kansas thesis. Compiles more than thousand terms from novel for use by the DAE; gives special attention to French and Indian terms used by Cable.

**3.195 Griffin, Hazel.** 1967. Some folk expressions from northeastern North Carolina. North Carolina Folklore 15.56-57. Layman's collection of localisms, all well known.

**3.196 Grubb, Sam, Jr.** 1969. The opposite of white: a glossary of reference names for Negroes. Commerce: East Texas State University thesis. 130 pp. Glossary of 500 terms collected in four towns in NE TX.

**3.197 Gunn, Larry.** 1971. Some slang terms of the south Mississippi sawmill industry. MFR 5.84-86. Explains sawmill terms current in early 20th century.

**3.198 Guthrie, Charles S.** 1966. Corn: the mainstay of the Cumberland valley. KFR 13.87-91. Includes comments on localisms.

**3.199 Guthrie, Charles S.** 1968. Tobacco: cash crop of the Cumberland valley. KFR 14.38-43. Tobacco lexicon used in CENT KY.

**3.200 Hale, Morrie Smith.** 1931. The vocabulary of Negro high school pupils. Nashville: George Peabody College thesis. [102 B high school students, Tampa, FL]. Studies frequency of words in written vocabulary.

**3.201 Hall, Joan.** 1986. Black speech: lexical evidence from <u>DARE</u>. Language variety in the south: perspectives in black and white, ed. by Michael Montgomery and Guy Bailey, 319-32. University: University of Alabama Press. 7 maps. Outlines criteria used by DARE for considering words characteristic of black speech and discusses six terms and their variants that qualify for this label.

**3.202 Hall, Joseph S.** 1972. Sayings from old smoky. Asheville, NC: Cataloochee. 149 pp. [S Appalachia]. Comprehensive dictionary (pp. 36-144) based on personal interviews and observations, as well as on other printed sources. **Reviews:** L. Montell. 1972. KFR 18.87; C. Williams. 1973. AJ 1.61.

**3.203 Hall, Joseph S.** 1978. Glossary. Yarns and tales from the Great Smokies, 74-76. Asheville, NC: Cataloochee. [S Appalachia]. Fifty-four items. **Review:** K. B. Harder. 1980. TFSB 46.144-45.

**3.204 Halpert, Herbert.** 1951. The blue hen's chickens. AS 26.196-98. [TN, TX, W KY]. Reports phrase in folk speech as referring to unusually conceited person or unusually cold day. Cf. Dunlap (**2.128**).

**3.205 Harder, Kelsie B.** 1953. The mammary "weed." AS 28.236-37. [CENT TN]. An unrecorded meaning of <u>weed</u> denoting an inflamation in udder of animals.

**3.206 Harder, Kelsie B.** 1955. Musseling terms from Tennessee. AS 30.74-76. [CENT TN]. Discussion and brief glossary of terms in fresh-water clam industry on Tennessee River.

**3.207 Harder, Kelsie B.** 1955. A "tub" of corn. AS 30.76-77. [CENT TN]. Terms used for measuring and marketing corn.

**3.208 Harder, Kelsie B.** 1956. Home remedies in Perry County. TFSB 22.97-98. [CENT TN]. Seventeen names for diseases and cures.

**3.209 Harder, Kelsie B.** 1957. The baby's "dinnel." AS 32.158. [CENT TN]. An unrecorded term meaning "breast milk" and "to suckle" reported from Perry County, TN.

**3.210 Harder, Kelsie B.** 1957. Pert nigh almost: folk measurement. TFSB 23.6-12. [CENT TN]. Formations with -<u>ful</u>, <u>deep</u>, <u>high</u>, <u>thick</u>, and other measure terms in Perry County, TN.

**3.211 Harder, Kelsie B.** 1957. Weather expressions and beliefs in Perry County, Tennessee. TFSB 23.83-86. [CENT TN]. Terms for hot spells, cold spells, storms, and clouds.

**3.212 Harder, Kelsie B.** 1959. The vocabulary of hog-killing. TFSB

25.111-15. [CENT TN]. Ninety-five terms used in Perry County from 1930s to 1950s.

**3.213 Harder, Kelsie B.** 1961. The jake leg. TFSB 27.45-47. [CENT TN]. Term used in Perry and Gibson Counties, TN, meaning "a crippled leg."

**3.214 Harder, Kelsie B.** 1962. A vocabulary of wagon parts. TFSB 28.12-20. [CENT TN]. 138 terms from Perry County, TN.

**3.215 Harder, Kelsie B.** 1967. Hay-making terms in Perry County. TFSB 33.41-48. [CENT TN]. 125 terms used in Cedar Creek community, TN, from 1930s to 1950s.

**3.216 Harper, Francis.** 1941. The way we see it. North Georgia Review 6.129-30. Glossary of twenty-nine expressions mainly from S Appalachian area.

**3.217 Harper, Francis, and Delma E. Presley.** 1981. Swamp talk. Okefinokee Album, 135-45. Athens: University of Georgia Press. [SE GA]. Glossary of terms current in swamp area, culled from Harper's notebooks.

**3.218 Hatteras, Owen III [Raven I. McDavid, Jr.]** 1981. "Pinto" as "coffin." AS 56.308. Says model of Ford car would not have sold well in SC Sea Islands, given local meaning of term.

**3.219 Hayes, Francis C.** 1944. A word-list from North Carolina. PADS 2.32-37. [CENT NC]. Ninety-eight items, including two notes on pronunciation.

**3.220 Haynes, Randolph A., Jr.** 1954. A vocabulary study of Travis County, Texas. Austin: University of Texas thesis. 181 pp. [CENT TX, 10 speakers]. Analyzes heterogeneity of vocabulary in county, especially with reference to Spanish, Swedish, and German borrowings.

**3.221 Hazouri, Jeanette, Douglas Martin, and Arthur J. Palin.** 1952. The argot of soda jerks, car hops, and restaurant waiters in the vicinity of Gainesville, Florida. AS 27.231-33. [N FL]. Sixty-nine items for beverages and foods.

**3.222 Heald, Ann R. B.** 1979. A partial black word list from east Texas. Linguistics and literary studies in honor of Archibald A. Hill. Vol. IV: Linguistics and literature/sociolinguistics and applied linguistics, ed. by Mohammad Ali Jazayery et al., 259-63. The Hague: Mouton.

**3.223 Heap, Norman A.** 1959. A vocabulary of burley tobacco growing in Fayette County, Kentucky. Baton Rouge: Louisiana State University thesis. [N CENT KY]. Compiles list of 275 terms from burley tobacco growers in order to show usefulness of topical study of vocabulary of local occupation.

**3.224 Heap, Norman A.** 1966. A burley tobacco word list from Lexington, Kentucky. PADS 45.1-27. [N CENT KY]. Revision of preceding item.

**3.225 Hench, Atcheson L.** 1939. To come to fetch fire. JAF 53.123-24. Says the Chaucerian idiom, meaning "to come for a moment and then leave," is still used in VA and elsewhere in the South.

**3.226 Hench, Atcheson L.** 1941. The survival of "start-naked" in the South. Humanistic studies in honor of John Calvin Metcalf. University of Virginia Studies 1.48-64. Charlottesville, VA. Etymology and geographical range of term in South, with appendix of personal reports and testimonies of use.

**3.227 Hench, Atcheson L.** 1941. "To light a shuck" and "to come to fetch fire." AS 16.259. Cites examples of first phrase meaning "to clear out fast."

**3.228 Hench, Atcheson L.** 1944. Start-naked. AS 19.227. Cites two 1863 written uses of term.

**3.229 Hench, Atcheson L.** 1949. Swamp angel, 1947. AS 24.281. Says term means a worthless person and originally referred to Confederate deserter who lived in swamps of NC and VA.

**3.230 Hench, Atcheson L.** 1949. Mummly, mummly, buck!--a reply. AS 24.314. Says children's game exists in VA with name <u>bucketty buck</u>.

**3.231 Hench, Atcheson L.** 1951. "Arab"--a Baltimore word. AS 26.70-72. Says word refers to a street huckster.

**3.232 Hench, Atcheson L.** 1956. Baltimore's "Arab": a further note. AS 31.310-11. Discusses uses of the word as verb.

**3.233 Hicks, Joseph Leon.** 1940. Florida and Tennessee. AS 15.215-16. FL uses of terms cited by T. J. Farr from TN (**3.164**).

**3.234 Hicks, Michael.** 1982. Speaking southern. The South made simple, 12-13. Austin: Texas Monthly Press. Short notes on nine linguistic forms and practices in the South, such as <u>y'all</u>, <u>hisself</u>, and forms of address for one's parents.

**3.235 Higginbotham, W. R.** 1974. The real nitty gritty. AS 49.90-93. Discusses origin of Southern black phrase.

**3.236 Hines, Carole P., and David L. Shores.** 1984. The vocabulary of the watermen of the Chesapeake Bay. Abstract in NADS 16.3.4. [MD, VA]. Character, origins, geographical and social limits of, and variations in, working vocabulary of Chesapeake watermen.

**3.237 [Hinton, Elmer.]** 1961. Some more examples of Southern folk idiom. TFSB 27.35-36. Reprint of Nashville Tennessean column on vocabulary; contains little but citations.

**3.238 Hintze, S. J., and L. Oukada.** 1977. The lexical item "creole" in Louisiana. Journal of the Linguistic Association of the Southwest 2.143-61. Sketches semantic development of word in LA over four centuries and says term has clear denotation now only for scholars.

**3.239 Hirshberg, Jeffrey.** 1982. Towards a dictionary of black American English on historical principles. AS 57.163-82. Says that such a proposed dictionary must involve "systematic comparison of black speech and white over identical sociolinguistic domains" and presents forty-nine prototypical entries based on DARE data.

**3.240 Hogan, Charles H.** 1945. A Yankee comments on Texas speech. AS 20.81-84. Comments by native Missourian about characteristic TX usages after two-year residence in Lone Star state.

**3.241 Hogrefe, Pearl.** 1934. Notes from Louisiana. AS 9.79. Bumble-bee cotton, gumbo file, infare, might could, mirate, the missus, the mister, second-day dress, tignon, tom walker, until.

**3.242 Howard, Francesca S.** 1972. Terms from Ocean Springs seafood industry. MFR 6.139. [S MS]. List of twenty-one terms.

**3.243 Howard, Martha C.** 1981. Fifty years later and less: dialect loss in West Virginia. Abstract in NADS 13.3.7. Claims degree of lexical dialect loss in state since Woofter's study (3.554) can be correlated with degree of speakers' education and with educational level of school teachers in local area.

**3.244 Howell, Elmo.** 1967. William Faulkner's "Christmas gift." KFR 13.37-40. [MS]. Discusses uses of term in antebellum South and its symbolic nature in The Sound and the Fury.

**3.245 Howell, Ralph.** 1972. "Dominicker": a regional racial term. AS 47.305-06. [W FL]. Term refers to person of mixed ancestry.

**3.246 Hudson, Benjamin F.** 1963. Another view of "Uncle Tom." Phylon 24.79-87. Says term, as drawn on and used in Harriet Beecher Stowe novel, originally connoted goodness, compassion, and faith.

**3.247 Hughes, Herbert L.** 1951. A word-list from Louisiana. PADS 15.69-71. Thirty-seven items from N LA.

**3.248 Hughes, Herbert L., and W. Clayton Beeson.** 1936. Older English in Louisiana. AS 11.368-69. [Monroe, LA]. Twenty-six N LA expressions.

**3.249 Hunter, Edwin R.** 1943. Picturesque speech. TFSB 9.4.10. Three phrases, including Old Huldy meaning "sun."

**3.250 Hurlbut, Marilyn.** 1976. Folk synonyms from Argyle, Texas. AS 51.63-75. [17 speakers, ages 35-79, N CENT TX]. Comparison of selected terms used in Denton County, TX, with Atwood and Tarpley glossaries (**3.17, 3.465**) showing localisms are rapidly being replaced by general TX usage.

**3.251 Hurston, Zora Neale.** 1935. Mules and men. Philadelphia: Lippincott. Reprinted in 1963 by University of Illinois Press, Urbana. Pp. 253-56, glossary and discussion of speech acts woofing and testifying and nickname blue baby.

**3.252 Ivey-Dillard, Margie.** 1980. "Larrupin": from nautical word to multiregionalism. Perspectives on American English, ed. by J. L. Dillard, 131-33. The Hague: Mouton. Says term referring to sweetness of syrup is known throughout South, although it is viewed as localism everywhere.

**3.253 Jackson, Bruce,** collector and ed. 1972. Glossary. Wake up dead man: Afro-American worksongs from Texas prisons, 311-16. Cambridge: Harvard University Press.

**3.254 Jarnagan, Bert, and Fred Eikel, Jr.** 1948. North Texas Agricultural college slang. AS 23.248-50. [Arlington, TX]. Glossary of ninety-two terms used at the school, most of which are from the military.

**3.255 Jenson, Kathryn.** 1983. Sayin' the right thing and sayin' it right: talkin' redneck style. Redneckin': a hell-raisin', foot-stompin' guide to dancin', dippin' and doin' around in a GEN-U-WINE country way!, 19-39. New York: Putnam. Phrases handy as a pocket on a shirt, 19-33, miscellaneous phrases with comments on social uses; The tars on far burn mainly in the flars, 33-36, pronouncing glossary of 108 terms; For the first thing, there ain't no "g" in "fixin'", 37-38, eleven rules of pronunciation.

**3.256 Johnson, Kenneth.** 1972. The vocabulary of race. Rappin' and stylin' out: communication in urban black America, ed. by Thomas Kochman, 140-51. Urbana: University of Illinois Press. Discussion of peckerwood, honkey, cracker, etc.

**3.257 Jones, Phyllis R.** 1944. A glossary of the speech of Virginia north of the James river. Providence: Brown University thesis. [VA]. Takes 443 terms from eighteen VA records of LAMSAS and studies their regional spread in U.S. and in British Isles.

**3.258 Jordan, Terry G.** 1972. The origin of "motte" and "island" in Texas vegetational terminology. SFQ 36.121-35. As synonyms for "grove," motte probably came from Irish English, and island from Cajun French. **Revised**

as "The origin of <u>mott</u> in Anglo-Texan vegetational terminology" in J. L. Dillard 1980(**1.197**).163-73.

**3.259 Kaimen, Audrey A.** 1965. The Southern fiddling convention--a study: part I music and musicians. TFSB 31.7-16. [NC. VA]. Includes comments on vocabulary.

**3.260 Kay, Donald.** 1972. "Tea-hounds" in Carolina: British fops and American hair. [Anderson, SC]. AS 47.155-57. Says term originated in early 20th century to refer to bushy sideburns.

**3.261 Keller, Dean H.** 1963. Junesey. Word Study 39.1.7. Speculates that term, used in Chesnutt's <u>The Conjure Woman</u> and meaning "sweetheart," derives from French <u>jeunesse</u>.

**3.262 Kelly, Claire.** 1961. Comment on "Brief lexical notes." KFR 7.77-78. [KY]. Comments on eight items in Woodbridge's article (**3.551**, KFR 5.107-10 (1959).

**3.263 Kephart, Horace.** 1917. A word-list from the mountains of western North Carolina. DN 4.407-19. Extensive list, most items discussed in Kephart's <u>Our Southern Highlanders</u> (**1.357**).

**3.264 Killion, Ronald G., and Charles T. Waller.** 1983. Old time Negro expressions. A treasury of Georgia folklore, 159-61. Atlanta, GA: Cherokee. List of twenty GA phrases and idioms.

**3.265 King, Arthur T.** 1947. Oil refinery terms in Oklahoma. PADS 9.3-64. Extended glossary of terms from oil industry, including scattered entries from TX.

**3.266 King, Duane H., and Laura H. King.** 1976. Old words for new ideas: linguistic acculturation in modern Cherokee. Tennessee Anthropologist 1.58-62. Discusses borrowings of NC Cherokee from English and other languages.

**3.267 King, Viola.** 1974. Wha' hapnin'?: a dictionary of terms and expressions frequently occurring in the informal speech of young black adults in New Orleans. New Orleans, LA: privately printed. 17 pp. Glossary of expressions from Southern University students, compiled to "provide the teacher of black children a means of familiarizing herself with the language that she is obligated to understand if she wishes to teach them."

**3.268 Kniffen, Fred.** 1954. Geographic sayings from Louisiana. JAF 67.78. [S LA]. Explains four expressions that embody folk beliefs and are expressed in proverbial form.

**3.269 Kolin, Philip C.** 1980. "Blackneck." AS 55.294. [MS]. Says term refers to "a rural black Southerner whose desires and political views may be essentially the same as his white (redneck) counterpart."

**3.270 Krapp, George Philip.** 1926. Query no. 155. American Mercury 8.240. Speculates that coon, referring to a black person, derives from Spanish barracoon, "slave quarters."

**3.271 Krumpelmann, John T.** 1939. West Virginia peculiarities. AS 14.155-56. A dozen lexical items.

**3.272 Kuethe, J. Louis.** 1935. Runs, creeks, and branches in Maryland. AS 10.256-59. Says three terms tend to correspond with three regions of state--mountains, plateau, and coastal area.

**3.273 Kuethe, J. Louis.** 1937. Pocosin. MLN 52.210-11. [MD]. Term, referring to low, swampy ground, dates back to at least 1673.

**3.274 Kurath, Hans.** 1946. A glossary of Virginia words. PADS 5.3-6. Preface to Phyllis J. Nixon (**3.358**). Praises Nixon's work and calls for a Dictionary of Spoken American English.

**3.275 Kurath, Hans.** 1949. A word geography of the eastern United States. Ann Arbor: University of Michigan Press. xii + 252 pp. Based on LANE and LAMSAS, this atlas shows principally geographical distribution of traditional vocabulary from ME to SC on 163 maps and subdivides eastern states into eighteen primary dialect areas based on distinctive vocabulary patterns. First study of dialect geography of Atlantic states using Linguistic Atlas records; first conclusive demonstration of three principal Eastern dialect areas--Northern, Midland, and Southern--and their subareas. **Reprinted** in 1966. **Excerpted** in E. Kerr and R. Aderman 1971(**1.358**).182-90. **Reviews:** E. B. Atwood. 1950. Word 6.194-97; E. B. Atwood. 1950. Geographical Review 40.510-12; G. Bonfante. 1951. AA 53.103-05; A. L. Davis. 1950. JEGP 49.431-32; E. Dieth. 1953. English Studies 34.122-26; N. E. Eliason. 1951. MLN 66.487-89; H. M. Flasdieck. 1951. Anglia 70.335-36; L. Florez. 1952. Thesaurus 8.217-18; W. C. Greet. 1950. New York Times, p. 22 (Jan. 22); L. Grootaaers. 1954. Leuvense Bijdragen 44.17; S. B. Liljegren. 1952-53. Studia Neophilogica 25.193; R. I. McDavid, Jr. 1950. New York History 31.442-44; J. B. McMillan. 1951. Language 27.423-29; R. J. Menner. 1950. AS 25.122-26; F. Mosse. 1951. Bulletin de la Société Linguistique de Paris 46.154-55; V. Pisane. 1952. Paideia 7.317-18; C. E. Reed. 1951. MLQ 12.245-47; H. L. Smith, Jr. 1951. Studies in Linguistics 9.7-12; A. Sommerfelt. 1954. Norsk Tidsskrift for Sprogvidenskap 17.564-66; C. K. Thomas. 1950. QJS 36.262; J. N. Tidwell. 1954. JAF 67.222-23; H. Whitehall. 1950. Yale Review n.s. 39.556-58; R. M. Wilson. 1951. YWES 30.37.

**3.276 Kurath, Hans.** 1949. What do you call it? Michigan Alumnus Quarterly Review 55.293-99. 2 maps. Discusses patterns of folk vocabulary in

Eastern U.S., as revealed by Linguistic Atlas records, and says differences define regions corresponding to settlement history of the country. **Reprinted** in J. Williamson and V. Burke 1971(**1.823**).245-54.

**3.277 La Pin, Deirdre.** 1982. Johnson family words and expressions. Hogs in the bottom: family folklore in Arkansas, 107. Little Rock, AR: August House. Twelve AR terms, including family vocabulary.

**3.278 Laubscher, G. G.** 1916. Terms from Lynchburg, Virginia. DN 4.302. Fifteen items.

**3.279 Laughlin, Hugh C.** 1944. A word-list from Buncombe County, North Carolina. PADS 2.24-27. [W NC]. Glossary of items common to Buncombe Co., NC and Logan County, OH.

**3.280 Law, Robert Adger.** 1927. A note on four Negro words. Texas and southwestern lore, ed. by J. Frank Dobie, 119-20. Texas Folklore Society Publication 6. Dallas: Southern Methodist University Press. Comments on buckra, pinder, goober, and broadus.

**3.281 Lawson, Marvin.** 1977. Appendix: colloquial words, phrases and sayings. By gum, I made it!: life in the Ozark hills of Arkansas, 1900-1925, 115-26. Branson, MO: Ozarks Mountaineer. [NW AR]. List of expressions indigenous to area.

**3.282 Leas, Susan.** 1981. A preliminary survey of terms in the LAGS urban supplement. LAGS Working Papers, 1st series, no. 7. Microfilm 1186. Addendum to Pederson, et al. 1981(**1.594**). 72 pp. Compiles terms based on 111 interviews in urban areas.

**3.283 LeCompte, Nolan.** 1962. A word atlas of Terrebone Parish. Baton Rouge: Louisiana State University thesis. iv + 359 pp. [32 adults, SE LA]. Studies "number and distribution of synonymous terms" for 375 items and gauges "extent to which standard French and the local patois terms have become part of the natural English idiom of the area"; includes maps.

**3.284 LeCompte, Nolan.** 1967. A word atlas of Lafourche Parish and Grand Isle, Louisiana. Baton Rouge: Louisiana State University dissertation. Abstract in DAI 28.1808A. [21 speakers in two groups--older, less educated speakers and college students, SE LA]. Presents social and generational distribution of 305 items and details French influence on vocabulary.

**3.285 Ledford, Ted Roland.** 1975-76. Folk vocabulary of western North Carolina: some recent changes. AJ 3.277-84. [100 natives, ages 18-20, W NC]. Investigates extent to which folk vocabulary is still known in four areas of terminology: the house, the farm, common animals, and food; finds "a striking loss of some local terms."

**3.286 Little, Bert.** 1982. Prison lingo: a style of American English slang. AnL 24.206-44. Ethnographic study of social, psychological, and political functions of prison language at county farm in SE U.S.; includes glossary.

**3.287 [Long, Percy W.]** 1916. South Carolina. DN 4.344. Six Charleston items.

**3.288 [Long, Percy W.]** 1922. Negro lingo. DN 5.189. Cites fourteen words from Thomas W. Talley, Negro Folk Rhymes, Wise and Otherwise (New York, 1922).

**3.289 Long, Richard A.** 1959. "Man" and "evil" in American Negro speech. AS 34.305-06. Suggests black origin of two terms, man used only by men, especially by jazz musicians, evil meaning "unpleasant, disagreeable" in black community. Cf. A. F. Moe 3.343 for earlier citations of man.

**3.290 Louisiana Heritage Dictionary.** 1984. Gretna, LA: HER Publications. 64 pp.

**3.291 Lucke, Jessie Ryon.** 1960. A dozen with a black cat, a pair of hobos, and a fin. AS 35.237-38. [New Orleans, LA]. Argot of black truckers.

**3.292 Lumiansky, Robert M.** 1948. "Freezmobile." AS 23.158. Reports term from Pawleys Island, SC, for truck hauling cold drinks and frozen foods for sale.

**3.293 Lumpkin, Ben Gray.** 1962. Comments on "A lexical appendix." KFR 8.141-42. MS usage of terms reported by Woodbridge (3.553) from KY.

**3.294 Lyman, Dean B.** 1936. Idioms in West Virginia. AS 11.63. Six miscellaneous items.

**3.295 McAtee, W. L.** 1943. Samples of the speech of a few old timers. AS 18.237-38. Includes (from MS) entertain "gossip," jumped up "extemporized," make miration "admire," put your feet in the road, raise, rest.

**3.296 McAtee, W. L.** 1955. Names for sugar-cane beer. AS 30.158. Notes soocat and five other terms for beverage made from skimmings of sugar-cane juice as it is boiled into syrup.

**3.297 McCluskey, John.** 1982. Americanisms in the writings of Thomas Nelson Page. AS 57.44-47. Glossary of forty-two items unrecorded elsewhere and taken from novels and dialect tales of the VA writer.

**3.298 McCutchan, J. Wilson.** 1936. Virginia expressions. AS 11.372-73. Fairydiddle, shun, stile, reverent, scenery.

**3.299 McCutcheon, Mary Lou.** 1940. A lexicographical study of the north Florida vocabulary set forth in Marjorie Rawlings' The Yearling. Charlottesville: University of Virginia thesis. Compiles 500 words and meanings from the novel not found in five comprehensive dictionaries.

**3.300 McDaniel, Susan L[eas].** 1985. "Dry sitting." AS 60.95-96. [Haleyville, AL]. Reports custom of silent visit to newcomers to welcome them to community.

**3.301 McDavid, Raven I., Jr.** 1939. A Citadel glossary. AS 14.23-32. [Charleston, SC]. Extensive list of cadet vocabulary from Military College of South Carolina.

**3.302 McDavid, Raven I., Jr.** 1942. A new meaning for "heave." AS 17. 284. Cites use of term by Nashville Tennessean as transitive verb with animate object.

**3.303 McDavid, Raven I., Jr.** 1943. Provincial sayings and regional distributions. AS 18.66-68. Southern currency of items reported from IN.

**3.304 McDavid, Raven I., Jr.** 1943. Miscellaneous notes on recent articles. AS 18.152-53. [SC]. Light a rag, brass ankle, dead wagon.

**3.305 McDavid, Raven I., Jr.** 1949. Grist from the atlas mill. AS 24.105-14. Compilation of "interesting folk terms of very local distribution" in SC, GA, FL.

**3.306 McDavid, Raven I., Jr.** 1972. Carry you home once more. Studies presented to Tauno Mustanoja. Neuphilologisches Mitteilungen 12.192-95. 1 map. Says linguistic data show verb carry in sense of "to take" is current throughout Atlantic states, especially in New England.

**3.307 McDavid, Raven I., Jr., and Virginia G. McDavid.** 1969. The late unpleasantness: folk names for the Civil War. SSJ 34.194-204. Surveys terms for conflict in Eastern U.S., as recorded in Linguistic Atlas records, and discusses their regional and social distribution. **Reprinted** in R. McDavid 1979(**1.454**).309-14.

**3.308 McDavid, Raven I., Jr. and Virginia G. McDavid.** 1973. The folk vocabulary of eastern Kentucky. Lexicography and dialect geography: festgabe for Hans Kurath, ed. by Harald Scholler and John Reidy, 147-64. Wiesbaden: Franz Steiner Verlag. Same as ZDL heft 9. 13 maps. Analyzes distribution of Midland and Southern vocabulary in E KY, using data from LANCS records made in 1950s. **Reprinted** in R. McDavid 1980(**1.456**).92-113.

**3.309 McDonald, Richard R., and Walburga von Raffler-Engel.** 1975. A semantic analysis of some religious terms of a snake-handling sect in

Appalachia. Views on language, ed. by Reza Ordoubadian and Walburga von Raffler-Engel, 182-91. Murfreesboro: Middle Tennessee State University. Based on research in four pentecostal churches in TN, studies terminology used in the pentecostal experience called "anointing."

**3.310 McDonough, Nancy M.** 1975. Sayings. Garden sass: a catalog of Arkansas folkways, 253-63. New York: Coward, McCann and Geoghegan. [AR]. Anecdotes about local usages.

**3.311 McEwen, Ruth Estelle.** 1933. The vocabulary of William Byrd's A Journey to the Land of Eden. Charlottesville: University of Virginia thesis. xv + 135 pp. Comprehensive glossary of terms from book identified as Americanisms, coinages, obsolete terms, or British usages by reference to OED.

**3.312 McIver, Zadie Runkels.** 1939. Linguistic borrowings from the Spanish as reflected in writing of the Southwest. Austin: University of Texas thesis. v + 77 pp. [SW TX, NM]. 138 words from Bentley (**3.38**) and other writers, and forty-two colloquial expressions from folklore.

**3.313 McJimsey, George D.** 1940. Topographic terms in Virginia. AS reprints and monographs, no. 3. New York: Columbia University Press. Also in AS 15.1-38, 149-79, 262-300, 381-419 (1940). Bibliography, 413-19. New York: Columbia University dissertation. Extensive dictionary, with illustrative definitions and explanatory analysis, of topographic terms in state. **Review:** H. B. Woolf. 1941. Language 17.275-77.

**3.314 McMillan, James B.** 1986. Short end of the stick. AS 61.306. Traces origin of expression to logging industry.

**3.315 McMullen, Edwin Wallace.** 1953. English topographic terms in Florida 1563-1874. Gainesville: University of Florida Press. Abstract in DAI 10.204-05. New York: Columbia University dissertation, 1950. Bibliography, 223-27. Studies words applied to topographic features which exist in their natural state. Identifies parts of topographic vocabulary borrowed from Indian, French, Spanish sources and from British dialects, and classifies terms as Americanisms, Southernisms, or FL localisms. **Reviews:** M. M. Bryant. 1954. Names 1.142-43; F. G. Cassidy. 1954. Language 30.554-56; R. I. McDavid, Jr. 1955. AS 30.53-54; M. M. Mathews. 1955. AS 30.58-60.

**3.316 Major, Clarence.** 1970. Dictionary of Afro-American slang. New York: International. 127 pp. Extensive dictionary, including some "Southern Negro college slang" of 1940's; says black slang stems from "the rejection of the life-styles, social patterns, and thinking in general of the Euro-American sensibility." **Reviews:** R. Abrahams and J. Szwed. 1977. AA 77.329-35; A. L. Smith. 1971. QJS 57.231-32.

**3.317 Malin, H.** 1974. A questionnaire of lexical items used by New Orleans speakers. New Orleans: University of New Orleans thesis.

**3.318 Maloney, William E.** 1977. The Jimmy Carter dictionary: how to understand your president and learn to speak English. New York: Push Pin Press. 146 pp. Popular dictionary of seventy items in modified spelling with illustrative photographs.

**3.319 Man, A. P., Jr.** 1914. Virginia. DN 4.158-60. [CENT VA]. Seventy-three terms from Louisa County.

**3.320 Martin, Elizabeth K.** 1969. Lexicon of the Texas oilfields. Commerce: East Texas State University thesis.

**3.321 Martin, Elizabeth K.** 1971. Name patterns in Texas oil fields. Of Edsels and Marauders, ed. by Fred Tarpley and Ann Moseley, 13-18. Publication 1, South Central Names Institute. Commerce, TX: Names Institute Press. Metaphorical vocabulary in TX oil business.

**3.322 Mason, Julian.** 1960. The etymology of "buckaroo." AS 35.51-55. Proposes derivation of word from Gullah buckra.

**3.323 Mathews, Mitford M.** 1952. Of matters lexicographical. AS 27.199-203. Discusses July, Red Bone, Walker, potlicker, hush-puppy, and Trigg as names for breeds of hounds.

**3.324 Matthias, Virginia P.** 1946. Folk speech of Pine Mountain, Kentucky. AS 21.188-92. [SE KY]. Glossary, with explanatory notes, of twenty-seven terms observed in two summers in the KY mountains.

**3.325 Matthias, Virginia P.** 1952. A wordcatcher asks your help. Mountain Life and Work 28.3.23-24. Appeals for help in recording Southern Appalachian speech.

**3.326 Maurer, David W.** 1949. The argot of the moonshiner. AS 24.3-13. Glossary of hundred items, prefaced by comments on manufacture and prevalence of illegal whisky in KY.

**3.327 Maurer, David W.** 1974. Kentucky moonshine. Lexington: University Press of Kentucky. The argot of the craft, 105-11; Glossary, 113-27. **Reviews:** Anonymous. 1975. JSH 41.284-85; C. S. Guthrie. 1975. KFR 21.2.63-64; L. Pederson. 1979. AS 54.52-55.

**3.328 Maurer, David W.** 1981. Language in the underworld. Lexington: University Press of Kentucky. 417 pp. Includes scattered Southern material, including chapter on KY moonshiner argot (pp. 370-80) revised and expanded from Maurer 3.327. **Reviews:** A. Burgess. 1982. Times Literary Supplement, p. 74 (Jan. 22); J. R. Gaskin. 1984. Sewanee Review

92.114-21; J. Hall. 1983. SAQ 82.341-42; K. B. Harder. 1982. AS 58.288; R. I. McDavid, Jr. 1983. American Studies 24.115; J. B. McMillan. 1982. SECOL Review 6.138-39; W. K. McNeil. 1982. Mid-America Folklore 10; G. Nunberg. 1982. NYTBR, May 2, p. 9; L. Pederson. 1983. MP 81.105-07; M. Salovesh. 1982. AA 84.456-57; L. E. Seits. 1983. Names 31.211-13.

**3.329 Mead, Leon.** 1902. Provincialisms and Americanese. Word-coinage, 192-210. New York: Crowell. Potpourri of terms used in Eastern states, many of them current in the South.

**3.330 Meredith, Mamie J.** 1954. "Twinkley twinkle" or "on the dab." AS 29.232. Expressions for ways to serve fritters recorded in Jackson, TN, during Civil War period.

**3.331 Meredith, Mamie J.** 1955. "Poorboy," a verb used in the Texas oil fields. AS 30.71. In addition to its use as a noun and an adjective, the word is used as verb meaning "to beg or steal."

**3.332 Meyer, Peggy L.** 1976. Slang in the hallowed halls of learning: a sociolinguistic analysis. ED 142 081. 52 pp. Preliminary survey of problems in collection and sociological analysis of student slang at the University of Virginia.

**3.333 Meyers, Walter E.** 1975. "Cute": an underground meaning. AS 50.135-37. Says term in sense of "bow-legged" has been spread widely through linguistic folklore of children but has been ignored by dictionaries.

**3.334 Miles, Kay W.** n.d. The Ozark dictionary: "how to talk right around hyar." Clinton, MO: The Printery. 15 pp. Glossary of 138 terms in modified spelling, with citations.

**3.335 Miller, Jim Wayne.** 1969. The vocabulary and methods of raising burley tobacco in western North Carolina. North Carolina Folklore 17.1.27-38. Explains terminology used in production and marketing of tobacco.

**3.336 Miller, Jim Wayne.** 1979. An interview with Jim Wayne Miller. AJ 6.207-25. [S Appalachia]. P. 214, discusses treatment of taboo word bull and explains substitutes for it.

**3.337 Miller, Melba Lou.** 1935. The vocabulary of the rice industry of Louisiana. Baton Rouge: Louisiana State University thesis. [SW LA]. Dictionary of 159 terms from rice industry of state, with transcriptions of phonetic variants, including Cajun French and black pronunciations.

**3.338 Miller, Michael I.** 1983. Editing Green's word-book. Papers of the Dictionary Society of North America, ed. by Yeatman Anderson III, 77-87. Terre Haute: Indiana State University. Abstract in NADS 13.2.4. Reports on proposed editing of Green's massive wordbook (**3.193**) using LAUSC and

DARE data and listing words that characterize VA dialect areas.

**3.339 Miller, Michael I.** 1986. Virginia words: historical and geographical perspectives. Proceedings of the Third April Conference of University Teachers of English, Cracow 1984, ed. by Teresa Baluk-Ulewiczowa and Maria Korosadowicz, 11-21. Krakow, Poland: Jagiellonskiego University. 3 maps. Surveys known facts about origins, development, and spread of VA vocabulary, principally from work of linguistic geographers, and makes suggestions for future research.

**3.340 Mitchell, Steve.** 1976. How to speak Southern. New York: Bantam. 64 pp. Popular dictionary, with cartoons.

**3.341 Mitchell, Steve.** 1980. More how to speak Southern. New York: Bantam. 64 pp. Popular dictionary sequel to preceding item, with cartoons.

**3.342 Mockler, William E.** 1940. Localisms. AS 15.83. Nine miscellaneous items from mountains of WV and PA.

**3.343 Moe, Albert F.** 1961. "Man" as a form of direct address. AS 36.136-37. Notes use predating jazz era and going back in U.S. as far as 1822; cf. R. A. Long (**3.289**).

**3.344 Monaghan, Jay.** 1957. Civil war slang and humor. Civil War History 3.2.125-33. Expressions primarily from Union soldiers but some items used by Confederates.

**3.345 Montell, William Lynwood.** 1975. Glossary. Ghosts along the Cumberland: death lore in the Kentucky foothills, 217-20. Knoxville: University of Tennessee Press. [S CENT KY]. Forty-six items.

**3.346 Montell, William Lynwood.** 1983. Glossary. Don't go up Kettle Creek: verbal legacy in the upper Cumberlands, 197-201. Knoxville: University of Tennessee Press. [S CENT KY]. **Reviews:** R. E. Corlew. 1984. JSH 50.143-44; G. B. McKinney. 1984. AJ 11.255-59; J. H. Speer. 1984. JAF 97.480-81.

**3.347 Moon, Jake.** 1976. Dixie-doodle dictionary: how to understand a southerner: a handy, disorganized guide, an unscholarly lingual tour, a deep-south smorgasbord, mush-mouf McGee from a-z. New York: Two Continents. 112 pp. Popular, fanciful dictionary of Southern speech with pronunciation of each item in informal transcription.

**3.348 Moore, Arthur K.** 1941. "Jouk." AS 16.319-20. Agrees with Scottish etymology of word in <u>Webster's New International Dictionary, Second Edition</u> and speculates about possible Latin etymology; cites examples of word as noun and verb collected by Alan Lomax from throughout South, especially from blacks in FL.

**3.349 Moore, Arthur K.** 1947. Southern dialect notes. AS 22.73-74. Notes drunk potatoes and staggle in S GA and cooning (for fish) in KY.

**3.350 Morris, Robert L.** 1948. More Ozark speech. AS 23.304-05. [Fayetteville, AR]. Oddities from student writing and from local speech.

**3.351 Mountain English: collection of mountain expressions reproduced for your enlightenment.** n.d. Asheville, NC: Tarmac Audio Visual Company. 10 pp. Popular glossary of mountain terms in modified spelling with definitions; most items identical to Weals (**3.498**).

**3.352 Mull, J. Alexander, and Gordon Boger.** 1983. Sayin's and meanin's. Recollections of the Catawba Valley, 63-64. Boone, NC: Appalachian Consortium. Thirty-seven NC terms that author says are misunderstood in the North.

**3.353 Nashvillese.** 1986. The Tennessee sampler, ed. by Peter Jenkins et al., 272. Nashville: Thomas Nelson. [Nashville, TN]. Twenty-four terms and their "translations."

**3.354 Neal, Marvin H.** 1957. The word-book of a backwoodsman. Ceres, VA: Backwoods Press. xi + 49 pp.

**3.355 Neitzel, Stuart.** 1936. Tennessee expressions. AS 11.373. Notes "Shakespearean phrases" poke, proud, admire, stob, as well as novel expressions in Cumberland Valley.

**3.356 Newburger, Gabriel F.** 1938. Glossary. Ozark anthology, 181-85. Cedar Rapids, IA: Torch Press. Glossary of terms from Ozarks in modified spelling to show pronunciation to reader, who should "bear in mind that embodied in this idiom is all that is still extant of pre-Elizabethan English as spoken by the first settlers in America."

**3.357 Newton, Mary C.** 1958. A comparative study of the dialect vocabulary of East Tennessee and Western North Carolina using selected words: a report of a special study. Maryville, TN: Maryville College. [99 speakers, most natives, E TN, W NC]. Based on local questionnaires and on data from Linguistic Atlas, finds predominant Midland usage but that education had little correlation with use and recognition of vocabulary; also finds some differences between NC and TN.

**3.358 Nixon, Phyllis J.** 1946. A glossary of Virginia words. PADS 5.3-43. Preface by Hans Kurath. Based on 138 VA LAMSAS field records; notes geographical and social distribution of terms; gives thorough picture of VA usage and greatly supplements Green (**3.193**). **Reviews:** R. I. McDavid, Jr. 1947. Studies in Linguistics 5.21-24; B. J. Whiting. 1946. PADS 6.44-46. Comments and additions by T. A. Kirby, W. L. McAtee, W. M. Miller, R. V. Mills, F. W. Palmer, and H. H. Petit. 1947. PADS 8.11-38.

**3.359 Norman, Arthur M. Z.** 1952. Food names from Austin, Texas. AS 27.155. Chuckburger, someburger, cheesedog, bubble, and squeak.

**3.360 Norman, Arthur M. Z.** 1956. Migration to southeast Texas: people and words. Southwestern Social Science Quarterly 37.149-58. [12 natives, 10 W, 2 B, of SE TX]. Analyzes sources of E TX dialect vocabulary in other regional dialects of American English and concludes that it "is made up of about five parts Southern terms, two parts Midland expressions, and one part Northern words." Based on 1.544.

**3.361 North Carolina Department of Commerce.** n.d. A dictionary of the queen's English. Raleigh, NC. 24 pp. [NC]. Booklet for tourists with three short glossaries stressing archaic expressions still heard in state, where English spoken is "not prose but metaphor."

**3.362 Nye, Hermes.** 1961. Folksay of lawyers. Singers and story tellers, ed. by Mody C. Boatright et al., 92-97. Dallas: Southern Methodist University Press. Idioms and figures of speech used by Southwestern lawyers.

**3.363 O'Cain, Raymond K., and John B. Hopkins.** 1977. The southern mountain vocabulary in the low country of South Carolina and Georgia. An Appalachian symposium: essays written in honor of Cratis D. Williams, 215-23. Boone: Appalachian State University. Detailed study of "the geographical distribution of the ten vocabulary items that were . . . most frequently cited in early word lists of mountain speech" and speculates whether their occurrence in the low country is due to common sources in England or to diffusion in colonial times.

**3.364 Oliver, George J.** 1980. Language variation in New Orleans: the semantics of naming housetypes. Baton Rouge: Louisiana State University thesis. [20 informants, photographic questionnaire]. Study of lexical variation that finds "at least 14 housetype lexemes, and at least 5 porchtype lexemes are necessary to account for all the responses given by all 20 informants to all the photos."

**3.365 Oliver, George, and Frank Parker.** 1981. A semantic analysis of terms for New Orleans housetypes. Abstract in NADS 13.3.10-11. [20 natives of New Orleans, LA]. Reports results of photoquestionnaire of terms for fourteen housetypes and presents general argument for usefulness of photoquestionnaire for terms for household objects.

**3.366 Olmstead, George C.** 1934. Testimonies. AS 9.236. Reports goober grabber in Chattanooga for "an Alabamian" and hairydick, "maverick," and Indian River chicken, "mullet," in FL.

**3.367 O'Quinn, Trueman E.** 1937. Colloquialisms along the Sabine. Texas Folklore Society Publication 13.245-49. [W LA, E TX]. Forty-one terms from Sabine River country.

**3.368 Orrick, Allan H.** 1955. Gritted and gritter. PADS 23.49-50. Says Ozark dialect word <u>gritted</u>, reported by Randolph and Wilson (**1.630**) is derived from verb <u>to grit</u> rather than from <u>grated</u>.

**3.369 Outer banks dialect.** 1974. North Carolina English Teacher 36.2.9. [E NC]. Four terms: <u>mommick</u>, <u>winter lights</u>, <u>snuff coffee</u>, and <u>coolin'</u> <u>board</u>.

**3.370 Owens, Bess Alice.** 1931. Folk speech of the Cumberland. AS 7.89-95. [Pikeville, KY]. 116 terms that have "a Shakespeare flavor" collected in E KY around 1930.

**3.371 Parler, Mary Celestia.** 1930. Word-list from Wedgefield, South Carolina. DN 6.79-85. Identifies geographical and social distribution of items.

**3.372 Parler, Mary Celestia.** 1945. "Lay-by time" and "protracted meetings." AS 20.306-07. [SC Low Country]. Terms refer to time in late summer between cotton cultivation and harvesting devoted to relaxation and religious revivals.

**3.373 Pederson, Lee A.** 1975. Sourmilk. AS 50.49. [TN]. Reports term for clabber having primary-secondary stress pattern.

**3.374 Pederson, Lee A.** 1976. A datum for "podunk." AS 51.108. [Houston, TX]. Cites term <u>poor dunks</u> referring to prejudiced, close-minded people.

**3.375 Pederson, Lee A.** 1976. American "rap": three more times. AS 51.279-81. [Wilkinson Co., MS]. Cites term as meaning "to accompany musically."

**3.376 Pederson, Lee A.** 1977. The dugout dairy. TFSB 43.88-89. [E TN]. Notes several senses of word <u>dairy</u>, including reference to room in dugout area.
**3.377 Pederson, Lee A.** 1978. Right on. AS 53.80. [Clanton, AL]. Says adverb has "radical . . . durative" sense in South.

**3.378 Pederson, Lee A.** 1978. Flying jenny. AS 53.198. [Mena, AR]. Suggests etymology for term, with <u>jenny</u> referring to a mule.

**3.379 Pederson, Lee A.** 1980. Calvary camels and the knockaway tree. AS 55.158-59. [Victoria, TX]. Two folk etymologies.

**3.380 Pederson, Lee A.** 1980. Lexical data from the gulf states. AS 55.195-203. Describes three aspects of LAGS: regional word geography, urban geography, and inventorial research, and their implications for future research; lists collection of 222 terms referring to ethnic groups in South.

**3.381 Pederson, Lee A.** 1981. Hey, Lucy. AS 56.63. [Jacksboro, TN]. Points out difficulty of ordering senses in LAGS legendry, dictionary component of the atlas.

**3.382 Pederson, Lee A.** 1981. E-80 "Negro": argot from the game of life. AS 56.78. [Birmingham, AL]. Cites expression as euphemism in insurance business for black person.

**3.383 Pendleton, Paul E.** 1930. How the "wood hicks" speak. DN 6.86-89. Words and phrases from Buckhannon, WV.

**3.384 Pennington, Eunice.** 1978. Ozark folkways. Piedmont, MO: Piedmont Printers. 56 pp. Folkwords: glossary of Ozark terms and expressions, 51.

**3.385 Petit, Herbert H.** 1947. Terms in a word-list from Virginia and North Carolina (PADS 6) common in the Blue Grass region of Kentucky. PADS 8.21-23. Confirmation of Woodard's (3.539) findings by KY native.

**3.386 Pierce, Marvin.** 1959. Slang at the University of Virginia. Abstract in SAB 24.3.4. Reports slang vocabulary at University of Virginia consists of 150 items and cites their principal characteristics.

**3.387 Pollard, Mary O.** 1915. Terms from the Tennessee mountains. DN 4.242-43. Twenty-four items from Gatlinburg; brief note on phonological and grammatical tendencies.

**3.388 Poston, Lawrence.** 1964. Some problems in the study of campus slang. AS 39.114-23. Compares University of Florida slang (from Boone, 3.42) with slang at U.S. schools elsewhere.

**3.389 Powers, Nick, and Wilann Powers.** 1975. Speakin suthern like it should be spoke: a dixie dictionary. Lindale, GA: Country Originals. 44 pp. Popular dictionary of Southern speech.

**3.390 Prescott, R. T.** 1938. Calls to animals. SFQ 2.39-42. Calls for hogs, cows, sheep, chickens, and dogs in Midwest and South.

**3.391 Preston, Dennis R.** 1969. Bituminous coal mining vocabulary of the eastern United States: a pilot study in the collecting of geographically distributed occupational vocabulary. Madison: University of Wisconsin dissertation. Abstract in DAI 39.3929-30A. Reprinted in 1973 as Bituminous coal mining vocabulary of the eastern United States. PADS 59. 128 pp. Lexicon of 489 terms used by bituminous coal miners in ten states in Midland and Midwest regions. Finds northern coal-mining areas preserve more British terms while southern areas have more native American ones. Review: K. Hameyer. 1980. ZDL 47.108-11.

**3.392 Preston, Elaine Lucile.** 1969. Lexical variations in the speech of Mid-South Carolina. Columbia: University of South Carolina thesis. [21 W, 14 B adult natives from 7 counties, CENT SC]. Uses 143-item survey based on Linguistic Atlas worksheets; finds age, sex, and county of residence correlate less with lexical variation than race, level of education, and urbanness.

**3.393 Pritchard, Constance J.** 1978. Flinging slang: women's prison language. Columbia: University of South Carolina thesis. [Columbia, SC]. Analyzes function and formation of language of minimum-security women's prison and how this language depicts social structure of community, including its subcultures, and reveals its speakers' values.

**3.394 Pritchard, Constance J.** 1978. Getting acclimated: language in a women's prison. ED 157 398. 13 pp. [Columbia, SC]. Describes prison language, primarily the lexicon, in women's correctional institution, and discusses how this language reflects social structure and values of prison.

**3.395 R., F.** 1933. Coonjining. AS 8.1.77-78. Word for old-fashioned gait or shuffle, reported from lower Mississippi River.

**3.396 Ragaway, Martin A.** 1977. We don't tawuk funny . . . yew all lissen funny!: how to really understand the South. Beverly Hills, CA: Laughter Library. 48 pp. Glossary of 134 terms compiled for amusement, with appendices "Southern Descriptions," "Southern Expressions," and "Southern Similes."

**3.397 Raine, James Watt.** 1924. The speech of the land of saddle-bags. QJS 10.230-37. Reports KY localisms and calls for more respect for area's speech, which "is more closely akin to Elizabethan English than any other dialect spoken today."

**3.398 Randolph, Vance.** 1926. A word-list from the Ozarks. DN 5.397-405. [NW AR, SW MO]. Compiled as supplement to Jay Taylor 1923 (**3.466**); list of nearly 1,000 items.

**3.399 Randolph, Vance.** 1927. More words from the Ozarks. DN 5.472-79. [NW AR, SW MO]. Glossary of more than 200 terms.

**3.400 Randolph, Vance.** 1928. Literary words in the Ozarks. AS 4.56-57. Says archaisms in Ozark speech are preserved only in literary usage elsewhere. **Reprinted** in M. Williams, ed. 1981. Ozark, Ozark: a hillside reader, 41-43. Columbia: University of Missouri Press.

**3.401 Randolph, Vance.** 1928. A possible source of some Ozark neologisms. AS 4.116-17. Says that it "seems quite probable that a number of otherwise inexplicable words and phrases, particularly those confined to very restricted areas, owe their existence to the hillman's tendency to imitate the speech of his feeble-minded [mentally defective] fellows."

**3.402 Randolph, Vance.** 1929. A third Ozark word-list. AS 5.16-21. [NW AR, SW MO]. List of a hundred items.

**3.403 Randolph, Vance.** 1933. A fourth Ozark word-list. AS 8.1.47-53. [Benton, Washington, Carroll, and Boone Counties, AR, SW MO]. Adds items to preceding lists.

**3.404 Randolph, Vance, and Nancy Clemens.** 1936. A fifth Ozark word list. AS 11.314-18. [NW AR, SW MO]. Glossary of a hundred items. See N. Wilt (**3.526**), for disagreements.

**3.405 Randolph, Vance, and Patti Sankee.** 1930. Dialectical survivals in the Ozarks, III archaic vocabulary. AS 5.424-30. Discusses analogues of unusual Ozark usages in writing of Shakespeare, Chaucer, and other British writers.

**3.406 [Rayburn, Otto Ernest].** 1943. "Bustle-fight." Rayburn's Ozark Guide 1.3.15. Term refers to street boxing with bustles rather than gloves.

**3.407 [Rayburn, Otto Ernest].** 1943. Christmas in the Ozarks. Rayburn's Ozark Guide 1.3.15. Origin and currency of term "Old Christmas."

**3.408 [Rayburn, Otto Ernest].** 1954. "I'm from Missouri." Rayburn's Ozark Guide 12.40.25. Recounts story explaining origin of phrase.

**3.409 [Rayburn, Otto Ernest].** 1960. Hillfolks vocabulary. Rayburn's Ozark Guide 18.66.21. Cites list of expressive local terms and claims they are gaining popularity elsewhere in country.

**3.410 Rayburn, Otto Ernest.** 1966. Old Ozark customs. Rayburn's Ozark Yearbook 1966. Reed Springs, MO. Same as Rayburn's Ozark Guide 18.63.9-10. Discussion of old-fashioned expressions like cobbing and slicking.

**3.411 Read, William A.** 1926. Creole and "Cajun." AS 1.483. Notes different senses of creole and says that Louisianans are divided over its application to Cajuns.

**3.412 Reagan, Patty S.** 1979. A word atlas of Central Texas. Commerce: East Texas State University dissertation. Abstract in DAI 40.5841-42A. [200 speakers in 12 counties]. Surveys folk expressions for 129 concepts; finds age is "the most significant variable in the study" and sex, education, urbanness, and national origin also correlate with terms; includes maps.

**3.413 Reid, William W.** 1969. The agricultural idiom of the North Carolina coastal plain. North Carolina Folklore 17.1.9-11. [E NC]. Notes how expressions and old-fashioned agricultural practices have acquired new local meanings.

**3.414 Reinecke, George F.** 1970. Mardi gras, chooka lapai, a probable meaning. Louisiana Folklore Miscellany 3.77-79. [New Orleans, LA]. Proposes that <u>chooka lapai</u> derives from a Choctaw expression meaning "a vagrant."

**3.415 Reinecke, John A.** 1965. The language of marbles games in New Orleans. Louisiana Folklore Miscellany 2.2.107-09. Discusses pre-1940 marbles terms whose meanings have undergone little change, although the game has diminished in popularity.

**3.416 Reynolds, Ollye.** 1982. A bluegrassspeak primer [or] how to tawk kin-tuckee: a beginner's glossary, for visitors to the commonwealth. Kentucky Monthly (Apr.), p. 43. Glossary of thirty-three "words and phrases peculiar to Kentuckians."

**3.417 Riedel, E.** 1916. New Orleans word-list. DN 4.268-70. Items used by non-French, white population.

**3.418 Ringe, Donald A.** 1959. "Pike": to be nosy, to pry. AS 34.306-07. Reports the verb in New Orleans.

**3.419 Roach, Polly S.** 1975. A lexical study of the speech of Lauderdale County, Alabama. Tuscaloosa: Unversity of Alabama thesis. [9 W adults, interviews based on 342 items from LAGS worksheets, NW AL]. Study finds that older, more poorly educated speakers use more Southern forms and that younger, better educated speakers use more Midland and Northern forms.

**3.420 Roberts, Hermese E.** 1971. The third ear: a black glossary. Chicago: English-Language Institute of America. 14 pp. Lexicon of contemporary black slang.

**3.421 Roberts, Leonard.** 1962. Additional notes on Archer Taylor's <u>On Troublesome Creek</u>. KFR 8.142-44. [KY]. Explains six terms cited by Woodbridge (**3.553**) that come from James Still's fiction, including <u>bunty bird</u> and <u>corn capping</u>.

**3.422 Robinson, Roy.** 1984. Inquiry: "we'll see you later." AS 59.69. [GA]. Speculates that expression <u>We'll see you later</u>, used by single, unaccompanied person, is related to Southern <u>you all</u>; calls usage the "Protective Plural."

**3.423 Routh, James.** 1916. Louisiana. DN 4.346-47. Twenty-four local expressions, most from New Orleans.

**3.424 Routh, James.** 1917. Terms from New Orleans. DN 4.420-21. Twenty-one items.

**3.425 Routh, James.** 1923. Louisiana gleaning. DN 5.243-44. Sixty-nine items, including some from GA and NC.

**3.426 Rushing, Nellie Georgia.** 1929. A word study of Mary Noailles Murfree's stories of the Tennessee mountains. Chicago: University of Chicago thesis. Analyzes and compiles regional vocabulary from seven of Murfree's novels.

**3.427 Ryder, Tex S.** 1982. Cowboy/English, English/cowboy dictionary. New York: Ballantine. 81 pp. Popular dictionary of words in Southwestern speech in modified spelling; appendix with ninety-five connotations of shee-ut.

**3.428 Saxon, Lyle, Edward Dreyer, and Robert Tallant,** compilers. 1945. Glossary. Gumbo ya-ya, 559-68. Boston: Houghton Mifflin. Potpourri of folk terms from LA, including items from hunting, fishing, and farming, similes, adages, creole, Cajun, Gumbo, and black expressions. **Reviews:** D. L. Cohn. 1945. Saturday Review of Literature 28.11 (Dec. 22); E. Welty. 1946. New York Times, p. 5 (Jan. 20).

**3.429 Schneidemesser, Luanne von.** 1980. "Purse" and its synonyms. AS 55.74-76. Discusses regional distribution of billfold, wallet, change purse, and coin purse throughout country.

**3.430 Schneider, Edgar W.** 1987. Dialect analysis and automatic cartography by means of a microcomputer. Literary and Linguistic Computing 2.2.80-85. 4 maps. Exemplifies how typical lexical responses from LAGS informants in AL and GA can be mapped by microcomputer.

**3.431 Schulman, Steven A.** 1973. Logging terms from the upper Cumberland river. TFSB 39.35-36. [W KY]. Twenty-seven terms from the logging industry.

**3.432 Seymour, Richard K.** 1969. Collegiate slang. PADS 51.13-22. Examples of word formation and semantic change compiled at Duke University in 1964-67.

**3.433 Shearin, Hubert G.** 1911. An eastern Kentucky dialect word-list. DN 3.537-40. 150 items, many in modified phonetic transcription.

**3.434 Sherry, Denver William.** 1970. A dialect study of Caroline Miller's Lamb in His Bosom. Gainesville: University of Florida thesis. 122 pp. Identifies dialect nouns, verbs, and other types of vocabulary used by Pulitzer Prize-winning GA novelist.

**3.435 Shott, Hugh Ike, II.** 1951. A lexical study of the vocabulary of Alberta Pierson Hannum's regional novel Thursday April. Charlottesville: University of Virginia thesis. Identifies dialect expressions and unusual words used by W NC novelist and crossreferences them to eight dictionaries.

**3.436 Shulman, David.** 1937. Words from the southern Negro. AS 12.243. Requests information on copesetic and cuffy.

**3.437 Simpkins, Karen L.** 1969, Terminology used in selected local settings. Chapel Hill: University of North Carolina thesis. 39 pp. [Chapel Hill, NC]. Study of terms of reference and address for different social and ethnic groups based on research in laundromat and other locales; finds "terms increased in number as a relationship was more personal and informal."

**3.438 Simpson, William F.** 1959. Tobacco words. KFR 5.136,148. [Shelby Co., KY]. Twenty-one items.

**3.439 Skillman, Billy G.** 1966. A Cleburne County, Arkansas, word list. PADS 46.24-30. [N CENT AR]. Glossary of localisms and "sayings" collected in 1952.

**3.440 Smith, C. Alphonso.** 1916. North Carolina. DN 4.343-44. Eight Chapel Hill student terms.

**3.441 Smith, Fabia R., and Charles Rayford.** 1976. Southern words and sayings. Jackson, MS: Office Supply Company. 28 pp. Popular lexicon of words, weather expressions, names for food, sayings, and figures of speech.

**3.442 Smith, Gerald J.** 1981. Response. AS 56.160. [GA]. Note on the infix by God.

**3.443 Smith, Harley, and Hosea Phillips.** 1939. The influence of English on Louisiana "Cajun" French in Evangeline Parish. AS 14.198-201. Glossaries of English words borrowed into LA French, most maintaining English pronunciation, and of French words taking on meanings of corresponding English words.

**3.444 South Carolina.** 1916. DN 4.344. Six vocabulary items from Charleston.

**3.445 Sparkman, Evelyn P.** 1940. A study of high school slang in Jonesboro, Arkansas. Nashville: George Peabody College thesis. [NE AR]. 117 pp. Based on surveys in 1930 and 1940, presents 765 expressions for nicknames, emotions, food and drink, drunkenness, money, disapproval, and other domains.

**3.446 Spears, James E.** 1970. Some Negro folk pregnancy euphemisms and birth superstitions. MFR 4.24-27. Shows how expressions for pregnancy and birth reflect folk beliefs.

**3.447 Spears, James E.** 1972. Southern folk by-words, intensifiers, and reinforcement phrases. MFR 6.115-17. Lists and comments on eighty-nine euphemistic expletives.

**3.448 Spears, James.** 1986. A note on folk medical terms. TFSB 52.11-13. Cites folk etymology, redundancy, and other popular medical usages.

**3.449 Starr, Fred.** 1938. From an Ozark hillside. Siloam Springs, AR: Bar-D-Press. Pp. 35-39, Ozark hillbilly lingo.

**3.450 Starr, Fred.** 1968. Deep hollows, and tall tales of the Ozarks. Fayetteville, AR: Southwest Printing. 24 pp. Popular lexicon of Ozark dialect.

**3.451 Steadman, John M., Jr.** 1918. A North Carolina word list. DN 5.18-21. Words and phrases reported by students at Chapel Hill.

**3.452 Steele, Pauline Davis.** 1976. Hill country sayin's and Ozark folklore. West Fork, AR: Hutcheson Press. 40 pp. Popular compendium of folk speech, sayings, place-names, tales, jokes, songs, and other items.

**3.453 Steele, Pauline Davis.** 1977. Hill country sayin's and Ozark folklore: book two. West Fork, AR: Hutcheson Press. 41 pp. Popular compendium of over 200 items of folk speech and sayings.

**3.454 Stern, Henry R.** 1980. Carolina "fish camps." AS 55.80. Cites term as referring to restaurants specializing in fish dishes in Carolinas and speculates on development of this sense of term.

**3.455 Strainchamps, Ethel Reed.** 1958. Language note. Ozarks Mountaineer 7.3.2. Discusses rock, stone, and dornick.

**3.456 St. Martin, Thad.** 1937. Cajuns. Yale Review, n.s. 26.859-62. [LA]. Letter with incidental comments on language.

**3.457 "Swamp angel" again.** 1951. AS 26.301. Supplementary note to Hench (**3.229**) noting citation from Mamie Meredith indicating that the term referred to a regular soldier, not a deserter, or to a Parrott gun.

**3.458 Tackett, Santa.** 1930. Words, words, words which show homely philosophy, keen wit, utter absurdity, or no sense at all. Some Mississippi Negro oddities, 38-52. Nashville: George Peabody College thesis. Compendium of malapropisms.

**3.459 Tallichet, H.** 1892. A contribution towards a vocabulary of Spanish and Mexican words used in Texas. DN 1.185-95. Supplementary notes by E. S. Sheldon and G. Hempl, 195-96. Glossary of 160 terms, nearly all collected by author personally.

**3.460 Tallichet, H.** 1893. Addenda to the vocabulary of Spanish and Mexican words used in Texas. DN 1.243-53. Glossary of 200 additional items.

**3.461 Tallichet, H.** 1894. A vocabulary of Spanish and Mexican words used in Texas--additions and corrections. DN 1.324-26. Forty-three items adding or correcting information in preceding two lists.

**3.462 Tanner, Jeri.** 1971. The nomenclature of tobacco. North Carolina Folklore 19.116-22. Etymology of tobacco and nicotine, and terms for varieties of the plant and from languages other than English.

**3.463 Tanner, Jeri.** 1973. The nomenclature of tobacco. Love and wrestling, butch and o.k., ed. by Fred Tarpley, 14-20. Commerce, TX: South Central Names Institute.

**3.464 Tarpley, Fred A.** 1960. A word atlas of Northeast Texas. Baton Rouge: Louisiana State University dissertation. Abstract in DAI 21.2289A. 506 pp. [200 native adults in 26 counties]. Studies "the geographical distribution of folk synonyms of 126 concepts"; compares findings with Kurath's (3.275) and finds vocabulary predominantly South Midland; says vocabulary "for the most part . . . is highly homogeneous" and presents maps with isoglosses showing that the southeastern counties of region adjoining LA differ from the rest of NE TX.

**3.465 Tarpley, Fred A.** 1970. From blinky to blue-john: a word atlas of Northeast Texas. Austin: University of Texas Press. Revision of preceding item.

**3.466 Taylor, Jay L. B.** 1923. Snake County talk. DN 5.197-225. Ozark mountain glossary, primarily from McDonald Co., MO.

**3.467 Teaford, Ruth Romine.** 1980. Southern homespun. Huntsville, AL: Strode. Country lingo, 17-36; Expressions, 37-46.

**3.468 Thanet, Octave.** 1892. Folk-lore in Arkansas. JAF 5.121-25. Brief notes on vocabulary. **Reprinted** in W. K. McNeil, ed. 1984. The charm is broken: readings in Arkansas and Missouri folklore, 30-35. Little Rock, AR: August House.

**3.469 Thomas, Roy Edwin.** 1972. Popular folk dictionary of Ozarks talk. Little Rock, AR: Dox Books. 96 pp. [NW AR]. Comprehensive dictionary of vocabulary from Ozarks region, based on 248 interviews by the author, a schoolteacher.

**3.470 Thomas, Roy Edwin.** 1972. Glossary. Authentic Ozarks stories about big varmints: bears wolves panthers, collected, transcribed, and edited by Roy Edwin Thomas, 45-48. Little Rock, AR: Dox Books. Seventy-four items in modified spelling in appendix to collection of short stories.

**3.471 Thomas, Roy Edwin.** 1972. Glossary. Authentic Ozarks stories about bee huntin and stingin insects, 46-48. Little Rock, AR: Dox Books. Sixty-three items in modified spelling in appendix to collection of short stories.

**3.472 Thomas, Roy Edwin.** 1972. Glossary. Authentic Ozarks stories about bird hunting and trapping, 44-48. Little Rock, AR: Dox Books. 106 items in modified spelling in appendix to collection of short stories.

**3.473 Thomas, Roy Edwin.** 1972. Glossary. Authentic Ozarks stories about fox huntin' and fox dogs, 43-48. Little Rock, AR: Dox Books. 151 items in modified spelling in appendix to collection of short stories.

**3.474 Thomas, Roy Edwin.** 1972. Glossary. Authentic Ozarks stories about hunting and trapping possums-skunks-mink-bobcats, 42-48. Little Rock, AR: Dox Books. 157 items in modified spelling in appendix to collection of short stories.

**3.475 Thomas, Roy Edwin.** 1972. Glossary. Authentic Ozarks stories about coon hunting, 46-48. Little Rock, AR: Dox Books. Eighty-four items in modified spelling in appendix to collection of short stories.

**3.476 Thompson, Doris E.** 1961. "Off like a jar handle"--an Ozark simile. AS 36.156. [AR]. Term refers to person who has left town suddenly and unexpectedly.

**3.477 Thompson, Lawrence S.** 1958. Mitching. KFR 4.100. [Ohio Co., KY]. Query about localism meaning "playing hooky."

**3.478 Thompson, Marion Cross.** 1951. A study of yeoman speech of Leon County, Florida, and near-by areas: a contribution to a dialect dictionary. Tallahassee: Florida State University thesis. [15F, 6M older natives, W FL]. Finds that on 143-item questionnaire only "on less than than one-third of the items was there any appreciable agreement of all responses."

**3.479 Thornton, Richard H.** 1916. Comment on "A word-list from Virginia." DN 4.349-50. [SW VA]. Discusses seven older items. Cf. Dingus (**1.200**).

**3.480 Tidgwell, Flo M.** 1974. Genteel speech seems ever more desirable. Ozarks Mountaineer 22.6.32-33. Short essay on prudishness and delicateness of Ozark speech in early 20th century, at which time a privy was called Mrs. Jones.

**3.481 Tidwell, James Nathan.** 1949. A word-list from West Texas. PADS 11.3-15. Includes Southern items and three pages of "sayings."

**3.482 Tidwell, James Nathan.** 1950. Comments on word-lists. PADS 13.16-21. Report on usage in Runnels Co., TX, 1911-29, supplementing earlier reports in PADS.

**3.483 Tresidder, Argus.** 1940. Some Virginia provincialisms. QJS 26.262-69. Notes terms in old-fashioned VA speech of Tidewater, Piedmont, and mountain areas; discusses German contributions to VA speech.

**3.484 Underwood, Gary N.** 1975. Razorback slang. AS 50.50-69. Discussion and glossary of slang collected at University of Arkansas, Fayetteville, in 1970-72.

**3.485 Underwood, Gary N.** 1976. Some characteristics of slang used at the University of Arkansas at Fayetteville. Mid-South Folklore 4.49-54.

**3.486 Underwood, Josephine Key.** 1931. Quaint sayings and peculiar expressions. Joel Chandler Harris's portrayal of Negro life after the war, 70-75. Nashville: George Peabody College thesis. Short list of unusual sayings from nine stories and collections.

**3.487 W., F.** 1891. Two Virginianisms. Critic 18.10. Letter defending raised and tote. Reprinted in American Notes and Queries 6.129 (Jan. 10, 1891).

**3.488 Walker, Andrew Jackson.** 1962. The life and death of buttermilk or changing habits of Georgia Tech students. Abstract in SAB 27.4. On change in college student slang.

**3.489 Walker, Saunders.** 1956. A dictionary of the folk speech of the East Alabama Negro. Cleveland: Western Reserve University dissertation. Abstract in Bibliography of Publications and Abstracts of Dissertations, 1956-58 (p. 403), Western Reserve University; uses Linguistic Atlas questionnaire.

**3.490 Walton, Gerald W.** 1967. Some southern farm terms in Faulkner's Go Down, Moses. PADS 47.23-29. [MS]. Detailed definitions of twenty-three terms and comparison of them to current dictionaries.

**3.491 Walton, Gerald W.** 1972. A word list of Southern farm terms from Faulkner's The Hamlet. MFR 6.60-75. [MS]. Detailed glossary of twenty-nine terms.

**3.492 Warner, James H.** 1938. A word-list from southeast Arkansas. AS 13.3-7. [Monticello, AR]. Sixty-five words considered distinctive to the region.

**3.493 Warnick, Florence.** 1942. The dialect of Garrett County, Maryland. Privately printed. 16 pp. [W MD]. Popular glossary of words and phrases collected in Appalachian area of MD in 1900-1918.

**3.494 Warnock, Elsie.** 1912. Terms of approbation and eulogy in American dialect speech. Lincoln: University of Nebraska thesis. 25 pp. [Mostly from Nebraska, but some collected from Southern fiction writers]. Compilation and brief analysis of fanciful terms like "humgumptious."

**3.495 Waterman, Margaret.** 1975. DARE: a showcase of linguistic change. ED 117 700. 28 pp. Discusses covered dish, dinner on the grounds, and pounding as regional terms.

**3.496 Watkins, Floyd C.** 1963. Yesterday in the hills. Chicago: Quadrangle. Folk culture, including lexicon, from Cherokee County, GA.

**3.497 Watson, George.** 1938. Nahuatl words in American English. AS 13.108-21. Discusses terms for flora and fauna and terms for food, like cacao, that have come into American English, especially in the Southwest, through Mexican Spanish.

**3.498 Weals, Vic.** n.d. Hillbilly dictionary (revised): an edifying collection of mountain expressions. Gatlinburg, TN: privately printed. Dictionary of 175 items.

**3.499 Weeks, Abigail.** 1910. A word list from Barbourville, Kentucky. DN 3.456-57. Forty-five items.

**3.500 Weilenman, W. E.** 1950. Southern plantation terms. AS 25.230. [Stoneville, MS]. Twenty-three terms.

**3.501 Wentworth, Harold.** 1944. American dialect dictionary. New York: Crowell. 747 pp. Large volume containing more than 15,000 terms (many not appearing in another index or dictionary) that vary geographically in pronunciation, form, or meaning, these terms compiled from wordlists published in Dialect Notes and American Speech and from unpublished collections. **Reviews:** 1944. Christian Science Monitor, July 22, p. 11; 1944. New York Times, July 23, p. 25; 1944. New Yorker, July 29, p. 64; 1944. Wisconsin Library Bulletin, Nov., p. 144.

**3.502 West, Don.** 1957. "Hill-billy," "plowboy," "wool-hats," and "crackers." Southern Newsletter 2.10.6-8. Says four terms are used in prejudicial and erroneous way to imply that poor whites are responsible for persecution of blacks.

**3.503 White, Alice Melton.** 1977. A "good scald" on colloquialisms. Ozarks Mountaineer 25.7.31. Explains a good scald, haw-bushing, and other terms.

**3.504 White, Edward M.** 1963. The vocabulary of marbles in eastern Kentucky. KFR 9.57-74. 4 maps.

**3.505 White, Linda C.** 1975. Unemphatic love. Western Folklore 34.154.

Describes use of word <u>love</u> in "an unemotional, often negative vein" in Cumberland County, KY.

**3.506 Whitley, Edna Talbott.** 1958. What was bettywood? KFR 4.175-76. Etymologies for <u>bettywood</u>, name of tree in KY.

**3.507 Whittaker, Della S.** 1969. What is DARE doing? Maryland English Journal 8.1.15-17. Preview of DARE and its usefulness to English teachers, especially in MD.

**3.508 Wilder, Roy, Jr.** 1975. You all spoken here: a handy, illustrated guide to carryin' on in the South. First verse. Spring Hope, NC: Gourd Hollow Press. 20 pp. Popular "collation of words and phrases and expressions in common and ordinary day-by-day use in the South"; includes many figures of speech.

**3.509 Wilder, Roy, Jr.** 1976. You all spoken here: a handy, illustrated guide to carryin' on in the South. Second verse. Spring Hope, NC: Gourd Hollow Press. 20 pp. Sequel to preceding item, with same kind of material.

**3.510 Wilder, Roy, Jr.** 1977. You all spoken here: a handy, illustrated guide to carryin' on in the South. Third verse. Spring Hope, NC: Gourd Hollow Press. Sequel to preceding item, with same kind of material.

**3.511 Wilder, Roy, Jr.** 1984. You all spoken here. New York: Morrow. 213 pp. Lengthy compilation of colorful expressions, collected by personal observation and from reading newspapers, books, and magazines; no information on regional or social distribution or on source of material. **Review:** J. Burges. 1986. Southern English Newsletter 4.5-6.

**3.512 Wilgus, D. K.** 1959. Down our way: who's in town? KFR 5.1-8. Describes eight children's games and their unusual terminology.

**3.513 Wilgus, D. K., and L. Montell.** 1959. Notes: "uker." KFR 5.130. Describes marble game by the name.

**3.514 Williams, Cratis D.** 1944. A word-list from the mountains of Kentucky and North Carolina. PADS 2.28-31. [Mainly E KY, W NC]. Fifty-two items.

**3.515 Wilson, Charles M.** 1935. Backwoods language. Scholastic 26.8-9. Comments on Southern mountain speech.

**3.516 Wilson, George P.** 1944. Introduction to word-lists from the South. PADS 2.3-5. Introduces eight word-lists from Southern states as contributions to dialect dictionary of American English.

**3.517 Wilson, George P.** 1944. A word-list from Virginia and North

Carolina. PADS 2.38-52. Glossary of items crossreferenced to OED and EDD where possible.

**3.518 Wilson, George P.**, ed. 1945. Comments on word-lists from the South. PADS 3.7-12. Compilation of comments by six people about items in earlier lists.

**3.519 Wilson, George P.** 1958. Some folk sayings from North Carolina. North Carolina Folklore 6.2.7-18.

**3.520 Wilson, Gordon.** 1963. Studying folklore in a small region--IV: regional words. TFSB 29.79-86. Discusses rustic vocabulary and place names; calls for more interest in folk language.

**3.521 Wilson, Gordon.** 1964. Words relating to plants and animals in the Mammoth Cave region. PADS 42.11-25. **Reprinted** in Folklore of the Mammoth Cave Region (Bowling Green: Kentucky Folklore Society, 1968), pp. 12-26. More than 200 items collected in W KY.

**3.522 Wilson, Gordon.** 1965-66. Mammoth Cave words. KFR 11. Sections: I Around the house. KFR 11.5-8; II Around the house some more. KFR 11.28-31 (Apr.-June 1965); III Neighborhood doings. KFR 11.52-55 (July-Sept. 1965); IV More neighborhood doings. KFR 11.78-81 (Oct.-Dec. 1965); V Some good regional verbs. KFR 12.15-20 (Jan.-Mar. 1966); VI Some folk nouns. KFR 12.67-71 (Apr.-June 1966); VII Some more folk nouns. KFR 12.93-98 (July-Sept. 1966); VIII Some useful adjectives. KFR 12.119-22 (Oct.-Dec. 1966). First four articles reprinted in Folklore of the Mammoth Cave Region, edited by Lawrence Thompson (Bowling Green: Kentucky Folklore Society, 1968).

**3.523 Wilson, Gordon.** 1969. Some Mammoth Cave sayings: I. Sayings with a farm flavor. KFR 15.12-21; 15.37-44 (Apr.-June 1969): 15.69-74 (July-Sept. 1969).

**3.524 Wilson, Gordon.** 1970-71. Origins of the people of the Mammoth Cave region as shown by their surnames and regional words. KFR 16.73-78, surnames; 17.10-18, regional words I; 17.31-39, regional words II.

**3.525 Wilson, M. L.** 1973. A vocabulary study of St. Tammany Parish using the New Orleans questionnaire. New Orleans: University of New Orleans thesis.

**3.526 Wilt, Napier.** 1937. Ozark words again. AS 12.234-35. Critique of Randolph and Clemens item (**3.404**).

**3.527 Withers, A. M.** 1941. Provincialisms and illiteracies. Word Study 23.1.5. Reports right much and right smart from educated Virginians.

**3.528 Wood, Gordon R.** 1955-62. Heard in the South. TFSB 21.42-45; 21.111-16 (Dec. 1955); 23.33-38 (June, 1957); 24.95-101 (Sept. 1958); 26.1-7 (Mar. 1960); 27.69-71 (Dec. 1961); 28.90-92 (Dec. 1962). Informal discussions of regionalisms and requests for information on localisms.

**3.529 Wood, Gordon R.** 1958. A list of words from Tennessee. PADS 29.3-18. 152 items, submitted mostly by the public in response to newspaper solicitations from the writer.

**3.530 Wood, Gordon R.** 1959. Report on dialect collecting in Tennessee. Abstract in SAB 24.3.4. Progress report on postal questionnaire.

**3.531 Wood, Gordon R.** 1960. Heard in the South: the progress of a word geography. TFSB 26.1-7. Discusses early stages of author's large-scale postal survey of Southern vocabulary.

**3.532 Wood, Gordon R.** 1961. Heard in the south: the present distribution of "headcheese." TFSB 27.69-71. Shows the term spread along rivers rather than overland.

**3.533 Wood, Gordon R.** 1961. Word distribution in the interior South. PADS 35.1-16. 7 maps. Preliminary statement about Upper South-Lower South dialect boundaries in the interior South, using vocabulary.

**3.534 Wood, Gordon R.** 1962. Word mapping in the South. SAB 27.1-4. 3 maps. Preliminary report on project surveying vocabulary of mid-South, with examples of plum peach, batter bread, and gunny sack.

**3.535 Wood, Gordon R.** 1962. Word patterns of the South. Round Table of the South Central Modern Language Association 3.1-2.

**3.536 Wood, Gordon R.** 1963. Dialect contours in the Southern states. AS 38.243-56. 7 maps. Discusses major lexical isoglosses showing Midland-Southern boundary in eight states in interior South that were settled after 1800 and correlates vocabulary with three stages of settlement history of region: advancing frontier, growth of towns, and increase of regional communication. **Reprinted** in H. Allen and G. Underwood 1971(**1.12**).122-34; in D. Shores and C. Hines 1977(**1.689**).103-18.

**3.537 Wood, Gordon R.** 1971. Vocabulary change: a study of variation in regional words in eight of the Southern states. Carbondale: Southern Illinois University Press. 392 pp. Comprehensive work based mainly on postal survey of over 1,000 informants that studies generational and subregional patterns of nearly 1,200 words and expressions in the mid-South; uses ninety-four figures and maps to relate these patterns to agricultural regions and to 19th-century migration across South. **Reviews:** W. J. Griffin. 1972. TFSB 38.82-83; J. B. McMillan. 1972. Mississippi Quarterly 8.101-04; H. W. Marshall. 1974. JAF 87.101-02; L. Pederson. 1973. Language 49.184-87.

**3.538 Wood, Gordon R.** 1977. Refinements in tabular models of variation in regional American English. Computational and mathematical linguistics. Proceedings of the International Conference on Computational Linguistics, Pisa 27.8-1.9.1973, Firenze, 343-47. Discusses evolution of computer analysis of data in preceding item and compares this to linguistic atlas approaches.

**3.539 Woodard, C. M.** 1946. A word-list from Virginia and North Carolina. PADS 6.4-43. [mainly Pamplico Co., NC, Salem, VA]. Extended wordlist, with notes of frequency of use; includes a ten-page list of sayings and similes.

**3.540 Woodbridge, Hensley C.** 1955. A note on dogtrot. KFR 1.80-81. Cites use of term in 1920, thirteen years before earliest citation in any dictionary.

**3.541 Woodbridge, Hensley C.** 1955. More on dogtrot. KFR 1.107-08. Cites 1912 use of <u>dogtrot</u> and 1904 use of <u>dog run</u>.

**3.542 Woodbridge, Hensley C.** 1956. Americanisms in Felix Holt's <u>Gabriel Horn</u>. KFR 2.15-22. Cites two dozen terms from historical novelist that do not appear in dictionaries of Americanisms.

**3.543 Woodbridge, Hensley C.** 1956. Queries. KFR 2.147-48. Discusses possibility that term <u>rake-down</u> refers to type of square dance.

**3.544 Woodbridge, Hensley C.** 1956. 1. "To funk." 2. "Dog run." AS 31.309-10. First term used in KY meaning "to spoil tobacco"; second cited from AR and FL and refers to dogs trotting over loose, dry boards.

**3.545 Woodbridge, Hensley C.** 1957. Eleven Kentucky tobacco words. KFR 3.59-66. Proposes a dictionary of tobacco grower's vocabulary on historical principles and provides twelve sample entries.

**3.546 Woodbridge, Hensley C.** 1957. To top cotton. KFR 3.74. Traces use of term, meaning "to be very angry," to pre-Civil War days when slaves picked cotton.

**3.547 Woodbridge, Hensley C.** 1957. Some unrecorded hunting terms found in Kentucky. KFR 3.153-58. Discusses twenty-nine terms, most from Harriette Arnow's <u>Hunter's Horn</u>; based on Armstrong (**3.12**), Cauthern (**3.77**), and Dominick (**3.133**).

**3.548 Woodbridge, Hensley C.** 1958. Americanisms in James Still's <u>The Nest</u>. KFR 4.63-64. [KY]. Six terms, including <u>crawdabber</u> and <u>battle out</u>, not appearing in Mitford M. Mathews' <u>Dictionary of Americanisms</u>.

**3.549 Woodbridge, Hensley C.** 1958. Lexicographical note on <u>Song on the</u>

River. KFR 4.111-13. Discusses <u>hunker</u>, <u>joeboat</u>, <u>nib</u>, <u>staggon</u>, and <u>trotline</u> from novel by Billy Clark.

**3.550 Woodbridge, Hensley C.** 1958. Flats and bottoms. KFR 4.175. Use of these terms, referring to land bordering water, in Hopkins County, KY.

**3.551 Woodbridge, Hensley C.** 1959. Brief lexical notes. KFR 5.107-10. See Claire Kelly, KFR 7.77-78 (**3.262**). Discusses KY items, including <u>crawdad</u>, <u>john</u>, <u>Yankee dime</u>, and <u>shotgun.</u>

**3.552 Woodbridge, Hensley C.** 1962. Notes. KFR 8.56. Lexical citations: <u>dinky boat</u>, <u>jow boat</u>, <u>harricane</u>.

**3.553 Woodbridge, Hensley, C.** 1962. Lexical appendix. KFR 8.95-96.

**3.554 Woofter, Carey.** 1927. Dialect words and phrases from West-Central West Virginia. AS 2.347-67. [CENT WV]. Extended word-list from Little Kanawha Valley.

**3.555 Woolf, Henry Bosley.** 1942. The DAE and topographic terms. AS 17.177-78. Words from McJimsey's list (**3.313**) of terms from VA not in the DAE.

**3.556 Work Projects Administration.** 1940. Glossary. South Carolina folk tales: stories of animals and supernatural beings, 115-16. Columbia: University of South Carolina. Forty-eight terms.

**3.557 [Wright, Cecil A. and WPA Writer's Project (Louisiana)].** 1980. Slang and words with their origin on the river. Perspectives on American English, ed. by J. L. Dillard, 43-46. **Excerpted** in Lyle Saxon et al., eds. 1945. Gumbo ya ya. WPA Writer's Project. Glossary of fifty-eight items in LA collected by WPA in 1930s.

**3.558 Wyllie, John.** 1936. Short dictionary of slang, jargon, cant, and popular customs now or formerly current at the University of Virginia. University of Virginia Alumni News 24.80-81.

**3.559 Zimmerman, H. E.** 1916. Maryland. DN 4.343. [Frederick Co., MD]. Twenty-three terms.

**3.560 Zinderman, Zeek.** 1967. Hill Latin: Ozark hillbilly lingo dictionary. Cabool, MO: Hickoryville. 44 pp. Popular dictionary of Ozark speech. with cartoons, mostly in eye dialect.


See Also


1.9 Alexander; 1.14 Arkansas; 1.42 Baird; 1.44 Bandy; 1.61 Bell; 1.63 Benar-

# 4 Phonology and Phonetics

**4.1 Abel, James W.** 1950. A study of the speech of six freshmen from Southern University (Negro). Baton Rouge: Louisiana State University dissertation. xi + 942 pp. 57 tables. Abstract in Louisiana State University Bulletin n.s. 42.24–25 (1950); in Speech Monographs 17.302–03 (1950). [New Orleans, LA]. Compares pronunciation of speakers to "standard southern American pronunciation."

**4.2 Abel, James W.** 1951. About the pronunciation of six freshmen from Southern University. SSJ 16.259–67. [LA] Condensed version of preceding item.

**4.3 Abel, James W.** 1952. Standard southern American. Le Maître Phonétique, third series, 98.35–37. [LA]. Specimen transcription of a black university student's speech.

**4.4 Adams, George C. S.** 1953. On the speech of Carroll County, Georgia. Abstract in SAB 18.3.5. [NW GA]. Says the speech of the county "shows marked similarity to the Georgia-Alabama dialect used somewhat to the south of the county."

**4.5 Allison, Vernon C.** 1929. On the Ozark pronunciation of "it." AS 4.205–06. Says Ozark speakers use <u>hit</u> pronunciation of pronoun only at beginning of a clause or for emphasis and that Vance Randolph violates this principle in representing Ozark dialect.

**4.6 Ansberry, Clare.** 1987. Cannagijut to a burlitz? or, take those Sonys out of your ears and listen up. AJ 14.216. Discusses short course to acquaint Japanese workers in KY with pronunciation of local, informal variety of English.

**4.7 Anshen, Frank.** 1969. Speech variation among Negroes in a small Southern community. New York: New York University dissertation.

Abstract in DAI 30.2509-10A. [272W, 87B, Hillsborough, NC]. Finds that whites use standard forms more than blacks but that speech in both white and black communities is heterogeneous and patterns socially in same way-- older speakers, more educated speakers, and women in both communities use more standard pronunciation.

**4.8 Anshen, Frank.** 1970. A sociolinguistic analysis of a sound change. Language Sciences 9.20-21. [87 B adults, Hillsborough, NC]. Finds pronunciation of postvocalic /r/ correlates with youth and educational level of speakers; says race of interviewer also influences frequency of feature.

**4.9 Armour, Malcolm.** 1983. The social stratification of (e) in Midlothian, Texas. Research Papers of the Texas Summer Institute of Linguistics 13. Pilot studies in sociolinguistics: variation, use and attitudes, ed. by Jerold A. Edmondson, 2-21. Dallas: SIL. [24 W adults]. Finds /e/-lowering correlates in words like ache, wage, and age with decreasing age, that it is more advanced in women than men, and that it has taken place about twenty years earlier for women than men.

**4.10 Atherton, H. E., and Darrell L. Gregg.** 1929. A study of dialect differences. AS 4.216-23. [NC]. Early acoustic comparison of phonograph recordings of speakers from NC and South England, analyzing length of words in millimeters of film per second, frequency of double vibrations, and pitch level.

**4.11 Atwood, E. Bagby.** 1950. Grease and greasy: a study of geographical variation. University of Texas Studies in English 29.249-60. Analyzes distribution of [s] and [z] pronunciations in New England and Atlantic states and finds [z] pronunciations dominate from W PA southward; compares results to Hempl (**1.314**) and Thomas (**4.340**). **Reprinted** in H. B. Allen. 1958. Readings in Applied English Linguistics. 1st ed., 158-67; 1964. 2nd ed., 242-51; in H. Allen and G. Underwood 1971(**1.12**).160-68; in Bobbs-Merrill Reprint Series, Language-2.

**4.12 Atwood, E. Bagby.** 1950. The pronunciation of "Mrs." AS 25.10-18. 1 map. Based on Linguistic Atlas records, delineates areas in South where "mistriz" and "miziz" pronunciations are used, the latter pronunciation dominating.

**4.13 Atwood, E. Bagby.** 1951. Some eastern Virginia pronunciation features. English studies for James Southall Wilson, ed. by Fredson Bowers, 111-24. University of Virginia Studies no. 4, Charlottesville. 7 maps. Using LAMSAS records, analyzes extension of Tidewater VA features in South Atlantic states. **Reprinted** in J. Williamson and V. Burke 1971 (**1.823**).255-67. **Review:** E. V. K. Dobbie. 1953. AS 28.121.

**4.14 Austin, William M.** 1972. Nonverbal communication. Culture, class, and language variety, ed. by A. L. Davis, 140-69. Urbana: NCTE. P. 163, notes that the drawl "is often used for sarcasm or threat" in the South.

**4.15 Avis, Walter S.** 1956. The mid-back vowels in the English of the eastern United States. Ann Arbor: University of Michigan dissertation. Abstract in DAI 17.140. Includes Middle and South Atlantic states; finds more than one mid-back vowel phoneme only in New England.

**4.16 Ayres, Harry Morgan, and W. Cabell Greet.** 1930. American speech records at Columbia University. AS 5.333-58. Includes transcriptions from GA, NC, SC, TX, and VA, and list of records in collection.

**4.17 Bailey, Charles-James N.** 1967. Syllabic, semisyllabic, and unsyllabic in English: a ternary distinction. Chicago Journal of Linguistics 1.53-84. Revised as "Dialectal differences in the syllabification of non-nasal sonorants in American English" in General Linguistics 8.1.79-91 (1968). Says Southern American speech differences from English in Northern states in syllabification of /l, y, r, w/ justify a two-way dialect distinction in Eastern states, supported by acoustic evidence.

**4.18 Bailey, Charles-James N.** 1969. An exploratory investigation of variations in the accented outputs of underlying short vowels in a dialect of Southern states English. UHWPL 1.1.57-64. Spectrographic and phonetic study of variation in the low central unrounded vowel, showing a clear differentiation in vowels of cot and cop.

**4.19 Bailey, Charles-James N.** 1969. Ternary-valued phonetic features: a third approximation. UHWPL 1.4.63-79. Argues that ternary phonetic features are more valid than binary ones.

**4.20 Bailey, Charles-James N.** 1969. Chapter one: introduction to Southern states phonetics. UHWPL 1.4.81-96. Introduces linguistic framework and terminology for lengthy description of phonetics of consonants and vowels and syllable structure of Southern American speech. Addenda and corrigenda in UHWPL 1.6.105-08; 1.7.71-73; 1.10.101-02; 2.2.163-66. Further installments annotated below (**4.21-26**).

**4.21 Bailey, Charles-James N.** 1969. Chapter two: the speech tract, articulatory mechanism, and the classification of sounds. UHWPL 1.4.97-144. Introduces phonetic framework and symbols for lengthy description of phonetics of Southern American speech.

**4.22 Bailey, Charles-James N.** 1969. Chapter three: acoustics and perception. UHWPL 1.5.107-33. Introduces acoustic framework and terminology for author's description of phonetics of Southern American speech.

**4.23 Bailey, Charles-James N.** 1969. Chapter four: the obstruents. UHWPL 1.5.135-84. Discusses patterning of obstruent consonants in Southern American English.

**4.24 Bailey, Charles-James N.** 1969. Chapter five: the accented non-complex nuclei. UHWPL 1.6.105-66. Discusses phonetics of monophthongs in stressed syllables for Southern states.

**4.25 Bailey, Charles-James N.** 1969. Chapter six: the sonorants--nasals, liquids, and glides. UHWPL 1.6.169-203. Discusses assimilation to place of articulation and other features of sonorant consonants.

**4.26 Bailey, Charles-James N.** 1969. Chapter seven: unaccented simple and complex nuclei. UHWPL 1.7.75-95. Discusses weakly accented monophthongs and diphthongs in Southern American English.

**4.27 Bailey, Charles-James N.** 1969. Syllabic boundaries. UHWPL 1.9. 205-08.

**4.28 Bailey, Charles-James N.** 1969. Introduction to Southern states phonetics. UHWPL 1.10.101-23. Addenda, corrigenda, and appendix to earlier item (**4.20**).

**4.29 Bailey, Charles-James N.** 1970. Black English. UHWPL 2.2.167-68. Says his analysis of phonetics and phonology of Southern American should serve as basis for analyzing patterns of black speech and preparing materials for teachers of reading and writing.

**4.30 Bailey, Charles-James N.** 1970. A new intonation theory to account for Pan-English and idiom-particular patterns. UHWPL 2.3.1-83. Also in Papers in Linguistics 2.522-604.

**4.31 Bailey, Charles-James N.** 1970. Building rate into a dynamic theory of linguistic description. UHWPL 2.9.161-234. Shows how rate of change governed by a "calculus of weighted environments" for variable pronunciation of diphthongs in Southern American English can be built into his wave model of linguistic change.

**4.32 Bailey, Charles-James N.** 1971. Vowel reduction and syllabic sonorants in English (parts of two recently revised chapters of "Southern states phonetics"). UHWPL 3.2.35-104.

**4.33 Bailey, Charles-James N.** 1971. Tempo and phrasing. UHWPL 3.2.105-14.

**4.34 Bailey, Charles-James N.** 1971. Intonation (excerpt from revised chapter ten of <u>Southern States Phonetics</u>). UHWPL 3.5.43-117. Part of chapter 10 of revised version of Southern States Phonetics. Introduces Bailey's system for analyzing intonation in Southern American and other varieties of English.

**4.35 Bailey, Charles-James N.** 1973. Variation resulting from different rule orderings in English phonology. New ways of analyzing variation in English, ed. by Charles-James N. Bailey and Roger W. Shuy, 211-52. Washington: Georgetown University Press. Presents reorderings of fifty-five pairs of phonological rules in American English, many from Southern varieties.

**4.36 Bailey, Charles-James N.** 1974. The giddy and gaudy but guileful glamor of gadfly glottometry bzw. tell me not in mirthful numbers. Lectological Newsletter 2.3.1-5. Says native-speaker introspection best identifies phonological change, as for pronunciation of [aɪ] in the South.

**4.37 Bailey, Charles-James N.** 1978. Gradience in English syllabization and a revised concept of unmarked syllabization. Bloomington: Indiana University Linguistics Club. 49 pp. Proposes rules for syllabization and says it is normally gradient. Corrigenda et addenda in TUB-Arbeitspapiere zur Linguistik 6.222.

**4.38 Bailey, Charles-James N.** 1978. Suggestions for improving the transcription of English phonetic segments. Journal of Phonetics 6.141-49. Proposes notational conventions for improved transcription, especially of offglides, a "brief prolegomenon to English phonetology." Corrigenda in TUB-Arbeitspapiere zur Linguistik 3.118.

**4.39 Bailey, Charles-James N.** 1978. System of English intonation with gradient models. Bloomington: Indiana University Linguistic Club. 59 pp. Reduces Bolinger's semantically based intonational patterns to two gradient pitch increments. Corrigenda et addenda in TUB-Arbeitspapiere zur Linguistik 6.222.

**4.40 Bailey, Charles-James N.** 1980. Evidence for variable syllabic boundaries in English. The melody of language: intonation and prosody, ed. by L. R. Waugh and C. H. van Schooneveld, 25-39. Baltimore: University Park Press. Draws on Southern English in proposing gradient framework for syllable analysis. Corrigenda in TUB-Arbeitspapiere zur Linguistik 10.229.

**4.41 Bailey, Charles-James N.** 1980. The patterning of sonorant gemination in English lects. Language use and the uses of language, ed. by Roger W. Shuy and Anna Shnukal, 1-11. Washington: Georgetown University Press. Contrasts gemination of nonnasal sonorants across word, formative, and syllable boundaries in Southern American and Northern American English.

**4.42 Bailey, Charles-James N.** 1981. Restructuring of nuclear length in "r-less" Southern states English. Arbeiten aus Anglistik und Amerikanistik 6.119-25. Discusses differences in vowel length "occasioned by the dropping or desulcalization of //r//, by the dropping of //l//, or by the dropping of //h//," outlines these differences between Southern American English and Southern British English.

**4.43 Bailey, Charles-James N.** 1981. Supplement to "laterals and trills." Zeitschrift für Phonetik, Sprachwissenschaft und Kommunikationsforschung 34.352-53. Includes notes on Southern pronunciation of postvocalic and intervocalic /l/.

**4.44 Bailey, Charles-James N.** 1984. Workbook for English transcriptional phonetics: syllabus of exercises for Southern states English. Aufsätze und andere Materialien zum Sprachunterricht: Phonetik und historische Linguistik by Charles-James N. Bailey, 49-101. Arbeitspapiere zur Linguistik 21. Berlin: Institut für Linguistik. Supplement to following item; contains introduction and twelve chapters with exercises.

**4.45 Bailey, Charles-James N.** 1985. English phonetic transcription. Dallas: SIL. 265 pp. Textbook on phonetics for students of linguistics, with many examples from Southern English; includes suprasegmentals and intonation. **Review:** G. Bailey. 1989. Southern English Newsletter 5.

**4.46 Bailey, Charles-James N.** 1986. Even dialectologists get the blues: inadequate phonetic transcription of English. Papiere zur Linguistik 35.3-38. Concludes that "if we want real descriptions that are of assistance either to the comparatist or to the explanatory-predictive theorist or to the language teacher, we have got to rid phonetics of unenlightening phonemics."

**4.47 Bailey, Guy.** 1979. Folk speech on the Cumberland plateau: a phonological analysis. Knoxville: University of Tennessee dissertation. Abstract in DAI 40.5031A. [Type IA W, E TN]. Outlines segmental phonemic structure of speech of area, describing phonological processes and offering phonetic, contextual, and historical explanations for variants.

**4.48 Bailey, Guy.** 1981. The phonological content of a field record. LAGS Working Papers, 1st series, no. 6. Microfiche 1185. Addendum to Pederson, et al. 1981(1.594). 20 pp. Study of constraints on /t/ and /d/ deletion after /l/ and /n/ in LAGS field record of 76-year-old man from Gantt, AL.

**4.49 Bailey, Guy.** 1986. Phonetic constraints on the restoration of postvocalic /r/: evidence from LAGS. NADS 18.3.11-12. Says that /r/ represents a prestige feature for LAGS informants but that for younger speakers it is more common after front vowels than after back vowels.

**4.50 Bailey, Nina V.** 1930. Pitch and time variations in certain American dialects. Ames: Iowa State University thesis. Finds that "the voices of the Southerners had a wider pitch range than did those of the Easterners" and that Southerners had more frequent pitch changes within "phonations" and Easterners more frequent shifts between "phonations."

**4.51 Baird, Allyne Higgason.** 1982. Rural southwest Georgia speech: a phonological analysis. Atlanta: Georgia State University dissertation. Abstract in DAI 43.1956A. 193 pp. [40 B, 40 W, age over 65, 40 "better educated," 40 "lesser educated," SW GA]. Uses data from Dialect Survey of Rural Georgia. Outlines allophonic and subregional phonemic variation and concludes "the dialect can be described in terms of one phonemic system"; finds "no stratification of data along racial lines" and no subregional dialect patterns.

**4.52 Barrett, Madie Ward.** 1948. A phonology of southeast Alabama speech. Chapel Hill: University of North Carolina dissertation. Cf. Madie Belle Ward (**4.366**).

**4.53 Barrett, Madie Ward.** 1952. Southeast Alabama speech. Abstract in SAB 17.1.5 (Jan. 1952). Variation in phonology of the Wiregrass region.

**4.54 Bloch, Bernard.** 1934. The American vowel in bird. Le Maître Phonétique, third series, 45.9-11. Argues that symbol /ɝ/ is needed to represent vowels in several American dialects, especially Southern American.

**4.55 Blunt, Jerry.** 1967. An American Southern. Stage dialects, 40-50. New York: Harper and Row. Directions for actors in imitating accents.

**4.56 Blunt, Jerry.** 1980. More stage dialects. New York: Harper and Row.

**4.57 Boiarsky, Carolyn.** 1969. Consistency of spelling and pronunciation deviations in Appalachian students. MLJ 53.347-50. [High school students, WV]. Studies "pronunciation of certain words by Appalachian students and analyzes the consistency between the Appalachian dialectal pronunciation of certain vowels and the spelling of words in which they appear"; identifies four "vowel shifts" in Appalachian speech, three dealing with pronunciation of front vowels before /l/.

**4.58 Boiarsky, Carolyn.** 1970. Improving oral communication of Appalachian youth through rhyme. MLJ 54.188-89. Discusses a model "from which Appalachian students can learn to differentiate between their dialectal pronunciation of certain vowels and pronunciation of those vowels in Standard American English" and reports on project using five pilot lessons, based on an aural-oral approach, to assist such students.

**4.59 Borchers, Gladys L., and Claude M. Wise.** 1949. Modern speech. New York: Harcourt, Brace. Notes on Southern speech, 93-94; The Southern drawl, 171-76.

**4.60 Bronstein, Arthur.** 1960. The pronunciation of American English: an introduction to phonetics. Englewood Cliffs, NJ: Prentice-Hall. Pp. 40-51, summary of regional speech characteristics. **Reviews:** R. I. McDavid, Jr. 1966. Language 42.149-55 (reprinted in McDavid 1979(**1.454**).381-84); W. L. Thurman. 1963. JSHD 28.409-10.

**4.61 Buckingham, Andrew.** 1983. The stratification of the sociolinguistic variable (e) in the speech of residents of Midlothian, Texas. Research Papers of the Texas Summer Institute of Linguistics 13. Pilot studies in sociolinguistics: variation, use and attitudes, ed. by Jerold A. Edmondson, 22-36. Dallas: SIL. Contrasts /e/-lowering in speech of male and female teenagers and in conversational, reading, and word-list style.

**4.62 Burger, Carl R.** 1975. A comparative phonology of the stressed vowel systems of Texas English and modern high German. Houston: Rice University thesis. 48 pp. A contrastive analysis, with TX English material based on Klipple (**4.187**), T. Lawrence (**4.202**), and Sawyer (**1.671**).

**4.63 Burrows, Evelyn Honor.** 1976. Some correlates of speech in Tallahassee, Florida. Columbus: Ohio State University dissertation. Abstract in DAI 37.714B. [20 B college students, Tallahassee, FL]. Finds educational background, rather than sex or social status, correlates with choice of phonological variants.

**4.64 Butters, Ronald R.** 1981. Unstressed vowels in Appalachian English. AS 56.104-10. Discusses constraints on raising of final unstressed schwa in Appalachian speech and tries to unite interpretations of Wolfram and Christian (**1.852**) and Kurath and McDavid (**4.197**). **Reprinted** in H. Allen and M. Linn 1986(**1.11**).198-203.

**4.65 Caffee, Nathaniel M.** 1935. A phonological study of the speech of a homogeneous group in Charlottesville, Virginia. Charlottesville: University of Virginia dissertation. Abstract in University of Virginia Abstracts of Dissertations (1935), pp. 3-4.

**4.66 Caffee, Nathaniel M.** 1935. Transcription of a phonograph record of the speech of a Negro between 70 and 75 years old and a life-long resident of Charlottesville, VA. AS 10.298-99. Transcription and commentary.

**4.67 Caffee, Nathaniel M.** 1940. Some notes on consonant pronunciation in the South. Studies for William A. Read, ed. by N. M. Caffee and Thomas A. Kirby, 125-32. Baton Rouge: Louisiana State University Press. Notes variations in pronunciation of consonants which "are possibly peculiar to southern states," including nonplosion of word-final stop consonants.

**4.68 Caffee, Nathaniel M.** 1940. Southern "l" plus a consonant. AS 15.259-61. Consonant is vocalized to back vowel, not to schwa, in Southern American speech.

**4.69 Callary, Robert E.** 1971. Dialectology and linguistic theory. AS 46.200-09. Comments briefly on Charleston, SC, and Roanoke, VA.

**4.70 Callary, Robert E.** 1973. Indications of regular sound shifting in an Appalachian dialect. AJ 1.238-40. Says dialect spellings in Dargan's 1932

Appalachian novel <u>Call Home the Heart</u> reveal systematic differences between Appalachian dialect and standard English that can demonstrate phonological rules.

**4.71 Campbell, Ellen.** 1934. A study of words mispronounced in the high schools of West Texas. Lubbock: Texas Technological College thesis.

**4.72 Cassano, P. V.** 1980. Language interaction in Louisiana: sound systems in contact, English and French. Orbis 29.206-33. Examines vowel phonology, stress, and intonation in LA French and English to determine the effect of each language's contact on the other.

**4.73 Cavender, Anthony Patterson.** 1974. A phonemic and phonetic analysis of the folk speech of Bedford County, Tennessee. Knoxville: University of Tennessee thesis. [5 W Type IA over 70, S CENT TN]. Study undertaken to provide baseline data for LAGS and other work in Middle TN; no comparison with speech elsewhere. Uses approach developed by Harold Orton.

**4.74 Ching, Marvin, K. L.** 1982. The question intonation in assertions. AS 57.95-107. [14 Southerners, mostly from Memphis, TN]. Discusses variety of speaker intentions conveyed by high final level intonation in statements, including topicalization, deference, and politeness.

**4.75 Clifton, Ernest S.** 1959. Some [u]-[ju] variations in Texas. AS 34.190-93. [484 students at North Texas State College, Denton, from 101 counties]. Says monophthongal variant is gaining in Dallas, but variation in feature in general does not divide E TX from W TX, though monophthong is more common in E TX.

**4.76 Cogdill, Cindy A., Judith Harkins, and Karl Nicholas.** 1978. A good mill will make you fill better. SECOL Bulletin 2.62-66. [91 W NC, ages 7 to 79]. Investigates laxing of /i/ before /l/ as change in progress; finds /i/ when spelled <ea> more likely to lax than when spelled <ee>.

**4.77 Coye, Dale Fincher.** 1979. A linguistic guide to the pronunciation of English for actors: standard American and selected dialects. Princeton, NJ: Princeton University dissertation. Pp. 116-23, short description of Southern American pronunciation, with reference to postvocalic /r/ and to vowel quality.

**4.78 Crane, L[indsay] Ben[jamin, Jr.]** 1973. The death of a prestige form, or the social stratification of /R/ in Tuscaloosa, Alabama. ED 100 174. 25 pp. [ages 8-86]. Finds postvocalic /r/ stratified by both class and age and that fully constricted /r/ is incoming norm of pronunciation.

**4.79 Crane, Lindsay Benjamin, Jr.** 1973. Social stratification of English among white speakers in Tuscaloosa, Alabama. Amherst: University of

Massachusetts dissertation. Abstract in DAI 34.6615A. [56 W adults, in 3 social classes]. Investigates five vowel variables and postvocalic /r/; finds all variables show social stratification but that only /r/ shows stratification by age within social classes (with /r/-constriction becoming the norm); evidence conflicting whether Tuscaloosa speech moving in direction of "broadcast standard pronunciation."

**4.80 Crane, [Lindsay] Ben[jamin, Jr.]** 1975. /ɪ/-raising as a social marker in the deep South. Views on language, ed. by Reza Ordoubadian and Walburga von Raffler-Engel, 127-37. Murfreesboro: Middle Tennessee State University. [56 W adults, Tuscaloosa, AL]. Studies linguistic, age, and social class constraints on raising of /ɪ/ to /i/ in words like bitter, dig, timber, and brick; finds younger speakers have more raising than older ones and working-class speakers less than upper-middle-class ones.

**4.81 Crane, L[indsay] Ben[jamin, Jr.]** 1977. The social stratification of /aɪ/ in Tuscaloosa, Alabama. Papers in language variation, ed. by David L. Shores and Carole P. Hines, 189-200. University: University of Alabama Press. [56 native W, 3 social classes, ages 8-86]. Finds wide gap between upper and lower class pronunciation of diphthong in oldest age group but much narrower gap in youngest group.

**4.82 Crockett, Harry J., Jr., and Lewis Levine.** 1967. Friends' influences on speech. Sociological Inquiry 57.109-28. [216 W, CENT NC]. Statistical study examining correlation of gender, style, and social factors with pronunciation of postvocalic /r/ and final -ing; finds influence of friends on pronunciation stronger than other social forces, although "the strength if not also the quality of such influences seems to be different for speech traits for different social significance" and that "women seem more affected by such influences than men."

**4.83 Crow, Porter J.** 1950. Standardization of American speech: reflected by one Texas family of five generations. Dallas: Southern Methodist University thesis. 57 pp. [5 F, ages 7-87, Dallas, TX]. Finds little movement toward standard pronunciation across five generations of one family.

**4.84 Current, Richard N.** 1983. Northernizing the South. Athens: University of Georgia Press. Scattered comments on Southern accent.

**4.85 Dalgert, Stanley M.** 1951. Ms., miss, and mrs. Word Study 26.4.5-6. Notes that Southerners have used the [miz] pronunciation for both married and unmarried women when using surname, thus obviating need for Ms. as term of address; notes Southerners also use Miss [mɪs] with both married and unmarried women but only with a first name.

**4.86 Dandy, Evelyn B.** 1982. A dialect rejection. Georgia Journal of Reading 7.22. Reports anecdote about how a child's reading of street and stretched as skreet and sketched led to correction and inhibitions about his speech.

**4.87 Darrow, Anne.** 1937. Phonetic studies in folk speech and broken English: for use on stage, screen, radio, platform and in school and college. Boston, MA: Expression. American Negro English, 57-63.

**4.88 Davis, Arthur Kyle, Jr., and Archibald A. Hill.** 1933. Dialect notes on records of folk songs from Virginia. AS 8.4.52-56. [SW VA]. Discriminates which features of recorded folk songs are due to rhythm and other effects of singing and which are of genuine interest to dialectologists; focuses on vowel quality, postvocalic /r/, pronunciation of normally unstressed function words when stressed, verb principal parts, and other features.

**4.89 Davis, Margaret B.** 1975. A study of East Tennessee regional phonology: its influence on reading performance. Knoxville: University of Tennessee dissertation. 88 pp. Abstract in DAI 36.7183A. [20 W 1st, 3rd graders, 20 W elementary teachers, Sevier Co., E TN]. Finds that both students and teachers differed from expected pronunciations and that both groups showed wide variation in pronunciation.

**4.90 Davis, Mary A.** 1904. Causes of dialects and tonal variations. Out West 22.213-20. Argues fundamental effect of climate and topography on languages and dialects; attributes purity of MD and VA speech to education "aided by a salubrious climate."

**4.91 de Camp, L. Sprague.** 1941. Specimen: Southern American English. Le Maître Phonétique 73.6. [NW TN]. Transcription and comments on passage read by native of Dyer County.

**4.92 de Camp, L. Sprague.** 1979. American English from Central Texas. Journal of the International Phonetic Association 8.81-82. Analyzes vowels and other features; includes transcription.

**4.93 DeLattre, Pierre, and Donald C. Freeman.** 1968. A dialect study of American r's by x-ray motion picture. Linguistics 44.29-68. [46 adults, including 5 Southerners]. Identifies eight distinct types of American /r/, based on acoustic and x-ray analysis.

**4.94 Dickson, Lee Anne, and Fred Tarpley.** 1982. Age as a factor in the use of /hw/. Abstract in NADS 14.3.3. [50 adults in TX]. Reports age more strongly influences use of /hw/ than occupation, length of residence, or education.

**4.95 Dodd, Celeste V.** 1938. The speech of a San Antonio American family: a study in Texas pronunciation. Austin: University of Texas thesis. 93 pp. Compares pronunciation of four generations of San Antonio natives.

**4.96 Dorrill, George T.** 1975. A comparison of Negro and white speech in central South Carolina. Columbia: University of South Carolina thesis. [1 B, 1 W from Newberry Co., 1 B, 1 W from Sumter Co.] 62 pp. Using four LAMSAS records of two pairs of comparable black and white informants, finds differences in white and black speech but only "of a minor statistical nature rather than categorial."

**4.97 Dorrill, George T.** 1982. Black and white speech in the South: evidence from the Linguistic Atlas of the Middle and South Atlantic States. Columbia: University of South Carolina dissertation. Abstract in DAI 43.2335A. [16 W, 16 B, older LAMSAS speakers from NC, VA, MD]. Reprinted in 1986 as Bamberger Beiträge zur Englischen Sprachwissenschaft 19. New York: Peter Lang. 246 pp. Finds that blacks have greater tendency to use pure vowels than whites and that black speech is much more homogeneous than white speech in the three-state region. **Review:** E. Schneider. 1987. EWW 8.140-43.

**4.98 Dorrill, George.** 1986. A comparison of stressed vowels of black and white speakers in the South. Language Variety in the South: perspectives in black and white, ed. by Michael Montgomery and Guy Bailey, 149-57. University: University of Alabama Press. Condensed version of preceding item.

**4.99 Doss, Sandra F.** 1981. A survey of the speech of certain black students at Tulane University. New Orleans: Tulane University thesis. [40 B, ages 18-22, New Orleans]. Using Schaffer's (**4.301**) word and sentence list, finds upper and middle class students have pronunciations significantly different from lower class students.

**4.100 Dozier, Judy Burges.** 1984. Deletion and relexicalization in Charleston speech. Columbia: University of South Carolina thesis. 54 pp. [10 UMC W, ages 10-85, Charleston, SC]. Examines the deletion of unstressed initial syllables of four types; says that "the Charleston dialect is one of those in which the deletion process operates relatively frequently," but that the frequency of deletion is decreasing sharply for younger generations.

**4.101 Dozier, Judy B.** 1985. Language change in Charleston: deletion and relexicalization. SECOL Review 9.217-35. Condensed version of preceding item.

**4.102 Ducote, Charlotte Anne.** 1983. A study of the reading and speaking fundamental vocal frequency of aging black adults. Baton Rouge: Louisiana State University dissertation. [277 B speakers, 133 M, 144 F, ages 50-79]. Finds fundamental vocal frequency decreases with age for black women but not for black men.

**4.103 Duke, Francis J.** 1938. A phonetic study of Italo-American speech in Richmond, Virginia. Charlottesville: University of Virginia thesis.

Explores which traits of American speech are most difficult, and which easiest, for immigrants to learn.

**4.104 Duke, Francis J.** 1941. "Long i" in Richmond speech. Humanistic studies in honor of John Calvin Metcalf, 314-18. University of Virginia Studies no. 1., Charlottesville. Discusses different pronunciations of diphthong /aɪ/ in VA, with emphasis on Richmond.

**4.105 Edelsky, Carole.** 1979. Question intonation and sex roles. LIS 8.15-32. [154 M, 165 F]. Doubts that geographic background of speakers is tenable explanation for differences in use of high rising final intonation in statements.

**4.106 Edgerton, William.** 1935. Another note on the Southern pronunciation of "long i." AS 10.190. Says diphthong has longer and more frequent offglides before unvoiced consonants than before voiced ones.

**4.107 Edgerton, William.** 1948. A note on "spigot" and "spicket." AS 23.33-35. Says "spicket" is standard pronunciation throughout the South.

**4.108 Elders, Roy.** 1949. The stressed back vowels in the speech of Parker County. Denton: North Texas State University thesis. 77 pp. [N CENT TX]. Compares local pronunciation to that given in standard dictionaries.

**4.109 Ericson, Eston E.** 1937. American pronunciation. Notes and Queries n.s. 172.413 (June 5). Notes on Southern r̲. Reports Southern college students are /r/-less speakers but tend to spell words with adventitious /r/'s, as ballard for ballad.

**4.110 Evans, Medford.** 1935. Southern "long i." AS 10.188-90. Extreme defense of Southern pronunciation; says "Southern long i̲ is a simple vowel, not a diphthong."

**4.111 Everett, Russell I.** 1958. The speech of the tri-racial group composing the community of Clifton, Louisiana. Baton Rouge: Louisiana State University dissertation. [3 speakers]. Compares speech of community to "standard and substandard characteristics of Southern and General American speech"; finds substandard Southern speech most noticeably influential and points out nine features he believes unique to community.

**4.112 Farrison, William Edward.** 1936. The phonology of the illiterate Negro dialect of Guilford County, North Carolina. Columbus: Ohio State University dissertation. Descriptive study; makes no reference to African survivals in NC.

**4.113 Feagin, Crawford.** 1985. A new approach to variation in the Southern drawl: a sociolinguistic analysis of Alabama talk. Abstract in NADS 17.3.5-6. [Anniston, AL]. Discusses sociolinguistic constraints on the drawl.

**4.114 Feagin, Crawford.** 1986. More evidence for major vowel change in the South. Diversity and diachrony, ed. by David Sankoff, 83-95. Amsterdam: John Benjamins. [7 speakers from Anniston, AL]. Presents evidence that supports view that "the vowels of the American South are undergoing an extensive rearrangement in their configuration as a result of a series of chain shifts in which the traditional back vowels have moved to the front, followed by the shift of the traditionally short or lax nuclei to peripheral position."

**4.115 Feagin, Crawford.** 1987. A closer look at the southern drawl: variation taken to extremes. Variation in language NWAV-XV at Stanford: proceedings of the fifteenth annual conference on new ways of analyzing variation, ed. by Keith M. Denning, Sharon Inkelas, Faye C. McNair-Knox, and John R. Rickford, 137-50. Stanford: Stanford University Department of Linguistics. Discusses difficulty of defining the drawl on phonetic or acoustic basis and analyzes phonetic elements of the drawl--vowel lengthening, gliding, and intonational contours.

**4.116 Fenn, Johnnye A.** 1938. The speech of Haynesville, Louisiana at three age levels. Baton Rouge: Louisiana State University dissertation. 324 pp. [3 adult natives, NW LA]. Linguistic atlas type study to determine "General American" and Southern speech characteristics of three informants, generational differences, consistency of each informant's speech, and relation between community's speech and earlier British pronunciation.

**4.117 Fetscher, Margaret Elisabeth.** 1971. The speech of Atlanta school children: a phonological study. Athens: University of Georgia dissertation. Abstract in DAI 32.5762A. [36 5th-graders, 9 UMC B, 9 UMC W, 9 LC B, 9 LC W]. Compares speech of students to "standard Southern speech" as described by C. M. Wise, finding that most frequent vowel variations were made by lower-class students, both black and white, and that most frequent consonant variations were made only by blacks.

**4.118 Fisher, Hilda Brannon.** 1938. A study of the speech of Jackson, Louisiana, at three age levels. Baton Rouge: Louisiana State University thesis. Abstract in Louisiana State University Bulletin, n.s. 31.161 (1939). [SE LA]. Compares data with "standard Southern" and "nonstandard Southern" and points out intergenerational trends.

**4.119 Fisher, Hilda Brannon.** 1949. A study of the speech of East Feliciana Parish, Louisiana. Baton Rouge: Louisiana State University dissertation. Abstract in Louisiana State University Bulletin n.s. 42.31-32 (1950). [17 informants, SE LA]. Analysis of phonetic data, showing "geographical spread of phonemic variants, and comparing phonetic characteristics with the standard southern dialect"; explores British and American correspondences to dialectal forms of area.

**4.120 Fluke, Dorotha Louise.** 1938. A descriptive study of the speech of

Dutchtown, Louisiana, at three age levels. Baton Rouge: Louisiana State University thesis. vii + 139 pp. Abstract in Louisiana State University Bulletin, n.s. 31.78 (1939). [Ascension Parish, SE LA]. Investigates Southern, "General American," and Cajun French influences on pronunciation of different generations.

**4.121 Frazer, Timothy C.** 1978. South midland pronunciation in the north central states. AS 53.40-48. 3 maps. Investigates distribution of North Midland, South Midland, and Southern variants of six vowels and diphthongs in LANCS data; includes coverage of KY.

**4.122 Freiman, Howard A.** 1979. Speech rate as a function of dialect geography. Applied sociolinguistics, ed. by Robert N. St. Clair, 128-36. Lawrence, KY: Coronado. [35 W M students at Vanderbilt University]. Experimental study that concludes "the popular notion that Southerners talk slower than Northerners is false" although it "might be true that the individual phonemes pronounced by Southerners are said at a slower rate."

**4.123 Fruit, John P.** [with notes by C. H. Grandgent]. 1892. Uncle Remus in phonetic spelling. DN 1.196-98. Transcription of text read as if by a Southern black.

**4.124 Fujii, Kenzo.** 1979. Amerika no LAGS keikaku no genkyo to igi [Progress and significance of LAGS]. The Bulletin, the Phonetic Society of Japan 160.16-18.

**4.125 Furbee, N. Louanna.** 1972. Transcription of Appalachian child's English. Culture, class, and language variety: a resource book for teachers, ed. by A. L. Davis, 212-13. Urbana, IL: NCTE. Orthographic and brief phonetic transcript of ten-year-old child from Barboursville, KY.

**4.126 Gebelin, Elizabeth Gertrude.** 1932. Prevalent errors of speech among the children of Baton Rouge, Louisiana, and means for their correction. Baton Rouge: Louisiana State University dissertation. 174 pp. [385 children, 35 each from grades 1-11 in Baton Rouge]. Attempts "to discover what errors of pronunciation are prevalent among the children of a typical Louisiana community," using standard oral reading of sentences.

**4.127 George, Albert D.** 1951. Some Louisiana isoglosses, based on the workbooks of the Louisiana Dialect Atlas. Baton Rouge: Louisiana State University thesis. v + 169 pp. [68 informants, 38 communities]. Using interview records from the Louisiana Dialect Atlas, finds four dialects of LA speech: "general American," "southern," "French-colored English," and "mountain."

**4.128 George, Albert Donald.** 1952. Graduate study and research in linguistic geography: some Louisiana isoglosses. SSJ 18.87-95. 13 maps. [80 natives, 33 parishes]. Examines use of postvocalic /r/ in field records of th

Linguistic Atlas of Louisiana and draws isoglosses; find areas of /r/-lessness extend up Mississippi, Red, and Ouachita rivers.

**4.129 Gilbert, Glenn.** 1987. Phonological variation among blacks, Brandywines, and whites in Charles Co., Maryland. Variation in language NWAV-XV at Stanford: proceedings of the fifteenth annual conference on new ways of analyzing variation, ed. by Keith M. Denning, Sharon Inkelas, Faye C. McNair-Knox, and John R. Rickford, 160-72. Stanford, CA: Stanford University Department of Linguistics. 3 maps. [14 B, 9 W, 6 Brandywine 2nd-graders, 3 B, 5 W, 8 Brandywine teachers]. Examines postvocalic /r/ and final consonant cluster simplification, finding that adult Brandywines, an isolated tri-racial group of speakers, have lower level of /r/ in every environment than blacks or whites but that Brandywine and black children have similar levels of /r/.

**4.130 Gingiss, Peter, and Valerie Sheppard.** 1976. Stress variation in Texas English. Southwest areal linguistics then and now: proceedings of the fifth southwest areal language and linguistics workshop, ed. by Bates Hoffer and Betty Lou Dubois, 152-61. San Antonio: Trinity University. Investigates variability of stress in Thanksgiving, umbrella, and insurance in TX pronunciation and discusses whether this should be handled in the lexicon or in the phonological rules of a grammar.

**4.131 Glenn, Ethel C.** 1977. Articulation habits of North Carolina sixth grade students. North Carolina Journal of Speech and Drama 10.4.2-9. [430 6th-graders]. Says "percentage of nonstandard [i.e., Southern] pronunciation" of six vowel and two consonant features ranges from 46.7% to 20.8% for NC pupils.

**4.132 Glowka, Wayne, and Ellen Glowka.** 1986. Talking through a smile: high school cheerleader talk in middle Georgia. Abstract in NADS 18.3.11. Discusses rhythm, pausing, syllabification, liaison, and consonant reduction in high school football cheers; says white female cheerleaders tend "to adopt the phonological features of black speakers or older white speakers of the area."

**4.133 Goodwin, Thelma.** 1960. Observations on speech patterns in fifteen areas of Alabama. Nashville: George Peabody College specialist thesis. [34 older natives, 11 M, 23 F, from 15 counties throughout AL]. Surveys vowel and consonant pronunciation in state and classifies into four groups of "deviations from so-called standard Southern speech."

**4.134 Grace, Eugene.** 1977. Southern Louisiana English and the substratum theory. Abstract in NADS 9.3.8. Suggests substratal influence from French in nasalization of vowels in LA English.

**4.135 Grandgent, Charles H.** 1890. English sentences in American mouths. DN 1.198-204. Transcriptions of a text from H. Sweet's Elementarbuch des gesprochenen Englisch as read by speakers from various regions; includes one MD and one KY speaker.

**4.136 Grandgent, Charles H.** 1890. HAF and HAEF. DN 1.269-75. Reports on national survey of pronunciation of 130 words with /ɑ/ ∼ /æ/ alternation.

**4.137 Grandgent, Charles H.** 1891. Notes on American pronunciation. MLN 6.41-44. Comments on regional distribution of vowel and diphthong pronunciations, especially before /r/, based on 180 questionnaires sent to ADS and MLA members; uses early ADS transcription system.

**4.138 Grandgent, Charles H.** 1891. More notes on American pronunciation. MLN 6.229-34. Survey of regional distribution of vowel pronunciations, based on 160 questionnaires sent to scholars.

**4.139 Grandgent, Charles H.** 1894. English in America. Die Neueren Sprachen 2.443-69. Detailed analysis of American English pronunciation, with notes on regional variants, covering vowel and segmental phonemes, vowels before /r/, stress, consonant and vowel length, syllabication, and intonation; based on five questionnaires distributed to members while author was secretary of the Phonetic Section of the MLA.

**4.140 Grandgent, Charles H.** 1894. Unaccented I. DN 1.319-23. Reports on national survey of 150 educated speakers to determine percentages of three variants in eight regions of the country, including the South.

**4.141 Grandgent, Charles H.** 1894. The phonetic section. MLN 9.95-96. Reports results from fifth postal questionnaire on pronunciation of -ful with vowel plus /l/ or with vocalic /l/, latter being decidedly preferred in the South.

**4.142 Grandgent, Charles H.** 1894. Teat-yure. MLN 9.136-38. Variation in palatalization of alveolar consonants before high-front vowels in words in eight regions, including the South.

**4.143 Grandgent, Charles H.** 1903. American pronunciation again. MLN 18.137-41. Reports on regional patterns of pronunciation, based on 192 questionnaires sent to MLA members; discusses types of /r/, aspiration of initial "wh," and vowels of words like period and haunt.

**4.144 Gray, Giles W., and Claude M. Wise.** 1959. The southern drawl. The bases of speech, 293. 3rd ed. New York: Harper.

**4.145 Greet, William Cabell.** 1931. A phonographic expedition to Williamsburg, Virginia. AS 6.161-72. Reports on project to record 170 speakers in Tidewater area of VA and makes forty-two observations about usages; concludes that "drawl and laxness is not characteristic of Tidewater

Virginia" and that "there is not so strong a tendency to diphthongs as is found inland in the South."

**4.146 Greet, William Cabell.** 1933. Delmarva speech. AS 8.4.56-63. Based on fifty-nine phonograph records of residents of peninsula, surveys pronunciation of vowel and consonant phonemes; includes two transcripts.

**4.147 Greet, William Cabell, and W. B. Meloney.** 1930. Two notes on Virginia speech. AS 6.94-96. Pronunciation of house, houses; speech of Guinea Neck, Gloucester County.

**4.148 Greibesland, Solveig C.** 1970. A comparison of uncultivated black and white speech in the Upper South. Chicago: University of Chicago thesis. 87 pp. [3 B and 3 W paired for education, age, and socioeconomic position, Northern Neck of VA and MD Eastern Shore]. Using LAMSAS field records, finds reduction of final consonant clusters more common in black speech and /w/ glide as bilabial fricative and certain allophones of labiodental fricatives only in black speech, but finds vowel pronunciation correlates with geographical region and not race.

**4.149 Habick, Timothy.** 1980. Sound change in farmer city: a sociolinguistic study based on acoustic data. Urbana: University of Illinois dissertation. Abstract in DAI 41.655A. 441 pp. [7 speakers, 3 generations, Somerset, KY, 40 speakers from IL]. Spectrographic analysis of generational differences in vowel offglides and placement of /u/ vowel. Includes comments on Southern drawl.

**4.150 Hackett, William A.** 1940. An analysis and suggested solution of the educational problem resultant from dialectal pronunciations in the southern Appalachians. Columbus: Ohio State University dissertation.

**4.151 Hale, Lulu Cooper.** 1930. A study of English pronunciation in Kentucky. Lexington: University of Kentucky thesis. 60 pp. [44 University of Kentucky students from 33 counties]. Discusses pronunciation of vowels, diphthongs, and two consonants (postvocalic /r/ and final velar nasal); includes alphabetical list of words.

**4.152 Hall, Joan Huston.** 1976. Rural southeast Georgia speech: a phonological analysis. Atlanta: Emory University dissertation. Abstract in DAI 37.2830A. [32 W, 32 B]. Finds "no systematic differences based solely on race" and that most subregional allophonic and incidental phonemic variations are due to different settlement patterns and economic histories; finds Savannah not to be focal area.

**4.153 Hall, Joseph S.** 1942. The phonetics of Great Smoky Mountain speech. New York: Columbia University dissertation. Also in AS 17 (Apr. 1942), part 2. Same as AS Reprints and Monographs no. 4. New York: Columbia University Press. Bibliography, 107-10. [TN, NC]. Study based on seventy-three recordings of "Arthur the Rat" and on folk and local stories recorded between 1937 and 1940, covering stressed vowels, unstressed vowels, and consonants, but little attention to social variation. **Reviews:** R I. McDavid, Jr. 1943. Language 19.184-95 (reprinted in **1.454**); A. H Marckwardt. 1942. QJS 28.487; D. Whitelock. 1944. YWES 23.28-29.

**4.154 Hamilton, Ruth Steagall.** 1942. A study of deviations from standard Southern speech as shown by Louisiana State University freshmen born in Louisiana. Baton Rouge: Louisiana State University thesis. 41 pp. Abstract in Louisiana State University Bulletin n.s. 35.100 (1943). [107 college freshman native to LA]. Finds widespread "sub-standard southern" pronunciations but says they are "not characteristic of any particular group."

**4.155 Hamilton, Westley H.** 1977. Phonological variations observed in San Antonio, Texas. Journal of the Linguistic Association of the Southwest 2.83-93. [23 Anglos, 2 blacks, 35 Mexican-Americans]. Investigates same features as Sawyer (**1.671**) and finds that Mexican-American speech i evolving toward that of Anglo-Americans in San Antonio.

**4.156 Hanley, Miles L.** 1923. The Texas L. DN 5.247. Discusses inter vocalic dental /l/ common in South in words like Dallas and Helen.

**4.157 Hanley, Theodore D.** 1950. An analysis of vocal frequency and duration characteristics of selected samples of speech from General American, Eastern American, and Southern American dialect regions. Iowa City: University of Iowa dissertation. 76 pp. [67 M]. Acoustic study o vocal frequency and duration characteristics of selected samples of speech "from General American, Southern American and Eastern American"; find that "sounds which are stressed tend to be relatively greater in duration fo the Southern American group, while unstressed sounds" tend to be relatively greater in duration for Eastern Americans.

**4.158 Harris, Alberta.** 1948. Southern mountain dialect. Baton Rouge Louisiana State University thesis. Abstract in Louisiana State University Bulletin, n.s. 41.87 (1949). 116 pp. [S Appalachia, Ozarks, E TX]. States there is little difference in pronunciation between three areas, based or evidence collected from personal observation, classroom teaching, published literature, and recordings made by author.

**4.159 Harris, Maverick Marvin.** 1969. The retroflexion of postvocalic /r/ in Austin. AS 44.263-71. Based on fieldwork in department stores ir Austin, TX, finds that retroflexion of postvocalic /r/ varies "socially occupationally, and to a lesser degree stylistically, slight retroflexion being the prestige model of older people"; says that "almost exclusive use of the heavily retroflexed form appears likely in the not too distant future."

**4.160 Hartman, Erika.** 1981. The front vowels before r of the north-central states. Chicago: Illinois Institute of Technology dissertation.

Abstract in DAI 42.3137A. [Includes KY]. Discusses diminishing contrasts in phonemic system as revealed in LANCS field records.

**4.161 Hartman, James W.** 1985. Guide to pronunciation. Dictionary of American Regional English, ed. by Frederic G. Cassidy, xli-lxi. Cambridge: Harvard University Press. Discusses present-day variation in American English pronunciation and historical influences on this variation; describes twenty-three types of "alternation between sound units" and twenty-seven types of "variation within sound units" and summarizes major regional variants.

**4.162 Hastings, Pat.** 1983. Age stratification of (u) in Lillian, Texas. Research Papers of the Texas Summer Institute of Linguistics 13. Pilot studies in sociolinguistics: variation, use and attitudes, ed. by Jerold A. Edmondson, 37-57. Dallas: SIL. [19 adults, NE TX]. Finds use of glide [j] after initial consonant in words like <u>tune, duke</u>, and <u>new</u> to be decreasing.

**4.163 Heard, Betty Ruth.** 1969. A phonological analysis of the speech of Hays County, Texas. Baton Rouge: Louisiana State University dissertation. Abstract in DAI 30.1546A. Abstract reprinted in J. Williamson and V. Burke 1971(1.823).680-81. [27 speakers, CENT TX]. Studies phonology of different age and education levels; finds more Midland and Northern features in pronunciation than Southern ones but vocabulary is basically Southern.

**4.164 Hempl, George.** 1892. Unstressed wh. MLN 6.155-56. Has brief reference to Southern usage of unaspirated variant in unstressed syllables.

**4.165 Herman, Lewis H., and Marguerite S. Herman.** 1947. American dialects: a manual for actors, directors, and writers. New York: Theatre Arts. 2nd ed. 1949. Southern dialect, 61-100; Delmarva dialect, 101-03; Tidewater dialect, 103-05; East Texas dialect, 109-24; Louisiana French dialect, 125-26; Cajun dialect, 126-42; New Orleans creole dialect 142-47; Mountain dialect 148-84; Negro dialect, 185-223; Gullah dialect, 224-41. Nontechnical and not based on linguistic literature, a guide for dialect interpretation of stage characters.

**4.166 Hill, Archibald A., ed.** 1962. First Texas conference on problems of linguistic analysis in English. Studies in American English. Austin: University of Texas Press. Confrontation of Southern vowels and Trager-Smith system. **Reviews:** C. J. Fillmore. 1964. Word 20.126-55; G. C. Lepsch. 1966. Linguistics 23.104-13.

**4.167 Hollien, Harry, and E. Malcik.** 1962. Adolescent voice change in southern Negro males. Speech Monographs 29.53-58. Finds that the reading fundamental vocal frequency of Southern black males ages 10, 14, and 18 is lower than for Southern and Northern white males in the same age groups, but not to a statistically significant degree.

**4.168 Hollien, Harry, and Patricia Paul.** 1969. A second evaluation of the speaking fundamental frequency characteristics of post-adolescent girls. Language and Speech 12.119-24. [160 F teenagers, Gainesville, FL]. Finds most females attain relatively stable adult voices immediately after puberty.

**4.169 Hopkins, John Rathbone.** 1975. The white middle class speech of Savannah, Georgia: a phonological analysis. Columbia: University of South Carolina dissertation. Abstract in DAI 37.265A. Finds that Savannah speech has many similarities with Charleston speech but that some prestigious Charleston pronunciations are stigmatized in Savannah because they are associated with Jewish and Irish speakers there.

**4.170 Huckleberry, Alan W.** 1970. The disappearing postvocalic r of "General American" English speech. Proceedings of the Sixth International Congress of Phonetic Sciences. Prague: Czech Academy of Sciences. Says "post-vocalic r" is misnomer, since acoustically it is vowel coloring; compares "General American" and other varieties of English.

**4.171 Hudson, Amelia L., and Anthony Holbrook.** 1982. Fundamental frequency characteristics of young black adults: spontaneous speaking and oral reading. JSHR 25.25-28. [100 M, 100 F, B students, ages 18-29, at Florida A and M University]. Finds that black adults have a lower mean fundamental frequency than whites in other studies.

**4.172 Hunt, Hazel Elise.** 1938. A study of the speech of Haynesville, Louisiana, at three age levels. Baton Rouge: Louisiana State University thesis. Abstract in Louisiana State University Bulletin n.s. 31.79 (1939). [NW LA]. Studies generational differences to "see which changes come first, which come last," and which pronunciations remain same; finds differences in postvocalic /r/ but not in the drawl or other features.

**4.173 Huss, Veronica, and Evelyn Werner.** 1940. The conchs of Riviera, Florida. SFQ 4.141-51. [S FL]. Says Conch speech is mixture of Southern American and Bahamian and that Conch pronunciation has variable initial /h/ and variable initial /v/ and /w/; includes sample conversations.

**4.174 Idol, Harriet R.** 1936. A strobophotographic study of Southern intonation. Baton Rouge: Louisiana State University dissertation. [18 speakers]. Exploratory acoustic study of Southern intonational patterns.

**4.175 Ingledue, Grace.** 1938. A study of the speech of three generations in one family and in like generations of three different families in Monroe, Louisiana. Baton Rouge: Louisiana State University dissertation. Abstract in Louisiana State University Bulletin n.s. 31.19-20 (1939). [3 older F, 3 middle-aged M, 3 younger F, LA natives]. Finds that oldest generation used "more nearly pure standard southern American speech," while middle-aged speakers "deviated from standard southern American pronunciation more than their elders"; finds youngest speakers have "more frequent use of the southern drawl" and "more deviations from the standard southern speech" than oldest speakers, but "more deviations from ['General American'] standard than the second generation."

**4.176 Istre, Giles Lothar.** 1966. An investigation of the pronunciation of English by persons of Slavic descent in parts of Plaquemines Parish, Louisiana. Baton Rouge: Louisiana State University thesis. 139 pp. [9 speakers of South Slavic descent, ages 21-70, S CENT LA]. Finds homogeneous phonemic structure in group and that "the speech of the younger generation with advanced education was characterized by more precision than that of the older generation."

**4.177 Ives, Sumner.** 1952. American pronunciation in the linguistic atlas. Tulane Studies in English 3.179-93. Analyzes extent to which American English pronunciation is sampled in LAUSC field records by examining records from W PA, Asheville, NC, and Atlanta, GA; considers how atlas fieldwork procedures and previous knowledge of American English phonemic system affected data gathered by the project.

**4.178 Ives, Sumner.** 1953. Pronunciation of "can't" in the eastern states. AS 28.149-57. 2 maps. Using LANE and LAMSAS records, finds subregional differences in South in raising, lengthening, and diphthongizing of vowel in word, raising being found mostly in mountain areas. **Reprinted** in H. Allen and G. Underwood 1971(**1.12**).169-77.

**4.179 Ives, Sumner.** 1953. Vowel transcriptions in a Georgia field record. Tulane Studies in English 4.147-69. Detailed catalog of incidence of stressed vowels in transcriptions of one LAMSAS record from Atlanta, GA, with notes on unstressed vowels and consonants.

**4.180 Johnson, T. Earle.** 1951. Nasality in Southern speech. SSJ 17.30-39. Defines nasality as "excessive, unpleasant, or improper nasal resonance given to non-nasal sounds" and declares that it is "quite prevalent" in Southern speech.

**4.181 Joos, Martin.** 1934. Regional and personal variations in general American. Le Maître Phonétique, third series 49.45.3-6 (Jan.-Mar.). Compares "General American" to standard Eastern and Southern pronunciation.

**4.182 Kane, Elisha K.** 1925. The Negro dialects along the Savannah River. DN 5.354-67. [GA-SC border area]. Distinguishes three different dialects and portrays pronunciation and syntax of black speech in three stories and accompanying transcription.

**4.183 Kantner, Claude E.** 1944. Variant Louisiana pronunciations of the word "pecan." AS 19.148. Documents eleven variant pronunciations of word.

**4.184 Kenyon, John Samuel.** 1926. Some notes on American r. AS 1.329-39. Surveys pronunciation of consonant in U.S. and Britain; includes extensive comments on Southern American speech.

**4.185 Kerr, Nora Fields.** 1963. Baltimore city English. Washington: Georgetown University thesis. See item below.

**4.186 Kerr, Nora Fields.** 1966. The pronunciation of Baltimore city English. Occasional Papers in TESL 1.2.13-21,66-68. [10 adults, 8 in 20s, 2 in 40s]. Based on reading wordlist, compares findings with data in Kurath and McDavid 1949 (**4.197**). Documents replacement of Southern features with Mid-Atlantic ones for all social classes in city and decreasing prestige of Southern features as they become associated with more recent immigrants from rural South rather than with older, more affluent immigrants from MD Eastern Shore.

**4.187 Klipple, Florence Carmelita.** 1944. A study of the speech of Spicewood, Texas. Austin: University of Texas thesis. [10 speakers, CENT TX]. Study of segmental phonology and intonational characteristics; condensed in following item.

**4.188 Klipple, Florence Carmelita.** 1945. The speech of Spicewood, Texas. AS 20.187-91. [CENT TX]. Finds "an extremely retroflex [r], the preservation of numerous archaisms, and the total lack of any main features of 'plantation-southern' speech"; discusses intonation and finds some evidence for high level final intonation in declarative sentences.

**4.189 Konold, Florence.** 1937. Sectional dialect. A workbook in speech correction for high school teachers, 152-68. Baton Rouge: Louisiana State University thesis. Catalogs "deviations from standard" American speech and presents exercises for correcting them.

**4.190 Krieger, Robert W.** 1963. A phonological study of the speech of mid-city New Orleans, Louisiana. Baton Rouge: Louisiana State University thesis. [18 speakers, ages 15-68]. Based on reading passage, finds "a metropolitan dialect which contains features of Southern, Eastern, and General American English" but which "possesses fewer Southern characteristics than it does features of the other two."

**4.191 Kriger, Albert.** 1942. A study of the speech of Clinton, Louisiana, at three age levels. Baton Rouge: Louisiana State University thesis. Abstract in Louisiana State University Bulletin 35.100-01 (1943). [3 adults, ages 19, 35, 69]. Finds speech of community is chiefly Southern standard; oldest speaker has postvocalic /r/ but youngest speaker does not.

**4.192 Kruse, Vernon David.** 1972. The pronunciation of English in Kentucky, based on the records of the Linguistic Atlas of the North-Central states. Chicago: Illinois Institute of Technology dissertation. Abstract in

DAI 33.4388A. Describes vowels of KY speech, using binary analysis; includes chapter on methods of field work, informants, settlement history, and dialect areas.

**4.193 Kurath, Hans.** 1928. Southern pronunciation. American pronunciation. Society for Pure English Tract 30.291-97. Early, tentative sketch of main features of Southern pronunciation, based on scattered and largely unsystematic research at the time, the description of some of these features needing revision after atlas investigations; calls for systematic study of spoken American English.

**4.194 Kurath, Hans.** 1940. Mourning and morning. Studies for William A. Read, ed. by Nathaniel M. Caffee and Thomas A. Kirby, 166-73. University: Louisiana State University Press. 1 map. Summarizes linguistic atlas findings from Atlantic coast on pronunciation of word pairs like hoarse-horse with low back vowels; finds difference in pronunciation in MD, but not in VA or any other South Atlantic states.

**4.195 Kurath, Hans.** 1962. Regional features in cultivated American pronunciation. Michigan Quarterly Review 1.239-48. 4 maps. Discusses briefly prominent differences in pronunciation of educated Americans and divides differences into three types--systemic, phonic, and incidental.

**4.196 Kurath, Hans.** 1964. A phonology and prosody of modern English. Ann Arbor: University of Michigan Press. 158 pp. Detailed description and comparison of American English (based on LAUSC findings) and standard British English, with most attention to incidence of phonemes; also discusses grammatical intonation, word, phrase, and sentence stress, juncture, and syllabification. **Reviews:** L. F. Brosnahan. 1966. Journal of Australasian Universities Language and Literature Association 26.341-43; A. A. T. Davies. 1968. Archiv für das Studium der Neueren Sprachen 204.376-77; K. Hansen. 1965. ZAA 1.409-11; A. A. Hill. 1967. JEL 1.74-75; C. L. Laird. 1966. English Language Notes 4.315; J. W. Lewis. 1967. English Studies 48.180-83; R. I. McDavid, Jr. 1966. MP 64.182-84; E. Siversten. 1966. Phonetica 14.115-20; J. H. Sledd. 1965. AS 60.201-05; H. O. Thieme. 1966. Die Neueren Sprachen 15.40-41; R. M. Wilson. 1966. YWES 45.43.

**4.197 Kurath, Hans, and Raven I. McDavid, Jr.** 1961. The pronunciation of English in the Atlantic States. Ann Arbor: University of Michigan Press. xi + 364 pp. 180 maps. Paperback edition 1982 published by University of Alabama Press. [Includes MD, WV, VA, NC, SC, GA]. Authoritative phonological demarcation of dialect areas based on field records of LAMSAS and LANE interviews. Presents pronunciation of educated natives in series of seventy synoptic charts of pronunciation of individual speakers, detailed descriptions of how specific words are pronounced throughout the Atlantic states, and 180 large maps that show distribution of various pronunciations of key words. **Reviews:** W. S. Avis. 1965. CJL 11.63-70; F. H. Beukema. 1967. Orbis 16.577-79; A. J. Bronstein. 1962. QJS 68.440-41; R. M.

Dorson. 1963. Ohio History 72.73-75; N. E. Eliason. 1962. SAQ 61.121-22; T. Hill. 1962. MLR 58.624-25; S. J. Keyser. 1963. Language 39.303-16; L'Année Sociologique. 1963. Third series, 531; Leuvense Bijdragen. 1963. 52.180-81; F. F. Lewis. 1962. Professional Geographer 14.35; J. Y. Mather. 1963. Review of English Studies 14.216-18; J. E. Medcalf. 1962. Notes and Queries n.s. 9.402-03; G. Scherer. 1962. Beiträge zur Geschichte der Deutschen Sprache und Literatur 84; A. W. Stanforth. 1963-64. ZFM 30.374-75; B. Trnka. 1962. Philologica Pragensia 5.176-77; B. Trnka. 1962. Casopis pro Moderni Filologii 44.188-90; E. T. Uldall. 1962. Le Maître Phonétique 117.29-31; W. Viereck. 1967. Lebende Sprachen 12.58-59; R. M. Wilson. 1963. YWES 42.51; K-H Wirzburger. 1966. ZAA 14.215-16.

**4.198 La Ban, Frank K.** 1965. Phonological study of the speech of the Conchs, early inhabitants of the Florida Keys, at three age levels. Louisiana State University dissertation. Abstract in DAI 26.3318-19A. Finds characteristic British pronunciations in speech of older Conchs, unique community descended from early 19th-century settlers of FL Keys, but Southern and "General American" pronunciations among younger informants.

**4.199 La Ban, Frank K.** 1971. From cockney to conch. A various language: perspectives on American dialects, ed. by Juanita V. Williamson and Virginia M. Burke, 301-08. New York: Holt, Rinehart and Winston. [Key West, FL]. Condensed from preceding item. Says pronunciation of FL Keys noticeably differs from rest of southern FL; compares it to British, general Southern, and "General American" patterns.

**4.200 Labov, William.** 1969. Contraction, deletion, and inherent variability in the English copula. Language 45.715-62. Discusses internal linguistic constraints on phonological processes affecting copula verb in black speech and proposes variable rules to account for these processes.

**4.201 Lass, Roger.** 1987. The shape of English. London: J. M. Dent. North America, Canada and the U.S.A., 280-95. Summary of main features of Southern pronunciation, based primarily on McDavid 1958 (**1.418**).

**4.202 Lawrence, Telete Zorayda.** 1963. An analysis of the speech of twenty students at Texas Christian University. Fort Worth: Texas Christian University thesis.

**4.203 Lawrence, Telete Zorayda.** 1970. Certain phonetic tendencies perceived in the idiolects of selected native Texans. Proceedings of the sixth international congress on the phonetic sciences, September 7-13, 1967, Prague, 527-30. Prague: Czechoslovakian Academy of Sciences.

**4.204 Lawrence, Telete Zorayda.** 1970. Regional speech of Texas: a description of certain paralinguistic features. Actes du Xe congrès international des linguistes, Bucarest, 28 août-2 septembre 1967, 125-30. Vol. 2. Bucarest: Editions de l'Académie de la République Socialiste de

Roumanie. Summarizes findings of acoustic study of nasality in TX speech; includes transcript of discussion following paper.

**4.205 Leas, Susan E.** 1981. A pronunciation of "Negro." AS 56.154. Says pronunciation with final schwa is typical of whites and is not considered pejorative by many blacks. Editor's response (by Charles Clay Doyle), AS 56.154-55.

**4.206 Levine, Lewis, and Harry J. Crockett, Jr.** 1966. Speech variation in a piedmont community: postvocalic r. Sociological Inquiry 36.204-26. Also issued as IJAL 33, no. 2, part 2 (1967), pp. 76-98. [216 W, CENT NC]. Finds younger people, newer residents, and middle-class speakers closer to national norm than men, older people, long-term residents, and blue-collar speakers, the latter closer to traditional Southern pattern of not pronouncing /r/ after vowels. **Reprinted** in J. Williamson and V. Burke 1971(**1.823**).437-60; in Explorations in Sociolinguistics, ed. by S. Lieberson. Indiana University Publications in Anthropology and Linguistics no. 44 (1967).

**4.207 Levine, Lewis, and Harry J. Crockett, Jr.** 1979. Modal and modish pronunciations: some sex differences in speech. Language and society: anthropological issues, ed. by William C. McCormack and Stephen A. Wurm, 209-20. The Hague: Mouton. [30 W, CENT NC]. Studies extent to which cross-section of speakers pronounce sixty-seven words identically to one another, based on sentence-list and word-list passages to examine conformity of different social groups in their pronunciation.

**4.208 Loman, Bengt.** 1967. Intonation patterns in a Negro-American dialect: a preliminary report. Washington: CAL. 292 pp.

**4.209 Loman, Bengt.** 1967. Conversations in a Negro American dialect. Washington: CAL. 164 pp. [3 adults, 5 children, Washington, DC]. Transcriptions of fourteen texts of eight black speakers in modified standard spelling with accompanying stress notations.

**4.210 Loman, Bengt.** 1980. Prosodic patterns in a Negro American dialect. Style and text: studies presented to Nils Erik Enkvist, ed. by Hakan Ringbom et al., 219-42. Stockholm: Sprakfolaget Skriptor. [10-year-old children, Washington, DC]. Detailed analysis of juncture, stress, pitch, and intonation of black speech contours from recorded conversations, with extensive illustrations.

**4.211 Lomax, Alan.** 1973. Cross cultural factors in phonological change. LIS 2.161-75. Connects "frequencies of vowels in one set of songs and the severity of sexual sanctions in that community . . ."; discusses Southern Appalachian and Southern black songs and cultures.

**4.212 Lomax, Alan, and Edith Caldwell Trager.** 1964. Phonotactique du chant populaire. L'Homme 4.5-55. Compares aspects of phonotactics of folk songs from many countries and languages, including three from Southern mountains and one from AL.

**4.213 Lowman, Guy S.** 1936. The treatment of /au/ in Virginia. Proceedings of the second international congress on phonetic sciences, 122-25. Cambridge, UK: Cambridge University Press. Seven types of /au/ described, with well-defined areal boundaries, from Linguistic Atlas evidence.

**4.214 Luelsdorff, Philip A.** 1971. A segmental phonology of black English. Washington: Georgetown University dissertation. Abstract in DAI 33.742A. Published in 1975 by Mouton, The Hague. Constructs segmental phonology of English spoken by black adolescents in Washington, DC, based on one principal informant.

**4.215 McAtee, W. L.** 1945. A pronunciation of sedge. AS 20.306. Sage grass.

**4.216 McCarthy, Janice.** 1963. A phonological study of the speech of Rayville, Louisiana, at three age levels. Baton Rouge: Louisiana State University thesis. 138 pp. [3 natives, ages 18, 50, and 71, NE LA]. Says that community "lies on the edge of the Southern speech region where General American and, to a lesser extent, Mountain speech influences can be felt but do not predominate"; finds raising, drawling, and nasalizing of vowels at all age levels.

**4.217 McCormick, S. D.** 1900. The Virginia dialect. Bookman 11.446-50. Pronunciation.

**4.218 McDavid, Raven I., Jr.** 1940. Low-back vowels in the South Carolina Piedmont. AS 15.144-48. [75 natives, NW SC]. Examines frequency of occurrence of low-back vowels in 158 words; finds SC Piedmont speech "quite different" from Midwestern speech, especially when vowel is followed by an intervocalic /r/.

**4.219 McDavid, Raven I., Jr.** 1941. SAMLA and Southern pronunciation. SAB 6.4.17-18. Notes little research done on standard Southern speech (as opposed to more exotic, relic varieties) and calls on Southerners to help dictionaries compile material on standard Southern.

**4.220 McDavid, Raven I., Jr.** 1943. Review of The phonetics of Great Smoky Mountain speech by Joseph S. Hall. Language 19.84-95. Extended review criticizing Hall's fieldwork and presentation of material. **Reprinted** in R. McDavid 1979(**1.454**).317-24.

**4.221 McDavid, Raven I., Jr.** 1943. /ɪzənt/ and /ɪdənt/: addenda. Studies in Linguistics 1.17.6. Points out replacement of /z/ by /d/ before nasals, as in isn't and cousin in South, especially in Middle TN.

**4.222 McDavid, Raven I., Jr.** 1944. The unstressed syllabic phonemes of a Southern dialect: a problem of analysis. Studies in Linguistics 2.51-55. Discusses vowels in unstressed syllables of /r/-less speech in Greenville, SC. **Reprinted** in R. McDavid 1979(**1.454**).267-69.

**4.223 McDavid, Raven I., Jr.** 1948. Postvocalic /-r/ in South Carolina: a social analysis. AS 23.194-203. Shows how lack of /r/ in white speech spread from low-country plantation belt with influence and migration of Charlestonians and how pronunciation of /r/ was preserved in areas of state populated by working-class whites and few blacks; although absence of /r/ has traditionally been a prestigious feature, McDavid finds it giving way in communities having military bases with Northern personnel. **Reprinted** in D. Hymes, ed. 1964. Language in Culture and Society, 473-80; in M. Lourie and N. Conklin 1978(**1.397**).178-86; in R. McDavid 1979(**1.454**).136-42; in R. McDavid 1980(**1.456**).1-14.

**4.224 McDavid, Raven I., Jr.** 1949. Derivatives of Middle English [o:] in the South Atlantic area. QJS 35.496-504. Outlines regional distribution of [u] and [ʊ] for twenty words in South Atlantic states.

**4.225 McDavid, Raven I., Jr.** 1949. /r/ and /y/ in the South. Studies in Linguistics 7.1.18-19. Notes that pronunciation of stressed vowels in words like <u>worm</u> and <u>thirty</u> with [y] offglide rather than [r] is scattered throughout South Atlantic states. **Reprinted** in McDavid 1979(**1.454**).270-71.

**4.226 McDavid, Raven I., Jr.** 1949. Review of Phonetics of American English by Charles K. Thomas. Studies in Linguistics 7.89-99. **Reprinted** in McDavid 1979(**1.454**).335-39.

**4.227 McDavid, Raven I., Jr.** 1949-1950. Our initial consonant "h." CE 11.458-59. Summarizes LANE and LAMSAS findings for use of initial aspirant before /y/ and /w/ in words like <u>humor, whip, wharf</u>, and <u>whoa</u>; says most speakers in South Atlantic states lack aspirant but that this pronunciation has no social stigma.

**4.228 McDavid, Raven I., Jr.** 1952-53. Some social differences in pronunciation. LL 4.102-16. Includes Southern features. **Reprinted** in H. B. Allen. 1958. Readings in Applied English Linguistics, 1st ed., 174-85, 2nd ed. (1964), 251-61; in R. McDavid 1979(**1.454**).114-20; in D. Shores 1972(**1.685**).42-52.

**4.229 McDavid, Raven I., Jr.** 1953. Notes on the pronunciation of "catch." CE 14.290-91. Geographical distribution of pronunciation "ketch" in cultivated speech. Also in EJ 42.98-99 (Feb. 1953). **Reprinted** as "The Pronunciation of 'Catch,'" in J. D. Barry and W. U. McDonald, Language into Literature (1965), 174-76; in H. B. Allen, ed. 1958. Readings in Applied English Linguistics, 167-69. 1st ed. New York: Appleton Century Crofts.

**4.230 McDavid, Raven I., Jr.** 1956. Social differences in pronunciation: a problem in methodology. General Linguistics 2.15-21.

**4.231 McDavid, Raven I., Jr.** 1967. A checklist of significant features for discriminating social dialect. Dimensions of dialect, ed. by Eldonna Evertts. Champaign, IL: NCTE. **Reprinted** in A. L. Davis 1969(**1.159**).133-39.

**4.232 McDavid, Raven I., Jr.** 1970. Some problems of over-all patterning. Proceedings of the Sixth International Congress on Phonetic Sciences, 7-13 September, 1967, Prague, 631-32. Prague: Czechoslovakian Academy of Sciences. Points out that vowel and diphthong contrasts in Southeast cannot be accommodated in Trager-Smith vowel system.

**4.233 McDavid, Raven I., Jr.** 1977. Notes on the pronunciation of "American." AS 52.98-104. 4 maps. Discusses variant pronunciations of each vowel and intervocalic /r/ in the word in Atlantic states and in Midwest.

**4.234 McDavid, Raven I., Jr.** 1979. Confederate overalls: or a little Southern sweetening. Dialects in Culture: essays in general dialectology by Raven I. McDavid, Jr., ed. by William A. Kretzschmar et al., 282-87. University: University of Alabama Press. [Charleston and Greenville, SC]. Paper written in 1961. Presents detailed case that overall pattern of analyzing long syllabic nuclei designed by Trager and Smith cannot accommodate observable phonological contrasts in Southern speech.

**4.235 McDavid, Raven I., Jr., and Virginia Glenn McDavid.** 1952. h before semivowels in the eastern United States. Language 28.41-62. Initial consonants in whip, whetstone, wheelbarrow, whinny, wharf, whoa, and humor in Linguistic Atlas records; includes MD, VA, WV, NC, SC, and E GA. **Reprinted** in R. McDavid 1979(**1.454**).185-98.

**4.236 McDavid, Raven I., Jr. and Virginia G. McDavid.** 1978. Intuitive rules and factual evidence: /-sp, -st, -sk/ plus -Z. Linguistic and literary studies in honor of Archibald A. Hill, volume 2, ed. by M. A. Jazayery, Edgar C. Polome, and Werner Winter, 73-90. The Hague: Mouton. 9 maps. Investigates occurrence of disyllabic plurals of words like post and wasp and finds pronunciations from both black and white speech; discusses analogous British dialect features.

**4.237 McDowell, John, and Susan McRae.** 1972. Differential response of the class and ethnic components of the Austin speech community to marked phonological variables. AnL 14.228-39. [20 Anglo, 13 Chicano, 13 B]. Examines social, ethnic, and stylistic variation in postvocalic /r/ and offglides of /ay/ diphthong.

**4.238 McMillan, James B.** 1939. Vowel nasality as a sandhi-form of the morphemes "-nt" and "-ing" in Southern American. AS 14.120-23. Discusses variation in pronunciation of negative auxiliary verbs like don't, in which both final consonants are frequently lost and vowel is usually nasalized. **Reprinted** in J. Williamson and V. Burke 1971(**1.823**).489-96.

**4.239 McMillan, James B.** 1946. Phonology of the standard English of east central Alabama. Chicago: University of Chicago dissertation. Description of phonemes and phonotactics of standard white pronunciation in AL piedmont. Synopsized in H. L. Mencken, The American Language, Supplement Two (1948), pp. 130-31.

**4.240 McMillan, James B.** 1968. Unsyllabic schwa in Southern American English. Abstract in PADS 49.40. Says boa and via are homophonous with bore and veer in the South and discusses implications of this for phonological identity of American dialects and for representating pronunciation in dictionaries.

**4.241 Magovern, Anita L.** 1968. The social stratification of the phoneme /r/ in Washington, DC. Washington: Georgetown University thesis.

**4.242 Markel, Norman N., and Clair Ann Sharpless.** 1972. Socio-economic and ethnic correlates of dialect differences. Studies in linguistics in honor of George L. Trager, ed. by M. Estelle Smith, 313-23. The Hague: Mouton. Same as ED 031 703. [Gainesville, FL]. Finds higher-class whites and blacks of higher and lower class use mixture of "General American" and Southern features, but lower-class whites use only Southern features; finds overall cleavage between classes for whites but not for blacks.

**4.243 Meese, Elizabeth A.** 1968. The art of the tale teller: a study of the suprasegmental phonemes in a folktale. KFR 14.25-37. Discusses how to represent pitch, stress, juncture in ghost story from Harlan, KY; includes transcription.

**4.244 Merritt, Francine.** 1943. West Texas pronunciation--an investigation. SSJ 9.59-62. [120 natives, students at Hardin-Simmons University, Abilene, TX]. Investigates typical features of W TX pronunciation, extent of substandard features, influence of "General American" and Southern speech, and effect of speech training on pronunciation.

**4.245 Metfessel, Milton.** 1928. Phonophotography in folk music. Chapel Hill: University of North Carolina Press. Dialect in Negro songs, 137-41, compares quality of vowels and diphthongs and division of syllables in African languages and American black folk songs.

**4.246 Michel, John F., Harry Hollien, and Paul Moore.** 1966. Speaking fundamental frequency characteristics of 15, 16 and 17 year old girls. Language and Speech 9.46-51. [307 FL teenagers]. Finds no significant difference in speaking fundamental frequencies (voice pitch levels) across three teenage groups.

**4.247 Miller, Michael I.** 1982. Umlaut and analogy. Abstract in NADS 14.2.2. Investigates plural variants of <u>tooth</u>, <u>foot</u>, and <u>mouse</u> in LAMSAS records.

**4.248 Minchew, E. R.** 1938. A survey of speech anomalies among teachers of Bienville, Jackson, and Red River Parishes of Louisiana. Baton Rouge: Louisiana State University thesis. [NW LA]. Says that eighty percent of the public school teachers of area "showed sufficient errors [in pronunciation, articulation or voice quality] to be classed as 'unsatisfactory'."

**4.249 Minderhout, David.** 1972. Final consonant cluster reduction. Language and linguistics working papers number 5: sociolinguistics, ed. by Richard J. O'Brien, 8-15. Washington: Georgetown University Press. [22 B, Washington, DC]. Analyzes effect of following liquid or glide on final consonant cluster reduction, finding that /l/ and /w/ acted like consonants and /y/ like a vowel; also finds consonant cluster reduction tends to correlate with class and age distinctions, but not with sex.

**4.250 Mock, Carol C.** 1977. Concurrent shifting of /ay/ and /ey/ in the speech of four generations of an Ozark family. Abstract in NADS 9.3.8. ED 150 882. 24 pp. [9 speakers, ages 7-86 in Christian Co., SW MO]. Says differences in speech between generations "indicates that even in rural settings the family may be only a minor influence on the phonetic character of speech"; finds /ey/ becoming more centralized and developing "strong prosodic conditioning," while /ay/, rather than varying along generational lines, is becoming a gender marker.

**4.251 Mock, Carol C.** 1981. Phonological change in an Ozark family: results of a four-generation study. Abstract in NADS 13.3.5. Says that influence of stylistic and social factors is significant for some phonological variables and for some speakers, but not for entire community.

**4.252 Montgomery, Michael.** 1983. The southern drawl as a research problem. Abstract in NADS 15.3.5-6. Hypothesizes that Southern drawl is feature of special register of emphatic or exaggerated Southern English rather than feature of typical speech.

**4.253 Morgan, Lucia C.** 1970. The status of /r/ among North Carolina speakers. Essays in honor of Claude M. Wise, ed. by Arthur J. Bronstein, Claude L. Shaver, and C. Stevens, 167-86. New York: Speech Association of America. [120 W, 15 B native to NC, ages 5-87]. 21 maps. Analyzes regional and age differences in pronunciation of postvocalic /r/ within state.

**4.254 Nail, William A.** 1948. The phonology of the speech of Crawford, Texas. Austin: University of Texas thesis. 134 pp. [12 natives, E TX]. Analyzes phonology of community; includes transcripts.

**4.255 Nicholas, Karl.** 1982. Think you for the wedding rang. SECOL

Review 6.131-37. [77 W, W NC, 25 W, CENT NC]. Finds raising of vowel before nasal in words like __thank__ and __sang__ is strong in lower working class mountain speech and is increasing in NC Piedmont.

**4.256 Nixon, Cynthia Delmar.** 1945. Negro speech in Haynesville, Ruston, and Baton Rouge, Louisiana. Baton Rouge: Louisiana State University thesis. 85 pp. [8 B F]. Abstract in Louisiana State University Bulletin 39.65-66 (1945). Compares N LA with Baton Rouge residents to identify "errors of substitution, omission, insertion, and those related to general American speech."

**4.257 Nobbelin, Kent G.** 1980. The low-back vowels of the north-central states. Chicago: Illinois Institute of Technology dissertation. Abstract in DAI 41.2089-90A. [Includes KY]. Interprets phonic character of vowel patterns in LANCS field records.

**4.258 O'Cain, Raymond K.** 1972. A social dialect survey of Charleston, South Carolina. Chicago: University of Chicago dissertation. Condensed in item below.

**4.259 O'Cain, Raymond K.** 1977. A diachronic view of the speech of Charleston, South Carolina. Papers in language variation, ed. by David L. Shores and Carole P. Hines, 135-50. University: University of Alabama Press. [77 natives]. Intensive study comparing pronunciation of native and nonnative Charlestonians to LAMSAS evidence generation earlier; finds Charleston speech less homogeneous than before, with some traditional pronunciations yielding to Midland forms, others diffusing throughout region, still others, especially centralization of diphthongs, being used by only natives even though they are stereotyped.

**4.260 Parker, Frank.** 1979. "There," "their," and "they." USF LangQ 19.3-4.46-48. Reviews and clarifies proposals for phonological and morphological derivation of possessive __they__ and __you__ and existential __they__.

**4.261 Patrick, Gail.** 1935. Training of the voice and diction of a Southerner for moving pictures. Southern Speech Bulletin 1.24-25. Says Hollywood has double standard in considering Southern accent as "soothing and delightful" but in offering few roles for Southern speakers, all of which are stereotyped; explains how Southerners in Hollywood must shed their accents in order to succeed in acting.

**4.262 Pederson, Lee A.** 1964. The pronunciation of English in metropolitan Chicago: vowels and consonants. Chicago: University of Chicago dissertation. [33 B, 103 W natives of Chicago, IL].

**4.263 Pederson, Lee A.** 1964. Non-standard Negro speech in Chicago. Non-standard speech and the teaching of English, ed. by William A. Stewart, 16-23. Washington: CAL. Compares vowel and consonant features in urban black and white speech and pronunciation of final consonant in greasy in speech of Chicago-born, Midland-born, and Southern-born blacks.

**4.264 Pederson, Lee.** 1977. Structural description in linguistic geography. Papers in language variation: SAMLA-ADS collection, ed. by David L. Shores and Carole P. Hines, 19-24. University: University of Alabama Press.

**4.265 Pederson, Lee.** 1977. Studies of American pronunciation since 1945. AS 52.262-327. Detailed literature survey, with emphasis on linguistic atlas studies. Pp. 300-27, bibliography.

**4.266 Pederson, Lee.** 1985. Systematic phonetics. JEL 18.14-24. Outlines method of classification of phonetic segments to analyze consonants to represent system enabling computer-assisted analysis of consonants and vowels for LAGS.

**4.267 Pederson, Lee.** 1986. An English technical alphabet. LAGS Working Paper, third series, no. 1. Addendum to Pederson, McDaniel, and Bassett 1986(1.600). 17 pp. Discusses six intersecting transcription systems for converting LAGS data from orthographics to "systematics."

**4.268 Pederson, Lee.** 1986. A survey in deductive phonetics. LAGS Working Paper, third series, no. 2. Addendum to Pederson, McDaniel, and Bassett 1986(1.600). 29 pp. Published in ZDL 53.289-309. Discusses development of phonetic code for computer analysis of LAGS data.

**4.269 Pederson, Lee, and Susan Leas McDaniel.** 1986. Mapping phonetics in the gulf states. LAGS Working Paper, third series, no. 5. Addendum to Pederson, McDaniel, and Bassett 1986(1.600). 25 pp. Explains LAGS microcomputer programs for analysis of phonological items.

**4.270 Pence, James W., and Sterling S. Ruffin.** 1972. Vowel phonemes of the black dialect in Ahoskie, North Carolina. North Carolina Journal of Speech and Drama 6.1.28-30. [1 B 47 year old, NE NC]. Discusses quality and incidence of vowels in monosyllables.

**4.271 Pennington, Martha [Carswell].** 1973. A phonology of the speech of Floyd County, Georgia. Penn Review of Linguistics 1.1-12. [NE GA]. Detailed analysis of vowels in stressed syllables and sibilants and phonological processes affecting them.

**4.272 Pennington, Martha Carswell.** 1982. The story of "s" or everything you always wanted to know about sibilants but were afraid to ask. Philadelphia: University of Pennsylvania dissertation. Abstract in DAI 43.3585. [Rome, GA]. Investigates form and phonological and social distribution of sibilants in Rome, GA, area; finds that backing of some types of sibilants expresses "local and rural identity and solidarity, particularly among males," that these sibilants "may be an expression of an American country-western image and so may be increasing in frequency."

**4.273 Perritt, Margaret F.** 1942. A study of the usage of the /r/ phoneme by freshmen students at Louisiana State University. Baton Rouge: Louisiana State University thesis. Abstract in Louisiana State University Bulletin 35.101-02 (1943). [120 students]. Compares pronunciation of students on basis of sex, speech training, educational background, geography, and other factors, but finds "little consistency of pronunciation of r among various groups or within any single group."

**4.274 Perritt, Margaret F.** 1944. The Louisiana "r." SSJ 9.102-06. Summary of preceding item; includes six tables.

**4.275 Phillips, Betty S.** 1981. Lexical diffusion and Southern "tune," "duke," "news." AS 56.72-78. [60 GA natives, ages 18-21]. Based on reading wordlist, finds that use of glide pronunciation ([ju]) by Southern university students correlates closely with frequency of word.

**4.276 Pike, Kenneth L.** 1945. The intonation of American English. Ann Arbor: University of Michigan Press. Comment on the Southern drawl, 106.

**4.277 Pilch, Herbert.** 1980. The rise of the American English vowel pattern. Perspectives in American English, ed. by J. L. Dillard, 37-70. The Hague: Mouton. Attempts to outline history of American English vowel pattern from time of its geographical separation from British English.

**4.278 Pitts, Ann.** 1986. Flip-flop prestige in American "tune," "duke," "news." AS 61.130-38. [3704 citations from radio and television announcers]. Says that both glided and glideless pronunciations are prestigious for broadcasters, the former for non-Southern male announcers adopting or maintaining glide in a small number of frequent words, the latter for women and Southern announcers not as well established in the media.

**4.279 Plank, Grace G.** 1930. Pronunciation in American speech. Rochester: University of Rochester thesis. 101 pp. The Southern dialect, 19-41. Attempts to "sum up, on the basis of such materials as are available, the present state of American dialects."

**4.280 Pulley, Michael L.** 1982. Stylistic shifting in the Missouri Ozarks. Abstract in NADS 14.3.4. [12 natives]. Discusses stylistic shifting in Ozark speech and compares four phonological features to findings of W. Wolfram and D. Christian (**1.852**)..

**4.281 Randolph, Vance, and Anna A. Ingleman.** 1928. Pronunciation in the Ozark dialect. AS 3.401-07. Surveys Ozark pronunciation and says it is, after vocabulary, most distinctive part of region's speech.

**4.282 Randolph, Vance, and Patti Sankee.** 1930. Dialectical survivals in the Ozarks, I archaic pronunciation. AS 5.198-208. Surveys analogues between Ozark pronunciation and earlier British speech.

**4.283 Raubichek, Letitia, Estelle H. Davis, and L. Adele Carll.** 1931. Voice and speech problems. New York: Prentice-Hall. Pp, 317-18, list of Southern pronunciations considered "provincial" and needing correction, including diphthongs and vowels before /r/ and /l/.

**4.284 [Rayburn, Otto E.].** 1956. A: in Ozark dialect. Rayburn's Ozark Guide 14.47.28-29. Says that the "first letter of the English alphabet is corrupted in various ways" in Ozark speech but that British and Bostonian "broad a" has never caught on in region, despite efforts of at least one determined teacher.

**4.285 Read, William A.** 1909. The vowel system of the Southern United States. Englische Studien 41.70-78. Broad description of six classes of vowel sounds in speech of educated native Southerners; compares qualities of vowels to British English and European languages, but makes no distinctions within South.

**4.286 Read, William A.** 1910. The Southern r. Louisiana School Review, Feb. Essay on qualities of the consonant in variety of phonological environments in the South; compares Southern patterns with British and other American patterns and discusses historical aspects of the consonant. **Reprinted** in Louisiana State University Bulletin 1.2.3-13 (1910).

**4.287 Read, William A.** 1911. Some variant pronunciations in the new South. DN 3.497-536. [General South, 11 states except SC]. Detailed presentation of findings from 241 mail questionnaires concerning variant pronunciations of thirty words and comparisons of them with Middle and Early Modern English pronunciations. **Reprinted** in Louisiana State University Bulletin 3.5. (1912). **Review:** O. Glode. 1912. Englische Studien 45.439-40.

**4.288 Read, William A.** 1923. Some phases of American pronunciation. JEGP 22.217-44. Examines archaizing and innovating features of vowel and consonant phonology in American English as compared to British English.

**4.289 Reese, George H.** 1941. Pronunciation of "shrimp," "shrub," and similar words. AS 16.251-55. [VA]. History and explanation of variation between "sr" and "shr".

**4.290 Reese, James Robert.** 1983. Intonational variation in southern Appalachian English. Abstract in NADS 15.2.5. Suggests computer analysis of pitch, stress, vowel length, and juncture can be used to identify and classify dialects in Southern Appalachian region.

**4.291 Reinecke, George Francis.** 1951. New Orleans pronunciation among school children and educated adults. New Orleans: Tulane University thesis. 166 pp. Abstract in Tulane University Bulletin, series 52, 13.72 (1951). [42 children, 20 adults from New Orleans]. Describes pronunciation of educated white speech in New Orleans and attempts to abstract a standard; includes all transcribed data.

**4.292 Reynolds, Jack A.** 1934. The pronunciation of English in southern Louisiana. Baton Rouge: Louisiana State University thesis. Surveys English pronunciation of predominantly French-speaking areas of the state.

**4.293 Rice, B. W.** 1936. Note on the Ozark dialect. Rayburn's Arcadian Life, Sulphur Springs, TX. 2.6.3 (Mar.) Old-time pronunciations in the Ozarks.

**4.294 Ripman, Walter.** 1918. The sounds of spoken English. New York: Dutton. Pp. 24-29, Brer Rabbit story in phonetic transcription with notes.

**4.295 Rizzo, Sr., Mary Joanna.** 1945. The speech of New Orleans, Louisiana at three age levels. Baton Rouge: Louisiana State University thesis. xiv + 201 pp. Abstract in Louisiana State University Bulletin 39.66 (1947). [3 speakers, ages 21, 48, and 78]. Finds youngest speaker has "more precision" and older speaker "more substandardisms" and that components of New Orleans pronunciation, in order of prominence, are "standard southern American," "standard general American," "standard eastern American," and substandard.

**4.296 Roberts, Margaret M.** 1966. The pronunciation of vowels in Negro speech. Columbus: Ohio State University dissertation. Abstract in DAI 27.3328B. ix + 98 pp. [20 W, 20 B teenagers from Columbus, OH]. Compares vowels and diphthongs of white and black high school students and examines whether race of a speaker can be determined from tape recorded speech; subjective cues reported by listeners to distinguish black speech "included nasality, vowel prolongation, lower pitch, and slower rate" and to distinguish white speech "higher pitch, faster rate, and precise articulation."

**4.297 Rubrecht, August Weston.** 1971. Regional phonological variants in Louisiana speech. Gainesville: University of Florida dissertation. Abstract in DAI 32.6958A. [28 native English speakers from 18 communities throughout LA, ages 11-88]. Describes phonetic features characteristic of four subregions; provides maps for all stressed vowels and some consonants.

**4.298 Rudorf, E. Hugh, and Richard T. Graham.** 1970. An investigation of the effect of dialect variation upon the learning of phoneme-grapheme relationships in American English spelling. Final report, U.S. Dept. of HEW. ED 039 259. Focuses on whether spelling mistakes of sixth-graders from four different regions are related to the dialects of the students.

**4.299 Rueter, Grace S.** 1975. Vowel nasality in the speech of rural middle Georgia. Atlanta: Emory University dissertation. Abstract in DAI 36.8027-28A. [3 adults]. Says vowel nasality cannot be accounted for by conventional phonemic model; finds nasality more frequent for blacks than for whites and slightly more frequent for higher class whites than for poor whites.

**4.300 Sanders, Sara L.** 1978. The speech of Fairfax, South Carolina, in its sub-regional context: selected phonological features. Columbia: University of South Carolina thesis. [12 W, 12 B adults, Allendale Co., SC]. Compares six phonological features of Fairfax, SC, a small rural community, with that of Augusta, Savannah, and Charleston, three equidistant cities; finds Fairfax most like Charleston and that innovations in white speech move upward from bottom of social structure, while innovations in black speech begin at top of the social structure and move down.

**4.301 Schaffer, James E.** 1964. A survey of the speech of certain students at Xavier University of Louisiana in New Orleans. New Orleans: Tulane University thesis. [519 B undergraduates in New Orleans]. Finds that speakers of black English scored lower on a test of "correctness" in pronunciation than speakers of LA Creole French.

**4.302 Schnitzer, Marc L.** 1972. The Baltimore /o/ and generative phonology. General Linguistics 12.86-93. Shows how sequence of generative phonological rules describes fronting of all back vowels in Baltimore, MD, speech.

**4.303 Searles, Charlotte L.** 1938. A study of the speech of Minden, Louisiana, at three age levels. Baton Rouge: Louisiana State University thesis. Abstract in Louisiana State University Bulletin n.s. 31.164 (1939). [3 adults, ages 17, 40, and 66, NW LA] 187 pp. Finds little use of postvocalic /r/ and in general "more resemblance of the speech of the three informants to sub-standard southern than any other dialectal form."

**4.304 Sharpless, Clair Ann.** 1966. Pronunciation characteristics of Negro and white sixth-grade children from different socio-economic levels. Gainesville: University of Florida thesis. [20 B, 20 W 6th graders, from highest and lowest class, Gainesville, FL]. Studies ten phonological features and finds blacks of different social classes were similar, while whites of different classes were different in five features; finds lower-class white pronunciation all Southern but that higher-class white and higher and lower class black speech showed some non-Southern features.

**4.305 Shayer, Howard V.** 1972. The stressed vowels of Negro and white speech of the Southern states: a comparison. ED 057 640. 61 pp. Describes stressed vowels in terms of the "chorophone," "an overall pattern unit based on Daniel Jones's 'diaphone'," and says that "some monophthongs tend to be fronter in Southern white speech" and that "the vowels of Southern Negro speech are much more likely to be nearer to the corresponding Gullah vowels than the vowels of Southern white speech are."

**4.306 Sherman, Josephine Elmerine.** 1942. An objective study of the nasalization of diphthongs in the speech of natives of Alabama. Tuscaloosa: University of Alabama thesis. 122 pp. [University of Alabama freshmen from all 67 counties of state]. Acoustic study showing that "diphthong nasality is general throughout the state of Alabama" and that nasality is particularly strong in three subregions of the state.

**4.307 Shewmake, Edwin Francis.** 1925. Laws of pronunciation in eastern Virginia. MLN 40.489-92. Quality and distribution of [au] and [aɪ].

**4.308 Shewmake, Edwin Francis.** 1927. English pronunciation in Virginia. Davidson, NC: privately printed. University of Virginia dissertation, 1920. Though using makeshift transcription, a comprehensive description of pronunciation in VA, covering both contemporary and historical patterns and how VA speech is represented in literature. **Review:** H. Kurath. 1928. AS 3.478-79.

**4.309 Shewmake, Edwin Francis.** 1943. Distinctive Virginia pronunciation. AS 18.33-38. [E VA]. Discusses diphthongs /aɪ/ and /aʊ/ and vowel /o/ before /r/; says cultivated speech in E and W parts of state are distinguishable by pronunciation of diphthongs.

**4.310 Shewmake, Edwin Francis.** 1945. How to find [ʌɪ] in eastern Virginia. AS 20.152-53. Caveats about accurately identifying centralized pronunciation of diphthong /aɪ/ before voiceless consonants in E VA.

**4.311 Shores, David L.** 1984. The stressed vowels of the speech of Tangier Island, Virginia. JEL 17.37-56. [Chesapeake Bay, E VA]. Outlines vowel characteristics of relic speech area and discusses relative influences of surrounding territories on it.

**4.312 Shores, David L.** 1985. Vowels before /l/ and /r/ in the Tangier dialect. JEL 18.124-26. [Chesapeake Bay, E VA]. Says "Tangier speech has /r/ in all positions and that it is notable in that sharp constriction occurs even in the intervocalic and unstressed positions"; finds that "fewer vowels occur before /l/ in the Tangier dialect than in other dialects."

**4.313 Shores, David L.** 1986. "Porchmouth" for "Portsmouth." AS 61.147-52. [SE VA]. Says the "porchmouth" pronunciation occurs for all social classes in Hampton Roads area of VA and that it is apparently a relic from British folk speech.

**4.314 Shores, David L.** 1986. Unstressed vowels in the Tangier dialect. Abstract in NADS 18.3.6. [Chesapeake Bay, E VA]. Examines vowels in final syllables and compares findings to Appalachian speech.

**4.315 Sledd, James H.** 1955. Review: George L. Trager and Henry Lee Smith. An outline of English structure. Language 31.312-35. Reprinted as Bobbs-Merrill Reprint Series, Language-83. Argues that Trager-Smith phonology is inadequate for representing vowels of Southern speech.

**4.316 Sledd, James H.** 1958. Some questions of English phonology. Language 34.252-58. Responds to H. Kurath critique of preceding item and says that "for some dialects, a unit analysis must include an absolute minimum of twenty-four vowel phonemes and . . . at least tenuous arguments might be advanced for over forty."

**4.317 Sledd, James H.** 1959. Footnote for rebels. A short introduction to English grammar, 48. Chicago: Scott Foresman. Notes "low front unround, somewhat retracted" vowel /a/, especially as first element of diphthongs in words like fire and tire, in speech of SE U.S. but not elsewhere.

**4.318 Sledd, James H.** 1966. Breaking, umlaut, and the Southern drawl. Language 42.18-41. Describes in detail and formulates phonological rules for Southern drawl and compares it to more general patterns of American pronunciation. **Reprinted** in H. Hungerford et al., eds. 1970. English linguistics, 244-70; in J. Williamson and V. Burke 1971(**1.823**).461-88.

**4.319 Sledd, James H.** 1987. The last blast of the trumpet against unbelievers; or, instrumental evidence of breaking and umlaut in the one genuine U. S. English. Abstract in NADS 19.3.6. Says that "instrumental analysis shows that breaking and umlaut can produce phonetic differences between manifestations of the same phoneme which are greater than differences between distinct phonemes in some other American dialects."

**4.320 Smith, H. A.** 1974. How to talk Texian in tin easy lessons. Smithsonian 5.108. Says raised [ı] pronunciation of front short vowel in words like ten and pen is most distinctive pronunciation of Texans.

**4.321 Smith, Harley A.** 1936. A recording of English speech sounds at three age levels in Ville Platte, Louisiana. Baton Rouge: Louisiana State University dissertation. Abstract in Louisiana State University Bulletin n.s. 28.67-68. [4 speakers, ages 25, 43, 53, 70, SW LA]. Studies relation of local speech to French, Southern English, and "General American" English; finds pronounced French tendencies in all speakers, "General American" English influence greater among older speakers, Southern English greater among younger.

**4.322 Smith, Riley B.** 1973. Some phonological rules in the Negro speech of East Texas. Austin: University of Texas dissertation. Abstract in DAI 34.5949A. [30 B adults, 5 NE TX communities]. Presents thirty-one generative phonological rules for vowels and consonants in black speech.

**4.323 Smith, Riley B.** 1974. Hyperformation and basilect reconstruction.

JEL 8.48-56. Prefers term to "hypercorrection" because it avoids question of existence of conscious process; discusses hyperform pronunciations in E TX and elsewhere.

**4.324 Smith, Voncile Marshall.** 1963. An analysis of the pronunciation of life-long Florida residents who have enrolled in Florida colleges, 1938-63. Gainesville: University of Florida thesis.

**4.325 Stanley, George Edward.** 1971. Phonoaesthetics and west Texas dialect. Linguistics 71.95-102. [Lubbock, TX]. Investigates relations between incidence of phonological features and their classification by native speakers as "ugly" or "uneducated" (i.e., as "not aesthetically pleasing").

**4.326 Stanley, Oma.** 1937. The speech of East Texas. AS monograph no. 2. New York: Columbia University Press. Also in AS 11.3-36; 145-66; 232-52; 327-53 (1936). New York: Columbia University dissertation, 1937. **Reviews:** K. Malone. 1939. MLN 54.536-37; C. K. Thomas. 1938. QJS 24.698; L. Wilson. 1937. Rural Sociology 2.352.

**4.327 Steetle, Ralph Waldo.** 1938. A study of the speech of Lake Charles, Louisiana, at three occupational levels. Baton Rouge: Louisiana State University thesis. Abstract in Louisiana State University Bulletin n.s. 31.80-81 (1939). x + 204 pp. [SW LA]. Compares pronunciation of a business-man, a waterfront worker, and a farmer.

**4.328 Stephenson, Edward A.** 1970. Linguistic predictions and the waning of Southern [ju] in tune, duke, news. AS 45.297-300.

**4.329 Summerlin, Nan Jo Corbitt.** 1972. A dialect study: affective parameters in the deletion and substitution of consonants in the Deep South. Tallahassee: Florida State University dissertation. Abstract in DAI 33.4394A. [39 LC high school students, 20 B, 19 W; 24 MC teachers, 12 B, 12 W, SW GA, NW FL]. Based on Labov quantitative paradigm, studies variables of final consonant cluster reduction, /r/-lessness and /l/-lessness, and consonant substitutions; finds correlations with education, race, age, and sex.

**4.330 Summerlin, Nan Jo C.** 1972. The regional standard/standards: variations from it/them in oral language of lower socio-economic black and white students in a rural Deep South county. Abstract in NADS 5.2.6. [SW GA, NW FL]. Compares consonant features, such as consonant cluster simplification, final devoicing, /r/-lessness and /l/-lessness in speech of lower-class white and black students.

**4.331 Summerlin, Nan Jo C.** 1973. Some systematic phonological variations from the regional standard in the oral language of lower socio-economic white and Negro students in a rural deep south county. Final Report. 154 pp. National Center for Educational Research and Development. Washington: Dept. of HEW. Project 1-D-066. ED 096 669. Version of **4.329**.

**4.332 Summerlin, Nan Jo C.** 1974. Black English in the rural southeast. Sociolinguistics in the southwest, ed. by Bates L. Hoffer and Jacob Ornstein, 23-48. San Antonio: Trinity University. [52 speakers in SW GA, NW FL, schoolteachers, high school students, and second graders]. Condensed version of author's dissertation (**4.329**).

**4.333 Sutton, Vida R.** 1936. The speech of the announcer in radio. Southern Speech Bulletin 1.2.15-17. Discusses preferable features of speech for radio announcers and praises "good Southern speech" for having "a rhythm that makes the most of vowel values and gives time for the voice to emerge. It has a melody that few Southern imitators can reproduce, and at the same time gives diphthongs their value, and not lose essential consonants."

**4.334 Talbert, Bob.** 1968. You orter node that! Sandlapper 1.4.52-53. [SC]. Cites cases of Northerners misunderstanding Southern pronunciation and provides list of SC words in modified spelling that "could possibly be of great help for confused Yankees."

**4.335 Thomas, Charles Kenneth.** 1939. A composite transcription from Knox County, Tennessee. AS 14.125-26; 15.85 (Feb. 1940). Composite transcription of twenty-six Knox County natives who were students at the University of Tennessee.

**4.336 Thomas, Charles Kenneth.** 1944. The dialect significance of the non-phonemic low-back vowel variants before r. Studies in speech and drama in honor of Alexander M. Drummond, 244-54. Ithaca: Cornell University Press. Map showing isogloss and discussion of regional occurrence of stressed vowel variants in words like forest, horrid, borrow, quarry.

**4.337 Thomas, Charles Kenneth.** 1946. Notes on the pronunciation of "hurry." AS 21.112-15. Shows line running from VT to CENT TX separating [ʌ] and [ɜ] pronunciations, noting similarity to line for forest, horrid, orange, etc.

**4.338 Thomas, Charles Kenneth.** 1947. Notes on the pronunciation of "on." AS 22.104-07. Boundary between /ɑn/ and /ɔn/ runs from NJ to W TX.

**4.339 Thomas, Charles Kenneth.** 1948. Mississippi "honey chile." QJS 34.369-70. Transcription of speech of MS college student.

**4.340 Thomas, Charles Kenneth.** 1958. The linguistic Mason and Dixon Line. The rhetorical idiom, ed. by Donald Cross Bryant, 251-55. Ithaca: Cornell University Press. Reissued, New York: Russell and Russell, 1966. Includes map with isoglosses for on, greasy, and grease.

**4.341 Thomas, Charles Kenneth.** 1958. Phonetics of American English.

2nd ed. New York: Ronald Press. 1st ed. 1947. Ch. 21, "Regional variations in American pronunciation," has many comments on Southern features
passim. **Reviews:** Y. H. Frank and A. L. Davis. 1948. LL 1.27-29; R. I.
McDavid, Jr. 1949. Studies in Linguistics 7.89-99 (reprinted in R. I. McDavid 1979(**1.454**).335-39); R. I. McDavid, Jr. 1966. Language 42.149-55 (reprinted in R. McDavid 1979(**1.454**).381-84); R. West. 1948. JSHD 13.145.

**4.342 Thomas, Charles Kenneth.** 1968. Florida pronunciation. SSJ 33.223-
29. [1,117 native W students at 4 FL universities]. Sketches settlement
history and variation in vowels and consonants and compares pronunciation
with rest of South. **Reprinted** in J. Williamson and V. Burke 1971(**1.823**).294-
300.

**4.343 Thompson, Roger M.** 1971. Language loyalty in Austin, Texas: a
study of a bilingual neighborhood. Austin: University of Texas dissertation.
Abstract in DAI 32.6408A. [136 Mexican-American male heads of
household, Austin, TX]. Finds that Mexican-Americans "who believe that
occupational advancement depends on education and ability are adopting
Northern speech patterns" but that those "who feel that their accent is important are adopting a Southern accent."

**4.344 Thompson, Roger M.** 1975. Mexican-American English: social correlates of regional pronunciation. AS 50.18-24. [Austin, TX]. Finds adult
male Mexican-Americans who have adopted regional (Southern or Midland)
pronunciation are better educated, have higher socioeconomic status, are
more likely to have service occupations, and have stronger feeling that
accent is socially important than those who have adopted nonregional or
"standard" pronunciation. **Reprinted** in H. Allen and M. Linn 1986(**1.11**).500-
07.

**4.345 Todd, Julia M.** 1965. A phonological analysis of the speech of aged
citizens of Claiborne County, Mississippi. Baton Rouge: Louisiana State
University dissertation. Abstract in DAI 26.4894. 263 pp. [9 older speakers,
SW MS]. Investigates diphthongs and other phonological phenomena,
presents vowel chart for each informant, based on model in Kurath and
McDavid (**4.197**) and finds post-vocalic /r/ pronounced more often than not
and [ɪ] before nasals in words like pen is categorical.

**4.346 Townsend, Howard W.** 1952. A Texas accent in Brooklyn. Word
Study 27.5.1-3. Testament of Texan who taught speech for year in
Brooklyn; says speech students should learn fundamental features of
American main accents and contrasts Eastern and Southern accents to show
how they might be taught.

**4.347 Trager, George, and Henry L. Smith.** 1957. Outline of linguistic
analysis. Washington: American Council of Learned Societies. 91 pp.
Scattered comments on Southern pronunciations and justification of fitting
Southern vowel phonology into nine-vowel Trager-Smith framework.

**4.348 Tresidder, Argus.** 1941. Notes on Virginia speech. AS 16.112-20. [101 F teenagers from Tidewater, Piedmont, mountain areas of VA]. Examines regional variation in diphthongs /ai/ and /aʊ/, in central and low-back vowels, and postvocalic /r/, saying last feature is main one distinguishing regions of state.

**4.349 Tresidder, Argus.** 1943. The sounds of Virginia speech. AS 18.261-72. Analysis of a passage of 195 words recorded by 254 college students representing all sections of VA; some disagreement with Shewmake (**4.308**).

**4.350 Troike, Rudolph C.** 1971. Overall pattern and generative phonology. Readings in American dialectology, ed. by Harold B. Allen and Gary N. Underwood, 324-42. New York: Appleton-Century Crofts. Proposes generative model for dialect comparison and discusses implications of its adoption, including its handling of Sledd's "tenth vowel" argument (cf. **4.317**).

**4.351 Troike, Rudolph C.** 1986. McDavid's law. JEL 19.177-205. Abstract in NADS 17.3.2. Gives examples and assesses status of sound change of [z] to [d] before a nasal, as in isn't, first discussed by R. McDavid (**4.221**).

**4.352 Tucker, R. Whitney.** 1966. Vibrate. AS 41.77-78. Vibrate pronounced as vabberate in N VA.

**4.353 Underwood, Gary N.** 1971. Some rules for the pronunciation of English in Northwest Arkansas. ED 057 652. 16 pp. Presents set of ordered rules for vowels, based on underlying system of diaphonemes.

**4.354 Underwood, Gary N.** 1977. The pronunciation of "r" in Arkansas. Abstract in NADS 10.2.6. Says distribution of postvocalic /r/ in AR does not support traditional dialect boundaries drawn through state.

**4.355 Underwood, Gary N.** 1980. The orthoepy of Jim Everhart, or how to talk like the proverbial good old boy from Texas. Speaking, singing and teaching: a multidisciplinary approach to language variation: proceedings of the eighth annual Southwestern areal language and linguistics workshop, ed. by Florence Barkin and Elizabeth Brandt, 205-14. Anthropological Research Papers no. 20. Tempe: Arizona State University. Contends literary dialect in Everhart's popular lexicons of Texas English is "surprisingly consistent and realistic" and is hardly an exaggeration; less than ten percent of words in first four volumes are either eye dialect or otherwise improbable representations of regional pronunciation and most words exhibit consistent, well-known phonological features; claims Everhart's work is in class by itself among popular lexicons.

**4.356 Underwood, Gary N.** 1982. Arkansawyer postvocalic /r/. AS 57.32-43. 2 maps. [6 B, 18 W adults, from 8 randomly chosen counties in AR]. Finds /r/-lessness not valid "marker of geographic dialects in Arkansas, but it does identify black and white varieties of Arkansas English."

**4.357 Van Riper, Charles G., and Dorothy E. Smith.** 1962. An introduction to general American phonetics. 2nd ed. New York: Harper and Row. Pp. 215-17, brief description of Southern speech, with transcript and exercises.

**4.358 Van Riper, William R.** 1958. The loss of post-vocalic r in the Eastern United States. Ann Arbor: University of Michigan dissertation. Abstract in DAI 19.806. Based on Linguistic Atlas data from 1930s and 1940s, including South Atlantic states; details geographical and social variation in pronunciation of /r/ after vowels, finding "r-lessness" to pattern differently in Upper South (VA and MD) and Lower South (NC and SC) but to be prestigious and spreading in both areas.

**4.359 Vaughn-Cooke, Anna Fay.** 1976. The implementation of a phonological change: the case of resyllabification in Black English (Parts I and II). Washington: Georgetown University dissertation. Abstract in DAI 38.234-35A. [40 LC B, 29 younger, 6 middle-aged, 5 older, SW MS; 34 LC W observed]. Analyzes variable deletion and replacement in unstressed initial syllables as ongoing change in black speech.

**4.360 Vaughn-Cooke, Fay Boyd.** 1986. Lexical diffusion: evidence from a decreolizing variety of black English. Language variety in the South: perspectives in black and white, ed. by Michael Montgomery and Guy Bailey, 111-30. University: University of Alabama Press. Condensed version of preceding item.

**4.361 von Raffler-Engel, Walburga.** 1972. Intonational and vowel correlates in contrasting dialects: a suggestion for further research. Proceedings of the seventh international congress of phonetic sciences, ed. by Andre Rigault and Rene Charbonnean, 768-73. The Hague: Mouton. [B, W, 60 4th graders, Nashville, TN]. Says that speech of black children has longer consonant duration, generally shorter breath groups, and sharper pitch variations than speech of white children.

**4.362 Wacker, Marilynn A. Z.** 1942. A study in the speech of a group of freshmen in the University of San Antonio. Austin: University of Texas thesis. [24 college freshmen from San Antonio, TX]. Finds little variation in patterns of pronunciation of students.

**4.363 Walsh, Chad.** 1938. Phonetic transcription, II. AS 13.51-52. Compares a Boston and a Williamsburg, VA, reading.

**4.364 Walsh, Chad.** 1940. Broad "a" in Virginia. AS 15.38. Impressionistic note on recession of old feature.

**4.365 Walsh, Harry, and Victor L. Mote.** 1974. A Texas dialect feature: origins and distribution. AS 49.40-53. 4 maps. Attempts to draw isophone bisecting TX into two major dialect regions on basis of neutralization of low back vowels and variation in three degrees of retroflexion of postvocalic /r/.

**4.366 Ward, Madie Belle.** 1946. The treatment of r in southeast Alabama speech. Chapel Hill: University of North Carolina thesis. xlviii + 60 pp. [22 natives, ages 17-72]. Analyzes epithesis, epenthesis, and metathesis of /r/.

**4.367 Wells, J. C.** 1982. Accents of English 3: beyond the British Isles. New York: Cambridge University Press. The South, 527-53, discusses heterogeneity of Southern white English and surveys its principal phonetic characteristics and phonological processes. Black English, 553-59. **Reviews:** J. Connolly. 1983. EWW 4.103-06; H. Rogers. 1983. CJL 28.199-207.

**4.368 Wetmore, Thomas H.** 1959. The low-central and low-back vowels in the English of the Eastern United States. PADS 32. 131 pp. Abstract in DAI 18.1423. Ann Arbor: University of Michigan dissertation, 1957. Analyzes and describes low-central and low-back vowel phonemes, their phonic characteristics, and their incidence in the Eastern U.S., based on LANE and LAMSAS field records. Includes W NC, 59-68; E VA, 69-83; E SC, 84-97. **Excerpted** in J. Williamson and V. Burke 1971.406-16. **Reviews:** M. L. Gateau. 1963. Word 18.362; C. K. Thomas. 1961. AS 36.201-03; K. Wittig. 1962. Anglia 80.161-64.

**4.369 Wheatley, Katherine E.** 1934. Southern standards. AS 9.36-45. Early, wide-ranging, but unsystematic discussion of standard pronunciation of mid-South [particularly in Austin, TX], written to counter prejudice against cultivated Southern speech and to supplement scanty discussion of Southern speech in books on American pronunciation of the day.

**4.370 Wheatley, Katherine E., and Oma Stanley.** 1959. Three generations of East Texas speech. AS 34.84-94. [9 W, Nacogdoches, TX]. Examines prevalence of plantation Southern and hill Southern features of pronunciation in E TX speech.

**4.371 White, Dorothy.** 1934. Improving the pronunciation of high school seniors. Morgantown: West Virginia University thesis. [WV]. Discusses nonstandard pronunciations of supervisors, teachers, and students at university laboratory high school.

**4.372 Williams, Cratis D.** 1961. The "r" in mountain speech. Mountain Life and Work 37.5-8. Argues "a heavy r is a general characteristic" of Appalachian speech that sets "it apart, quantitatively rather than qualitatively, from that of other Southern and Midwestern groups descended from similar pioneer stock"; exemplifies epenthesis and other processes and discusses pronunciation of vowels and diphthongs before /r/.

**4.373 Willis, Clodius.** 1971. Synthetic vowel categorization and dialectology. Language and Speech 14.213-28. [VA]. Studies feasibility of using a test to categorize vowels and tests hypothesis that differences in manner of categorization correlate with differences in dialect.

**4.374 Wilson, George P.** 1934. Some unrecorded Southern vowels. AS 9.209-13. Lists twenty-three pronunciations of vowels, diphthongs, and nasal vowels in Southern speech that he says have been neglected by other scholars.

**4.375 Wilson, George P.** 1936. Three North Carolina letters showing occasional spellings. AS 11.223-26. Presents occasional spellings from three letters written in 1927 by residents of NC Piedmont and cautions that such spellings must be analyzed with discretion.

**4.376 Wilson, George P.** 1938. American dictionaries and pronunciation. AS 13.243-54. Criticism of dictionary practices, including their representation of Southern American speech.

**4.377 Wilson, Gordon.** 1964. Studying folklore in a small region--V: pronunciation. TFSB 30.119-26. **Reprinted** in Folklore of the Mammoth Cave Region, pp. 45-53. Bowling Green: Kentucky Folklore Society, 1968. Informal catalog of features of W KY pronunciation.

**4.378 Wise, Claude Merton.** 1933. Negro dialect. QJS 19.522-28. Early, sound overview of black pronunciation in South and of social and educational characteristics of black community; points out social and regional differences in black speech.

**4.379 Wise, Claude Merton.** 1933. A specimen of Louisiana French-English, or "Cajan" . . . dialect in phonetic transcription. AS 8.3.63-64. A text in broad phonetic transcription.

**4.380 Wise, Claude Merton.** 1933. Southern American dialect. AS 8.2.37-43. Overview of typical educated pronunciation in Deep South, with comments on Southern intonation, Southern drawl, and characteristic black pronunciations.

**4.381 Wise, C[laude] M[erton].** 1933. The Southern American drawl. Le Maître Phonétique, third series 48.44.69-71. Brief description of phonological character and constraints on the drawl.

**4.382 Wise, Claude M[erton].** 1936. Common errors in our daily speech. SSJ 2.1-8. Lists common American pronunciations and labels them as errors; does not distinguish clearly between regional and "incorrect" speech.

**4.383 Wise, C[laude] M[erton].** 1936. A comparison of certain features of British and American pronunciation. Proceedings of the second international congress on the phonetic sciences, London, 22-26, July, 1935, 285-91. Cambridge, UK: Cambridge University Press. Descriptive commentary on features of American and British pronunciation, with particular reference to comparison of such words as derby and those ending in -ile, phonemic shifts, phonemes with noncongruent boundaries, and pseudo-phonetic shifts used by literary authors; appends four-way list comparing "General American," Southern, Eastern, and British pronunciations.

**4.384 Wise, C[laude] M[erton].** 1939. Militarism and pacifism among phonemes in American English. Proceedings of the third international congress on the phonetic sciences, 18-22 July, 1938, Ghent. Ghent: Laboratory of Phonetics of the University of Ghent. Identifies vowel correspondences between substandard and standard speech, especially in the South, concluding that "/ɛ/ may be thought of as a very aggressive phoneme, its characteristic spellings having attacked its neighbors on every side and appropriated pronunciations from /ĭ/, /æ/, and /e/".

**4.385 Wise, Claude Merton.** 1957. Applied phonetics. Englewood Cliffs, N.J.: Prentice Hall. Southern American English: standard and substandard, 205-20; Substandard Southern Negro speech, 293-302; Mountain speech, 303-21; Presents inventories of phonetic and phonological features for each variety, with transcription exercises.

**4.386 Wise, Claude Merton.** 1957. Introduction to phonetics. Englewood Cliffs, NJ: Prentice-Hall. Deviations from standard General American, Southern, and Eastern speech, 193-204; Southern American English: standard and substandard, 205-20. Inventories of phonetic and phonological features for each variety, with transcription exercises.

**4.387 Wise, Claude M[erton], James H. McBurney, Louis A. Malloy, and others.** 1942. Foundations of speech. New York: Prentice-Hall. Pp. 17-18, notes on Southern speech.

**4.388 Wise, Claude Merton, W. Scott Nobles, and Herbert Metz.** 1954. The Southern American diphthong /ai/. SSJ 19.304-12. [79 college students from South, mainly from MS and LA]. Finds monophthongal pronunciation most common before voiced consonant, less common syllable final, and least common before voiceless consonants; finds [ɑ] pronunciation only once and concludes popular notion of its alternation with [aɪ] to be misconception perpetuated by dialect writers.

**4.389 Wise, Harry Stephen.** 1937. A phonetic study of the Southern American (aɪ) phoneme. Baton Rouge: Louisiana State University thesis. [16 speakers, 13 from LA, 2 from MS, 1 from GA, ages 15-22]. Studies [a] and [aɪ] variants of phoneme, finding that pronominal forms most frequently have a monophthong, that diphthong occurs at higher percentage before voiced consonants than voiceless ones and that reverse is true after voiceless and voiced consonants.

**4.390 Wolfram, Walt.** 1970. Underlying representations in black English phonology. Language Sciences 10.7-12.

**4.391 Womack, Alma Belle.** 1940. Drill book in Southern pronunciation for intermediate grades. Baton Rouge: Louisiana State University thesis. Discusses pronunciations of vowels, diphthongs, and /r/ that C. M. Wise classifies as "deviations from standard Southern" and provides drills for modifying these pronunciations.

**4.392 Wood, Gordon R.** 1989. The Southern drawl. Encyclopedia of Southern culture, ed. by William Ferris and Charles Wilson. Chapel Hill: University of North Carolina Press. Brief comments on social distribution, assessment, and phonetic features of the Southern drawl.

**4.393 Zimmerman, Jane Dorsey,** ed. 1939. Phonetic transcriptions from "American Speech." AS reprints and monographs no. 1, revised ed., New York: Columbia University Press. Includes IPA transcriptions of speech from VA, NC, SC, GA, and TX; see AS annual indexes through 1945 for later transcriptions. **Review:** B. Bloch. 1940. Language 16.172-75.

## See Also

1.7 Adams; 1.9 Alexander; 1.26 Bailey; 1.42 Baird; 1.61 Bell; 1.63 Benardete; 1.65 Berrey; 1.72 Blake; 1.78 Bond; 1.84 Boswell; 1.87 Boswell; 1.89 Bountress; 1.98 Brandes; 1.99 Bray; 1.100 Brewer; 1.115 Butters; 1.116 Butters; 1.124 Carpenter; 1.126 Carpenter; 1.132 Cassidy; 1.144-45 Combs; 1.152 Currie; 1.168 Davis; 1.177 Dennis; 1.200-01 Dingus; 1.205 Dumas; 1.213 Dumas; 1.225 Ellis; 1.229 Faneuf; 1.235 Fasold; 1.244 Foley; 1.245 Folk; 1.251-52 Fruit; 1.261 Gibson; 1.264 Gilbert; 1.276 Green; 1.280 Greene; 1.281 Greet; 1.284 Guest; 1.288 Hall; 1.295 Hanners; 1.301 Harper; 1.304 Harper; 1.306 Harris; 1.308 Hartman; 1.314 Hempl; 1.318 Higgins; 1.323 Hoff; 1.329 Houston; 1.334-35 Howren; 1.342 Jackson; 1.344 Jaffe; 1.349 Jones; 1.350 Jones; 1.353 Keener; 1.370-71 Kurath; 1.375 Kwachka; 1.380 Labov; 1.389 LeCompte; 1.390 Lemotte; 1.406 McBride; 1.410 McDavid; 1.417-19 McDavid; 1.432 McDavid; 1.434 McDavid; 1.438 McDavid; 1.443 McDavid; 1.468 McDavid; 1.473 McDavid; 1.481 McGreevy; 1.482 McGuire; 1.500 Maynor; 1.508 Mencken; 1.510 Midgett; 1.513 Miller; 1.517 Miller; 1.532-34 Morgan; 1.538 Nelson; 1.543 Nix; 1.544-45 Norman; 1.546 Oettenger; 1.547 Oomen; 1.555 Payne; 1.564 Pederson; 1.583 Pederson; 1.608 Pietras; 1.618 Primer; 1.621 Putnam; 1.630 Randolph; 1.632 Rash; 1.645 Reese; 1.660 Rodgers; 1.663 Rubrecht; 1.665 Rueter; 1.667 Sackett; 1.670 Satterfield; 1.671 Sawyer; 1.679 Schrock; 1.682 Shands; 1.687 Shores; 1.694 Skillman; 1.700 Sledd; 1.702 Smith; 1.738 Stolz; 1.760 Tinkler; 1.764 Tozer; 1.768 Troike; 1.783 Vickers; 1.790 Vinson; 1.793 Walker; 1.804 Whiteman; 1.813 Williams; 1.815 Williams; 1.816 Williamson; 1.818 Williamson; 1.830 Wilson; 1.832 Wilson; 1.835 Wolfram; 1.837 Wolfram; 1.839 Wolfram; 1.850 Wolfram; 1.854 Wolfram; 1.858 Wood; 2.5 Allen; 2.7 Alleyne; 2.8 Ames; 2.23 Berger; 2.33 Boyette; 2.43 Bronstein; 2.44 Brooks; 2.53 Bruce; 2.57 Burt; 2.76 Clemens; 2.77 Cobb; 2.102 Dalton; 2.129 Eanes; 2.132 Eliason; 2.160 Godfrey; 2.167 Hall; 2.187 Harrison; 2.192 Hawkins; 2.209 Hisley; 2.212 Holmberg; 2.220 Jeremiah; 2.222 Johnson; 2.225 Johnson; 2.231-32 Jones-

Jackson; 2.250 Kurath; 2.253 Kurath; 2.255-56 Kurath; 2.260 Lang; 2.265 Lewis; 2.270 Lucke; 2.277 McDavid; 2.283 Mack; 2.292 Mathews; 2.325 Nies; 2.333 Page; 2.335-36 Pardoe; 2.349-52 Primer; 2.357 Read; 2.392 Smallfry; 3.405-409 Stephenson; 2.428 Thrower; 2.432 Traugott; 2.435 Turner; 2.437 Turner; 2.463 Williams; 2.475 Woofter; 3.219 Hayes; 3.255 Jenson; 3.337 Miller; 5.170 Miller; 5.226 Terrebonne; 6.17 Aschbacher; 6.94 Bryson; 6.254 Goff; 6.297 Hill; 6.307 In; 6.322 Jones; 6.354 LaBorde; 6.376 McDavid; 6.378 McDavid; 6.452 Neuffer; 6.469 Pace; 6.490 Plummer; 6.494 Pronunciation; 6.502 Read; 6.503 Read; 6.563 Smith; 6.572 Stewart; 6.574-75 Stokes; 6.621 Underwood; 6.641 West; 6.642 Whaley; 7.15 Bolton; 9.15 Boykin; 9.17 Brooks; 9.48 Foster; 9.61 Haskell; 9.66 Holmberg; 9.70 Ives; 9.87 Mitchell; 9.94 Nixon; 9.102 Peppers; 9.106 Preston; 9.116 Rulon; 9.132 Stockton; 9.134 Tidwell; 9.143 Williams; 10.3 Baird; 10.7 Bryden; 10.10 Coe; 10.54 Shields; 10.67 Underwood; 10.79 Willis.

# 5 Morphology and Syntax

**5.1 Adamko, Jerzy.** 1978. Some remarks on tense and aspect in black English. Lubelskie Materialy Neofilologiczne 1976.145-52. Says understanding of tense and aspect systems of standard English discounts contention by Dillard and Fickett that black English systems are different from them on deep level.

**5.2 Allen, Edward A.** 1899. You-uns. Nation 68.476 (June 22). Cites use of term in Tyndale's New Testament translation (1525) and reports <u>we-dem</u> and <u>you-dem</u> in Lancaster County, VA.

**5.3 Armstrong, Mary Sheila.** 1953. Survivals in Kentucky. AS 28.306-07. [KY]. Reports compound adjectives like <u>disgraceful indecent</u> in novel by Kentuckian Harriet Arnow that are similar to Shakespearian usages.

**5.4 Atwood, E. Bagby.** 1953. A survey of verb forms in the Eastern United States. Ann Arbor: University of Michigan Press. [Maine to NE FL]. Using records from LANE and LAMSAS, details regional patterns in eighty-eight verb features, including principal parts, subject-verb agreement, negative constructions, infinitives, and modals. **Reviews:** H. B. Allen. 1954. AA 56.315; A. L. Davis. 1955. AS 30.121-23; N. E. Eliason. 1954. MLN 69.282; H. M. Flasdick. 1955. Anglia 73.76-77; L. Grootaers. 1954. Leuvense Bijdragen 44.17; S. Ives. 1953. JEGP 52.391-92; R. I. McDavid, Jr. 1954. IJAL 20.74-78; A. H. Marckwardt. 1954. Language 30.426-28; P. Mossé. 1954. Bulletin de la Société de Linguistique de Paris 50.143; R. Quirk. 1954. MLR 49.390-91; A. Sommerfelt. 1955. Norsk Tidsskrift for Sprogvidenskap 17.564-66; C. K. Thomas. 1954. QJS 40.81-82; J. N. Tidwell. 1954. JAF 57.222-23; R. M. Wilson. 1955. YWES 34.40; C. M. Wise. 1954. SSJ 19.341-42; J. S. Woodley. 1953. Archivum Linguisticum 5.118-19.

**5.5 Axley, Lowry.** 1927. "You all" and "we all" again. AS 2.343-45. Comments on use of <u>you'uns</u> and <u>you all</u>; says in lifetime of experience he has "never heard any person of any degree of education or station of life use the expression <u>you all</u>" as singular.

**5.6 Axley, Lowry.** 1928. West Virginia dialect. AS 3.456. Notes many items in Carey Woofter (**3.554**) article that he finds in Savannah, GA and are therefore not unique to WV.

**5.7 Axley, Lowry.** 1928. Y'all. AS 4.103. Disagrees with Fischer's statement (**5.107**) that "owing to sentence stress, the <u>all</u> may lose its own accent completely so that the phonetic penultimate is something like <u>you'll</u>."

**5.8 Axley, Lowry.** 1929. One word more on "you all." AS 4.347-51. Continues debate on whether term can be used as singular; answers Morrison (**5.179**) and expresses skepticism about existence of singular usage since he has never heard it, despite lifetime of observation.

**5.9 B., G.** 1927. "You all." AS 2.476. Says in lifetime of observation in SC, GA, and New Orleans, he has never heard singular usage.

**5.10 Bachmann, James K.** 1970. A comparison of nonstandard grammatical usage in some Negro and white working-class families in Alexandria, Virginia. Washington: Georgetown University dissertation. Abstract in DAI 31.2364A. [12 W, 12 B, 12 adults, 12 children, Alexandria, VA]. Finds children use more nonstandard forms than adults, but no significant difference in usage between white and black adults.

**5.11 Bachmann, James K.** 1970. Field techniques in an urban language study. TESOL Quarterly 4.255-60. [12 W, 12 B, 12 adults, 12 children, Alexandria, VA]. Analyzes eight pronoun, verb, and other features and finds that they "while not exclusive to Negroes, are used more often by them than by whites."

**5.12 Bailey, Beryl Loftman.** 1968. Some aspects of the impact of linguistics on language teaching in disadvantaged communities. EE 45.570-78,626. [MS]. Discusses language patterns of black freshman at Tougaloo College. **Reprinted** in A. L. Davis 1969(**1.159**).15-24.

**5.13 Bailey, Guy, and Marvin Bassett.** 1986. Invariant "be" in the lower South. Language variety in the South: perspectives in black and white, ed. by Michael Montgomery and Guy Bailey, 158-79. University: University of Alabama Press. [39 B, 83 W, 51 Type I, 48 Type II, 23 Type III, S MS, SE LA]. Shows verb has same meaning, function, and social distribution for both blacks and older whites.

**5.14 Bailey, Guy, and Natalie Maynor.** 1985. The present tense of "be" in Southern black folk speech. AS 60.195-213. [7 B Type I, Brazos Valley, E TX, B Type I, Oktibbeha Co., MS]. Finds nonsystematic contrast between unmarked <u>be</u> and other uses of copula verb in black folk speech, but finds distinctive person/number distribution of unmarked <u>be</u> verb that reflects influence of English superstratum.

**5.15 Bailey, Guy, and Natalie Maynor.** 1985. The present tense of "be" in white folk speech of the Southern United States. EWW 6.199-216. [10 W over 65, 5 F, 5 M, Brazos Valley, TX]. Finds only quantitative differences between black and white folk speech in distribution of present tense forms of <u>be</u> and that both blacks and whites use same forms in same way.

**5.16 Bailey, Guy, and Natalie Maynor.** 1986. The sources of durative/ habitual "be" in the present-day black English vernacular. NADS 18.2.4. Claims that habitual <u>be</u> "is the consequence of an independent syntactic reanalysis of the earlier invariant <u>be</u>, motivated by the lack of transparency in present tense forms, the anomalous nature of the English progressive, and the social insularity of blacks that resulted from the Great Migration [of blacks to Northern cities following World War I]."

**5.17 Bassett, Marvin W.** 1983. Social differences in the grammar of lower Alabama. Atlanta: Emory University dissertation. Abstract in DAI 44.2460-61A. 360 pp. [16 adults, S AL]. Presents morphological and syntactic variants used by LAGS informants; finds work-sheet sample not entirely adequate "for recognizing the influence of the social factors of caste and education in a grammatical description."

**5.18 Baugh, John G., Jr.** 1980. A re-examination of the black English copula. Locating language in time and space, ed. by William Labov, 83-106. New York: Academic Press. Same as Working Papers in Sociolinguistics 66. 1979. Austin: Southwest Regional Laboratory. Based on twenty-six interviews with adolescent black males in Labov et al. (1.380-81); shows variable use of copula verb depending on following different grammatical environments and discusses theoretical implications. **Reprinted** in J. Baugh and J. Sherzer 1984(**1.58**).247-67; in H. Allen and M. Linn 1986(**1.11**).474-99.

**5.19 Baugh, John.** 1986. Linguistic divergence or linguistic innovation: a review of suffix {-s} variation in vernacular black English. Abstract in NADS 18.3.5. Says that Labov's claim that black vernacular English and white vernacular English are diverging is either limited to Philadelphia or is premature.

**5.20 Baugh, John.** 1987. Beyond linguistic divergence in black American English: competing norms of linguistic prestige and variation. Abstract in NADS 19.2.9. Says that much variation in black speech is situational and "accommodates to alternative prestige norms in different social circumstances."

**5.21 Beitscher, Diane.** 1973. Observations of standard and non-standard English as used by some lower socioeconomic level high school students. Nashville: Tennessee State University thesis.

**5.22 Bergin, Kendall Russell.** 1984. The relationship of English composition grades to oral (social) dialect: an analysis of dialectal and non-dialectal writing errors. Cultural language differences: their educational and clinical-professional implications, ed. by Sol Adler, 29-43. Springfield, IL: Charles Thomas. [9 B, 26 W University of Tennessee students]. Claims strong correlation between oral dialect use (based on instructor rating) and errors in written composition (based on Harbrace College Handbook).

**5.23 Bernstein, Cynthia.** 1986. A variant of the "invariant be." Abstract in NADS 18.3.11. Examines distribution of inflected form bees in LAGS field records.

**5.24 Bernstein, Herbert B.** 1929. Mr. Axley and "you all." AS 5.173. Says he heard term used as singular in Atlanta and that all is added to you for dramatic reasons, as a "verbal gesture."

**5.25 Billiard, Charles E.** Correlates among social dialects, language development, and reading achievement of urban children. Language variety in the South: perspectives in black and white, ed. by Michael Montgomery and Guy Bailey, 365-72. University: University of Alabama Press. Concludes that "given the strong positive correlations between function-word scores (language development) and reading achievement, and only moderate correlations between standard English usage and reading achievement, the content of language . . . appears more important than the form . . . for developing reading comprehension."

**5.26 Blaisdell, Thomas C.** 1931. More "you all" testimony. AS 6.390-91. Says term in NC "clearly was used . . . to mean only the single individual addressed."

**5.27 Blanton, Linda L.** 1974. The verb system in Breathitt County, Kentucky: a sociolinguistic analysis. Chicago: Illinois Institute of Technology dissertation. Abstract in DAI 35.7888-89A. [22 speakers, E KY]. Analyzes dialect patterns of subject-verb concord, auxiliary deletion, tense marking, and negation and finds all very frequent; concludes "that the verb system, as a whole, has undergone a great deal of morphological leveling."

**5.28 Blanton, Linda L.** 1975. The verb system in Breathitt County, Kentucky: a sociolinguistic analysis. Reviewed in NADS 8.3.13. Finds disagreements in studies of Appalachian English in WV and KY and reasons to doubt such an entity as Appalachian English exists.

**5.29 Blanton, Linda.** 1977. How nonstandard is "Appalachian English"? Abstract in NADS 9.3.7-8. Argues that most previous descriptions of Appalachian speech were distorted by focusing on only nonstandard forms, and claims that for grammatical categories Appalachian speech is far less nonstandard than generally thought.

**5.30 Boertien, Harmon S.** 1979. The double modal construction in Texas. Texas Linguistic Forum 13, ed. by Carlota S. Smith and Susan F. Schmerling, 14-33. Austin: University of Texas. [5 college students native to TX]. Outlines acceptable sequences of double modals and phrase-structure and transformational rules for forming negatives, yes-no questions, contraction, and niching with them; concludes there are at least two double-modal dialects, one treating the structures as inseparable and the other treating modals as separable and second modal as tensed.

**5.31 Boertien, Harmon S.** 1986. Constituent structure of double modals. Language variety in the South: perspectives in black and white, ed. by Michael Montgomery and Guy Bailey, 294-318. University: University of Alabama Press. [5 college students native to TX]. Revision of preceding item; concludes phrase-structure and transformational rules for single-modal and double-modal dialects are the same.

**5.32 Boertien, Harmon S., and Sally Said.** 1980. Syntactic variation in double modal dialects. Journal of the Linguistic Association of the Southwest 3.210-22. [TX]. Examines patterning and variation of double modal structures in contraction, yes-no question inversion, quantifier floating, and negative placement, and tag question formation; finds evidence that two syntactic features, modal tense and modal position, govern application of these rules.

**5.33 Bonner, Patricia Elaine.** 1982. A morphological and syntactic analysis of a Mantua, Alabama idiolect. Atlanta: Atlanta University thesis. 97 pp. [1 elderly B M, S AL]. Analyzes morphology, subject deletion, non-third-person you, "syntactic divergences," and other features.

**5.34 Boock, Darwin F.** 1933. You-all in the Bible. American Mercury 28.246. Disputes with S. A. H. (**1.285**) that the form of you all found in New Testament is same as in American South, since Southerners can use it as singular or plural.

**5.35 Briggs, Dolores Griffin.** 1968. Deviations from standard English in papers of selected Alabama Negro high school students. Tuscaloosa: University of Alabama dissertation. Abstract in DAI 29.3595A. [10 B high-school students, 5 M, 5 F, Birmingham, AL]. Using Walter Loban's Problems in Oral English error taxonomy, finds greatest difficulties were with nonstandard verb forms and inflectional morphology and that only spelling and vocabulary correlated with grade level.

**5.36 Briggs, Olin DeWitt.** 1968. A study of deviations from standard English in papers of Negro freshmen at an Alabama college. Tuscaloosa: University of Alabama dissertation. Abstract in DAI 29.3596A. [6 junior-college students]. Analyzes thirty essays, using Loban's Problems in Oral English taxonomy; finds more errors, particularly with word endings, in writing than Loban found in speech.

**5.37 Brown, Bertram H.** 1933. The truth about "you-all." American Mercury 29.116. [NC]. Disagrees with Boock (5.34) about singular usage and says apparent singular uses are always associative; says am is never used by blacks and is an artificial stage and screen dialect feature.

**5.38 Brown, Rebecca Ann.** 1982. The double modal dialect: issue update and syntactic analysis. Baton Rouge: Louisiana State University thesis. v + 72 pp. Analyzing forms in published literature, proposes that "the surface form of double modals is generated from two underlying sentences, a matrix and an embedding, on which the Raising to Subject transformation applies."

**5.39 Bush, Clara B.** 1899. Done. Nation 58.476. [LA]. Says use of done in I's gwine done do it is literary dialect, not actual usage of blacks.

**5.40 Butters, Ronald R.** 1973. Black English {-Z}: some theoretical implications. AS 48.37-45. Reviews principal notions of Labovian variation theory and discusses how third-person-singular ending in black speech is analyzed in this framework.

**5.41 Butters, Ronald R.** 1973. Acceptability judgments for double modals in Southern dialects. New Ways of Analyzing Variation in Linguistics, ed. by C.-J. N. Bailey and Roger Shuy, 276-86. Washington: Georgetown University Press. [NC]. Finds negatives are formed with second element of double modal and concludes first auxiliary verb is an adverbial element.

**5.42 Butters, Ronald R.** 1974. Variability in indirect questions. AS 49.230-34. Abstract in NADS 8.3.12-13. Suggests inverted word order in indirect questions, usually associated with black speakers, has an Anglo-Irish origin and that even "Standard English" speakers use pattern variably.

**5.43 Butters, Ronald R.** 1975. Variation in some Southern black idiolects. ED 120 767. 10 pp. [Wilmington, NC]. Says use of inversion in indirect question formation is variable for both blacks and whites and is therefore not a feature of black English; says categorical use of inversion reflects age-grading or hypercorrection.

**5.44 Butters, Ronald R.** 1976. More on indirect questions. AS 51.57-62. [8 B F, ages 65-81, Wilmington, NC]. Revision of preceding item. Finds limited use of inversion in indirect questions in older blacks and says it represents stylistic variant for most speakers of American English.

**5.45 Butters, Ronald R.** 1987. The historical present as evidence of black/white convergence/divergence. Abstract in NADS 19.2.9. Counters argument that white and black vernaculars are diverging put forth by Labov and others by reinterpreting Labov's evidence as representing borrowing of historical present marker into black vernacular speech.

**5.46 Butters, Ronald R.** 1987. Verbal -s as past-time indication in various narratives. Proceedings of the annual linguistics colloquium, University of North Carolina at Chapel Hill, 9-17. Chapel Hill: UNC Linguistics Circle. Surveys possibilities other than Labov's divergence hypothesis for use of suffix in past-tense narratives; uses data from Wilmington, NC, and elsewhere.

**5.47 Butters, Ronald R., and S. C. A.** 1987. More on singular "y'all." AS 62.191-92. Says humorous use of y'all in movies has promoted popular misconception of singular use of term.

**5.48 Butters, Ronald R., and Kristin Stettler.** 1986. Causative and existential "have . . . to." AS 61.184-90. [57 Duke University students]. Finds structure used almost exclusively by Southerners and South Midlanders and less by females than males.

**5.49 Callary, Robert E.** 1971. Syntactic correlates of social stratification. Baton Rouge: Louisiana State University dissertation. Abstract in DAI 32.3975A. [12 Louisiana State University students]. Based on inclass speeches, finds that higher status students use more complex sentences than lower status ones.

**5.50 Callary, Robert E.** 1975. Syntax and social class. Linguistics 143.5-16. [12 Louisiana State University students, 2 social classes]. Examines speech of lower-class and higher-class students on fourteen measures of syntactic complexity and patterning; finds lower-class speech more homogeneous and characterizes higher-class speech as more elaborate and complex.

**5.51 Canine, Karen M.** 1979. The case hierarchy and Faulkner's relatives in Absalom, Absalom! SECOL Bulletin 3.63-80. Criticizes Edward Keenan's Case Hierarchy as too simple to account for complex uses of relative clauses in the Faulkner novel.

**5.52 Canine, Karen M.** 1981. Faulkner's theory of relativity: non-restrictives in Absalom, Absalom! SECOL Bulletin 5.118-34. Says lack of clearcut distinctions between restrictive and non-restrictive relative clauses in Faulkner novel indicate author's intention to "withhold meaning or make perspectives conditional or ambiguous."

**5.53 Canine, Karen M.** 1983. Faulkner's theory of relative clauses in Absalom, Absalom! Greensboro: University of North Carolina dissertation. Abstract in DAI 45.182A. 179 pp. Says that Faulkner used relative clauses to construct "a level of meaning beyond the 'story'" and that "linguistic analysis of literature can illustrate precisely how style and meaning are interrelated."

**5.54 Catlett, L. C.** 1888. "We-uns" and "you-uns." Century 36.477-78. [VA]. Says he has never heard forms in state, even though writers about VA put them in mouths of their characters.

**5.55 Chomsky, Noam, and Howard Lasnik.** 1977. Filters and control. Linguistic Inquiry 8.425-504. P. 454, cites for to infinitives in Ozark English as crucial to argument for complementizer structure in English.

**5.56 Christian, Donna.** 1975. Non-participle "done" and non-productive classification. ED 116 499. 26 pp. Examines proposals for classifying auxiliary done and, using data from Appalachian English, says that both semantic information (perfectiveness) and pragmatic information (emphasis) must be added to the syntactic information before classifying it.

**5.57 Christian, Donna M.** 1978. Aspects of verb usage in Appalachian speech. Washington: Georgetown University dissertation. Abstract in DAI 39.7317A. [26 M, 26 F, ages 7-93, S WV]. Examines patterns in irregular verb principal parts and subject-verb concord and provides evidence for language change in progress. Classifies verbs with nonstandard principal parts into five categories and finds nonstandard subject-verb concord "occurs only with plural subjects, with the exception of the item don't."

**5.58 Christian, Donna.** 1982. The personal dative in Appalachian speech. Abstract in NADS 14.3.6. [WV]. Describes characteristics of personal dative and compares it to for-dative construction.

**5.59 Cohen, Gerald L.** 1982. "That don't make me never no mind." AS 57.76-79. [756 Ozark residents]. Speculates on origin of term used to express anger and humor.

**5.60 Coleman, William L.** 1975. Multiple modals in Southern states English. Bloomington: Indiana University dissertation. Abstract in DAI 36.2174-75A. Using quantitative analysis and implicational scaling, identifies three regional patterns of multiple modal variation in NC with range of acceptable modal combinations increasing from east to west.

**5.61 Coleman, William L.** 1975. Regional distribution of double modals usage in North Carolina. Abstract in NADS 8.3.10. [179 informants from NC, mostly from Piedmont area]. Uses implicational scales to show how acceptability of double-modal constructions is regionally distributed.

**5.62 Cooley, Marianne.** 1982. Complementation in West Texas. Abstract in NADS 14.3.9-10. Shows how indirect questions and other complements are double marked with conjunction and that and claims this is archaic feature, as in he asked how that I could afford to come.

**5.63 Dabney, John M.** 1899. You-all. Nation 68.436 (June 8). [MS]. Defends you-all as refined and useful expression; notes you-uns rarely heard in MS.

**5.64 Davis, Marianna W.** 1970. Verb patterns in the written sentences of a group of students enrolled in a pre-college curriculum. CLAJ 14.197-204.

[83 B college freshmen, 68 from SC]. Description of modals and forms of be, have, and get as auxiliary and main verbs in student essays.

**5.65 DeBose, Charles.** 1976. Be insertion: a zero copula analysis of black English deep structure. Abstract in NADS 8.4.13. Claims that black speech has no copula verb in deep structure and that copula must be inserted into surface structure.

**5.66 DeVere, Louise.** 1971. Non-standard English in Norfolk city schools. Norfolk: Old Dominion University thesis. 145 pp. [40 B, W students in 1st, 6th, 8th, 10th grades, Norfolk, VA]. ED 082 554. Investigates nonstandard morphology and syntax of black and white speech and finds many nonstandard features occur in speech of whites as well as blacks, but some features of copula and auxiliary verbs, inflections, and pronouns are restricted to blacks; concludes preponderance of similarities between races indicates dialect variations are apparently regional rather than social.

**5.67 Dietrich, Julia C.** 1981. The Gaelic roots of a-prefixing in Appalachian English. AS 56.314. Says form reported by Wolfram (**5.247**) derives from influence of Gaelic verbal noun construction and results "not from a careless handling of English grammar but from a careful preservation of Scottish Gaelic grammar, learned generations ago and applied to English long before the migration to America."

**5.68 Dillard, J. L., James Sledd, Eric P. Hamp, and Archibald A. Hill.** 1979. Joinder and rejoinder. AS 54.113-19. Polemical note by Dillard on durative be in Irish English (and its possible relation to black English use of be), with responses by Hamp, Hill, and Sledd.

**5.69 DiPaolo, Marianna.** 1982. A cross-dialect comparison of double modals. Abstract in NADS 14.3.3. [NC, AL, TX]. Claims double-modal patterns in Southern white speech distinguish it from black speech, Caribbean creoles, and Scots English.

**5.70 DiPaolo, Marianna.** 1986. A study of double modals in Texas English. Austin: University of Texas dissertation. Abstract in DAI 47.2143-44A. [62 informants, ages 11-81, E TX, W TX]. Syntactic analysis of double modals and study of social factors related to their acceptability; finds double modals are not stigmatized and that gender and region less important in acceptability than age, with middle-age speakers accepting them least.

**5.71 DiPaolo, Marianna, Charles L. McClenon, and Kenneth C. Ranson.** 1979. A survey of double modals in Texas. Texas Linguistic Forum 13.40-49. 5 maps. [750 native Texans]. Surveys usage of double modals mainly in E TX and compares rural vs. urban and younger vs. older speakers; finds older and more rural speakers use structures more but that "double modals may be part of standard Urban speech in Texas."

**5.72 Duke, Alba W.** 1933. "You-all" once again. American Mercury 29.377. [MS]. Disagrees with Boock (**5.34**); says that the form of you all in the Bible is not same as that used in South and that you all is never used as singular by Southern speakers.

**5.73 Dumas, Bethany K.** 1975. The morphology of Newton County, Arkansas: an exercise in studying Ozark dialect. Mid-South Folklore 3.115-25. Explores retention of archaic verb and noun forms in Ozarks and finds that age and lack of exposure outside community correlate with retention, but that amount of formal education does not.

**5.74 Dumas, Bethany K.** 1980. Grammatical patterns in the folk speech of the Arkansas Ozarks. Abstract in NADS 12.3.5. [Newton Co., AR]. Reports morphology and syntax of AR Ozark speech to be identical to that of MO Ozarks and very similar to S Appalachia.

**5.75 Dumas, Bethany K.** 1980. Variation in Ozark English. Abstract in NADS 12.3.12. See preceding item.

**5.76 Dunlap, Howard G.** 1973. Social aspects of a verb form: native Atlanta fifth-grade speech--the present tense of "be." Atlanta: Emory University dissertation. Abstract in DAI 34.4230A. Disputes Labov/Wolfram methodology for distinguishing between copula deletion and contraction, a methodology that "creates the appearance of far greater divergence from standard English" than is the case and says that invariant be "cannot be accounted for solely in terms of intermittent action or the deletion of an underlying will or would" and that invariant be is used "for a constant state, for the present moment, and for past occurrences."

**5.77 Dunlap, Howard G.** 1974. Social aspects of a verb form: native Atlanta fifth-grade speech--the present tense of "be." PADS 61-62. 96 pp. [96 Atlanta, GA, fifth-grade children]. Marked by methodological clarity, finds white and black speech to be very similar except that lower-class blacks use invariant be, though in more varied way than Northern blacks.

**5.78 Dunlap, Howard G.** 1977. Some methodological problems in recent investigations of the Ø copula and invariant "be." Papers in language variation, ed. by David L. Shores and Carole P. Hines, 151-59. University: University of Alabama Press. Abstract in NADS 6.1-2.27. [96 Atlanta fifth-graders, 48 B, 48 W, 48 UMC, 48 LC]. Disputes Labov/Wolfram distinction between copula deletion and contraction and says that invariant be "cannot be accounted for solely in terms of intermittent action or the deletion of an underlying will or would."

**5.79 Earle, Mary T.** 1899. You-all. Nation 68.436 (June 8). Says that singular use of pronoun occurs "in the everyday speech of cultivated people" and that "in the ordinary give-and-take of greeting and gossip it is as characteristic as the accent of the South."

**5.80 Elgin, Suzette [H].** 1972. The crossover constraint and Ozark English. Syntax and semantics I, ed. by John Kimball, 267-75. New York: Academic Press. Claims that many well-formed sentences in Ozark English, especially sentences with reflexive pronouns, violate Paul Postal's doctrinaire "crossover constraint" and cannot be derived from American English according to standard generative analysis.

**5.81 Elgin, Suzette H.** 1979. What in the world is "that"? Georgetown University papers on languages and linguistics 16.33-44. Washington: Georgetown University Press. Analyzes variable relativization system in Ozark English speech to argue that relativizer that is a pronoun, not a conjunction.

**5.82 Elgin, Suzette H.** 1981. The Ozark WHICH/THAT, which/that I wish you lots of luck. Lonesome Node 1.2.2-7. Further comments in Supplement, pp. 1-3. Analyzes pronoun-antecedent relationships in Ozark English, especially with reflexives and relative clauses.

**5.83 Elgin, Suzette H.** 1982. [Of and to]. Lonesome Node 2.1.11. Says "crucial semantic distinction in Ozark English that controls the choice between "of" and "to" as the case markers for the possessive is whether the possessed item is or can be a separate entity."

**5.84 Elgin, Suzette H.** 1983. [For-to and to]. Lonesome Node 2.4-5.18. Argues I expect for the roads to get icy differs in meaning from I expect the roads to get icy in Ozark English.

**5.85 Elgin, Suzette H.** 1983. [For-to and to]. Lonesome Node 3.1.3-4. Distinguishes between Do you need me to come help you? and Do you need for me to come help you?

**5.86 Elgin, Suzette H.** 1983. ["Him" and "his" before gerunds]. Lonesome Node 3.1.4. Says I hate him leaving and I hate his leaving are not synonymous in Ozark English.

**5.87 Elgin, Suzette H.** 1983. On cows, and the Ozark English auxiliary. Lonesome Node 3.2.9-16. Analyzes auxiliary verbs in terms of four layers of Ronald Langacker's Space Grammar model.

**5.88 Elgin, Suzette H.** 1984. [Need + past participle]. Lonesome Node 3.5.2. Reports patterns like the device needs destroyed and they need fixed in Ozark speech.

**5.89 Elgin, Suzette H.** 1984. ["Said . . ."] Lonesome Node 4.1.9. Points out single word said is used to introduce reported speech in Ozark English.

**5.90 Elgin, Suzette H.** 1987. [For-to and to]. Lonesome Node 7.1.14. Points out subtle distinction between I didn't intend for the subscription to *expire* and I didn't intend the subscription to expire in Ozark English.

**5.91 Elgin, Suzette H.** 1988. [Double modals in Ozark English.] Lonesome Node 7.3.2. Argues that might could be and maybe are distinct in meaning.

**5.92 Elifson, Joan M.** 1976. Effecting bidialectal shift in speakers of nonstandard English through a sequenced curriculum. Atlanta: Georgia State University dissertation. Abstract in DAI 37.5091A. Same as ED 140 311. Pp., 14-16, black dialect defined by nine features: deletion of copula, possessive, plural, third-person singular; consonant cluster reduction and substitution; invariant be; "negative spread"; and left dislocation. Cf. Rubadeau item **10.49**.

**5.93 Fasold, Ralph W.** 1969. Tense and the form "be" in black English. Language 45.763-76. Says black English has distinctive use of be as main verb, expressing iteration rather than instantaneous or constant states.

**5.94 Fasold, Ralph W.** 1970. Two models of socially significant linguistic variation. Language 46.551-63. Argues that observation of frequency of variants leads to generalizations not revealed by use of scalogram analysis alone.

**5.95 Fasold, Ralph W.** 1972. Tense marking in black English: a linguistic and social analysis. Arlington: CAL. xviii + 254 pp. [19 children, 18 adolescents, 14 adults; 32 M, 19 F, Washington, DC]. Detailed analysis of interaction of phonological and morphological constraints on marking of tense in black speech and correlation of this marking with age, sex, social class of speakers and race of interviewers; includes coverage of distributive be. **Reviews:** W. Labov. 1975. LIS 4.222-27; R. S. Macaulay. 1974. Language 50.758-62; L. Pederson. 1975. AS 50.98-110.

**5.96 Fasold, Ralph W., and Walter W. Wolfram.** 1970. Some linguistic features of Negro dialect. Teaching standard English in the inner city, ed. by Ralph W. Fasold and Roger W. Shuy, 41-86. Washington: CAL. **Reprinted** in J. DeStefano 1973(**1.179**).116-48; in D. Shores 1972(**1.685**).53-85; in P. Stoller 1975(**1.737**).49-83; in Language, Speech, and Hearing Services in Schools 1972.3.16-49,72.

**5.97 Feagin, Crawford.** 1975. Southern white and black English: verb agreement. Abstract in NADS 8.3.10. [58 W, Anniston, AL]. Finds two divergent varieties of Southern white English, both of which are closer to regional British and older English than to black speech and Caribbean creoles in verb agreement patterns.

**5.98 Feagin, Louise C[rawford].** 1976. A sociolinguistic study of Alabama white English: the verb phrase in Anniston. 2 vols. Washington: Georgetown University dissertation. Abstract in DAI 38.3445A. Published in abridged form as **5.100**.

**5.99 Feagin, Crawford.** 1976. Southern white English: the changing verb phrase. ED 135 261. 16 pp. [65 W teenagers and adults over 65, UC and LC, Anniston, AL]. Discusses which of fourteen verb-phrase features are increasing, which are decreasing, and which are stable across generations within the community; discounts age-grading as explanation for generational differences.

**5.100 Feagin, Crawford.** 1979. Variation and change in Alabama English: a sociolinguistic study of the white community. Washington: Georgetown University Press. Foreword by William Labov. 395 pp. [82 W; 67 urban, 15 rural; 34 teenaged, 5 middle aged, 43 older; 44 F, 38 M; Anniston, AL]. Comprehensive analysis of linguistic and social (class, urban/rural, age, gender) constraints on features of verb phrase (tense, aspect, person-number agreement, modality, negation, etc.) in white speech in Anniston, AL, comparing it to black and to British speech. Excerpted in Allen and Linn 1986(1.11).259-83. **Reviews:** R. Butters. 1981. Language 57.735-38; B. Davis. 1982. LIS 11.139-41; T. C. Frazer. 1980. JEL 14.41-44; R. McDavid, Jr. 1982. EWW 2.99-110; J. B. McMillan. 1980. SECOL Bulletin 4. 86-88; M. I. Miller. 1981. AS 56.288-95; B. Rigsby. 1981. Australian Journal of Linguistics 1.122-27; H. Ulherr. 1982. Anglia 100.484-85; H. B. Woods. 1981. CJL 26.250-51.

**5.101 Feagin, Crawford.** 1980. Woman's place in nonstandard Southern white English: not so simple. Language use and the uses of language, ed. by Roger W. Shuy and Anna Shnukal, 88-97. Washington: Georgetown University Press. [26 WC, teenagers and older adults, 15 rural older adults, Anniston, AL]. Finds speech of older urban working-class men is no different from that of women but that rural men and urban boys are more nonstandard than their female counterparts.

**5.102 Feagin, Crawford.** 1986. Competing norms in the white speech of Anniston, Alabama. Language variety in the South: perspectives in black and white, ed. by Michael Montgomery and Guy Bailey, 216-34. University: University of Alabama Press. Compares how thirteen grammatical features of the verb phrase pattern in local prestige norm and in local vernacular or solidarity norm of speech as revealed in different social groups and in style shifting; employs Leslie Milroy's network framework.

**5.103 Fickett, Joan.** 1970. Aspects of morphemics, syntax, and semology of an inner-city dialect (Merican). Buffalo: State University of New York dissertation. [Buffalo, NY]. Reprinted by Meadowood Publishers, New York, 1972; by Department of Anthropology, Southern Illinois University, Carbondale, 1974.

**5.104 Fickett, Joan.** 1972. Tense and aspect in black English. JEL 6.17-19. Says "Black English has five aspects, four relative past tenses, two relative future tenses, and a true present tense."

**5.105 Fickett, Joan G.** 1975. 'Merican: an inner-city dialect: aspects of morphemics, syntax, and semology. Studies in Linguistics occasional paper 13. 99 pp. [Buffalo, NY]. Revision of **5.103.**

**5.106 Fickett, Joan G.** 1975. "Ain't," "not," and "don't" in black English. Perspectives on black English, ed. by J. L. Dillard, 86-90. The Hague: Mouton. Argues that black English has six tense forms which may be "phased" to the present, and illustrates negative and nonnegative expressions of them.

**5.107 Fischer, W.** 1927. "You all." AS 2.496. Summarizes C. A. Smith (item **5.213**).

**5.108 Fitzgerald, Alma Annette.** 1976. The uses of negative concord by ten black graduate students. Chapel Hill: University of North Carolina thesis. iv + 78 pp. [10 B adults, CENT AL]. Finds that negative concord and negative inversion are used by college-educated, standard-speaking black graduate students for expressive and stylistic purposes.

**5.109 Fitzgerald, [Mary] Carol.** 1977. Double subjects in conversational English. Reviewed in NADS 10.1.8. Finds blacks and nonstandard speakers both use double subjects, unlike whites and standard speakers, but differed in types of construction they use.

**5.110 Fitzgerald, Mary Carol.** 1977. Double subjects in conversational English. Columbia: University of South Carolina thesis. 117 pp. [23 W, 4 B primary informants]. Outlines three distinct double subject patterns, analyzes 171 examples of these patterns, and characterizes double subject construction as "a feature of conversational standard English" rather than marker of nonstandard or black English.

**5.111 Fitzgerald, Carol.** n.d. The double subject in conversational English. University of North Carolina at Greensboro Papers in Language and Discourse. 13 pp. Short version of preceding item; says "double subject does not carry the strong social penalty in speech that some educators and linguists have maintained it does" and that it "helps to bring order and clarity to often complex, spontaneous conversational narration."

**5.112 Foster, Joseph F.** 1976. Of natural and unnatural dialect differences: when the standard is the deviant. Language Today 2.46-56. ED 129 103. 23 pp. [AR]. Says case marking of subject pronouns in "Southern Highland English" contrasts with patterns of "Prescribed Standard English" taught in schools and that teaching of latter may be effective only to extent it appreciates systematicness of differences between two varieties.

**5.113 Foster, Joseph F.** 1979. Agents, accessories, and owners: the cultural base and the rise of ergative structures, with particular reference to Ozark English. Ergativity: toward a theory of grammatical relations, ed. by Frans

Plank, 489-510. New York: Academic Press. Hypothesizes that "Ozark English is accommodating a cultural preference for clear identification of wilful responsible agents through an increasing tendency to identify that semantic and pragmatic notion with the syntactic category of transitive active subject and that this has resulted in the re-analysis of passive sentences and the rise in OZ [Ozark English] of structures which seem very like . . . ergative."

**5.114 G.** 1899. Youse. Nation 68.476 (June 22). [Chicago]. Contrasts use of second-person-plural pronoun with Southern variants.

**5.115 Gantt, Walter.** 1977. Black dialect: myth and reality. ED 163 490. 20 pp. [174 B children, kindergarten through intermediate grades, Washington, Baltimore]. Says nonstandard speech of black children in urban areas is neither consistent nor homogeneous, nor does it justify being called a separate dialect.

**5.116 Gantt, Walter, and Robert M. Wilson.** 1972. Syntactical speech patterns of black children from a depressed urban area: educators look at linguistic findings. ED 070 079. 27 pp. [78 B children grades, K-6, Baltimore, MD]. Finds occurrence of eight inflectional and other features in speech of children of different achievement levels.

**5.117 Garner, Samuel.** 1899. You all. Nation 68.436 (June 8). [MD]. Says "no educated Southerners ever use you-all as applied to one person"; notes all you, all your, we-dem and you-dem among uneducated speakers.

**5.118 Gilman, Charles.** 1985. Had've: a new auxiliary. SECOL Review 9.9-23. Theoretical discussion of development of structures like I wish I had've gone, with citations from TN and MS.

**5.119 Graves, Richard L.** 1967. Language differences among upper- and lower-class Negro and white eighth graders in east central Alabama. Tallahassee: Florida State University dissertation. Abstract in DAI 28.3657A. Abstract reprinted in J. Williamson and V. Burke 1971(1.823).675-76. [20 UC white, 20 UC black, 20 LC W, 20 LC B 8th-graders in Auburn, AL]. Compares written and spoken patterns of usage and syntactic complexity of upper-class and lower-class students; finds some features to correlate with social class but others, including uninflected verbs and nouns and double negatives, more characteristic of lower-class students than of blacks or whites and more common in writing than in speech, thus casting doubt on assumption that dialect forms pattern according to social or regional background.

**5.120 H., J. C.** 1899. [You-uns]. Nation 68.436 (June 8). Says you-uns and we-uns are prevalent in Southern mountain and piedmont areas settled originally from PA.

**5.121 Hackenberg, Robert G.** 1973. Appalachian English: a sociolinguistic study. Washington: Georgetown University dissertation. Abstract in DAI 33.6893A. [39 speakers, Nicholas Co., WV]. Finds subject-verb concord is grammatical feature with most nonstandard forms, subject relative pronoun deletion is heavily favored by existential there, and a-prefixing "is most likely to occur when there is a stress on the duration of the action"; provides rough correlations of nonstandard forms with educational and occupational indexes.

**5.122 Hackenberg, Robert.** 1977. Language variation in Appalachia. Abstract in NADS 9.3.9. [75 speakers in Nicholas Co., WV]. Finds that nonstandard subject-verb agreement and nonstandard subject relative pronoun deletion correlate with social class of speakers.

**5.123 Harder, Kelsie B.** 1957. Let it go it. AS 32.240. [S CENT TN]. Reports expression means "don't bother" in Perry County, TN.

**5.124 Hill, Archibald A.** 1975. The habituative aspect of verbs in black English, Irish English, and standard English. AS 50.323-24. Says black English and Irish English habitual forms developed from standard English through analogy; there is no need to posit black English-Irish English connection.

**5.125 Hills, E. C.** 1926. The plural forms of "you." AS 2.133. Notes you all used by cultivated speakers in FL and NC, you'uns used by uncultivated speakers in NC and TN mountains.

**5.126 Hilobow, Marian.** 1981. An examination of black English as found in spiritual texts. Montreal, Ontario: Concordia University thesis.

**5.127 Hirshberg, Jeffrey.** 1981. Regional morphology in American English: evidence from DARE. AS 56.33-52. 22 maps. Using DARE records, examines regional distribution of derivational affixes like -fest and other morphemes.

**5.128 Holm, John.** 1984. Variability of the copula in black English and its creole kin. AS 59.291-309. Examines quantitative effects of different following syntactic environments (verb, adjective, locative adverb, or noun phrase) on deletion of be in black English, compares them in Jamaican, Gullah, and other creoles, and examines possible substratal influence from Yoruba and other African languages.

**5.129 Howell, Ralph D.** 1971. Morphological features of the speech of white and Negro students in a southern Mississippi community. Tallahassee: Florida State University dissertation. Abstract in DAI 32.5212-13A. [100 W, 100 B, 50 1st, 3rd, 5th, and 7th graders]. Investigates knowledge of fifteen inflectional and four derivational endings; concludes that both white and black children "enter school without a mastery of the common forms of

English morphology. . . . but the whites become proficient earlier."

**5.130 Huber, Robin H.** 1973. The syntax of the written language of urban (Tallahassee) black and white fourth graders. Tallahassee: Florida State University dissertation. Abstract in DAI 34.5945A. Finds minimal racial differences in syntactic development, as measured by length and complexity of clauses and sentences in compositions, but several significant differences in morphological patterns.

**5.131 Jackson, Alma F.** 1978. The uses of negative concord by ten college educated blacks. Greensboro: University of North Carolina at Greensboro Papers in Language and Discourse. 7 pp. [10 B graduate students at University of North Carolina at Chapel Hill]. Finds speakers use negative concord "frequently and competently" and that females use it more in all-female groups than in mixed-gender groups.

**5.132 Johnson, Guy B.** 1931. "Belong to." AS 6.390. Reports use of modal verb among whites of NC and blacks of SC Sea Islands.

**5.133 Jones, Nancy Nell Alsobrook.** 1972. "Be" in Dallas black English. Denton: North Texas State University dissertation. Abstract in DAI 33.4386A. Proposes a transformational-generative analysis of the auxiliary, saying that do functions as modal auxiliary but that otherwise black speech in Dallas resembles that elsewhere in country.

**5.134 Jones, Nancy.** 1974. Black English in Dallas. Sociolinguistics in the Southwest, ed. by Bates L. Hoffer and Jacob Ornstein, 13-18. San Antonio: Trinity University. Be, do, and other syntactic features.

**5.135 Kenny, Hamill.** 1935. "To" in West Virginia. AS 10.314-15. Preposition equivalent to stative at and equivalent to with/under in phrase take a course to a professor.

**5.136 Kessler, Carolyn.** 1972. Noun plural absence. Annex to Tense marking in black English: a linguistic and social analysis, by Ralph W. Fasold, 223-37 (5.95). Arlington: CAL. [6 M, 6 F, 3 UMC, 3 LMC, 3 UWC, 3 LWC, Washington, DC]. Examines social and generational differences in use of noun plural -s in black speech; finds large percentage of indeterminate cases of plural use.

**5.137 Kester, Barbara D.** 1986. Appalachian and urban grammatical patterns: a note on standardized tests. Athens, OH: Ohio University Working Papers in Linguistics and Language Teaching 8.58-62.

**5.138 Lanier, Dorothy.** 1974. Selected grammatical patterns in the language of Jarvis students. Sociolinguistics in the Southwest, ed. by Bates L. Hoffer and Jacob Ornstein, 19-22. San Antonio, TX: Trinity University. [129 pre-college students]. Examines five features, including subject-verb agreement and past tense verb forms, and classifies students as standard or nonstandard and compares their speech to their attitudes on language.

**5.139 Lee, Adrienne Chingkwei, and Michael Montgomery.** 1987. Relative clauses in written and spoken English. Proceedings of the annual linguistics colloquium, University of North Carolina at Chapel Hill, 33-42. Chapel Hill: UNC Linguistics Circle. [3 older natives, E TN]. Contrasts relative clause features of spoken English of E TN with those in John Lyons' Introduction to Theoretical Linguistics.

**5.140 Light, Richard L.** 1969. Syntactic structures in a corpus of nonstandard English. Washington: Georgetown University dissertation. Abstract in DAI 30.4438-39A. [5 B children, ages 6-11, Washington DC]. Quantitative analysis of multiple negation and of plural, possessive, and third-person-singular suffixes, and correlation of their occurrence with presence or absence of an adult interviewer, sex and race of interviewer, and ages of children.

**5.141 Loflin, Marvin D.** 1966. A note on the deep structure of nonstandard English in Washington, D.C. Washington: CAL. **Reprinted** as Glossa 1.26-32. Same as ED 010 875. 9 pp. [1 B, 14 years old, Washington, DC]. Posits deep-structure habituative category for sentences with copula verb in black speech.

**5.142 Loflin, Marvin D.** 1968. Negro nonstandard and standard English: same or different deep structures? Orbis 18.74-91. Discusses whether standard English and black vernacular English have same or different deep structure.

**5.143 Loflin, Marvin D.** 1969. On the passive in nonstandard Negro English. Journal of English as a Second Language 4.19-23. Constructs partial phrase-structure grammar to account for passive formation in black speech.

**5.144 Loflin, Marvin D.** 1970. On the structure of the verb in a dialect of American Negro English. Linguistics 59.14-28. [1 B, 14 years old, Washington, DC]. Contrasts auxiliary verb system with "Standard English"; finds Black English has no <u>have</u> present perfect structure, no subject-verb agreement other than with <u>be</u>, and marginal use of -<u>ed</u> marker for past-tense verbs. **Reprinted** in H. Allen and G. Underwood 1971(**1.12**).428-43.

**5.145 Loflin, Marvin D.** 1975. Black American English: independent motivation for the auxiliary hypothesis. Linguistic perspectives on black English, ed. by Philip A. Luelsdorff, 45-59. Regensburg: Verlag Hans Carl. Argues that phrase structure rules of black American speech show it has a certain underlying structure and "provide indirect evidence for the hypothesis that the tense structures of Black and Standard English are different at a fundamental level."

**5.146 Loflin, Marvin D.** 1975. Black American English and syntactic dialectology. Perspectives on black English, ed. by J. L. Dillard, 65-73. The Hague: Mouton. Critiques linguistic atlas methodology and argues that it has "no theory"; discusses "additional independent syntactic motivation for the auxiliary hypothesis" presented in preceding item.

**5.147 Loflin, Marvin D.** 1976. Black English deep structure. Assessing linguistic arguments, ed. by Jessica R. Wirth, 269-73. Washington, DC: Hemisphere.

**5.148 Loflin, Marvin D., Nicholas J. Sobin, and J. L. Dillard.** 1973. Auxiliary structures and time adverbs in black American English. AS 48.22-28. Says co-occurrence of time adverbials and auxiliary verbs differs in black English and standard English and thus the former cannot be derived from the latter through phonological contraction and deletion.

**5.149 Long, E. Hudson.** 1943. Ancestry of the Southerner's "you all." Southern Literary Messenger 5.518. Reported from Orangeburg and elsewhere in SC. List of citations of compound pronoun in literary sources from Old English to present.

**5.150 McCain, John Walker, Jr.** 1939. "Any more." AS 14.304. Cites use of form in positive sentences in Orangeburg and surrounding counties in SC.

**5.151 McCardle, Peggy.** 1982. The deep structure of indirect questions in vernacular black English: its relation to language acquisition. SECOL Bulletin 6.25-34. [26 B children, 26 W children, 17 B adults, Orangeburg, SC, 17 W adults, Columbia, SC]. Explores development of subject-auxiliary inversion in four age groups of whites and blacks.

**5.152 McDavid, Raven I., Jr.** 1942. "Oughtn't" and "hadn't ought." CE 14.472-73 and EJ 42.273-74. Uses Linguistic Atlas data and finds oughtn't is nearly universal form south of Mason-Dixon line. **Reprinted** in Readings in applied English linguistics ed. by Harold B. Allen 1969.169-71.

**5.153 McDavid, Raven I., Jr.** 1960. Grammatical differences in the north central states. AS 35.5-19. 4 maps. Plots variants of Midland and Northern verb principal parts in North Central states, including KY. **Reprinted** in R. McDavid 1979(**1.454**).245-53.

**5.154 McDavid, Raven I., Jr., and Virginia G. McDavid.** 1964. Plurals of nouns of measure in the United States. Studies in languages and linguistics in honor of Charles C. Fries, ed. by Albert H. Marchwardt, 271-301. Ann Arbor: University of Michigan English Language Institute. 12 maps. Examines distribution of zero plurals of seven nouns (including foot, pound, and bushel) in LANE, LAMSAS, LANCS, and LAUM data; finds regional variation more significant than social variation and no black-white differences. **Reprinted** in R. McDavid 1979(**1.454**).199-218.

**5.155 McDavid, Raven I., Jr. and Virginia G. McDavid.** 1986. Kentucky verb forms. Language variety in the South: perspectives in black and white, ed. by Michael Montgomery and Guy Bailey, 264-93. University: University of Alabama Press. Details social and regional distribution of variant principal parts for thirty-eight strong verbs among ninety-six LANCS informants in KY; compares data to LAMSAS and LANE.

**5.156 McDavid, Raven I., Jr., and Raymond K. O'Cain.** 1977. "Existential" there and it: an essay on method and interpretation of data. James B. McMillan: essays in linguistics by his friends and colleagues, ed. by James C. Raymond and I. Willis Russell, 29-40. University: University of Alabama Press. Examines variation between it and there and in pronunciation of there in Atlantic states as revealed in LANE and LAMSAS records; finds recessive use of it and they and says more evidence for them is to be found in taped interviews.

**5.157 McDavid, Virginia Glenn.** 1958. Verb forms of the North Central states and Upper Midwest. Minneapolis: University of Minnesota dissertation. Includes KY data.

**5.158 McDavid, Virginia Glenn.** 1963. "To" as a preposition of location in linguistic atlas materials. PADS 40.12-19. 3 maps. Studies alternation of to with at and in in five phrases in Atlantic states from New England to GA.

**5.159 McDavid, Virginia G[lenn].** 1977. Patterns of grammatical variation in the North-Central states. Abstract in NADS 9.3.6. Progress report on editing of LANCS; discusses how regional and social distribution of patterns extends westward from Atlantic seaboard.

**5.160 McDavid, Virginia G[lenn].** 1977. The social distribution of selected verb forms in the Linguistic Atlas of the North Central states. James B. McMillan: essays in linguistics by his friends and colleagues, ed. by James C. Raymond and I. Willis Russell, 41-50. University: University of Alabama Press. Examines principal parts for ten strong verbs in LANCS; finds "a generally lower use of standard forms" and "a higher use of relic forms" in KY.

**5.161 McKay, June Rumery.** 1969. A partial analysis of a variety of non-standard Negro English. Berkeley: University of California dissertation. Abstract in DAI 30.4967A. Generative-transformational analysis of negatives, relatives, existentials, and questions in speech of elderly black woman originally from LA and comparison of these structures to "standard English."

**5.162 Mandina, Genevieve Hogue.** 1969. Composition problems of Negro students in four East Texas high schools. Commerce: East Texas State University thesis.

**5.163 Martin, S. Rudolph, Jr.** 1960. Four undescribed verb forms in

American Negro English. AS 35.238-39. Josh, toch (or taught), jonah, slow around, reported in San Francisco from children of Southerners.

**5.164 Michael, Rebecca J.** 1981. Preterite and participial irregular verbs on Tilghman Island. Pittsburgh: University of Pittsburgh thesis. [Chesapeake Bay, E VA].

**5.165 Miles, Celia H.** 1980. Selected verb features in Haywood County, North Carolina: a generational study. Indiana: Indiana University of Pennsylvania dissertation. Abstract in DAI 41.2089A. [30 speakers, ages 10-75, W NC]. Studies retention of older verb forms such as a-prefixing and variation in principal parts of twenty-four irregular verbs in three generations and finds that "while the dialect is not preserving older forms to any large extent, it is maintaining a high degree of nonstandard usage in irregular verb forms."

**5.166 Miller, Joy L.** 1972. Be, finite and absence: features of speech--black and white? Orbis 21.22-27. Cites absence of be and occurrence of finite be, two features characterized as "black speech," as common in speech of white Southerners, based on personal observation and literary dialect evidence.

**5.167 Miller, Michael I.** 1978. Inflectional morphology in Augusta, Georgia: a sociolinguistic description. Chicago: University of Chicago dissertation. [20 W, 17 B, 22 M, 15 F, ages 18-83, Augusta, GA]. Extensive study of nominal and verbal morphology, using Linguistic Atlas methodology; compares patterns of verb principal parts to statements in usage guides and dictionaries for validity of latter; calls on linguists to challenge reference works to reflect popular usage accurately.

**5.168 Miller, Michael I.** 1982. Irregular English plurals: nouns of measure once again. Abstract in NADS 14.3.7. Studies plurals of nine measure nouns; finds unique history for each and says use of each word, increased literacy, and urbanization account for spread of inflected forms.

**5.169 Miller, Michael I.** 1984. Arrant solecisms. AS 59.131-48. [20 W, 17 B, 22 M, 15 F, ages 18-83, Augusta, GA]. Investigates variation in past tense forms of run and dive in order to make suggestions for how lexicographers might use data from field studies to improve dictionaries.

**5.170 Miller, Michael I.** 1986. The greatest blemish: plurals in "-sp," "-st," "-sk." Language variety in the South: perspectives in black and white, ed. by Michael Montgomery and Guy Bailey, 235-53. University: University of Alabama Press. [20 W, 17 B, 22 M, 15 F, ages 18-83, Augusta, GA]. Examines plurals for wasp, fist, ghost, post, desk, and tusk; finds disyllabic plurals in both white and black speech of older generations and that unmarked plurals are the norm for both blacks and whites.

**5.171 Miller, Michael I.** 1987. Three changing verbs: "bite," "ride," and "shrink." JEL 20.3-12. [Augusta, GA]. Finds that dialect forms of verbs have leveled since World War II, that relic forms are found usually in black speech, that mass education and urbanization are factors correlating best with standard forms, and that "leveling to a contemporary literary standard seems to increase from east to west, the direction of population movement."

**5.172 Montgomery, Michael B.** 1978. Left dislocation: its nature in Appalachian speech. SECOL Bulletin 2.55-61. [20 W, S WV]. Using data from W. Wolfram-D. Christian study (**1.852**), shows functions and varieties of patterns in which left dislocation occurs.

**5.173 Montgomery, Michael B.** 1979. A discourse analysis of expository Appalachian English. Gainesville: University of Florida dissertation. Abstract in DAI 40.5036A. [40 W, 18 M, 22 F, ages 16-87, E TN]. Studies distribution and discourse functions of grammatical and rhetorical devices such as left dislocation, deictic pronouns, and conjunctions.

**5.174 Montgomery, Michael B.** 1979. The discourse organization of explanatory Appalachian speech. Papers of the 1978 Mid-America Linguistics Conference, ed. by Ralph E. Cooley, et al., 293-302. Norman: University of Oklahoma. Excerpt of preceding item. [40 W, 18 M, 22 F, ages 16-87, E TN]. Examines patterning of left dislocation and other syntactic patterns for presenting new information in discourse.

**5.175 Montgomery, Michael B.** 1980. Inchoative verbs in East Tennessee English. SECOL Bulletin 4.77-85. [40 W, E TN]. Study of syntax and semantics of verbs <u>go to</u>, <u>get to</u>, and <u>get to be</u>.

**5.176 Montgomery, Michael B.** 1983. The functions of left dislocation in spontaneous discourse. The ninth LACUS forum, ed. by John Morreall, 425-32. Columbia, SC: Hornbeam Press. Based on Montgomery 1979 (**5.173**), showing subtleties of syntactic patterning of left dislocation.

**5.177 Montgomery, Michael B.** 1987. The roots of Appalachian English. Abstract in NADS 19.2.12. Outlines research project to compare verbal auxiliaries in Southern Appalachian and Scotch-Irish English.

**5.178 Morgan, Argire L.** 1967. An analytical study of the oral language of culturally disadvantaged children in the New Orleans area. New Orleans: Louisiana State University in New Orleans thesis.

**5.179 Morrison, Estelle Rees.** 1926. "You all" and "we all." AS 2.133. First term used by less educated speakers for respect; both forms used in general for courtesy and solidarity.

**5.180 Morrison, Estelle Rees.** 1928. "You all" again. AS 4.54-55. Continues controversy; cites cases of apparent singular usage in VA and MO.

**5.181 Mufwene, Salikoko S.** 1983. Some observations on the verb in black English vernacular. African and Afro-American studies and research center papers: series 2. Austin: University of Texas. 47 pp. Thorough assessment of scholarly literature on origin of Black English Vernacular in attempt to support and highlight creolist hypothesis, without assuming African linguistic substratum or suggesting Gullah as only ancestor of BEV; gives special attention to time reference system and copula in BEV.

**5.182 Nesom, W. E.** 1933. You-all again. American Mercury 29.248-49. Disputes claim of Boock (**5.34**) that you all is used as singular and asserts that no native-born Southerner of any class or ethnicity ever uses it in that fashion.

**5.183 Nichols, Patricia C.** 1986. Prepositions in black and white English of coastal South Carolina. Language variety in the South: perspectives in black and white, ed. by Michael Montgomery and Guy Bailey, 73-84. University: University of Alabama Press. [16 B, 13 W, 14 F, 15 M, Waccamaw Neck, E SC]. Finds different patterns of preposition usage for two insular communities, one black and one white, but that speech of both communities reflects ongoing processes of linguistic change in direction of national norm.

**5.184 Pampell, John R.** 1975. More on double modals. Texas Linguistic Forum 2, ed. by Susan F. Schmerling and Robert D. King, 110-21. Austin: University of Texas. [6 speakers]. Discusses methodological issues and problems inherent in studying double modals, lists modal structures found through series of test questions, and discusses syntactic and semantic aspects of double modals and implications for theory of variability.

**5.185 Parker, Frank.** 1975. A comment on "anymore." AS 50.305-10. Negative restriction on occurrence of anymore has been relaxed in many dialects, but temporal restriction to present tense has not; includes bibliography.

**5.186 Pederson, Lee [A].** 1977. Grassroots grammar in the gulf states. James B. McMillan: essays in linguistics by his friends and colleagues, ed. by James C. Raymond and I. Willis Russell, 91-112. University: University of Alabama Press. Presents range and variety of Southern morphological and syntactic features that LAGS was designed to collect. **Reprinted** in H. Allen and M. Linn 1986(**1.11**).162-79.

**5.187 Perkins, T. W.** 1931. "You all" again. AS 6.304-05. Cites use of term as singular in novel by AR native Charles Morrow Wilson.

**5.188 Perry, Louise Sublette.** 1941. A study of the pronoun "hit" in Grassy Branch, North Carolina. Baton Rouge: Louisiana State University thesis. [62 speakers, ages 5-87, W NC]. 58 pp. Says aspirated variant of it appears most often in initial positions, after a pause, and in stressed and emphatic contexts, and is used primarily by older, less educated speakers.

**5.189 Pickens, William.** 1975. Black vernacular in the Sea Islands of South Carolina. Trends in Southern sociolinguistics, ed. by William G. Pickens, 17-25. Lakemont, GA: CSA Printing and Bindery. [15 B children, grades 5 through 8, Daufuskie Island, SC]. Analyzes nonstandard morphology of nouns, verbs, and other structures in compositions.

**5.190 Pitts, Walter.** 1981. Beyond hypercorrection: the use of emphatic -Z in BEV. Papers from the seventeenth regional meeting Chicago Linguistics Society, ed. by Roberta A. Hendrick et al., 303-10. Chicago: University of Chicago. Says use of verbal -s has an emphatic, stylistic function in black English that derives ultimately from African languages and that its use serves the function of dialect loyalty.

**5.191 Pitts, Walter.** 1985. Linguistic variation as a function of ritual structure in the Afro-Baptist church. Papers from the Berkeley Linguistics Society 11. Berkeley, CA. [CENT TX]. Examines normal speech and prayer speech in black church services to compare variation in multiple negation, copula deletion, deletion of auxiliary have, and four other syntactic features; finds them twice as common in normal speech as in prayers.

**5.192 Pope, Mike.** 1969. The syntax of the speech of urban (Tallahassee) Negro and white fourth graders. Tallahassee: Florida State University dissertation. Abstract in DAI 31.1252A. [30 B, 30 W 4th-graders, Tallahassee, FL]. Finds little difference in syntactic maturity in speech between whites and blacks.

**5.193 Potts, Richard Earl.** 1982. The effects of a proofreading and editing strategy on detecting and selfcorrecting specific nonstandard errors in the writing of tenth-grade students. Memphis: Memphis State University dissertation. Abstract in DAI 44.93A. 152 pp. [76 B 10th graders, Memphis, TN]. Experimental study that finds teaching of proofreading strategies has positive effect on "students' ability to detect and self-correct specific nonstandard errors in writing."

**5.194 Randolph, Vance.** 1927. The grammar of the Ozark dialect. AS 3.1-11. Says grammatical peculiarities of Ozark speech are not as striking as pronunciation or vocabulary, but discusses verb principal parts, case and forms of personal pronouns, relative pronouns, adverb and adjective usage, and other grammatical matters.

**5.195 Randolph, Vance, and Patti Sankee.** 1930. Dialectal survivals in the Ozarks, II: grammatical peculiarities. AS 5.264-69. Discusses verb principal parts, possessive pronoun forms, comparative and superlative forms, multiple negatives, and other features, and exemplifies them in Elizabethan and other writers.

**5.196 Richardson, Gina.** 1984. Can "y'all" function as a singular pronoun in

Southern dialect? AS 59.51-59. Abstract in NADS 14.3.6. [112 residents of Greenville, Spartanburg, SC]. Concludes pronoun can be only plural and claims confusion over its interpretation arises because it is often used by Southerners who deliberately exaggerate their dialect for social effect.

**5.197 Rickford, John R.** 1975. Carrying the new wave into syntax: the case of black English BIN. Analyzing variation in language, ed. by Ralph W. Fasold and Roger W. Shuy, 162-83. Washington: Georgetown University Press. [Philadelphia, Sea Islands of SC]. Says that "eliciting judgments of the equivalence or acceptability of various sentences, and arranging the results in implicational arrays" can supplement data from interviews and personal observation for infrequent syntactic forms such as "remote phase," stressed been. **Reprinted** in R. W. Fasold 1983(1.236).

**5.198 Robert, Martha Jane Godfrey.** 1967. An analysis of the verb forms in a corpus of English spoken by Negroes of south central Louisiana. Baton Rouge: Louisiana State University thesis. Examines features of verbs from corpus of black English obtained from official court transcript recorded in S CENT LA, focusing on -s suffix, strong and weak verb forms, and -ing verb forms and finding -s suffix "is often extended to the first person singular present and omitted from the third person singular."

**5.199 Robinson, Roy.** 1984. Inquiry: we'll see you later. AS 59.69. [GA]. Speculates that expression We'll see you later, used by single, unaccompanied person, is related to Southern you all; calls usage the "Protective Plural."

**5.200 Rouquette, Hyta M.** 1975. On nominal constructions. Gainesville: University of Florida thesis. Notes regional differences in whether try and attempt can take gerund complements.

**5.201 Rulon, C. M., and N. Ongroongraung.** 1981. Texas verb inflection: novel methods of elicitation and interpretation. Abstract in NADS 13.2.8. [N TX]. Discusses recent changes in verb principal parts in terms of linguistic system rather than as social or regional phenomena.

**5.202 Russell, I. Willis.** 1941. Notes on American usage. AS 16.17-20. Notes on like for + pronoun + infinitive in the South, anymore in the affirmative (noted in WV and elsewhere), and shambles.

**5.203 Sackett, S. J.** 1959. "Any more" once more. Word Study 35.4-5. Says readers report use of form in affirmative sentences in thirty-one states, that form "seems most common in the mid-Atlantic and Midwest states and is least common in New England, the deep South, the Southwest, the Far West, and the Northwest."

**5.204 Sanders, Willease S.** 1978. Selected grammatical features of the speech of blacks in Columbia, S.C. Columbia: University of South Carolina dissertation. Abstract in DAI 39.1521A. 123 pp. [43 B adults, Columbia,

SC]. Investigates in careful speech of black adults grammatical "features classified in the literature as nonstandard," which include absence of past tense marker, superfluous past tense marker, deletion of auxiliary have/has, auxiliary done, invariant be, ain't, and others.

**5.205 Schrock, Earl F., Jr.** 1986. Some features of the "be" verb in the speech of Pope County, Arkansas. Language variety in the South: perspectives in black and white, ed. by Michael Montgomery and Guy Bailey, 202-15. University: University of Alabama Press. Explores verb be--its deletion, its use as an invariant form, and its agreement with subjects--and finds black speakers in AR hills are closer to standard forms than are black speakers investigated in Northern cities.

**5.206 Schur, G. S.** 1978. Concerning some peculiarities of the perfect in English. Sprache in gegenwart und geschichte: festschrift für Heinrich Matthias Heinrichs zum 65. geburtstag, ed. by Dietrich Hartmann et al., 174-87. Cologne: Bohlau Verlag. Argues that omission of auxiliary have in some varieties of English represents natural development of Germanic languages and that the pattern in American black speech most likely derived from speakers of Scottish English in Southern colonies.

**5.207 Schur, G. S., and N. V. Svavolya.** 1976. On one peculiarity of the verb of the English language in the U.S.A. (with special reference to black English). Studia Anglica Posnaniensia 7.21-28. Disputes claims that deletion of auxiliary have and use of perfective done are unique to black speech or show creole substratum and says these features have been common in many other varieties of English.

**5.208 Scott, Jerrie.** 1973. The need for semantic consideration in accounting for verb forms in black dialects of English (BDE). University of Michigan Papers in Linguistics 1.2.140-45. Says that "phonological and grammatical rules that deal with surface structure representations fail to convey certain subtle but important semantic distinctions that help to determine variable usage" in black dialects, distinctions between continuative and noncontinuative verbs and between future, momentary, habitual, and durative "temporal aspects."

**5.209 Shay, James F.** 1981. Still more on double modals. Journal of the Linguistic Association of the Southwest 4.313-19. Argues that ought to "does not belong in the analysis of double modal construction" and that "the first modal in a double modal construction is always epistemic."

**5.210 Shewmake, Edwin F.** 1938. Shakespeare and Southern "you all." AS 13.163-68. Says Shakespeare's use of phrase in three plays had second syllable stress, emphasized inclusiveness, and differed from Southern American usage in being formal in style.

**5.211 Sledd, James H.** 1973. A note on buckra philology. AS 48.144-46.

Criticizes Loflin, Stewart, and Dillard for saying black dialect has distinctive, creole-like, habitual use of be; points out that similar usage in British and Irish English has been noted since at least 1910.

**5.212 Slotkin, Alan Robert.** 1969. A survey of verb forms in the midlands of South Carolina. Columbia: University of South Carolina thesis. vi + 134 pp. [21 M, 14 F, 7 counties, CENT SC]. Examines principal parts, subject-verb concord, negatives, infinitives, participles, and other verb forms, using questionnaire based on Atwood (3.17) and comparing results to Atwood.

**5.213 Smith, C. Alphonso.** 1907. "You all" as used in the South. Uncle Remus's Magazine. Also in the Kit-Kat (1920), pp. 27-40. Columbus, OH; in Southern Review 30.41-44 (1920). Discusses use and history of form and contends that its stress on second syllable in Elizabethan times has evolved to first-syllable stress in the American South. **Reviews:** W. Fischer. 1922. Beiblatt zur Anglia 23.168; O. Jesperson. 1914. Modern English Grammar. Vol. I, Item 2.88.

**5.214 Smith, C. Alphonso.** 1916. "Ordinary North-Carolinese," or "I had rather stay than to go with you." Studies in Philology 13.95-99. Argues that the unusual infinitive structure is common in NC and cites precedents from Shakespeare and King James Version to refute OED editor's statement that structure "is not English."

**5.215 Smith, Riley B.** 1969. Interrelatedness of certain deviant grammatical structures in Negro nonstandard dialects. JEL 3.82-88. [170 B, 83 W speakers in E TX]. Claims that in black speech use of "pleonastic pronouns" as in My mother she . . . and deletion of subject relative pronoun as in I have a brother work . . . are related in that the extra personal pronoun after a subject disambiguates sentences with a deleted relative pronoun. Reprinted in R. Abrahams and R. Troike 1972(1.4).291-94; in R. Bentley and S. Crawford 1973(1.64).90-96; in J. L. Dillard 1980(1.197).393-99.

**5.216 Sommer, Elisabeth.** 1980. Prepositions and determiners: some dialectal variations. Abstract in NADS 12.3.8. [9 UMC whites, 9 UMC blacks, 9 LC whites, 9 LC blacks in Atlanta, GA]. Discusses nonstandard uses of function words and correlates them with ethnic and socioeconomic factors; discusses historical and social dimensions of black dialect in the U.S.

**5.217 Sommer, Elisabeth.** 1981. Methodology and data generalizability in dialect research: the study of black American English. Aspects of linguistic variation: proceedings of the conference on language varieties, July 1980, ed. by Steve Lander and Ken Reah, 11-19. Sheffield, UK: University of Sheffield.

**5.218 Sommer, Elisabeth.** 1986. Variation in Southern urban English. Language variety in the South: perspectives in black and white, ed. by Michael Montgomery and Guy Bailey, 180-201. University: University of

Alabama Press. [96 5th-graders, 48 B, 48 W, Atlanta, GA, 32 UMC, 32 LMC, 32 LC]. Contrasts black-white use of distributive be, subject-verb agreement with be, and third-person singular marker -s and finds ethnic as well as class differences.

**5.219 Spears, Arthur [K].** 1978. The black English modal "come." Abstract in NADS 10.2.6. Distinguishes modal come from main verb come and explores its syntactic features and pragmatic use to express disapproval.

**5.220 Spears, Arthur K.** 1980. The other "come" in black English. Working Papers in Sociolinguistics 77. Austin: Southwest Educational Development Laboratory. 14 pp. Preliminary version of following item.

**5.221 Spears, Arthur K.** 1982. The black English semi-auxiliary "come." Language 58.850-72. Says black dialect has use of come as an auxiliary to express speaker indignation and that it is post-creole, "camouflaged" form that is "phonologically similar or identical to" a form in base language, but has different semantic values.

**5.222 Spencer, Nancy J.** 1975. Singular "y'all." AS 50.315-17. [Richmond, VA]. Says pronoun is used as singular in referring to an entire group as a single body and that "for some speakers y'all denotes the second person, singular or inclusive plural, and connotes informal social dialogue of a friendly nature."

**5.223 Starnes, Val W.** 1888. [Comment]. Century 36.799. Cites use of we-uns and you-uns in SC, TN, and by "piney-wood tackeys" in GA; also notes your-all and our-all.

**5.224 Stewart, William.** 1973. Is you or is you ain't my decreolization? Lectological Newsletter 9.2. Notes because that "in speech of "lower-class black speakers. . . particularly in the Gullah region."

**5.225 Strite, Victor.** 1979. Focusing and control in black English pronouns. Papers of the 1978 Mid-America Linguistics Conference, ed. by Ralph B. Cooley, et al., 436-43. Norman: University of Oklahoma. Says grammatical descriptions of "personal pronoun repetition" (as in This boy he stole) miss the fact that pronouns "are usually found at the beginning of narratives"; exemplifies feature in published fiction and speculates it has a creole origin.

**5.226 Terrebonne, Robert A.** 1973. A variable rule analysis of the indefinite article "an." ED 095 713. 27 pp. [35 college students, 13 W from LA, 12 B and 10 W from OH]. Using variable rule program, finds much variation in indefinite articles before vowels, with schwa variant common and zero variant occasional, but that variation between schwa and an does not show style shifting for black speakers.

**5.227 Thompson, Carolyn McLendon.** 1981. A comparative study of standard and nonstandard English syntactic features in the language of lower socioeconomic children. Columbus: Ohio State University dissertation. Abstract in DAI 42.2005A. [60 B, 60 W, LC rural schoolchildren in grades 2, 4, 6]. Based on sentence repetition, examines five syntactic variables; finds racial differences in "copula absence, possessive marker, and subject-verb agreement" but no sex or grade level differences.

**5.228 Tucker, R. Whitney.** 1966. Contraction of "was." AS 41.76-77. Says I's is a contraction for I was in rural Southern black English and should be distinguished from I'se in dialect literature, which is a present-tense form.

**5.229 Turner, Kathleen Denise.** 1981. A unified description of the systematic nature of double modals. Tuscaloosa: University of Alabama thesis. viii + 123 pp. Discusses history, semantics, and syntactic behavior of double modal patterns, and proposes new analysis of them based on X-bar model of syntax.

**5.230 Tyson, Adele.** 1976. Pleonastic pronouns in black English. JEL 10.54-59. Repeats Smith's argument (**5.215**) of the relatedness of deletion of subject relative pronoun and use of pleonastic pronoun, and says that major function of extra pronoun is to serve as agreement marker with main verb of sentence (as in I have one nephew that he stays here with me).

**5.231 Underwood, Gary N.** 1983. Mid-South, midwestern teachers, and middle-of-the-road textbooks. Black English: educational equity and the law, ed. by John Chambers, Jr., 81-96. Ann Arbor, MI: Karoma. Examines ten common syntactic features in the "Mid-South" (KY, TN, AR, southern MO) that are socially marked when speakers move to Midwest, and finds features are rarely mentioned in school textbooks.

**5.232 Van Riper, William R.** 1971. Dialect features and grammatical depth. Abstract in NADS 3.2.25-26. Says many of most striking dialect features lie near the grammatical surface.

**5.233 Vincent, Opal.** 1945. Certain language habits and needs of the senior class of Harrisville high school. Morgantown: West Virginia University thesis. Studies nonstandard usage of verbs and pronouns.

**5.234 Vowles, Guy R.** 1944. A few observations on Southern "you-all." AS 19.146-47. Criticizes Northern magazines for using term indiscriminately for both singular and plural and says he has "never heard anyone say 'you all,' unless the plural was definitely and distinctly intended."

**5.235 White, Grover Gene.** 1985. Black dialect in student writing: a correlation analysis of reading achievement, syntactic maturity, intelligence, grade level, and sex. Auburn: Auburn University dissertation. Abstract in DAI 46.3639A. 95 pp. [375 B 7th-8th graders]. Finds reading achievement correlates with invariant be, copula absence, and multiple negation but grade level, intelligence, and syntactic maturity correlate only with "suffixal z."

**5.236 Whiteman, Marcia F.** 1981. Dialect influence in writing. Variation in writing: functional and linguistic-cultural differences, ed. by Marcia Farr Whiteman, 153-66. Hillsdale, NJ: Erlbaum. [B, W, 32 8th-graders, S MD]. Finds blacks omit inflectional endings verb -ed, verb -s, and noun -s more than whites, but that blacks omit them more in speech than in writing, while whites omit them more in writing than in speech, thus providing evidence against dialect interference hypothesis.

**5.237 Whitley, M. Stanley.** 1975. Dialectal syntax: plurals and modals in Southern American. Linguistics 161.89-108. Investigates patterns of modals and associative pronouns in Southern English and their relation to phrase structure rules of other American English dialect systems; concludes that Southern English and other systems can all be classified as dialects of one language.

**5.238 Whittaker, Della Silverman.** 1972. A content analysis of black English markers in compositions of community-college freshmen. College Park: University of Maryland dissertation. Abstract in DAI 34.756A. [72 B college students, ages 18-45, MD]. Collects and categorizes black English markers in compositions of black freshmen; finds different rates of markers for students assigned to different levels of writing classes but no difference in rate between younger and older students or between males and females

**5.239 Wilkins, Harriet.** 1975. A study of perfective verb markers in a corpus of black English. Baton Rouge: Louisiana State University thesis. 63 pp. [5 elderly, rural B, S CENT LA]. Describes verbal auxiliaries done, have, had, and has, compares them to speech of other black Americans and to literary representations and suggests sources for done, an "invariant preverbal marker."

**5.240 Williams, Cratis D.** 1962. Verbs in mountain speech. Mountain Life and Work 38.15-19 (Spring). [S Appalachia]. Discusses verb principal parts and says that the "primitive strength of mountaineer speech is exerted largely in verbs and the spare economy with which they function."

**5.241 Williams, Cratis D.** 1964. Prepositions in mountain speech. Mountain Life and Work 40.53-55 (Spring). [S Appalachia]. Says mountain speakers rely heavily on prepositions to express themselves rather than Latinate words and that mountain grammar tends not to have "distinctions between prepositions and subordinate conjunctives and, frequently, relative pronouns."

**5.242 Williamson, Juanita V.** 1969. A note on "it is"/"there is." Word Study 45.506. Argues that use of it in existential sentences is not distinctive to speech of black ghetto children, in that it dates back at least to 1300, is reported by Atwood (5.4) as prevalent in WV and Chesapeake Bay area and is observed by author in TN, MS, KY, and TX. **Reprinted** in J. Williamson and V. Burke 1971(**1.823**).434-36.

**5.243 Williamson, Juanita V.** 1972. A look at the direct question. Studies in linguistics in honor of Raven I. McDavid, Jr., ed. by Lawrence M. Davis, 207-14. University: University of Alabama Press. Argues that noninversion in yes-no and Wh-questions is characteristic of standard and white English as well as of black speech, citing examples from dialogue of fictional works, speech reported in Memphis, TN, newspapers, and personal observation primarily in the South.

**5.244 Williamson, Juanita V.** 1973. On the embedded question. Lexicography and dialect geography: festgabe for Hans Kurath, ed. by Harald Scholler and John Reidy, 260-67. Same as ZDL heft 9. Wiesbaden: Franz Steiner Verlag. Says inversion in indirect question formation is often found in white speech, especially in the South.

**5.245 Wilson, George P.** 1960. "You all." Georgia Review 14.38-54. Documents use of expression in English literature and in Southern speech, investigates its singular use, and speculates on its origin.

**5.246 Wilson, Gordon.** 1967. Studying folklore in a small region XII: some folk grammar. TFSB 33.27-35. [Mammoth Cave, KY]. Survey of noun, pronoun, and other morphological features from W KY, gleaned from freshman compositions and from lifetime of personal observation.

**5.247 Wolfram, Walt.** 1976. Toward a description of "a"-prefixing in Appalachian English. AS 51.45-56. [100+ children and adults, S WV]. Examines syntactic properties, phonological constraints, and semantic aspects of prefix; finds that it occurs mainly with -ing progressive verbs and before stressed syllables beginning with a consonant and that it has no apparent semantic content of indefiniteness or remoteness (contrary to Stewart **1.727**) or of continuousness or intermittentness (contrary to Hackenberg **5.121**).

**5.248 Wolfram, Walt.** 1980. "A"-prefixing in Appalachian English. Locating language in time and space, ed. by William Labov, 107-42. New York: Academic Press. [S WV]. Detailed analysis of syntactic and phonological constraints on use of prefix; finds no evidence for semantic content.

**5.249 Wolfram, Walt.** 1982. Language knowledge and other dialects. AS 57.3-18. Theoretical essay examining how accurately nonnative speakers of a-prefixing and distributive be judge syntactic constraints for these features, in attempt to support view that speakers may have more than one grammar for different styles of their language.

**5.250 Wolfram, Walter A., and Ralph W. Fasold.** 1969. A black English translation of John 3:1-21 with grammatical annotations. Bible Translator 20.48-54. Discusses linguistic and sociological factors in translation of New

Testament passage into oral, ethnic variety of English having low status; includes annotations on wide range of morphological and syntactic features.

**5.251 Wright, Barbara Helen White.** 1985. Hypercorrections and dialect forms in the compositions of native-born college students from Georgia. New York: City University of New York dissertation. Abstract in DAI 46.3340A. [94 B, 52 W]. Explores nonstandard morphological and syntactic features in college writing and finds eleven features distinctive of black writers. Says main sources of errors in compositions of both black and white remedial college students are "hypercorrections and dialect forms."

**5.252 Wright, Barbara Helen White.** 1986. Hypercorrections and dialect forms in compositions of native-born college students in Georgia. Standard English as a Second Dialect Newsletter 5.2.1-2. Condensed version of preceding item.

**5.253 Youmans, Gilbert.** 1986. Anymore on "anymore"?: evidence from a Missouri dialect survey. AS 61.61-75. [926 informants at University of Missouri at Columbia]. 1 map. Finds usage of form in affirmative declarative sentences and in wh-questions almost equally divided in acceptability; includes marginal discussion of use in KY and elsewhere, especially as reported by DARE.

## See Also

1.9 Alexander; 1.15 Armstrong; 1.21 Austin; 1.33 Bailey; 1.37 Bailey; 1.61 Bell; 1.63 Benardete; 1.65 Berrey; 1.74 Blanton; 1.84 Boswell; 1.89 Bountress; 1.98 Brandes; 1.99 Bray; 1.111 Burling; 1.115-16 Butters; 1.119 Campbell; 1.124 Carpenter; 1.126 Carpenter; 1.132 Cassidy; 1.139 Christian; 1.144-45 Combs; 1.168 Davis; 1.178 Dent; 1.188-90 Dillard; 1.200-01 Dingus; 1.205 Dumas; 1.213 Dumas; 1.221 Edson; 1.225 Ellis; 1.229 Faneuf; 1.235 Fasold; 1.251-52 Fruit; 1.261 Gibson; 1.264 Gilbert; 1.280 Greene; 1.284 Guest; 1.287 S.A.H.; 1.294-95 Hanners; 1.304 Harper; 1.318 Higgins; 1.329 Houston; 1.334 Howren; 1.344 Jaffe; 1.349 Jones; 1.350 Jones; 1.351 Jones; 1.353 Keener; 1.371 Kurath; 1.373 Kurath; 1.380 Labov; 1.389 LeCompte; 1.399 Lucas; 1.406 McBride; 1.417-18 McDavid; 1.423 McDavid; 1.432 McDavid; 1.434 McDavid; 1.438 McDavid; 1.443 McDavid; 1.473 McDavid; 1.481 McGreevy; 1.482 McGuire; 1.498 Massey; 1.508 Mencken; 1.513 Miller; 1.536 Muehl; 1.538 Nelson; 1.543 Nix; 1.541-42 Norman; 1.546 Oettenger; 1.550 Park; 1.555 Payne; 1.564 Pederson; 1.583 Pederson; 1.608 Pietras; 1.621 Putnam; 1.630 Randolph; 1.632 Rash; 1.645 Reese; 1.653 Reirdon; 1.655 Richert; 1.656-57 Rickford; 1.660 Rodgers; 1.661 Roebuck; 1.665 Rueter; 1.670 Satterfield; 1.671 Sawyer; 1.679 Schrock; 1.680 Scott; 1.707 Smith; 1.722 Stewart; 1.738 Stolz; 1.743 Street; 1.764 Tozer; 1.768 Troike; 1.770 Twiggs; 1.793 Walker; 1.794 Walker; 1.804 Whiteman; 1.813 Williams; 1.815 Williams; 1.816 Williamson; 1.818-19 Williamson; 1.830 Wilson; 1.835 Wolfram; 1.837 Wolfram; 1.839 Wolfram; 1.850 Wolfram; 1.854 Wolfram;

1.858 Wood; 2.5 Allen; 2.7 Alleyne; 2.10 Asante; 2.13 Bailey; 2.22 Berdan; 2.25 Birmingham; 2.36-38 Brewer; 2.40 Brewer; 2.86 Combs; 2.95 Cunningham; 2.102 Dalton; 2.132 Eliason; 2.140 Fasold; 2.142 Fitzhugh; 2.148 Frajzyngier; 2.169 Hancock; 2.177 Hancock; 2.179 Hancock; 2.181-82 Hancock; 2.187 Harrison; 2.192 Hawkins; 2.194 Haynes; 2.219-20 Jeremiah; 2.222 Johnson; 2.227 Johnson; 2.231-35 Jones-Jackson; 2.238 Joyner; 2.254 Kurath; 2.257 Kurath; 2.265 Lewis; 2.310-12 Mufwene; 2.316 Nichols; 2.318 Nichols; 2.320 Nichols; 2.322 Nichols; 2.347-48 Poplack; 2.366-69 Rickford; 2.380-84 Schneider; 2.394 Smith; 2.396 Smith; 2.432 Traugott; 2.437 Turner; 2.465 Williams; 2.475 Woofter; 2.479 Ziegler; 3.84 Ching; 3.522 Wilson; 4.209 Labov; 4.255 Miller; 9.15 Boykin; 9.16 Briggs; 9.29 De Spain; 9.45-46 Fine; 9.63 Hensley; 9.85 Meyer; 9.87 Mitchell; 9.94 Nixon; 9.102 Peppers; 9.116 Rulon; 9.132 Stockton; 9.143 Williams; 10.10 Coe; 10.49 Rubadeau.

# 6 Place Name Studies

**6.1 Abernathy, Edgar.** 1943. Unusual names. [NC] State Magazine 10.14–15.

**6.2 Adams, John D.** 1921. Coosa County: present day place names showing aboriginal influence. Arrow Points 2.73-75. [E CENT AL].

**6.3 Alabama County names.** 1917. Magazine of History 25.54-59.

**6.4 Alford, Terry L.** 1968. An interesting place-name. MFR 2.3.76-78. Speculates on origin and spread of Indianola, MS.

**6.5 Alleman, Elise A.** 1936. The legend and history of place names of Assumption Parish. Baton Rouge: Louisiana State University thesis. xiii + 104 pp. [SE LA]. Classifies 167 names according to Indian, German, Spanish, French, or English/Celtic origin; discusses settlement of each parish locality, etymology of local names, and popular legends behind them.

**6.6 Allsopp, Fred W.** 1931. Folklore in romantic Arkansas. New York: Grolier Society. 2 vols. P. 36, on the name <u>Arkansas</u>; pp. 59-108, on AR place names.

**6.7 Alsup, Lynda S.** 1977. Plantations and clubs of Jasper County. NSC 24.27-30. [SE SC].

**6.8 Anderson, James L.** 1956. The house that named the town. American Motorist 24.3. On Owingsville, KY.

**6.9 Anderson, John Q.** 1958. Some mythical places in Louisiana. Louisiana Folklore Miscellany 1.3.1-10. Names for mythical towns, rivers, and bayous in state.

**6.10 Anderson, John Q.** 1962. From Flygap to Whybark: some unusual

Texas place names. The golden log, ed. by Mody C. Boatright, et al., 73-98. Texas Folklore Society Publication 31. Dallas: Southern Methodist University Press.

**6.11 Anderson, John Q.** 1964. Texas stream names. A good tale and a bonnie tune, ed. by Mody C. Boatright, Wilson M. Hudson, and Allen Maxwell, 112-47. Texas Folklore Society Publication 32. Dallas: Southern Methodist University Press.

**6.12 Anderson, Jolane Springston.** 1980. The place names of Lamar County, Mississippi. Hattiesburg: University of Southern Mississippi thesis.

**6.13 Anderson, Jolane Springston.** 1981. Lamar County place-names: land features and water bodies. MFR 15.1-12. [SE MS]. List and analysis of twenty-seven descriptive names.

**6.14 Anderson, Sallie B.** 1968-70. Some names in Clarendon County. Part 1, NSC 15.32-36. Part 2, NSC 16.31-36. Part 3, NSC 17.30-33. [E CENT SC]. Names of plantations.

**6.15 Ariail, Robert L.** 1974. Ariail, Rial Hill, and Ariel Crossroads. NSC 21.30-31. [Pickens Co., NW SC].

**6.16 Arkansas geographic names.** 1981. Reston, VA: U.S. Geological Survey. 2 vols. 449 pp. Alphabetical listing of over 22,000 place names with identification of their nature--locale, church, cemetery, stream, etc.

**6.17 Aschbacher, Frances M.** 1953. Pronouncing directory of cities, towns, and counties in Texas. San Antonio: privately printed. 32 pp. Pronunciation of localities, with more than 500 sources of county names.

**6.18 Associated Stamp Clubs of the Chesapeake Area.** 1960. Postal markings of Maryland, 1766-1855. The Maryland postal history catalog, ed. by Edgar T. Powers. Baltimore. 100 pp. Lists more than 600 names of MD offices and specifies their period of operation.

**6.19 Avery, Sharon.** 1983. Fairfield County towns and communities. NSC 30.34-40. [N CENT SC].

**6.20 B., J. C.** 1881. Origin of the name of Texas. Magazine of American History 7.149.

**6.21 Babcock, W. H.** 1888. Notes on local names near Washington. JAF 1.146-47. The origin and changes of several place names around Washington, DC.

**6.22 Ball, Frank.** 1975. Place names in W. Va. Preacher changed the name to Poca-to-Hell-you-go. West Virginia Hillbilly 17.1.

**6.23 Ball, Frank.** 1975. West Virginia: state with funny names. West Virginia Hillbilly 17.1.

**6.24 Barbour, Philip L.** 1967. Chickahominy place names in Captain John Smith's True Relation. Names 15.60-71. Indian names of Chickahominy River basin in SE VA in 1607. Comments by Hamill Kenny, 225-26.

**6.25 Barbour, Philip L.** 1971. The earliest reconnaissance of Chesapeake Bay area: Captain John Smith's map and Indian vocabulary. Virginia Magazine of History and Biography 79.280-302. Bibliography, 283-84. Lists and analyzes Indian place names (mostly Powhatan) recorded by John Smith in his writings.

**6.26 Barto, Karen, and other students of John L. Idol.** 1981. Pickens County rural roads: a representative list. NSC 28.43-45. [NW SC].

**6.27 Bass, Mary Frances.** 1942. A study of place names of Clarke County, Mississippi. Tuscaloosa: University of Alabama thesis. 173 pp. [E CENT MS]. Compiles dictionary of Clarke County names, classifies names into six types according to origin, and discusses their special features.

**6.28 Bass, Robert D.** 1977. Some names in Britton's Neck. NSC 24.19-21. [E SC]. Portion of land extending twenty-five miles to confluence of Peedee and Little Peedee rivers, Marion County.

**6.29 Battle, Kemp P.** 1888. The names of the counties of North Carolina and the history involved in them. Winston, NC: W. A. Blair. 38 pp.

**6.30 Battle, Kemp P.** 1906. Glimpses of history in the names of our counties. North Carolina Booklet 6.27-48.

**6.31 Battle, Kemp P.** 1908. North Carolina county names. Magazine of History 7.208-22.

**6.32 Bayer, Henry G.** 1930. French names in our geography. Romanic Review 21.195-203. Includes names from AR, MO, and other states.

**6.33 Bentley, Harold W.** 1932. A dictionary of Spanish terms in English. New York. Pp. x + 243. Pp. 221-35, lists placenames of Spanish origin in AL, AR, FL, GA, KY, LA, MS, TN, TX.

**6.34 Benton, John T.** 1965. Names and places on Cooper River. NSC 12.22-31. Names in Charleston area and surrounding SC low country.

**6.35 Berkeley, Francis L.** 1935. "Purton." Virginia Magazine of History and Biography 43.150-52. [SE VA]. Aspects of name of estate in Gloucester County.

**6.36 Berkley, Henry J.** 1924. Extinct river towns of the Chesapeake Bay region. Maryland Historical Magazine 19.125-34.

**6.37 Berry, C. B.** 1970. Cemetery names in Horry County. NSC 17.21-22. [E SC].

**6.38 Berry, C. B.** 1980. Grand strand place names. NSC 27.30-31. [E SC]. Names in Myrtle Beach and environs.

**6.39 Berry, C. B.** 1981. From Cainhoy to Izardtown. NSC 28.24-27. Names of area between Cooper and Santee rivers in Charleston and Berkeley Counties.

**6.40 Berry, Earl.** 1977. History of Marion County [AR]. Little Rock: Marion County Historical Association. Pp. 331-37, discusses all known post offices in county; 342-405, surveys town names and reports how they were coined.

**6.41 Berry, Nora.** 1935. Place names of Natchitoches Parish. Baton Rouge: Louisiana State University thesis. [NW LA]. Glossary of 203 names.

**6.42 Bevan, Edith Rossiter.** 1952. Some Maryland towns have odd place names. Maryland Gardener 6.19-20.

**6.43 Bibb, J. Porter.** 1921. Montgomery County: present day place names showing aboriginal influence. Arrow Points 2.14-17. [CENT AL].

**6.44 Bigbee, Janet H.** 1970. 17th century place names: culture and process on the Eastern Shore. College Park: University of Maryland thesis. [E MD].

**6.45 Biggs, Thomas H.** 1974. Geographical and cultural names in Virginia. Information circular 20. Richmond: Virginia Division of Mineral Resources. 374 pp. Index to information on U. S. Geological Survey maps, divided by placenames, water features, landforms, and religious institutions. **Review:** P. B. Rogers. 1975. Names 23.215.

**6.46 Bigham, John A.** 1974. Names in the greater Columbia area. NSC 21.31-32. [CENT SC].

**6.47 Bigham, John A.** 1975. Names in southeast Chester County. NSC 22.14-17. [N CENT SC].

**6.48 Bigham, John A.** 1976. Columbia area names prior to World War II. NSC 23.14-16. [CENT SC].

**6.49 Bigham, John A.** 1977. Names in Winnsboro and vicinity. NSC 24.30-31. [N CENT SC].

**6.50 Bigham, John A.** 1978. Chapin section names. NSC 25.12-14. [CENT SC]. Names in Dutch Fork area of Lexington County.

**6.51 Bigham, John A.** 1980. Calhoun County place names. NSC 27.13-15. [CENT SC].

**6.52 Bigham, John A.** 1981. Names in Newberry County. NSC 28.22-24. [CENT SC].

**6.53 Bloodworth, Bertha Ernestine.** 1959. Florida placenames. Gainesville: University of Florida dissertation. 260 pp. Abstract in DAI 20.2790. Details origins, meanings, modifications, and connotations of 2,400 placenames and classifies them as commemorative, descriptive, or cultural.

**6.54 Bloodworth, Bertha E., and Alton C. Morris.** 1978. Places in the sun: the history and romance of Florida placenames. Gainesville: University Presses of Florida. x + 209 pp. Narrates history of naming in FL and classifies 2,500 names into "commemorative, descriptive, and cultural" categories; attributes lack of pejorative names to activities of promoters in state. **Reviews:** P. A. Bulger. 1982. JAF 95.363-64; M. L. Chapman. 1979-80. Florida Historical Quarterly 58.332-33; K. B. Harder. 1979. TFSB 45.130-33; E. B. Vest. 1979. Names 27.274.

**6.55 Boland, Rendy L.** 1977. Bowman place names. NSC 24.37-38. [Orangeburg Co., CENT SC].

**6.56 Bonham, Milledge Louis, Jr.** 1926. Notes on place names. AS 1.625. LA and SC names.

**6.57 Bonner, Jessie Lee.** 1926. Where Oak Hill [AL] got its name. Arrow Points 12.23. Legendary account.

**6.58 Boone, Lalia Phipps.** 1958. Florida, the land of epithets. SFQ 22.86-92. Nicknames of locations.

**6.59 Boozer, Herman W.** 1972. Bethany church and related names in upper Richland County. NSC 19.17-21. [CENT SC].

**6.60 Boswell, George W.** 1976. A selection of Mississippi place names. American Name Society Bulletin 45.4.11.

**6.61 Boyd, Mark F.** 1939. Mission sites in Florida; an attempt to approximately identify the sites of Spanish mission settlements of the seventeenth century in northern Florida. Florida Historical Quarterly 17.255-80. Lists names from old manuscripts and maps.

**6.62 Braake, Alex L.** 1968. What's in a name: the three Charlestowns. West Virginia History 30.351-57. Three early WV towns had the name.

**6.63 Bradley, A. G.** 1897. Sketches from old Virginia. London: Macmillan. Notes on names in VA mountains, 154.

**6.64 Bragg, Marion.** 1977. Historical names and places on the lower Mississippi River. Vicksburg: Mississippi River Commission, U.S. Army, Corps of Engineers. Locales south of junction of Ohio and Mississippi rivers.

**6.65 Brame, J. Y.** 1921. Lowndes County: present day place names showing aboriginal influence. Arrow Points 2.55-56. [S CENT AL].

**6.66 Branner, John Casper.** 1899. Some old French place names in the state of Arkansas. MLN 14.33-40. **Reprinted** in W. K. McNeil, ed. 1984. The charm is broken: readings in Arkansas and Missouri folklore, 69-81. Little Rock, AR: August House.

**6.67 Brannon, Peter A.** 1921. Pike County: present day place names suggesting aboriginal influence. Arrow Points 3.18-19. [SE AL].

**6.68 Brannon, Peter A.** 1922. Tallapoosa County; present day place names suggesting aboriginal influence. Arrow Points 3.46-49; 5.104-08. [E CENT AL].

**6.69 Brannon, Peter A.** 1922. Clay County: place names showing aboriginal influence. Arrow Points 3.56-58; 4.96-98. [E CENT AL].

**6.70 Brannon, Peter A.** 1922. Aboriginal towns in Alabama: showing locations by present county boundary lines. Arrow Points 4.26-28.

**6.71 Brannon, Peter A.** 1922. Elmore County; present day place names suggesting aboriginal influence. Arrow Points 4.46-51. [CENT AL].

**6.72 Brannon, Peter A.** 1922. Macon County; present day place names suggesting aboriginal influence. Arrow Points 5.5-9. [SE AL].

**6.73 Brannon, Peter A.** 1922. Barbour County; present day place names showing aboriginal influence. Arrow Points 5.32-37. [SE AL].

**6.74 Brannon, Peter A.** 1922. Alabama post office and stream names. Arrow Points 6.3-7. Discusses locations having aboriginal significance and lists names of modern post offices with their present-day spellings as well as according to language of origin; also lists rivers and largest streams still called by their Indian names.

**6.75 Brannon, Peter A.** 1923. County names in Alabama history. Arrow Points 6.33-34.

**6.76 Brannon, Peter A.** 1923. Place names in Clarke County. Arrow Points 6.103-07. [SW AL].

**6.77 Brannon, Peter A.** 1924. Monroe County; some sketches of its places. Arrow Points 8.39-42. [SW AL].

**6.78 Brannon, Peter A.** 1925. The name "Alabama." Arrow Points 10.19-21. Analyzes etymology and history of state's name; discredits traditional translation, "Here we rest."

**6.79 Brannon, Peter A.** 1925. Certain place names in Choctaw County [AL]. Arrow Points 11.8-12. [SW AL].

**6.80 Brannon, Peter A.** 1928. Jackson County place names; a study of the names, suggesting the aboriginal history of the county. Arrow Points 13.9-11. [NE AL].

**6.81 Brannon, Peter A.** 1951. Name places affected by the Indian War of 1813-14. Alabama Historical Quarterly 13.132-35.

**6.82 Brannon, Peter A.** 1959. Russell County place names; present day names perpetuating aboriginal and early historic points in the county. Alabama Historical Quarterly 21.96-103. [SE AL].

**6.83 Brawley, James S.** 1974. Towns and communities: their origins and development. Rowan County: a brief history, 161-68. Raleigh: North Carolina Department of Cultural Resources. [CENT NC].

**6.84 Brennecke, Marguerite.** 1961. Some Oconee County names. NSC 8.12-15. [NW SC].

**6.85 Brinegar, Bonnie.** 1977. Choctaw place-names in Mississippi. MFR 11.142-50.

**6.86 Brinkley, Hal E.** 1973. How Georgia got her names. Atlanta, GA: Educational Supply. 190 pp. Glossary of 1500 brief entries of town and other names. **Reviews:** Anonymous. 1974. GHQ 58.379-80; K. B. Harder. 1976. TFSB 42.47-48; R. M. Rennick. 1976. Names 24.318.

**6.87 Bristol, Roger P.** 1974. Greene County place names. Virginia Place Name Society Occasional Papers 17. Charlottesville: University of Virginia. 32 pp. [CENT VA].

**6.88 Bristol, Roger P.** 1974. Approved place names in Virginia, an index to Virginia names approved by the United States Board of Geographic Names from 1970 through 1973. Virginia Place Name Society Occasional Papers 18. Charlottesville: University of Virginia. 16 pp. Cf. Biggs (**6.45**) and Topping (**6.616**).

**6.89 Brock, Clifton.** 1984. In honor of the occasion. Verbatim 11.2.16-17. Casual essay on "quaint" place names in NC, especially Whynot, Erect, and Climax.

**6.90 Brown, Alexander Crosby.** 1951. Wolf Trap, the baptism of a Chesapeake Bay shoal. Virginia Magazine of History and Biography 39.176-83.

**6.91 Brown, Virginia Pounds, and Jane Porter Nabers.** 1952. The origin of certain place names in Jefferson County, Alabama. Alabama Review 5.177-202. [CENT AL].

**6.92 Brunn, Stanley D. B., and James O. Wheeler.** 1966. Notes on the geography of religious town names in the U.S. Names 14.197-202.

**6.93 Bryson, Artemisia Baer.** 1928. [Contrasting American names compared with the Spanish names found in Texas]. AS 3.436. Points out unusual names for counties, towns, and natural formations in TX that suggest development of the country after American settlement of the state.

**6.94 Bryson, Fred R.** 1945. The spelling and pronunciation of Arkansas. Arkansas Historical Quarterly 4.175-79. Variation in AR's name revealed in 18th- and 19th-century records.

**6.95 Bull, Elias B.** 1964. Community and neighborhood names in Berkeley County. Part 1, NSC 11.11-24. Part 2, NSC 12.32-39. [SE SC]. Attempts to record and preserve names of small, dying rural communities.

**6.96 Bull, Elias B.** 1969-71. Coastal island names. Part 1, NSC 16.22-29. Part 2, NSC 17.11-15. Part 3, NSC 18.25-28. [E SC].

**6.97 Bull, Elias B.** 1976. Old postal routes, 1855. NSC 23.34-38.

**6.98 Bull, Elias B.** 1981. Random names from South Carolina Gazette. NSC 28.51-54. 18th-century newspaper citations of Charleston locations.

**6.99 Bull, Elias B.** 1983. Gleanings from old Charleston newspapers. NSC 30.17-21. Reports of extinct neighborhoods and localities in SC.

**6.100 Bullard, David F.** 1956. Haughabook swamp. NSC 3.7-8. Located in Lexington County. [CENT SC].

**6.101 Bullard, Helen, and Joseph Marshall Krechniak.** 1956. Cumberland County's first hundred years. Crossville, TN: Centennial Committee. [E TN]. P. 32, notes on family and place names in county.

**6.102 Bump, Charles Weathers.** 1907. Indian place names in Maryland. Maryland Historical Magazine 2.287-93.

**6.103 Burke, John E.** 1981. Eudora Welty's use of character and place names in sixteen of her short stories. The scope of names, ed. by Fred Tarpley, 87-105. Commerce, TX: Names Institute Press.

**6.104 Burnside, Ronald.** 1981. Towns and communities in Laurens County. NSC 28.19-22. [NW SC].

**6.105 Burrill, Meredith F.** 1957. Terminology of Virginia's geographic features. Virginia Geographical Society Bulletin 9.12-20.

**6.106 Bushnell, David Ives.** 1909. The Choctaw of Bayou Lacomb, St. Tammany Parish, Louisiana. Bulletin of American Ethnology Bulletin 48. Washington: Government Printing Office. Pp. 6-7, place names in St. Tammany Parish. [SE LA].

**6.107 Butt, Marshall W.** 1971. Place names of early Portsmouth. Portsmouth, VA: Portsmouth American Revolution Bicentennial Committee. [SE VA]. Covers names of towns, natural features, streets, and squares. **Review:** P. B. Rogers. 1974. Names 22.75.

**6.108 Cain, Cyril E.** 1949. The first hundred years of post offices on the Pascagoula River. Journal of Mississippi History 11.178-84. [SE MS].

**6.109 Caldwell, Norman W.** 1944. Place names and place name study. Arkansas Historical Quarterly 3.28-36. Outlines main influences on state's place names--French, German, Indian--and discusses possibilities for conducting serious place name research in AR.

**6.110 Cameron, Minnie B.** 1950. [County of Bexar, TX.] Southwestern Historical Quarterly 53.477-79. Corrects material on origin of name, ibid., 49.275 (Oct. 1946).

**6.111 Carpenter, Charles.** 1929. Our place names. West Virginia Review 6.422,440. Surveys names of WV rivers, towns, and other places and shows how they preserve state history.

**6.112 Chapman, H. H.** 1924. Why the town of McNary moved. American Forests and Forest Life 30.589-92. Describes renaming of town after inhabitants abandoned McNary, LA, and moved to AZ.

**6.113 Chappell, Buford S.** 1974. Names--old, new, and forgotten--along Monticello Road and Little River. NSC 21.15-19. [CENT SC]. Names of landmarks from Columbia to Monticello.

**6.114 Chardon, Roland.** 1977. Notes on south Florida place names: Norris Cut. Tequesta: Journal of the Historical Society of South Florida 37.51-61. Says the cut was the waterway into Biscayne Bay and Miami until 1905.

**6.115 Chrisman, Lewis H.** 1930. The origin of the names of the county seats of West Virginia. West Virginia Review 8.44-45,62.

**6.116 Chrisman, Lewis H.** 1946. The origin of place names in West Virginia. West Virginia History 7.77-88.

**6.117 Clark, Thelma Chiles.** 1981. Marion County townships. NSC 28.41-43. [E SC].

**6.118 Cleaves, Mildred P.** 1948. Kentucky towns and their mark. In Kentucky 11.39.

**6.119 Clover, Margaret.** 1952. The place names of Atascosa County, Texas. Austin: University of Texas thesis. 230 pp. [S CENT TX]. Pp. 61-202, dictionary.

**6.120 Cocke, Charles Francis.** 1964. Parish lines, Diocese of Southern Virginia. Richmond: Virginia State Library. 287 pp. Pp. 235-46, lists and gives origin of town and county names.

**6.121 Cohen, Hennig.** 1953. A colonial topographical poem. Names 1.252-58. SC place names, especially rivers, in 1753 poem, "C. W. in Carolina to E. J. at Gosport."

**6.122 Collitz, Hermann.** 1934. Baltimore--what does the name mean? Johns Hopkins Alumni Magazine 22.133-34. [MD].

**6.123 Cooper, Elizabeth Scott.** 1956. How Ocracoke got its name. North Carolina Folklore 4.19-21. [E NC]. Verse account deriving name from "O crow, cock."

**6.124 Corbitt, David Leroy.** 1950. The formation of the North Carolina counties: 1663-1943. Raleigh: North Carolina Department of Archives and History.

**6.125 Corse, Herbert M.** 1942. Names of the St. Johns River. Florida Historical Quarterly 21.127-34. [NE FL].

**6.126 Coumes, Bertha Davis.** 1962. A study of some place names in Calhoun County, Alabama. Auburn: Auburn University thesis. [NE AL].

**6.127 Coumes, John Valsin.** 1967. A study of some place-names in Tangipahoa Parish, Louisiana. Auburn: Auburn University thesis. [SE LA].

**6.128 Counties in Kentucky and origin of their names.** 1903. Kentucky State Historical Society Register 1.34-37.

**6.129 Cox, William E.** 1942. Southern sidelights: a record of personal experience. Raleigh, NC: Edwards and Broughten. Names and their oddities, 162-70.

**6.130 Craig, Marjorie.** 1946. Western North Carolina place names. North Carolina English Teacher 3.3.12-15.

**6.131 Crenshaw, Mrs. William.** 1966. Origins of Butler County place names. Butler County Historical Society Publications 2.1-13 (Mar.); 2.1-5 (June). [S CENT AL].

**6.132 Cridlin, William Broadus.** 1923. A history of colonial Virginia, the first permanent colony in America, to which is added the genealogy of the several shires and counties and population in Virginia from the first Spanish colony to the present time. Richmond, VA: Williams. 181 pp. **Review:** Virginia Magazine of History 32.207.

**6.133 Crockett, Nancy.** 1983. Place names in the Waxhaws. NSC 30.50-53. [N CENT SC]. Names from area in Lancaster County.

**6.134 Cumming, Willian Patterson.** 1945. Naming Carolina. North Carolina Historical Review 22.34-42. Development of nomenclature for the two adjacent colonies in 16th and 17th centuries, based on close scrutiny and analysis of old maps.

**6.135 Cumming, William P.** 1962. Naming Carolina. NSC 9.14-18. Historical account of naming and founding of American colony; includes discussion of earlier unsuccessful European habitations.

**6.136 Curtis, Rosalee M.** 1973. Texas counties named for South Carolinians. NSC 20.39-46.

**6.137 Danton, Emily Miller.** 1956. Alabama place names: a selection. Alabama Review 9.68-69. List of "picturesque" names.

**6.138 [Dart, Henry P.]** 1931. Note on the origin of Natchez. Louisiana Historical Quarterly 14.515. Quotes Albert S. Gatschet as now opining that it is a Caddo word.

**6.139 Dau, Frederick W.** 1934. Indian and other names in Florida, their meaning and derivation. Florida old and new, 336. New York: Putnam.

**6.140 Davidson, Chalmers P.** 1970. Chester County plantation names. NSC 17.22-25. [N CENT SC].

**6.141 Davis, T. N.** 1965. Of many things. America 112.407. Comments on names in KY.

**6.142 Davis, Ted M.** 1965. Place names in and around Walhalla. NSC 12.15-

17. [NW SC]. Names from area founded by German Colonization Society of Charleston.

**6.143 Deal, N. Harvey.** 1962. Ah sid. Virginia Place Name Society Occasional Papers 5.1-6 (June 13). Charlottesville: University of Virginia.

**6.144 Deal, N. Harvey.** 1964. The mountains of Virginia. Virginia Place Name Society Occasional Papers 10. Charlottesville: University of Virginia. 40 pp. **Review:** P. M. Strain. 1965. SLA Geography and Map Division Bulletin 59.23-24.

**6.145 Deane, Ernie.** 1978. Ozarks country: a collection of articles about folklore, places, people, customs, history and other Ozarks subjects. Republic, MO: Western. Why we say "Arkansaw," 15-16; How Yellville was named, 18-19; Missouri place name origins, 21-22; "Hillbilly," 26-27; The noble "hillbilly," 27-28.

**6.146 Deane, Ernie.** 1986. Arkansas place names. Branson, MO: Ozarks Mountaineer. 201 pp. Discusses names of counties and county seats and more than 400 other place names. **Review:** K. B. Harder. 1987. Names 35.110-11.

**6.147 Derrick, Barbara.** 1950. A name for a state. South Carolina Magazine 13.12,23-24. Traces origin of term Palmetto State to 1776.

**6.148 Detro, R[andall] A.** 1970. Generic terms in Louisiana place names: an index to the cultural landscape. Baton Rouge: Louisiana State University dissertation. Abstract in DAI 31.5417B. Examines origin, three hundred years of spread, and present distribution of generic toponyms in effort to delimit French LA and Anglo-American LA cultural areas.

**6.149 Detro, Randall A.** 1984. Louisiana toponymic generics delimit culture areas. Names 32.367-91. Based on preceding item.

**6.150 Doar, David.** 1982. Plantations at St. James, Santee. NSC 29.21-23. [SE SC].

**6.151 Dobie, James Frank.** 1936. Stories in Texas names. Southwest Review 21.125-36, 278-94, 411-17. Origins of many TX place names. **Reprinted** in Texas Folklore Society Publications 13.1-78 (1937).

**6.152 Donnell, Marianne,** comp. 1978. Toponyms in Florida: an alphabetical listing of names approved by the U. S. Board of Geographic Names through 1976 with 1977 addendum. Gainesville: University Presses of Florida. 56 pp.

**6.153 Dorrance, Ward Allison.** 1938. We're from Missouri. Richmond, MO:

Missourian Press. Change the name of Arkansas?, 17-21; Senator's revenge, 31-35.

**6.154 Douglas, Lillian.** 1932. Place-names of East Feliciana Parish. Baton Rouge: Louisiana State University thesis. 30 pp. [SE LA]. Discussion of forty-six names, drawn mostly from local histories.

**6.155 Drew, Frank.** 1926. Some Florida names of Indian origin. Florida Historical Quarterly 4.181-82; Part 2, 6.197-205 (Apr. 1928).

**6.156 Drew, Shelley.** 1962. Place names of ten northeastern counties of Florida. AS 37.255-65.

**6.157 Duckson, Don W., Jr.** 1981. Toponymic generics in Maryland. Names 28.163-69. Analyzes generic names for topographic features.

**6.158 Duckson, Don W., Jr.** 1983. A creek is a creek . . . or is it? Names 31.51-59. [MD and elsewhere]. Says perceptions in geographical names for streams of water have been applied consistently, but according to different scales in U.S.

**6.159 du Gard, Rene Coulet.** 1986. Dictionary of French names in the U.S.A. Newark, DE: Edition des Deux Mondes. vi + 431 pp. **Review:** K. Harder. 1986. TFSB 42.24.

**6.160 Dugas, Tomie Dawkins.** 1978. Place name origins. Alabama Life 1.1.56-58. [E CENT AL]. On Chambers Co., AL.

**6.161 Dugas, Tomie Dawkins.** 1978. Place name origins. Alabama Life 1.2.78-80. [S CENT AL]. On Butler Co., AL.

**6.162 Dugas, Tomie Dawkins.** 1979. Place name origins. Alabama Life 1.5.86-88. [E CENT AL]. On Tallapoosa Co., AL.

**6.163 Dugas, Tomie Dawkins.** 1980. Place name origins. Alabama Life 2.1.94-98. [S CENT AL]. On Monroe Co., AL.

**6.164 Dunbar, Gary S.** 1962. Some notes on bison in early Virginia. Virginia Place Name Society Occasional Paper 4, (Jan. 30). Charlottesville: University of Virginia. 10 pp. 1 map. Discusses line of buffalo names that runs across VA, east of which the animals had ceased to range by advent of European settlers.

**6.165 Duncan, Alderman.** 1971. Feminine place names. NSC 18.32-36. SC towns and locations named after females.

**6.166 Duncan, Alderman.** 1974. Random place names in the state. NSC 21.33-35.

**6.167 Duncan, Alderman.** 1978. Extinct place names. NSC 25.17. Names on 1850 map of SC that no longer exist.

**6.168 Duncan, Alderman.** 1979. Place names of Scottish origin. NSC 26.19-21. Counties, towns, and communities in SC, mainly in the Up Country, named after Scots.

**6.169 Dunlap, A. R.** 1955. Names for Delaware. Names 3.230-35. Names given to area, from "Nieu Nederland" and "Virginia" to the "Delaware State" in 1776.

**6.170 Dunlap, A. R.** 1956. Dutch and Swedish place-names in Delaware. Newark: Institute of Delaware History and Culture. 66 pp. Bibliography and maps. Finds thirteen percent of 103 names from 17th-century documents and maps still surviving; sixty percent of names treated are of Dutch origin, forty percent are Swedish. **Review:** C. A. Weslager. 1957. Names 5.182-83.

**6.171 Dunlap, A. R., and C. A. Weslager.** 1950. Indian place-names in Delaware. Wilmington: Archaeological Society of Delaware. 61 pp. **Review:** J. B. McMillan. 1952. AS 27.190-91.

**6.172 Dunlap, A. R., and C. A. Weslager.** 1967. Two Delaware Valley Indian place names. Names 15.41-46.

**6.173 Edwards, Roy.** 1959. Cut'n Shoot, Texas. Western Folklore 18.33-34. Folklore surrounding and origin of name of nonexistent town.

**6.174 Edwards, Thomas H.** 1921. Lee County: present day place names showing aboriginal influence. Arrow Points 2.112-14. [E CENT AL].

**6.175 Eisiminger, Sterling.** 1979. Joketowns in South Carolina. AS 54.145-48. Analysis of sixty SC placenames, real and imaginary, that Clemson University students use for a joketown, "a real or imaginary place that arouses mirth at its mention."

**6.176 Eleazar, J. M.** 1971. Name origins of some places in the Dutch Fork area. NSC 18.10-13. [CENT SC]. Dutch Fork area was settled by Germans and is located in parts of Richland, Lexington, and Newberry Counties.

**6.177 Elmore, Frank H.** 1922. Baldwin County; present day place names showing aboriginal influence. Arrow Points 4.13-15. [SW AL].

**6.178 Fant, Christie Z.** 1978. Historic landmarks: part I. NSC 25.23-26. [NW SC]. Places on National Register in Greenville, Spartanburg, Chester, and Union Counties.

**6.179 Fant, Christie Z.** 1979. Historic landmarks of Fairfield County. NSC 26.28-30. [N CENT SC].

**6.180 Fant, Christie Z.** 1981. Historic landmarks in Lexington and Newberry Counties. NSC 28.45-51. [CENT SC].

**6.181 Fant, Christie Z.** 1983. Abbeville--McCormick landmarks. NSC 30.40-44. [W NC].

**6.182 Fenno, Cheryl Barnwell.** 1970. The place names of Benton County, Arkansas. Fayetteville: University of Arkansas dissertation. Abstract in DAI 39.3553A. Records place names in county, determines linguistic trends in their selection, and analyzes "origin of the names to learn what they reveal about the culture, history, and language of the area."

**6.183 Ficklen, John Rose.** 1919. Origin of the name Louisiana. Louisiana Historical Quarterly 2.230-32.

**6.184 Field, Thomas P.** 1959. The Indian place names of Kentucky. Names 7.154-66. **Reprinted** in the Filson Club Historical Quarterly 24.237-47 (July 1960). **Review:** H. Carlson. 1962. Names 10.190.

**6.185 Field, Thomas P.** 1961. A guide to Kentucky place names. Lexington: Kentucky Geological Survey. 246 pp. **Review:** H. Carlson. 1962. Names 10.190-92.

**6.186 Field, Thomas P.** 1972. Religious place-names in Kentucky. Names 20.26-47. Religious place names are plentiful, though random, everywhere in state except Eastern Coal Fields, which was last area settled; includes three appendices.

**6.187 Filby, Vera Ruth.** 1976. From Forest to Friendship. Maryland Historical Magazine 71.93-102.

**6.188 Fink, Paul M.** 1934. Smoky mountain history as told in place names. ETHSP 6.3-11. [E TN].

**6.189 Fink, Paul M.** 1941. Some East Tennessee place names. TFSB 7.40-50.

**6.190 Fink, Paul M.** 1956. That's why they call it. . . . The names and lore of the Great Smokies. Have you ever wondered why the mountains and valleys of the Smokies were so named? These are the romantic stories behind them. Jonesboro: privately printed. 20 pp. **Reprinted** in 1972 by the Great Smoky Mountains Natural History Association, Gatlinburg, TN.

**6.191 Fink, Paul M. and Mylon H. Avery.** 1937. The nomenclature of the Great Smoky Mountains. ETHSP 9.53-64. [E TN].

**6.192 Finnie, Bruce.** 1963. Ohio Valley localisms--topographic terms, 1750-1800. AS 38.178-87. Includes material from WV and KY.

**6.193 Finnie, W. Bruce.** 1970. Topographic terms in the Ohio Valley, 1748-1800. PADS 53. 119 pp. Based on diaries, journals, maps, correspondence, and other sources, analyzes terms for land forms and water forms and presents extensive glossary (pp. 38-110).

**6.194 FitzSimons, Frank L.** 1976. From the banks of the Oklawaha. n.p.: Golden Glow. [NE FL]. Pp. 65-68, naming of the new county; pp. 223-31, accounts of the origin of Battle Creek, Dana, and Uno.

**6.195 Florida Department of Agriculture.** 1945. The seventh census of the state of Florida. Nathan Mayo, Commissioner of Agriculture. Tallahassee. 141 pp. Pp. 7-8, origin and names of FL counties.

**6.196 Florida Division of Water Resources and Conservation.** 1966. Gazetteer of Florida streams. Tallahassee: Florida Board of Conservation. 88 pp.

**6.197 Florida Division of Water Resources and Conservation.** 1969. Florida lakes. Tallahassee: Florida Board of Conservation. 3 vols. Vol. 3: Gazetteer.

**6.198 Flowers, Paul.** 1960. Place names in Tennessee. WTHSP 14.113-23.

**6.199 Floyd, Viola Caston.** 1968. Lancaster County place names. NSC 15.39-42. [N CENT SC].

**6.200 Ford, Zillah.** 1947. The pronunciation of Spanish place names in the southwestern United States. Norman: University of Oklahoma thesis.

**6.201 Foscue, Virginia Oden.** 1960. Sumter County place-names: a selection. Alabama Review 13.52-67. Condensed from thesis, University of Alabama, Tuscaloosa, 1959. [W AL].

**6.202 Foscue, Virginia O.** 1978. The place names of Sumter County, Alabama. PADS 65. 75 pp. Analyzes types, linguistic aspects, and spreading of names in county and presents dictionary (pp. 17-66) of them. Reviews: K. B. Harder. 1979. TFSB 45.123-24; P. Munro. 1981. Language 57.510-11; M. Rennick. 1979. Names 27.280; W. Viereck. 1984. ZDL 51.108-09.

**6.203 Foscue, Virginia O[den].** 1989. Place names in Alabama. Tuscaloosa: University of Alabama Press. Comprehensive dictionary of toponymy of AL.

**6.204 Foscue, Virginia [Oden].** 1989. Place names. Encyclopedia of

Southern culture, ed. by William Ferris and Charles Wilson. Chapel Hill: University of North Carolina Press. Short essay surveying how place names in the South reflect concerns and interests of early inhabitants of the region.

**6.205 Fox, Edna R.** 1970. Streams and mill sites in Laurens County. NSC 17.25-30. [NW SC].

**6.206 France, Isabel.** 1959. Fascinating folk names of our hills and hollows. Ozarks Mountaineer 7.5. Explains names of mountains, gaps, bluffs, and hollows in AR Ozarks.

**6.207 Frazier, Evelyn, and W. E. Friff.** 1965. Names in Colleton County. NSC 12.11-13. [SE SC].

**6.208 Fullerton, Ralph.** 1974. Place names of Tennessee. Bulletin 73, State of Tennessee Department of Conservation, Division of Geology. Nashville. 421 pp. County by county list of place names in the state. **Review:** K. B. Harder. 1975. Names 23.124.

**6.209 Fulmore, Z. T.** 1915. History and geography of Texas in county names. Austin, TX: E. L. Steck. 312 pp. 2nd ed. **Reviews:** E. W. Winkler. 1916. Southwestern Historical Quarterly 19.209-11; E. W. Winkler. 1916. Southwestern Historical Quarterly 19.317-18.

**6.210 Gandee, Lee R.** 1961. Some Lexington County place names. NSC 8.15-21. [CENT SC]. Early names and settlement history of county.

**6.211 Gannett, Henry.** 1902. The origin of certain place names in the state of Mississippi. Publications of Mississippi Historical Society 6.339-49.

**6.212 Gannett, Henry.** 1904-06. Indian names--early geography of West Virginia. Charleston, WV: Department of Archives and History. Biennial report 1.251-68. Includes names of places on early maps as well as Indian names of WV rivers.

**6.213 Gannett, Henry.** 1947. American names: a guide to the origin of place names in the United States. Washington: Public Affairs Press. 334 pp. + appendix. **Review:** J. P. Moran. 1948. Catholic Historical Review 34.103-04.

**6.214 Gannett, Henry.** 1976. A gazetteer of Maryland and Delaware. Baltimore: Genealogical Publishing Co. Originally published in 1904 as U.S. Geological Survey Bulletin 230 and 231.

**6.215 Garrett, Patrick Posey.** 1963. A study of place names in Lincoln Parish, Louisiana. Auburn: Auburn University thesis. [NW LA].

**6.216 Gasque, Thomas J.** 1968. A rhyme, and a reason for naming our rivers. NSC 15.57-62.

**6.217 Gatschet, Albert Samuel.** 1901. Towns and villages of the Creek Confederacy in the XVIII and XIX centuries. Alabama Historical Society, Publication 1.386-415. Montgomery, AL: Brown Ptg. Co. Also published in Washington, 1901. Revision of list in Gatschet, A Migration Legend of the Creek Indians (Philadelphia, 1884-88), 1.120-50.

**6.218 Gatschet, Albert Samuel.** 1902. Onomatology of the Catawba River Basin. AA n.s. 4.52-56. [NC, SC]. Names along the Catawba/Wateree River from Catawba and Muskhogean sources.

**6.219 Gaut, John M.** 1901. Freedom's namesake, or, the origin and historic import of the name Cumberland. American Historical Magazine 6.99-117.

**6.220 Georgia's official register** 1923-   Atlanta: Georgia Department of Archives and History. Each issue has a section called "County Data," which discusses origin of county names.

**6.221 Gerard, William R.** 1905. Some Virginia Indian words. AA n.s. 7.222-49. Derivation and meaning of certain place names in VA; answer to criticisms by W. W. Tooker (**6.610**); see AA 6.670 (1904).

**6.222 Gettys, Paul M.** 1978. Some road names in Lexington County. NSC 25.37-38. [CENT SC].

**6.223 Gibbs, Lloyd G.,** ed. 1982. Will C. Lake's Union County: places and people. Union, SC: privately printed. Notes on a surname and etymology of county's name.

**6.224 Gibert, Anne C.** 1973. Abbeville district towns and plantations on the Savannah. NSC 20.34-37. [W NC].

**6.225 Gibert, Anne C.** 1974. The mystery of Nutshell plantation. NSC 21.27-30. [Richland Co., CENT SC].

**6.226 Gill, Donald Artley.** 1970. A linguistic analysis of the place names of the Texas Panhandle. Commerce: East Texas State University dissertation. Abstract in DAI 31.2368A. Classifies 1505 names in thirty-eight counties in TX Panhandle/South Plains area according to languages and sources from which they are derived.

**6.227 Gill, Donald A.** 1974. Louisiana place names with a touch of the unusual. They had to call it something, ed. by Fred Tarpley, 83-92. Commerce, TX: Names Institute Press. Glossary of forty-seven names whose form or origin is unusual.

**6.228 Gill, Donald A.** 1975. The onomastics of Louisiana river names. Naughty names, ed. by Fred Tarpley, 5-13. Publication 4, South Central Names Institute. Commerce, TX: Names Institute Press. Etymologies of forty LA river names.

**6.229 Gill, Donald A.** 1977. Louisiana place names of arboreal origin. Labeled for life, ed. by Fred Tarpley, 55-57. Publication 5, South Central Names Institute. Commerce, TX: Names Institute Press. Notes that and explains how more than 200 current LA place names derive from terms for trees or shrubs.

**6.230 Gill, Donald A.** 1978. Texas Panhandle place names of Spanish origin. Ethnic names, ed. by Fred Tarpley, 37-47. Commerce, TX: Names Institute Press. Categorizes and explains sixty-five names with Spanish elements from Gill 1970 (**6.226**).

**6.231 Gill, Donald A.** 1981. Place names of Bienville Parish, Louisiana. The scope of names, ed. by Fred Tarpley, 19-33. Commerce, TX: Names Institute Press. [N CENT LA]. Lists and gives origin of all place names on map of parish.

**6.232 Gilliam, Charles Edgar.** 1942. "Harrican" in colonial Virginia records. Virginia Magazine of History and Biography 50.337-44. Cites variant spellings of Hurricane as a place name in colonial records.

**6.233 Gilliam, Charles Edgar.** 1950. Geoethnology--Apamatuck (Mattica) and/or Appamattucks: the chief villages of the Appomattoc, 1607-1691. Archeological Society of Virginia Quarterly Bulletin 4.[8-9]. Discusses early spellings and meaning of name Appomattox.

**6.234 Gilliam, Charles Edgar.** 1953. Ethnic significance of the term: Appomattoc. Archeological Society of Virginia Quarterly Bulletin 7.[7-11].

**6.235 Gilliam, Charles Edgar.** 1953. Indicated portals of safe entry into Appomattox. Archeological Society of Virginia Quarterly Bulletin 7.14-15.

**6.236 Gilliam, Charles Edgar.** 1955. Tsenakcommacah. Archeological Society of Virginia Quarterly Bulletin 9.4-7.

**6.237 Gilliam, Charles Edgar.** 1957. The Algonquian term--Ajacan--its Indian and Spanish meaning. Archeological Society of Virginia Quarterly Bulletin 12.[2-11].

**6.238 Gilliam, Charles Edgar.** 1958. Ajacan, the Algonkian name for Hampton Roads, Virginia. Names 6.57-59.

**6.239 Gilliam, Charles Edgar.** 1960. Pagan Creek: ethnology of name. Archeological Society of Virginia Quarterly Bulletin 14.9.

**6.240 Gilliam, Charles Edgar.** 1962. Yellow jacket town. Virginia Place Name Society Occasional Paper 5.7-9 (June 18). Charlottesville: University of Virginia.

**6.241 Gilliam, Charles Edgar.** 1967. The Potomac debate. Extracts from his letter, September 1966. Names 15.242. [VA]. Disagrees with etymologies for river name meaning "emporium" or "place of trade" especially if trade along river was in steatite or buffalo skins.

**6.242 Glenn, Emily S.** 1971. Some names around Eutawville. NSC 18.39-41. [SE SC].

**6.243 Godley, Margaret W.** 1935. Georgia county place-names. Atlanta: Emory University thesis. 95 pp. Pronouncing dictionary of 159 names of counties; classifies names by origin.

**6.244 Goerch, Carl.** 1956. How it got its name. Ocracoke, 20-22. Winston-Salem, NC: Blair. [E NC].

**6.245 Goff, John Hedges.** 1953. Old Chattahoochee town, an early Muscogee Indian settlement. Georgia Mineral Newsletter 6.52-54. Discusses name and site of GA town.

**6.246 Goff, John Hedges.** 1954. Hog crawl creek. Georgia Mineral Newsletter 7.38-40. Study of the GA name.

**6.247 Goff, John Hedges.** 1954. The beaverdam creeks. Georgia Mineral Newsletter 7.117-22. Discusses the streams in GA that now have or once had beaver in their name.

**6.248 Goff, John.** 1955. The devil's half-acre. Georgia Review 9.290-96. Discusses Georgia names containing words devil and hell, like Devil's Elbow and Hell's Half Acre.

**6.249 Goff, John Hedges.** 1957. The buffalo in Georgia. Georgia Review 11.19-28. Georgia place names which include the element Buffalo.

**6.250 Goff, John Hedges.** 1958. The poor mouthing place names. Georgia Review 12.440-50. **Reprinted** in Georgia Mineral Newsletter 12.65-68 (Fall, 1959). Place names that reflect poverty.

**6.251 Goff, John Hedges.** 1958. Some old road names in Georgia. Emory University Quarterly 14.30-42. **Reprinted** in Georgia Mineral Newsletter 11.98-102 (Autumn, 1958).

**6.252 Goff, John Hedges.** 1961. The Creek village of "Cooccohapofe" on Flint River. Georgia Mineral Newsletter 14.34-35. Concerning location and derivation of name of GA town.

**6.253 Goff, John Hedges.** 1961. The derivations of Creek Indian place names. Georgia Mineral Newsletter 14.63-70.

**6.254 Goff, John H.** 1962-63. Pronunciations of Georgia place names. Georgia Magazine 6.4.13-15; 6.5.14-15,27; 6.6.12-13. Three-part series. Survey of unusual and variable pronunciations of towns, counties, and physical features in state.

**6.255 Goff, John Hedges.** 1964. The "Hurricane" place names in Georgia. Georgia Review 18.224-35.

**6.256 Goff, John H.** 1975. Placenames of Georgia: essays of John H. Goff, ed. by Francis L. Utley and Marion R. Hemperley. Athens: University of Georgia Press. 534 pp. **Reviews:** C. S. Brown. 1976. AS 51.153-57; K. B. Harder. 1976. TFSB 42.47-50; A. C. Morris. 1976. Florida Historical Quarterly 55.104-05; R. E. Rennick. 1976. Names 24.321-23; J. E. Talmadge. 1976. GHQ 60.68-69.

**6.257 Gordon, James Waddell, Jr.** 1933. French place names in Virginia. Charlottesville: University of Virginia thesis. 59 pp. Fifty-eight names, information based on personal oral accounts.

**6.258 Gordon, James Waddell, Jr.** 1975. French place names in Virginia. Virginia Place Name Society Occasional Paper 19. Charlottesville: University of Virginia. 20 pp.

**6.259 Gray, Jo Anne.** 1962. Place names of the Texas coastal bend. Commerce: East Texas State University thesis. 209 pp. [S TX]. Jackson, Calhoun, Victoria, Goliad, Nueces, and five other counties; each chapter alphabetically organized.

**6.260 Green, Bennett Wood.** 1907. How Newport's News got its name: Cui Bono? Richmond, VA: W. E. Jones. 142 pp.

**6.261 Green, Bennett Wood.** 1912. Word book of Virginia folk-speech. Richmond, VA: W. E. Jones' Sons. Some Virginia names spelt one way and pronounced another, 13-16.

**6.262 Grima, Edgar.** 1914. Les noms géographiques français en Louisiane. Société de Géographie de Quebec Bulletin 8.267-69.

**6.263 Gritzner, Janet H.** 1972. Seventeenth century generic place-names: culture and process on the eastern shore. Names 20.231-39. [Delmarva Peninsula]. Examines Eastern Shore naming practices in their cultural setting.

**6.264 Grubbs, Millard Dee.** 1949. Origin of historic place names. The 4 keys to Kentucky, 227-50. Louisville, KY: Slater and Gilroy. [KY].

**6.265 Haber, Tom Burns.** 1936. "Gulliver's travels" in America. AS 11.99-100. Name of Lulbegrud Creek in KY comes from Swift's book, according to record made by Daniel Boone.

**6.266 Hagood, Thomas Neal.** 1960. Place-name patterns in Jefferson County, Alabama. Birmingham, AL: Birmingham Southern College thesis. [N CENT AL].

**6.267 Halbert, Henry Sale.** 1898-1899. Choctaw Indian names in Alabama and Mississippi. Alabama Historical Society Transactions 3.64-77.

**6.268 Halbert, Henry Sale.** 1902. Bvlbancha, Choctaw word for the town of New Orleans. Gulf States Historical Magazine 1.53-54.

**6.269 Halbert, Henry Sale.** 1903. Origin of Mashulaville. Mississippi Historical Society Publications 7.389-97. An American village named after ancient Indian chief Moshulitubee.

**6.270 Halliday, Roy.** 1975. The heritage of place-names. ARK/OZARK, pp. 14-15 (Summer). Comments on unusual names for AR towns, including towns named after foreign locations.

**6.271 Halpert, Herbert.** 1961. Place name stories of Kentucky waterways and ponds. KFR 7.85-101. Stories from fourteen locations.

**6.272 Halpert, Violetta M., ed.** 1961. Place name stories about western Kentucky towns. KFR 7.103-16. Stories about fifteen names.

**6.273 Hamill, Alfred E.** 1934. The pronunciation of American place names. Notes and Queries 167.153. Includes note saying pronunciation of Arkansas is changing; speakers now put main stress on first syllable, rhyme last syllable with law.

**6.274 Hanson, Raus McDill.** 1970. Virginia place names: derivation, historical uses. Verona, VA: McClure. 253 pp. Comprehensive compendium of more than 2,000 names of counties, cities, regions, valleys, mountains, and other areas, with derivations. **Reviews:** E. Green. 1972. Names 20.207; V. C. Hall, Jr. 1970. Virginia Magazine of History and Biography 78.121-22; P. B. Rogers. 1969. Names 17.306-11.

**6.275 Hardaway, Billie Touchstone.** 1980. These hills my home: a Buffalo river story. Republic, MO: Western Printing. Some creeks along the Buffalo, 138-47, discusses names of twenty-two creeks that flow into NW AR river.

**6.276 Harder, Kelsie B.** 1977. The names of TVA dams. MFR 11.131-41. [TN, AL].

**6.277 Hardy, Emmett Layton.** 1949. An introduction to the study of the geographic nomenclature of Kentucky's counties, cities, and towns. Lexington: University of Kentucky thesis. 119 pp. Divides names into twelve categories based on origin; appendix gives complete alphabetical list of names.

**6.278 Harrelson, William L.** 1973. Ancient ferrymen on Little Pee Dee. NSC 20.23-29. [E SC]. Ferries and landings in Marion County.

**6.279 Harris, W. Stuart.** 1977. Dead towns of Alabama. University: University of Alabama Press. 165 pp. Anecdotal accounts of former Indian villages and colonial and territorial towns and forts. **Reviews:** H. C. Bailey. 1978. Alabama Review 31.230; K. B. Harder. 1977. TFSB 43.227-28; K. B. Harder. 1978. Names 26.118-21.

**6.280 Harris, [W.] Stuart.** 1982. Alabama place-names. Huntsville: Strode. Popular glossary of selected names, based mainly on secondary sources. **Reviews:** L. R. Atkins. 1984. Alabama Review 37.230; V. Foscue. 1985. Names 33.280-81.

**6.281 Hartsook, Richard.** 1955. A study of the personal interview method for determining the locally-accepted educated pronunciation of Alabama place names. Tuscaloosa: University of Alabama thesis. Includes list of names with transcriptions made in field interviews.

**6.282 Hayes, Lois.** 1969. Place names of Concholand. Commerce: East Texas State University thesis. Study of 345 place names from an eight-county ranch area of SW TX.

**6.283 Hayes, Lois.** 1971. Place names of Concholand. Of Edsels and marauders, ed. by Fred Tarpley and Ann Moseley, 51-57. Publication 1, South-Central Names Institute. Commerce, TX: Names Institute Press. Excerpt of preceding item, citing names of Indian, Spanish, German, and Anglo-American sources.

**6.284 Hazelip, Pauline.** 1960. Tales of Glasgow Junction: a town is named. KFR 6.1-3. [KY].

**6.285 Heckewelder, John Gottlieb Ernestus.** 1940. Names given by the Lenni Lenape or Delaware Indians to rivers, streams, and places. . . Pennsylvania German Folklore Society Publication 5.1-41. Also in American Philological Society Transactions 4.351-96 (1834), Historical Society of Pennsylvania, Bulletin 1.121-35, 139-54 (June, Sept., 1847), and Moravian Historical Society Transactions (1872), 275-33. Includes place names in MD and VA.

**6.286 Hemperley, M[arion] R.** 1973. Indian place names in Georgia. GHQ 57.562-79.

**6.287 Hemperley, Marion R.** 1979. Cities, towns, and communities of Georgia between 1849-1962. List of 8,500 names, giving place, county, date of references. **Reviews:** Anonymous. 1981. JSH 47.651; K. B. Harder. 1981. TFSB 47.185; K. B. Harder. 1981. Names 29.170-71.

**6.288 Hench, Atcheson L.** 1944. Virginia county names. AS 19.153. In Piedmont area of VA, custom is to omit word county whenever a speaker wishes to.

**6.289 Henderson, P. F.** 1960. Some Aiken County names. NSC 7.14-19. [W SC].

**6.290 Hensley, Cornelia H.** 1966. Some early place names in lower Richland [County]. NSC 13.16-26. [CENT SC].

**6.291 Hewell, Marion M.** 1963. Some Greenville names. NSC 10.24-28. [NW SC]. Early names in Greenville County.

**6.292 Hewell, Marion M.** 1979. Donaldson air base names. NSC 26.25-27. [NW SC]. Located six miles north of Greenville.

**6.293 Hewitt, John Napoleon Brinton.** 1908. The name "Kentucky." AA n.s. 10.339-42. Account of derivation and meaning of name.

**6.294 Hicks, Theresa M.** 1972. Streams of Florence County. NSC 19.32-35. [E SC].

**6.295 Hiden, Martha Woodroof.** 1957. How justice grew: Virginia counties, an abstract of their formation. Williamsburg, VA: 350th Anniversary Celebration Corp. Includes naming of counties.

**6.296 High, Ellesa Clay.** 1981. From pinch-em tight to the calaboose. Abstract in NADS 13.3.6-7. [E KY]. Discusses and classifies place names from Red River Gorge area.

**6.297 Hill, Robert T.** 1887. The pronunciation of Arkansas. Science 10.107-08. Complains that New Englanders, including lexicographers, are determined to mispronounce final syllable of name as "sass."

**6.298 Hodgkins, George W.** 1960-62. Naming the capitol and the capital. Columbia Historical Society Records 60-62.36-53.

**6.299 Hoppen, Harry E.** 1921. Randolph County: present day place names showing aboriginal influence. Arrow Points 2.86-87. [E CENT AL].

**6.300 Huddleston, Eugene L.** 1972. Place names in the writings of Jesse Stuart. Western Folklore 31.169-77. [KY]. Says Stuart's names are rich and expressive and important in establishing a sense of place.

**6.301 Hudson, A. P.** 1957. Buncombe--talking to Buncombe. North Carolina Folklore Journal 5.23. Popular etymology of the place name. [W NC].

**6.302 Hummel, Ray Orvin.** 1960. A list of places included in 19th century Virginia directories. Richmond: Virginia State Library. 153 pp.

**6.303 Hunter, J. Oscar.** 1975. Grist mills of Old Abbeville district. NSC 22.12-14. [W SC].

**6.304 Hunter, J. Oscar.** 1981. Abbeville County towns and communities. NSC 28.12-16. [W SC].

**6.305 Hutchins, Ailene W.** 1986. A study of some unusual names of people and places in early Maryland. Maryland Historical Magazine 81.94-95.

**6.306 Indian names--early geography of West Virginia.** 1904-06. Charleston: West Virginia Dept. of Archives and History. Biennial report 1.251-68. Discusses Indian names of WV rivers and names of locations on early maps.

**6.307 In relation to the pronunciation of the name "Arkansas."** 1908. Arkansas Historical Association 2.462-77. Reprint of 1880 pamphlet discussing variant pronunciations of the state name.

**6.308 Irvine, William Stafford.** 1937. Governor Wilson Lumpkin and the naming of Marthasville. Atlanta Historical Bulletin 2.46-56. [GA].

**6.309 Irvine, William Stafford.** 1938. Terminus and Deanville, local names of long ago, of the site of Atlanta. Atlanta Historical Bulletin 3.101-19. [GA].

**6.310 Irwin, Ned.** 1948. The legend of Eve Mills. TFSB 14.28-30. Story behind name of community in Monroe Co., TN.

**6.311 Jackson, Sarah Evelyn.** 1978. Place names in Ashe County, North Carolina. Names 26.96-105. Sources of names in county--surnames, animal names, farming, weather, topography; says few Indian names remain.

**6.312 Jacocks, W. P.** 1958. Bertie County stream names and their origins. Bertie County Historical Society Chronicle 6.3-4. [NC].

**6.313 Janssen, Quinith, and William Fernbach.** 1984. West Virginia place names: origins and history. Shepherdstown, WV: J. and F. Enterprises. 88 pp. **Review:** K. B. Harder. 1987. Names 35.42-43.

**6.314 Jenkins, William H.** 1959. Some Alabama "dead" towns. Alabama Review 12.281-85.

**6.315 Jimenez, Alma Delia.** 1981. Texas barrio names. The scope of names, ed. by Fred Tarpley, 11-18. Commerce, TX: Names Institute Press. Names of Mexican-American neighborhoods in Dallas and other TX towns and their origins.

**6.316 Johnson, F. Roy.** 1966. Legends and myths of North Carolina's Roanoke-Chowan area. Murfreesboro, NC: Johnson Publishing Company. Names and their origins (Part VI), 111-23.

**6.317 Johnson, Nexen B.** 1969. Some Williamsburg County names. NSC 16.36-40. [E SC].

**6.318 Johnson, Thomas Cary.** 1957-58. How Albemarle got its name. Magazine of Albemarle County History 16.20-24. [VA].

**6.319 Johnston, Ross B.** 1954. U.S. Board accedes to West Virginia wishes. West Virginia History 16.48. On naming Tygart Valley and Tygart Valley River.

**6.320 Jolly, James L., Jr.** 1987. The place names in Calhoun and Etowah Counties, Alabama. Tuscaloosa: University of Alabama dissertation. Historical and descriptive study of place names in two NE AL counties.

**6.321 Jones, Billie Walker.** 1957. Origin of the name Dry Branch, Georgia. Georgia Mineral Newsletter 10.69.

**6.322 Jones, Nancy.** 1967. Pronunciation patterns of place names in Northeast Texas. Commerce: East Texas State University thesis.

**6.323 Jordan, Terry G.** 1976. Place names of Texas. Atlas of Texas, ed. by Stanley A. Arbingast et al. Austin: University of Texas Bureau of Business Research.

**6.324 Jordan, Virginia.** 1962. A note on the place-name "Blacks and Whites" (present Blackstone, VA). Virginia Place Name Society Occasional Paper 2.10-11 (June 13). Charlottesville: University of Virginia.

**6.325 Kaltenbaugh, Louise P.** 1970. A study of the place names of St. Bernard Parish, Louisiana. New Orleans: University of New Orleans thesis. [SE LA].

**6.326 Kay, Carol McGinnis, and Donald Kay.** 1975. A preliminary survey of British-received place names in Alabama. Alabama Review 28.282-85. List of seventy-one AL town names that correspond to British place names.

**6.327 Kay, Donald.** 1974. British influence on Kentucky municipal place names. KFR 20.9-13. List of 131 KY place names that echo British place names.

**6.328 Kay, Donald.** 1974. Municipal British-received place names in Tennessee. AJ 2.78-80.

**6.329 Kay, Donald.** 1974. Texas: British through and through. Newsletter of the Indiana Place-Name Survey 4.2-6.

**6.330 Kay, Donald.** 1974. British influences on Mississippi municipal place names. Journal of Mississippi History 36.269-72.

**6.331 Keating, Ruth Aikman.** 1959. Spanish place-names in Texas. Fort Worth: Texas Christian University thesis.

**6.332 Kemper, Charles E.** 1937. Home names in the valley. Virginia Magazine of History and Biography 45.353-56. List of names, with notes, of antebellum homes of prominent residents in the Valley of Virginia.

**6.333 Kendall, K. M.** 1975. A study of placenames in Livingston Parish, Louisiana. New Orleans: University of New Orleans thesis. [SE LA].

**6.334 Kenny, Hamill.** 1940. The synthetic place name in West Virginia. AS 15.39-44. Analyzes thirty-five names formed by combining syllables or elements of other names or words.

**6.335 Kenny, Hamill.** 1945. West Virginia place names. Piedmont, WV: Place Name Press. Reprinted by West Virginia University Library, 1960. Bibliography, 699-720. 768 pp. **Reviews:** L. H. Chrisman. 1946. West Virginia History 7.341-44; E. G. Gudde. 1946. AS 21.206-08; J. B. McMillan. 1948. MP 45.279-82; J. J. Tierney. 1946. Maryland Historical Magazine 41.166; R. M. Wilson. 1947. YWES 27.50-51.

**6.336 Kenny, Hamill.** 1951. The origin and meaning of the Indian place-names of Maryland. 2 vols, College Park: University of Maryland dissertation. Reprinted, Baltimore: Waverly Press, 1961. Bibliography, 161-175. 186 pp. **Reviews:** A. R. Dunlap. 1962. AS 37.55-57; C. G. Holland. 1962. IJAL 28.296-99; V. J. Vogel. 1962. Names 10.65-69; C. A. Weslager. 1961. Maryland Historical Magazine 56.311-14; R. M. Wilson. 1963. YWES 42.50.

**6.337 Kenny, Hamill.** 1953. Cheat River and the "Horn Papers." AS 28.65-66. [WV]. Dismisses theory that river's name came from French trader Jacques Cheathe.

**6.338 Kenny, Hamill.** 1954. Baltimore: new light on the old name. Maryland Historical Magazine 49.116-21. Origin, history, and meaning of name.

**6.339 Kenny, Hamill.** 1961. Settling Laurel's business. Names 9.160-62. Origin of Laurel in Laurel Hill in WV.

**6.340 Kenny, Hamill.** 1965. Behold these names. Maryland English Journal 4.1-11. MD place names.

**6.341 Kenny, Hamill.** 1967. Alias Pangayo. Names 15.238-39. [S MD]. An alias of Zekiah Swamp in Charles County, MD.

**6.342 Kenny, Hamill.** 1970. Place names from surnames: Maryland. Names 18.137-54. Classifies 3,183 MD place names from Gannett's A Gazetteer of Maryland (1904), according to Anglo-Saxon elements in them and finds majority of them (1,731) are probably derived from surnames.

**6.343 Kenny, Hamill.** 1976. Place names and dialects: Algonquian. Names 24.86-100. Uses Bloomfield's proposed proto-Algonkian phonemes to identify Anglo-Algonkian place names in Eastern states.

**6.344 Kenny, Hamill.** 1984. The placenames of Maryland, their origin and meaning. Baltimore: Maryland Historical Society. xii + 352 pp. Comprehensive analysis of state's place names, with special attention to names of Indian origin. **Review:** C. R. Sleeth. 1985. Names 33.277-79.

**6.345 Kerney, Ellen.** 1944. American ghost towns. American Notes and Queries n.s. 4.32. Snowhill and Furnace, MD.

**6.346 Kibler, James E.** 1983. Dutch Fork names (with map). NSC 30.24-31. [CENT SC]. Dutch Fork names in O. B. Mayer's fiction.

**6.347 Kibler, James, and Rene LaBorde.** 1973. South Carolina post offices, 1867. NSC 20.46-49.

**6.348 Kinard, James C.** 1964. Place-names in Newberry County. NSC 11.49-53. [CENT SC]. Names of communities.

**6.349 Kolin, Philip C.** 1977. Place-names, naming, and folklore. MFR 11.72-73. Introduction to special journal issue on folk naming.

**6.350 Kolin, Philip C.** 1977. State names used as city and county names. MFR 11.164-73. National survey of cities and towns named after states.

**6.351 Krakow, Kenneth K.** 1975. Georgia place-names. Macon, GA: Winship Press. 272 pp. Dictionary of over 5,000 names. **Reviews:** P. Dobson. 1975. Florida Historical Quarterly 54.95-96; K. B. Harder. 1976. TFSB 42.47-48; R. M. Rennick. 1975. Names 23.306; W. Tate. 1975. GHQ 59.460-62.

**6.352 Krakow, Kenneth K.** 1975. Georgia place names with South Carolina derivations. NSC 22.17-24.

**6.353 LaBorde, Rene.** 1974. Southernisms in D.A.R.E. NSC 21.32-33.

**6.354 LaBorde, Rene.** 1976. Correct mispronunciations of some South Carolina names. NSC 23.38-40.

**6.355 LaBorde, Rene.** 1983. Thirty years. NSC 30.21-23. Reviews career of Claude H. Neuffer and thirty years of publication of onomastic journal Names in South Carolina.

**6.356 Lachicotte, Alberta Morel.** 1956. Georgetown plantation names. NSC 3.10-14. [E SC]. Names reflect homes or regions planters or their ancestors were from.

**6.357 Lagoudakis, Charilaos.** 1963. Greece in Georgia. GHQ 47.189-92. Presents place names in GA with Greek derivations and list of twenty-one changed names.

**6.358 Lanman, Charles.** 1914. The Catawba country of North Carolina. Magazine of History 19.92-100. Names of Ginger Cake Mountain and Roan Mountain in NC.

**6.359 Lanman, Charles.** 1914. The falls of Tallulah. Magazine of History 19.249-53. Meaning of Tallulah and three other GA names.

**6.360 Laurent, Lubin F.** 1924. History of St. John the Baptist Parish. Louisiana Historical Quarterly 7.316-31. Origin of several LA place names.

**6.361 Lawrence, James Walton, Sr.** 1979. How Landrum gets a name. Shadows and Hogback, 30-34. Landrum, SC: New Leader.

**6.362 Lawrence, R. C.** 1944. Many changes in names. [NC] State Magazine 11.6.

**6.363 Leeper, Clare D'Artois.** 1976. Louisiana places: a collection of the columns from the Baton Rouge Sunday Advocate 1960-1974. Baton Rouge: Legacy. 296 pp. Includes many columns on local names. **Reviews:** K. B. Harder. 1976. TFSB 42.207-08; R. M. Rennick. 1977. Names 25.39.

**6.364 Leighly, John.** 1982. German family names in Kentucky place names. American Name Society monograph no. 2. New York.

**6.365 Leighly, John.** 1986. Biblical place-names in the United States. Names and their varieties: a collection of essays in onomastics, ed. by Kelsie B. Harder, 291-304. Surveys density of biblical names in eastern half of country and contrasts Northern and Southern states.

**6.366 Lipscomb, J. M.** 1983. Cherokee County towns and communities. NSC 30.46-49. [NW SC].

**6.367 Long, Charles M.** 1908. Virginia county names: two hundred years of Virginia history. New York: Neale.

**6.368 Lorio, Elaine C.** 1932. The place-names of Pointe-Coupee Parish. Baton Rouge: Louisiana State University thesis. [SE LA].

**6.369 Louisiana Department of Public Works.** 1971. Directory of Louisiana cities, towns, and villages. Baton Rouge. 167 pp.

**6.370 McCampbell, Coleman.** 1954. Texas history as revealed by town and community name origins. Southwestern Historical Quarterly 58.91-97.

**6.371 McCarthy, Kevin.** 1978. South Carolina names as Florida place names. NSC 25.35-36.

**6.372 McClendon, Carlee T.** 1964. Names of plantations and homes in Edgefield County. NSC 11.38-45. [W SC].

**6.373 McClendon, Carlee T.** 1983. Edgefield County towns and communities. NSC 30.31-32. [W SC].

**6.374 McColl, Eleanor T.** 1969. Place names in Marlboro County. Part I. NSC 16.12-19. [NE SC].

**6.375 McDavid, Raven I., Jr., and Raymond K. O'Cain.** 1976. The name researcher and the Linguistic Atlas. NSC 23.23-28.

**6.376 McDavid, Raven I., Jr., and Raymond K. O'Cain.** 1978. Louisiana and New Orleans: notes on the pronunciation of proper names. MFR 11.76-92. 6 maps. Based on LAMSAS material; distribution of variants of two names in Atlantic states.

**6.377 McDavid, Raven I., Jr., and Raymond K. O'Cain.** 1978. South Carolina county names: unreconstructed individualism. Names 26.106-15. Principles followed in naming SC counties.

**6.378 McDavid, Raven I., Jr., and Raymond K. O'Cain.** 1980. Some notes on Maryland and Baltimore. AS 55.278-87. Surveys social and regional pronunciation of two place names in LAMSAS territory and points out importance of place names in dialect geography.

**6.379 McDavid, Raven I., Jr., Raymond O'Cain, George T. Dorrill, and David Fischer.** 1985. Names not on the map. Names 33.216-24. Discusses place names reported in Linguistic Atlas records but not found on maps or in other records and difficulties of verifying these names; includes South Atlantic states.

**6.380 McDermott, John Francis.** 1979. The French impress on place names in the Mississippi valley. Journal of the Illinois State Historical Society 72.225-34.

**6.381 McDonald, Fred Lochlan.** 1961. A study of place names in Lowndes County, Georgia. Auburn: Auburn University thesis. [S CENT AL].

**6.382 MacDonough, Nancy M.** 1975. Place names. Garden sass: a catalog of Arkansas folkways, 242-47. New York: Coward, McCann and Geoghegan. Folklore of unusual AR names, including name of state.

**6.383 McIntosh, Bethel W.** 1979. Summerville place names. NSC 26.24-25. [SE SC].

**6.384 McIver, Petrona.** 1966. Some towns and settlements of Christ Church Parish. NSC 13.46-50. [SE SC]. Names found in Charleston County.

**6.385 McKay, Henry Bacon.** 1978. Springs of Greenville. NSC 25.34-35. [NW SC].

**6.386 Mackintosh, Robert H., Jr.** 1977. Historic names in York County c1760-1860. NSC 24.32-37. Map.

**6.387 McMillan, James B.** 1985. Toponymic lapses. Names 33.58-67. [NE AL]. Sources of errors on maps and in official records of Talladega County, AL.

**6.388 McMillan, James B.** 1985. Dictionary of place names in Talladega County, Alabama. x + 179 pp. Copies in University of Alabama Library, Tuscaloosa, and State Dept. of Archives and History, Montgomery.

**6.389 McMillan, James B.** 1986. The name of Sleeping Giant mountain. Talladega [AL] Historical Association Newsletter 169.7. Report of action of U.S. Board on Geographic Names to correct official name of mountain.

**6.390 McMillan, James B.** 1987. The name of Shocco Springs. Talladega County [AL] Historical Association Newsletter 181.5. Derivation from Shoccoree tribe to Shocco Creek (NC), to Shocco Springs, NC, to Shocco Springs, AL.

**6.391 McMullen, Edwin Wallace.** 1964. Cape Canaveral and Chicago. Names 12.128-29. Reports discussion of name change of Cape Canaveral to Cape Kennedy, FL, a discussion at meeting of the American Name Society in Chicago, Dec. 1963.

**6.392 McNeel, Allen.** 1921. Escambia County; present day place names showing aboriginal influence. Arrow Points 2.32-35. [S AL].

**6.393 McWhorter, A. W.** 1933. Classical place names in Tennessee. Word Study 9.7-8.

**6.394 Mahr, August C.** 1960. Shawnee names and migrations in Kentucky and West Virginia. Ohio Journal of Science 60.155-64. Traces migration of Shawnees from Cumberland River area west across KY, as revealed in place names of Shawnee origin.

**6.395 Manahan, John E.** 1961. Analysis of Virginia place-names as to origin. Virginia Place Name Society Occasional Paper 3. Charlottesville: University of Virginia. 8 pp.

**6.396 Manahan, John E.** 1966. British origins of names of some old Virginia homes. Virginia Place Name Society Occasional Paper 11 (new series no. 1, Jan. 25). Charlottesville: University of Virginia. 8 pp.

**6.397 Martel, Glenn.** 1952. Origin of Columbia's place names reviewed. Arkansas Historical Quarterly 11.1-14. [S AR]. Place names of Columbia County.

**6.398 Martin, Joseph.** 1836. A new and comprehensive gazetteer of Virginia, and the District of Columbia. To which is added a history of Virginia from its first settlement to the year 1754: with an abstract of the principal events from that period to the independence of Virginia, written expressly for the work by a citizen of Virginia (W. H. Brockenbrough). Charlottesville, VA: J. Martin. 636 pp.

**6.399 Marye, William Bose.** 1930, 1958. Place-names of Baltimore and Harford Counties. Maryland Historical Magazine 25.321-65; 53.34-57,238-52 (Mar.-Sept. 1958).

**6.400 Marye, William Bose.** 1939. The several Indian "Old Towns" on the upper Potomac River. Maryland Historical Magazine 34.325-33.

**6.401 Marye, William Bose.** 1959. Some Baltimore city place names. Maryland Historical Magazine 54.15-35,353-64; Part 2, 58.211-32 (1963); Part 3, 58.344-77 (Sept. 1963); Part 4, 59.52-93 (Mar. 1964). Part 2 titled "Huntington or Huntingdon, the two Liliendales and Sumwalt Run"; Parts 3-4 titled "Baltimore city place names: Stony Run, its plantations, farms, country seats and mills." Supplementary note by the author, ibid. 54.437-38 (1959).

**6.402 Maxwell, Claude W.** 1925. Indian names in West Virginia. West Virginia Review 2.286,291.

**6.403 Maxwell, Cordelia.** 1971. A place name study of Washington Parish. Louisiana Studies 10.170-86.

**6.404 May, Carl H.** 1978. Spartanburg County names. NSC 25.20-22. [NW SC].

**6.405 Mayrant, Drayton.** 1960. Place names on or near the Cooper River. NSC 7.11-13. [SE SC].

**6.406 Mayrant, Drayton.** 1961. More names of places on or near the Cooper River. NSC 8.8-10. [SE SC].

**6.407 Mayrant, Drayton.** 1963. South Carolina island names. Part 1, NSC 10.21-22; Part 2, NSC 11.34-37 (1964).

**6.408 Meaning of the Creek Indian name Eufaula.** 1962. Chronicles of Oklahoma 40.310-11. [AL, OK].

**6.409 Messick, Mary Ann.** 1973. History of Baxter County, 1873-1973. Little Rock, AR: Mountain Home Chamber of Commerce. Other towns and places--then and now, 77-96, names of old towns and post offices; In the sweet by and by, 194-208, names of cemeteries and churches.

**6.410 Meyer, Robert, Jr.** 1981. Names over Texas airports. The scope of names, ed. by Fred Tarpley, 145-52. Commerce, TX: Names Institute Press. Name patterns of commercial and military airports.

**6.411 Milbourne, Mrs. V. S.** 1930. The founding of Luray and the origin of its name. William and Mary College Quarterly Historical Magazine 2nd ser. 10.142-44. [VA].

**6.412 Miller, Aaron.** 1959. How Kettle Run was named. West Virginia Folklore 10.4-5.

**6.413 Miller, E. Joan Wilson.** 1969. The naming of the land in the Arkansas Ozarks: a study of culture processes. Annals of the Association of American Geographers 59.240-51.

**6.414 Miller, Mary R.** 1972. Teaching Maryland place names. Maryland English Journal 10.2.3-9.

**6.415 Miller, Mary R.** 1976. Place-names of the northern neck of Virginia: a proposal for a theory of place naming. Names 24.9-23. Surveys 350 years of names in narrow strip of NE VA between Potomac and Rappahannock rivers and discusses their purposes as revealed in sample of 2,500 names.

**6.416 Miller, Mary R.** 1980. Place names as noun phrases. Abstract in NADS 12.3.9. Identifies three types of noun phrases functioning as place names in the Northern Neck of VA.

**6.417 Miller, Mary R.** 1983. Place-names of the northern neck of Virginia from John Smith's 1606 map to the present. Richmond, VA: Virginia State Library. xiv + 183 pp. [NE VA]. Scholarly analysis of region's place-names, with special attention to historical and sociolinguistic aspects of names. **Reviews:** Anonymous. 1984. JSH 50.156; G. L. Cohen. 1984. AS 59.178-82; S. M. Embleton. 1985. LIS 14.145; K. B. Harder. 1983. TFSB 49.146; R. Ordoubadian. 1984. SECOL Review 8.214-16.

**6.418 [Mississippi] official and statistical register.** 1904-    Nashville: Mississippi Department of Archives and History. Each issue has list of state's counties, with date of establishment and origin of each name.

**6.419 Mitchell, Eugene M.** 1931. Queer place names in old Atlanta. Atlanta Historical Bulletin 5.22-31.

**6.420 Moffatt, James S., Jr.** 1958. Place names of the Abbeville area. NSC 5.3-8. [W SC].

**6.421 Montgomery, James R.** 1956. The nomenclature of the upper Tennessee River. ETHSP 28.46-57. **Reprinted** in ETHSP 51.151-62 (1979).

**6.422 Mooney, James.** 1889. Indian tribes of the District of Columbia. AA 2.259-66.

**6.423 Moore, M. V.** 1955. Southern rivers. Names 3.38-43. A poem.

**6.424 Morgan, Gordon D.** 1973. Black hillbillies of the Arkansas Ozarks: a report of the department of sociology, University of Arkansas. Naming the town, 66-67, discusses black contributions to Ozark place names.

**6.425 Morris, Alton.** 1974. Florida place names. Coral Gables: University of Miami Press. 160 pp. General work including alphabetical list of towns larger than 1,000 in population. **Reviews:** M. M. Bryant. 1975. Names 23.117; P. Dodson. 1974. Florida Historical Quarterly 54.95-96; K. B. Harder. 1976. TFSB 42.47; R. C. White. 1975. SLA Geography and Map Division Bulletin 100.138-39.

**6.426 Morris, Clay Louise.** 1970. You take the high road: a guide to the place names of colonial eastern shore of Maryland. Easton, MD: Easton. 48 pp.

**6.427 Morris, Robert L.** 1943. Ozark or Masserne. Arkansas Historical Quarterly 2.39-42. Earlier name for hills of AR was Masserne.

**6.428 Moss, Bobby G.** 1971. Post offices and voting precincts in Cherokee County, 1900. NSC 18.36-39. Map. [N SC].

**6.429 Murley, Olga.** 1966. Texas place names: voices from the historic past in a goodly land. Commerce: East Texas State University thesis. Four chapters--names from history, from geography, from language modifications (names derived from towns elsewhere or from people) and from other sources.

**6.430 Muth, Bell Rowan Stuart.** 1978. Place names on a family farm. KFR 24.15-17. [KY].

**6.431 Myers, Minnie Walker.** 1898. Romance and realism of the southern Gulf Coast. Cincinnati: Clarke. Pp. 40-42, notes on placenames of French and Indian origin, especially names of rivers.

**6.432 Myers, Sylvester.** 1915. History of West Virginia. Wheeling: News Lithograph Co. 2 vols. The counties of West Virginia, 2.2-14. Rivers of WV and how they were named, 2.395-408.

**6.433 Names.** 1937. Eastern Shore Magazine 1.5. Unusual names found on MD Eastern Shore.

**6.434 Naming of places in the Carolinas.** 1967. NSC 14.36-41. Unsigned article reprinted from The Southern and Western Monthly Magazine and Review, Dec. 1845.

**6.435 National Gazetteer of the United States.** In progress. Denver, CO: U. S. Geological Survey. Preliminary alphabetical listings for all fifty states, based on USGS topographic maps, are completed. Most state lists are available as bound volumes, microfiche, and magnetic tape. State gazetteers for AL, FL, and MS (and several non-Southern states) are in progress (Aug. 1987).

**6.436 Nelson, Mildred M.** 1950. Folk etymology of Alabama place-names. SFQ 14.193-214.

**6.437 Neuffer, Claude H., ed.** 1954-1983. Names in South Carolina. 30 vols. Columbia: University of South Carolina Department of English. Annual journal devoted to documenting names of places, people, events, and other aspects of South Carolina geography and history. Vols. 1-12 (1954-65) reprinted, bound with index. Reprinted in 1976, 1983. Volumes 13-18 (1966-71) reprinted in 1983. Volumes 19-24 (1972-77) reprinted in 1983. Index to volumes 19-24 (1972-77) compiled by Rene LaBorde Neuffer in 1978. Volumes 25-30 (1978-83) reprinted in 1984. **Reviews:** Vol. 10: K. B. Harder. 1964. Names 12.64-65; Vol. 12: M. M. Bryant. 1966. Names 14.126-27; T. Pyles. 1966. Georgia Review 20.370-71; Vol. 1-13: K. B. Harder. 1968. Names 16.194-95; J. I. Waring. 1966. South Carolina Historical Magazine 67.119-20; Vol 25: K. B. Harder. 1979. TFSB 45.123-24.

**6.438 Neuffer, Claude H.** 1962. Names beneath man and the land. South Carolina Librarian 6.10-12.

**6.439 Neuffer, Claude H.** 1965. Names in South Carolina: a study of its origin and development. University of South Carolina Magazine 1.14-15.

**6.440 Neuffer, Claude H.** 1965. The first ten years of Names in South Carolina. University of South Carolina Alumni Quarterly 1.14-15,25.

**6.441 Neuffer, Claude H.** 1965. Calhoun County plantations of St. Matthew's Parish near the Congaree-Santee River. NSC 12.45-48.

**6.442 Neuffer, Claude H.** 1966. Folk etymology in South Carolina place names. AS 41.274-77. Place names based primarily on forgotten surnames.

**6.443 Neuffer, Claude H.** 1966. Rich source of picturesque names. Columbia, SC: The State. 75th anniversary edition, Feb. 13, p. 7A.

**6.444 Neuffer, Claude H.** 1967. S.C. place names: from Gobbler's Knob to Whooping Island. South Carolina Magazine 31.23-26.

**6.445 Neuffer, Claude H.** 1968. The origin and development of a state onomastic periodical. Names 16.127-29. About the journal Names in South Carolina.

**6.446 Neuffer, Claude H.** 1968. Names in South Carolina. Sandlapper 2.3.60-61. History, scope, and purposes of the state onomastic journal Names in South Carolina.

**6.447 Neuffer, Claude H.** 1969. Place names related to the Lords Proprietors and their associates. The State, Columbia, S.C. Prepared for special issue observing tricentennial South Carolina.

**6.448 Neuffer, Claude H.** 1970. The Lord's Proprietors and their influence on South Carolina place names. NSC 17.49-50.

**6.449 Neuffer, Claude H.** 1975. South Carolina firsts. NSC 22.42-45. Famous men and achievements in SC.

**6.450 Neuffer, Claude H.** 1976. Place names in South Carolina. Sandlapper 9.10.27-28. Legends behind unusual names in SC.

**6.451 Neuffer, Claude H., and Irene L. Neuffer.** 1972. The name game: from Oyster Point to Keowee. Book introducing children to place name study. Columbia, SC: Sandlapper Press. **Review:** Anonymous. 1972. South Carolina Historical Magazine 73.224.

**6.452 Neuffer, Claude H., and Irene L. Neuffer.** 1983. Correct mispronunciations of some South Carolina names. Columbia: University of South Carolina Press. 182 pp. Glossary of place and family names whose pronunciation differs from their spellings, with short history of each name.

Reviews: K. B. Harder. 1984. Names 32.331-33; R. I. McDavid, Jr. 1984. Bulletin of the Illinois Name Society, pp. 12-19.

**6.453 Norona, Delf.** 1958. Wheeling; a West Virginia place name of Indian origin. Moundsville, WV: West Virginia Archeological Society.

**6.454 Norris, Walter B.** 1959. Origin of some interesting Maryland place names. Maryland and Delaware Genealogist 1.16.

**6.455 Norris, Walter B.** 1960. More Maryland place names: "Maryland Point." Maryland and Delaware Genealogist 1.63.

**6.456 Nostalgia in place names.** 1979. Cumberland 3.3.38-40. [TN]. Short accounts of history and naming of Red Boiling Springs, Hohenwald, and Indian Mound.

**6.457 Note on the origin of Natchez.** 1931. Louisiana Historical Quarterly 14.515.

**6.458 Oakley, Bruce C.** 1969. A postal history of Mississippi's stampless period, 1799-1860. Baldwyn, MS: Magnolia Publishers. 290 pp. Maps. Records names of post offices in the MS Territory and the State of MS.

**6.459 O'Bannon, Joyce S.** 1968. Names in Barnwell County. NSC 15.10-18. [W SC].

**6.460 O'Bannon, Joyce S.** 1971. Disappearing place names in Barnwell County. NSC 18.41-49. [W SC].

**6.461 O'Cain, Raymond K.** 1966. Some place names here and there in Orangeburg County. NSC 13.51-57. [S CENT SC].

**6.462 Ordoubadian, Reza.** 1968. Rutherford County: a study in onomastics. Auburn: Auburn University dissertation. Abstract in DAI 29.890A. Classifies place names in Middle TN county into six groups.

**6.463 Ordoubadian, Reza.** 1977. Rutherford County onomastics: a bicentennial reminiscence. The third LACUS forum 1976, ed. by Robert J. Di Pietro and Edward L. Blansitt, Jr., 228-33. Columbia, SC: Hornbeam. [CENT TN].

**6.464 Origin of the name of Newport News.** 1901. William and Mary College Quarterly Historical Magazine 9.233-37. [VA].

**6.465 Ott, Ruby M.** 1978. Some names of resorts and springs. NSC 25.14-16.

**6.466 Owen, Thomas M.** 1921. Jefferson County: present day place names showing aboriginal influence.    Arrow Points 3.10-11.    [CENT AL].

**6.467 Owens, Harry P.** 1985. Steamboat landings of the Yazoo and Talla-hatchie rivers (1876-86). Journal of Mississippi History 47.266-83. [MS]. Includes list of landings recorded in 1875-82.

**6.468 Owens, Tony J.** 1980. Cherokee place names in upper South Carolina. NSC 27.28-30. [NW SC].

**6.469 Pace, George B.** 1960. Linguistic geography and names ending in <i>. AS 35.175-87. 2 maps. Linguistic Atlas evidence for pronunciation of final vowel in _Missouri_ and _Cincinnati_; includes South Atlantic States. **Reprinted** in H. Allen and G. Underwood 1971(**1.12**).216-27.

**6.470 Pap, Leo.** 1972. The Portuguese adstratum in North American place-names. Names 20.111-30. Town and county names throughout country.

**6.471 Parkerson, Codman.** 1969. Those strange Louisiana names; a glos-sary. Baton Rouge, LA: Claitor's Book Store. 22 pp. + map. Mostly Indian names.

**6.472 Patterson, Lucy Adelaide Holloway.** 1963. A study of some place names of southeastern Lee County, Alabama. Auburn: Auburn University thesis. [E CENT AL].

**6.473 Patton, Eugene E.** 1952. First territory named for Washington. D.A.R. Magazine 86.139-40,251. [E TN]. See Williams (**6.656**).

**6.474 Payne, Roger L.** 1985. Place names of the Outer Banks. Washing-ton, NC: Thomas A. Williamson. Dictionary listing over 1,000 names found on maps of NC barrier islands, with detailed locations, alternate names, and historical notes. **Review:** R. R. Randall. 1988. Names 34.114-15.

**6.475 Pearson, Bruce L.** 1978. On the Indian place names of South Caro-lina. Names 26.58-67. Many patterns in 230 Indian place names; short appendix of major river and other place names.

**6.476 Peden, Ann.** 1971. Place names in Humphreys County. MFR 5.39-49. [W CENT MS].

**6.477 Peeples, Robert E. H.** 1972. Old Hilton Head Island names. NSC 19.38-53. [SE SC].

**6.478 Percy, Alfred.** 1950. Old place names, west central Piedmont and Blue Ridge Mountains. Madison Heights, VA: Percy Press. [VA].

**6.479 Pettus, Louise.** 1983. Streams and roads of Catawba Indian lands. NSC 30.32-34. [N CENT SC]. SC Up Country, particularly Lancaster Co.

**6.480 Pfister, Fred.** 1975. What's in a name? Ozark Highways (Summer), 29-30. Discusses place names in AR-MO Ozarks.

**6.481 Phelps, Dawson A., and Edward Hunter Ross.** 1952. Names please: place-names along the Natchez Trace. Journal of Mississippi History 14.217-56.

**6.482 Phillips, George H.** 1979. Handling the mail in Benton County, Arkansas, 1836-1976. Siloam Springs, AR: Benton County Historical Society. Instructions relative to names of post offices, 22-25. Gives brief accounts of origins of many post office names.

**6.483 Phillips, S. T.** 1980. A study of placenames in St. Charles Parish, Louisiana. New Orleans: University of New Orleans thesis.

**6.484 Pickens, A. L.** 1937. Dictionary of Indian place names in upper S.C. Greenwood, SC: S.C. Natural History, no. 51-57.

**6.485 Pickens, A. L.** 1961. Indian place names in South Carolina. NSC 8.3-7. Extensive glossary of names from Choctaw, Catawba, Cherokee, and other sources.

**6.486 Pickens County stream names: a selective list.** 1980. NSC 27.12-13. [NW SC].

**6.487 Place name origins.** 1967. Foxfire 1.62-72. NE GA names derived from Cherokee.

**6.488 Place name pride.** 1979. Cumberland 3.1.12-14. Survey of locations in TN with name of Cumberland in them.

**6.489 Place name pride.** 1980. Cumberland 4.1.26-27. Short accounts of history and naming of Rheatown, Castalian Springs, Chuckey, and Cheatham County, TN.

**6.490 Plummer, Niel.** 1949. Guide to the pronunciation of Kentucky towns and cities. Lexington: University of Kentucky Dept. of Journalism. 52 pp.

**6.491 Pope, Harold Clay.** 1954. The lighter side of Texas place naming. Western Folklore 13.125-29.

**6.492 Powell, William S.** 1968. The North Carolina gazetteer. Chapel Hill: University of North Carolina Press. 561 pp. Glossary of NC placenames; very little on etymology, but more on local history. **Reviews:** Anonymous. 1972. North Carolina Folklore 20.94-96; F. N. Cheney. 1969. Wilson Library Bulletin 43.673; C. Crittenden. 1969. NCHR 46.58-59; B. H. Granger. 1969. Names 17.312-14.

**6.493 Presnall, Clifford C.** n.d. Names of waters bordering the Northern Neck. Northern Neck of Virginia Historical Magazine 21.1.33-34. [NE VA].

**6.494 Pronunciation guide to West Virginia place names.** 1951. Morgantown: West Virginia University School of Journalism. 51 pp. Alphabetical listing of state's placenames, giving pronunciations and stress patterns.

**6.495 Randolph, Jennings.** 1970. Dogbone and other towns represent strength in America--place names present quaint and original quality of life in West Virginia. Congressional Record 116.41683.

**6.496 Randolph, Vance.** 1976. Senator Johnson's great speech. Pissing in the snow, 171-73. New York: Avon. Note on proposal to change the pronunciation of the name of AR to rhyme with Kansas.

**6.497 Rawlings, James Scott.** 1963. Virginia's colonial churches: an architectural guide together with their surviving books, silver and furnishings. Richmond, VA: Garrett and Massie. xi + 286 pp. Discusses forty-eight colonial churches and origin of name of each parish. **Reviews**: J. M. Jennings. 1964. Virginia Magazine of History and Biography 72.211-12; C. W. Warterfield, Jr. 1965. Tennessee Historical Quarterly 24.89-90.

**6.498 [Rayburn, Otto E.]** 1956. Place names in the Ozarks. Rayburn's Ozark Guide 14.48.65. Notes dozen metaphorical names in AR.

**6.499 [Rayburn, Otto E.]** 1958. The legend of Petit Jean. Rayburn's Ozark Guide 16.55.27. [CENT AR]. Stories about origin of mountain name in Conway County.

**6.500 [Rayburn, Otto E.]** 1960. [The gentleman from Arkansas. . .] Rayburn's Ozark Guide 18.63.11-12. Says pronunciation of final syllable of state name was disputed until 1883, when AR legislature established official version.

**6.501 [Rayburn, Otto E.]** 1966. The name--Ozarks. Rayburn's Ozark Guide 18.66.6. Says name derives from French aux arcs.

**6.502 Read, Allen W.** 1933. The basis of correctness in the pronunciation of place-names. AS 8.1.42-46. Considers spelling, etymology, legislative resolutions, and other criteria as bases for correct pronunciation of place names but rejects them.

**6.503 Read, William Alexander.** 1913. A Vernerian sound change in English. Englische Studien 47.169-74. Discusses pronunciation and spelling of Missouri and Mississippi.

**6.504 Read, William Alexander.** 1927. Louisiana place-names of Indian origin. Louisiana State University Bulletin, no. 19, n.s., no. 2, Baton Rouge. 72 pp.

**6.505 Read, William Alexander.** 1928. More Indian place names in Louisiana. Louisiana Historical Quarterly 11.445-62. Additions and corrections to preceding item.

**6.506 Read, William Alexander.** 1931. Geographical names. Louisiana-French, 152-201. Baton Rouge: Louisiana State University Press. **Reprinted** as Louisiana State University Studies, no. 5, 1963. Includes three alphabetical lists: Indian, French, and Spanish; first list supplements author's Louisiana Place-Names of Indian Origin (**5.504**).

**6.507 Read, William Alexander.** 1931. Istrouma. Louisiana Historical Quarterly 14.503-15. Says Indian word, which means "red post," is source for name Baton Rouge.

**6.508 Read, William Alexander.** 1934. Florida place names of Indian origin and Seminole personal names. Louisiana State University Studies, no. 11, Baton Rouge. 83 pp. **Reviews:** J. A. Robertson. 1934. Florida Historical Society Quarterly 13.111-12; J. R. Swanton. 1934. AS 9.218-20.

**6.509 Read, William Alexander.** 1937. Indian place-names in Alabama. Baton Rouge: Louisiana State University Press. 84 pp. Bibliography, 80-84. Supplemented in AS 13.79-80 (Feb. 1938). Revised ed., with a foreword, appendix (pp. 85-102), and index by James B. McMillan, published in 1984 by the University of Alabama Press. xvi + 107 pp. Exhaustive identification and etymological analysis of AL place names from Creek, Choctaw, and Cherokee. **Reviews:** Anonymous. 1985. Florida Historical Quarterly 63.377; M. Bryant. 1984. Names 32.187-88; M. J. McDaniel. 1985. Alabama Review 38.309; W. E. H. Nicolaisen. 1986. AS 61.179-81; B. Pearson. 1986. SECOL Review 10.135-37; J. R. Swanton. 1937. AS 12.212-15; J. B. Whisker. 1987. The Reprint Bulletin 32.2.37.

**6.510 Read, William Alexander.** 1938. The Hitchiti name of Silver Springs, Florida. MLN 53.513-14. Translates Indian name of springs as "wells of light."

**6.511 Read, William Alexander.** 1938. Ten Alabama place names. AS 13.79-80. Sumter County names derived from Choctaw.

**6.512 Read, William Alexander.** 1940. Caxambas, a Florida geographic name. Language 16.210-13.

**6.513 Read, William Alexander.** 1949. Indian stream-names in Georgia. IJAL 15.128-32; 16.203-07 (Oct. 1950).

**6.514 Reeves, Paschal.** 1963. Thomas Wolfe's "Old Catawba." Names 11.254-56. Origin of Wolfe's fictional name for NC.

**6.515 Reid, Maude.** 1954. Origin of some place names in southwest Louisiana. McNeese Review 6.105-20.

**6.516 Renault, Raoul.** 1899. Correspondence: some old French place-names in the state of Arkansas. MLN 14.96.

**6.517 Rennick, Robert.** 1984. Kentucky place names. Lexington: University Press of Kentucky. xxiv + 375 pp. Bibliography, 329-75. **Reviews:** C. E. Martin. 1985. KFR 30.127-28; L. E. Seits. 1985. Names 33.271-72.

**6.518 Rennick, Robert M.** 1984. How Bone Cave got its name: a legend from Wayne County, Kentucky. TFSB 50.75-78. [S CENT KY].

**6.519 Rennick, Robert M.** 1985. A note on Shakerag as a place name. TFSB 51.22-24. Discusses three locations in KY with the name and others in TN, TX, FL.

**6.520 Rennick, Robert M.** 1985. Traditional accounts of some Eastern Kentucky place names. Appalachian Notes 13.2-17. Discusses place names based on associations with fanciful, literary, and personal names.

**6.521 Rennick, Robert M.** 1987. Some Pike County place names: Leonard Roberts' contributions to the Kentucky place name survey. Appalachian Heritage 15.2.51-55.

**6.522 Rennick, Robert M.** 1988. Place name derivations are not always what they seem. Appalachian Heritage 16.1.50-62. [KY].

**6.523 Reynolds, Jack Adolphe.** 1942. Louisiana place-names of romance origin. Baton Rouge: Louisiana State University dissertation. Abstract in Louisiana State University Bulletin, n.s. 35.9-10 (1943).

**6.524 Reynolds, T. N.** 1964. Born of the mountains. Highlands, NC: privately printed. [S Appalachia]. Peculiar names in mountain states, 83-131; More about Indian names, 148-50; More about derogatory names, 154-55; [Miscellaneous names], 162-64. Information on place names of W NC. **Review:** K. B. Harder. 1965. Names 13.133-35.

**6.525 Reynolds, T. N.** 1964. High lands. Highlands, NC: privately printed. [W NC]. That name Cashiers with some sidelights, 29-36; Bohaynee and other place names of the area, 37-46; How Burnington got its name, 79; [Indian place names], 97-102. Tour guide of region, including place name lore. **Review:** K. Harder. 1965. Names 13.133-35.

**6.526 Rich, John Stanley.** 1980. The place names of Greene and Tuscaloosa

Counties, Alabama. Tuscaloosa: University of Alabama dissertation. Abstract in DAI 40.4576-77A. 660 pp. [W CENT AL]. Classifies, discusses naming processes and grammar of, and includes dictionary of 2,500 place-names in two counties.

**6.527 Rich, John Stanley.** 1981. Landscapes and the imagination: the interplay of folk etymology and place names. SFQ 45.155-62. [Greene, Tuscaloosa Cos., W AL]. Folk etymologies revealed in names of communities, churches, bodies of water, and other places.

**6.528 Rich, John Stanley.** 1982. South Carolina names in West Alabama. NSC 29.19-21.

**6.529 Richardson, Thomas J.** 1977. Current place-names of Jasper County, Mississippi. MFR 11.101-30. [SE MS].

**6.530 Riddle, Billie Jean.** 1951. Creeks, branches, forks, licks, runs, sloughs and hollows in Kentucky. Kentucky Historical Society Register 49.280-330. Compilation of names, based on county maps of Kentucky Geological Society.

**6.531 Riley, Franklin L.** 1902. Extinct towns and villages of Mississippi. Mississippi Historical Society Publications 5.311-83.

**6.532 Robb, Kenneth A.** 1969. Names of grants in colonial Maryland. Names 17.263-77. Study of 4,108 names given to land tracts.

**6.533 Robertson, Ann Elizabeth Worcester.** 1931. Some Choctaw names. Arrow Points 19.15-16. Etymology of name Alabama.

**6.534 Robertson, Ben.** 1942. Red hills and cotton, an upcountry memory. New York: Knopf. Pp. 53-55, names in the red hills of NW SC.

**6.535 Robinson, M. P.** 1916. Virginia county names. Bulletin of the Virginia State Library 9.1-283. Includes origins of county names.

**6.536 Roden, Jerry, Jr.** 1978. Place name origins. Alabama Life 1.3.52-53. On Marshall Co., NE AL.

**6.537 Rogers, Elzia Guy.** 1936. Stories and legends of Marshall County north of Duck River. Nashville: George Peabody College thesis. [CENT TN]. Place names, 191-94.

**6.538 Rogers, P. Burwell.** 1954. Place names on the Virginia peninsula. AS 29.241-56.

**6.539 Rogers, P. Burwell.** 1956. Indian names in Tidewater, Virginia. Names 4.155-59.

**6.540 Rogers, P. Burwell.** 1967. The first names of Virginia. Virginia Place Name Society Occasional Papers 12 (new series no. 2, Feb. 10). Charlottesville: University of Virginia. 14 pp.

**6.541 Rogers, P. Burwell.** 1972. Virginia counties. Virginia Place Name Society Occasional Paper 16. Charlottesville: University of Virginia. 10 pp.

**6.542 Rothert, Otto A.** 1927. Origin of the names Beargrass Creek, The Point, and Thruston Square. Filson Society History Quarterly 2.19-21. Names of sections of Louisville, KY.

**6.543 Rutherford, Philip Roland.** 1964. Place name study of five southeast Texas counties. Commerce: East Texas State University thesis. 638 names from five counties. Discusses origins, variation in names, changes in names and spellings, and effect of immigration on names.

**6.544 Salley, A. S.** 1926. The origin of Carolina. South Carolina Historical Commission Bulletin no. 8. 26 pp.

**6.545 Schwartz, Janet.** 1980. The poet and the naming of suburbia. Names 28.231-54. Categories and patterns of subdivision names in Atlanta, GA.

**6.546 Scomp, H. A.** 1908. Kentucky county names. Magazine of History 7.144-54.

**6.547 Scroggs, William O.** 1917. Origin of the name Baton Rouge. Proceedings of the Historical Society of East and West Baton Rouge 1.20-24. [LA].

**6.548 Seale, Lea Leslie.** 1939. Indian place-names in Mississippi. Baton Rouge: Louisiana State University dissertation. Abstracted in Louisiana State University Bulletin, n.s. 32.5-7 (1940). 225 pp. List of names, 33-215. Studies origin and meaning of geographic names derived from languages spoken by "tribes that at some time were settled within the Mississippi Territory"; most names from Choctaw.

**6.549 Shampine, William J.** 1970. Gazetteer of Louisiana lakes and reservoirs. Baton Rouge: Louisiana Department of Public Works, Basic records report no. 4. U.S. Geological Survey.

**6.550 Shannon, Karr.** 1947. History of Izard County, Arkansas. Little Rock, AR: Democrat Printing. [N CENT AR]. Pp. 61-78, place names.

**6.551 Shellans, Herbert.** 1956. Tarheel place names. North Carolina Folklore 4.28-32. Eleven names including Barbecue, Snakebite, and Old Trap.

**6.552 Shellans, Herbert.** 1963. Table d'hote: towns, counties and places, North Carolina. Names 11.270-71. Names of places listed in the form of menus.

**6.553 Sheppard, Harvey.** 1972. Town name changes in Virginia. Virginia Postal History Society Way Markings. Item noted in Sealock et al. **(12.30)**.

**6.554 Sherwood, Adiel.** 1827. A gazetteer of the state of Georgia. Charleston; 2nd ed., Philadelphia, 1829; 3rd ed., Washington, 1837; 4th ed., Macon, GA: S. Boykin.

**6.555 Sherwood, Adiel.** 1939. A gazetteer of the state of Georgia, by Rev. Adiel Sherwood; biographical sketch by John B. Clark; foreword by President Spright Dowell, Mercer University. 143 pp. The present edition being a facsimile reprint of the original 1827 publication, with a map of Georgia from the 1829 edition and a portrait of the author. Athens: University of Georgia Press.

**6.556 Shields, Carla Smith.** 1966. Spanish influences on East Texas place names and vocabulary. Commerce: East Texas State University thesis.

**6.557 Shores, David L.** 1982. "Porchmouth" for Portsmouth. Abstract in NADS 14.3.5-6. Surveys history of, and attitudes toward the affricate pronunciation of [ts] in city's name.

**6.558 Shulman, David.** 1952. Nicknames of states and their inhabitants. AS 27.183-85.

**6.559 Siler, Tom.** 1975. Tennessee towns: from Adams to Yorkville. Knoxville: East Tennessee Historical Society. 108 pp. Capsule history and etymology of 334 town names.

**6.560 Simpson, James Clarence.** 1946. Middle Florida place names. Apalachee 3.68-77.

**6.561 Simpson, James Clarence.** 1956. A provisional gazetteer of Florida place-names of Indian derivation, together with others of recent application. Ed. by Mark F. Boyd. Tallahassee: Florida Geological Survey. 158 pp. Names of Indian origin. **Reviews:** J. W. Griffin. 1956. Florida Historical Quarterly 35.194; E. W. McMullen. 1956. Names 4.249-52.

**6.562 Smith, Jack.** 1968. The Mississippi place-name repository. MFR 2.1.19-26. Describes operations of the repository.

**6.563 Smith, Jack A.** 1969. A study of place-names in Forrest County, Mississippi. Auburn: Auburn University dissertation. Abstract in DAI 30.709A. 193 pp. [SE MS]. Studies "the pronunciation, spelling, origin, period of popularity, and changes of application" of 325 names.**6.564 Smith,**

**John Gettys.** 1976. York County's Sutton Springs and families involved. NSC 23.17-20. [N CENT SC].

**6.565 Sockwell, Sandra M.** 1985. The place names of Colbert and Lauderdale Counties, Alabama. Tuscaloosa: University of Alabama dissertation. Abstract in DAI 47.890A. Historical study of toponymy of two NW AL counties.

**6.566 Some Virginia names and their meanings.** 1904. Virginia Magazine of History and Biography 11.317-21.

**6.567 Spence, Dorothy Clark.** 1961. How Tolu, Kentucky, got its name. KFR 7.119-20. Folk etymologies for town on Ohio River.

**6.568 Spiro, Robert.** 1955. Place names in Mississippi. Mississippi Magazine 1.6-8.

**6.569 Springston, Jolane.** 1980. Place-names in Lamar County. Hattiesburg: University of Southern Mississippi thesis. 97 pp. [S MS]. Place name list, 16-71. Finds most town and community names derive from names of people and most names of natural features from names of local people or from descriptions of terrain.

**6.570 Starnes, D. T.** 1966. Bulls Gap and some other related place names. Names 14.41-42. [E TN].

**6.571 Sternberg, Hilgard O'Reilly.** 1948. The names "False River" and "Pointe Coupee," an inquiry in historical geography. Louisiana Historical Quarterly 31.598-605.

**6.572 Stewart, George R.** 1945. [The "Change the name of Arkansas" controversy]. Names on the land, 335-40. New York: Random House.

**6.573 Still, James A.** 1929. Place names in the Cumberland Mountains. AS 5.113. [SE KY]. Twenty-two names of creeks, ridges, hollows, and villages in the Cumberland Gap area.

**6.574 Stokes, George Mitchell.** 1947. A study of the pronunciation of Texas towns. Waco: Baylor University thesis.

**6.575 Stokes, George M.** 1977. A guide to the pronunciation of Texas towns. Waco, TX: Texian Press. xii + 141 pp. Pronouncing dictionary for broadcasters, with pronunciation of more than 3200 place names listed in IPA symbols. **Review:** K. B. Harder. 1979. TFSB 45.123-24.

**6.576 Strecker, John K.** 1929. Animals and streams: a contribution to the study of Texas folk names. Baylor University contributions to folk-lore 2. 23 pp.

**6.577 Street, Oliver Day.** 1900. Cherokee towns and villages in Alabama. Alabama History Commission Report 1.416-21.

**6.578 Stuart, Elsie Rast.** 1981. Roads, railroads, and bridges in southern Lexington County. NSC 28.27-32. [CENT SC].

**6.579 Stubbs, Thomas M., and James L. Haynesworth.** 1970. Early ferries on the Wateree and Catawba rivers. NSC 17.9-11.

**6.580 Swift, Lucie.** 1961. Who'd a thought it and other Paducah place-names. KFR 7.117-19. [KY]. Discussion of twelve names, edited by Herbert Halpert.

**6.581 Swint, Henry Lee.** 1944. Ezekiel Birdseye and the free state of Frankland. Tennessee Historical Quarterly 3.226-36. [E TN].

**6.582 Tanner, Douglas W.** 1975-76. From the Albemarle bookshelf: Charlottesville's royal namesake, Britain's Queen Charlotte. Magazine of Albemarle County History 33-34.173-80. [CENT VA]. Also includes references to other places named for the Queen.

**6.583 Tanner, Douglas W.** 1976. Place name research in Virginia: a handbook. Virginia Place Name Society Occasional Paper 20. Charlottesville: University of Virginia. iii + 52 pp. Comprehensive manual for state survey of place names; includes lists of terms and bibliographical aids. **Review:** K. B. Harder. 1976. TFSB 42.107-12.

**6.584 Tanner, Douglas W.** 1978. Madison County place names. Virginia Place Name Society Occasional Paper 21. Charlottesville: University of Virginia. xiv + 119 pp.

**6.585 Tarpley, Fred.** 1969. Place names of northeast Texas. Commerce: East Texas State University Educational Research and Field Services. xxi + 245 pp. Classifies and discusses origins of names in twenty-six county area. **Review:** L. P. Boone. 1970. Names 18.318-20.

**6.586 Tarpley, Fred.** 1970. Principles of place-name studies outlined. Humanities in the South 32.3.4. Says TX names can be classified in ten categories according to origins.

**6.587 Tarpley, Fred,** ed. 1973. Love and wrestling: butch and o.k. South Central Names Institute Publication 2. Commerce, TX: Names Institute Press. 126 pp.

**6.588 Tarpley, Fred,** ed. 1974. They had to call it something. Publication 3, South Central Names Institute. Commerce, TX: Names Institute Press. **Review:** K. B. Harder. 1976. TFSB 40.110-11.

**6.589 Tarpley, Fred**, ed. 1975. Naughty names. Publication 4, South Central Names Institute. Commerce, TX: East Texas State University and American Name Society. 66 pp. **Review:** K. B. Harder. 1976. TFSB 42.150-51.

**6.590 Tarpley, Fred**, ed. 1977. Labeled for life. Publication 5, South Central Names Institute. Commerce, TX: Names Institute Press. 92 pp.

**6.591 Tarpley, Fred.** 1980. 1001 Texas place names. Austin: University of Texas Press. 236 pp. Encyclopedia of names from 254 counties of state having unique, significant, or appealing stories behind their origin.

**6.592 Tarpley, Fred**, ed. 1981. The scope of names. Commerce, TX: Names Institute Press. 198 pp. **Review:** K. B. Harder. 1982. TFSB 43.34-37.

**6.593 Tarpley, Fred**, ed. 1982. Names and popular culture: selected papers of the South Central Names Institute. Irvington, TX: Names Institute Press.

**6.594 Tarpley, Fred, and Ann Moseley**, eds. 1971. Of Edsels and marauders. Publication 1, South-Central Names Institute. Commerce, TX: Names Institute Press. 126 pp.

**6.595 Tennessee blue book.** 1961-  Nashville: Secretary of State. Features section "The Origin of County Name" in each volume.

**6.596 ter Braake, Alex L.** 1968. What's in a name: the three Charlestowns. West Virginia History 30.351-57.

**6.597 Terry, George D.** 1979. Eighteenth century plantation names in Upper St. John's, Berkeley. NSC 26.15-19. [SE SC]. Names from Monck's Corner in northwestwardly direction along Santee River.

**6.598 Thigpen, Samuel Grady.** 1965. Next door to heaven. Kingsport, TN: Kingsport Press. 247 pp. [NE TN]. The romance of names of Hancock County, 10-17.

**6.599 Thomas, Charles E.** 1965. Some Fairfield County names of plantations and houseseats. NSC 12.49-54. [N CENT SC].

**6.600 Thompson, Lawrence S.** 1969. The meaning of Kentucky. American Notes and Queries 7.68-71.

**6.601 Thompson, T. P.** 1916. Origin of the various names of the Mississippi River. Louisiana Historical Society Publications 9.92-95. Traces names in chronological order from early maps.

**6.602 Tindall, William.** 1920. Naming the seat of government of the

United States; a legislative paradox. Columbia Historical Society Records 23.10-25.

**6.603 Tolbert, Marguerite.** 1977. Gray Court and related names in Laurens County. NSC 24.23. [NW SC].

**6.604 Tompkins, D. A.** 1903. History of Mecklenburg County and the city of Charlotte from 1740 to 1903. Charlotte, NC: Charlotte Observer. Pp. 28-30, origin of names of county and city of Charlotte.

**6.605 Tooker, William Wallace.** 1891. Some Indian names of places on Long Island, N.Y. and their correspondence in Virginia, as mentioned by Capt. John Smith and associates. Magazine of New England History 1.154-58.

**6.606 Tooker, William Wallace.** 1893. The Kuskarawaokes of Captain John Smith. AA ser. 1, 6.409-14. [E VA].

**6.607 Tooker, William Wallace.** 1894. On the meaning of the name Anacostia. AA ser. 1., 7.389-93. [DC].

**6.608 Tooker, William Wallace.** 1895. Chickahominy, its origin and etymology. AA ser. 1., 8.257-63. [E VA].

**6.609 Tooker, William Wallace.** 1895. [No title.] American Antiquarian 17.289-93. [E VA].

**6.610 Tooker, William Wallace.** 1901. The names Chickahominy, Pamunkey, and the Kuskarawaokes of Captain John Smith; with historical and ethnological notes. New York: F. P. Harper. Reprinting of items (**6.606, 6.607, 6.608**). [E VA].

**6.611 Tooker, William Wallace.** 1904. Derivation of the name Powhatan. AA n.s. 6.464-68. [E VA]. Says name means "hill of divination," not "falls in a stream," as generally believed.

**6.612 Tooker, William Wallace.** 1904. Some Powhatan names. AA n.s. 6.670-94. [E VA]. Detailed refutation of Gerard's (**2.155**) etymologies.

**6.613 Tooker, William Wallace.** 1905. Meaning of some Indian names in Virginia. William and Mary College Quarterly Historical Magazine 14.62-64. Etymologies of six names.

**6.614 Tooker, William Wallace.** 1905. Some more about Virginia names. AA n.s. 7.524-28. Answers criticisms of W. R. Gerard with regard to author's preceding essay (item **6.613**).

**6.615 Tooker, William Wallace.** 1906. The Powhatan name for Virginia. Lancaster, PA: New Era. Reprint 1906. AA n.s. 8.23-27.

**6.616 Topping, Mary.** 1971. Approved place names in Virginia, an index to Virginia names approved by the United States Board on Geographic Names through 1969. Virginia Place Name Society Occasional Paper 15. Charlottesville: University of Virginia. Reprinted by University of Virginia Press. viii + 167 pp. Alphabetical list identifying and locating names and giving their date of approval by the board.

**6.617 Trumbull, James Hammond.** 1870. Indian names in Virginia. Historical Magazine, second series, 7.47-48.

**6.618 Turner, Sarah Anne.** 1935. Place-names of Webster Parish--a linguistic historical study. Baton Rouge: Louisiana State University thesis. [NW LA].

**6.619 Two place-name pronunciations.** 1928. AS 4.156-57. Cites local usage, rather than spelling, as guide in pronunciation of Staunton, VA, and Houston, TX.

**6.620 Underwood, Lawrence Eugene.** 1980. Overland stages: a sociolinguistic study of place names along a portion of Arkansas' Southwest Trail. Commerce: East Texas State University dissertation. Abstract in DAI 41.4387A. Studies "effects of history and the conscious and unconscious linguistic practices of the people upon the place names" of five-county section of AR; shows how distribution of place names in area was affected by sequences of social and demographic factors.

**6.621 Underwood, [Lawrence] Eugene.** 1981. Place name pronunciations in White County, Arkansas. The scope of names, ed. by Fred Tarpley, 35-41. Commerce, TX: Names Institute Press. [CENT AR]. Finds twenty-five place names have uniform pronunciation in county, but twenty names have two or more different pronunciations.

**6.622 Union County communities.** 1975. NSC 22.24-26. Reprint from Union [SC] Daily Times.

**6.623 U. S. Writers' Program, North Carolina.** 1941. How they began--the story of North Carolina county, town and other place names, compiled by workers of the Writers' Program of the Work Projects Administration in the State of North Carolina. Sponsored by North Carolina Dept. of Conservation and Development, Raleigh, NC. New York: Harian Publications. 73 pp.

**6.624 Utley, Francis Lee.** 1973. Hog Crawl Creek again. Names 21.179-95. [GA]. Proposal that hog-crawl is an etymological blend.

**6.625 Utley, George Burwell.** 1908. Origin of the county names of Florida. Magazine of History 8.77-81. **Reprinted** in Florida State Historical Society Publications 1.29-35 (1908).

**6.626 Villiers du Terrage, Marc, Baron de.** 1929. La Louisiane, histoire de son nom et de ses frontières successives (1681-1819). Paris: Adrien-Maisonneuve. 74 pp.

**6.627 Virginia Division of Planning and Economic Development.** 1951. Index of the surface waters of Virginia. Richmond. 1st ed. 1949. Lists names and approximate locations of state's surface waters; includes additions and corrections for Bedford County.

**6.628 Virginia Division of Water Resources.** 1960. Index of the surface waters of Virginia. Richmond. Incorporates additions for Bedford County made by Kenneth E. Crouch.

**6.629 Virginia Place Name Society.** 1961. Virginia place names 1676. Occasional Paper 2 (Sept. 20). Charlottesville: University of Virginia. 8 pp. An index to John Speed's 1676 Map of Virginia and Maryland.

**6.630 Virginia Place Name Society.** 1969. Prospectus June 1969. Occasional Paper 14. Charlottesville: University of Virginia Library. 18 pp.

**6.631 Virginia Place Name Society.** 1972- . Newsletter. No. [1]- . Charlottesville: University of Virginia. Information on state's place name survey and requests for information.

**6.632 Walker, Norman M.** 1883. The geographical nomenclature of Louisiana. Magazine of American History 10.211-22.

**6.633 Walls, David S.** 1977. On the naming of Appalachia. An Appalachian Symposium, ed. by J. S. Williamson, 56-76. Boone, NC: Appalachian Consortium. 7 maps. Explores etymology and use of name Appalachia and surveys official and unofficial names for the mountain region.

**6.634 Watson, Harry L.** 1960. Greenwood County place names. NSC 7.7-10. [W CENT SC].

**6.635 Welborn, George E.** 1964. Some Pickens County names. NSC 11.27-32. [NW SC].

**6.636 Weslager, C. A.** 1954. Place names on Ocracoke island. North Carolina Historical Review 31.41-49. [E NC].

**6.637 West, Robert C.** 1954. The term "bayou" in the United States; a study in the geography of place names. Association of American Geographers Annals 44.63-74. Abstract in Annals 43.197-98 (June 1953).

**6.638 West, Roy A.** 1952. West Virginia place names. West Virginia Folklore 3.15-16.

**6.639 West Virginia.** 1939? Constitutional convention, 1861-1863. Debates and proceedings. Huntington, WV: Gentry Bros. 1.81-107. Recounts debate by convention to choose name of state.

**6.640 West Virginia Heritage Foundation,** comp. and ed. 1967. Origin of place names in West Virginia. West Virginia heritage volume one. Richwood, WV.

**6.641 West Virginia University School of Journalism.** 1951. Pronunciation guide to West Virginia place names. Morgantown, WV. 51 pp. Foreword by Paul Krakowski.

**6.642 Whaley, Storm.** 1951. They call it: a guide to the pronunciation of Arkansas place names. Siloam Spring, AR: Associated Press (Radio Station KUOA). 48 pp.

**6.643 What's in a name, being a continuation of the origin of various place names in counties of North Carolina.** 1944. State Magazine 11.3.

**6.644 What's in a place name? History--legend--pride.** 1978. Cumberland 2.4.41-43. [TN]. Short accounts of history and naming of Cheap Hill, Wartrace, Bell Buckle, Eighty Eight, Bon Aqua, and other names.

**6.645 Whitbeck, R. H.** 1911. Regional peculiarities in place names. Bulletin of the American Geographical Society 43.273-81. Includes VA and mountain areas of TN and KY.

**6.646 Whitbread, L. G.** 1968. Louisiana place names. Louisiana Studies 7.228-51. A plea for systematic study in LA.

**6.647 Whitbread, L. G.** 1975. Place names of Jefferson Parish, Louisiana, an introductory account. Gretna, LA: La Pelican Press. Unpaged.

**6.648 Whitbread, Leslie George.** 1977. Placenames of Jefferson Parish, Louisiana: an introductory essay. Metairie, LA: Jefferson Parish Historical Commission. [SE LA].

**6.649 Who named the Ozarks and when?** 1938. Missouri Historical Review 32.523-33. Argues that explorer Stephen Long is source of name around 1820.

**6.650 Wilburn, Hiram C.** 1952. Judaculla place names and the Judaculla tales. Southern Indian Studies 4.23. [NC]. Deals with geographical location and meaning of names derived from stories about the giant mythological creature Judaculla.

**6.651 Wildes, Jeffrey.** 1981. Names along Black River (with map). NSC 28.16-19. [SE SC]. Rivers and creeks of Black River in Williamsburg County.

**6.652 Wilkinson, Herbert James.** 1938. The Florida place name "Jupiter." AS 13.233-34.

**6.653 Williams, Coral.** 1930. Names of places in White County. Legends and stories of White County, Tennessee. [16 pages]. Nashville: George Peabody College thesis.

**6.654 Williams, David A.** 1963. Manassas gap. Virginia Place Name Society Occasional Papers 8. Charlottesville: University of Virginia. 7 pp.

**6.655 Williams, Horace G.** 1963. Anderson County place names. Part 1, NSC 10.5-20. Part 2, NSC 11.54-63 (1964). [NW SC].

**6.656 Williams, Samuel C.** 1932. The first territorial division named for Washington. Tennessee Historical Magazine n.s. 2.153-64. Asserts priority of Washington County, NC (now in TN) as first locality in U.S. to bear Washington's name.

**6.657 Wilson, E. W.** 1943. Names in the mountains. [NC] State Magazine 10.4.

**6.658 Wilson, Gordon.** 1968. Place names in the Mammoth Cave region. KFR 14.8-13. [W KY]. **Reprinted** in Lawrence Thompson, ed. 1968. Folklore of the Mammoth Cave Region, 27-31. Bowling Green: Kentucky Folklore Society.

**6.659 Wilson, Jerome.** 1972. Landings on the Savannah in Allendale County. NSC 19.54-55. [S SC].

**6.660 Wilson, T. E.** 1956. Names in Darlington County. NSC 3.8-9. [E SC].

**6.661 Wilstach, Paul.** 1938. Potomac landings. New York: Tudor. Pp. 25-27, origin of river name; pp. 73-75, origin of names of inlets and adjacent locations.

**6.662 Witty, Elizabeth.** 1970. Legends of two Mississippi place names. MFR 4.105-07.

**6.663 Woods, William S.** 1951. L'abbé Prévost and the gender of New Orleans. MLN 66.259-61. Reply by Leo Spitzer, MLN 66.571-72, (Dec. 1951). Discusses gender of name New Orleans in French.

**6.664 Work Projects Administration.** 1941. Palmetto place names. Columbia: South Carolina Education Association. **Reprinted** in 1975 by the Reprint Co., Spartanburg, SC. 158 pp. Names and their etymologies divided into three lists--Counties, Towns and Cities, and Islands and Streams.

**6.665 Wright, Esther Clark.** 1957. The naming of Monkton Mills. Maryland Historical Magazine 52.148-50. Named after township in Nova Scotia.

**6.666 Wright, Muriel H.** 1928. The naming of the Mississippi River. Chronicles of Oklahoma 6.529-31.

**6.667 Writings on Tennessee counties.** 1971. Nashville: Tennessee State Library and Archives.

**6.668 Wyllie, John C.** 1962. Meadow Branch, the stream east of Monticello, lately called Tufton Branch, with some notes on the nearby surface waters. Virginia Place Name Society Occasional Papers 7. Charlottesville: University of Virginia. 7 pp. Advocates return to earlier name of stream in Albemarle Co.

**6.669 Wyllie, John C.** 1963. Totier Creek, a first-families-of-Albemarle place name. Virginia Place Name Society Occasional Paper 9. Charlottesville: University of Virginia. 10 pp. [CENT VA]. Documents early use of name and says it derives from name of Siouan tribe, the Toteros (Tutelos).

**6.670 Yount, W. H.** 1926. Origin of the name Ozark mountains. Missouri Historical Magazine 20.587-88. Asserts name derives from French term "Azoic Arc Monts."

## See Also

1.84 Boswell; 1.87 Boswell; 1.117 Byron; 1.122 Carey; 1.202 Doran; 1.271 Goodner; 1.298 Hannum; 1.342 Jackson; 1.499 Masterson; 1.508 Mencken; 1.551 Parris; 1.702 Smith; 1.756 Thompson; 1.830 Wilson; 2.102 Dale; 2.135 Eubanks; 2.154 Gerard; 2.286 McMullen; 2.443 Vass; 2.469 Williams; 3.193 Green; 3.313 McJimsey; 3.315 McMullen; 3.452 Steele; 3.520 Wilson; 4.55 Baird; 4.136 Goff; 4.245 McDavid; 12.8 Dunbar; 12.12 Harrington; 12.23 Rajec; 12.24 Randolph; 12.29 Sealock.

# 7 Personal and Miscellaneous Name Studies

7.1 **Aimar, Caroline Picault.** 1959. Saint Domingan names in Charleston. NSC 6.8-10. Pronunciation of names of descendants of refugees from Saint Domingue (Haiti) who came in 1790s.

7.2 **Algeo, John.** 1978. From classic to classy: changing fashions in street names. Names 26.80-95. Contrasts early 19th-century commemorative names with decorative, artificial, and slick names of post-1960 in Athens, GA. **Reprinted** in K. Harder, ed. 1986. Names and their varieties: a collection of essays in onomastics, 230-45. Lanham, MD: University Press of America.

7.3 **Algeo, John, and Adele Algeo.** 1983. Bible Belt onomastics revisited. Names 31.103-16. Changes in Southern naming practices since Pyles study of 1959 (**7.163**).

7.4 **Ames, Karl.** 1981. Austin and Travis county forebears: glimpses of our past in the census of 1860. The scope of names, ed. by Fred Tarpley, 161-68. Commerce, TX: Names Institute Press. [TX]. Ranks surnames according to frequency.

7.5 **Arthur, Stanley Clisby.** 1917. Bird names in Terms from Louisiana. DN 4.422-31. Compiler's name was incorrectly printed as Archer in the byline; nearly 300 common local names.

7.6 **Arthur, Stanley Clisby.** 1917. Animal names in Terms from Louisiana. DN 4.431. Compiler's name was incorrectly printed as Archer in the byline; eleven local names.

7.7 **Bailey, J. D.** 1927. History of Grindal Shoals and some early adjacent families. Gaffney, SC: Ledger. Reprinted 1981. Greenville, SC: A. Press. [NW SC]. Pp. 10-12, origin of names Grindal and Pacolet.

**7.8 Baird, Scott.** 1985. English dialects in San Antonio. Names 33.232-42. Fine-meshed study of pronunciation of street names revealing three dialects of English in San Antonio, TX.

**7.9 Barker, Howard F.** 1939. The family names of American Negroes. AS 14.163-74. Discusses social factors in adoption of surnames by ex-slaves and speculates on reasons for inconsistent proportions of many names between white and black populations in the South.

**7.10 Beckham, Charles W.** 1885. List of birds of Nelson County. Frankfurt: Kentucky Geological Survey, ser. 2, vol. 6, part 3. 58 pp. Scientific and common names for 171 birds.

**7.11 Bedichek, Roy.** 1953. Folklore in natural history. Folk travelers: ballads, tales, and talk, ed. by Mody Boatright, et al. 18-39. Austin: Texas Folklore Society. Pp. 22-23, notes on animal names.

**7.12 Beers, H. Dwight.** 1977. African names and naming practices. Library of Congress Information Bulletin 76.206-07.

**7.13 Bergen, Fanny D.** 1892-98. Popular American plant-names. JAF 5.89-106; 6.135-42; 7.89-104; 9.179-93; 10.49-54,143-48; 11.221-30,273-83. Scattered citations from the South.

**7.14 Berry, Brewton.** 1945. The mestizos of South Carolina. American Journal of Sociology 51.34-41. Discusses origin of names, attitudes toward, and social plight of mixed-race groups like the Brass Ankles, Red Bones, and Turks.

**7.15 Bolton, Henry Carrington.** 1891. The pronunciation of folk names in South Carolina. JAF 4.270-72. Modifications of English, German, and French surnames.

**7.16 Booker, Louise.** 1976. Why North Carolinians are called Tarheels. The New East 17.

**7.17 Boone, Lalia Phipps.** 1955. Folk names for blooming plants. SFQ 19.230-36. Collection made in Gainesville, FL.

**7.18 Boswell, George W., and Thomas M. Pullen.** 1976. Mississippi folk names of plants. KFR 22.3.64-69. List of 103 folk names for flowering plants, with their common name and scientific name equivalents, collected by the WPA and University of Mississippi students and grouped into fifteen classes according to their imagery.

**7.19 Bouton, E. H.** 1919. A competition in street naming. Landscape Architecture 9.125-28. Contest for naming streets in Sparrows Point, MD.

**7.20 Boyet, Aggie.** 1973. What siblings call each other. Love and wrestling, butch and o.k., ed. by Fred Tarpley, 21-27. Commerce, TX: South Central Names Institute. Finds brothers have and use more nicknames than sisters do.

**7.21 Brewer, John Mason**, ed. 1968. American Negro folklore. Chicago: Quadrangle. Names, 355-58. Unusual given names.

**7.22 Bull, Elias B.** 1972. Names of houses on Folly Beach. NSC 19.25-28. [E SC].

**7.23 Bull, Elias B.** 1973. Transient yachts at Charleston Municipal Marina. NSC 20.30-34.

**7.24 Bull, Gertrude C.** 1970. Georgetown street names, 1734-1970. NSC 17.15-21. [E SC].

**7.25 Buych, Mark W., Jr.** 1977. House names along Florence's Cherokee Road. NSC 24.26-27. [E SC].

**7.26 Byrd, James W.** 1978. Dracula! What kind of name is that for a niggah? Ethnic names, ed. by Fred Tarpley, 19-26. Commerce, TX: Names Institute Press. Anecdotal survey of given names of blacks, drawing from J. Mason Brewer and other sources; says black American "has always been less disposed to remain conventional, traditional, and unimaginative in his choice of names and, especially nicknames" but that contemporary names are difficult to distinguish by race.

**7.27 Casey, Joseph J.** 1933. Personal names in Hening's statutes at large of Virginia and Shepard's continuation. Bridgewater, VA: Green Bookman.

**7.28 Chappell, Naomi C.** 1929. Negro names. AS 4.272-75. Anecdotal discussion of given names: supplemented by Myron item (**7.138**).

**7.29 Chase, John Churchhill.** 1949. Frenchmen, Desire, Good Children, and other streets of New Orleans, in words and pictures. New Orleans, LA: Crager. 246 pp. History of the city as revealed in its street names.

**7.30 Cohen, Hennig.** 1952. Slave names in colonial South Carolina. AS 27.102-07. Cites South Carolina Gazette, colonial newspaper in Charleston, as source for early citations of Americanisms, including Gullah terms, and for naming patterns. Says newspaper reveals "tacit recognition by white owners of a dual naming system among Negro slaves in the eighteenth century," a system of African and English names described later by Turner. See Williams (**7.209**) for supplement.

**7.31 Cohen, Hennig.** 1953. On the word Georgian. GHQ 37.347-48. 1735 citation of adjective Georgian.

**7.32 Combs, Josiah H.** 1976. Combs: a study in comparative philology and genealogy. Pensacola, FL: privately printed. Traces naming patterns in Combs family since 18th century.

**7.33 Coppock, Paul R.** 1957. History in Memphis street names. WTHSP 11.93-111. [W TN].

**7.34 Coulthard, A. R.** 1984. Flannery O'Connor's names. Southern Humanities Review 18.97-105. Discusses how O'Connor uses names with religious significance, triple names for women, last names as given names, and "un-Southern" names for irony.

**7.35 Craig, James C.** 1954. Origins of street names. Jacksonville Historical Society Papers 3.7-11. [NE FL].

**7.36 Currer-Briggs, Noel.** 1970. Similarity of surnames in York County, Virginia, and County Norfolk, England. Virginia Magazine of History and Biography 78.[442]-46.

**7.37 Darden, Donna Kelleher.** 1969. A study in Louisiana French onomastics. Baton Rouge: Louisiana State University thesis. [Breaux Bridge, S LA]. Finds correlation between adoption of English infant naming patterns, based on baptismal records from 1877 to 1960, and shift from English to French language use; finds different tendencies in shifts away from French in assigning first and middle names.

**7.38 Dark, Harry, and Phyl Dark.** 1979. The greatest Ozarks guidebook. Springfield, MO: Greatest Graphics. Pp. 11-18, debates Ozarker vs. Ozarkian as best designation for resident of the region.

**7.39 Dean, Florine.** 1971. Names viewed through the racial looking glass. Of Edsels and marauders, ed. by Fred Tarpley and Ann Moseley, 40-42. Publication 1, South Central Names Institute. Commerce, TX: Names Institute Press. Reports on TX survey collected 590 terms for black Americans and classifies terms into seventeen groups.

**7.40 Dean, Florine.** 1973. Little Hope and New Hope: names of Southern Baptist churches. Love and wrestling, butch and o.k., ed. by Fred Tarpley, 101-05. Commerce, TX: South Central Names Institute. Analyzes names of 180 Baptist churches in NE TX and classifies them according to their origin.

**7.41 Dean, Florine.** 1981. Autumn leaves: names for homes for the elderly in five Texas cities. The scope of names, ed. by Fred Tarpley, 107-16. Commerce, TX: Names Institute Press. Identifies main elements and patterns of 117 names for nursing homes in state.

**7.42 Dean, Patricia E.** 1981. Names in Larry McMurtry's Thalia trilogy. Papers of the north central names institute, 1981: the dangerous, secret name of god; fartley's compressed gas company; the "barf 'n' choke" and other matters onomastic, ed. by Laurence E. Seits, 71-76. Sugar Grove, IL: Waubonsee Community College.

**7.43 Deiler, J. Hanno.** 1909. Settlement of the German coast of Louisiana. German American Annals, n.s. 8.192. Changes of family names from German to Spanish.

**7.44 Dignowity, Hartman.** 1927. Nicknames in Texas oil fields. Texas and southwestern lore, ed. by J. Frank Dobie, 98-101. Texas Folklore Society Publication 6. Dallas: Southern Methodist University Press. Nicknames of pipe liners and other classes of oil men in NE TX.

**7.45 Dillard, J. L.** 1968. On the grammar of Afro-American naming practices. Names 16.230-37. Nontraditional naming of store-front churches in Washington, DC, area. **Reprinted** in K. Harder, ed. 1986. Names and their varieties: a collection of essays in onomastics, 310-17. Lanham, MD: University Press of America.

**7.46 Dillard, Joe [L].** 1970. Names or slogans: some problems from the Cameroun, the Caribbean, Burundi, and the United States. Caribbean Studies 9.4.104-10. Addresses theoretical question of making distinctions between slogans and types of names, using examples from Africa, Caribbean, and Southern U.S., drawing on work of Ambrose Gonzales, William Stewart, and others.

**7.47 Dillard, J. L.** 1976. Black names. Mouton: The Hague. 114 pp. **Reviews:** K. B. Harder. 1980. MFR 14.41-45; W. K. McNeil. 1978. JAF 91.727; R. Price. 1980. Ethnohistory 27.99-101.

**7.48 Donald, Henderson Hamilton.** 1952. The Negro freedman. New York: Schuman. Pp. 149-51, comments on naming of freed slaves.

**7.49 Duncan, Alderman.** 1972. Sobriquets of famous South Carolinians. NSC 19.21-23.

**7.50 Dunlap, A. R., and C. A. Weslager.** 1947. Trends in the naming of tri-racial mixed-blood groups in the Eastern United States. AS 22.81-87. No formal proper name for tri-racial groups has emerged; informal, often metaphorical, names have been applied by dominant white society; includes glossary of forty names.

**7.51 Dunlap, Fayette.** 1913. A tragedy of surnames. DN 4.7-8. On Americanization of family names of early settlers from PA in Boyle Co., KY.

**7.52 Eastman, Jean.** 1972. Colloquial names of South Carolina plants. NSC 19.28-32.

**7.53 Eby, Cecil D., Jr.** 1961. Classical names among Southern Negro slaves. AS 36.140-41. Suggests that practice of 18th-century English gentlemen of giving classical names to their hunting dogs was transferred to black slaves, thus accounting for large numbers of slaves with Roman names.

**7.54 Eisiminger, Sterling.** 1979. South Carolina nicknames. NSC 26.22-24. Nicknames for the state and for its residents, including sandlapper and clayeater (cf. Bradley **3.49**).

**7.55 Emerson, O. B., and John P. Hermann.** 1986. William Faulkner and the Faulkner family name. Names 34.255-65. History and proposed explanation of change in spelling from Falkner to Faulkner.

**7.56 Evans, William W.** 1982. Naming day in old New Orleans: charactonyms and colloquialisms in George Washington Cable's The Grandissimes and Old Creole Days. Names 30.183-91. Says Cable's personal naming patterns give subtle insights into the relationship between the races.

**7.57 Fairclough, G. Thomas.** 1960. "New light" on "Old Zion": names of white and Negro Baptist churches in New Orleans. Names 8.76-86. Finds "white congregations take their names primarily from 'this present world,' and particularly from their own immediate neighborhoods," while black church names usually have a religious, often a Biblical, element in them. **Reprinted** in K. Harder, ed. 1986. Names and their varieties: a collection of essays in onomastics, 89-99. Lanham, MD: University Press of America.

**7.58 Fawcett, Bill.** 1976. How slaves were named. KFR 22.100. Anecdotes on naming two slaves "Bottoms" because they worked at stripping bottom leaves from tobacco plants.

**7.59 Fitzsimons, Mabel Trott.** 1958-59. Colorful and curious names on eighteenth-century Charleston street signs. NSC 5.14-18; 6.12-14.

**7.60 France, Isabel.** 1958. Folklore survivals of plant names in Arkansas hills. Ozarks Mountaineer 6.4. Names of mullein.

**7.61 Gandee, Lee R.** 1978. Names of state-owned holdings and buildings in Richland County. NSC 25.17-20; 26.39-41. [CENT SC].

**7.62 Gaskins, Avery F.** 1970. The epithet "Guinea" in central West Virginia. Philological Papers 17.41-44. Presents accounts of origin of term as it has become applied to isolated triracial group in Barbour and Taylor Counties, WV.

**7.63 Genovese, Eugene D.** 1974. The naming of cats. Roll, Jordan, roll, 443-50. New York: Pantheon. Essay by historian on personal naming patterns in antebellum slave society.

**7.64 Gilpin, George H.** 1970. Street names in San Antonio: Signposts to history. Names 18.191-200. [TX].

**7.65 Gordon, Douglas H.** 1948. Hero worship as expressed in Baltimore street names. Maryland Historical Magazine 43.121-26.

**7.66 Greear, Yvonne E.** 1973. At the corner of Pecan and Congress: street names of Austin, Texas. Love and wrestling, butch and o.k., ed. by Fred Tarpley, 95-100. Commerce, TX: South Central Names Institute. Explains how city was laid out in 1839 and how original naming patterns of city streets patterned.

**7.67 Greear, Yvonne E.** 1977. The name of the game: street names. Labeled for life, ed. by Fred Tarpley, 29-33. Publication 5, South Central Names Institute. Commerce, TX: Names Institute Press. Street names in Abilene, TX.

**7.68 Green, Lola Beth.** 1974. Names in the Bible Belt: a study from Faulkner's Go Down Moses. They had to call it something, ed. by Fred Tarpley, 117-20. Commerce, TX: Names Institute Press. Argues that characters in the novel were shaped by their given names.

**7.69 Grise, George C.** 1959. Patterns of child naming in Tennessee during the depression years. SFQ 23.150-54. Sources of given names of 700 white freshmen at Austin Peay College in Clarksville, TN.

**7.70 Grubbs, Sam.** 1969. The opposite of white: a glossary of reference names for Negroes. Commerce: East Texas State University thesis. [4 towns, NE TX]. Glossary of 500 first names for blacks.

**7.71 Grubbs, Sam.** 1971. The opposite of white: names for black Americans. Of Edsels and marauders, ed. by Fred Tarpley and Ann Moseley, 25-32. Commerce, TX: Names Institute Press. Discusses evolution of terms to refer to members of the black race.

**7.72 Gutman, Herbert.** 1976. The black family in slavery and freedom, 1750-1925. Aunts and uncles and swap-dog kin, 185-229, discusses development of given name patterns in black community; Somebody knew my name, 230-56, discusses development of surname patterns in black community.

**7.73 Hagner, Alexander Burton.** 1904. Street nomenclature of Washington City. Columbia Historical Society Records 7.237-61. Suggests names and methods for naming streets in federal capital to replace current system of designating streets by letters.

**7.74 Harris, Maverick.** 1973. Psychological implications of Austin [TX] apartment names. Love and wrestling, butch and o.k., ed. by Fred Tarpley,

33-45. Commerce, TX: Names Institute Press. Finds widespread use of botanical and foreign names.

**7.75 Hartley, Dan Manville.** 1970. Streets of Barnwell. NSC 17.45-49. [SW SC].

**7.76 Hearn, Lafcadio.** 1925. The curious nomenclature of New Orleans streets. Occidental gleanings, sketches and essays now first collected by Albert Mordell, vol. 1.263-75. New York: Dodd, Mead, and Co.

**7.77 Heller, Murray.** 1974. Black names in America: history and meaning. 2 vols. Ohio State University dissertation. Abstract in DAI 38.3446A. Dictionary of African origins, 374-470. Published in 1975 by G. K. Hall. 561 pp. Surveys 340,000 names of black Americans from 1619 to 1940s, classifies them by source, and lists them "to reveal patterns of name usage and to suggest possible areas of future investigation on the basis of these patterns"; organizes material in seven chronological periods; based primarily on material collected by Newbell Niles Puckett. **Reviews:** B. H. Granger. 1976. Names 24.61; K. B. Harder. 1975. TFSB 41.192.

**7.78 Hensley, Lee R.** 1981. Bars, taverns, and cocktail lounges: current names for public drinking establishments in Texas cities. The scope of names, ed. by Fred Tarpley, 117-44. Commerce, TX: Names Institute Press. Explores extent to which name of a drinking establishment gives "an indication of what goes on beyond those swinging doors" in ten largest TX cities.

**7.79 Herskovits, Melville J.** 1941. The myth of the Negro past. Boston: Beacon Press. Pp. 190-94, naming practices.

**7.80 Hewell, Marion M.** 1970. Nineteenth-century academies and seminaries. NSC 17.39-44.

**7.81 Holmes, Urban T.** 1930. A study in Negro onomastics. AS 5.463-67. Classified list of given names from Rockingham Co., NC.

**7.82 Howell, Elmo.** 1973. Eudora Welty and the poetry of names: a note on <u>Delta Wedding</u>. Love and wrestling, butch and o.k., ed. by Fred Tarpley, 73-78. Commerce, TX: South Central Names Institute. Examines names of characters in the novel.

**7.83 Hudson, Arthur Palmer.** 1938. Some curious Negro names. SFQ 2.179-93. Given names classified by type and source.

**7.84 Idol, John L., Jr.** 1979. Street names in Clemson: a representative list. NSC 26.27-28. [NW SC].

**7.85 Idol, John, Glenn Marsch, Steve Simmons, and Valerie Speegle.** 1980. Street names in Pendleton. NSC 27.26-27. [NW SC].

**7.86 Inscoe, John C.** 1983. Carolina slave names: an index to acculturation. JSH 49.527-54. Sources of names of slaves and changes after emancipation.

**7.87 Jackson, Bruce.** 1967. Prison nicknames. Western Folklore 26.48-54. On nicknames in AR, LA, MS, and TX prisons.

**7.88 Jeffreys, M. D. W.** 1948. Names of American Negro slaves. AA 50.571-73. Notes similarities between naming patterns of the Ibo, Fanti, and Efik and American black slaves; discusses ways these names have been disguised in the U.S.

**7.89 Johnson, E. D.** 1955. Family names in French Louisiana. Names 3.165-68. Americanization of French surnames.

**7.90 Johnson, E. D.** 1956. First names in French Louisiana. Names 4.49-53. Says fashion in 19th century was to give children names from Greek and Roman mythology, in 20th century to give English names.

**7.91 Jones, James P.** 1962. Southern newspaper names. Names 10.115-26.

**7.92 Jones, W. M.** 1958. Name and symbol in the prose of Eudora Welty. SFQ 22.173-85. Welty's use of symbols from myth and folklore.

**7.93 Jottings.** 1944. AS 19.151. Note from a 1943 Saturday Evening Post article by Jeanne Douglas and Liz Wharton about J. Frank Dobie and term "Texian."

**7.94 Kimbrough, Marvin G.** 1981. Wanted: a foreign language consultant for street namers. The scope of names, ed. by Fred Tarpley, 43-48. Commerce, TX: Names Institute Press. Classifies and illustrates the grammatical formation of Spanish-derived streetnames in Austin, TX.

**7.95 King, G. Wayne.** 1982. Streets of Florence. NSC 29.27-31. [E SC].

**7.96 Kinnier, C. L.** 1959. The renaming of Arlington streets. Arlington Historical Magazine 1.41-51. [NE VA]. Describes work of Arlington's Street Names Committee, appointed in 1932, and system worked out for relieving confusion in street and highway names in Arlington County.

**7.97 Kolin, Philip C.** 1977. Jefferson Davis: from president to place-name. Names 25.158-73. Davis' name has been applied to schools, highways, organizations, and numerous other items.

**7.98 Kolin, Philip C.** 1989. Personal names in the South. Encyclopedia of Southern Culture, ed. by William Ferris and Charles Wilson. Chapel Hill:

University of North Carolina Press. Discusses patterns of given naming prevalent in South--commemorative names after military heroes and classical and Biblical characters, folksy and metaphorical nicknames, initials, and double names for males and females.

**7.99 Krumpelmann, John T.** 1951. The renaming of Berlin Street and Berlin Streets. AS 26.156-57. [New Orleans, LA].

**7.100 Kuethe, J. Louis.** 1936. A list of Maryland mills, taverns, forges and furnaces in 1795. Maryland Historical Magazine 31.155-69.

**7.101 Lewis, Margaret Jane.** 1970. Some nicknames and their derivations. MFR 4.52-57.

**7.102 Linton, Albert C.** 1944. New Orleans street names record history. Illinois Central Magazine 32.5-6.

**7.103 Lipscomb, Terry W.** 1973. South Carolina Revolutionary battles. Part I, NSC 20.18-23; Part II, 21.23-27 (1974); Part III, 22.33-39 (1975); Part IV, 23.30-33 (1976); Part V, 24.13-18 (1977); Part VI, 25.26-33 (1978); Part VII, 26.31-38 (1979); Part VIII, 27.16-19 (1980); Part IX, 28.33-41 (1981).

**7.104 Lomax, Ruby T.** 1943. Negro nicknames. Backwoods to border, ed. by Mody C. Boatright and Donald Day, 163-71. Texas Folklore Society Publication no. 18. Dallas: Southern Methodist University Press. Unusual patterns of given names among black males, based on research among convict population in TX.

**7.105 Lowry, Lillian.** 1953. Christian names in western Kentucky. Midwest Folklore 3.131-36.

**7.106 Lynchburg, Va. Ordinances, etc.** 1958. Ordinance naming and describing streets of the city of Lynchburg, Va., amended to Aug. 26, 1958. 66 pp.

**7.107 McAtee, W. L.** 1923. Local names of migratory game birds. Washington: U.S. Dept. of Agriculture. Miscellaneous circular no. 13. National list; includes South.

**7.108 McAtee, W. L.** 1951. Some folk and scientific names for plants. PADS 15.3-25. Includes names from GA, KY, LA, MS, NC, SC, TN, TX, and VA.

**7.109 McAtee, W. L.** 1957. Folk names of birds in Kentucky. Kentucky Warbler 33.27-37. Lists common, folk, and scientific names for birds in state.

7.110 McDavid, Raven I., Jr. 1949. Berlin Street in New Orleans. AS 24.238. On change of name to General Pershing Street.

7.111 McDavid, Raven I., Jr. and Samuel R. Levin. 1964. The Levys of New Orleans: an old myth and a new problem. Names 12.82-88. On New Orleans surnames.

7.112 McDavid, Raven I., Jr., and Virginia McDavid. 1973. Cracker and hoosier. Names 21.161-67. Relationship and geographical spread of two nicknames.

7.113 McDavid, Raven I., Jr. and Sarah Ann Witham. 1974. Poor whites and rustics. Names 22.93-103. Names used for lower-class whites recorded in LANE and LAMSAS. Reprinted in R. McDavid 1980(1.456).337-52.

7.114 McDermott, John Francis. 1934. French surnames in the Mississippi Valley. AS 9.28-30. Includes notes on early LA names.

7.115 McIlwaine, Shields. 1939. Introduction. The Southern poor-white from lumberland to tobacco, xiii-xxv. Norman: University of Oklahoma Press. Discusses Cohee, Tuckahoe, Cracker, buckra, and other designations for poor whites.

7.116 McIver, Petrona R. 1972. Names of streets in Mount Pleasant. NSC 19.35-37. [SE SC].

7.117 McWhiney, Grady, and Forrest McDonald. 1983. Celtic names in the antebellum southern United States. Names 31.89-102. Argues tendency "was for Celts in the north to become anglicized and for Englishmen in the south to become celticized."

7.118 Martin, Daniel S. 1951. A guide to street naming and property numbering. Nashville: Tennessee State Planning Commission. 47 pp.

7.119 Mayrant, Drayton. 1955. Early Charleston street names. NSC 2.6-7. [SE SC].

7.120 Medford, W. Clark. 1969. Finis and farewell, 4-10. Waynesville, NC: privately printed. [Haywood Co., NC]. Analyzes early and most common surnames in county.

7.121 Meeks, Elizabeth. 1981. Reflections of the milieu in names of William Faulkner's characters. Southern Studies 20.91-96.

7.122 Mencken, Henry Louis. 1940. Some southern given-names. Saturday Review of Literature 22.21.11 (Sept. 14). Notes penchants of Southerners for double names and deriving female names from male ones; also notes that a preponderance of members of Congress with nicknames are Southern.

**7.123 Meyer, Robert, Jr.** 1975. Names over New Orleans public schools. New Orleans, LA: Namesake Press. More than 100 names in compendium; mostly a biographical dictionary of individuals after whom schools were named. **Reviews:** K. B. Harder. 1975. TFSB 41.135-36; K. B. Harder. 1975. Names 23.304.

**7.124 Meyer, Robert, Jr.** 1977. Names over New Orleans public schools. Labeled for life, ed. by Fred Tarpley, 35-40. Commerce: Names Institute Press. Stories about how schools were given names of prominent social and political figures.

**7.125 Meyer, Robert, Jr.** 1981. Names over Texas airports. The scope of names, ed. by Fred Tarpley, 145-52. Commerce, TX: Names Institute Press. Name patterns of commercial and military airports.

**7.126 Miler, Joyce C.** 1972. House names around the world. Detroit: Gale. 135 pp. **Review:** Kelsie B. Harder. 1975. TFSB 41.39.

**7.127 Milling, Chapman J.** 1975. Savannah and Shawnee: same people. NSC 22.26-27. Replies to Pearson (**7.153**) and says same Indian tribe was variably referred to as Savannah and Shawnee.

**7.128 Mockler, William E.** 1955. The source of "Ku Klux." Names 3.14-18. Names derives from Kyklos Adelphon, antebellum secret society at Southern colleges, dissolved in 1855.

**7.129 Mockler, William Emmett Morgan.** 1955. The surnames of trans-Allegheny Virginia: 1750-1800. Columbus: Ohio State University dissertation. Abstract in DAI 16.960A. Investigates etymology and phonology of surnames of early WV north of the Kanawha, based on official public records, and includes dictionary. Reprinted in 1973 as West Virginia Surnames: the Pioneers. Parsons, WV: West Virginia Dialect Society. 197 pp. **Reviews:** Raven I. McDavid, Jr. 1974. AS 49.149-51; Elsdon C. Smith. 1975. Names 23.53.

**7.130 Mockler, William E.** 1956. Surnames of Trans-Allegheny Virginia, 1750-1800. Part I, Names 4.1-17. Part II, Names 4.96-118 (1957). Based on preceding item.

**7.131 Moffatt, James S., Jr.** 1962. Names of Associate Reformed Presbyterian churches in South Carolina. NSC 9.6-11.

**7.132 Moore, J. Brewer and Bruce S. Trant.** 1962. Street renaming is no cinch, but it solves a lot of problems, as the colorful experience of Portsmouth, VA, demonstrates. American City 77.82-84.

**7.133 Morrall, John F., and Thomas M. Stubbs.** 1969. The original streets of Beaufort town: Part I, NSC 16.43-45. [SE SC].

**7.134 Morrall, John F., and Thomas M. Stubbs.** 1970. The original streets of Beaufort town: Beaufort expands: Part II, 17.50-53. [SE SC].

**7.135 Moseley, Ann.** 1971. The opposite of black: names for white Americans. Of Edsels and marauders, ed. by Fred Tarpley and Ann Moseley, 33-39. Commerce, TX: Names Institute Press. Survey of usage and evaluation of terms for white people by black students at East Texas State University.

**7.136 Moses, Herbert A.** 1967. Some street names in Sumter. NSC 14.42-44. [CENT SC].

**7.137 Mufwene, Salikoko.** 1985. The linguistic significance of African proper names in Gullah. New West Indian Guide 59.149-66. Compares pronunciations of Turner's African proper names in Gullah with their proposed possible African etyma and concludes on basis of phonetic evidence they provide limited evidence supporting Turner's African substrate hypothesis.

**7.138 Myron, H. B. Jr.** 1929. Another Negro name. AS 5.177-78. [Atlanta, GA]. Notes Cumsy from "Come-see-the-world-and-go" for name of infant. Supplement to article on black given names by Naomi C. Chappell 7.28.

**7.139 Nall, Kline A.** 1973. Love and wrestling, butch and o.k. Love and wrestling, butch and o.k., ed. by Fred Tarpley, 1-6. Commerce, TX: South Central Names Institute. Compares Puritan names with those of Lubbock, TX, residents.

**7.140 Negro names.** 1927. American Mercury 33.303-04. List of unusual names from NC reported in the American Medical Association Journal.

**7.141 Neuffer, Claude Henry.** 1965. The Bottle Alley song. SFQ 29.234-38. Origin of name of alley in Charleston, SC, with material about song in which it is featured.

**7.142 Neuffer, Claude H.** 1965. Alleys, lanes, and courts of Charleston. NSC 12.18-21. [SE SC].

**7.143 Neuffer, Claude Henry.** 1975. Four-year colleges. NSC 22.29-33. [SC].

**7.144 Neuffer, Claude Henry.** 1976. A sampling of festivals. NSC 23.28-30.

**7.145 Norman, Walter H.** 1979. Nicknames and conch tales. Tavernier, FL: W. H. Norman. Nicknames, 95-117, list of approximately 900 nicknames, with full names of individuals to whom they apply.

**7.146 Old slave names.** 1890. Atlantic 66.428. Disagrees with earlier anonymous writer (Atlantic 65.430-31, Mar. 1890) that fanciful names are given to white children but says unusual names have been especially common among black children.

**7.147 Oliphant, Mary Chevillotte Simms.** 1940. Some French names in Charleston District, South Carolina. Chapel Hill: University of North Carolina thesis. [SC]. Compiles list of 300 French surnames from 18th-century Charleston, discusses their etymologies and compares them to continental names, and says in 20th century they have "been Anglicized beyond recognition" in pronunciation but have with very few exceptions kept original spellings.

**7.148 Osborn, John.** 1976. White house watch: glimpses of Jimmy. New Republic 175.12.9. Note on Jimmy Carter's preference of names for himself.

**7.149 Otto, John Solomon.** 1987. Cracker: the history of a Southeastern ethnic, economic, and racial epithet. Names 35.28-39. Discusses roots of term among Scotch-Irish settlers of the Piedmont South and accounts for how it has become strongly associated with white rustics in GA and FL.

**7.150 P., C. D.** 1944. "Abused Spanish" place names in Texas. AS 19.238. Street names in Bunavista, TX.

**7.151 Pate, Frances Willard.** 1969. Names of characters in Faulkner's Mississippi. Atlanta: Emory University dissertation. Abstract in DAI 30.2036-37A. 326 pp. Study of naming as an art and as a literary device; includes alphabetical list of all names in Faulkner's Mississippi works; says the novelist successfully chose names that are descriptive and provide a sense of culture.

**7.152 Paustian, P. Robert.** 1978. The evolution of personal naming practices among American blacks. Names 26.177-91. Principal historical tendencies.

**7.153 Pearson, Bruce L.** 1974. Savannah and Shawnee: same or different? NSC 21.19-22. Says that two names are not etymologically related, contrary to wide belief, that name of city is derived from Spanish borrowing and not from name of Indian tribe.

**7.154 Pearson, Bruce L.** 1976. Savannah and Shawnee: same people, different names. NSC 23.20-22. Answers Milling (7.127) objection by clarifying original point that two names are etymologically unrelated, even though same Indians were often called both names.

**7.155 Pearson, Bruce L.** 1987. Savannah and Shawnee: the end of a mini-controversy. IJAL 53.183-93. Cites historical and linguistic evidence for separate derivations for name of river and name of tribe.

**7.156 Pender, Virginia.** 1973. Six historic homes of Newberry. NSC 20.37-38. [CENT SC].

**7.157 Petrea, H. S.** 1970. Names of early Lutheran churches. NSC 17.33-35. 18th- and 19th-century churches in SC.

**7.158 Powell, William S.** 1977. When the past refused to die: a history of Caswell County, North Carolina, 1777-1977. Durham, NC: Moore. [N CENT NC]. Pp. 41-43, roster of surnames in early county history.

**7.159 Powell, William S.** 1982. What's in a name?: why we're all called tar heels. Tar Heel. Chapel Hill: University of North Carolina.

**7.160 Pruett, Jean.** 1979. Camden street names. NSC 26.10-15. [CENT SC].

**7.161 Puckett, Newbell Niles.** 1937. Names of American Negro slaves. Studies in the science of society presented to Albert Galloway Keller, ed. by G. P. Murdock, 471-94. New Haven, CT: Yale University Press. Surveys and discusses main trends in 12,000 slave names (including 5,600 from Lowndes Co., MS) from 17th through 19th centuries.

**7.162 Puckett, Newbell Niles.** 1938. American Negro names. JNH 23.35-48. Compares trends in given names of three groups--slaves from 17th to 19th century, free blacks in South before 1830, and 20th-century black college students.

**7.163 Pyles, Thomas.** 1959. Bible belt onomastics, or some curiosities of anti-pedobaptist nomenclature. Names 7.84-101. Tour, both scholarly and comic, through eccentricities and excesses of Southern namegiving; shows how Southerners fashion nicknames, who Southerners name children after, and how Southerners devise names that are unique, fashionable, and folksy. Excerpt in C. Laird and R. M. Gorrell. 1961. English as Language, 98-103. New York: Harcourt Brace Jovanovich. **Reprinted** in Bobbs-Merrill Reprint Series, Language-77; in John Algeo, ed. 1979. Thomas Pyles: Selected Essays on English Usage, 152-66. Gainesville: University Presses of Florida; in Kelsie Harder, ed. 1986. Names and their varieties: a collection of essays in onomastics, 73-88. Lanham, MD: University Press of America.

**7.164 Quarles, Garland R.** n.d. The streets of Winchester, Virginia: the origin and significance of their names. Winchester, VA: Farmers and Merchants National Bank. 47 pp.

**7.165 Quave, Mackie.** 1947. Elm in South Carolina. AS 22.76. Reports "Ellumwood" pronunciation of street name in Columbia.

**7.166 Rainey, Frank L.** 1938. Some folk names of plants. Bulletin of the Kentucky Folklore Society, pp. 7-13.

**7.167 Randolph, Vance.** 1954. The names of Ozark fiddle tunes. Midwest Folklore 4.81-86.

**7.168 Randolph, Vance, and Isabel Spradley.** 1933. Quilt names in the Ozarks. AS 8.1.33-36. Classifies and discusses more than 200 quilt names.

**7.169 Reed, Louis.** 1967. Family names. Warning in Appalachia: a study of Wirt County, West Virginia, 15-32. Morgantown: West Virginia University Library.

**7.170 Reid, Alice C.** 1941. Gee's Bend: a Negro community in transition. Nashville: Fisk University thesis. [AL]. Lists unusual folk names given to men and women. Excerpted in 7.21.

**7.171 Reid, Bessie M.** 1951. Vernacular names for Texas plants. PADS 15.26-50. Folk names and folklore associated with 208 plants.

**7.172 Rennick, R. M.** 1982. The alleged "Hogg Sisters," or simple ground rules for collectors of "odd" names. Names 30.193-97. Warns onomastic researchers that proliferation of apochryphal stories about unusual names such as those of TX sisters can easily mislead them.

**7.173 Roberts, Betty.** 1977. Who's who in a family. Labeled for life, ed. by Fred Tarpley, 59-62. Commerce, TX: Names Institute Press. [Garland, TX]. Surveys variation in terms high school students use to refer to relatives.

**7.174 Robinson, Lynn C.** 1977. Street names in Orangeburg. NSC 24.24-26. [CENT SC]. Study of patterns in naming homes.

**7.175 Rogers, P. Burwell.** 1956. Changes in Virginia names. AS 31.21-24. Changes in pronunciation of personal and place names.

**7.176 Rogers, P. Burwell.** 1959. Tidewater Virginians name their homes. AS 34.251-57. Principles, practices, and elements of house naming in the state of VA.

**7.177 Saxon, Lyle.** 1943. Fabulous New Orleans. New York: Appleton Century. Street name notes, 82-83; History in street names, 184-88.

**7.178 Schabel, Elizabeth Smith.** 1981. The historical significance of patchwork quilt names as a reflection of the emerging social consciousness of the American woman. TFSB 47.1-6.

**7.179 Schele de Vere, M.** 1887. A few Virginia names. MLN 7.97-103. Surveys surnames of state and assesses contributions by different linguistic and ethnic groups to state's name pool.

**7.180 Schuricht, Herman.** 1911. Anglicized and corrupted German names in Virginia. Pennsylvania-German 12.305-06.

**7.181 Siler, James H.** 1975. Surnames of possible French origin in early Appalachian Kentucky. Appalachian Notes 3.4.49-53.

**7.182 Simons, Katherine Drayton Mayrant.** 1958. French Huguenot names and their mispronunciation. NSC 5.11-12.

**7.183 Simons, Mary Louise.** 1949. Nicknaming in southwestern Kentucky. Hoosier Folklore 30.8.1-6.

**7.184 Sizer, Miriam M.** 1933. Christian names in the Blue Ridge of Virginia. AS 8.2.34-37. Finds "little conscious attempt to preserve in Christian names the family relationship of different individuals."

**7.185 Skinner, James C.** 1986. Nicknames, coal miners and group solidarity. Names 34.134-45. [33 M, 6 F, W]. Surveys prevalence and functions of nicknames at four WV and two SW VA coal mines.

**7.186 Slavick, William H.** 1973. Dubose Heyward's names. Love and wrestling, butch and o.k., ed. by Fred Tarpley, 85-90. Commerce, TX: South Central Names Institute. Says that Heyward's fiction "reflects an early and increasingly sophisticated interest in character names as a vehicle for suggesting personality traits and roles."

**7.187 Spears, James E.** 1972. Folk children's pejorative nicknames and epithets. KFR 18.3.70-74.

**7.188 Spratt, Nellie McMaster.** 1978. Rural churches of Fairfield County. NSC 25.22-23. [N CENT SC].

**7.189 Springston, Jolane.** 1987. The naming of the streets in Purvis, Mississippi. MFR 21.89-105. [SW MS]. Discusses how streets were named in the county seat of Lamar County and extent to which haphazard records in typical small town can provide onomastic material.

**7.190 Stanley, Marion E.** 1927. Name-lore from New Orleans. AS 2.412. Notes on three unusual names.

**7.191 Stephens, J. C.** 1978. What did Hiawatha call his son? An analysis of given names of 1,271 junior high school students in Richardson, Texas. Ethnic names, ed. by Fred Tarpley, 105-14. Commerce, TX: Names Institute Press. 8 tables. Examines frequency and variant spellings of given names, shortened names, and nicknames.

**7.192 Still, James A.** 1930. Christian names in the Cumberlands. AS 5.306-07. [E KY]. Main sources of given names and unusual naming practices.

**7.193 Stoudemire, Sterling.** 1980. Names of girls (and boys) in colonial Virginia. Names 28.98-100. Frequency of given names in The Register of Ancestors for the years 1607-20.

**7.194 Stubbs, Thomas M.** 1968. More about Sumter street names. NSC 15.43-47. [CENT SC].

**7.195 Stubbs, Thomas M., and Wade T. Batson.** 1974. South Carolina botanists remembered by names of plants. NSC 21.12-15.

**7.196 Tabor, Paul.** 1968. Bermuda Grass, a Georgian name? GHQ 52.199-202. Originated in vicinity of Sunbury, GA, around 1800.

**7.197 Tanner, Jeri.** 1977. Miss Tumbleweed and her peers: or, Miss Informed. Labeled for life, ed. by Fred Tarpley, 5-9. Commerce, TX: Names Institute Press. Unusual names for beauty pageants in TX.

**7.198 "Tar Heels."** 1926. AS 1.355. Explanation in talk by Maj. William A. Graham, April 25, 1915, of how North Carolinians came to be called by epithet.

**7.199 Tarpley, Fred A.** 1963. Southern cemeteries: neglected archives for the folklorist. SFQ 27.323-33. Includes brief reference to personal names on New Orleans tombstones.

**7.200 Tarpley, Fred A., ed.** 1978. Ethnic names. South Central Names Institute Publication 6. Commerce, TX: South Central Names Institute. **Review:** K. B. Harder. 1978. TFSB 44.214-16.

**7.201 Taylor, Balma C.** 1974. They had to call it something: names for Texas beauty shops. They had to call it something, ed. by Fred Tarpley, 1-11. Commerce, TX: Names Institute Press. Surveys unusual beauty shop names from large and small towns around the state.

**7.202 Vickers, Ovid.** 1983. Mississippi Choctaw names and naming: a diachronic view. Names 31.117-22. [E CENT MS]. Patterns of given names.

**7.203 Wages, Jack D.** 1973. Names in Eudora Welty's fiction: an onomatological prolegomenon. Love and wrestling, butch and o.k., ed. by Fred Tarpley, 65-72. Commerce, TX: South Central Names Institute. Says Welty is "consistently expert" in naming her characters.

**7.204 Walser, Richard, and Julia Montgomery Street.** 1966. We are called "tar heels." North Carolina parade: stories of history and people, 120-24. Chapel Hill: University of North Carolina Press. Surveys epithets for NC residents referring to use of tar in state--Tar-boiler, Tar-burner, and Tar-heel.

**7.205 Watson, Ellen B.** 1959. Names of early Baptist churches in South Carolina. NSC 6.14-19.

**7.206 West, Robert C.** 1986. An atlas of Louisiana surnames of French and Spanish origin. Baton Rouge: Geoscience Publications, Louisiana State University. ix + 217 pp. History and distribution (shown on maps) of 100 important surnames and hundreds of related names. **Reviews:** J. Jordan. 1987. Names 35.95-98; J. B. McMillan. 1988. Alabama Review 41.239-40.

**7.207 Who is a hillbilly?** 1968. ARK/OZARK 1 (Fall). Traces negative stereotype associated with term since Henry Schoolcraft's days.

**7.208 Who is a hillbilly (continued)?** 1974. ARK/OZARK 7.27-29 (Spring). Cites legal case over whether term hillbilly is an insult; court ruled it is, on the contrary, "an expression of envy."

**7.209 Williams, George Walton.** 1958. Slave names in antebellum South Carolina. AS 33.294-95. Supplements Cohen **7.30.**

**7.210 Wilson, Gordon.** 1970-71. Origins of the people of the Mammoth Cave region as shown by their surnames and regional words. KFR 16.73-78. Surnames.

**7.211 Winkler, J. S.** 1972. Whence the name Dula? One plausibility. North Carolina Folklore 22.84-86.

**7.212 Zelinsky, Wilbur.** 1970. Cultural variation in personal name patterns in the Eastern United States. Annals of the Association of American Geographers 60.743-69. Finds regional patterns in choice of given names, which confirm "the existence of three basic early American culture areas: New England, the Midland, and the South." Based on frequency of principal male names in sixteen selected counties in eastern U.S. in 1790 and 1968.

### See Also

1.122 Carey; 1.123 Carpenter; 1.202 Doran; 1.261 Genovese; 1.321 Hiller; 1.653 Reirdon; 1.702 Smith; 1.756 Thompson; 2.31 Botume; 2.166 Hair; 2.203 Herskovits; 2.237 Joyner; 2.239 Kahn; 2.437 Turner; 3.196 Grubb; 3.307 McDavid; 3.321 Martin; 3.445 Sparkman; 3.502 West; 6.103 Burke; 6.342 Kenny; 6.508 Read; 12.23 Rajec.

# 8 Figurative Language, Exaggerations, and Word-Play

**8.1 Adams, Henry J.** 1976. Speech patterns. TFSB 41.70-71. 104 figures of speech from GA, AL, TN, and KY.

**8.2 Atkinson, Mary J.** 1926. Familiar sayings of oldtime Texans. Texas Folklore Society Publications 5.78-92. Sayings, similes, proverbs, nicknames, and exclamations. Excerpted in Texas folk and folklore, ed. by Mody C. Boatright et al., 213-18. Dallas: Southern Methodist University Press.

**8.3 Berry, Earl.** 1977. History of Marion County. Little Rock, AR: Marion County Historical Association. [N CENT AR]. Pp. 47-48, sayings and metaphors.

**8.4 Berry, Pearlleen D., and Mary Eva Repass**, compilers. 1980. Granpa says: superstitions and sayings from Eastern Kentucky, 18-21. Fredericksburg, VA: Foxhound Enterprises. Cites sayings and idioms.

**8.5 Blair, Marion E.** 1938. The prevalence of older English proverbs in Blount County, Tennessee. TFSB 4.1-24. [34 natives, E TN]. Investigates how many proverbs prevalent before 1500 are recognized by heterogeneous group of Blount County, TN, natives.

**8.6 Boatright, Mody C.** 1949. Free speech. Folk laughter on the American frontier, 146-58. New York: Macmillan. Essay on tall talk, fanciful language and comparisons, and other types of extravagant speech of early 19th-century West.

**8.7 Boshears, Frances, and Herbert Halpert.** 1954. Proverbial comparisons from an East Tennessee county. TFSB 20.27-41. [E TN]. List of 1045 comparisons compiled in Scott Co.

**8.8 Boswell, George W.** 1972. Tongue twisters and a few other examples of linguistic folklore. KFR 18.49-51. Three dozen folk expressions, mostly tongue twisters, from MS and KY.

**8.9 Bradley, F. W.** 1937. South Carolina proverbs. SFQ 1.99-101 passim. Includes several Gullah specimens.

**8.10 Brewer, J. Mason.** 1954. Old-time Negro proverbs. Texas folk and folklore, ed. by Mody C. Boatright et al., 219-23. Dallas: Southern Methodist University Press. Sayings from elderly blacks in CENT TX.

**8.11 Brinegar, Bonnie.** 1971. Metaphorical expressions from Adams County, Mississippi. MFR 5.124-31. [B and W, SW MS]. List of 124 folk comparisons and discussion of difficulty in comparing them.

**8.12 Broadrick, Estelle D.** 1978. Old folk sayings and home-cures. TFSB 44.35-36. One dozen proverbial sayings.

**8.13 Carey, George G.** 1970. Maryland folklore and folklife. Cambridge, MD: Tidewater. Proverbs and proverbial speech, 63-67, proverbs, similes, riddles, and tongue twisters.

**8.14 Clark, J. D.** 1940. Similes from the folk speech of the South. SFQ 4.119-33. Discusses types of similes, with numerous examples.

**8.15 Clark, J. D.** 1940. Similes from the folk speech of the South: a supplement to Wilstach's compilation. SFQ 4.205-26. 2,026 items from students at North Carolina State College.

**8.16 Clarke, Mary Washington.** 1965. Proverbs, proverbial phrases, and proverbial comparisons in the writings of Jesse Stuart. SFQ 29.142-63. Glossary.

**8.17 Comeaux, Elizabeth Smallwood.** 1981. Let the cat die: a collection of folklore from the southern Alabama and southern Mississippi woodlands. Louisiana Folklore Miscellany 5.1.1-3. Brief notes on unusual idioms, folk expressions, boasts, proverbs, and blessings.

**8.18 Cox, Ernest.** 1947. Rustic imagery in Mississippi proverbs. SFQ 11.263-67. Figures of speech and proverbs.

**8.19 Crews, Jacquelyn.** 1973. On being pretty as a speckled pup under a red wagon and other Southern expressions. English Review 1.2.43-62.

**8.20 Deaton, Mary B.** 1973. Folk expressions. MFR 7.51. [MS]. List of similes.

**8.21 de Carion, Flavia J.** 1948. Some Florida proverbs and their literary background. Gainesville: University of Florida thesis. vi + 192 pp. Culls proverbs from FL fiction writers, classifies them, and discusses origin and foreign language sources of them.

**8.22 Dick, Everett.** 1974. Frontier speech. The Dixie frontier: a social history of the southern frontier from the first transmontane beginnings to the Civil War, 310-20. New York: Octagon Books. Popular account of tall talk, fanciful metaphors, and other verbal play and allusions along late 18th- and early 19th-century frontier in the South.

**8.23 Eastridge, Nancy Emilia.** 1939. Common comparisons and folk sayings. A study of folklore in Adair County, Kentucky, 114-34. Nashville: George Peabody College thesis. Anecdotal discussion of similes and list of 155 "epithets used to show surprise, anger, disgust, or unhappiness."

**8.24 Eddins, A. W.** 1954. Grandma's sayings. Texas folk and folklore, ed. by Mody C. Boatright et al., 218-19. Dallas: Southern Methodist University Press. [NE TX]. Oldtime sayings from pioneer Texan in Collin County.

**8.25 Gonzalez, Charles.** 1962. Rumno riddles. North Carolina Folklore 10.40-41.

**8.26 Greer, Dale.** 1964. Secret speech. KFR 10.35. [Berea, KY]. Description of "double Dutch."

**8.27 Halpert, Herbert.** 1945. Grapevine Warp an' Tobacco Stick Fillin'. SFQ 9.223-28. Songs, rimes, and sayings, most from KY.

**8.28 Halpert, Herbert.** 1951. A pattern of proverbial exaggeration from west Kentucky. Midwest Folklore 1.41-47. A glossary.

**8.29 Halpert, Herbert.** 1956. Some Wellerisms from Kentucky and Tennessee. JAF 69.115-22. Sixty-two specimens, most from KY and TN.

**8.30 Hamilton, Kim, and Dana Holcomb.** 1979. Ole time expressions. Foxfire 13.1.69-72. [NE GA]. List of similes collected by high school students from their grandparents.

**8.31 Hanford, G. L.** 1911. Metaphor and simile in American folk-speech. DN 5.149-80. Includes citations from the South.

**8.32 Harder, Kelsie B.** 1955. Rhyming names in Tennessee. SFQ 19.101-03. Short verses for remembering names from Perry County, TN.

**8.33 Harder, Kelsie B.** 1956. Jingle lore of pigtales, pals, and puppy love. TFSB 22.1-9. Folk verses from Perry County, TN.

**8.34 Harder, Kelsie B.** 1958. Proverbial snopeslore. TFSB 24.89-95. Proverbs and expressions used by Faulkner's I. O. Snopes.

**8.35 Hendricks, George D.** 1956. Texas Wellerisms. JAF 69.356. Brief note supplementing Halpert 1956 (**8.29**).

**8.36 Hendricks, George D.** 1960. Texas folk similes. Western Folklore 19.245-62. 639 similes from students at North Texas State College at Denton; sixty percent not recorded in comparable lists.

**8.37 Hopkins, Bessie Cooper.** 1957. Write folksay. Life and lore of the old Natchez region, 231-43. Nashville: George Peabody College thesis. [S MS]. Similes, proverbs, rhymes, and riddles.

**8.38 Jackson, Bruce.** 1965. Prison folklore. JAF 78.317-29. Has section on argot, slang, and nicknames heard in Southern prisons.

**8.39 Jackson, Bruce.** 1967. "Get your ass in the water and swim like me": narrative poetry from black oral tradition. Cambridge: Harvard University Press. **Reviews:** R. G. Alvery. 1976. TFSB 42.202-03; D. M. Axler. 1977. KFR 23.26-27; S. W. Fabio. 1976. Black World 25.81; P. B. Mullen. 1978. JAF 91.601-04; H. Spiller. 1975. CLAJ 19.105-07; H. Spiller. 1976. Black Scholar 7.5.44-46; H. Vendler. 1975. NYTBR, Sept. 7, p. 6; A. H. Walle. 1976. AA 78.666-67.

**8.40 Johnson, Helen Sewell.** 1968. "To give someone a Yankee dime": a Southern proverbial expression. JAF 81.71-72. Term offering inducement to a child for doing a small favor refers to a kiss, rather than to the coin, as the reward.

**8.41 Lamkin, Thelma L.**, collector, and **Herbert Halpert**, ed. 1952. Telling the time: some retorts from West Kentucky. Midwest Folklore 2.109-11.

**8.42 Leary, James P.** 1980. Recreational talk among white adolescents. Western Folklore 39.284-99. Stylistic and structural features of ritualized verbal play among whites in NC, IN, and WI.

**8.43 McNeil, W. K.**, annotater. 1981. Folklore from Big Flat, Arkansas, Part I: rhymes and riddles. Mid-American Folklore 9.9-21. Analyzes riddles, jump-rope rhymes, autograph album rhymes, counting-out rhymes, and other rhymes; discusses British, European, and American sources of items.

**8.44 Messick, Mary Ann.** 1973. History of Baxter County, 1873-1973. Little Rock, AR: Mountain Home Chamber of Commerce. [N CENT AR]. Cross questions and silly answers, 493-506. Local sayings, wisecracks and rhymes.

**8.45 Oxrieder, Julie.** 1976. Folklife and folklore from Amherst County, Virginia, told by Mrs. Lenis Foster Murphy. KFR 22.47-51. P. 50, proverbs and similes.

**8.46 Parler, Mary Celestia.** 1958. Folklore from the campus. Arkansas Folklore 8.4-9. Includes number of sayings and proverbs.

**8.47 Preston, Dennis R.** 1989. Folk speech. Encyclopedia of Southern culture, ed. by William Ferris and Charles Wilson. Chapel Hill: University of North Carolina Press. Discusses defining features, types, and major compilations of similes and other Southern folk expressions.

**8.48 Rayburn, Otto Ernest.** 1945. Heard in the Ozarks. Ozark Guide. Summer, p. 69. Item reported in Randolph **12.25** as containing "seventeen examples of the sayings and proverbs which Rayburn has collected. . . . [which], with two additional items, is reprinted in Ozark Guide (Autumn, 1950), p. 41, under the title 'Folk Proverbs'."

**8.49 [Rayburn, Otto E.]** 1958. Ozark folk-say. Rayburn's Ozark Guide 16.57.6-7. Gives sample of proverbs and sayings from AR Ozarks and asks readers for further examples.

**8.50 Roberts, Leonard.** 1952. Additional exaggerations from East Kentucky. Midwest Folklore 2.163-66. Ninety-four items listed in order "to show some insight into the way of life in the hilly, dissected third of the state, where the hills rise from choked valleys on a forty-five degree angle to sharp ridges."

**8.51 Robinson, Emma.** 1944. Two proverbial comparisons. Arkansas Folklore 3.2.

**8.52 Rogers, E. G.** 1950. Figurative language the folkway. TFSB 16.71-75. Catalog of folk similes in eleven classes and list of metaphors, synecdoches, and hyperboles.

**8.53 Rogers, E. G.** 1953. Some East Tennessee figurative exaggerations. TFSB 19.36-40. List of ninety exaggerations heard in E TN.

**8.54 Rountree, Thomas J.** 1970. More on the Southernism "Yankee dime." JAF 83.461. [SE AL]. Agrees with Johnson's account (**8.40**) in general, but says expression conveyed advance appreciation and kiss was seldom given.

**8.55 Sanders, Martha D.** 1951. Proverbial exaggerations from Paducah, Kentucky. Midwest Folklore 1.191-92.

**8.56 Smith, Mrs. Morgan, and A. W. Eddins.** 1937. Wise saws from Texas. Texas Folklore Society Publications 13.239-44. Riddles, proverbs, and other folk wisdom.

**8.57 Syatt, Dick.** 1980. Country talk. Secaucus, NJ: Citadel Press. 218 pp. Reprinted in 1987 as <u>Like we say back home: some examples of our colorful, humorous and imaginative American language</u>. Extended list of similes, mostly anonymous, grouped into chapters such as "Cotton-pickin' so-and-so," "The lone star state," and "Hell in Texas."

**8.58 Taylor, Archer.** 1958. Snakes in Virginia. Western Folklore 17.277. Reports simile <u>as sure as there are snakes in Virginia</u>.

**8.59 Taylor, Archer.** 1962. Proverbial comparisons and similes in <u>On Troublesome Creek</u>. KFR 8.87-95. Figures of speech in James Still novel, set in KY.

**8.60 White, Vallie Tinsley.** 1961. Proverbs and picturesque speech from Claiborne Parish, Louisiana. Louisiana Folklore Miscellany 2.1.85-87.

**8.61 Whitney, Milton.** 1935. Weather sayings from Maryland. JAF 48.195-96. Proverbial sayings.

**8.62 Wilgus, D. K.** 1960. Proverbial material from the Western Kentucky [University] folklore archive. KFR 6.47-49. Similes and proverbs from throughout KY.

**8.63 Wilkerson, Isabelle Jeanette.** 1963. A compilation of the proverbial expressions in the works of Charles Egbert Craddock. Knoxville: University of Tennessee thesis. Classifies material into twenty-eight categories.

**8.64 Williams, Cratis D.** 1962. Metaphor in mountain speech. Mountain Life and Work 38.4.9,11-12. **Reprinted** in Bobbs-Merrill Series, Language-100. Says "speech of Southern Mountaineers bristles with strong language, pungent metaphors, vivid similes, and vigorous personifications" and discusses social uses of these figures of speech; says similes far outnumber all other types of figurative expressions.

**8.65 Williams, Cratis D.** 1963. Metaphor in mountain speech. Mountain Life and Work 39.1.50-53. Discusses figures of speech and traditional expressions for characterizing great physical strength, unusual courage, honesty, strength of convictions, and other personal traits in Southern Appalachian speech.

**8.66 Williams, Cratis D.** 1963. Metaphor in mountain speech. Mountain Life and Work 39.2.51-53. Discusses and exemplifies exaggerations used in Southern mountains.

**8.67 Wilson, Gordon.** 1956. Down our way: tell us what it's like. KFR 2.1-3. Sample similes based on ten adjectives such as <u>big</u>, <u>crooked</u>, etc.

**8.68 Wilson, Gordon.** 1965. Proverbial lore. TFSB 31.99-104. [W KY]. Classified list of proverbs from Mammoth Cave region.

**8.69 Wilson, Gordon.** 1968. Similes from the Mammoth Cave region with a farm flavor. KFR 14.44-50; 14.69-75; 14.94-99. [W KY].

**8.70 Woodbridge, Hensley C.** 1957. Folklore in the works of Janice Holt Giles. Kentucky Historical Society Register 55.330-37. [KY]. Includes brief comments on similes.

**8.71 Woodson, Anthony.** 1925. Kentucky similes. Kentucky Folklore Bulletin, 8-11. Classification of more than one hundred similes based on comparisons to vegetables, animals, and minerals.

## See Also

1.87 Boswell; 1.101 Brookes; 1.117 Byron; 1.122 Carey; 1.145 Combs; 1.150 Cooper; 1.202 Doran; 1.215 Duncan; 1.338 Hurston; 1.404 McAtee; 1.504 Medford; 1.553 Parris; 1.630 Randolph; 1.720 Stephens; 1.805 Whitener; 1.830 Wilson; 1.832 Wilson; 2.296 Mathews; 2.396 Smith; 2.462 Wilkinson; 3.23 Ayres; 3.65 Campbell; 3.66 Carpenter; 3.72 Carter; 3.143 Dwyer; 3.193 Green; 3.281 Lawson; 3.362 Nye; 3.439 Skillman; 3.447 Spears; 3.452-53 Steele; 3.481 Tidwell; 3.486 Underwood; 3.519 Wilson; 3.523 Wilson; 3.539 Woodard; 8.38 Jackson; 9.40-41 Figh; 9.57 Harder; 9.128 Smith; 12.12 Harrington.

# 9 Literary Dialect

**9.1 Babcock, C. Merton.** 1963. A word-list from Zora Neale Hurston. PADS 40.1-11. Items from FL black novelist.

**9.2 Barnes, Verle.** 1980. Dialect in Southern fiction. Southern Conference on English in the Two-Year College Newsletter 13.1.44-45.

**9.3 Baskerville, Katherine Taylor.** 1929. A study of the life and writings of Irwin Russell. Nashville: George Peabody College thesis. P. 81, discusses Russell's attempt to represent dialect of MS blacks.

**9.4 Bell, H. M.** 1925. The development of dialect in the American short story. Columbus: Ohio State University thesis. 49 pp. The South, 26-37. Survey of eight writers, including George Washington Harris and George Washington Cable; says the South "is the most interesting and the most fertile in dialect of all the regions," in which "there are two languages very closely related, that of the Negro and that of the southern gentleman."

**9.5 Billups, Edgar P.** 1923. Some principles for the representation of Negro dialect in fiction. Texas Review 8.99-123. Condensed version of Emory University thesis, 1922; deals with George W. Cable, Octavus R. Cohen, Harris Dickson, Joel C. Harris, John Trotwood Moore, Thomas N. Page.

**9.6 Black, Jane M.** 1978. The language of Ben K. Green: Texas talks ahorseback. Commerce: East Texas State University dissertation. Abstract in DAI 39.6733A. Says Green was determined to keep "Western language" in his four books "despite well-intentioned interference by Eastern editors"; defines expressions used by Green's characters not found in standard or regional dictionaries, and analyzes Green's use of Americanisms.

**9.7 Black, Jane M.** 1978. Horse tradin' vocabulary in the works of Ben K. Green. Abstract in NADS 11.1.11. Examines vocabulary distinctive to the

Texas cowboy's books, much of which is not recorded in any existing dictionary.

**9.8 Blackwell, Louise.** 1966. Eudora Welty: proverbs and proverbial sayings in The Golden Apples. SFQ 30.332-37. Shows how Welty uses folk wisdom and folk expressions to advance characterization, plot, and atmosphere in her stories.

**9.9 Blair, Walter, and Raven I. McDavid, Jr.** 1983. The mirth of a nation: America's great dialect humor. Minneapolis: University of Minnesota Press. Anthology of 19th-century dialect fiction writers; includes "Linguistic Note" (pp. 279-83) by McDavid explaining editorial alteration of dialect to make stories more readable. **Reviews:** K. B. Harder. 1983. TFSB 49.47; R. Higgs. 1983. AJ 10.379-85; M. Dunne. 1984. SECOL Review 8.74-75; L. Pederson. 1984. JEL 17.97-102; R. B. Shulman. 1984. AS 59. 365-67.

**9.10 Boswell, George W.** 1968. Picturesque Faulknerisms. University of Mississippi Studies in English 9.47-56.

**9.11 Bowdre, Paul H.** 1964. A study of eye dialect. Gainesville: University of Florida dissertation. Abstract in DAI 29.887A. 127 pp. Defines "eye dialect" and discusses it "from the standpoint of its use as a literary device and from the standpoint of the science of graphics"; finds it used unconsciously, as by local colorists and creators of dialect characters, and consciously, as by writers trying to create special effects.

**9.12 Bowdre, Paul H., Jr.** 1977. Eye dialect as a literary device in the works of Sidney Lanier. Papers in language variation: SAMLA-ADS collection, ed. by David L. Shores and Carole P. Hines, 247-51. University: University of Alabama Press. Abstract in SAB 30.3 (1965). Finds that Lanier used eye dialect frequently in five of his seven dialect poems and freely in Tiger Lilies and that it is "mixed in with substandard dialect and regional dialect in his representation of the speech of mountaineers, crackers," and blacks.

**9.13 Bowman, Alberta O.** 1968. William Gilmore Simms' The Scout: a dialect study. Gainesville: University of Florida thesis.

**9.14 Boykin, Carol.** 1965. Sut's speech: the dialect of a 'nat'ral borned mountaineer. The Lovingood Papers 4.36-42. Knoxville: University of Tennessee Press. Reviews arguments over authenticity and purposes of George Washington Harris' portrayal of Sut Lovingood's speech and analyzes Harris' use of spelling to represent dialect pronunciation and Harris' use of dialect grammar and local terms and figures of speech.

**9.15 Boykin, Carol D.** 1966. A study of the phonology, morphology, and vocabulary of George Washington Harris' Sut Lovingood yarns. Knoxville: University of Tennessee thesis. v + 71 pp. Thorough study of dialect patterns in Harris' fiction; says Harris was "careful, accurate craftsman" in rendering E TN dialect and indulged in eye dialect much less than his contemporaries.

**9.16 Briggs, Cordell Augustus.** 1982. A study of syntactic variation in the dialect poetry of Paul Lawrence Dunbar. Washington: Howard University dissertation. Abstract in DAI 44.157A. 252 pp. Studies eleven dialect poems from each of three periods of Dunbar's poetry; finds "the 'middle years' is most syntactically varied period" and that nonstandard syntactic features are similar in frequency of occurrence to findings of sociolinguistic studies.

**9.17 Brooks, Cleanth.** 1979. Eudora Welty and the Southern idiom. Eudora Welty: a form of thanks, ed. by Louis Dollarhide and Ann J. Abadie, 3-24. Jackson: University Press of Mississippi. Says vocabulary, metaphor, idiom, and pronunciation of Welty's characters reflect speech of plain people of the South, whose pronunciation derives from southern counties of England.

**9.18 Bryant, Katie.** 1978-79. The slavery of dialect exemplified in Mark Twain's works. Mark Twain Journal 19.3.5-8. Says Twain used some of his best-known characters to protest prejudice against stigmatized dialects.

**9.19 Butters, Ronald R.** 1982. Dialect at work: Eudora Welty's artistic purposes. MFR 16.2.33-40. In story A Worn Path rustic characters speak a kind of charming country poetry.

**9.20 Campbell, Killis.** 1936. Poe's treatment of the Negro and of Negro dialect. University of Texas Studies in English 16.106-14. Says Poe attempted black dialect only in his story The Gold Bug and then managed it badly.

**9.21 Carkeet, David.** 1981. The source for the Arkansas gossips in Huckleberry Finn. American Literary Realism 14.90-92. Says source of language of gossiping ladies in chapter 41 of Twain's novel is imitation of Joel Chandler Harris story.

**9.22 Carson, W. P.** 1926. A descriptive study of literary dialect of the southern highlander. New York: Columbia University dissertation.

**9.23 Clarke, Mary Washington.** 1960. Folklore of the Cumberlands as reflected in the writings of Jesse Stuart. Philadelphia: University of Pennsylvania dissertation.

**9.24 Clarke, Mary Washington.** 1963. As Jesse Stuart heard it in Kentucky. KFR 9.85-86. Folk expressions in Stuart's writings.

**9.25 Cobb, Ima Willie.** 1941. A study of Negro dialects in American poetry. Los Angeles: University of Southern California thesis.

**9.26 Cole, Roger.** 1986. Literary representation of dialect. USF LangQ 24.3-4.3-8. Says literary representation of dialect "must be viewed primarily within a theoretical framework encompassing the literary representation of human speech in general," and demonstrates this by analysis of Joel Chandler Harris' dialect treatment.

**9.27 Curtis, Jay L.** 1942. The dialect writing of Charles Egbert Craddock in the light of the author's background. Chapel Hill: University of North Carolina thesis.

**9.28 Dean, Patricia.** 1980. Dialect in the fiction of Larry McMurtry. Abstract in NADS 12.3.3-4. [Thalia, TX]. Slang, Americanisms, and N TX vocabulary in McMurtry's fiction and their use in his characterization.

**9.29 De Spain, La Rene, and Roderick A. Jacobs.** 1977. Syntax and characterization in Faulkner's As I Lay Dying. JEL 11.1-8.

**9.30 Dunn, Durwood.** 1979. Mary Noailles Murfree: a reappraisal. AJ 6.197-206. P. 201, discusses early critical reception of author's portrayal of mountain speech.

**9.31 Edwards, Dorothy E.** 1935. The dialect of the southern highlander as recorded in North Carolina novels. Rochester: University of Rochester thesis. Discussion of Olive Dargon, Paul Green, DuBose Heyward.

**9.32 Elam, W. C.** 1895. Lingo of Negroes in literature. Lippincott's Magazine 55.286-88. Argues portrayal of black speech in literature is misconceived because typical black "talks more or less like the white persons he serves or comes most frequently in contact with" and that "the great body of the lingo commonly regarded as distinctively the [black's] is equally the lingo of the wholly uneducated whites."

**9.33 Esau, Helmut, Norma Bagnall, and Cheryl Ware.** 1980. Faulkner, literary criticism, and linguistics. Journal of the Linguistic Association of the Southwest 4.275-300. Reviews changing currents in study of literary dialects, finding that earlier analysts, including Ives, failed to appreciate social variation in literary dialects; analyzes social dialect used in Faulkner's Intruder in the Dust and shows how dialect shift indicates social status and attitudes in novel.

**9.34 Evans, William.** 1971. French-English literary dialect in The Grandissimes. AS 46.210-22. Says French-English dialect in the novel is reliable reflection of southern Louisiana creole speech of 19th century. Reprinted in D. Shores and C. Hines 1977.233-45; in Arlin Turner, ed. 1980. Critical essays on George W. Cable. Boston: G. K. Hall.

**9.35 Evans, William.** 1971. Cable, Poquelin, and Miss Burt: the difficulties of a dialect writer. Louisiana Studies 15.45-60. Abstract in NADS 3.2.26.

Discusses how Cable used flexible French-English dialect to emphasize character differences.

**9.36 Evans, William.** 1981. George Washington Cable's French-English dialect and the free indirect style. Abstract in NADS 13.3.3. Cable used indirect free style to suggest French speech and milieu.

**9.37 Evans, William W.** 1981. Dialect and diglossia in George Washington Cable's Belles Demoiselles Plantation. Journal of the Linguistic Association of the Southwest 4.254-59. Examines use and functions of English by characters whose native language is French.

**9.38 Evans, William W.** 1986. When English isn't English: yet another foray into George Washington Cable's linguistic variations in literature. Abstract in NADS 18.3.8. Discusses Cable's manipulation of literary English and French, as well as Creole French, in two stories.

**9.39 Evans, William W.** 1989. Literary dialects. Encyclopedia of Southern culture, ed. by William Ferris and Charles Wilson. Chapel Hill: University of North Carolina Press. Short essay surveying principal writers of literary dialect and their techniques of writing in dialect.

**9.40 Figh, Margaret Gillis.** 1947. Folklore and folk speech in the works of Marjorie Kinnan Rawlings. SFQ 11.201-09. Rustic epithets and similes in the FL novelist.

**9.41 Figh, Margaret Gillis.** 1949. Tall talk and folk sayings in Bill Arp's work. SFQ 13.206-12. Rustic epithets and similes.

**9.42 Figh, Margaret Gillis.** 1950. A word-list from "Bill Arp" and "Rufus Sanders." PADS 13.3-15. Wordlist from late 19th-century newspaper columnists from AL and GA whose writing reflected everyday speech of period.

**9.43 Figh, Margaret Gillis.** 1952. Bartow Lloyd, humorist and philosopher of the Alabama back country. Alabama Review 5.83-99. Includes brief discussion of Lloyd's use of hyperbole, boasting, and fantastic simile.

**9.44 Fine, Elizabeth.** 1983. In defense of literary dialect: a response to Dennis R. Preston. JAF 96.323-30. Detailed response to Preston (9.106); defends use of modified spelling by folklorists to represent speech in print.

**9.45 Fine, Marlene G., and Carolyn Anderson.** 1978. Dialect features in the language of black characters on American television programming. ED 162 519. 40 pp. Examines scripts and audiotapes of three black situation comedies for ten syntactic features; finds only three present--copula deletion, auxiliary deletion, and negative concord--and concludes that television programs are in the process of creating an artificial, homogenized dialect that "gives the impression of difference" from other varieties of English.

**9.46 Fine, M. G., and C. Anderson.** 1980. Dialectical features of black characters. Phylon 4.396-409. Condensed version of preceding item.

**9.47 Foster, Charles William.** 1968. The representation of Negro dialect in Charles W. Chesnutt's The Conjure Woman. Tuscaloosa: University of Alabama dissertation. Abstract in DAI 29.3596-97A. Abstract reprinted in J. Williamson and V. Burke 1971(**1.823**).672-73. Concludes Chesnutt was remarkably accurate in representing dialect of blacks in Cape Fear-Peedee River area of NC and that he used dialect to enhance character development.

**9.48 Foster, Charles W.** 1971. The phonology of the conjure tales of Charles W. Chesnutt. PADS 55. 43 pp. 11 maps. [6 W, 2 B LAMSAS informants in Cape Fear Valley, SE NC]. Phonemic reconstruction of Chesnutt's speech, based on LAMSAS field records and exploration of authenticity of Chesnutt's representation of dialect of his characters. **Reviews:** K. Hameyer. 1980. ZDL 47.108-11; P. Kolin. 1975. AS 50.115-20.

**9.49 Freimarck, Vincent.** 1953. Mark Twain and "infelicities" of Southern speech. AS 28.233-34. Discusses ain't and it don't in speech of cultivated Southern characters.

**9.50 Gillespie, Elizabeth.** 1939. The dialect of the Mississippi Negro in literature. Oxford: University of Mississippi thesis. 174 pp. Surveys use of black dialect in fiction, nonfiction, and poetry of 19th- and 20th-century writers of the state.

**9.51 Gregg, Alvin Lanier.** 1969. Style and dialect in Light in August and other works by William Faulkner. Austin: University of Texas dissertation. Abstract in DAI 30.3009A. Discusses social, conventional, and aesthetic factors in how Faulkner represented dialects, and differentiates five dialect styles in the white speech and three dialects in the black speech of Light in August.

**9.52 Gregg, Alvin L.** 1982. Faulkner's changing dialect styles. Abstract in NADS 14.3.5. Analyzes Faulkner's evolving portrayal of dialect features.

**9.53 Gwynn, Frederick L., and Joseph L. Blotner,** eds. 1958. William Faulkner on dialect. University of Virginia Magazine 2.7-13,32-37.

**9.54 Hall, Wade.** 1970. "The truth is funny": a study of Jesse Stuart's humor. ED 048 250. 79 pp. Also appears in Indiana English Journal 5.2-4. Examines ways Stuart uses material from his own life and observations as subject matter in his fiction, and focuses on Stuart's use of dialect and natural metaphors of folk speech.

**9.55 Haman, James B.** 1939. The growth of the use of Negro dialect in American verse and short story to 1900. Durham: Duke University thesis. 163 pp. Detailed descriptive study covering period from 1721 to 1900; includes 36-page bibliography.

**9.56 Hanson, Wyoline.** 1930. The Georgia cracker in the poetry of Frank L. Stanton. Nashville: George Peabody College thesis. P. 9, comments on the "cracker" dialect.

**9.57 Harder, Kelsie B.** 1959. Charactonyms in Faulkner's novels. Bucknell Review 8.189-201. Says Faulkner consciously chose names of characters to strengthen effects in his fiction, sometimes using allegory and sometimes relying on connotations from etymology.

**9.58 Harder, Kelsie B.** 1982. Dialect duplicity in Stark Young's So Red the Rose. MFR 16.41-44. Young differentiated three social classes of characters through use of dialect.

**9.59 Harris, Joel Chandler.** 1883. Nights with Uncle Remus: myths and legends of the old plantation. Boston: Osgood. Pp. xxviii-xxxi, says that use of dialect in Uncle Remus stories "is a part of the legends themselves, and to present them in any other way would be to rob them of everything that gives them vitality"; presents grammatical, lexical, and phonological notes on Sea Island dialect of his character Daddy Jack.

**9.60 Harris, Joel Chandler.** 1935. The Uncle Remus book. Retold by Miriam Blanton Huber. New York: Appleton-Century. Glossary, 145-51. Discusses his presentation of dialect, particularly the Gullah of his Daddy Jack character, and presents brief list of Daddy Jack's dialect forms (p. xxix).

**9.61 Haskell, Ann S.** 1964. The representation of Gullah-influenced dialect in twentieth century South Carolina prose: 1922-30. Philadelphia: University of Pennsylvania dissertation. Abstract in DAI 25.3562-63A. Abstract reprinted in J. Williamson and V. Burke 1971(1.823).679-80. 280 pp. Based on Ives' method (9.70), compares phonological and lexical items in six writers with LAMSAS records, Atlas-based studies, and Turner (2.437); finds a literary tradition for portraying Gullah that frequently differs from actual language patterns.

**9.62 Hays, Virgil.** 1950. Philology in the funnies. Word Study 25.5.8. Author contends that Southern mountaineers speak "Elizabethan English of the purest lineage" and suggests that this dialect can be found in comic strip such as Snuffy Smith, whose characters use the term bodacious.

**9.63 Hensley, Lee Rasbury.** 1975. Dialect research and prose fiction: use of a dialect survey in writing prose fiction. Commerce: East Texas State University dissertation. Abstract in DAI 36.6064A. [178 W adults in Cottle

Co., TX]. Shows that intensive survey of stock vocabulary and grammar of a dialect "can be used as a resource to portray that dialect selectively and realistically by the prose fiction writer who wishes to deemphasize the phonological features."

**9.64 Hoffer, Bates.** 1973. Use of black dialects by Faulkner. Abstract in NADS 5.2.6. Says Faulkner carefully discriminated regional and social dialects in his fiction.

**9.65 Hoffer, Bates.** 1980. Dialect shift in Twain, Faulkner, and Joyce. Abstract in NADS 12.3.3. Discusses literary effects achieved by Faulkner's use of dialect.

**9.66 Holmberg, Carl Bryan, and Gilbert D. Schneider.** 1986. Daniel Decatur Emmett's stump sermons: genuine Afro-American culture, language and rhetoric in the Negro minstrel show. Journal of Popular Culture 19.4.27-38. Analyzes Emmett's sermons for the minstrel stage to show evidence of African culture in such shows, the authenticity of African phonology Emmett incorporated in his spelling practice, and the rhetorical prowess of the sermons.

**9.67 Holton, Sylvia Wallace.** 1984. Down home and uptown: the representation of black speech in American fiction. Rutherford: Fairleigh Dickinson University Press. ix + 214 pp. Examines "the ways in which black English dialect has been used in American fiction, . . . the literary effects its uses have generated" and explores potential of black speech as an autonomous literary language in Chesnutt and Harris as well as for modern-day writers. **Review:** M. N. Simmons. 1985. LIS 14.398-403.

**9.68 Hunter, Edwin R.** 1925. The American colloquial idiom, 1830-1860. Chicago: University of Chicago dissertation. Based on, among others, work of Joseph G. Baldwin, William A. Caruthers, David Crockett, John Pendleton Kennedy, A. B. Longstreet, William Gilmore Simms, William T. Thompson, Thomas Bangs Thorpe.

**9.69 Inge, M. Thomas.** 1977. The Appalachian backgrounds of Billy de Beck's Snuffy Smith. AJ 4.120-32. Pp. 122-23, discusses George Washington Harris as primary source of de Beck portrayal of Snuffy Smith's speech.

**9.70 Ives, Sumner.** 1950. The Negro dialect of the Uncle Remus stories. Austin: University of Texas dissertation. Condensed in 1954 and published as The phonology of the Uncle Remus stories. PADS 22. 59 pp. Systematic description of phonology of the literary dialect, and authentification of Harris' practices by comparison to phonology of LAMSAS records from mid-GA; argues that "analysis of those literary dialects for which verifying evidence is available can quite possibly bring out clues to a more certain interpretation of evidence on historical developments."

**9.71 Ives, Sumner.** 1950. A theory of literary dialect. Tulane Studies in English 2.137-82. Seminal theoretical article on nature of dialects and dialect representation by fiction writers; detailed analysis of consistency and authenticity of Joel Chandler Harris' portrayal of Uncle Remus' speech. Revised in J. Williamson and V. Burke 1971(**1.823**).145-77.

**9.72 Ives, Sumner.** 1955. Dialect differentiation in the stories of Joel Chandler Harris. American Literature 27.88-96. Modern dialect studies show that Harris portrayed dialogue of his folk characters with skillful discrimination of both regional and social dialects. **Reprinted** in J. Williamson and V. Burke 1971(**1.823**).222-29.

**9.73 Jones, Bessie Washington.** 1967. Stylistic features of the Negro folktale: language. A descriptive and analytical study of the American Negro folktale, 47-57. Nashville: George Peabody College dissertation. Abstract in DAI 28.3673-74A. Presents "noteworthy stylistic features which help to establish the Negro's unique contributions to the oral tradition in literature."

**9.74 Krapp, George Philip.** 1926. The psychology of dialect writing. Bookman 63.522-27. Seminal essay on nature of devices used by literary artists to achieve characterization and other purposes through literary dialect; includes comments on black literary dialect.

**9.75 Landrum, Louise M.** 1930. A study of Kentucky mountain dialect based on Lucy Furman's Quare Women. Lexington: University of Kentucky thesis. 74 pp. [Knott Co.]. Study of peculiarities of speech of E KY mountains.

**9.76 Lanier, Sidney.** 1945. To Scribner's Monthly. Collected works of Sidney Lanier 10.156. Baltimore: Johns Hopkins University Press. Note the poet wrote to his publisher about his representation of black dialect; says commonest mistake in reproducing it is "to make it too consistent."

**9.77 Lloyd, John U.** 1901. The language of the Kentucky Negro. DN 2.179-84. Novelist's list of respellings to indicate pronunciation.

**9.78 Long, Richard A.** 1969. The Uncle Remus dialect: a preliminary linguistic view. ED 028 416. 7 pp. Cites Herskovits' claim that black speech had creole basis and says that Joel Chandler Harris was skilled recorder of creolized variety of Southern black speech.

**9.79 McClure, Paul E.** 1979. Dialectal variation in the work of Harry Stillwell Edwards. Abstract in NADS 11.3.6. Says Edwards portrays many different types of dialects in his fiction.

**9.80 McDowell, Tremaine.** 1926. The Negro in the Southern novel prior to 1850. JEGP 25.455-73. Surveys treatment of blacks in novels from 1824 to

1850, with particular attention to William Gilmore Simms; passing comments on and examples of black speech.

**9.81 McDowell, Tremaine.** 1930. Notes on Negro dialect in the American novel to 1821. AS 5.291-96. Says use of the dialect developed slowly before James Fenimore Cooper.

**9.82 McDowell, Tremaine.** 1931. The use of Negro dialect by Harriet Beecher Stowe. AS 6.322-26. Says dialect in Uncle Tom's Cabin is unsuccessful because it resembles lower-class white speech too closely and that Stowe's use of dialect in general is makeshift and a regression from earlier writers like William Gilmore Simms.

**9.83 Maiden, Emory Virgil, Jr.** 1968. A comparison of the Negro dialect poetry of Irwin Russell and Thomas Nelson Page. Charlottesville: University of Virginia thesis. Prefers Russell's treatment of dialect as more realistic than Page's romanticized portrayal.

**9.84 Marwell, D. E. S.** 1956. Language in the novel. Dublin Magazine 31.14-17. Praises Robert Penn Warren's resistance to uniformity of language.

**9.85 Meyer, Norma Lee.** 1971. Syntactic features of William Faulkner's narrative style. Lincoln: University of Nebraska dissertation. Abstract in DAI 32.6406A. Applies techniques of generative transformational grammar to three novels "to determine the syntactic choices underlying the 'full' style" and finds nominalization, conjunction, and right-branch embedding most central elements of Faulkner's style.

**9.86 Miller, Daisy.** 1924. Negro dialects in American literature. Opportunity 2.327-29. Surveys early portrayals of black dialect on minstrel stage and in literature and concludes they are all failures to one degree or another.

**9.87 Mitchell, Ruth D.** 1963. A study of Smoky Mountain regional speech as used in Lanier's Tiger Lilies. Columbia: University of South Carolina thesis. 117 pp. Detailed analysis of phonology, vocabulary, and grammar used in Lanier's story set in E TN and comparison of findings with linguistic research of Joseph Hall, Lester Berrey, Horace Kephart, James Tidwell, and linguistic studies.

**9.88 Montenyohl, Joseph.** 1986. The origins of Uncle Remus. Folklore Forum 18.136-67. Shows how Joel Chandler Harris' newspaper dialect sketches evolved from Harris' earlier work to become character studies and editorials on Southern life.

**9.89 Moore, Opal.** 1942. Negro dialect. The development of Negro character in Louisiana fiction, 18-41. Baton Rouge: Louisiana State University thesis. Surveys use of black dialect by American fiction writers, with special attention to writers from LA.

**9.90 Morris, J. Allen.** 1947. Gullah in the stories and novels of William Gilmore Simms. AS 22.46-53. Studies features in four short stories and nine novels, including A Scene of the Revolution, early story using Gullah dialect (1833).

**9.91 Negro folk-lore.** 1981. Critical essays on Joel Chandler Harris, ed. by R. Bruce Bickley, Jr., 3-6. Reprint of 1880 review of Uncle Remus: His Songs and His Sayings. Praises Harris' "fineness of ear" and expressive dialect writing; says he "shows cleverly the distinction between Middle Georgia and Southern Georgia Negro dialects."

**9.92 Nelson, John H.** 1926. The Negro character in American literature. University of Kansas Humanistic Studies 4.1. Based on Cornell University dissertation, 1923.

**9.93 Nelson, Lawrence E.** 1931. Vocabularies of nineteenth and twentieth-century American prose writers. Stanford: Stanford University dissertation. Discusses Poe, Simms, Mencken.

**9.94 Nixon, Nell Marie.** 1971. Gullah and backwoods dialect in selected works by William Gilmore Simms. Columbia: University of South Carolina dissertation. Abstract in DAI 32.2667-68A. Examines validity of Simms' portrayal of phonology, morphology, syntax, and vocabulary of Gullah and white backwoods characters in ten novels and short stories; says Simms used dialect to individualize rather than type characters and that his "Gullah dialect furnishes further evidence that Negro speech is almost wholly derived from speech of white illiterates or non-standard English speakers" of 17th and 18th centuries.

**9.95 Nott, C. William.** 1900. Irwin Russell, first dialect writer. Christmas-night in the quarters by Irwin Russell, v-xiii. Richmond, VA: Dietz Press. Essay on formative influences on Russell's dialect writing; praises Russell as "pioneer writer" of black dialect.

**9.96 Objecting to the Negro dialect.** 1916. Literary Digest 53.1253 (Nov. 11). Protest by Southerners against effort by New York music teachers to purge dialect forms from Southern songs.

**9.97 Olney, Clark.** 1934. Archaisms in the poetry of Sidney Lanier. Notes and Queries 166.292-94 (Apr. 28). Classifies archaic usages in Lanier's poetry into four groups and concludes "Lanier's use of obsoletisms and archaic and poetic forms was a characteristic of his poetry on both ancient and modern themes."

**9.98 Pederson, Lee.** 1966. Negro speech in the adventures of Huckleberry

Finn. Mark Twain Journal 13.1.1-4. Says Twain represented complicated dialect in Huckleberry Finn in skillful and consistent fashion.

**9.99 Pederson, Lee.** 1985. Language in the Uncle Remus tales. MP 82.292-98. Says that usual claims (such as Ives' **9.70**) of accuracy of Harris' representation of Southern black speech are based on phonetic features only and that they are belied by sentence patterns used by the Uncle Remus character, which are Ciceronian and Senecan in style and do not correspond to any spoken variety of American English.

**9.100 Pederson, Lee.** 1986-87. Rewriting dialect literature: "the wonderful tar-baby story." Atlanta Historical Journal 30.3-4.57-70. Examines four versions of Joel Chandler Harris story in dialect to discover how author revised grammar and spelling.

**9.101 Pennekamp, Arnold H. C.** 1938. The treatment of the Negro in the literary magazines of the South during the reconstruction period from 1865 to 1880. Chapel Hill: University of North Carolina thesis. Peculiarities of the Negro's speech, 94-100. Discusses how short stories in magazines of different parts of the South represented speech of slaves in fictional dialogue after the Civil War.

**9.102 Peppers, Wallace Ray.** 1979. Linguistic variation in the dialect poetry of Paul Lawrence Dunbar. Chapel Hill: University of North Carolina dissertation. Abstract in DAI 40.2639A. 204 pp. Analyzes five features (postvocalic /r/, final consonant clusters, multiple negation, third person singular -s, and initial, medial, and final "th") as function of poetic type, persona, and setting.

**9.103 Peterson, P. W.** 1978. The misuses and dangers of literary dialect as linguistic data. Papers in linguistics: 1974-1977: a collection of M.A. papers from students in the linguistics department of Northeastern Illinois University. ED 163 760. 27 pp. Assesses Bailey's (**1.24**) uncritical use of data from Warren Miller's novel The Cool World to differentiate Southern white and black speech; points out main function of literary dialect is artistic construction of narrative and discusses valid linguistic evaluation of such a dialect.

**9.104 Pollak, Gustav.** 1913. Dialect in literature. Nation 97.561 (Dec. 11). Praise for Stephen Foster's "Negro melodies" and "Uncle Remus's Negro prose."

**9.105 Pollard, Ella Townsend.** 1936. The Gullah Negroes in regional literature. Stillwater: Oklahoma A and M University thesis. 77 pp. Analyzes presentation of Gullah culture and language in fiction of Peterkin, Gonzales, Heyward, Simms, and other writers; outlines phonology, archaic usages, and grammar of Gullah, 49-68.

**9.106 Preston, Dennis R.** 1982. 'Ritin' fowklower daun 'rong: folklorists' failures in phonology. JAF 95.304-26. Argues that most folklorists lack linguistic expertise to represent details of pronunciation with spelling and therefore that serious distortions of texts and speakers result.

**9.107 Preston, Dennis R.** 1983. [Response]. JAF 96.330-39. A response to Fine 1983 (**9.44**). Says folklorists seek linguistic accuracy but do not use linguistic sophistication in the quest; cites many examples.

**9.108 Pugh, Griffith T.** 1960. George W. Cable's theory and use of folk speech. SFQ 24.287-93. Says Cable had theory of folk speech as device in his fiction and applied it with success.

**9.109 Pullen, Mabel G.** 1925. A comparative study of the dialect used in the poems of Frank L. Stanton and James W. Riley. Nashville: George Peabody College thesis. 141 pp. Examines dialect spellings, grammar, and expressions in two writers and concludes "the Hoosier dialect found in the poems of James Whitcomb Riley and the Cracker dialect in the poems of Frank L. Stanton are more than ninety percent the same dialect."

**9.110 Randolph, Vance.** 1927. The Ozark dialect in fiction. AS 2.283-89. Surveys fourteen novels prior to 1926; says much fiction set in Ozarks poorly represents local dialects and cites examples.

**9.111 Randolph, Vance.** 1931. Recent fiction and the Ozark dialect. AS 6.425-28. Surveys nine novels and says one using Ozark dialect best is by AR native Charles M. Wilson.

**9.112 Render, Sylvia Lyons.** 1967. North Carolina dialect: Chesnutt style. North Carolina Folklore 15.67-70. Black dialect and vocabulary in novels of Charles W. Chesnutt.

**9.113 Rhame, John M.** 1933. Flaming Youth, a story in Gullah dialect. AS 8.3.39-43. Reprinted from The State (Columbia, SC). Short story and section "Notes on the dialect" (p. 43).

**9.114 Riley, James Whitcomb.** 1892. Dialect in literature. Forum 14.465-73. Argues merits of using dialect in literature, using Joel Chandler Harris, Richard Malcolm Johnston, and Thomas Nelson Page as examples.

**9.115 Rollins, Hyder E.** 1916. The Negro in the Southern short story. Sewanee Review 24.42-60. Survey from John Pendleton Kennedy to Mrs. Stuart, with occasional comments on dialect.

**9.116 Rulon, Curt Morris.** 1967. The dialects in Huckleberry Finn. Iowa City: University of Iowa dissertation. Abstract in DAI 28.2232A. Finds novel has two basic dialects, one white, one black, and that they are distinguished most by phonology and verb morphology.

**9.117 Savannah Unit, Georgia Writer's Project, Work Projects Administration.** 1940. Athens: University of Georgia. Drums and shadows: survival studies among the Georgia coastal Negroes. Reprinted in 1986 with introduction by Charles H. Joyner, ix-xxviii. Notes to the reader, xxxix-xl. Notes on spellings and diacritical marks used to represent speech of ex-slaves.

**9.118 Scarborough, W. S.** 1890. The Negro element in fiction. Proceedings of the American Philological Association 21.42-44. Abstract of talk arguing that "Negro English" is not a homogeneous dialect.

**9.119 Schlager, Walter B.** 1974. A practical use for literary dialect applied to the works of Flannery O'Connor. Las Vegas: University of Nevada thesis. 63 pp. [CENT GA]. Proposes and exemplifies method for linguists to "use literary dialect as a source of data to reinforce through comparative methods what has already been collected in the field or will be collected in the future."

**9.120 Schrock, Earl F. Jr.** 1971. An examination of the dialect in This Day and Time. TFSB 37.31-39. [Sullivan Co., TN]. Examines validity of representation of dialect in Anne Armstrong's novel by comparing lexical and grammatical features to author's own ongoing research in E TN area in 1970s. **Reprinted** in Robert J. Higgs, and Ambrose N. Manning, eds. 1977. Voices from the hills: selected readings of Southern Appalachia, 460-73. New York: Ungar.

**9.121 Sharp, Ann Wyatt.** 1981. The literary dialect in the Simon Suggs stories of Johnson Jones Hooper. Tuscaloosa: University of Alabama dissertation. Abstract in DAI 43.170A. Analyzes Hooper's dialect "in order to contribute to a description of a variety of mid-nineteenth century Southern American English"; finds difference "in the extent, not in the presence, of certain patterns . . . between black and white speech" and that Suggs' dialect portrayal was very similar to that found in Uncle Remus stories.

**9.122 Simon, Charlie May.** 1945. Straw in the sun. New York: Dutton. P. 218, note on dialect writing in the Ozarks.

**9.123 Sledge, Mailande C.** 1985. The representation of the Gullah dialect in Francis Griswold's A Sea Island Lady. Tuscaloosa: University of Alabama dissertation. Abstract in DAI 46.1917A. [SC Sea Islands]. Compares Griswold's dialect spellings with Linguistic Atlas records of speakers in Griswold's home area and area of setting of novel.

**9.124 Sledge, Mailande C.** 1987. The verisimilitude of the Gullah dialect in Francis Griswold's A Sea Island Lady. Abstract in NADS 19.2.13. Compares Griswold's representation of Gullah dialect to data from Linguistic Atlas field records made by Turner (2.437) and claims it is "remarkably accurate."

**9.125 Smith, C. Alphonso.** 1891. The dialect of Miss Murfree's mountaineer. Christian Advocate 52.3.12-13 (Jan. 17).

**9.126 Smith, C. Alphonso.** 1918. Dialect writers. Cambridge history of American literature, vol. 2, ed. by W. P. Trent et al., 347-60. Cambridge, UK: Cambridge University Press. Discusses Joel Chandler Harris (pp. 347-58) and various writers of white dialect (pp. 360-66).

**9.127 Smith, Charles F.** 1885. Southern dialect in life and literature. Southern Bivouac 4.343-50. Denies there is a "Southern dialect" and discusses "peculiarities of Southern speech, especially as handled by literary artists."

**9.128 Smith, Raoul Lawrence.** 1977. The Gullah dialect and the Gullah-influenced writings of Ambrose Elliot Gonzales. Clemson: Clemson University thesis. 101 pp. Reviews background and literary uses of Gullah, presents short biography of Gonzales, and discusses metaphor, simile, and word play in Gonzales' Gullah-dialect writings.

**9.129 Snyder, Bob.** 1978. Colonial mimesis and the Appalachian renascence. AJ 5.340-49. Pp. 346-47, says liveliness and freshness of Appalachian writers comes from these qualities in the region's speech patterns.

**9.130 Sorrells, Mary Suzanne Kirkman.** 1971. Black dialect: current linguistic studies and black American novels. Commerce: East Texas State University dissertation. Abstract in DAI 33.742-43A. Says black American novelists have tried to represent black dialect accurately, despite pressures to conform to white stereotypes of black dialect.

**9.131 Southard, Bruce.** 1978. From black to white: William Faulkner's use of dialect in his Lucas Beauchamp stories. Abstract in NADS 11.1.13. Says Faulkner revised his representation of black dialect in preparing the Beauchamp stories for inclusion in Go Down, Moses.

**9.132 Stockton, Eric.** 1964. Poe's use of Negro dialect in The Gold Bug. Studies in languages and linguistics in honor of Charles C. Fries, ed. by Albert H. Marckwardt. Ann Arbor: University of Michigan English Language Institute. Examines representation of phonology of stressed vowels, unstressed vowels, and consonants, stress modification, morphology and syntax, and vocabulary of speech of character Jupiter in Poe short story. **Reprinted** in J. Williamson and V. Burke 1971(1.823).193-214.

**9.133 Tidwell, James Nathan.** 1942. Mark Twain's representation of Negro speech. AS 17.174-76. Says Twain represented distinctive features of Nigger Jim's speech by accurate, but not always consistent, spelling.

**9.134 Tidwell, James Nathan.** 1948. The literary representation of the phonology of the Southern dialect. Columbus: Ohio State University dissertation. Deals with Charles W. Chesnutt, Joel C. Harris, Richard M. Johnston, A. B. Longstreet, Mary N. Murfree, Thomas N. Page, William G. Simms.

**9.135 Tiller, Lessie.** 1923. Gullah in American literature. Columbia: University of South Carolina thesis.

**9.136 Todd, Hollis B.** 1965. An analysis of the literary dialect of Irwin Russell and a comparison with the spoken dialect of certain informants of West Central Mississippi. Baton Rouge: Louisiana State University dissertation. Abstract in DAI 26.4893-94A. Examines Russell's twenty-four poems in black dialect by classifying ten types of "departure from conventional literary English" in order to estimate accuracy of his dialect representation; compares findings with speech of six older black natives from Russell's hometown.

**9.137 Traugott, Elizabeth C.** 1978. Linguistic variation in Afro-American fiction. Abstract in NADS 10.2.4. Shows much of variability in fictional representation of black dialect can be understood as style-shifting.

**9.138 Traugott, Elizabeth Closs.** 1983. The sociostylistics of minority dialect in literary prose. Proceedings of the ninth annual meeting of the Berkeley Linguistics Society, ed. by Amy Dahlstrom et al., 308-16. Berkeley: University of California. Argues that minority writers' attempt to treat nonstandard language of minority characters as familiar and normal, as in Charles Chesnutt's work The Conjure Woman, brings about a loss of identity for a minority writer.

**9.139 Van Patten, Nathan.** 1931. The vocabulary of the American Negro as set forth in contemporary literature. AS 7.24-31. Includes one LA source. Catalog of vocabulary used by blacks in four books, including R. Emmett Kennedy's Gritny People in LA.

**9.140 Walser, Richard.** 1955. Negro dialect in eighteenth-century American drama. AS 30.269-76. Abundant black dialect in 18th-century American drama began tradition that became characteristic of much indigenous literature.

**9.141 Weaver, Constance Waltz.** 1970. Analyzing literary representation of recent Northern urban Negro speech: a technique with application to three books. East Lansing: Michigan State University dissertation. Abstract in DAI 32.416A. Same as ED 053 630. Says evidence from recent sociolinguistic studies are more valid than Linguistic Atlas data for testing validity of literary representation of Northern urban speech; finds, however, that novelists are routinely inaccurate in portraying black urban speech, usually exaggerating frequency of certain features.

**9.142 West, Harry C.** 1971. Negro folklore in Pierce's novels. North

Carolina Folklore 19.66-72. Comments on use of black dialect in Ovid William Pierce's novels.

**9.143 Williams, Barbara A. Gibbs.** 1971. A study of the Uncle Remus dialect. Atlanta: Atlanta University thesis. 86 pp. Phonological, phonotactic, and morphological characteristics of the dialect, based on tales from Joel Chandler Harris' Nights with Uncle Remus.

**9.144 Williams, Cratis D.** 1975-76. The southern mountaineer in fact and fiction. AJ 3.8-61,100-62,186-261,334-92. Pp. 101-02, discusses James Hall's handling of dialect in Harpe's Head: a Legend of Kentucky and Caroline M. S. Kirkland's handling of dialect in his A New Home--Who'll Follow? or, Glimpses of Western Life.

**9.145 Wilson, George P.** 1961. Lois Lenski's use of regional speech. North Carolina Folklore 9.2.1-3. Defends NC regional novelist's use of dialect in her children's novels.

**9.146 Woody, Lester G.** 1980. On dialect and style in the work of some Appalachian writers. Abstract in NADS 12.3.8. Details how treatment of mountain dialect by Appalachian writers has evolved since mid-19th century, when extreme eye dialect was prevalent, to present.

**9.147 Yates, Arminda Timmons.** 1948. O. Henry's use of dialect in portraying American character. Abilene: Hardin-Simmons University thesis. Analyzes author's representation of dialect of Cumberland Mountains, New Orleans, and TX.

**9.148 Zanger, Jules.** 1966. Literary dialect and social change. American Studies 7.2.40-48. Says "Guinee" dialect was "the conventional mode of indicating Negro speech in literature until approximately 1840, when it was replaced by new literary convention, the 'plantation' dialect."

**9.149 Ziegler, Mary E.** 1983. The lexicon of Richard Malcolm Johnston's Middle Georgia dialect. Athens: University of Georgia dissertation. Abstract in DAI 44.3375A. Discusses Johnston's vocabulary for natural terrains and characteristic plant and animal life.

## See Also

1.92 Bowman; 1.101 Brookes; 1.103-04 Brooks; 1.233 Farrison; 1.482 McGuire; 1.630 Randolph; 1.718 Spurlock; 1.745 Stuart; 2.104 Davis; 2.161 Gonzales; 2.333 Page; 2.342 Pickens; 2.365 Repka; 2.418-19 Stoddard; 2.466 Williams; 3.1-3 Adams; 3.12 Armstrong; 3.20 Austin; 3.44 Botkin; 3.77 Cauthern; 3.79-82 Chapman; 3.91 Clarke; 3.127 Dickinson; 3.133 Dominick; 3.152 Elton; 3.194 Gregg; 3.244 Howell; 3.297 McCluskey; 3.299 McCutcheon; 3.421 Roberts; 3.426 Rushing; 3.434 Sherry; 3.435 Shott; 3.486

Underwood; 3.490-91 Walton; 3.542 Woodbridge; 3.547 Woodbridge; 4.5 Allison; 4.73 Callary; 4.319 Shewmake; 5.51-53 Canine; 5.126 Hilobow; 6.103 Burke; 6.300 Huddleston; 7.34 Coulthard; 7.42 Dean; 7.56 Evans; 7.68 Green; 7.82 Howell; 7.92 Jones; 7.151 Pate; 7.186 Slavick; 7.203 Wages; 8.59 Taylor; Wilkerson 8.63.

# 10 Language Attitudes and Speech Perception

**10.1 Arahill, Edward Joseph.** 1970. The effect of differing dialects upon the comprehension and attitude of eighth grade children. Gainesville: University of Florida dissertation. Abstract in DAI 31.6030A. [80 B, 40 W 8th-graders, South Miami, FL]. Measures and compares comprehension of Midwestern, Northeastern, Southern white, and Southern black dialects; finds white students have lower comprehension overall and that black students have greater difficulty comprehending Southern black dialect than Southern white dialect.

**10.2 Badger, Andrew.** 1976. Subjective identification of social dialects. Abstract in NADS 8.3.3. [NW MS]. Responses to ten samples of taped speakers from different social strata in MS Delta region.

**10.3 Baird, Scott James.** 1969. Employment interview speech: a social dialect study in Austin, Texas. Austin: University of Texas dissertation. Abstract in DAI 30.1543A. Studies reactions of white college students to three phonological variables in speech of lower-class black females in job interviews.

**10.4 Berry, Lenora.** 1967. Attitudes toward the nature of language: a survey of informants of the Highland Hills community, Dallas, Texas. Commerce: East Texas State University thesis.

**10.5 Billiard, Charles, and Robert L. Driscoll.** 1979. A study of dialect preparation of student teachers in an urban teacher education center program. ED 177 099. 24 pp. [Atlanta, GA]. Finds attitudes of white middle class student teachers toward children speaking black dialect can be changed in a positive way and that their listening comprehension of such children can be improved.

**10.6 Bock, E. Rope, and James H. Pitts.** 1975. The effects of three levels of black dialect on perceived speaker image. Speech Teacher 24.218-25.

[114 B college students]. Finds a speaker of "jive" is rated more positively (i.e., having higher status, more audience confidence) than a speaker of "uneducated Southern Black" dialect or "the common dialect used by Blacks in most Black-White communication situations."

**10.7 Bryden, James D.** 1968. An acoustic and social dialect analysis of perceptual variables in listener identification and rating Negro speakers. Final Report. Project no. 7-C-003. Washington: U. S. Office of Education. ED 022 186. 147 pp. [43 W, 43 B]. Study to specify which variables function in the racial identification and speech quality rating of black and white speakers; finds black speakers "had consistently greater attentuation of formant amplitudes of [u] vowel than white speech."

**10.8 Carpenter, Gwendolyn Gail.** 1970. Social dialects in Louisiana. Baton Rouge: Louisiana State University thesis. 25 pp. [1 20-year-old Cajun, 1 35-year-old B from LA, judged by 59 university students]. Finds most LA natives cannot identify black and Cajun dialects and rate black speech higher on "authoritativeness."

**10.9 Carson, A. S., and A. I. Rabin.** 1960. Verbal comprehension and communication in Negro and white children. Journal of Educational Psychology 51.47-51. [30 Northern W, 30 Northern B, 30 Southern B, 4th, 5th, 6th graders]. Finds that on vocabulary comprehension test Northern whites score higher than Northern blacks, who score higher than Southern blacks; discusses possible racial and geographical factors accounting for this.

**10.10 Coe, Elizabeth Beaubien.** 1984. Assessing Afro-American English comprehension by student teachers whose mother tongue is mainstream English. Houston: University of Houston dissertation. Abstract in DAI 46.963A. Finds semantic and phonological differences cause more comprehension problems than syntactic and lexical differences.

**10.11 Cohen, Karen M., and Flo Gryn Kimmerling.** 1971. Attitudes based on English dialect differences: an analysis of current research report no. 4. Cambridge, MA: Language Research Foundation. ED 056 579. 54 pp. Evaluates and synopsizes eighteen studies that investigate attitudes based on language differences, especially attitudes of teachers toward speech of students; outlines purpose, speakers, judges, materials, measures, and findings of each study.

**10.12 Coleman, Cynthia.** 1985. Dominance patterns in the verbal interaction of black students at Frostburg State College. Indiana: Indiana University of Pennsylvania dissertation. Abstract in DAI 46.3704A. [55 B, MD]. Studies use and evaluation of argumentative strategies in single-sex and in cross-sex situations.

**10.13 Coleman, William L.** 1978. Sociolinguistic aspects of language attitudes towards Southern American English. Abstract in NADS 11.1.12.

[250 adults, NC]. Measures attitudes toward nonstandard Southern, standard Southern, and "Network English" with respect to sex of speaker and sex, education, and age of judge.

**10.14 Colquhoun, Ann.** 1978. Attitudes toward five dialects of English. ED 184 368. 12 pp. [457 residents of Toronto, Canada]. Examines listener assessment of twenty voices representing five varieties of English (including Southern) and finds, contrary to previous research, that the dialect factor is weakened "when combined with real personality differences and passage content variation."

**10.15 Crosthwait, Charles, and Charles E. Billiard.** 1978. Ethnic attitudes and language usage. ED 168 299. 23 pp. [162 adults, Atlanta, GA]. Finds no variables have predictive value for identification and evaluation of whites, but that combination of nonstandard speech patterns and black race predict high identification of blacks; includes some discussion of LAGS and Southern speech.

**10.16 Dickens, Milton, and Granville M. Sawyer.** 1952. An experimental comparison of vocal quality among mixed groups of whites and Negroes. SSJ 17.178-85. [5 W F, 5 B F, 5 W M, 5 B M, Austin TX]. Examines accuracy and quality of assessment of speaker's race from recordings; finds overall accuracy of identification is seventy percent, with whites more accurate in identifying race of speakers than blacks, each race better at identifying its own members, and race of males easier to identify than race of females.

**10.17 Dorne, William Padgett.** 1959. The comprehensibility of the speech of representative sixth-grade Negro children in the Lee County School System, Alabama. Gainesville: University of Florida dissertation. Abstract in Speech Monographs 27.81-82. [156 B 6th graders, E CENT AL]. Investigates comprehensibility of short-answer and free-speech samples of speech from black children; finds Southerners rate comprehensibility significantly higher than Northerners.

**10.18 Dundes, Alan.** 1977. Jokes and covert language attitudes: the curious case of the wide-mouth frog. LIS 6.141-47. Says the joke enables whites to covertly imitate blacks and old-fashioned Atlantic Coast speech, especially in the exaggerated lip-rounding of saying the punchline, as in pronouncing the vowel in the exclamation oh.

**10.19 Edwards, Charlye Mae.** 1972. Southern black dialect auditory discrimination test. Atlanta: Georgia State University dissertation.

**10.20 Elifson, Joan McCarty.** 1976. Effecting bidialectal shift in speakers of nonstandard English through a sequenced curriculum. Atlanta: Georgia State University dissertation. Abstract in DAI 37.5091A. Studies effect of formal study of language on teacher attitudes toward nonstandard dialects and effect of curriculum to foster bidialectalism among speakers of nonstandard English.

**10.21 Fraser, Bruce.** 1973. Some "unexpected" reactions to various American-English dialects. Language attitudes: current trends and prospects, ed. by Roger W. Shuy and Ralph W. Fasold, 28-35. Washington: Georgetown University Press. Uses modified version of Tucker and Lambert (**10.34**) research rating and identifying race of anonymous speakers; finds that blacks whose race is misidentified are rated lower on personal qualities but whites whose race was misidentified were not.

**10.22 Garner, T., and D. L. Rubin.** 1986. Middle-class blacks' perceptions of dialect and style-shifting: the case of Southern attorneys. Journal of Language and Social Psychology 5.33-48. Finds black professionals dissociate standard English from ethnic identification and value black English positively as marker of cultural identity.

**10.23 Gayer, Ave Maria.** 1976. Black attitudes toward white English. Commerce: East Texas State University thesis.

**10.24 Grinstead, Tamela, S. S. Krzyston, Nelleke Van Deusen, and Jerrie Scott.** 1987. Listener's response to regional and ethnic accents in broadcasting. SECOL Review 11.115-34. Examines how three blacks, three Southern whites, and three Northeastern whites rate their own and each other's varieties of English; discusses these ratings "in relation to educability and employability of dialect speakers in broadcasting"; finds black speech rated highest in believability and communication and Southern white speech highest in professionalism and education.

**10.25 Halaby, Raouf, and Carolyn Long.** 1979. Future shout: name-calling in the future. Maledicta 3.1.61-68. Attitudes toward name-calling and four-letter-words in E TX.

**10.26 Harms, L. S.** 1963. Status cues in speech: extra-race and extra-region identification. Lingua 12.300-06. Finds judges at Eastern and Midwestern universities are able to assess social status of twelve Washington, DC, speakers reading a passage across race boundaries.

**10.27 Hartman, John J., and William Labov.** 1971. Psychological conflict in Negro American language behavior: a case study. American Journal of Orthopsychiatry 41.627-35. With comment by William Labov 41.636-37. Abstract in LLBA 4.2298-99 (Oct. 1971). Case study of black graduate student from small Southern town.

**10.28 Haywood, Marye L.** 1970. Negro dialect: attitudes and actualities at East Texas State University. Commerce: East Texas State University thesis. [NE TX].

**10.29 Hopper, Robert, et al.** 1972. Speech characteristics and employability. Technical Report. Austin: University of Texas Center for Communication Research. ED 067 713. 24 pp. [76 employers in Austin, TX, judging speech of B, Anglo, Hispanic]. Concludes that "employers make stable judgments of the speech characteristics of persons being interviewed for employment" and that these judgments involve whether an applicant is competent, agreeable, and self-assured and involve speech only for white collar executive and supervisory positions.

**10.30 Hurst, Charles G. Jr.** 1965. Psychological correlates in dialectolalia. Washington: Howard University Communication Science Research Center. 122 pp. ED 003 481. [1209 Howard University freshmen, Washington, DC]. Proficiency in speech correlated with class and ethnic orientation.

**10.31 Irwin, Ruth Beckey.** 1977. Judgments of vocal quality, speech fluency, and confidence of Southern black and white speakers. Language and Speech 20.261-66. [36 W college students in Ohio]. Finds twenty-five blacks and twenty-five whites from NC were correctly identified by race and that vocal quality, speech fluency, and confidence of white speakers were perceived as significantly better.

**10.32 Jones, Gwendolyn Storrs.** 1972. Speech and language characteristics of Negro speakers. Lafayette, IN: Purdue University dissertation. Abstract in DAI 33.844A. [391 B freshmen at Tuskegee Institute, Tuskegee, AL]. Finds that while freshmen evaluated their speech and thought peers evaluated it as "satisfactory" and "average," they judged it inferior to speech of students enrolled in colleges outside the South.

**10.33 Kontstaal, C. W., and F. L. Jackson.** 1971. Race identification on the basis of biased speech samples. Ohio Journal of Speech and Hearing 6.1.48-51.

**10.34 Lambert, Wallace E., and G. Richard Tucker.** 1969. White and Negro listeners' reactions to various American-English dialects. Social Forces 47.463-68. Attitudes of selected groups toward each other's speech. **Reprinted** in R. Bailey and J. Robinson 1973(1.39).293-301.

**10.35 Lane, Harlan L. and others.** 1967. The perception of general American English by speakers of Southern dialect. Studies in Language Behavior 4.207-17. [20 B, 16 W college students in AL]. Finds blacks have significantly more difficulty in correctly perceiving phonemes of "General American English" than whites do.

**10.36 Lane, Harlan L., and others.** 1967. The perception of general American English by speakers of Southern dialects. ED 016 974. 11 pp. Also published by University of Michigan Center for Research in Language and Behavior, report BR-6-1784. [16 W, 25 B college students in AL]. Says that "it appears that speakers of the Southern Negro dialect commit more errors when attempting to correctly perceive ['General American English'] than do Caucasian students from the same geographic area and of the same social and economic level" although both Southern whites and Southern blacks make more errors of perception than "native speakers of GAE."

**10.37 Lass, Norman J., Pamela J. Mertz, and Karen L. Kimmel.** 1978. The effect of temporal speech alterations on speaker, race, sex identifications. Language and Speech 21.279-90. [30 W F college students, WV]. Finds subjects are more accurate in judging sex of speakers than their race.

**10.38 Lee, Richard R.** 1971. Dialect perception: a critical review and reevaluation. QJS 57.410-17. Reviews empirical work on dialect perception, takes view that "interpretation of the research in dialect perception has ranged beyond the limits of its data," and concludes that results of experiments "should not be generalized from the laboratory to characterize casual social perception in interpersonal communication."

**10.39 Lee, Richard R.** 1971. Effects of age on student perception of social dialects. Synopsized as ED 053 134. 12 pp. [10 2nd-graders, 19 9th-graders, 19 12th-graders, 50 college students rating 8 high-school students, 4 B, 4 W, 4 F, 4 M, from Tallahassee, FL]. Finds great variability across age groups and between test occasions in rating of the optimal job prospects for different voices and concludes that dialect is not a reliable cue in social perception.

**10.40 McDavid, Raven I., Jr., and Raymond K. O'Cain.** 1977. Prejudice and pride: linguistic acceptability in South Carolina. Acceptability in Language, ed. by Sidney Greenbaum, 103-32. The Hague: Mouton. Compares judgments of acceptability and currency of thirty-two cultivated SC LAMSAS informants with patterns of usage by all 144 LAMSAS in state; finds judgments on lexical items more accurate than on phonological and grammatical items. **Reprinted** in R. McDavid 1980(**1.456**).131-63.

**10.41 McDavid, Raven I. Jr., Raymond K. O'Cain, and Linda L. Barnes.** 1980. Subjective appraisal of phonological variants. Studies in English Linguistics: For Randolph Quirk, ed. by Sidney Greenbaum, Geoffrey Leech and Jan Svartvik, 264-70. New York: Longman.

**10.42 Markel, Norman N., Monte F. Bein, Wm. W. Campbell, and Marvin E. Shaw.** 1976. The relationship between selfrating of expressed inclusion and speaking time. Language and Speech 19.117-20. [90 Univ. of Florida students, Gainesville]. Finds amount of talk directly related to self-rating on scale of "expressed inclusion."

**10.43 Matthews, Horace.** 1980. Attitudes and classroom behaviors of Virginia middle school English teachers regarding black English and certain other usages. Charlottesville: University of Virginia dissertation. Abstract in DAI 41.3861-62A. 178 pp. [51 urban, 32 rural middle-school English teachers, VA]. Finds that "teachers are more critical in their attitude of Black English in classroom speaking situations than they are" of other nonstandard forms.

**10.44 Mulac, Anthony.** 1977. Effects of selected American regional dialects upon regional audience members. Communication Monographs 44.185-95. Examines how speakers from S CA, E KY, and Boston assess regionalness and other qualities of their own and each other's speech.

**10.45 Parks, Thomas Ilon.** 1976. A profile of the sociolinguistic attitudes of students, teachers, and home adults in four South Carolina school communities. Nashville: George Peabody College dissertation. Abstract in DAI 37.2159A. 102 pp. [160 high school students, 160 parents and adults, 40 high school teachers, SC]. ED 131 458. Finds black parents and teachers of both races preferred bidialectal approach in dealing with spoken dialect differences and that white parents and students of both races preferred tolerance of all dialect differences.

**10.46 Preston, Dennis R.** 1982. Perceptual dialectology: mental maps of United States dialects from a Hawaiian perspective. UHWPL 14.2.5-49. Explores extent to which Hawaiians perceive and stereotype mainland American dialects, including Southern American.

**10.47 Preston, Dennis R.** 1986. Five visions of America. LIS 15.221-40. 17 maps. Analyzes and compares how speakers in different areas (NY, IN, MI, HI) perceive U.S. dialect areas, including the South; compares perceptions with traditional maps of American dialects and with cultural zones of the country.

**10.48 Randall, Phyllis R.** 1976. Socio-cultural correlates of the comprehension of black English vernacular and edited American English. Chapel Hill: University of North Carolina dissertation. Abstract in DAI 36.4824-25A. [99 B college freshmen]. Investigates comprehension of "Black American English" and "Edited American English" by entering black college freshmen.

**10.49 Rubadeau, John W.** 1975. Attitudinal and behavioral changes in prospective teachers toward black English resulting from training in transformational grammar which illustrates the similarity between the deep and surface structures of black and standard English. Atlanta: Georgia State University dissertation. Abstract in DAI 36.2150A. Uses nine features to define black English.

**10.50 Rubin, Donald L., and Marie Wilson Nelson.** 1983. Multiple determinants of a stigmatized speech style: women's language, powerless language, or everyone's language? Language and Speech 26.273-99. [40 W tenth-graders, 20 M, 20 F, 4 different verbal ability groups, Atlanta, GA]. Examines "the effects of speaker sex, socio-economic status, ability, communication apprehension, rigidity, and question type on the incidence of 16 style markers and on verbosity in simulated job interviews" in attempt to characterize "women's language" and "powerless language."

**10.51 Rundell, Edward E.** 1973. Studies of the comprehension of black English. Austin: University of Texas dissertation. 255 pp. Abstract in DAI 34.2801-02A. ED 078 459. [16 B, 32 W adults]. Compares standard English and black English speakers for comprehension of their own speech, each other's speech, and artificial varieties with different mixes of standard English and black English segmental and suprasegmental phonemes.

**10.52 Rystrom, Richard.** 1974. Rystrom dialect test, and testing Negro-standard English dialect differences. ED 091 759. 17 pp. [120 B, 100 W]. Repetition test for elementary school children "designed to discriminate Negro dialect speech from standard English." **Reprinted** from Reading Research Quarterly 1969.

**10.53 Shamo, G. Wayne.** 1970. The psychological correlates of speech characteristics of sounding "disadvantaged": a Southern replication. ED 039 177. 13 pp. [54 B, 33 W teachers in Memphis, TN]. Discovers that "even after very short exposure to a child's speech, teacher judgments tended to classify a child as being 'culturally disadvantaged' if his verbal and grammatical patterns were not standard."

**10.54 Shields, Kenneth.** 1978. Language attitudes in the South. USF Lang Q 18.1-2.2-6. [68 W, 7 B, 30 M, 45 F, adults in Memphis]. Compares how three generations of Memphians assess speakers of five regional accents and finds Southern accent has increasingly less prestige the younger the judge.

**10.55 Shores, David.** 1974. Black English and black attitudes. SAB 39.104-12. Discusses attitudes of black educators toward eradicating and tolerating dialectal differences and toward bidialectalism. **Reprinted** in D. Shores and C. Hines 1977(1.689).177-87.

**10.56 Shuy, Roger W.** 1972. Sociolinguistics and teacher attitudes in a Southern school system. Sociolinguistics in cross-cultural analysis, ed. by David M. Smith and Roger W. Shuy, 67-81. Washington: Georgetown University Press. Describes seven-month program in Norfolk, VA, designed to help teachers appreciate linguistic diversity, recognize dialects as systematic and valuable, and understand pitfalls of disregarding socio-linguistic information.

**10.57 Shuy, Roger, Joan C. Baratz, and Walter A. Wolfram.** 1969. Socio-linguistic factors in speech identification. Final report. Research project no. MH 15048-01. Washington: National Institute of Mental Health. ED 083 616. 135 pp. Reprinted 1970 by the Center for Applied Linguistics. [Detroit, MI]. Finds that Detroiters can correctly identify race of twenty-one taped voices of black and white men from 74.4% to 86.2% of time.

**10.58 Shuy, Roger, and Frederick Williams.** 1973. Stereotyped attitudes of selected English dialect communities. Language attitudes: current trends and prospects, ed. by Roger W. Shuy and Ralph W. Fasold, 85-96. Washington: Georgetown University Press. Results of statistical analysis of subjective judgment data from preceding study.

**10.59 Sigelman, Carol Kimball.** 1972. Giving and taking directions: subcultural communication barriers and evaluative reactions to speech. Nashville: George Peabody College dissertation. Abstract in DAI 33.3623-24A. [48 B WC, 48 W MC 10th-graders in TN]. Finds that directions read by black working-class students were more comprehensible than directions by white middle-class students but that white listeners were more successful in following directions than blacks are.

**10.60 Smith, Michael K., and Guy H. Bailey.** 1980. Attitude and activity: contextual constraints on subjective judgments. Language: social psychological perspectives, ed. by Howard Giles, W. Peter Robinson, and Philip M. Smith, 209-15. Oxford: Pergamon. [31 W, 4 B, 19 M, 16 F freshmen at Univ. of Tennessee]. Explores effects differing activities have on evaluation of speakers of regional dialects within U.S.; finds most subjects varied in evaluation not only on different activities but also on different instances of same activity, only exceptions being evaluation of North Midland and Southern black speakers.

**10.61 Stevenson, Cindy.** 1987. Language attitude survey: subjective responses toward American regional dialects, gender, and activity. Abstract in NADS 19.3.8. Reports how speakers in College Station, TX, assess speakers from main dialect areas of U. S.

**10.62 Strauss, A., and L. Schatzman.** 1955. Cross-class interviewing: an analysis of interaction and communicative styles. Human Organization 14.2.28-31. [AR]. Explores effectiveness of different interviewing techniques with informants from different social classes.

**10.63 Swacker, Marjorie.** 1976. When [-native] is [-favorable]. Lektos: interdisciplinary working papers in language sciences, special issue. ED 135 254. 5 pp. Discusses need for foreign students learning English in U.S. to develop positive attitudes about regional and social dialect variation, while learning dialectal patterns that will best facilitate their widest possible acceptance with the target language community.

**10.64 Swacker, Marjorie.** 1977. Attitudes of native and non-native speakers toward varieties of American English. College Station: Texas A and M University dissertation. Abstract in DAI 38.6692-93A. Finds English as a Second Language students have clearly defined notions about dialect superiority, although they are inconsistent in evaluating and ranking speakers of regional dialects.

**10.65 Tate, Donna A.** 1978. A study of speaker disguise. Gainesville: University of Florida thesis. iv + 62 pp. Finds that listeners are able to distinguish between native and imitation Southern speech most, but not all, of the time, that dramatic training tends to improve ability of speakers to disguise their voice, and that training and regional residence of listeners only slightly influences ability to detect disguise.

**10.66 Toomb, J. Kevin, James G. Quiggins, Dennis L. Moore, Lynn B. MacNeill, and Charles M. Liddell.** 1972. The effects of regional dialects on initial source credibility. Normal: Illinois State University Communication Research Center. ED 062 828. 13 pp. [492 students at Illinois State Univ.]. Reports how students in IL rate speeches given by natives from five dialect regions on nineteen scales that measure four dimensions of credibility; finds Southern speaker rated lowest on "confidence" dimension.

**10.67 Underwood, Gary N.** 1974. How you sound to an Arkansawyer. AS 49.208-15. [24 Ozarkers, ages 29-74, ranking 10 accents on 10 traits]. Finds Ozark residents evaluate their own speech highest, that of KY next, and that of AR blacks and Charleston, SC, lowest; finds no consensus on which accent is most standard.

**10.68 Underwood, Gary N.** 1975. Subjective reactions of Ozarkers to their own English and the English of other Americans. Journal of the Linguistic Association of the Southwest 1.63-77. Finds linguistic insecurity of Ozark residents, as revealed in attitudes toward their own speech, is related to educational level, occupation, social class, and urbanness, but not to age or sex.

**10.69 Underwood, Gary N.** 1987. Accent and identity. Abstract in NADS 19.2.13. [TX]. Examines LePage's identity hypothesis with respect to accent variation in contemporary TX society.

**10.70 Van Antwerp, Caroline, and Monica Maxwell.** 1982. Speaker sex, regional dialect and employability: a study in language attitudes. Linguistics and the professions: proceedings of the second annual Delaware symposium on language studies, ed. by Robert Di Pietro, 227-42. Norwood, NJ: Ablex. [4 Southerners, 4 non-Southerners, judged by 20 Southerners]. Finds evidence for both overt and covert prestige in rating of Southern speakers.

**10.71 von Raffler-Engel, Walburga.** 1976. Homophonous self primers and back channel elicitors. ED 152 068. 13 pp. [36 B, ages 3-18, Nashville, TN]. Pilot study of interpretation of "back-channel elicitors" and "buffers," two types of hesitation forms in speech.

**10.72 Watson-Thompson, Ocie Betty.** 1986. An investigation of elementary school teachers' attitudes toward the use of black English in west Alabama. Tuscaloosa: University of Alabama dissertation. DAI 46.3249A. Concludes that "teachers need to be sensitized in teacher education programs and/or inservice programs to the diversity of language patterns found in the classroom."

**10.73 Wilbur, Verna Martin.** 1981. Language attitudes of teachers at selected historically black colleges as measured by the language attitude scale. Denton: Texas Women's University dissertation. Abstract in DAI 42.3487-88A. [73 teachers, 8 colleges in TX]. Finds language attitudes of teachers correlate with differences in college education but not with sex or race.

**10.74 Wilke, Walter H., and Joseph F. Snyder.** 1941. Attitudes toward American dialects. Journal of Social Psychology 14.349-62. Individual and group differences in attitudes toward twelve regional dialect recordings are great in all regions.

**10.75 Williams, Frederick.** 1970. Language, attitude, and social change. Language and poverty: perspectives on a theme, ed. by Frederick Williams, 380-99. Chicago: Markham. Reviews theory of social stereotyping and discusses the role language has in it, based on research into attitudes toward social and regional varieties of speech.

**10.76 Williams, Frederick.** 1976. Explorations of the linguistic attitudes of teachers. Rowley, MA: Newbury House. 130 pp. Monograph on linguistic and psychological dimensions of measuring and assessing teacher attitudes toward language of students, based on author's extensive research in Chicago and TX.

**10.77 Williams, Frederick, and G. Wayne Shamo.** 1972. Regional variation in teacher attitudes toward children's language. Central States Speech Journal 23.73-77. [54 B, 33 W teachers in Memphis, TN]. Finds few differences between Memphis and Chicago in how school teachers rate cultural advantageness/disadvantageness of black and white schoolchildren.

**10.78 Williams, Frederick, Jack L. Whitehead, and Jane Traupmann.** 1971. Teachers' evaluations of children's speech. Speech Teacher 20.247-54. Effect of stereotyping in formation of language judgments on three varieties of TX speech--black, Mexican-American, and white.

**10.79 Willis, Clodius.** 1970. The development of an automatic dialect classification test. ED 041 263. 181 pp. Institute of International Studies final report. Tests vowel perception of 196 teenagers, including some from VA.

**10.80 Woodard, Charles.** 1973. Children's comprehension of teachers' speech. Columbia: University of South Carolina thesis. 34 pp. [60 B and W 5th-graders, Columbia, SC]. Finds that teachers' speech is comprehended better by middle-class than by lower-class children and better by white children than black children.

See Also

1.48 Baratz; 1.111 Burling; 1.213 Dumas; 1.392 Levine; 1.679 Schrock.

# 11 Speech Act and Style

**11.1 Alderman, Pat.** 1972. Mountain hollerin. In the shadow of Big Bald: about the Appalachians and their people, 64. Jonesboro, TN: Tri-Cities Press.

**11.2 Anderson, Edward.** 1978. Language and stylistic influences of the black folk tradition of black literature. ED 163 511. 15 pp. Says that such persuasive techniques as improvisation, indirection, and exaggeration and such communicative styles as "call and response" are prevalent in the black community and can be used by teachers to enhance the teaching of composition.

**11.3 Bauman, Richard.** 1981. Dog-trading and storytelling at Canton. "And other neighborly names": social process and cultural image in Texas folklore, ed. by Richard Bauman and Roger D. Abrahams, 79-103. Austin: University of Texas Press.

**11.4 Bauman, Richard.** 1984. "Any man who keeps more'n one hound'll lie to you": dog trading and storytelling at Canton, Texas. Language in use: readings in sociolinguistics, ed. by John Baugh and Joel Sherzer, 198-210. Englewood Cliffs, NJ: Prentice-Hall.

**11.5 Beck, Kay.** 1979. Speech behavior and social environment: selective interactions in the American South. Discourse Processes 2.335-42. Examines how middle-class Southerners in Atlanta, GA, male and female, black and white, modify their speech and their behavior for foreigners.

**11.6 Berdie, R. F.** 1947. "Playing the dozens." Journal of Abnormal and Social Psychology 42.120-21. Description of the activity by psychologist who reports that 90% of blacks in the Navy know term while only whites who know it had extensive contact with blacks.

**11.7 Brearley, H. C.** 1939. Ba-ad nigger. SAQ 38.75-81. In black speech, the word **bad** may be used as an epithet of honor for a reckless rebel.

**11.8 Bronner, Simon J.** 1978. A re-examination of dozens among white American adolescents. Western Folklore 37.118-28. Compares performance structure and gives examples of dozens collected from three American communities, including black community in Greenville, MS; finds among young white males in N features of ritualized verbal insults and dueling previously documented only for blacks.

**11.9 Brown, H. Rap.** 1972. Street talk. Rappin' and stylin' out: communication in urban black America, ed. by Thomas Kochman, 205-08. Urbana: University of Illinois Press. Excerpt from Brown's autobiography about his childhood in Baton Rouge.

**11.10 Ching, Marvin K. L.** 1979. Dialectal variations of the dozens in Tennessee. TFSB 45.68-78. [Memphis]. Report of playing dozens by black females.

**11.11 Ching, Marvin K. L.** 1987. "Ma'am" and "sir": modes of mitigation and politeness in the Southern United States. Abstract in NADS 19.2.10. Discusses attitudes toward and use of two politeness markers.

**11.12 Dargan, Amanda, and Stephen Zeitlin.** 1983. American talkers: expressive styles and occupational choice. JAF 96.3-33. Describes street cries, auction chants, and sales speech of pitchmen, including some Southern specimens.

**11.13 Darwin, M. B.** 1973. A footnote on the rebel yell. AS 48.303-04. Disagrees with Read (**11.46**); says rebel yell more likely originated as yell of running rabbit chaser.

**11.14 Dazey, Mary Ann Tharp.** 1981. A stylistic study of the public addresses of Senator John C. Stennis of Mississippi. Hattiesburg: University of Southern Mississippi dissertation. Abstract in DAI 42.2113A. 175 pp. Applies a rhetorical and grammatical analysis to thirteen public addresses of Stennis.

**11.15 Dew, J. Harvie.** 1892. The Yankee and rebel yells. Century Illustrated Magazine 43.954-55. Says war yell used by Confederates in Civil War was product of "unbounded enthusiasm and ardor" of Southerners and habit of communicating over long distances between neighbors in the South.

**11.16 Dubner, Frances S.** 1972. Nonverbal aspects of black English. SSCJ 37.361-74. Nonverbal characteristics of black English identified by linguists, anthropologists, sociologists, and communicologists.

**11.17 Elton, William.** 1950. Playing the dozens. AS 25.148-49. Describes a "dialect of insult" practiced by blacks and Southern whites; cites term from

Erskine Caldwell to support claim that whites practiced verbal games of insult as well.

**11.18 Hannerz, Ulf.** 1967. Gossip, networks and culture in a black American ghetto. Ethnos 32.35-60. [Washington, DC]. Discusses patterns and functions of gossip in black community, especially among males.

**11.19 Hatley, Donald, and Kathleen Thomas Severance.** 1980. Communication in a frontier society. Perspectives in American English, ed. by J. L. Dillard, 175-79. The Hague: Mouton. [Red River Parish, LA]. Essay on how news was spread through personal contact and mail on American frontier and how hollering, other vocal sounds, and trail signs functioned as systems of communication.

**11.20 Heath, Shirley Brice.** 1981. Oral and literate traditions--endless linkages. Moving between practice and research in writing: proceedings of the NIE-FIPSE grantee workshop, ed. by Ann Humes et al., 21-34. Los Alamitos, CA: Southwest Regional Laboratory for Educational Research and Development. [SC Piedmont]. Examines oral traditions in white and black working-class mill communities and argues there is no simple dichotomy or even single continuum of traditions from oral to literate.

**11.21 Heath, Shirley Brice.** 1982. Questioning at home and at school: a comparative study. Doing the ethnography of schooling: educational anthropology in action, ed. by George Spindler, 102-31. New York: Holt, Rinehart and Winston. Analyzes types of questions children are asked and learn to use in working-class black and white communities, based on Heath longitudinal study (1.310).

**11.22 Heath, Shirley Brice.** 1982. What no bedtime story means: narrative skills at home and school. LIS 11.49-76. Examines meaning and development of literacy in the home and in school in three contrasting communities--white middle-class school-oriented culture, white mill community, and black mill community.

**11.23 Hughes, Langston.** 1951. Jokes Negroes tell on themselves. Negro Digest 9.8.21-25.

**11.24 James, Willis Laurence.** 1955. The romance of Negro folk cry in America. Phylon 16.15-30. Musical analysis and discussion of types and functions of cries, particularly in religious services.

**11.25 Johnson, James D.** 1981. An instance of toasts among Southern whites. Western Folklore 40.329-37. [CENT GA]. Reports use of verbal narrative insults by white rural Southerner.

**11.26 Jones, Alice.** 1942. The Negro folk sermon: a study in the sociology of folk culture. Nashville: Fisk University thesis.

**11.27 Jones-Jackson, Patricia.** 1982. Oral tradition of prayer in Gullah. Journal of Religious Thought 39.21-33. Structure and arrangement of sermons in Sea Island culture; sample sermon appended, pp. 27-33.

**11.28 Kochman, Thomas.** 1970. Towards an ethnography of black American speech behavior. Rappin' and stylin' out: communication in urban black America, ed. by Thomas Kochman, 241-64. Urbana: University of Illinois Press. Analyzes rapping, shucking and jiving, tomming, sounding, copping a plea, and other patterns of expressive verbal behavior. P. 246, discusses tomming and jeffing, role-playing verbal behavior of blacks in the South. **Reprinted** in M. Lourie and N. Conklin 1978(**1.397**).94-115; in A. L. Smith 1972(**1.701**).58-86; in Norman E. Whitten and John F. Szwed, eds. 1971. Afro-American anthropology, 145-62. New York: Free Press.

**11.29 Kochman, Thomas.** 1974. "Orality" and "literacy" as factors of "black" and "white" communicative behavior. Linguistics 136.91-115. On barriers to communication between literate and nonliterate groups.

**11.30 Kochman, Thomas.** 1979. Boasting and bragging: "black" and "white." Sociolinguistic Working Paper no. 58. Austin, TX: Southwest Educational Development Laboratory. Analyzes patterns of boasting and bragging in black society and how these conflict with dominant white patterns.

**11.31 Kochman, Thomas.** 1981. Black and white styles in conflict. Chicago: University of Chicago Press. 177 pp. Anthropological study of different ways blacks and whites use language, perform tasks, and attach meaning to their words and behavior. **Reviews:** K. Reisman. 1983. LIS 12. 521-27; D. Schiffrin. 1983. Language 59.455.

**11.32 Krapp, George Philip.** 1925. [Rhetoric of Kentucky]. The English language in America, vol. 2, 297-306. New York: Ungar. Discusses development of folk tradition of exuberant, exaggerated, and picturesque style in KY and Old Southwest region in first half of 19th century.

**11.33 Leary, James P.** 1980. Recreational talk among white adolescents. Western Folklore 39.284-99. Reports on verbal play among lower-class white male adolescents in NC, WI, and IN.

**11.34 Leeper, Faye.** 1978. Talking and touching: a function of storytelling. Paisano, a folklore miscellany, ed. by Francis Edward Abernathy. 137-46. Austin, TX: Encino.

**11.35 McWhiney, Grady, and Perry D. Jamieson.** 1982. Attack and die: Civil War military tactics and the Southern heritage. University: University of Alabama Press. Pp. 190-91, likens Rebel yell used in Civil War to Celtic war charge used by Irish and Scots and noted as long ago as by Romans in Gaul.

**11.36 Mitchell, Henry H.** 1970. Black English. Black preaching, 148-61. Philadelphia: Lippincott. Discusses value, functions, and linguistic features of black English in preaching and emphasizes need for black preachers to be fluent in two dialects to preach effectively to black churchgoers and to communicate with wider community.

**11.37 Niles, Lyndrey A.** 1984. Rhetorical characteristics of traditional black preaching. Journal of Black Studies 15.41-52. Identifies and describes characteristics, types, and elements of black sermons.

**11.38 Noonan-Wagner, Desley.** 1981. Possible effects of cultural differences on the rhetoric of black basic skills writers. Houston: University of Houston thesis.

**11.39 Pember, Ann P.** 1986. "It's not in the book it's between your ears." SECOL Review 10.75-88. Says "teachers use directives as frequently with black females, remedial level, as with boys, both in control behavior as to instruct. Their language variety and cultural backgrounds are in stark contrast to the school's Standard English and classroom culture."

**11.40 Peppin, Suzanne Marie.** 1976. The language of black ritual insults. College Park: University of Maryland thesis. Surveys literature to examine language of black ritual insults and its historical origins and documents verbal insult patterns among young blacks at suburban MD high school.

**11.41 Pitts, Walter F.** 1986. Linguistic variation as a function of ritual frames in the Afro-Baptist church in central Texas. Austin: University of Texas dissertation. Abstract in DAI 47.1715-16. Uses frame analysis to analyze two vernaculars used in the black church service, one an inflated style associated with preaching, the other a deflated style connected with music.

**11.42 [Quidnunc].** 1979. More on the rebel yell. AS 54.60. Cites evidence supporting view of Darwin (**11.13**) that rebel yell was originally hunter's yell to incite dogs.

**11.43 [Rayburn, Otto E.]** 1954. Yodeling in the Ozarks. Rayburn's Ozark Guide 16-17. Intricacies of yodels and remnants of the rebel yell.

**11.44 [Rayburn, Otto E.]** 1959. Calling hogs in the hills. Rayburn's Ozark Guide 17.61.33-34. Intricacies and folklore of calls for hogs in the Ozarks.

**11.45 [Rayburn, Otto E.]** 1960. The White River yell. Rayburn's Ozark Guide 18.65.7. Describes version of rebel yell found in N AR.

**11.46 Read, Allen Walker.** 1961. The rebel yell as a linguistic problem. AS 36.83-92. Chastises linguists for ignoring semilinguistic phenomena like yells and reviews the firsthand descriptions of now-forgotten battle cry of

Confederate soldiers in effort to characterize its features and to account for its terrorizing effect on the enemy.

**11.47 Rickford, John R., and Angela F. Rickford.** 1976. "Cut-eye" and "suck-teeth": African words and gestures in new world guise. JAF 89.294-309. **Reprinted in J. L. Dillard 1980(1.197).347-65.**

**11.48 Rosenberg, Bruce A.** 1970. The formulaic quality of spontaneous sermons. JAF 83.3-20. Analyzes formulaic and metaphoric aspects of black folk sermons.

**11.49 Rosenberg, Bruce A.** 1970. The art of the American folk preacher. New York: Oxford University Press. Based on fieldwork in NC, VA, KY, and CA.

**11.50 Smith, Arthur L.** 1970. Socio-historical perspectives on black history. QJS 56.264-69. Says "central to the understanding of the role of expressiveness within the black community are Mommo, the generative and dynamic quality of vocal expression, and slavery, the primary fact of black existence in America."

**11.51 Spears, James E.** 1969. Playing the dozen [sic]. MFR 3.127-29. Says ritualized verbal game is found exclusively among blacks and summarizes its main elements as discovered by research.

**11.52 Spears, James E.** 1974. Southern folk greetings and responses. MFR 8.218-20. Categorizes greetings on basis of formality of expression and age and ethnicity of speakers; says Southerners use greetings "more frequently and more freely" than other Americans.

**11.53 Tanner, Ralph M.** 1962. Senator Tom Heflin a storyteller. Alabama Review 15.54-60. Describes oratorical techniques of famous AL populist.

**11.54 Vaughn-Cooke, Anna Fay.** 1972. The black preaching style: historical development and characteristics. Languages and linguistics working papers no. 5: sociolinguistics, ed. by Richard J. O'Brien, 28-39. Washington: Georgetown University Press. Analyzes role of intonation in black preaching style and compares prominence of intonational patterns in different stages of sermons.

**11.55 von Allmann, Alex, and Walburga von Raffler-Engel.** 1983. The relation of verbal cues to the image of the speaker. Tennessee Linguistics 3.2.6-21. [79 undergraduates, Vanderbilt University]. Examines whether students can correctly match voices with slides of speakers.

**11.56 von Raffler-Engel, Walburga.** 1972. Some phono-stylistic features of black English. Phonetica 25.1.53-64.

**11.57 von Raffler-Engel, Walburga.** 1974. Language in context: situationally conditioned style change in black English. Proceedings of the XIth international congress of linguists, Bologna, Italy, ed. by Luigi Heilmann, 757-63. Bologna, Italy: Il Mulino.

**11.58 von Raffler-Engel, Walburga.** 1976. Linguistic and kinesic correlations in code switching. Language and man: anthropological issues, ed. by William C. McCormack and Stephen A. Wurm, 229-38. The Hague: Mouton.

**11.59 von Raffler-Engel, Walburga, and C. K. Sigelman.** 1971. Rhythm, narration, description in the speech of black and white school children. Language Sciences 18.9-14. [24 W MC, 17 B LC 4th-graders]. Compares how black and white children differ in fluency and syntactic maturity, narrative form, and thematic content in narrating stories and describing pictures.

**11.60 von Raffler-Engel, Walburga.** 1979. Verbal and nonverbal student interaction in the college classroom a function of group cohesion. Linguistic agency, University of Trier, series B, paper no. 52. Trier, Germany. 17 pp.

**11.61 Wiley, Bell Irvin.** 1943. The life of Johnny Reb. Indianapolis: Bobbs-Merrill. Note on the rebel yell. **Reprinted** in B. A. Botkin, ed. 1949. A treasury of Southern folklore, 71-72. New York: Crown.

**11.62 Woodward, James C.** 1976. Black southern signing. LIS 5.211-18. Discusses lexical and phonological (formational) variation among old and young black sign-language users.

**11.63 Wright, Richard Louis.** 1976. Language standards and communicative style in the black church. Austin: University of Texas dissertation. Abstract in DAI 37.5797A. [10 sermons from 2 Washington, DC, churches]. Compares linguistic form, communicative style, and use of rhetorical devices in middle-class and working-class black preachers; quantifies selected syntactic and phonological variables.

See Also

1.709 Smitherman; 3.67 Carpenter; 3.251 Hurston.

# 12 Bibliographies

**12.1 Appalachian bibliography.** 1980. Morgantown: West Virginia University Library.

**12.2 Bibliographie linguistique de l'année.** 1939–47, 1949–    Utrecht: Comité International Permanent des Linguistes.

**12.3 Bibliographie linguistischer literatur.** 1975–    Frankfurt am Main: Klostermann.

**12.4 Bobson, Sarah,** comp. 1974. Nonstandard dialects: an annotated bibliography of ERIC references. ERIC-IRCD urban disadvantaged series, no. 38. Washington: National Institute of Education. ED 905 227. 97 pp. Lists and briefly annotates 415 items in three areas: "Nonstandard Dialects in the Classroom," "Sociolinguistics and Phonology," and "General Dialect Studies."

**12.5 Brasch, Ila Wales, and Walter Milton Brasch,** eds. 1974. A comprehensive annotated bibliography of American black English. Baton Rouge: Louisiana State University Press. 289 pp. Arranged in one alphabetical listing by author, with no indexes or subject headings; includes many unpublished items and occasional lapses. **Review:** J. Algeo. 1974. AS 49.142-46.

**12.6 Brenni, Vita J.** 1964. American English: a bibliography. Philadelphia: University of Pennsylvania Press. An eclectic compilation marred by inaccuracies.

**12.7 Dillard, J. L.** 1963. Bibliographical research. Caribbean Studies 3.84-95. Contends valid bibliography of works on Caribbean linguistics must include works on creole languages of various derivations and gives lengthy annotated list of such works.

**12.8 Dissertation abstracts.** 1939- . Ann Arbor, MI: University Microfilms.

**12.9 Dunbar, Gary S.** 1961. A preliminary bibliography of Virginia place-name literature. Virginia Place Name Society Occasional Papers, no. 1. Charlottesville: University of Virginia.

**12.10 Dundes, Alan,** comp. 1976. Folklore theses and dissertations in the United States. Austin, TX: American Folklore Society.

**12.11 Goehring, Eleanor E.** 1982. Speech, proverbs, and names. Tennessee folk culture: an annotated bibliography, 69-79. Knoxville: University of Tennessee Press.

**12.12 Harder, Kelsie B.** 1983- . The Ehrensperger report. American Name Society. Annual report on place-name studies in progress and published, supplementing Sealock et al. **(12.30)**, begun in 1953 by Edward C. Ehrensperger, chairman of the Place-Name Committee of the ADS, continued by Kelsie B. Harder, State University College, Potsdam, NY.

**12.13 Harrington, Judith.** 1974. An annotated bibliography of recent work on black English. ED 091 931. 42 pp. A 125-item annotated bibliography of articles and reports published in 1971.

**12.14 Kennedy, Arthur G.** 1927. American sectional dialects. Bibliography of writings on the English language, from the beginning of printing to the end of 1922, 413-16. Cambridge: Harvard University Press. Reissued in 1961 by Hafter, New York.

**12.15 Lee, Ann Morton.** 1980. An annotated bibliography of southern mountain speech. Johnson City: East Tennessee State University thesis.

**12.16 Linguistics.** 1964- . MLA international bibliography. Vol. 3. New York: Modern Language Association.

**12.17 Linn, Michael D., and Maarit-Hannele Zuber.** 1984. The sound of English: a bibliography of language recordings. Urbana: NCTE. 84 pp. Annotated bibliography of recordings of historical varieties of English, American English, modern non-American dialects, voices of notable Americans, authors reading their own works, and regional music.

**12.18 Mack, Molly.** 1977. Black English and standard English: an annotated bibliography. ED 154 394. 27 pp. Contains more than 100 items, mostly journal articles from early 1970s.

**12.19 McMillan, James B.** 1969. Southern speech. A bibliography guide to the study of Southern literature, ed. by Louis D. Rubin, Jr., 128-34. Baton Rouge: Louisiana State University Press.

**12.20 McMillan, James B.**, ed. 1971. An annotated bibliography of Southern American English. Coral Gables: University of Miami Press. 173 pp. First edition of present work. Reviews: B. Carstensen. 1976. ZDL 43.217-18; H. C. Woodbridge. 1972. KFR 18.57-58.

**12.21 Meehan, Robert L.** 1980. Gullah: texts and descriptions. Annotated bibliography, with selective indexing. ED 198 725. 125 pp. Covers scholarly and popular books and periodical items.

**12.22 Pederson, Lee.** 1968. An annotated bibliography of Southern speech. Atlanta: Southeastern Educational Laboratory Monograph no. 1. Has 190 items, many annotated.

**12.23 Pickett, Penelope O.** 1975. A selected bibliography of recent dialect studies. CAL-ERIC/CLL series on languages and linguistics, no. 24. ED 111 176. 27 pp. Annotated bibliography of studies on language variation, most appearing in 1973 or 1974.

**12.24 Rajec, Elizabeth M.** 1978. A study of names in literature: a bibliography. New York: K. G. Saur.

**12.25 Randolph, Vance.** 1972. The Ozarks: a bibliography. Bloomington: Indiana University Press. Folk speech, 41-75; Place Names, 77-95. 2nd edition published in 1987 by University of Missouri Press, with assistance of Gordon McCann and with an introduction by William K. McNeil. Folk speech, 42-55; Place names, 56-68.

**12.26 Reinecke, John.** 1937. Gullah and American Negro English. Marginal languages: a sociological survey of the creole languages . . . part 2, 480-516. New Haven: Yale University dissertation.

**12.27 Reinecke, John, et al.**, eds. 1975. A bibliography of pidgin and creole languages. Honolulu: University Press of Hawaii. Also ED 121 121. Gullah, 468-80; Black English, 481-529. Annotated bibliographies of, respectively, 160 and 529 items on and in two varieties of American English.

**12.28 Ross, Charlotte T.**, ed. 1976. Bibliography of southern Appalachia. Boone, NC: Appalachian Consortium Press.

**12.29 St. Louis Public Library.** 1914. Books containing American local dialects. St. Louis Public Library Monthly Bulletin 11.57-58, 81-82, 107-08, 128, 152-53, 285, 310-11; 12.161-62.

**12.30 Sealock, Richard B., Margaret M. Sealock, and Margaret S. Powell**, eds. 1982. Bibliography of place-name literature: United States and Canada. Chicago: American Library Association. 2nd ed.

**12.31 Theses and dissertations for 19--.** 1936- . SAR. Annual listing of theses and dissertations completed at colleges and universities in the South Atlantic region.

**12.32 Twining, Mary A., and Keith E. Baird,** eds. 1980. Sea island culture. Special issue of Journal of Black Studies 10.4.

**12.33 Viereck, Wolfgang, Manfred Görlach, and Edgar Schneider,** eds. 1984. A bibliography of writings on varieties of English, 1965-1983. Philadelphia and Amsterdam: Benjamins. **Reviews:** R. Butters. 1985. AS 60.88; J. B. McMillan. 1986. JEL 19.135-36.

**12.34 West, Donda C. Williams.** 1973. Black English vernacular: an annotated bibliography 1962-1972. Atlanta: Atlanta University thesis.

**12.35 Woodbridge, Hensley C.** 1958. A tentative bibliography of Kentucky speech. PADS 30.17-37. Includes references to local magazines and newspapers.


See Also

1.10 Allen; 4.275 Pederson; 6.517 Rennick; 9.55 Haman.

# Index